PRAEGER SPECIAL STUDIES IN
INTERNATIONAL ECONOMICS AND DEVELOPMENT

KU-549-161

Rural Development Planning

SYSTEMS ANALYSIS AND WORKING METHOD

Earl M. Kulp

PRAEGER PUBLISHERS
New York · Washington · London

The purpose of Praeger Special Studies is to make specialized research in U.S. and international economics and politics available to the academic, business, and government communities. For further information, write to the Special Projects Division, Praeger Publishers, Inc., 111 Fourth Avenue, New York, N.Y. 10003.

PRAEGER PUBLISHERS
111 Fourth Avenue, New York, N.Y. 10003, U.S.A.
5, Cromwell Place, London S.W.7, England

Published in the United States of America in 1970
by Praeger Publishers, Inc.

Library of Congress Catalog Card Number: 70-77006

Printed in the United States of America

ERRATA

(Over)

PREFACE

This book was made possible by a fellowship in systems analysis under which the U.S. Government sent me to Princeton University for a year of study, research, and reflection on the new decision tools of the late twentieth century. It is based on experiences and observations in the Far East and South Asia, particularly on my own experience in applying some of the main planning techniques of this book in Cambodia, Vietnam, and Thailand. Discussions with experts in Africa and Latin America have convinced me that these techniques apply with equal validity to those regions as well. It should be noted that the observations and concepts presented here are my own and do not necessarily express the policy of any agency of the U.S. Government.

Some acknowledgements are due. I should like to thank the Thai and Vietnamese colleagues with whom I worked and from whom I learned. My colleagues in Thailand included Dr. Sala Dhasananda, Director General of the Department of Rice; Nai Chusak Himathongkam of the Bangkok Bank; and the men of the Office of Accelerated Rural Development (ARD), particularly Nai Prasong Sukhum (Secretary General of ARD), Dr. Phimon Jitman, Nai Santisak Limphabhand, and Nai Supayoke Panitchavid. My principal colleagues in Vietnam were Ton That Trinh, former Minister of Agriculture, and Bui Quang Tan, former Director General of Commerce. I am indebted to many of the faculty of the Woodrow Wilson School at Princeton University for advice and guidance, particularly Professors William J. Baumol and Shane Hunt. I would also like to thank the staff of the Princeton University Computer Center for their valuable assistance.

To the following officials of the U.S. Agency for International Development, who gave me the opportunity and the encouragement to test some of the techniques of this book, I owe a debt of gratitude: Clayton E. McManaway, Jr., Solomon Silver, Leroy S. Wehrle, and Charles D. Matthias. My greatest debt of gratitude, however, is to my mentor in agricultural development, Dr. F. Jamison Bell, who pioneered an exciting variety of technical and institutional innovations in the villages of Southeast Asia.

And finally, I would like to acknowledge my indebtedness to my wife, Shirley, for her enduring patience and steadfast encouragement.

CONTENTS

LIST OF TABLES

LIST OF FIGURES

ABBREVIATIONS

AID   Agency for International Development

APPC   Agricultural Production Planning Committee

BSD   Banque Senegalaise pour la Developpement

CD   Community Development

CER   Centre d'Expansion Rurale

CFDT   Compagnie Francaise pour le Developpement des Fibres Textiles

CINAM   Compagnie d'Industrialisation et d'Amenagement de Territoire

CRAD   Compagnie Regionale de l'Assistance pour le Developpement

EPADC   East Pakistan Agricultural Development Corporation

FA   Farmers Association

FAO   Food and Agricultural Organization

FLDA   Federal Land Development Authority

GPSS   General Purpose Systems Simulator

Ha.   Hectare

ICM   Informal Constrained Maximization

JCRR   Joint Commission on Rural Reconstruction

LOB   Line of Balance

MPS   Mathematical Programming System

OCA   Office de Commercialisation Agricole

PDAF	Provincial Department of Agriculture and Forestry
PERT	Program Evaluation and Review Technique
PMS	Project Management System
PPBS	Planning - Programming - Budgeting System
RRI	Rubber Research Institute
SATEC	Societe de l'Aide Technique et de la Cooperation
SERESA	Societe d'Etudes et de Recherches Economiques et Sociales en Agriculture
TCCA	Thana Cooperative Credit Association
UNESCO	United Nations Educational, Scientific and Cultural Organization

PART I: BASIC PROBLEMS AND CONCEPTS

CHAPTER **1** SCOPE AND FOCUS

"The victory was Templer's, " a retired English officer
of the Malayan Civil Service once remarked to the author,
while reminiscing about the role of the commanding general
in the struggle against the Communist insurgency in Malaya.
"Not that Templer had any original ideas, " he quickly added,
"But, " he continued, placing slow, careful emphasis on each
word, "Templer--instilled--working--method. "

It is the basic premise of this book that in any rural
development effort, sanguine or sanguinary, working method
is the essential starting point.

THE RURAL DEVELOPMENT
WORKING METHOD GAP

Over the years experts in economic development have
developed a considerable body of literature on working
methods for capital projects (major engineering and construction projects). In addition to innumerable articles and
texts on the subject, the major assistance donor agencies,
unilateral and multilateral, have issued manuals for capital
projects, setting forth in great detail the appropriate considerations, contents, and formats for feasibility studies,
project proposals, and assistance requests.

This guidance is almost invariably in terms of large
individual physical installations, such as factories, transportation facilities, power plants, irrigation dams and networks, and institutions of higher learning. For each such
installation it is worthwhile to have a detailed feasibility study,
quality engineering, review, and high-level evaluation.

How do these projects and these methods affect the great bulk of the population of developing nations, who gain their livelihood from farms of one to three hectares? Factories offer job opportunities to very few; only in rare countries has the draw-off of the industrial sector significantly reduced the rural labor surplus. Irrigation facilities are sometimes vital--and transport facilities are often vital--to rural development. Such facilities have no payoff, however, until individual farmers make innovations that earn more money on their own farms.

In rural development, action takes place on thousands or hundreds of thousands of miniscule farms. The development activities of these minute enterprises are far too numerous, dispersed, and small in payoff to make capital project planning techniques feasible or economic.

Despite the lack of planning techniques, almost every developing nation has had its rural development projects, its credit projects, extension projects, cooperative projects, and other agricultural projects. These activities have generally failed to reach most of the farmers. They have variously been misguided, miscoordinated, underfinanced, or under-staffed and basically have suffered from lack of working method.

Many planners will assert that it is impossible to apply the level of working method required on capital projects to rural development activities. Particularly they will maintain that it is impossible to apply a measure of economic payoff or cost-effectiveness to services for the rural area. One is then left with the ironic proposition that the very activities which can most directly affect the income of the bulk of the population cannot be evaluated in an economic context!

Yet there is no lack of literature on the economics of rural development.[1] The problems of subsistence agriculture and the proper policies and activities for advancing it have been very thoroughly analyzed and documented. The basic know-how exists. The developing nations are littered with the debris of unsuccessful rural development projects, but there have been some notable successes, some of which are described in Part II of this book.

What is lacking in the literature of rural development is
a text or manual which sets forth a complete procedure, a
full sequence of data collection, compilation, analysis, documentation, review, evaluation, and decision. What is needed,
in brief, is a working method, a procedure for bringing all
the existing know-how to bear in formulating a rural development program.

We are living in an age of gaps--missile gaps, credibility
gaps, investment gaps, manpower gaps. Walter Rostow has
identified the project gap, the gap between good ideas and
bankable projects.[2] Albert Waterston, in the most exhaustive
and definitive examination of development planning experience
to date, has concluded that the greatest shortcoming in the
field has been lack of project planning method and attention.[3]
Certainly this project gap is most acute in the rural sector of
developing nations, where the method is particularly weak and
the bankable projects have been particularly few.

This book attempts to fill that gap.

SOME BASIC CONCEPTS OF SYSTEMS ANALYSIS

In attempting to fill this working method gap, this book
relies heavily, though by no means exclusively, on that body
of concepts and decision tools generally labeled systems
analysis.

Over the past 25 years many activities other than rural
development have suffered from working method gaps. They
are simply too complex to be planned and managed by traditional working method. At the same time the evolution of the
computer has offered the possibility of massive data manipu-
lation on a previously inconceivable scale, inviting new
quantitative approaches to complex problems. Systems analysis
has arisen in response to these new challenges and new opportunities.

Originally applied, under the name of operations analysis,
to military problems, systems analysis has achieved breakthroughs in problem-solving and complex project management

in a widening variety of fields: production, marketing, public administration, development planning, information retrieval, education, and public health. It has been used to open a Broadway show on time, to determine optimum feed mixtures, and to determine which weapon works best in an ambush.

As the range of successful applications has broadened, however, a comprehensive definition of systems analysis has become more elusive. Some explanations of the term would appear to limit the definition to "a mathematician linked to a computer." It is, indeed, a level of discourse, of conceptualization, somewhere between pure mathematics and traditional academic and professional disciplines. Other explanations of the term are so broad as to imply that everyone is actively engaged in systems analysis from weaning to old age.

As an approach to a useful definition, one might start by saying that systems analysis is a body of decision tools for complex problems developed over the past 25 years, starting with model-building and cutting across traditional disciplines. Looking closer at the key words in this definition, one sees first that it is decision-oriented, not designed primarily to broaden or deepen basic understanding of phenomena. Second, it is based on model-building.* Third, it is for problems too complex to be solved without these techniques. Finally, it is interdisciplinary; its tools of analysis are not confined to one field alone.

The Systems Approach

In addition to utilizing a variety of specific analytical tools, systems analysis is characterized by a consistent overall approach to problems. It starts from a highly formalized, carefully formatted exercise in definition. It aims at the broadest feasible, most rigorous consideration of relevant objectives and interrelationships, at a "look at the total system." The approach follows, roughly, the following sequence:

---

*See Appendix C for definitions of this and other basic terms of systems analysis.

1.   Define the scope of the problem and its objectives.

2.   Define the relevant system and build a model of it.

3.   Formulate alternative solutions, which may be either combinations of different activity systems or different systems configurations.

4.   Select an optimum solution by applying the model and evaluating results on the basis of objectives and other criteria.[4]

Types of Models

The heart of systems analysis, then, is the use of models. These may be adaptations of a standardized analytical structure or they may be specially designed, cut from whole cloth to handle a specific problem.   One can distinguish three types of models:

Mathematical--At the top level, so to speak, are the advanced mathematical tools of operations research, used by the operations analyst. Paraphrasing Robert Dorfman's excellent description, an operations analyst is a man who tackles a problem by writing down some equations first.[5] Some of the principle standard tools of model-building at this level are linear programming, simulation, queueing theory, game theory, search theory, and information theory.[6]

Management--At the middle level are models which are fully quantitative but whose application do not necessarily require mathematical formulations. These include a variety of scheduling techniques based largely on networking; techniques known generally by their acronyms: CPM (critical path technique), PERT (program evaluation and review technique), and LOB (Line of Balance), among others.[7] Also at this level are the techniques of cost-benefit analysis.

Schematic--Finally, there are models used to handle mixed quantitative-qualitative problems. These are largely graphic devices, sundry types of matrix, grid, or network analyses of relationships and alternatives. Also at this level are techniques for improving conceptualization of relationships of activities to objectives; these techniques include definition of missions, hierarchies of objectives, cost-effectiveness analysis, and various aspects of PPBS (Planning-Programming-Budgeting System), the planning system for the U. S. Federal Budget.[8]

Planning as a System

The use of schematic models and basic systems concepts can be illustrated by applying them to a question which we must use as a starting point: What is planning?

Like many complex problems, the complexity of planning is concealed by the simplicity of its label. Planning is an everyday household word. People are generally quite confident they know its exact meaning. In reality the use of the term is highly confusing, and much of what passes for planning is not planning at all.

One might start by noting that any real activity or real processing system must have a control system like that in Figure 1.1.

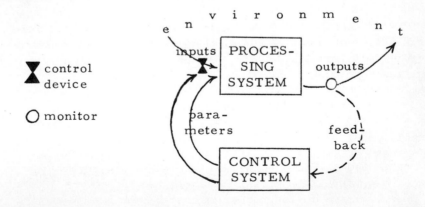

FIGURE 1.1.   Control System

The figure is something of a simplification of the full relationship. Using some of the standard systems terminology defined in Appendix C, the inputs to the control system are in part feedback from the output and in part data on the state of the processing system. The control system has two types of outputs: (1) regulation or changes in the flow of inputs and (2) changes in the parameters or systems structure of the processing system. The two systems are parts of each other's environment.

The entities (or elements) of the control system are decisions. Each decision can be, in turn, analyzed as a subsystem, having three types of attributes: rules, roles, and documents. The rules are the specified method of decision. They and their interrelationships generally constitute a model of the real processing system as well as a set of decision criteria. The roles are the people involved in the system and their relative responsibilities. Together they constitute an organizational system. The documents are the formats on which information and decisions are carried throughout the system; collectively, they constitute the paperwork system.

Three classes of decisions should be distinguished. Each class constitutes a subsystem of the total control system:

1. Policy decisions determine future responses to environmental conditions expected to reoccur: (Whenever x occurs, do A.)

2. Planning decisions determine a sequence of actions to take place at specified future times, given certain assumptions of the future state of the environment: (Based on assumed conditions x and y, do A in period t=1, B in t=2, 2B in t=3, etc.)

3. Coping decisions are responses to events that have just occurred: (Now that x has occurred, do A.)[9]

Coping is somewhat subordinated to planning, which in turn is subordinated to policy, as in Figure 1.2.

This book is concerned with the planning subsystem. Its purpose is to present a generalized design of an optimum planning system for rural development. It is thus concerned with policy and coping decisions only insofar as they constitute part of the environment of planning.

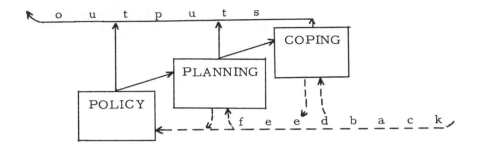

FIGURE 1.2.   The Total Control System

        The planning system by itself can thus be considered a
process-type system whose entities or elements are decision-
making operations.   These entities are structured in a network, connected by flows of documents.   Each operation conceived as a subsystem is composed of decision rules, or
decision steps, and the people involved in the operation.   The
participants have, in turn, subattributes of time available,
talent, and authority.* The decision rules (the model) and the
personnel and their attributes constitute the parameters of
the planning system as a whole and the parameters of each
subsystem.   These parameters are, in turn, set by some
broader governmental control system.

        The planning system is visualized schematically in Figure
1.3.

                    Some Words of Caution

        The above discussion of planning as a system illustrates,
hopefully, the use of general systems terminology and
schematic models to clarify and communicate concepts and
interrelationships.   It also helps illustrate some of the
dangers of systems analysis.

_____

        *Chapter 5 elaborates on these entities and attributes
and also provides criteria for evaluating the planning system.

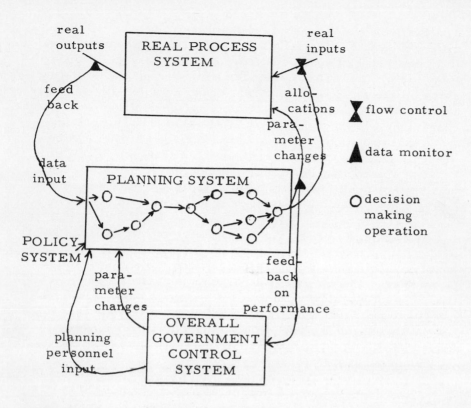

FIGURE 1.3.   The Planning System.

Systems techniques have the aura of tremendously powerful tools, at times in the panacea class. One hears: "What
the government needs is more systems analysis, " or "They
failed because they did not consider the total system. "
Systems analysis has grown up talking to computers and it
carries with it the programming jargon. This can give a
very false aura, a delusion of rigor, incisiveness, and
profundity--when one is actually saying nothing more than
"The knee bone's connected to the leg bone. " Worse, it can
at times gloss over very illogical propositions, particularly
in schematic diagrams in which entities of grossly different
levels of abstraction are treated uniformly.

It is easy, perhaps too easy, to draw a chart full of
boxes and arrows. But what are the specific interrelationships
represented by those arrows ? What counts is the concreteness of the statements of interrelationships.

Systems analysis is interdisciplinary, but its results always depend on the quality of the behavioral theory of the field in which it is being applied. It can only work on problems for which there are theories which can explain relationships between variables in terms of observable data. This is a problem for mathematical as well as schematic models. A coefficient as well as an arrow is of value only if it can be given quantification or some concrete meaning, that can be proven right or wrong by subsequent observations. For this reason, systems analysis is no revolutionary new tool that will replace traditional disciplines; it is completely dependent on traditional disciplines to provide the theory to make it work.

In addition to promoting a false aura of incisiveness and profundity, systems jargon can also get tedious. If every chapter of this book were spelled out completely in systems terminology, the words systems, entities, attributes, and environment would appear over ten times on each page. Many simple points would have to be spelled out with elaborate formal logic, and the book would be considerably longer. A human being can take a hint; a computer demands a mathematical demonstration every time.

For these reasons the jargon of systems analysis has been avoided in this book wherever possible. The most appropriate direct terminology for each problem and aspect of rural development is used; it may be the idiom of development economics or public administration, or it may be a special terminology best suited to the matter at hand. The systems idiom is used only where it is most appropriate, as in defining elusive concepts such as planning.

Systems tools and concepts, moreover, are used only where a simpler working method is inadequate. The book, indeed, derives much of its working method from successful techniques developed by planning staffs in some of the countries described in Part II and these planning staffs are by and large unacquainted with systems analysis. Where such methods are inadequate or display shortcomings, systems analysis techniques and concepts are applied.

RURAL DEVELOPMENT AS A SYSTEM

Scope

To define and delineate the process of rural development (the planning of which is the subject of this book), we must start with a view of the entire economic system of developing countries. The model commonly known as the Lewis model views developing countries as dual economies, each composed of a capitalist sector and a subsistence sector.[10] Each sector exhibits radically different behavior.

The subsistence sector--or, more broadly, the traditional sector--is composed of household-scale enterprises that follow pre-industrial commercial and production techniques. The sector consists largely of peasant farmers but also includes petty traders and artisans. Enterprises in this sector generally have surplus labor except at a few critical seasons of the year. The marginal revenue product of labor is zero for all practical purposes.

The capitalist sector--also called the modern sector-- consists of corporate enterprises or government agencies organized as in developed nations, with modern financing and technology. This sector is dispersed geographically, like islands in a sea of subsistence enterprises.

Attention in development planning originally focused on achieving an economic takeoff in the modern sector by expanding it until it absorbed all the surplus labor of the traditional sector, but this was found to be impossible. Feasible savings rates could rarely provide sufficient investment to furnish jobs for the natural increase in surplus labor in the traditional sector, let alone reduce and eliminate that pool. Moreover, unless the productivity and income of the traditional sector was raised, it could not provide the food or the markets to sustain a growing modern sector.

Attention has therefore focused more and more on raising productivity and income in the traditional sector. The planning system of this process is the subject of this book.

Rural development as a system may be defined for purposes of this book as that set of economic and social development activities peculiar to the process of transforming the
traditional sector as a whole. These activities require a set
of planning techniques different from those used for the
modern sector.

Basically, these activities fall within the agricultural
sector, as conventionally defined. Many activities of the
agricultural sector are excluded, however. This book does
not deal with development of plantations and commercial
farms, since these enterprises are in the modern sector.
Capital projects such as major roads, irrigation dams, and
main distribution channels are excluded from consideration,
unless they constitute part of the environment of rural
development; planning techniques of the modern sector are
suitable for such projects. Major institutional projects such
as research stations and agricultural schools are likewise
excluded except as part of the environment; capital project
techniques are more suited to them.

Since this book is about planning, policy actions in the
agricultural sector, such as monetary and fiscal controls,
market support, and regulation are not considered. The simulation techniques discussed in the final chapter, however, may
provide valuable insights for making policy decisions.

What is included, then, from the agricultural sector, is
a set of project activities that includes extension, credit, supply,
marketing, land-titling and engineering services, and promotion of particular crops.*

Rural development also includes activities outside the
agricultural sector which require rural community activity.
These include building and maintenance of small feeder roads,
village schools and clinics, and other community facilities.
All these are construction projects individually too small for
capital project planning techniques. It also includes the
critically important promotion of family-planning.

---

*"Crops" is used throughout this book as shorthand for
"crops and/or livestock varieties. "

Finally, rural development includes the paramilitary and civil aspects of counterinsurgency, the environment and the planning techniques of which are basically the same. In spite of the emphasis in today's headlines, the problem of maintaining rural security against a determined opposition is not peculiar to Vietnam. During the present decade India (in Nagaland), Kenya, Cameroun, Iraq, and several Latin American countries have been forced to engage in intensive counterinsurgency efforts. Because the environment and planning problems of counterinsurgency are so similar to those of rural development, the counterinsurgency efforts of British General Gerald Templer in Malaya, French Commandant David Galula in the Kabylia, and Ramon Magsaysay in Luzon provide valuable lessons for rural development planning as a whole.

Distinctive Features of Rural Development

The following special features of the rural development process and its environment make special planning techniques necessary:

Dispersed Responsibility--One agency or enterprise generally has full responsibility for a capital project. To get farmers in a region to grow a new crop may require projects by separate research, extension, and engineering departments of the Ministry of Agriculture, a project by a credit agency, and a project by a cooperative service. It may also require activity by a processing or exporting firm, involving government assistance or concessions. Finally, it requires the commitment of the ultimate decision-maker--the farmer himself. The increase in income is thus the result of projects by over half a dozen mutually independent agencies, plus the commitment and effort of the farmer. Projects in other sectors also require interproject coordination to some degree, but in rural development the payoff is almost invariably the result of a multiproject effort.

Small Units--Within a project there is a high degree of geographic dispersion in Rural Development. The activity of the agents of the project may take place simultaneously in

hundreds of separate locales. They may require local modification to meet different conditions. Coordination may take
place at several levels.

Homogeneous Units--In the industrial sector each producing unit must be treated as a unique project. The producing
units of the agricultural sector can, as we shall see, be treated
as identical units for many planning purposes. The more
primitive a country is, the fewer differences will be found
among the farms of a given agricultural region. This considerably simplifies the planning job. It means that the fewer
data available, due to the primitiveness of the country, the
fewer the data needed. Targets, strategy, and input requirements can be based on the average modular farm, modular
village, and modular district.

Pilot-Testing--Engineers work out the details of capital
projects before the work commences. In rural development
the details must be worked out by pilot-testing. No technology
can be transferred without adaptive research. New crop and
livestock varieties and new cultural practices must be tested
first on research stations within the region and often modified.
They must then be tried out on typical farms. The administrative routines of projects must be pilot-tested in one and
then in a few districts before they can be broadly applied.
Pilot-testing takes the place of engineering.

Cadre--Rural development needs large numbers of field
agents-of-change, that is, agents of various service institutions who contact the farmers and effect the services. The
educational systems of most developing nations produce very
few people with the qualifications required of the cadre (as
these agents are called in this book). The corps of cadre
grows slowly. The availability and capability of cadre will
generally limit rural development much more than the availability of financial resources.

Mobilization of Surplus Labor--An adult on a pure subsistence farm generally works a little over 100 days a year.
Except at the planting and harvest seasons of the basic crop,
there is plenty of surplus labor. The opportunity cost of off-
season labor is zero, on the farm or within the village. A
principle objective (in a sense, the principle objective) of a
rural development program is to exploit this prime natural

resource of a developing nation. All inputs to a capital
project must be paid in cash; the entire investment must be
covered by funds from the entrepreneur's cash savings or
from the development budget. Labor has a significant opportunity cost. In rural development, by contrast, the labor
opportunity cost is generally zero and the farmer contributes
a substantial "sweat equity, " the investment of his family's
labor. For these reasons the return per dollar of public
investment, in terms of increased gross national product
(GNP), should frequently if not generally be higher in rural
development than in other sectors.

There is a strong humanitarian reason for giving highest
priority to rural development. The more the increase in
GNP goes directly to the poorest families of a country, the
greater will be the immediate effect of that increase on the
welfare of the population. If income has a declining marginal
utility, then utility is maximized by directing increases in
income to the lowest income strata of the population. The
reality of this abstract proposition becomes quite vivid when
one considers the far greater utility of an additional $100 to
a family with an annual cash income of $175 than to a family
with an annual cash income of $2, 175.

There are other strong economic reasons for giving
priority to rural development. Two were mentioned above:
the mobilization of unused labor resources and the inducement
of "sweat equity investment. " In addition, the increased food
production makes it possible to support a greater urban population without using foreign exchange for food. The increased
cash in the village is rapidly converted into small consumer
goods, textiles, sewing machines, bicycles, radios, etc.,
all items that can be manufactured or assembled within small
developing nations. Rural development creates the market
and food supply to support this industrialization.

SPECIAL FEATURES OF THIS BOOK

Certain techniques and concepts of Rural Development
in this book represent new departures.

Single-Sheet Planning

Each decision step in the planning processes recommended in this book is documented by a single sheet, an all-on-one-page tabular/graphic format. This is "planning without narrative," a highly compact and fully quantified system. The critical importance of compactness and quantification is explained in Chapter 5. A complete project in this system is generally documented by one or two sheets. The individual project planning technique described in Chapter 12 is the heart of the book. It is a technique which the author has found useful in a wide variety of activities, including many outside the scope of Rural Development.

Simplified Systems Analysis

Appendix B includes a linear programming and mathematical simulation model of agricultural development. The book features, however, simplifications of linear programming and "critical path method," back-of-the-envelope techniques, which do not require computers and can be taught in a few weeks to typical planning staffs.

Modular Plan Building

Development economics makes extensive use of models for planning purposes. These models, however, are almost invariably based on observed historical relationships between macroanalytical variables (relationships between consumption, investment, production, etc.,) for the economy either as a whole or disaggregated into a few sectors. Planning thus works from the top down. This book takes a radically different approach. It builds the model from the bottom up. Its base is the individual farm and locale. It starts by defining activities in terms of standardized modules--the average or median farm, village, or district of a region. These modules become the units of increment, the building blocks of all plans. Plans are thus built up from detailed, concrete technical judgments. They are based on what can and should be done at the present, not on coefficients historically determined.

Management by Exception

Because feedback is the main input of the planning system, one of the vital concerns of this book is reporting. The reporting techniques it applies provide "management by exception," which is, basically, fast pinpointing of main problems of projects (Chapter 17).

Cost-Benefit Analysis of Institutions

The relationship between institutions and innovations in rural development has been subject to a good deal of confusion. Most rural development projects (extension projects, credit projects, community development projects, etc.) are concerned with institutions. Specific crop innovations, on the other hand, actually make money. This book provides an evaluation of the economic return on government services by systematically and quantitatively relating institutions to innovations.

The Development Curriculum

Development in the rural sector is conceived as an educational process, in which certain subjects must be mastered before others can be handled. Both villagers and planners must learn as they go. This book provides a procedure for planning that curriculum.

Cross-Disciplinary Thinking

One of the distinctive features of systems analysis is its interdisciplinary approach. Much of this book has been generated by a cross-fertilization of development economics and industrial engineering. Modular planning, scheduling techniques, reporting techniques, and forms management

are among the concerns and concepts it brings from industrial
engineering. The modular approach owes much to "ekistics,"
the synthesis of urban planning doctrines devised by C.
Doxiadis.[11]

APPROACH AND ORGANIZATION

This book, in effect, is concerned with two models.
Primarily it presents a model of a planning system for rural
development: organization, document flow, and logic.
The decision logic, however, is in itself a model, a simulation
of the real-world process of rural development. Al Maghraby
has outlined the process of model design in the schematic reproduced as Figure 1.4.

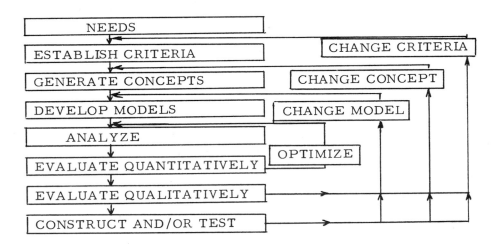

FIGURE 1.4.   The Process of Model Design

Source: (From S. Al Maghraby, "The Role of Modeling
in Industrial Engineering Design," Journal of Industrial Engineering, XIX, No. 6 (June 1968), 293).

This figure, very roughly, demonstrates the approach used in writing this book, although all the steps pictured are not explicit in the text.

Part I is dedicated to generating concepts and criteria. Chapters 2 through 4 provide concepts and criteria for the rural development system, the real-world model. Chapter 5 provides concepts and criteria for the planning system.

Part II evaluates the concepts by examining how they have been applied in four countries which have achieved some success in rural development: Taiwan, Malaysia, East Pakistan, and Senegal (with a brief postscript on Madagascar). The choice of these examples is not meant to imply that they have achieved perfect success, or that they are the only ones to achieve some success.* Rather, they were chosen as illustrative of certain types of successful techniques, and illustrative of progress in different stages under diverse conditions. As such they provide a basic test, a first validification, of the basic concepts of the model.

Part III develops a planning system model for agriculture, the core activity of rural development. This might be described as a middle-level management type model, designed for pencil-in-hand, back-of-envelope (preferably large envelopes) application.

In Appendix A, the model is tested and illustrated by application to a hypothetical region, the Southern Region of a hypothetical South Asian country, which has realistic data and problems drawn from a number of South Asian countries. The problems are realistic in terms of African and Latin American countries as well.

The data on this so-called Southern Region are easy to manipulate, since the region is composed of exactly 10 provinces, 50 districts, 5,000 villages, and 500,000 farms. The technical production possibilities and the institutional needs of the Southern Region, however, are much greater

---

*Indeed, since these chapters were written there have been serious political upsets in two of the countries, upsets which, in the opinion of the author, were delayed and mollified by the rural development program.

than those of most developing nations, and the resulting program is intentionally much more complex than those usually
undertaken, in order to present a maximum variety of planning
problems and to test the model by subjecting it to maximum
stress.

   While Part III and Appendix A were being written, all the
feedback loops shown in Figure 1.4 were actually demonstrated
in a comparable area of South Asia. Criteria, concepts, and
models were changed accordingly. The reasons for selecting
particular features of the models are explained in Part III and
related to criteria, but space prevents a full explanation of
the rejection of various alternatives.

   Part IV moves into the complementary activities of rural
development: education, health, family-planning, and transportation. First, additional concepts are generated. Then
one segment of the planning system in Part III--the individual
project planning system--is applied to these concepts. Then
a new planning system is developed for decentralized planning
of community facilities by the villagers themselves. This
system is, finally, applied to decentralized planning of
agriculture.

   Part V carries the model-building process as far as it
can go within the confines of this book. Chapters 20 and 21
present two supplementary techniques previously tested by
the author: project narrative and briefing; and simplified
PERT. Chapters 22 through 25 provide additional concepts
for some particularly difficult problems of rural development:
credit, the private sector, and that most agonizing of all
problems--counterinsurgency.

   The final chapter presents some techniques for computerization of Rural Development planning, including a mathematical model. Appendix B provides a linear programming
model whose coefficients are derived by simulation, a model
paralleling the management model in Part III and Appendix A.
The concluding chapter also suggests how both the manual
and the computer systems might be phased into the overall
planning system of a country.

   The state-of-the-art- of both rural development and
systems analysis are evolving rapidly. Rural development

evolved particularly rapidly during the time the book was being written. In 1966-67 the world food crisis was acute and the outlook was generally pessimistic. Then came the "green revolution" of 1967-68, in which the new high-yielding varieties of miracle rice and miracle wheat on a massive scale proved themselves out.* At about the same time SATEC (Société de l'Aide Technique et de la Coopération) in Senegal and Madagascar proved that cadre saturation can get results (see Chapter 9) and Pakistan proved that a large country can keep a family-planning program on schedule. Hopefully another breakthrough may be in the making--a "protein revolution" that will result in massive production of adequate protein diet in new food forms.

One important aspect of rural development that has been neglected in this book, namely research. It is neglected precisely because the state-of-art on allocation of resources to research is still primitive. Though there have been some dramatic results in agricultural research in recent years, the literature of rural development and systems analysis do not yet provide concepts adequate for a planning model. Operations research has been focusing increasingly, however, on problems of research and development in many fields. [12] There is reason to hope that in another few years a research planning model will be possible.

While this book was being written, some of the problems mentioned on the first page of this chapter received official recognition in the 1967 amendment to the U.S. Foreign Assistance Act:

Title IX--Utilization of Democratic Institutions in Development.

Sec. 281. a) In carrying out programs authorized in this chapter, emphasis shall be placed on assuring maximum participation in the task of economic development on the part of the people of the developing countries, through the encouragement of democratic private and local government institutions.

---

*Data in Appendix A are based on programs prior to the "Green Revolution."

b) In order to carry out the purpose of this title, programs under this chapter shall--

1) recognize the differing needs, desires, and
    capacities of the people of the respective develop-
    ing countries and areas;

2) use the intellectual resources of such countries
    and areas in conjunction with assistance provided
    under this Act so as to encourage the development
    of indigenous institutions that meet their particu-
    lar requirements for sustained economic and
    social progress; and

3) support civic education and training in skills re-
    quired for effective participation in governmental
    and political processes essential to self govern-
    ment.

This is a book on planning à la Title IX. The key to
successful planning is maximum participation as specified in
paragraph (a). In paragraph (b), the proposed system emphasizes skill training for effective participation: it treats
development as learning--a skill-training process, carefully
tailored to the needs of each region.

As specified in the new U.S. legislation, people are the
key variable of the rural development model of this book.

NOTES

1.   See particularly P. Gittinger, Notes on the Bibliography of Agricultural Development Planning (Washington, D.C.:
National Planning Association, 1965), a comprehensive
bibliography up to that date; and H. Southworth and B. Johnston,
eds., Agricultural Development and Economic Growth (Ithaca,
N.Y.: Cornell University Press, 1967), a more recent state-
of-the-art summary. See also the bibliography at the end of
this book.

2.   W. Rostow, "Unsolved Problems of Economic Development, " International Development Review (March, 1966),
pp. 2-3.

3.   A. Waterston, Development Planning: The Lessons
of Experience (Baltimore: Johns Hopkins Press, 1965);
summarized by the author in "What Do We Know About
Economic Planning?" International Development Review
(December, 1965), pp. 2-9.

4.   G. Black, "Systems Analysis in Government Operation, " Management Science, XIV, No. 1 (September, 1967),
B44-45.

5.   R. Dorfman, "Operations Research, " American
Economic Review, L, No. 4 (September, 1960), 577.

6.   H. Laue, "Operations Research as a Tool for Decision-Making, " Journal of Industrial Engineering, XVIII,
No. 9 (September, 1967), 539-49.

7.   K. F. Smith, Network Systems for Project Management (Fairfax, Va.: Program Management Associates, 1968),
a good introductory text.

8.   D. Novick, Program Budgeting (Cambridge, Mass.:
Harvard University Press, 1966).

9.   M. Starr, "Planning Models, " Management Science,
XIII, No. 4 (December, 1966), B147-48.

10.   A. Lewis, "Economic Development with Unlimited
Supplies of Labor, " in A. Agarwala and S. Singh, eds. , The
Economics of Underdevelopment (New York: Oxford University
Press, 1963), pp. 400-50.

11.   C. Doxiadis, Architecture in Transition (New York:
Oxford University Press, 1963).

12.   For a pioneering effort, see C. Gotsch, A Programming Approach to Some Agricultural Policy Problems
in West Pakistan, Economic Development Report No. 77
(Cambridge, Mass.: Development Advisory Service, Harvard
University, 1968).

CHAPTER **2** THE DEVELOPMENT
PROCESS: CONCEPTS
AND ELEMENTS

This and the two following chapters present the main concepts of the rural development system and the two main types
of systems which make up its environment: farm systems
and rural institutional systems. This chapter examines the
static structure of rural development, and the next chapter
examines its evolution through time.

The concepts are borrowed liberally from Arthur Mosher's
Getting Agriculture Moving,[1] which is the source of the section
on Essentials and Accelerators, and which is strongly recommended as background reading. This and the next chapter
touch very briefly on subjects about which volumes have already
been written. The concepts are treated therefore with the
minimum of detail necessary to establish their role in the
process.

FARM SYSTEMS AND FARM ENTERPRISES

In agricultural economics one conceives of a farm as a
system of several enterprises. Each crop* raised on the
farm constitutes one enterprise.

For example, a farm with 3.3 hectares of land might
have the following enterprises:

---

*"Crops" throughout this book, it should be remembered,
refers to livestock varieties as well as crops.

	Scale	Production
Rice	1.8 hectares	2,900 kg
Jute	0.7 hectares	850 kg
Vegetables	0.2 hectares	400 kg
Bananas	0.1 hectares	200 kg
Hogs	1 sow	10 head
Chickens	3 laying hens	30 head

The term enterprise is used because each of these product lines is conceived as a separate business. Farm management research attempts to isolate the costs of each separate business enterprise and determine its profitability.

The term "system" is used because the various enterprises conducted by one farm are very tightly interrelated, so tightly that it is extremely difficult to isolate the costs and profitability of separate enterprises. These inter-relationships are of three basic types:

Land--The same plot of land may be used for different enterprises in different seasons.

Labor--The same farm worker may give time to several different enterprises in one week or in one day. The farmer as a manager must select and scale his various enterprises so as to use the labor of his family most uniformly through the year.

Inputs--Different enterprises produce material inputs for each other, often with tight reciprocity. For instance, a corn grower may feed the sillage from the cornfield to cattle, which in turn will produce manure to fertilize the cornfields.

It is often the degree to which enterprises interchange resources that determines the profitability of the entire farm system. The more enterprises complement each other by using land and labor when they are not needed by others and by deriving their inputs from others, the more the limited land and labor resources of one farm can produce and earn.

Dimensions: The Individual Farm

A Taiwan farm with the same available labor and half the
available land of a Lao farm may earn five times as much;
it has several more enterprises and its yields are much higher.
Agricultural development may be conceived as a process of
enlarging the farm system by increasing the number of enterprises of a system and by increasing the income from each
enterprise.

One may visualize the farm system in terms of the graph
in Figure 2.1.

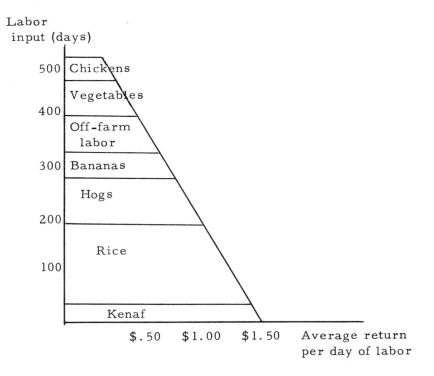

FIGURE 2.1.   A Farm System

On the vertical axis is plotted the input that varies most--the
labor input of a typical peasant family of four working members.   The area of the triangle represents the total income of

the farm, including on-farm consumption, in this case about
$400, a return of 80¢ per day of labor. The hypotenuse de-
fines the marginal revenue product of labor. The triangle is
truncated at the top because the marginal revenue product on
this farm is not zero but about 20¢ per day.

As the village economy develops, new enterprises, new
practices, and new material inputs will expand the farm
system in the manner shown in Figure 2.2 (the broken line
indicates the original system). Note that one new enterprise
has been added, sorghum, and several enterprises have
been expanded, particularly rice, vegetables, and chickens.
The average return per unit of labor has increased slightly
and the total input of labor by the family has increased considerably. (Note also that the graph indicates return from
labor, not return from land; one could draw the same type of
graph based on land input and get a radically different ranking
of relative returns.)

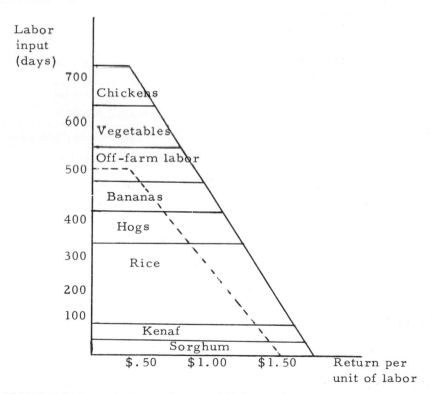

FIGURE 2.2. A Farm System Enlarged

Dimensions: The Agricultural Region

As mentioned in Chapter 1, the homogeneity of the village economy considerably facilitates planning. Over sizable regions one may find only a few truly different farm systems. With a description of two or three average farms one can describe 80 percent of the farms of many regions. For example, one can well describe the farm system of most of East Pakistan, with a rural population of 55 million, by analyzing the operation of an average farm there which would have 0.8 hectares of main-season rice, 0.3 hectares of jute, 0.1 hectares of vegetables for home consumption, and possibly 0.4 hectares of second-season rice. Farms with land and irrigation facilities substantially above or below the average might still have a basically similar operation.

There also are secondary farm systems in this or any other predominantly cereal growing region, of course. For example, there would be a lot of smaller units which grow primarily vegetables, fruit, or poultry, especially near urban areas. In the more sparsely settled fringes of the cereal growing area, one might find areas where farmers are predominantly upland field crop cultivators or livestock growers. In most developing nations these are numerically quite secondary to cereal growers, although in some regions the primary crop, coffee for example, is not for home consumption.

Perhaps the simplest way to characterize a particular system is by its main crop, its primary enterprise. Farms in developing nations in early stages of development which have the same primary enterprise will tend to have the same problems and potentials, in spite of some variations in side-line enterprises and in spite of some variations in the quantity and quality of land and labor available.

We then can add a third dimension to our graphic description of a farm system (Figure 2.3). The area enclosed now represents total income of the farmers of the region who follow the primary system. Under the solid line is the income of the system depicted in Figure 2.1: $400 X 400,000 farms = $160 million. Under the broken line is the enlarged system shown in Figure 2.2: $600 X 400,000 farms = $240 million.

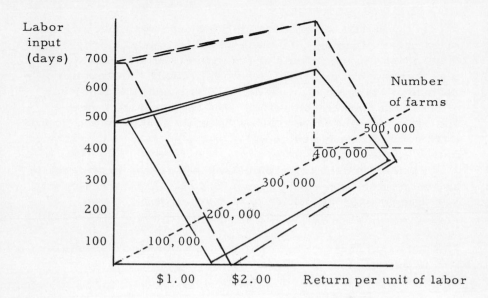

FIGURE 2.3. A Regional Farm System

In terms of these graphics, the object of any development program is to push the broken line as far out as possible from the solid line.

INNOVATIONS

It has been axiomatic in economics since Schumpeter that innovations are the basic motive forces, the basic elements of increment of economic development. Schumpeter defined innovations as new products, new techniques, new resources, or new markets. Innovations make development. No economist has challenged Schumpeter's proposition. Innovations have not, however, been a particularly useful tool of analysis or planning for industrial economies. The innovations that go to make up development in a developed society, even in the agricultural sector, are almost as numerous as the number of component firms and as varied in kind and in scale.

In the highly homogeneous village economy, innovations
are a useful planning tool. It is possible to plan a program
that will double the income of the farmers of a region with
less than a dozen major different innovations. In certain
regions of Malaysia, for example, improved rice seed, use
of fertilizer, better cultivation, double-cropping of rice,
and replanting of rubber trees will easily double income from
the principle farming system.

Figure 2.4 depicts graphically the increase in the area of
any enterprise segment in Figure 2.2 over Figure 2.1 as an
aggregate of innovations.

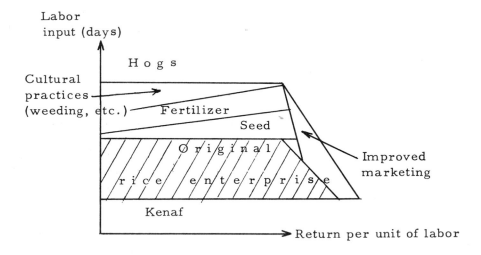

FIGURE 2.4.   The Expanded Rice Enterprise

The space taken by each innovation along the vertical axis
indicates the amount of increased labor required. The area
enclosed by each innovation measures the increased income
it provides, considered alone. Considering one such innovation alone, however, may be misleading; innovations often
require complementary innovations to realize their full benefit.

A minor cultural practice, such as weeding or treatment
of seeds against fungus, can constitute a complete innovation.

For planning purposes and, more important, for sales purposes, minor innovations must be grouped together or linked
to major cultural practices or new inputs, such as fertilizer
or vastly improved seed. They must be handled, in other
words, as an innovation package. Planning is greatly simplified when the number of separate innovation programs is
reduced by such packaging. The sales cost of each cultural
practice (and each innovation must be sold to the farmers,
the ultimate decision-makers) are greatly reduced when one
sales campaign covers them all.

Perhaps the most literal job of innovation packaging was
the rice campaign begun in the Philippines in 1966. Into one
plastic container were put the entire requirements for sowing
one acre with the "miracle seed" IRRI-8. In subcontainers
were placed the proper fertilizer for each application, the
proper pesticide for each application, the seed, and the instructions. Whether or not innovations are handled physically
in this manner, they should be handled in this manner con-
ceptually.

The sales problem of innovation must be strongly emphasized. The planning that counts for everything in the
end is that of the individual farmer. Agricultural development
planning of both government and of private agribusiness firms*
can usefully be conceived as sales planning.

One of the most important factors determining whether or
not the farmer will "buy" the innovation is its compatibility
with the present farm system. It must not interfere with other
profitable enterprises. To cite an extreme case, a new crop
that must be harvested at the same time as a main crop
essential to feeding the family is totally incompatible. It can
displace secondary crop only if it is clearly more profitable.
It must utilize labor and land not being utilized more profitably
by another enterprise.

Henceforth this book uses the term "innovation" as shorthand for: a new enterprise or a package of innovations in regard to an old enterprise, applied to all the farmers of the

---

*Processors or distributors of agricultural products·on a
national scale. This term will be further defined in Chapter 23.

region with the same farming system.   The innovation will be one of our key planning units.

ESSENTIALS AND ACCELERATORS

What causes farmers to adopt innovations? Arthur Mosher has given us a particularly clear and useful classification and definition of the motive factors, listing five essentials and five accelerators of agricultural development. [1] The essentials are factors which must be present for even one farmer to adopt an innovation. The accelerators (not to be confused with the accelerators used in Keynesian macroanalysis) are factors which may be necessary to get an innovation adopted by all the farmers of a region to which it is suited.

The Five Essentials

1.   Market for Farm Products--Mosher states that there must be a demand for the products, a system for distribution, and farmer confidence in the demand and in the system.

2.   Constantly Changing Technology--There must be a ready supply of innovations to offer farmers, proven as to their technical feasibility on farms of the region and their compatibility with the existing system.

3.   Local Availability of Supplies and Equipment--The necessary supplies and equipment must be available where and when needed, technically effective, dependable in quality, and fairly priced.

4.   Incentives--The price offered to farmers must make innovations sufficiently profitable to offset the uncertainties and risks inherent in all agriculture.

5.   Transportation--Transportation planning generally comes under another sector but is nevertheless essential to agriculture.

The Five Accelerators

1. Education for Development--This may be general
or specific, but Mosher emphasizes extension work on specific
innovations which are immediately and profitably applicable.

2. Credit--Credit must be carefully adapted to the needs
of the particular crop and coordinated with proper education
and technical supervision.

3. Group Action by Farmers--In LDCs, the individual
farmer is too small a unit to make the necessary services of
the public and private sector economical. A degree of organization is needed, so that an agent of a service can deal with
20 or 40 farmers in one visit to a village.

4. Improving and Expanding Agricultural Land--Land
resources can be expanded either by clearing uncultivated land
or by irrigating or otherwise improving land already cultivated to permit more production.

5. National Planning--Mosher stresses (a) that planning
should be on a region-by-region basis, (b) that production and
marketing possibilities should be considered jointly, and (c)
that emphasis should be on increasing farm income rather
than production.

Accelerators, unlike essentials, are not factors which,
in a passive manner, simply are or are not present in a given
locale. They are services which a public or private agency
applies actively to a specific innovation. Provision of any
given accelerator generally requires a major campaign by a
responsible agency. These campaigns must be carefully
timed and planned, like the marketing campaign that a large
corporation puts on for a new product. The seasonality of
agriculture makes timing particularly important. Farmers
can use soap all year round; they can use education and credit
only when preparing for a new crop.

Sometimes only one or two accelerators are required for
a major innovation. The rapid spread of corn production in
the Korat region of Thailand in the late fifties required only
land development and credit, both supplied by private sources.

In the early 1960's a highly profitable combination enterprise--
high-yield corn plus cattle--spread rapidly across central
Java with only one accelerator: education.

Other innovations require the whole range of accelerators.
Cotton in northeast Thailand has required all five: education,
credit, group action, land development, and planning.

Three factors determine the number of accelerators
needed and the intensity and complexity of the campaign behind
these accelerators:

1.   Novelty and Complexity--A highly novel or complex
innovation may require a great deal of group action and planning
to back up education.

2.   Capital--An innovation requiring substantial capital
inputs will require credit and may require planning and substantial group action to back up the credit campaign.

3.   Profitability--If the innovation offers sensational returns, as did the corn-cattle enterprise on Java, farmers will
adopt it without institutional credit and other accelerators.
They may find it pays even to borrow from the village moneylender at 10 percent a month. The higher the profitability,
the fewer the accelerators needed.

The essentials can be conceived as a set of vectors, lines
of force, which push the technical and economic frontier of a
given enterprise outward, as in Figure 2.5.

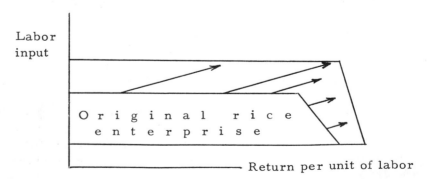

FIGURE 2.5. The Five Essentials: Vectors of the Expanded
Rice Enterprise

The accelerators can be conceived as a set of vectors moving in the direction of the third axis across all the farms of the region, ensuring that the innovation will be adopted throughout the region (Figure 2.6).

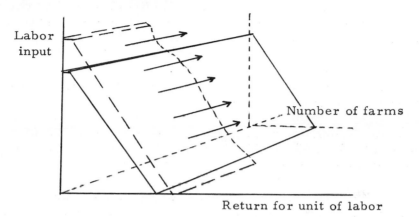

FIGURE 2.6.   The Accelerator Vectors

The Four Innovation Types

For some types of innovations, certain essentials and accelerators are the heart of the program. For other types, those same factors can be assumed as given. Their cogency and urgency depends on the type of innovation. Four types of innovation "packages" can usually be distinguished:

1.   Basic Cultivation--This package includes those elements necessary to raise production of an already existing enterprise: agricultural chemicals, improved seed, cultivation equipment, and cultivation practices. Fertilizer makes a good core element for such a package. It is easy to distribute, demonstrate, and supervise; one district can use sufficient quantities to support a variety of related services. It thus makes a good catalyst of development, a good starter for many of the development services we shall be examining shortly.

2. Basic Marketing--This package covers improvements
in the marketing of crops already grown. Frequently the main
element is the elimination of one middleman, giving the farmers the benefit of his margin. It may also include improved
storage processing, and transport, better market information,
purchase by grade, and better timing to eliminate the wide
seasonal variations of the flow of crops to market. The
"basic cultivation" package can generally be assumed as given.

3. New Enterprises--This package includes all the
elements necessary to get farmers into a particular new cash
production enterprise on a regular basis. Except for land
conditions, almost nothing can be assumed as given. (Note
the emphasis on regular cash production. A regular cash
sale enterprise is still considered new, even if the farmer,
as often happens, has already grown minute quantities of the
crop with poor cultural practices for home consumption.)

4. Land Improvement--This package covers any improvement to land already cultivated, from simple water
ponds to major irrigation systems.

Some innovations are combinations of the above types,
with all the features and problems of each component type.
Types 1 and 2 can be usefully combined to exploit complementary features. Land clearing is a combination of types
3 and 4. Land settlement combines all four types of innovations when properly done.

INSTITUTIONS AND INFRASTRUCTURE

Institutions

Behind each essential or accelerator stand the institutions
that give it its driving force:

Marketing   Local merchants, agribusinesses, coopera-
                     tives, marketing boards.

Technology   Research departments of ministries, agri-
                     businesses, agriculture faculties and
                     institutes.

Supplies and Equipment	Local merchants, cooperatives, agribusinesses, government-owned distribution authorities.
Incentives	Government price support agencies.
Transportation	National and local public works agencies, railroads, shipping firms.
Education	Extension services, community development services, agribusinesses.
Credit	Banks, cooperatives, agribusinesses.
Group Action	Farmers associations, cooperatives, local development committees.
Land Development	Irrigation departments, land cooperatives, settlement authorities.
Planning	Ministry of agriculture, planning commission, interagency planning committees.

One can see from the repetitions in the above list that many institutions* are multifunctional. We can see also that most essentials and accelerators can be provided by either public or private agencies. A major agribusiness may even do the entire planning for a particular crop.

This book will focus largely on the problems of the accelerator institutions. The planning techniques for essentials institutions have been fairly well worked out; it is among the accelerator institutions that planning methodology is badly needed. Institutions concerned with marketing and with supplies and equipment have some of the characteristics as accelerator institutions, however, so the generalities that follow may apply to them as well.

---

*The term "institution" as used in the preceding list and throughout this volume includes such diverse elements as local merchants, government agencies, business firms, community organizations, cooperatives, agricultural extension services, and banks.

The Three Elements of Institutional Development

The development of the institutions concerned with the
so-called accelerators can be analyzed and planned in terms
of three basic elements: (1) field service units, (2) staff,
and (3) program. They all are necessary to get the job done,
but each may have a different course and pace of development.
Each has its own bottlenecks.

1. Field Service Units--Every institution contacts and
deals with farmers through some kind of standardized field
service unit. This may consist merely of one man, such as
one extension agent in a district, or one mobile team, such
as a soil survey team, or it may be a branch with a physical
plant, a local bank office, or an engineering office. Generally
these units are established according to some standard ratio,
one per 1,000 (or 10,000 or 50,000) farmers or one per
province, district, or commune (see Chapter 4). Since these
units are the business end of every development institution,
any planning system should give them a lot of attention.

Three concepts are important to the planning of field service units. The first is cadre, the field agent-of-change, the
man with the greatest responsibility for effecting rural development. The agent-of-change label applies most frequently
to extension agents and community development workers. It
applies with equal validity to bank field loan officers, cooperative managers, private fertilizer salesmen, and village health
workers. Since middle-level manpower is so often the greatest
bottleneck to development in developing countries, the recruitment, training, and seasoning of these cadre often determines
the pace of the entire rural development program.

The term "cadre" has gained currency in English largely
through its use in Vietnam. It has some interesting and
colorful origins. The French have used the term to mean a
particular category of government employee (as in "le cadre
des ingénieurs agricoles"), any government employee, or all
government employees in general (as in "formation des
cadres," referring to training of government agents). In
Vietnam it has been used to translate the term "cán-bô," the
Vietnamese pronunciation of a Chinese Communist term.
The can-bo are the civilian shock troops of the red revolution,

all-purpose organizers with intense partisan motivation.
Saigon's can-bo of today are modeled somewhat on the can-bo
of its adversaries. They are oriented to both development
and politics. The current usage of the word cadre thus represents a meeting of East and West. In using the concept of
cadre, one should keep in mind both its development and its
political implications.

The second vital concept in analyzing and planning field
service units is coverage, the number or the percentage of
total farmers or villages or districts for whom field service
units have been provided. Here one must distinguish between
nominal and effective coverage. An agricultural bank may be
establishing one branch in each province, each with three
cadre. To date it may have established these branches in
half the provinces. Nominally, its coverage is 50 percent,
but is this effective coverage? If a province has, on the
average, 50,000 farms, are three cadre per 50,000 enough?
To provide effective service to all farmers may take three
cadre per 10,000. Determining what is effective coverage is
a key element in planning for the village economy.

The third vital concept is participation, the number of
farmers or the percentage of farmers responding positively
to coverage. A positive response may be either adoption of
an innovation or participation in a group activity. Participation is the direct immediate payoff of development effort.
Effective coverage should bring in 100 percent of the potential
participation in a few years. (The potential may be less than
100 percent of the farmers in a locale, depending on the nature
of the innovations or activities being promoted.)

2.   Staff--"Staff," as used here means supervisory and
supporting personnel and facilities behind the field service
units. This would include staffs of supervisory offices in
the organizational hierarchy; it would also include special
personnel and facilities for logistic support, demonstration,
training, planning, and troubleshooting.

Personnel at these levels require greater prior education, greater preservice and inservice training, and more
seasoning than the cadre. Higher-level manpower bottlenecks may make Staff development a pacing factor of rural
development. More field service units can be established

only if there is sufficient staff to supervise and service them.
More programs (below) can be articulated only with sufficient
staff.

3.   Program--The program of an institution can be
broken down into three elements: policy, strategy, and routines.
By policy we mean the roles and rules of servicing--or, in
broad terms, who does what and under what conditions? By
strategy here is meant the phasing of expansion of coverage
and services, and the relationships with other institutions.
(Another definition will be applied in Chapter 14, where
strategy is considered as a component of sector planning.)
By routines is meant the standard operating procedures of
internal administration and of actual service to farmers.

Policy and strategy can be set forth from the start.
Routines develop slowly. Those concerned with specific innovations must be closely coordinated with other agencies.

As institutions grow, they not only increase their coverage
by establishing more field service units, they also increase
the program content of each field service unit. A bank, for
example, may start out making loans for only a few purposes;
as it gains competence and experience and staff, it will make
loans for additional purposes. In our terminology, it is "expanding its program."

Infrastructure

The final payoff of development of village economy occurs
on the individual farm, with added income and a higher standard
of living. This comes largely through adoption of innovations
by individual farms. There is a great deal of important
activity that must be carried out on a scale larger than the
individual farm, however--activity which is not institution
building.

The most obvious example is road-building. Major roads
and waterways are generally built by the State; village access
roads may be constructed partly by farmer groups. The
physical facilities for marketing and research may be provided by the state or by agribusinesses. Irrigation and other
land development usually require group action.

This book refers to physical facilities in greater scale than the individual farm as infrastructure. This is a branch of development which requires planning techniques different from innovations and institutions. (Note that "infrastructure," as used elsewhere, but not in this book, often includes institutions.)

Infrastructure is defined to include rural welfare facilities also, such as schools, clinics, and potable water supply systems whose relation to agricultural development is uncertain. Indirectly they make a significant contribution. They are a vital part of the rural standard of living and must therefore be an integral part of planning for the village economy, but they cannot be categorized as essentials or accelerators.

The Interplay of Institutions and Innovations

Rural development proceeds from the dynamic interplay of institutions and innovations. Institutions provide the accelerators, which are the motive force of innovations; innovations, however, provide the program content for institutions and also the final payoff.

The latter is a point often overlooked. Project formulation generally centers around institutions, whereas development programs consist of so-called extension projects, credit projects, cooperative projects, etc. One often hears: "The farmers need credit. The farmers need better information. The farmers need water." These are half-truths. These elements are needed only in relation to a particular innovation.

One sees around the world repeated failures of institutions which were established with no particular innovations in mind. Without well-proven innovations, even with all five essentials present, extension services will have nothing to show, credit services will have no sound loan propositions to offer, and cooperatives nothing to buy or sell.

An institution must have specific innovations on which to work. At the same time, innovations can cover a region only insofar as the institutions responsible for the required

accelerators can provide the necessary coverage. Institutions
and innovations must move forward together in well-coordinated
campaigns.

Coordination services is a subject much like Mark Twain's
weather: everybody talks about it but nobody does anything
about it. As will be seen in Part III and in Chapter 21, the
innovation and the campaign are the prime instruments of
coordination in agricultural development.

THE CONCEPTS AND THE SYSTEM

At this point it may be worthwhile to see how some of the
concepts described in this chapter fit into the view of rural
development as a system.

Rural development is an incremental (or more properly
an increment-building) process, adding to the existing farm
systems and rural institutional systems. These systems, plus
other related sectors and the control system, constitute the
environment of the system. The entities of the system are
projects of three kinds: Innovation, Institution, and Infrastructure. As stated above, there is a very complex recip-
rocal action between these projects. The attributes of the
projects as entities and subsystems are numerous and varied;
among the principal common attributes are coverage, participation, and budget.

The essentials and accelerators can be regarded as the
functional relationships between innovation projects and other
projects (both institutional projects within rural development
and capital projects outside the scope of the system). Institutional projects have the additional major attributes of cadre
(or field service units), staff, and the crucial internal functional relationships determined by the program.

NOTES

1. A. Mosher, Getting Agriculture Moving, (New York:
Praeger, 1966).

CHAPTER **3** THE DEVELOPMENT
PROCESS: STAGES
AND PHASES

This chapter examines the long-run dynamics of the
rural development system and its environment, as well as
the short-run dynamics of its project subsystems. It de-
scribes the evolution of the rural milieu over time and also
the evolution of individual projects.

A word of caution: Descriptions of evolutionary processes
have a way of sounding inexorable, inevitable. The fact that
one stage logically follows another does not mean that each
stage automatically generates its successor. The fact that
the path leads from home plate to first, second, and third
base and then back to home does not mean the runner will
automatically make it around.

EVOLUTION OF AGRICULTURAL DEVELOPMENT

The core of the rural development system is the agricultural development process in which one can distinguish
four main stages:

I.   Traditional subsistence agriculture

II.   Institution-building development

III. Institution-based development

IV.   Capital intensive development[1]

Traditional Subsistence Agriculture (Stage I)

The distinguishing characteristics of this stage is the subsistence orientation of farmers and the absence of accelerator
institutions, as defined in the previous chapter.

Generally the primary enterprise of the farm system is
cereal production. The primary cereal crop and a few sidelines are scaled to provide a safe margin for home consumption.
In a good year there will be some surplus to sell; in a bad
year there will be barely enough to eat. Manufactured items
are purchased only if crops are better than average. The
household economy is geared to autonomy from the national
economy.

Agricultural chemicals, selected seeds, and other purchased production inputs are not used. Credit, used only for
emergency consumption requirements, is available only at
interest rates of 5 to 10 percent per month. Marketing
is largely through general-purpose merchants; agricultural
products pass through the hands of several middlemen.

The average adult works about 100 days a year. Additional
land resources may or may not be available, but substantial
unused labor resources are always available except during the
weeks of planting and harvest. Some of this idle time may be
used for pre-agricultural food gathering, such as the collection
of wild edibles.

Traditional agriculture is not necessarily static, but
progress is exceedingly slow without the push of government
services or modern private service institutions.

Almost every nation today, with the possible exception of
the minor states of the Arabian peninsula, is provided with
some sort of agricultural services, although they do not always
reach every region. It should be noted that the general concepts regarding stages of development in this chapter apply
primarily at the regional level. In this sense, traditional
agriculture is confined to scattered regions of underdeveloped
countries. It is important to understand this stage of agricultural development, however, since it is the starting point
of the development process.

Institution-Building Development (Stage II)

In this stage government and modern private institutions begin promoting innovations which result in more intensive labor application. (Note that "institution," as defined in the preceding chapter, includes a variety of organizations, businesses, and activities.) Some institutions expand their coverage to most of the villages. Most regions of developing nations today are in this stage, which can be further divided into (a) a preparatory stage and (b) a coverage expansion stage.

Stage IIA: Preparatory--Most countries go through a period of experimentation before institutions begin to achieve effective coverage. Institutions grow by fits and starts during this stage, many never getting out of the pilot phase. If an innovation moves well in a particular area, supporting institutions may increase their coverage. After that particular innovation is adopted, however, farmers may lose interest and the institutional coverage remains only on paper.

Typically, in this stage the extension services work with group action institutions in 10 to 20 percent of the villages. Credit and land development services reach a smaller number of villages. Infrastructure projects may reach most villages, however, since infrastructure is easier to plan than agricultural development (see Part IV).

In spite of the limited coverage of accelerator institutions, some simple innovations do spread across regions by a pure multiplier effect, farmers emulating what is being done in other villages. Improved seed for the basic cereal crop may be introduced by the extension services in a few villages and spread from there. Vegetable varieties for home consumption and cash sale may be introduced in the same way. Animals may be protected against certain diseases. Modern marketing firms may attempt their first tentative penetration of the traditional sector.

Stage IIb: Coverage Expansion--During this stage some institutions, typically extension and supply, expand effective coverage to most of the villages, which probably requires that field service units operate in all the districts of the region.

At least one innovation package reaches all the villages, through not necessarily all (or even most) of the farmers.

Throughout stage II, real per capita income may or may not grow, depending on the density and rate of growth of population. Farmers do begin to diversify a bit, and the average labor input per year begins to rise. If the number of mouths to be fed per hectare of food crop land is increasing rapidly, however, it takes a greater effort than stage II can provide to push the rate of production growth beyond the rate of population growth. Development, in effect, may become involuted, and per capita income may decline, as in some rice-growing deltas of Southeast Asia, particularly on Java.[2]

Institution-Based Development (Stage III)

This is the stage at which the process of rural development "takes off," and acquires a self-sustaining momentum. It may or may not coincide with the Rostovian takeoff point for the whole national economy, depending on what is happening in other sectors. In this stage the rural institutional development is completed and farmers push labor intensification to the maximum. Rural income rises fairly steadily, discounting the vicissitudes of weather and prices.

One might question why the completion of institutional development should assure rising innovation and income. It must be remembered that agricultural service institutions can be established and sustained only on the basis of innovations. The process of establishing institutions requires the promotion of innovations that will increase income.

Innovation without modern institutions is possible. Farmers have gone into coffee, cocoa, and other cash perennials while staying within the traditional milieu, because the profitability and the simplicity of these innovations eliminated the need for accelerators. Competition from institution-based innovating regions, however, has forced down prices on these older cash crops and kept their growers at a subsistence income level.

Innovation and investment in stage III are oriented to the
availability of surplus labor. The average work year may
reach 200 days. Farmers diversify. Cash crops overtake
consumption production in total value, and traditional cereal
crops become a minor part of gross income. There is a
shift to fiber crops, vegetables, and, particularly, to feed
grains and livestock, following the worldwide shift to more
protein production and consumption. There is some investment in labor-saving equipment but only to eliminate seasonal
bottlenecks and permit greater year-round utilization of labor.

Stage III can be subdivided into two stages: IIIa, in which
all agricultural services complete their coverage and secure
participation of most farmers; and IIIb, in which sustained
labor-intensive development continues on the basis of completed coverage.

Stage IIIa--Based on more complex innovations, the institutions and services which did not get under way in stage
IIb are launched and complete their coverage in stage IIIa.
These more complex services typically include modern
marketing (with purchasing by grade and crop storage
financing), engineering services (such as soil testing and
conservation), and medium-term credit (the most difficult
of all services--see Chapter 22). Short-term credit may be
launched in stage IIb but is frequently postponed to IIIa.

Stage IIIb--Institutions now develop their own momentum.
They demand new innovations each year in order to survive.
Innovation is recognized by all, particularly by group action
institutions, as a concrete, immediate source of profit.
Modern private supply and marketing firms now find the rural
economy lucrative and aggressively promote new farm supplies and seek production of new crops. Central planning
decreases in importance as a motive force of development
relative to local and commercial initiative.

The rural development planning model of this book is
designed to get the regional farm systems and agricultural
institutional systems from stage IIa to IIIb.

Capital Intensive Development (Stage IV)

In this stage, investment and innovation turn to substituting capital for labor. Rural labor shortages appear; the price of farm labor goes up, and farmers apply capital to reduce the labor requirement per hectare.

The onset of this stage depends primarily on the urban sector. Throughout the developmental process the cities are drawing labor from the countryside, but this draw-off is generally not enough to reduce the labor available per hectare. The urban sector, like the rural sector, develops at a gradually accelerating rate. At some point its draw-off of rural labor begins to have an impact on the farm system.

The impact of the urban draw-off will depend on the stage reached by rural development. In stage II the result is likely to be a decline in food production; the system is not yet capable of handling the labor-saving innovations necessary to maintain production with declining labor. Neither the service institutions nor the peasants remaining on the land have the know-how or the credit structure to acquire and use expensive equipment and intensive agricultural chemical application. A positive response to rising labor opportunity costs can come only in stage III.

The clearest example of the transition to stage IV is Japan. In the mid-fifties Japanese agriculture was still labor-intensive; it had been in stage III for decades, but the urban draw-off had not previously been felt. Faced with an accelerating draw-off and rising labor costs, Japanese farms became fully mechanized in less than 10 years, thanks to special equipment adapted to small fields and paddies. Silk production and other highly labor-intensive enterprises declined.

In stage IV the homogeneity of the village economy disappears. A multitude of new farm systems appear in every district. Farmers meet the labor shortage not only with labor-saving equipment but with specialized high-volume enterprises. Each farmer decides for himself how best to utilize expensive inputs and equipment. Not only farm labor but farm operators find jobs in the city; neighbors buy them out and become large farm operators. The distinctiveness of the rural development process fades away.

EVOLUTION OF RURAL MIND AND SOCIETY

Important psychological and sociological changes accom-
pany the rural economic evolution. These changes are both
the result of previous innovations and institutional developments and, in some measure, the cause of subsequent innovations and developments. The general trend is the assumption
of more initiative for development by the rural community and
the individual.

Steps in the Development of Village Organization

Four stages can be identified in the evolution of community organization. These stages do not necessarily follow
in chronological order; many countries undertake the advanced
steps before the earlier steps. The four stages do, however,
represent stages of ascending complexity of community
activity. Many of the difficulties that some countries have
had with village organization might have been avoided had
they followed the steps in chronological order.

1.   Consultation and Small Project Management--(Corresponds to rural development stages I and II.) In the earliest
and simplest form of village organization, village headmen
and elders regularly meet with cadre. At times the cadre
meet with the entire village. There is effective two-way
consultation. Some committees are formed. Some farm
leaders and volunteers are given special training. Village
committees undertake demonstration projects and self-help
construction of infrastructure facilities at irregular intervals.

2.   Infrastructure Management--(Corresponds to stage
II of rural development.) The village or commune* organization moves on from managing occasional projects to managing
annual programs. It has a council with a variety of permanent
committees concerned with specific aspects of development.
It has an annual budget which it may allocate to a variety of
infrastructure projects of its own choosing. It assumes the

---

*Definitions district, commune, etc., will be found in
Chapter 4.

initiative for infrastructure management. The leaders have
learned the ropes; they know how to get larger budgets for
local projects by working out the details well and presenting
them soundly.

3.   Business Management--(Corresponds to stage IIIa.)
Village leadership now moves up from project competence
to business competence. A cooperative or farmers association
now acts as collective business agent for the community. It
has a professional manager and staff, but the farmer directors
are very much in control of policy. It develops business
initiative and actively seeks new markets and new farm supplies
for its members in order to expand the group business.

4.   Service Management--(Corresponds to stages IIIb
and IV.) The community business complex now takes responsibility for providing a variety of accelerator services
to its members. In addition to short- and medium-term
credit it provides specialized technical services, employing
its own extension agents and even engineers. It has now taken
the initiative for providing all the accelerators. It takes this
initiative simply as an organizational necessity, to spread the
overhead of the community business over an increasing volume and to serve the increasingly specialized needs of its
members.

Evolution of Farmer Psychology

One may say that in the evolution of the village economy
and the village community, the individual farmer evolves
from a peasant into a competent businessman and into a full-
fledged entrepreneur. The peasant in rural development
stage I has full entrepreneurial authority to make production
and marketing decisions, but he does not have the competence
and the financial resources to respond to new technical and
economic opportunities and to thus use his land and labor to
maximize income. In stages I and II the farmer lacks the
institutional support to function as a full-fledged entrepreneur.

He becomes a full-fledged, innovation-oriented, income-
maximizing entrepreneur partly through individual and partly
through social action. Individually, he adopts innovations on

his farm. The first innovation is the hardest. He has full institutional support, but he lacks confidence in the cadre, in the village leaders, and, above all, in himself. Success builds confidence, and encourages risk-taking. The peasant is constrained to growing traditional crops to assure his family its calories, but as the margin over home consumption needs grows, he feels more free to grow whatever crops and use whatever practices will maximize cash income.

Socially, the peasant develops entrepreneurial compe- tence by participation in community activity, which is growing steadily in complexity. He learns what the government can and cannot provide, and how to get the most out of government agencies. He learns where to go for a loan and how to present the case for a loan. He learns how to take initiative in deal- ing with farm supply and marketing businesses and how to get the most for his money.

Through the development process the peasant develops his confidence, know-how, and basic mental capability. Successful innovation and community activity gives him con- fidence not only in himself but in his cadre and community leaders. This confidence in community leaders is particularly vital in that it enables the community to take initiative in in- creasingly complex activities. Successful innovation gives the farmer a credit rating; a businessman needs not only self- confidence but banker confidence. The development process is also an excellent on-the-job agricultural education.

The process goes deeper than this however; it affects the peasant's basic mental capacity and attitudes. Lawrence Doob points out that as people undergo a process of economic development, their mental processes and attitudes improve.[3] They value initiative and independence more. They judge time better. They become more proficient in handling novel ex- periences, more proficient in using language to describe and express reactions, and more proficient in abstracting from their experience.

These profound changes gradually transfer development initiative to the individual farmer. The distinction between the farmer and other entrepreneurs fades, and he takes on the same role as other businessmen in the economy.

EVOLUTION OF PLANNING AND FINANCING

As the village economy passes through the four stages of
agricultural development, planning and financing problems
and procedures change substantially. There is a transition
from institutional to financial issues.

Stage II

The major problems in stage II are finding the most
successful pattern of accelerator institutions and finding
some simple innovations with high profitability and broad
applicability, on which institutional coverage can expand.
Perhaps most project activity at the beginning of this stage
is in its experimental phase. The critical bottleneck is
cadre to expand the institutions.

Cost-benefit analysis and the various quantitative macroanalytic tools used by economists in comprehensive sector
planning are only partially applicable at this state. They are
applicable if sufficient proven innovations are available to
carry a particular region's institutional development forward
to stage III. The main purpose of this book is to provide a
system for applying innovations to such regions. There is a
good deal of institutional and infrastructure development which
must precede such a move forward, however. Most innovation research cannot be evaluated quantitatively. Until innovations are proven out for a region, that region's transport
infrastructure cannot be fully evaluated. Investment in education and health cannot be evaluated in the same way as
industrial, agricultural, and related service investments.

It would appear that the first investment priority at this
stage is the research necessary to provide all regions with
the basic biological potential for agricultural development
and with the necessary innovations. Of almost equal urgency
is investment in education, to provide sufficient staff and
cadre for the future. A good deal of infrastructure, particularly transport infrastructure, cannot wait for research to
provide a reasonably accurate means of evaluating the payoff.
Such infrastructure is likely to be costly. Investment in

roads in stage II is likely to be many times the direct investment in agriculture.

Direct investment in agriculture will be limited at first,
even in regions ready to move forward to stage III. Projects
must accelerate slowly. Capacity to absorb investment increases gradually.

Stage III

Once accelerator institutions begin to cover a region
(note that regions will reach stage III at different times), it
is ready for substantial direct investment in agriculture.
Problems of institutional strategy have been largely solved.
The major problem is now the allocation of limited investment funds over a wide variety of sound projects, whose
payoff can be adequately measured.

The payoff on investment in agriculture in regions in or
entering into stage III is likely to be quite high in terms of
increase in farmer income. As long as development is labor-
intensive, monetary investments are accompanied by a substantial investment of "sweat equity" by the farmers. Not
all labor cost of these investments has to be born by the investment budget; it is contributed by the farmers themselves.

As regions approach stage III, loan financing takes on
increasing importance. Credit to farmers grows to a significant volume. It becomes feasible for the country to seek
international loan financing for agricultural credit and for
rural infrastructure. The importance of regular budget outlays for the rural sector declines relative to the importance
of credit expansion.

Stage IV

In stage IV bank credit largely replaces government
projects for financing of innovation. Expansion of the rural
economy, now fully monetized and fully integrated into the
urban commercial economy, is promoted largely by banking

and monetary policy. Development planning, indeed, becomes
somewhat obsolete with the declining importance of development projects.

EVOLUTION OF A PROJECT: POINT; LINE; NETWORK

Regional or national projects which have activity at the
village level go through distinct phases in their development,
like the village economy as a whole. These phases may be
labeled:

Point   --trial in one place

Line   --trial in several places under varying
           conditions

Network --expansion at maximum speed as resources
           allow

The terms point, line, network are taken from the Chinese;
the principle has been best articulated and most scrupulously
followed by the JCRR of Taiwan.

These phases are applied here only to regional or national
projects down to the village level. This type of project is the
primary concern of this book. It excludes many types, such
as local projects and village self-help projects, which will
be considered later. It also excludes capital projects and
central educational and research facilities, which will be
treated only incidentally.

One may divide the projects to which this section does
apply into two categories: institutions and innovations. An
institution project generally has the objective of bringing a
farmer-servicing agency, public or private, up to a broader
level of coverage and/or servicing. Its end-point is effective
coverage and a variety of services. An innovation project
has a somewhat simpler end--the adoption of an innovation by
a certain number of farmers. Chapter 10 will delineate these
projects further.

Now let us examine the three phases--point, line, and
network.

Point--Trial in One Place

The most impressive and oppressive reality at the beginning of any rural development project is ignorance. One
can and, indeed, must make projections and cost-benefits
analysis before embarking on the project. One may even try
out an innovation on a few farms first. Later chapters will
go thoroughly into the planning procedures that are necessary
before embarking on project implementation. The only way
to find out how a project will fit into all relevant systems
(farm system, rural institutional system, and rural development system) is to try it out in a few locales. No amount of
engineering work at the drafting boards can substitute for
pilot-testing. There are too many social imponderables involved. Fortunately, in contrast to capital projects, it is
possible to test the entire project meaningfully in a few locales.
The tryout should first be made in one or at the most two
adjoining locales under high-level supervision. The trial
should be as realistic as possible. There are, however, some
limits to its realism. First, high-level personnel will have
to run the trial rather than ordinary field cadre. This is unavoidable; innumerable unforeseen problems will crop up
which will require the highest level of judgment. The operation at this stage must be "played by ear." It is too early to
write standard procedures for guidance of cadre. Second,
the volume of production involved will probably not be
economical for efficient marketing. It will be below a break-
even point, but may provide the necessary experience on
which to determine the break-even point. Finally, not all
participating institutions may be involved. A government
agency may have to play the role of a private banker or merchant, for example, although it may be possible to get the
cooperation of private firms in experimental operations.

In spite of these limitations, the so-called point phase
should give a clear indication of the probability of success on
a broader scale. Staff personnel involved should keep careful
records of costs, personnel requirements, and problems.
They should use the point phase to train cadre for the line

phase. A written evaluation will serve as a guide for the next phase.

Line--Trial in Several Places

The project should now be undertaken in several different locales representative of different general conditions under which the project will have to be applied. The mode of operation should be fully realistic; volume should be economical and the cadre and field supervisors of all concerned institutions should do the job. At this stage some alternatives to the mode of operation of the point phase may be tested.

In preparation, preliminary standard operating procedures (SOP'S) should be written. Cadre should be given the kind of training, including observation of the point phase, which will be similar to that envisioned for the network phase. Cadre and field supervisors should be left on their own as much as possible to see what kinds of problems will arise with minimum supervision. The staff personnel responsible for the point phase should observe what is happening in all locales and be available for troubleshooting. They should write an evaluation and fairly definitive SOP's and training programs for the network phase.

One can anticipate that operations will go wrong in some of the locales. At this stage, however, mistakes are a welcome source of understanding. They should not inhibit moving on to the network phase, if the problems and their solutions are understood.

Network--Expansion at Maximum Speed

Sufficient experience has now been gathered. The project can be expanded at as fast a pace as resources will allow. The pacing factor will now be the bottleneck resource, which may be personnel, training facilities, production of certain inputs, or funds.

Field cadre should be trained, if possible, at the sites of the line phase operations. SOP's and other guidance and publicity material should be distributed to all field cadre.

A word should be said on the importance of written manuals of procedures and programs. Many organizations do not bother with them and may keep SOP's in a variety of documents or in people's heads. The service institutions of the countries with the greatest success stories described in Part II of this book do, however, have particularly thorough operations manuals. The size and thoroughness of an institution's manual is a good indication of the degree of articulation of the institution's program and of the competence of its staff.

The manuals should cover specific innovation programs and general procedures and should cover personnel, client relations, accounting, reporting, logistical support, etc. Each procedure should be tested in point and line phase before it is put into the manual. Issuance of guidance which has not been tried under varying conditions will soon relegate the manual to a never-opened file drawer. More will be said later on manual orders when the subject of decentralization is taken up.

Project Pathology

Having covered the salient features of project anatomy, it is time we looked at the salient features of project pathology. Innumerable things can and do go wrong with projects. The four following ailments are particularly common:

1.   Crash Operation--Frequently all parties agree that the situation is so urgent and the needs are so great that there is no time for point or line phases. The project is launched immediately at the network phase, on the maximum possible scale. Operations grind rapidly to a halt, as problems arise which field cadre are not prepared or authorized to handle. Higher-level staff run around solving problems and succeed in restoring momentum in a few places. Results are meager; the operation is a success only where personal attention of the staff has moved the project, as in the point or line phase.

There is no opportunity for systematic evaluation and planning
for a continually expanding operation. In locales where the
project has not moved, cadre and their clients are badly
disillusioned.

Everyone agrees, however, that the gravity of the situation called for a crash program.

A word should be said about political motivation of project
choices. Governments frequently have the choice of two or
more sound and feasible alternatives and choose not the alternative with the greatest cash return on the investment but
the alternative with the greatest political return. This makes
good sense; money isn't everything. It does not make good
political sense, however, to choose an alternative for political
reasons which is economically unsound or operationally
unfeasible. Sooner or later (quite often sooner) such a choice
will result in a political loss.

2.   Model-village-itis--The network phase can be ignored
just as easily as the point or line phase. It is frequently proposed that if a model village were set up, neighboring villagers
would imitate it and progress would radiate steadily outward
from the model village. The proposition has an inspiring
ring of airtight logic. It is very attractive because it does
not require mass campaigns, effective coverage, and adequate
inputs. Economics are ignored. Sufficient resources and
sufficient high-level staff attention are concentrated on one
village to show results, come what may.

Imitation, of course, does not occur, because education
is only one of 10 essentials and accelerators. In contrast to
the crash operation, this ailment is relatively painless.
VIP's and sundry guests are regularly escorted through the
model village and everyone is happy because the model village
is a success.

It is a good idea to develop a pilot area and initiate a
complex of projects in the same locale and see how they
interrelate through the point phase and whether this particular
project mix makes for progress. This pilot program must not,
however, be considered a complete program in itself. There
is no substitute for mass campaigns, applying all the essentials and enough of the accelerators.

3. <u>Unburied Fatalities</u>--Living organisms either grow
to maturity or die. Institutions can go dead at an early stage
and survive as walking zombies. Most underdeveloped countries have agencies which stopped growing before they served
10 percent of their potential clientele, yet remained on the
budget years afterward. For institutions death comes easy,
but burial is excruciating for all concerned. Admitting that
an institution has failed and must be replaced is painful. It
means admitting mistakes; it may mean abolishing jobs.

Frequently at the line or initial network phase an institution shows signs of not producing results. The staff of the
institution then announces that for the next year or so, it is
not going to expand but "consolidate, " "improve management, "
or "stress membership education. " Training is frequently
offered as a panacea. Since it is universally recognized that
training is a good thing, the institution wins approval by
announcing its determination to concentrate on better training.
It thus avoids having to examine any other possible fundamental
causes of failure in order to determine precisely what went
wrong.

One way to avoid unburied fatalities is to keep institutional arrangements loose in the early phases. Definitive
legislation establishing an institution should be postponed
until the network phase. Until then it should operate under
temporary statutes, an arrangement that will permit easy
burial of mistakes. Timely burial facilitates reevaluation
of development strategy and trial of new institutional arrangements that have profited from past mistakes.

4. <u>Cream Skimming</u>--It is frequently pointed out that
cadre must work first with the leading, top-income farmers.
This is valid up to a point, but it is often used as an excuse
for failure to make plans and to allocate resources to other
farmers. An institution may field enough cadre to service
only 5 to 10 percent of the farmers in a district. The cadre
will show personal results by working with that top layer of
farmers who are out of the peasant class, the larger semi-
commercial operators. The institution will justify its failure
to field enough cadre or to provide services to all farmers
on two grounds. First, it may point out that the few farmers
it is servicing will set an example that other farmers will
imitate. This is model village fallacy again. Or it may argue

that the other farmers lack the education and resources to
make them suitable clients for its services and that some
other agency should handle the charity cases. As the countries discussed in Part II have demonstrated, the average
peasant farmer is not a charity case. The sweat equity he
brings to well-planned development projects give these projects a handsome return, in terms of increase in gross national
income.

DEVELOPMENT AS A LEARNING PROCESS

This chapter has examined a variety of developmental sequences: the rural economy, the rural community and individual, and the institution or innovation development project.
All these diverse sequences have one thing in common: they
can be viewed as learning processes, as educational curricula,
in which the more advanced phases and stages build on the
lessons learned in earlier stages.

Development is indeed a learning process for everyone
involved, for the peasant, the cadre, the staff, the planners,
and even for the aid donors. It is an education for master-
minds as well as simple minds. Both must learn step by
step what will work and what will not. Avoiding homework,
cutting classes, or taking too many courses can lead to
disaster in the final exams. The learning rate can be as
great a constraint to development as the savings rate.

All this has important bearing on certain widely discussed
issues of economics. First of all, it explains and even permits quantification of the concept of limited capacity to absorb
investment. In stage II of rural development a country is
extremely limited in the amount of investment its agricultural
sector can absorb. First, there must be proven innovations
which can enlarge the farm system. Let us suppose that
proven innovations can increase the average farm income of
a region by $100, with an average investment of $100. If the
region has 100,000 farms and all the accelerator institutions
are functioning in every locale of the region, then it can
absorb $10 million of investment funds. If, however, accele-
rator institutions reach only 20 percent of the farmers, then

the region can only absorb $2 million. Moreover, if research
has lagged and has only proven out innovations warranting an
average investment of $50, then the region can absorb only
$1 million. These are very real limitations in the many
countries which today find themselves in stage II.

This analysis also helps explain, in terms of the Lewis
model, the phenomenon of arrested development due to un-
balanced growth. If the urban draw-off of rural surplus
labor exhausts that surplus when the rural economy is in
stage III, it will respond by moving immediately into stage
IV. There are no problems of transition. Farmers in stage
III can easily make the shift to labor-saving investment,
maintaining (and even increasing) food production. The real
price of food stays the same, and farmers can devote increasing surplus income to buying the products of the urban sector.
Urban costs do not rise and its market expands. Growth is
sustained.

If, however, the urban draw-off absorbs the labor surplus
when the economy is in stage II, the problem is serious. The
transition out of stage II is the most difficult; even with the
best of planning and implementation it takes many years to
develop the innovations and spread the accelerator institutions
across the countryside. It is a particularly slow process if
research has lagged. An urban draw-off of all surplus labor
in stage II, therefore, will inevitably lead to a drop in food
production per capita (in terms of the total national population). Urban food and production costs will rise, and the rural
economy will not be able to devote a significant cash surplus
to buying the products of the urban sector, since it will still
be operating close to the subsistence level. With rising costs
and no expanding markets to provide economies of scale,
industrial profits and investments will decline.

Such are the consequences of neglect of the agricultural
sector.

NOTES

1.   Based partly on B. Johnston, "The Role of Agriculture in Economic Development, " American Economic Review, LI (1961), 575.

2.   C. Geertz, Agricultural Involution: The Process of Ecological Change in Indonesia (Berkeley: University of California Press, 1963).

3.   L. Doob, Becoming More Civilized (New Haven: Yale University Press, 1960).

CHAPTER **4** INSTITUTIONAL STRUC-
TURES AND OPTIONS

The various institutions servicing farmers (which were
itemized in Chapter 2 and which, together with the farm
systems, constitute the environment of the rural development
system) can themselves be conceived of as a single system,
in which each institution constitutes a subsystem. Rural
development institutional projects, then, have the function
of expanding the institutional system's capacity to promote
and support innovations.

This chapter will first look more closely at the standard
functions of the various types of institutions that, in effect,
constitute the outputs of the institutional system. The typical
administrative structure of a developing nation will then be
examined; this structure constitutes the basic environment
and also a major planning dimension of the institutional system.
The various structural options of rural development (alternative institutional structures and institutional project
structures) will then be discussed.

FUNCTIONS

Services

The direct services to farmers described below are vital
to rural development. Some provide essentials and other
accelerators, as these terms have been defined in Chapter 2.
Some of the essentials and accelerators listed in that chapter
are not included in the following list of services, because they
are not in the form of services by cadre to farmers.

Education--This service is generally performed by an
agricultural extension service. The extension agents may be
deployed as generalists or as specialists responsible for
certain crops only. Community development workers may
also perform this function. Another important and sometimes
overlooked source of education is the sales force of commercial firms. The sales organizations of agricultural chemical
distributors or the buying organizations of agribusiness
firms may often have extension agents with a routine quite
similar to that of government agents. Extension can pay; it
can be directly profitable to a firm or cooperative engaged
in the supply or marketing business.

Supply--The provision of seed, fertilizer, pesticides,
breedstock, and farm equipment may be performed by (1)
local merchants, (2) nationwide manufacturing and/or distribution firms, (3) cooperatives, or (4) government-owned
distribution authorities or corporations. Occasionally government extension services perform supply functions. When the
quantity of material they are distributing grows beyond that
needed for demonstration, however, the supply function de-
tracts heavily from their education function.

Two particular problems of the organization of the supply
function should be noted: economic volume and adequate
sales push. If the supply function is not organized to handle
supplies in carload and truckload lots, the handling costs
may make the products uneconomical for the farmers to use.
The function must be organized so as to give people at the
wholesale and retail level incentive to sell hard. A general-
purpose merchant, who carries a few bags of fertilizer along
with yardgoods, canned milk, biscuits, and other household
items, is not going to devote a lot of time to working with
the farmers to get them to use more fertilizer. Distribution
must be reasonably specialized, so that distributor incomes
are largely dependent on the quantity of supplies sold.

Marketing--"Marketing," as used in this book, refers to
crop marketing only; it excludes the supply business. As in
the supply business, however, economic lots are important.
Marketing may be viewed as a collection process in which
progressively larger lots are assembled at several echelons
for efficient distribution. For this reason the price to the
farmer may be less than the margins of all the middlemen in

the process. The closer to the farmer the truckload and carload lots can be assembled on a regular schedule, the lower the price to the farmer.

The marketing function has other important aspects, among which are grading, packaging, transport, processing, and storage. The last is particularly important in order to balance the flow of crops onto the final market, which must absorb an annual harvest over a 12-month period.

Credit--This is the most difficult of all services to provide to farmers. Chapter 22 is devoted to the difficulties, the problems, and some of the solutions to the problems of the credit function. In terms of institutional structural problems, one must distinguish carefully between three basic types of credit:

1.   Short-term Credit. Loans to be paid off at the next harvest are used mainly to finance agricultural chemicals and other production needs. Some special supervision may be necessary in the beginning to educate farmers to credit discipline, but in the long run this credit function can be combined with the supply (or better yet, supply plus marketing) function for economical administration.

2.   Medium-term Credit. Loans to be paid off over several harvests are used to finance equipment and other capital investments. These investments in any given locale will be quite varied; each will require skilled evaluation and some on-the-spot supervision. They require particularly competent and skilled cadre, working closely with the farmers.

3.   Long-term Credit. Loans for periods of over five years are generally for land purchase or major land improvements. These are capital investments involving all the problems of medium-term loans. Administration is somewhat simplified by two factors. First, demand for these loans should arise out of fairly sizable land development projects; a group of farmers will borrow large amounts and the group investment can be handled by the bank as one transaction for all practical purposes. Secondly, such projects make it possible to secure a lien on land.

Engineering--This function includes the technical preparation and supervision of land development and infrastructure.
It requires the best-educated cadre of any function. The service may be performed by a public works department, an
agricultural engineering department, an irrigation department,
a land development department, or a special irrigation or land
development authority.

Group Action

Group action can be viewed in one sense as a service
provided by cadre directly to farmers. This is, indeed, the
main function of a community development department. This
service should result, however, in the formation of local institutions (development committees, cooperatives, farmers
associations, etc.), which in turn perform important functions. They may themselves perform service functions.
They are unique in the following respects:

1.   Economy of Servicing. One cadre, from any service
institution, can service more farmers if they are organized
as a group.

2.   Sale of Ideas. Farmers accept new activities and
innovations much more readily if they participate in the
planning of programs.

3.   Labor Contribution Mobilization. Infrastructure
can be provided much more cheaply if the community can
organize voluntary contributions of labor from its members.
It provides a community "sweat equity."

4.   Upward Communication. Service institutions and
planners can get a much clearer picture of rural needs and
potential if community discussions, deliberations, decisions,
and petitions regularly express what the farmers are thinking.

5.   Democracy. Responsible community-level decision-
making trains farmers for more effective participation in
national decision-making.

Support

So far this chapter has dealt with functions performed at the local level. Behind the cadre, the branch offices, and the farmer groups at the local level must stand a national or regional organizational structure. The functions of this structure may be classified as

Regulation

Research

Subsidy

Logistic support

Guidance

Planning

Financing

There is no need to elaborate on the specific institutional problems of these functions. The main options and problems of rural development strategy concern the local level. Suffice it to say that they may be performed either by parent organizations of the cadre or by separate organizations.

ADMINISTRATIVE ECHELONS

The institutional structure of rural development is intimately related to the country's administrative structure. Since each country has its own administrative nomenclature, and since the same term often denotes radically different administrative units, confusion will be avoided by adopting a standard administrative nomenclature for use throughout this volume.

Administration: National Level

This is the main locus of the regulation, subsidy, planning, and financing functions. It shares with the regional level

the research, logistic support, and guidance functions. Three
types of government bodies are found at this level:

Ministries are the conventional primary agencies of government. They are in turn (using the standard nomenclature
of this book) subdivided into departments, divisions, and
sections, going down the administrative scale. Several
ministries may be concerned with rural development.

Central bodies, such as planning commissions or budget
offices, are distinguished from ministries by having no field
operations, no branches, and no cadre. Often they consist
of an interagency committee with a secretariat. They often
have important planning, regulation, subsidy, and financing
functions.

Authorities and public corporations are government agencies structured and authorized to function as commercial
enterprises. Being free from regular government civil service and budgetary regulations, and being often much more
insulated from political pressures than ministries, they have
many advantages over ministries in rural development activity.
They are much more able than conventional departments to
attract and motivate competent personnel, to secure necessary financing, to meet targets of opportunity, and to get jobs
done quickly. Agricultural credit is generally handled through
such an agency. This type of organization, however, like
any type of organization, is no panacea; its relative effectiveness depends on national circumstances.

Agribusinesses, in the private sector, can play a major
role in rural development. For purposes of this book, an
agribusiness is defined as a nationwide or regionwide agricultural development-oriented processing or distribution
firm, willing and able to invest money and technical talent in
increased agricultural production. These may be major
agricultural chemical distributors, canneries, textile mills,
millers, or crop exporters. They may be foreign firms.
They may have their own local branches or work through
local agents and merchants. Chapter 23 will examine the
possibilities and techniques of incorporating agribusinesses
into development plans. Also in the private sector are local
merchants who can play a role in agricultural development
but who themselves generally need a great deal of guidance
and often additional financing.

Administration: Regional Level

Only a brief word need be said about the regional level. This is the main locus of logistic support, research, and field supervision. Some countries have fairly autonomous regional programs; authorities or public corporations are often established at the regional rather than the national level.

Administration: Local Level

In some respects the local administrative structure varies greatly from country to country. Each country has its distinctive names for the administrative echelons. Because population densities vary so widely, average populations of types of administrative units may vary widely. Certainly the average areas of these units vary widely. The quantity and quality of cadre at various levels varies likewise. In spite of these differences, there is some consistency in the pattern of rural administrative organization. The hypothetical structure described below is typical of Southeast Asia and is not very different from that found in Latin America and Africa. References to administrative units throughout the book will assume the sizes and populations described below.*

Villages typically have about 100 families and a population of 600 in a compact settlement, either clustered around a center point or strung out along a road or canal. Very rarely does a village have full-time cadre or administrators. Some regions do not have villages; the population lives in homesteads scattered over the countryside.

Communes typically consist of 10 villages (1,000 families and a population of 6,000). The administrative status varies

---

*If the structure described appears to have an excessively unreal decimal progression, it should be remembered that some 32 centuries ago Moses appointed "rulers of thousands, rulers of hundreds, rulers of fifties, and rulers of tens" (Exod. 18:25).

widely. In some countries communes have no functions. In
others they are all-important. When the term "village" is
used in Vietnam and Cambodia, it refers to the commune,
the heart of local government. As the rural economy develops, the commune becomes increasingly the locus of services, absorbing functions formerly at village and district
level.

Districts typically consist of 10 communes (100 villages,
10,000 families, population 60,000). The main town is always a marketing center; it is often the only urbanized point
in the district. It generally maintains the lowest level of
full-time cadre and administrators, particularly in stage II
of rural development, as defined in the preceding chapter.

Provinces may be assumed to consist of 5 districts (50
communes, 500 villages, population 300,000). At this level
the full range of government services and cadre will be found,
even in early stage II. It is an important level of guidance
and logistic support for lower level cadre.

PROJECT STRUCTURE OPTIONS

Basic Organization of Services

There are five basic alternative structures, that is,
five basic ways of subdividing the total institutional system.

1.   One Agency, One Service--The extension department, the agricultural credit department, the community
development department, and the agricultural engineering
department each handle their service exclusively.

2.   One Agency, Several Services--The extension function is divided among several different departments of the
ministry of agriculture; each department also provides other
services to farmers. This results in some duplication of
services.

3.   Public Authorities and Corporations--Marketing boards, such as are found throughout former British Africa, may perform a variety of production promotion activities in addition to marketing. Supply-oriented public corporations, such as the East Pakistan Agricultural Development Corporation, may combine education and credit with the supply function. In brief, these autonomous public bodies may provide all the services necessary to complement their primary service.

4.   Private Firms--These may play a major role in agricultural development, again providing all the services necessary to complement their primary supply or marketing service.

5.   Farmer-Controlled Services--Following the Taiwan model, farmer-controlled services can supply all necessary services. A farmers association at a level between district and commune has supply, marketing, credit, and extension departments, all serving a variety of crops. Peoples irrigation associations provide all services necessary to make irrigation work. Crops such as bananas, which require a strongly vertically integrated organization, are handled by regional cooperatives.

The optimum structure for most countries is probably a combination of the above alternatives. The choice must be made on the basis of the stage of development, economies of horizontal versus vertical integration, social pressures, and availability of talent.

In stage II of rural development there is a lack of farmer and agribusiness entrepreneurial talent. Talent is something that comes with increased development. In its absence, the government is obliged to take the initiative. It should gear its policies, however, to encourage increased farmer and increased agribusiness initiative. More will be said on this subject later.

Social pressures will determine the choice between ministries and public authorities. In some countries one form is more insulated from political pressures and can operate more efficiently than the other.

Cadre Options

One cadre, of any service, can rarely service over 1,000 clients directly. Yet countries in stage II find it difficult to provide competent cadre for all services in every district, let alone in every commune. Moreover, even if manpower were available, the results obtainable from 1,000 farmers or less may not justify a full-time fully qualified cadre. There are five basic alternatives which can expand the reach of the district level cadre.

1. Multipurpose Workers--A fully competent generalist may be stationed in each commune to stimulate and guide group action and to serve as a point of contact between the farmers and the specialized district level cadre. He is generally called a community development worker or a village level worker. He has the same level of education and training as the district level specialized cadre.

This system has some advantages. There is a fully competent cadre close to the people. He gets to know their personalities, problems, and needs well. This approach has chalked up a great many disappointments, however. The village level worker is generally infrastructure-oriented; it is easier for him to get credit for a completed physical infrastructure project than for his work on an innovation campaign. The district level cadre, in turn, are reluctant to rely on him because he works for another agency.

There is a further problem which affects district level cadre in general. Education has been looked upon in underdeveloped countries as a means of escape from farm and field. Cadre with higher education (and even with secondary education in some countries) are quickly demoralized by living in the countryside and may spend their time in the office scheming to get back to the metropolis. Though education is generally a good thing, there often is such a thing as too much education for rural cadre.

2. Commune Assistants--Specialized agencies may hire assistants in each commune. With limited available manpower and funds, they are of necessity more poorly educated, trained, and paid than district level cadre. If the routines

are simple enough, and if they are closely supervised, the system may work. A farm youth with four years education may work very hard at this job. It is his one chance to earn a salary.

3.   Village Monitors--Part-time monitors may be hired in each village. Their problems are similar to those of commune assistants only more so. The routines they follow must be particularly simple, as if they had--almost literally-- been designed by a genius for the use of idiots.

4.   Village Volunteers--Programs may offer sufficiently attractive benefits to farmers to get them to organize and volunteer part-time services. District and province officers then train them in the necessary routines. It takes a high degree of community solidarity to get the farmers to organize and volunteer such services. It may work if the routines are simple enough, require minimal supervision, and do not require work at planting or harvest time.

5.   Mobile Cadre--Institutions may send competent cadre into every commune or hamlet of a target district. When activities are under way, they move on to a new district, leaving behind trained and tested assistants, monitors, volunteers.

Again, the best solution for a particular region will probably be a combination of the above options. The choice will depend on what cadre is already deployed, what manpower can be recruited, what functions can be combined, and what kind of cadre the particular innovations being promoted need. If the innovation to be promoted requires close and constant supervision--silk raising, for example--it may be necessary to have cadre in each village.

Cadre, like any scarce resource, should be used realistically but economically. The optimum program is that which gives effective coverage with the fewest cadre, having the least possible education and training. At the beginning of any project or program, however, one must be very cautious about cadre economy. Extra talent and extra manpower are needed to compensate for the mistakes that will be made.

The supporting staff options are somewhat simpler than the cadre options. Middle level personnel can either be trained and deployed as generalist supervisors at province and district levels or trained and grouped as teams of specialists at regional and province levels. In the same manner, funds for logistic support can be spent either on more common-purpose facilities at lower echelons or more specialized facilities at higher echelons. In earlier stages close supervision by generalists is more important; as the program grows in complexity more specialized support will be needed.

Geographic Expansion Options

Any new project must start in a few locales and spread gradually to others. There is never enough budget, man-power, and supervisory capacity to start everywhere at once. Interrelated projects, moreover, will have to follow the same geographic pattern of expansion, to provide necessary complementary services in the same locales. This is a difficult decision to make and at times a rather politically hot decision. Everyone wants new projects in his locale first. Again, there is a variety of alternatives, and the solution will probably be a compromise.

Oilspot or Vector--A project starts in one district, or a group of contiguous districts or communes, and expands into contiguous locales, forming either an ever-expanding circle (oilspot) or a continuous path (vector). This is probably the best alternative from the point of view of the project planners and managers. Supervision and logistic support is easy, since the project is located in a compact area in the early stages. Cadre and farm leaders in newly added districts can easily be brought in to observe what is being done in the original districts. Success in the original districts makes the selling job easier in neighboring districts.

There are many advantages to concentrating all rural development activities in one oilspot or vector. It creates a pole of growth which can develop its own momentum. Even activities indirectly related tend to build on each other. Each successful innovation makes it easier to sell other innovations.

Private enterprise is encouraged to take risks in a rapidly developing area.

Against the economic advantages must be weighed a significant political disadvantage. The government may make enemies by concentrating activities in a few provinces. To reduce the political risks of concentrating agricultural development, other development activities, such as construction of welfare facilities, may be concentrated in areas outside the oilspot of agricultural development.

Even Spread--Once out of the point stage, a project is started in one district or commune of each province and expanded at a uniform rate in each province. Politically, this is the easiest solution. It has the added advantage of getting the maximum number of provincial level officers involved. It is difficult to supervise and support, however, and it does not create a pole of growth.

Greatest Payoff First--Projects are concentrated in areas with the greatest production and growth potential, the areas which will give the greatest return on project efforts. This is a variation on the oilspot approach. If a country is really in desperate need of more food production, this may be the only approach.

Greatest Need First--Development is concentrated in the poorest, the most needy areas, even though these are areas of lesser production potential. If the particular poverty or backwardness of certain areas is a major political problem, this may be the essential solution.

Highest Bidder--Projects are given first to those districts offering the greatest local financial and labor contribution and showing good performance on previous projects. This is the approach of JCRR on Taiwan. It is particularly suited to countries in stage III, when the development initiative should be moving rapidly into local hands.

Political Payoff--Development is concentrated in certain areas in exchange for support of measures benefiting principally other areas. In the early 19th century the U.S. concentrated rural infrastructure construction in the West, in exchange for support of tariffs benefiting manufacturing in

the East.   Again, the general caution on politically based development decisions should be remembered; they don't have
to be economically optimum, but if they are not economically
sound they will backfire.

INTERPROJECT STRUCTURE OPTIONS

There are two basic alternate strategies or policies for
relating the project subsystems of a rural development
system to each other.   The degree to which projects must
be coordinated and interrelated can also be varied.

Simplicity vs. Comprehensiveness

Simplicity--Start with the fewest and simplest innovations possible, preferably just one.   An extension service,
a cooperative, and a bank might start servicing the farmers
with nothing but promotion of fertilizer for the basic cereal
crop.   Gradually, additional, more complex innovations are
added.   Cadre, training, and planning problems are minimized.
The simplicity of the operation makes it easy to move into the
network stage.   Coverage can be expanded rapidly.   The
major drawback of this approach is that one or two innovations
may not produce adequate business or adequate results to
make the services economical.

Comprehensiveness--Start with as broad as possible a
range of innovations and services.   Good cadre, much planning,
and much training and supervision are required.   It takes a
long time to move out of the point-line phases.   In any commune
or district in which the program does operate, however, business volume and increase in production will be substantial
during the first year.

It is interesting and instructive to note that two neighbors,
Thailand and Malaya, have used precisely these opposite
approaches in establishing farmers associations and related
crop promotions based on the Taiwan model.   Thailand, with
its relative lack of manpower and highly homogeneous

agriculture in the northeast pilot area, chose simplicity. It
launched 14 district level farmers associations on the basis
of one innovation--fertilizer for rice--using existing extension and community development cadre and existing commercial banks. The project was out of the point phase into the
line phase less than a year after the start of planning.

Malaysia, with greater manpower resources and a
highly heterogeneous agriculture, chose comprehensiveness.
It started with thorough surveys of 12 pilot communes and
provided five specially trained cadre to each as temporary
management. Each commune had a custom-designed program
covering all services and most enterprises. It has taken
over two years to get into the line phase.

While neither of the two programs have proven themselves and evolved into the network phase as yet, one can
say that each country has chosen the approaches suited to
its own needs and capabilities.

Tight vs. Loose Structure

One can be rigorous or relaxed about the degree to which
projects and project stages must follow each other in a set
sequence. It can be said that education and group action
must precede other services. No matter what the innovations
being promoted, those two accelerators must precede others,
as surely as sales effort must precede purchase and delivery.

Tight Structure--A program extending over a certain
number of annual stages is set up for the development of each
district, and each project is introduced into a district at its
designated stage. This is the policy followed in the system
described in Part III of this book. It is the essential approach
when simplicy is the strategy. Each succeeding innovation
builds on the institutional capability developed by previous
innovations.

Loose Structure--If adequate innovations have been developed, and adequate cadre and supervisors are available to
tailor-make a program for each local, a looser structure can
be permitted. A loose structure is preferable in stage III.

In such a case local cadre and farmers should choose the program content.

Chapter 14 presents a systematic procedure for considering all the options discussed in this chapter. It weighs the
pros and cons and settles on what may be called a strategy of
rural development. It will be based partly on a review of
quantitative data, but ultimately it will be based on the judgment of all those involved and on the "feel" they have for
conditions. There is no neat, mechanical way to apply this
feel for conditions to the choice among options. A well-
organized planning system can, however, assure that this
feel for conditions is brought to bear on decisions at the point
where it is most relevant.

CHAPTER 5 PLANNING SYSTEMS: CONCEPTS AND CRITERIA

Chapter 1 pointed out that the design of a rural development planning system requires the building of two models,
one of the activity and one of the planning sector of the control system. The three intervening chapters have generated
concepts for a model of the rural development activity
system. This chapter returns to a consideration of planning
systems and examines the concepts and criteria relevant to
such systems.

Reviewing briefly the structure of planning systems described in Chapter 1, we find that the system is conceived as
a network of decision-making operations. The input is policy
and data; the output is a set of decisions regarding a sequence
of actions to be taken to achieve a given set of objectives.
Each operation has three types of attributes: logical, social,
and documental.

There are thus two types of subsystems within the planning system. Each operation is a subsystem, an interplay
of logic and people connected by documentation. Each type of
attribute collectively forms the second type of subsystem--
the logical, social and documentational subsystems of the
planning system. Such is the complex, multifaceted nature
of planning. This chapter will first examine the main dimensions of the system, then the three basic subsystems.

Finally this chapter will attempt to specify some useful
performance criteria for a rural development planning system.
Like any control system, such a planning system has, in
simplest terms, the objective of optimum performance of the
real activity system at minimum investment in the control
system itself. The first criterion, then, is optimum results
in rural development with a minimum investment of personnel

time and talent in the planning system. Since the planning
system itself may be defective in defining optimum results in
the real activity, such a criterion is not very useful.

One must therefore step back a bit and define the main
criterion of the planning system. It can be defined as the
range of alternatives among which it executes optimization,
based on specific criteria, for a given investment in time and
talent. To this must be added two performance criteria. The
first is the reliability of the predictions of the planning system.
Every plan is a prognostication, a specification of future
actions and anticipated results. A planning system can be
judged by the correlation between actions and results. The
second additional criterion is the absence of system breakdown.
Poor planning systems may be overwhelmed by the number of
decisions to be made within a limited time and may fail to
provide the necessary outputs. The "coping system" must
then take over. More will be said on the coping system later.

Because of the complex interrelationships between these
three criteria, this chapter will approach the subject of performance criteria by first examining the things that go wrong
in development planning in general. Then it will specify the
features that indicate a good planning system.

DIMENSIONS OF PLANNING

Like any complex activity, planning can be conceived as
a network of operations spread over a hyperspace of more
than three dimensions, measurable along many axes. It has
its social dimension. It moves up and down an organizational
hierarchy. It has a time dimension since decisions follow a
time sequence and successively reduce the number of remaining alternatives so that planning must be measured along an
axis with a logarithmically decreasing number of decisions.

Two dimensions are particularly useful: the level of
aggregation and the sequence of documentation and decision.
The social dimension will roughly parallel the level of planning aggregation. The sequence dimension takes in the time
dimension and the decreasing number of alternatives.

With this two-dimensional view of planning, one can clarify
the use of many of the standard terms of planning which are
often used in an overlapping or contradictory sense--terms
such as sector, program, project, strategy, policy, and
programming.

Level of Aggregation

In this book rural development has the following levels
of aggregation:

> Total rural economy
>
> Sector
>
> Region
>
> Project
>
> Local module
>
> Farm

The bottom level and the top three levels are fairly
obvious. The sectors of rural development might be designated as agriculture and its complements (transportation,
education, health, family-planning, etc.). Regions could
either precede sectors or follow projects. Within a region
there are important intersectoral relationships to be considered, but within the agricultural sector some projects
and marketing problems must be multiregional.

Projects and local modules require further explanation.

Projects--In a hamlet in Vietnam $50 worth of geese are
distributed; a completed project is recorded on the books of
the commune, the district, and the province. The Federation of Malaysia seeks about $68 million from various sources
to provide irrigation on 261,000 acres under what it calls the
Muda River Project.[1] How can these both be called projects?

Projects, of course, are subsystems of the rural development system and may be further subdivided into subsystems.

As subsystems they should have common objectives and a greater density of activity within boundaries than across boundaries. Basically, however, projects are like a bookkeeper's accounts. The value units used are those most convenient and revealing from the point of view of a particular agency. If the agency is a village or commune, it is convenient to have projects ranging in value from $50 up. If the program is controlled by a national planning commission, it may not make sense to have projects with annual expenditures under $100,000; it may be best to consolidate smaller projects.

In general one should try to structure projects so as to avoid mixing very large and very small projects. One frequently sees programs which have a few large projects, each requiring some millions of dollars and thousands of cadre, listed together with a number of miniprojects, such as "Repair of Yakyak Experimentation Station." The megaprojects have goals too numerous to sort out and relate to costs, while the results of the miniprojects are too insignificant to relate to any goals.

Modules--A project is no better than its parts. The label "module" applies to the standard detail plans which are the building blocks of rural development activity. Examples are:

A standardized routine for a cadre.

A standard design for an infrastructure facility such as a school or a clinic.

Standard cost and design factors for village roads.

A standard plan for a commune or district level crop promotion.

A standard plan for development of a local institution, including

    standard staffing in various phases,
    standard training of cadre and farmers,
    standard structures and equipment, and
    targets and budgets for each phase or stage.

Standardized interchangeable parts are the key to modern industrial development; without them mass production and economies of scale would be impossible. Standardized designs and plans play the same role in rural development. They make it possible to mass-produce the necessary services at a price that is economical for a two-hectare farm. They make it possible to get the development job done with semiskilled cadre, when seasoned artisans of rural development are not available to service every locality.

It may seem that this is laboring the obvious. Yet one reads and hears a great deal about a customized approach to rural development. Articles and books by farm management experts recommend a complete survey and a unique farm management plan for each peasant holding. Many writers and speakers emphasize the importance of treating each farm and each village as a unique entity. Such statements have a wholesome ring and invite assent, but they are deceptive. The more all farms can be treated alike and serviced with a standardized operation, the more can be done for all farms.

Modular planning is planning from the bottom up, in the sense that it starts with a look at an individual farm, an individual village, or an individual district. Stating a plan in terms of individual units makes it possible to visualize what is happening. If we refer to "300 agents," we convey no picture. If we say "one agent per 10 villages," we begin to get a picture of the activity and a feel for the effectiveness of the coverage. Likewise, a 10,000-hectare increase in sorghum production conveys no picture, but a plan calling for 25 percent of the farms in a village to plant two hectares of sorghum each relates the increase to people and places.

Time should also be modularized. The farm and the locality should be conceived as going through standard "stages" of approximately equal length, with specific characteristics and activities. As Part III will show, the stage, in this sense, is a concept vital to coordination.

The Sequence of Decision and Documentation

One can roughly divide the planning process into three broad time phases: data preparation, structuring, and programming.

In the data preparation phase, the raw data on conditions, on problems, and on policies is organized in a fashion useful for decision-making. In the structuring phase, decisions are made regarding the structure of the activities, in particular the choice of the options discussed in the previous chapter. The sequence and interrelationships of projects is decided. Programming, properly speaking, means allocation of limited resources to achieve optimum results.

These phases have some overlap and a good deal of feed-back, particularly between structuring and programming. Many decisions are a combination of structure and program decisions. One decides to use a certain type of cadre, for example, because other types are in short supply. The structure of an activity is determined in part by the resource constraints. The structural decisions determine, in turn, the coefficients used in programming. It is for this reason, of course, that they must come first, but programming analysis often leads to restructuring of an activity in order to make better use of resources. With such feedback, the spiral process of planning goes on.

Running parallel to the decision sequence is a documen-tation sequence: data, strategy, project, program. Data here means the "givens" (the literal meaning of the word in Latin): the policies, the conditions, the resources, and the technical possibilities. Strategy means the choice of the options enumerated in Chapter 4. Strategy generally denotes planning under conditions of particularly high uncertainty; this point will be elaborated in Chapter 6. "Project" was ex-plained above. The program is the document setting forth the proposed or authorized allocation of resources among projects at the sector or regional level.

The Centrality of Projects

Project formulation is the indispensable element of the total planning process. In some countries, such as Taiwan, a great deal has been achieved with little formal planning (in the beginning) above the project level. In some cases the higher levels of planning can be handled largely by informal means; there is no substitute for rigorous working method and documentation at the project level.

One can, indeed, conceive of all the other decisions and
documents feeding into the project formulation. The data
and strategy documents are preparation for project formulation; the subsequent higher-level program documents have
as their object the authorization of projects.

THE THREE BASIC SUBSYSTEMS OF PLANNING

The Logical System

At the heart of each operation of a planning process is a
logical series of analytical operations leading to a decision.
Ideally it should be possible to spell out this logic in a computer program; Annex 25.1 (at the end of Chapter 25) gives
an example of the logic of one decision-making operation
programmed for a computer.

It can be said that the main function of each decision-
making operation is to eliminate some of the present or potential alternatives. It is important, therefore, in the
interest of overall system speed and efficiency, to sequence
the decision operations so as to narrow the range of possible
alternatives rapidly. This means considering the process
as the search for the optimum branch on a decision tree,
speeding that search by eliminating major trunk lines full of
branches early in the process. More will be said on this
in Chapter 13.

Each operation breaks down into steps or suboperations
of three types. The first are the computations, which may
be simple arithmetic or full-scale linear program solutions.
The second are the logical operations, usually of the form
"if x is true (or not true), do y." These generally involve
the comparison of data on real conditions with some test or
criterion data: "If return on investment is greater than the
prescribed minimum, continue examining the project."
Finally, there are the operations that are purely or largely
judgment and cannot be programmed for a computer. Authorized decision-makers say that, from a combination of rational
analysis and visceral feel for the situation, they prefer the
first of the three types.

The Social System

Planning is a social activity. Its participants function within a specific administrative system, which forms an important part of the planning environment. As a rule, people become involved in planning according to their position in the administrative system.

The organizational structure of the planning process varies widely from country to country. In general one can distinguish four basic structural elements:

Authorities--The legislature, the ministers (individually or in council), and department chiefs are authorized to name objectives, to set priorities, to allocate resources, and to determine roles and relationships of those who will implement programs. It is they who have the authority to decide what is feasible. Those who draft plans rarely have the authority to make these decisions, and authorities rarely have the time or the detailed knowledge to draft plans. Moreover, the higher the authority the less time he can devote to the planning process.

The authorities thus have broad powers to select among the alternatives offered them, but they must be presented with adequate and timely alternatives and information if they are to exercise their full prerogatives.

Local Leadership--The local community leaders, sometimes with the help of local officials, decide what the local labor and financial contribution to projects will be and decide how the program should be modified to suit local needs.

The system should provide local leaders with the widest possible choice of program content. In stage II of rural development, however, this choice is limited by several factors: The number of proven innovations is limited. The ability of the government and the private sector to service a wide variety of programs in stage II is particularly limited. As was pointed out in the previous chapter, decentralized planning must come gradually.

Staff--Generally the middle-level planning specialists and
project managers are responsible for drafting all planning
documents, policy papers, project plans, and guidance for
local planning. This book is directed particularly to the professionals of that group, who have the main responsibility
for making a planning system work.

Within that group two sharply different roles can be distinguished: The project staff works within specific operating
departments or divisions and is generally responsible for
drafting and implementing project documents. The planning
staff works within ministry special planning units or for
planning commissions and committees; they are full-time
planning specialists par excellence, who have the responsibility for designing the planning system and keeping it working.
Their role is to assist the project staff, particularly in plan
drafting by supplying them with adequate guidelines. They
then consolidate and screen project submissions and pass
them up to the authorities. They play devil's advocate and
probe hard for weak points in plans. They also have the
responsibility for sector planning. Their most important
task, however, is to make the system work.

In principle the two staffs are devoid of authority. If
they do their job properly, they make almost no decisions
themselves but they do influence the effectiveness of decision-
making. They determine the range and quality of the alternatives presented to authorities and local leaders. Paradoxically, the poorer a job the project and planning staffs do, the
more they concentrate power in their own hands.

The Paperwork System

Planning systems are generally described in terms of
their flow of documentation. Planning instructions are
usually in the form of instructions for filling out a series of
forms. The act of authorization takes the form of signing
a particular document.

Paperwork flow is the bloodstream of any planning
system. It links operations, brings in data, and carries off
decisions. Within each operation it is the link between the

logical system and the social system. It is on paper that
people bring logic to bear. Whatever the number of logical
steps required for a sound decision, the authorities can give
only a limited amount of time to any operation. If the paperwork system is inefficient, they may not be able to exercise
the prescribed steps on all relevant alternatives before the
deadline.

Thus the performance of the total planning system is
heavily, if not primarily, dependent on the design of the
paperwork system. Considering the three types of steps
mentioned above, the system should first provide for all
computations to be made in proper sequence, as part of the
process of completing any required document. Second, it
should speed the logical operations by exhibiting the figures
or variables relevant to such operations prominently. For
example, return on investment should be easy to spot in
final project documents, to speed the decision based on the
rule that a project must have some required minimum return.
Finally, data relevant to judgment-type decisions should be
displayed concisely and compactly.

If the paperwork is not efficiently designed, the authorities must either do staff work themselves or skip many of
the steps of the operation. They must make snap judgments,
based on inadequate data and computation. While intuitive
judgments have their place in planning, and more particularly
in coping, they are poor substitutes for proper data assembly,
computation, and quantitative evaluation. Failure to consider alternatives, failure to consider essential collateral
actions, and underestimation of time requirements are a few
of the consequences.

The paperwork system has important physical characteristics which should be considered. Authorities can peruse
no more than two sheets at a time. The contents of these
sheets are limited by their mechanical means of reproduction,
the typewriter and the stencil. The largest stencil is 14 inches
long. The typewriter prints 6 lines to the inch. This provides room for a great deal of information if it is carefully
laid out. Compact column headings are particularly important.
The planner responsible for design of the system must take
determined action to prevent paperwork sprawl. Essential
interrelated detail that sprawls over several pages forces the
reader to shift back and forth between pages.

Closely related to the design of the paperwork is the
structuring of the planning meetings. These are of three
types. The first is the predocumentation meeting, at which
preliminary concepts and decisions are generated on which
documentation is based. The second is the postdocumentation
meeting, at which planning documents are reviewed for
modification and approval. The third is the coordination
meeting to assure that all parties are working along the same
lines.

PLANNING PATHOLOGY--A PARTIAL LISTING

Unconnected Sector and Project Planning--There is a
popular fallacy that planning is a one-direction, straight-line
process, from the general to the particular, from high
policy to low-level detail. Many development planning systems
therefore start with an aggregate plan and complete programming before moving on to project planning. They start with
macroanalysis, input-output models of the entire economy,
analysis of capital-output ratios, etc. From these they determine goals and allocation of resources for each sector.

Some preliminary analysis of this type is necessary to
get an idea of the order of magnitude of available financial
resources and existing market demand for the products of
each sector. One must not, however, try to determine sector
goals and allocations of resources before planning projects.
Realistic planning is not a straight-line but a spiral process,
oscillating between the general and the particular. The pace
of development will be determined not only by overall resource constraints but also (perhaps more so) by intraproject
and interproject constraints. Administrative and personnel
bottlenecks within projects can be a greater detriment to
development than the overall lack of investment funds. Development is as much a learning process as an investment
process. Macroanalysis can determine the savings rate, but
only microanalysis can determine the learning rate.

It is therefore a fallacy to say: "Here are the goals and
resources. Now submit projects." Goals and resource allocation must be based on project analysis.

Incomplete Projects--Project managers often raise strong objections to multiyear planning on two grounds. One is that they see the development of their institutions as a process continuing over an indefinite period of time, rather than as a project ending on a certain date. The other is that they see so many problems and uncertainties in the coming year's operations they are unwilling to make concrete projections into subsequent years.

Yet year-to-year planning of rural development is meaningless. Efforts this year bring a payoff several years hence. One cannot consider the relations between inputs and outputs except on a multiyear basis.

Undefined Targets--Many development projects define their goals as "to improve and expand the services of the---- department." This is a semantically empty statement, telling nothing about what is to be accomplished. Unless the objectives and targets of a project are quantified, there is no way of evaluating its worth.

To be sure, qualitative goals are important. Upgrading of skills is important to development. This can be expressed quantitatively, however, in terms of numbers of people trained and performing new functions.

A word should be said about three terms often confused: objectives, goals, and targets. There is some overlap in the way these terms can be used, but they should be distinguished. Objective should denote the ends to which the whole development program can be directed (more income, more jobs, more exports, better welfare facilities, less severe poverty, better nutrition, etc.). Goals are specific quantitative end-points of a multiyear project or sector program (x dollars of increased income, y number of new jobs, z miles of roads). Targets are short-run results (annual benchmarks of accomplishment, x number of cadre trained by year's end, etc.).

Unrelated Inputs and Outputs--Project drafters may define concrete targets on the basis of what is required to meet the goals of a previously issued sector plan. They then may propose inputs, budget, and personnel allotments, without relating them systematically to the targets. Budget and personnel may be revised during the review process without changing

targets. Unless targets are systematically related to inputs,
they are meaningless.

Lack of Interproject Coordination--Innovations often require services of several institutions to make them a success.
Institutions may have to build on the services of other institutions. This means that the projects must be tightly coordinated
and phased into each locale according to a plan.

Project managers and planning staff are generally in
favor of coordination as a matter of principle, but they are
held back from meaningful coordination for three reasons.
First, they may not feel authorized to commit their agency
to assist another agency, feeling that such a decision is over
their heads. Secondly, they may be unwilling to let the success of their project depend on the assistance of another
agency. Finally, they may lack coordination method. Coordination is achieved by method, not meetings. Coordination
method will be spelled out in later chapters.

Two common results flow from lack of coordination. The
first is that different institutions locate in different locales
and then run into difficulties due to lack of complementary
services. The second is that institutions build up cadre with
duplicating functions, in an effort to do the complete job of
servicing innovations with no help from other agencies.

No Consideration of Alternatives--Planning systems often
provide the authorities with no opportunity to consider the
alternative institutional options listed in Chapter 4. First
they are presented with sector plans which deal only with
the economic macroanalytic variables--investments, inputs,
increases in production, etc. Then they receive completed
project plans from various agencies based on those agencies'
present institutional structures. Authorities do not have the
capacity for detail to modify project proposals to provide
other institutional options. At the project review stage the
authorities can only reduce the funding proposed or change a
few project details. Consideration of the institutional options
requires a system that provides expressly for such planning.

Some of the most common results are the "unburied
fatalities, " described in Chapter 4. No alternative is found
for institutions with fundamental difficulties.

The Budget Game--Planning is frequently conceived as strictly a bargaining process, something of a game between the implementing agencies and the planning and budgetary agencies. The operators judge their success by the size of the budget they secure, and the budgeteers play their roles like fiscal blackjack dealers, concerned with keeping the players' winnings to a minimum.

Documentation and discussion begin and end with the question of the size of the allotment. Operating agency staffs feel compelled to write the plans so as to justify the largest possible budget and keep outside control to a minimum. Budgeteers concentrate on finding errors in the financial calculations rather than on relating inputs to outputs.

This is a game that nobody wins. In the earlier stages of development the nonfinancial aspects are most important. Good planning can get an agency further than oversize budgets. Coming up with one set of plans is difficult enough without the added burden of presenting plans to fool the planning and budgeting authorities. Those who keep books to fool outsiders often end up fooling themselves.

Premature Detail--Planning and budgeting agencies often try to win the budget game by demanding exhaustive details from agencies. They require minute details on personnel and equipment in multiyear documents. This detail only gets in the way of meaningful drafting and review. Detail in multiyear documents should be kept to the minimum necessary to judge the relationship between inputs and outputs.

Premature Decentralization--"Planning from the bottom up" is a sound proposition that is sometimes adopted prematurely. It requires a great deal of preparation. At times local groups are asked to submit programs without preparation and without local leader training, local experience at project management, adequate cadre, adequate guidelines, or adequate institutional development. Under the guise of "letting the people decide," staff and authorities avoid the hard institutional and innovation planning they would otherwise have to face. The result is widespread disillusionment, as local plans become dead letters.

Instant Obsolescence--"You can't go by that plan document; it was written five months ago" is sometimes heard.
The educated guesses which inevitably make up a large part
of any plan have been rendered obsolete by further experience
and investigation, and the organization is faced with three
choices: ignoring realities and proceeding on the basis of the
approved plan, getting the plan revised and updated, or
operating informally without a plan. Planning systems often
have no provision for rapid revision. Original approval may
have taken six months. Authorities and staff are unwilling
to repeat the original procedure. They must then proceed
with an unrealistic plan or operate informally.

This brings us to one of the most common types of plan
pathology, the breakdown of the formal system. It is axiomatic in Sociology that when a formal system of interaction
breaks down the informal system takes over. This means
that planning is replaced by coping with problems as they
arise. Systematic decision-making goes out the window.
The decisions adopted are those which can go through the informal system most quickly, and these may be quite different
from the decisions which can best achieve program objectives.

CRITERIA OF A GOOD PLANNING SYSTEM

Having considered some of the functions planning must
perform and some of the dysfunctions it can display, one can
now establish a set of criteria for any rural development
planning system. It is against these criteria that one should
judge the system set forth in Part III of this book.

Concreteness--A plan is a quantification of a government's
program and policies. It's cutting edge is its tables and
figures, which tell specifically what is to be accomplished
and what is authorized. Plans should essentially consist of
tables supplemented by narrative, not the reverse as is often
the case. Not only inputs and outputs but also steps and
schedules should be set forth in tabular form. One can
measure actual results against a table and see exactly how
performance has measured up to plan; it is almost impossible
to go back over a narrative and see to what extent it has been
carried out.

Consideration of Alternatives--At some point in the
planning process, the system should provide explicitly for
consideration of all the options described in Chapter 4. Some
of the popular second-choice options should be explicitly included in the program as possible alternative strategy, to be
tested along with the first-choice options. Programming
alternatives should also be explicit. Documents should clearly
identify the incremental units, their cost, and marginal revenue
or products.

Compactness--The less paperwork the better. Only the
detail absolutely essential to multiyear decisions should be
included in a multiyear plan document. Further detail may
be submitted later, as documentation for annual and quarterly
releases of funds. The essentials of a project should be
summarized on one page, with some subordinate tables. The
compactness of the documentation required by a system is its
guarantee of on-time submission, evaluation, and revision.

Issues Identified--The planning procedure and formats
should focus attention on the big decisions. They should high-
light the options and the bottlenecks. They should also make
clear collateral actions, such as reforms and general economic
policy, that are essential to the success of a program.

Broad Participation--A plan should be drafted to the
maximum extent possible by the operators who will take responsibility for its implementation. It should be their plan
and directly incorporate the judgments of the experts of
technical implementing agencies. As the economy evolves,
more and more local leaders should participate in planning.

Easy Evaluation--The format and presentation should
speed the work of the authorities. The main factors and the
interrelationships of elements should be highlighted. All
projects should be submitted on formats with the same organization, so that the authorities know exactly where to look for
what. The format should provide a clear model of the structure
of the activity and enable the authorities to probe the value
and soundness of projects as quickly as possible. Note that
the format does not have to tell everything or be self-
explanatory. The presentation to the authorities may be a
combination of documentation and oral briefing. Compactness
makes for easy and speedy evaluation; documents can be slimmed
down considerably if they are supplemented by oral explanations.

Input-Output Functional Relationship--Each project should
have a clear functional relationship between its inputs (costs)
and its outputs (results). Its outputs should be a function, in
the mathematical sense, of its inputs. This does not mean
that outputs should be proportional to inputs. Any project will
obviously have a large fixed cost component that will not vary
with outputs. There will also be discontinuities in the functional realtionship; outputs may not rise smoothly with increases in the variable element of project costs but may rise
in uneven steps. Nevertheless, the project drafters should
be able to show some functional relationship.

Completeness--The planning system should cover all
rural development activities and all decisions necessary to
get action under way. Frequently activities or agencies are
not included in the rural development program, and the
budgeting agency or ministry of finance has a completely independent reviewing process, to which all activities are submitted after the plan is approved. The civil service commission may refuse to authorize positions essential to approved
projects. The system should bring all operating agencies and
all reviewing agencies into the process.

Revisability--Provision should be made for midperiod
adjustments. Inevitably unforeseen needs and opportunities
will arise, on the one hand, calling for unplanned allotments;
on the other hand, planned activities will prove unfeasible,
leaving budget available for other activities. Experience will
provide more realistic cost factors, personnel requirements,
and output relationships. There should be a procedure for
rapid systematic project and program revisions. If the plan
documents are not revised to reflect the realities of the situation, they will rapidly become dead letters.

Reportability--Plans are meaningless unless related to
reports of progress. Reports are meaningless unless they
can be compared with some standard of performance, and the
plan is far and away the best standard of what should be
accomplished. The original plan, therefore, should have a
format which will match quarterly or annual reports of
quantitative progress.

Teachability--The system should provide for educating
drafters in the techniques of project planning. The broader

the participation, the more education and guidance is needed.
Classes and lectures are not a satisfactory way of teaching
planning. The drafting process should be broken down into
easy steps, and the central planning group should work closely
with the drafters on their first efforts at each step. Adequate
time should be allowed for this education process, the first
time new techniques are required.

Enforceability--The system should provide incentives and
rewards for high-quality on-time planning and penalties for
low-quality late submissions. This means, first of all, that
the deadlines, the quality, standards, and the planning training techniques must be realistic. There are, however, some
problems in providing planning incentives and sanctions. A
central planning group has little control over the personnel
of operating agencies, nor can it withhold money from an
agency purely on the basis of poor or late documentation.
What it can do is let top authorities know who has done a good
job and who has not. A staff official's planning performance
should be reflected in his career dossier.

THE KEY ELEMENTS OF A
GOOD PLANNING SYSTEM

This chapter has viewed planning as the interaction of
logic, people, and paper, with paperwork as the pacesetter of
the interaction. This makes two features of the documentation
particularly important.

First, the documentation should be mainly tables, backed
up by a minimum of narrative. This is the reverse of most
planning systems, which rely heavily on narrative type documentation. Tabular formats force concreteness. They force
quantification. They are vastly easier to revise and update
than narratives and facilitate comparison with reports of progress.

Second, each decision step should be limited to one page per
project or program and should include only one table. Thus, a
project would have one sheet giving the local module and another
for the total project description. Compactness is the key to
meeting many of the other criteria of a good system, particularly concreteness, teachability, broad participation, easy
evaluation, revisability, reportability, and enforceability.

NOTES

1.   First Malaysia Plan: 1966-1970, (Kuala Lumpur:
Jabatan Chetak Kerajaan, 1965) p. 116.

PART II: FOUR CASE STUDIES

CHAPTER **6** TAIWAN

Taiwan is an island of enormous interest to planners, not so much for its working method as for its finished product. Taiwan is the rural development finished product. The structure of rural development institutions is complete. The average farm family has an average income of $740,* higher than that of Taiwan industrial workers and almost as high as government employees.[1] Rural production and income has been rising at a rate of about 6 percent a year.[2] All primary school children are in school and most of them go on to secondary school. At least 67 percent of the homes are electrified. Sales of motorcycles and heavy appliances to farmers are accelerating.

All this on average farms of 1.05 hectares! The land pressure on Taiwan is comparable to that of Bengal. Taiwan is in stage IIIb of its rural evolution, but it is not yet in stage IV. The 1968 target for mechanization by power tiller was less than 3 percent;[3] agricultural research is still oriented to increasing labor-intensive production. The industrial sector is growing at about 13 percent a year, and the urban sector has now surpassed the rural sector in production and employment, but it will be many years before industrialization starts reducing rural surplus labor.

The great lesson of Taiwan is what can be done, what can be done with resource limitations comparable to those of most developing nations.

---

*For purposes of simplicity, clarity, and consistency, the U. S. dollar is used as the sole monetary measure throughout this book; all costs, prices, etc., are translated into US$ equivalents.

THE PRESENT CONDITION OF
TAIWAN AGRICULTURE

The Taiwan Farm

In Taiwan 854,000 families, with an average of about
seven members and three employees, live on farms averaging
1.05 hectares. The land yields an average of 1.89 crops a
year. Although Taiwan has achieved extraordinary feats of
multiple cropping--in some cases by growing five or six
crops a year on a field by relay cropping (planting seedlings
between rows before the previous crop is harvested)--this
cropping ratio has been rising at a rate of less than 1 per cent
a year.

An average farm raises one to two crops of rice, plus
some other crop, three or four hogs, and some 35 to 45
chickens or ducks. Farmers, particularly the smaller ones,
increasingly turn to highly lucrative sidelines requiring
little land, such as commercial hog production, mushroom
production, or horticulture. Rice production is generally a
minor part of the cash income.

Services of the Farmer Association

Most services to farmers are provided by a local institution owned and operated by the farmers themselves, the
township-level farmers association (FA). The township on
Taiwan is about the size of two and a half communes in the
standard terminology of this book (Chapter 4, p. 71), but it
has more services and facilities of all kinds than a district
in most developing countries. There are some 324 of these
township FA's on Taiwan.[4] These are, in turn, federated
into 22 prefectural FA's and a provincial FA (Taiwan is a
province of the Republic of China), but this chapter uses
the term FA to mean exclusively the township FA.

The average FA has about 2,400 members. These, in
turn, are organized in an average of 15 village small agricultural units of an average of 160 members each.

The settled portions of the island have a good network of
roads; most villages are within 20 minutes of the township
office by motorcycle.

The average FA has 23.3 employees, 7.5 in supply and
marketing, 5.1 in credit, 4.1 in extension, and 6.6 in general
office work. Two percent are university graduates and 56
percent have completed secondary school. Taiwan is richly
endowed with talented manpower with advanced degrees, but
these are not what make the FA's operate. Indeed, many
successful FA's are staffed almost entirely with primary
school graduates, although this has some drawbacks. Credit
officers with only a primary education tend to be excessively
mechanical in their work.

Supply and Marketing--The average FA has almost one
ton of storage capacity per member, in addition to milling
and feed-mixing equipment. The heart of the FA business is
what is called on Taiwan "government entrusted services, "
combined supply, provision, and crop marketing on a compulsory or contractual basis. Through the FA's the provincial
food bureau provides all fertilizers for rice and all soybean
cake for hog feed, in exchange for compulsory rice deliveries.
The bureau also furnishes some other supplies and collects
other crops. Some other agencies conduct similar business
with the farmers through the FA's. All this business is on
commission. Altogether the FA's market about a third of
the Taiwan rice crop, for delivery to the provincial farm
bureau in payment of farmer land taxes and land purchase
under the land reform, and for ordinary marketing.

The FA's earn 75 percent of their gross margin on supply
and marketing from the more lucrative, self-initiated business. (Lucrative is a relative term here; rarely do FA's or
their competitors make over 5 percent gross margin on a
supply or marketing line.) In addition to rice, FA's have
successfully marketed hogs, eggs, poultry, corn, water-
melon, and vegetables. Mushrooms have proved particularly
lucrative to the farmers, to the township FA's, and to the
provincial FA. Supplies for other crops, sale and rental of
sprayers and other small tools, and livestock inoculation and
insurance round out the business. Some FA's do a significant
business in consumer goods, successfully selling motorcycles and large appliances on installment.

It must not be imagined, however, that all FA's are so broadly diversified. A few are, but most are in the rice business plus a few other supply and marketing lines.

Credit--Perhaps one of the most extraordinary accomplishments of Taiwan is comprehensive credit service coverage, which supplies farmers with all their needs. A few farmers in the bottom 10 percent have not yet been reached by the Taiwan "war on poverty" (see below), and occasionally an FA has a run on loan funds and has to ration credit for a month or so; otherwise the farmers can get what they need.

Short-term credit is essentially in the form of credit sales of farm supplies at the FA, payable at harvest. Everyone has a credit rating which is reviewed annually, on the basis of which terms are given for purchases of supplies.

Other credit is handled by the FA credit section under the Unified Credit Program. This is supervised credit; a credit officer inspects the farm and the investment proposition before each loan, and a credit or extension officer follows up the loan with an inspection visit within a month after it is extended.

No collateral is required for loans under a maximum set by each FA, usually around $1,200. Two cosigners are required, however. The average loan is $100 to $150. The main uses of loans under the Unified Credit Program up to 1963 were as follows:

	Percent
Land purchase and land improvement	29
Drying grounds, compost pits, and other farm installations	12
Farm equipment	12
Livestock and poultry	25
Seeds and seedlings	2

	Percent
Fertilizer and feeds	11
Wages for production	3
Materials for production	5

The FA's charge 14 percent per annum on loans and pay their depositors 11 percent. On this 3 percent gross margin they make most of their total profits. This rate structure is considerably lower than it was 15 years ago and is due to drop further now; in many FA's deposits outrace loans. The rate structure is attracting more money than it can loan out, and there are those who think that many good farm investments are not being made because the interest rate is too high.

An interesting indicator of the level of advancement of the Taiwan rural economy is the fact that it now has its own "war on poverty, " a special program for the bottom 10 percent of farmers, whose incomes are below Taiwan's poverty line of $180 a year and generally farm less than 0.3 hectares.[5] Under a spreading program, the small agricultural unit undertakes to assist a few of its members who are below the poverty line each year, guaranteeing a sizable loan for them and supervising them closely. The loan is usually for a hog or poultry enterprise, which can provide an adequate income on very little land. Extension agents and village farm leaders give the recipient almost daily supervision as the enterprise gets under way.

Extension--In Taiwan the extension agents are employed by the farmers themselves through their FA's; the government subsidizes about 35 percent of the extension expenses. The FA runs some township-level demonstration field days and contests, but the main locus of extension activity is the small agricultural unit, which organizes discussion groups, demonstration plots, contests, and distribution of improved seed.

In addition to working with these groups on demonstration of improved practices, extension agents work directly with farmers on new enterprises, particularly those under contract or package programs. Farmers interested in getting into such enterprises as bananas, mushrooms, asparagus, or

commercial hog or poultry production file applications. The
extension agent then checks their farm and its suitability and
the quantity and quality of land available. He lays out the
specifications and precise location of the new enterprise and
visits the farmer regularly after the loan is approved to provide guidance in getting the new enterprise started.

Other Local Services

Other Cooperatives--Alongside the FA's there are
special-purpose cooperatives, particularly for certain fruits
and vegetables. Perhaps the largest are the banana cooperatives, which handle banana distribution in a tightly integrated
vertical structure. The area of each local unit will differ
considerable from regular administrative boundaries, following the optimum limits of coverage of one local unit to the
growers. The banana cooperative structure in particular has
considerably increased the price to the growers. These
cooperatives provide production supplies in addition to marketing the crop.

Irrigation is managed by people's irrigation societies,
watershed-wide units which maintain the water distribution
system, determine the distribution of water to the farmers,
and collect water fees.

Government Monopolies--Credit, supply, and marketing
for several crops is provided by large government-owned
processing monopolies. The largest is the Taiwan Sugar
Corporation. There is also the Taiwan Pineapple Corporation, Taiwan Tea Corporation, and Taiwan Tobacco and Wine
Monopoly Bureau. The last-named works through the FA's,
but the others have their own field agents, contracting with
the farmers. They also have their own extension agents.

Private Firms--The comprehensive role of the government and cooperative sectors, far from shutting out private
agricultural services, has stimulated private efforts. Much
of the rice is milled and marketed by private firms. Private
farm supply stores, such as one rarely sees in market towns
in developing nations, do a thriving business, particularly on
specialized fertilizers and pesticides and farm tools. Some

FA's have gone out of these lines when private competition
eliminated their profit.

Supply and marketing of certain crops, particularly
vegetables, is dominated by private firms. The provincial
FA battled in vain to capture the asparagus market, but the
private firms were able to offer the farmers a better deal
for their crop. These private firms provide the farmer with
his farm supplies on contract and often employ extension agents.

THE EVOLUTION OF TAIWAN
RURAL DEVELOPMENT

Taiwan's rural development is now at the end of a long
road. It has been on that road a long time. Indeed, serious
intensive development of peasant agriculture probably had a
longer history on Taiwan than in any other developing country.

The Japanese Occupation (1895-1945)

The Japanese were determined to turn Taiwan into a major
source of food for their crowded, rapidly industrializing islands.
Farmer associations (FA's) modeled on those in Japan were
organized at the prefectural level in the first decade of the
century; cooperatives were organized in the next decade.
By the 1930's every township had its cooperative and FA,
generally managed by Japanese. There were extention agents
in practically every village. The Japanese stressed use of
improved seed, agrichemicals, rotation practices, and new
crops such as sugar, sweet potatoes, and jute. From 1924
to 1938 a vast irrigation network was built, along with roads
and schools. About 77 percent of the children went to primary
school.[6]
The Japanese held the Taiwanese in a state of helotry,
however. All responsible positions were reserved to the
Japanese. The Taiwanese lived close to subsistence. Very
few received more than a primary education. After about
two decades Japanese profits from the island were exceeding
new investments.

With World War II the provision of supplies were inter-
rupted, transportation was disrupted, and finally the Japanese
management and the Japanese market disappeared. Production and income nosedived.

Chinese Recovery and Reform (1946-1953)

The first years of Chinese postwar sovereignty over the
island were dominated by major reforms.

The story begins on the Chinese mainland, where the Joint
Commission on Rural Reconstruction (JCRR) was organized
in the fall of 1948. The Chinese and American governments
endowed it with a broad charter for rural development and
channeled into it all development funds for the rural sector.
Its five commissioners, Chinese and American, had a high
degree of autonomy. Subject to broad program approval by
the two governments, they could hire and fire on their own
terms employees of either nationality, and they could write
project agreements with government or cooperative agencies
at any echelon. After 10 months of operation with some success in a few provinces of the mainland, JCRR moved to
Taipei.

There the first order of business was land reform, which
moved forward in three successive stages. [7] The first,
launched in 1949, was limitation of rent to 37.5 percent of
the value of the crop. Then about 60,000 hectares of public
land were sold to landless farmers. Finally the land-to-the-
tiller program was launched in 1953, compulsorily purchasing
about 150,000 hectares of land and reselling it to 240,000
tenant families. Landlords received land bonds, payable in
rice as a hedge against inflation, and government enterprise
stocks. With this the basic character of farming on the island
changed from sharecropping to operator tenure, and many
new investments were made feasible and attractive to the
farmers.

The second reform was in farmer organization. The
FA's and cooperatives were dominated by local businessmen;
they lacked the capital, the management, and the motivation
to serve farmers. On the basis of a report by Professor D. A.

Anderson of Cornell, the FA's and cooperatives were consolidated and reorganized. The reform stressed two principles:

1.   Farmer Ownership--Voting membership was limited
to those deriving at least 50 percent of their income from
farming.

2. Separation of Ability and Authority -- Management was
entrusted to a professional general manager and staff, hired
by the FA board of directors and answerable to it.

By 1953 the basic reforms were under way, the economy
had reached its prewar level, and the stage was set for rapid
growth.

Productivity Growth (1953-1965)

With an increase of total crop area of less than 1 percent
a year and a growing population, the amount of land per farm
employee was dropping steadily. Before the war it had been
a bit under 1 hectare. In 1952 it was down to 0.49 hectares;
in the midsixties it leveled off at about 0.44 hectares. Yet
during this period productivity per employee doubled. An
annual increase of production and income of about 6 percent
was sustained.

The main increases in production were due to higher
yields; the yields on most crops rose impressively, due to
improved seed (the product of intensive research), improved
practices, and greater inputs of agricultural chemicals. The
fertilizer application per hectare of rice rose from 461 to
853 kilos. There was also considerable diversification and
transfer of marginal rice lands to other crops. Investment
in agriculture during this period amounted to $360 million.
A third of this went into water resource development, and the
rest was widely scattered.

FA's underwent further evolution. They doubled their
warehouse capacity to handle the increased productivity and
their credit outstanding rose from $1 to $50 million. Supervised credit was introduced in the late 1950's. Starting in
the midfifties extension officers were transferred to the FA's.

Integrated livestock programs were launched in the early 1960's. Commercial hog operation, mushrooms, asparagus, citrus, bananas, onions, and other new sidelines enabled farmers with very little land to make a comfortable living. Commercial poultry operation is just getting started.

In 1965 the American aid program was terminated, an important milestone in Taiwan's development. Some continuing sales of Public Law 480 commodities now sustain the JCRR program, currently running about $8 million a year.

The Current Strategy (1964-1974)

Ten-year projections, based on a conservative anticipation of about 4 percent annual growth, follow these main lines of strategy:

Land--Increases must come from marginal lands.

1.   Upland slopes. The island has relatively substantial upland slope areas that can be suited to some horticultural crops where the soil is good and to pasturage. Much conservation work must be done.

2.   Tidelands and riverbeds. With fairly substantial investments these lands can be adapted to crops requiring minimal soil conditions.

Rice--The current emphasis is on complete package demonstrations.

Multiple Cropping--Relay cropping and adaptation of varieties with shorter growing seasons is being pushed. Oil and feed crops are stressed.

Rural Sidelines--Entrepreneurial concentration on sideline activities, such as commercial hog production which has already been extended, is stressed. Farmers are encouraged to step up from garden and barnyard to commercial-scale activity based on purchased feed. Poultry and dairy production are promoted.

Cooperative Farming--Joint seedbeds, equipment use, and pest control can utilize farm labor more efficiently.

Rural Industries--Attempts will be made to move packing and processing closer to the farmer.

Food Technology--Freezing and other new processing methods are being supported to further upgrade the quality of Taiwan's exports.

Family-Planning--The birthrate has already been reduced. The target is 600,000 loop insertions by 1970.

Research--All the above activities will require increased research effort to achieve new heights of production efficiency in a developing nation. [8]

THE PLANNING AND INNOVATION PROMOTION SYSTEM

Taiwan has an efficient system of planning and promotion of innovations from the level of multiyear national development plans to the level of village farmer discussion groups. It can perhaps best be understood in terms of the roles and relationships of what the author considers to be the two key figures in the process, the JCRR specialist and the FA manager.

The Function of the JCRR Specialist

The Sino-American Joint Commission on Rural Reconstruction is a combination assistance donor agency and planning board. Under the direction of six commissioners, one of whom is an American at present, 120 specialists carry out a variety of planning and project management roles.

The organizational structure is simple. Technical specialists are organized in two types of divisions, those concerned with production--plant, animal, forestry, fisheries-- and those concerned with services--credit, irrigation, health, and farmer services. Technical specialists may be U. S. or Chinese; at present all are Chinese. JCRR has its own pay scale unrelated to those of the host governments. Salaries are

modest but high enough to command the best talent on Taiwan
in specialized fields. An engineer with a master's degree
and five years' experience makes about $100 a month.

Within a well-disciplined structure of project planning
and management, a specialist has wide latitude of operation
and plays a variety of roles. If the internal structure of
JCRR is simple, its external relationships are exceedingly
complex. It finances projects with government and cooperative agencies at all possible echelons and also with universi-
ties and private firms. The specialist's work occupies him
at the office, in conference in Taipei, and in villages and
offices throughout the island. He spends a good deal of time
consulting with farm dealers, FA managers, and government
officials at all echelons. To put it bluntly, he has a wide
latitude to wheel and deal within the discipline of a good planning system. He is in touch with the farmers and in touch
with all the decision-makers.

Development Planning--The committees and working
groups which do the planning of the rural sector of the Taiwan
economy are made up of JCRR specialists.

Taiwan now has a complete planning system, including
long-range econometric models, five-year development plans
updated annually, and annual production plans which are taken
quite seriously. This highly sophisticated plan structure was
built up gradually; initially the emphasis was on high-quality
project plans.

The man who is the specialist at JCRR on, let us say,
corn production, would draft the five-year plan for corn. He
would project production goals and set forth the measures
necessary to achieve these goals. The final plan documents
contain only a descriptive listing of the measures necessary,
but the working papers and the annual food plan contain full
quantification.

The overall planning work is under the Agricultural Production Planning Committee (APPC) of the Council for International Economic Cooperation and Development. The
Committee includes top-rank agricultural officials and senior
specialists. One of the JCRR commissioners serves as the
Committee's convener, and the JCRR Office of Planning and

Programming serves as its secretariat. The specialist does his drafting (including the projections of the econometric long-term model) under APPC policy, technical, and financial guidance.

Under the APPC eight working groups review and revise subsector plans. These working groups include a variety of government, university, public and private enterprise, and foreign advisory personalities. The JCRR Program Office compiles and coordinates the subsector plans, evaluating them in relation to market prospects and complementary subsectors, and reduces them as necessary to match the total financial requirements to total expected financial resources. All this is then reviewed by a variety of committees and then submitted for approval to the national and provincial governments, particularly the provincial assembly.

A word should be said about the participating agencies. The Provincial Department of Agriculture and Forestry (PDAF) has main responsibility for research and for extension guidance and training, as well as for agricultural administration and regulation. The Provincial Food Bureau is concerned with economic measures such as market stabilization, fertilizer allocation, and foodstuffs and feed distribution. Irrigation comes under the Provincial Water Conservancy Bureau. Other concerned agencies are the Provincial Land Bureau, the Land Bank, the Cooperative Bank, public enterprises, farmers organizations, and agricultural colleges. All are involved in the planning and all may receive JCRR loans and grants.

Annual Production Planning--The JCRR staff has a major role in the annual target setting and programming of the Provincial Food Bureau. These are discussed at a series of provincial conferences. The targets are then broken down by prefecture and discussed at prefectural conferences. There they are broken down by township and discussed at township conferences. These echeloned production conferences provide effective two-way planning communication.

The Provincial Agricultural Budget--Over half the annual investment in agriculture comes from the provincial budget. JCRR provides another 8-9 percent and the rest comes from the private sector, including the growing deposits of FA

members. Provincial officials generally look to the JCRR
specialists to play a role in drafting the agriculture budget,
knowing they are properly insulated from political pressures
and are knowledgeable authorities in their fields. The specialists, in turn, get most of the budget detail by consultation
with budget and technical officials. Each measure, set forth
in purely descriptive terms in the five-year plan, becomes
one paragraph in the provincial food plan and a one-line item
in the provincial budget.

The budget then goes through the provincial assembly and
often comes out quite different from what it was when submitted.

JCRR Program Formulation--The program of JCRR itself
is designed to complement the regular government annual budgets and guide the overall development program in a manner
roughly similar to that of a major aid donor mission. It tries
to use limited funds to gain maximum leverage over the total
development program. It promotes activities in areas that
have been neglected in the regular budgets. It finances
initiatives not suited to the regular budget because they are in
the early pilot stage. It structures its program to stimulate
government and local cooperative and private spending in de-
sirable directions. Its objectives, main lines of action, and
budget by subsector is submitted annually for government
approval.

JCRR Project Formulation--Within the framework of the
policies, objectives, courses of action, and budget of the program for his field contained in the annual program submission,
the specialist formulates specific projects. JCRR, with a
Program Office staff of nine, including clerks, operates about
250 projects. It maintains a steady level of projects, each
year phasing out some 50 or 60 and adding about the same
number. A field such as corn production might have six or
eight separate projects. One project might be with a university or research institute. Another might be with the Provincial Food Bureau. Another might be with three county
FA's. Another might be with over 200 township FA's.

In the process of managing previous-year projects, the
specialist is constantly in touch with a wide variety of project
sponsoring agencies. When he visits them to discuss current
project operations, he informally discusses future plans.

Corn production, for example, has been largely a JCRR concern. JCRR identified a need to replace feed imports with
domestic production, but it recognized the need to develop
varieties and cultivation practices suited to the unique intensive agriculture of the island. Like most JCRR innovations,
this one started with research grants, then grants were added
for adaptation and regional demonstration, followed by projects with prefectural and township FA's for pilot (and later
mass) demonstrations. In large measure the corn specialist
has had to be a salesman, presenting the opportunity to local
FA's, hoping that suitable FA's would respond with a substantial self-help contribution.

In some cases the initiative has come from the farmers
themselves. The livestock insurance program germinated in
the discussion groups of the farmers and then in spontaneous
requests to JCRR for assistance.

The detailed design of projects, particularly the relative
inputs of JCRR and the sponsoring agencies, thus grows
largely out of informal discussions. On the basis of these,
the specialist drafts project agreements. They are generally
standard for all sponsoring agencies of one project, with a
few minor individual variations.

Project drafting actually starts while the program submission is being drafted and submitted for approval. Proposed projects are advertised widely, by informal and
sometimes formal means. Those sponsoring agencies showing the most interest, the most suitability, the most competence, and the most substantial financial contribution get the
project. Ten out of 30 interested FA's might be given JCRR
assistance in a particular activity in the so-called line (or
secondary) phase of a project (see Chapter 3, p. 58).

Project Management--One of the unique features of JCRR
is its application of capital project financial management to
rural development. First, programs are, in effect, based on
detailed feasibility studies. Proposals are subject to critical
review of engineers and economists. Where applicable, releases are often contingent on completion of engineering or on
submission of detailed plans. Project agreements often set
up specific conditions for phased release of funds. Releases
are paced to the amount of work actually performed.

The JCRR specialist thus has a good deal of leverage in
maintaining project discipline. Sponsoring agencies are re-
ceptive to his advice on problems of project implementation.
Some of the larger projects, much as the Unified Credit
Project, have several field agents under the specialist managing the project.

Sponsoring agencies are constrained to perform well on
JCRR projects for two reasons. First, succeeding releases
on the project depend on their performance. Second, awards
of future projects depend on their performance on current
projects. Ordinary budget or planning offices do not have
this leverage; they cannot refuse future projects to a ministry
because it has not performed. JCRR can live without
project participation by 10 or 20 of the 324 FA's; it can refuse
projects to an FA which has not performed, and every FA
knows it.

The Role of the FA Manager

Taiwan has, in the farmers association, a local point of
development initiative complementing the central initiative
from JCRR: The FA manager thus becomes the second key
personality in the total rural development system.

The Local Decision Environment--The annual general
meeting of the FA elects members of the 11 to 21 man board
to staggered four-year terms. It also elects and dismisses
the manager, but he generally looks to the board as his direct
bosses. They are concerned with FA profits and also with FA
services to farmers, but since services are heavily dependent
on profits, the enterprise is almost as profit-oriented as a
private business.

The FA works within a framework of comprehensive regulation. The Provincial Department of Agriculture and Forestry
(PDAF) has issued about seven volumes of regulations and
standard operating procedures; Chinese is a very compact
means of written communication; in English the regulations
would fill several more volumes. FA's are frequently inspected by PDAF and by the provincial FA. They are required to submit a comprehensive annual report and annual

plan in matching formats. These documents run over 100
pages and give budgets and operational targets in great detail.
The extension section, for example, has a subsection on each
crop, with all the details on planned demonstrations, training
and discussion sessions, and other activities, and budgets
for each activity.

Within this framework it is the manager who makes the
operation go. He is the full time entrepreneur. His section
chiefs can generally run their operations with little routine
supervision. A good manager devotes much of his time to
seeking new business, and to seeking PDAF and JCRR aid
for new activities. Most of the new business must come
from the farmers' adoption of new innovations.

The FA manager thus has a unique entrepreneurial
interest in rural development. No other business manager
in the world has such full control over all the agricultural
services in his locale. What the FA extension section promotes makes money for its supply, marketing, and credit
services. The prize example of this is the Integrated Hog
Program, which gives the FA seven sources of income:
credit, sale of purebred sows, stud fees, sale of feed blended
in-house, inoculation fees, insurance fees, and marketing.

The extension service, then, is the FA manager's sales
force. The author found a fairly good correlation in the FA's
he examined between the number of extension agents per
thousand farmers and the percentage of members applying
for loans in a year. Experts at JCRR confirmed his observation. The denser the extension coverage, the more farmers
making innovations and borrowing money. One should remember that the credit service is the main source of income
for the FA's. The author found one FA with particularly
light extension coverage whose loans were falling so far behind its deposits that it was in danger of not earning enough
interest to pay its depositors.

Diversity within Regulations--As noted above, FA's are
tightly regulated and guided. All FA's use the same formats,
keep the same books, and follow the same standard operating
procedures. Yet within this standardization of operating procedures, the FA's show remarkable diversity.

The author had the opportunity to examine four FA's in
depth. Only one was operating a significant consumer goods
business; that FA was stressing consumer goods services
as the most dynamic part of its business. Another was emphasizing a wide variety of loans for farm improvements.
Another was building a substantial new horticulture, supply
and marketing business on watermelons, tomatoes, and
garlic. Another was emphasizing peanuts, feed growing and
marketing, and livestock. Each, in other words, was following a different growth strategy.

The Pu-tze Case--One FA illustrates particularly clearly
the role of the manager as a source of development initiative.
Pu-tze is an area of three-year rotation of sugar, rice, and
other crops. Its hog operation had been particularly successful and the FA was marketing most of the hogs produced. The
farmers and the FA were also doing well with a new variety
of high-yielding peanuts, and they were beginning to get into
corn production. The manager and some of the farm leaders
had seen a poultry demonstration that interested them, and
the manager began to think about ways of making poultry
production more attractive by reducing the cost of feed to the
growers. Having had some success with the hog feed blend-
ing operation and having pushed increased corn production,
the manager decided to look into poultry feed processing.

He went to JCRR for help. JCRR had had no experience
with this, but it made inquiries and found a suitable type of
pelletized feed processing equipment made in the U.S. The
manager then ordered an $11,000 pelletized feed plant from
the U.S., the first on Taiwan, with a $2,500 subsidy from
JCRR. He also laid plans to hire an additional extension
officer to push the poultry business.

Poultry production was thus initiated on a significant
scale in Pu-tze because the manager saw many ways to make
money from it: from credit, from sale of chicks, from possible future breeding of chicks, from improving the local
market for corn, from sale of feed in and around Pu-tze,
from sale of eggs, and from sale of birds.

The main lesson of Taiwan is its clear demonstration
of what can be done with one- and two-hectare farms. Taiwan
has demonstrated clearly that the peasant economy is something

more than a miserable waiting place for the labor reserves
of a growing industrial sector. The one-hectare farm can
be a source of wealth and strength to a nation, providing as
good a livelihood as industrial labor opportunities. The one-
hectare farm can provide expanding exports and an expanding
market for domestically manufactured goods.

The main lesson is one of hope. The Taiwan farmer on
one hectare is building new solid brick homes, sending his
children to secondary school, and buying motorcycles and an
increasing variety of electrical appliances. That this can be
done is an important lesson to all developing nations.

NOTES

1. C. Chang and A. Hinrichs, "Personal Income Distribution and Consumption Patterns in Taiwan, 1964, "
Industry of Free China (Taipei: November, 1967), p. 40.

2. Taiwan Statistical Year Book, 1967 (Taipei: Council
for International Economic Cooperation and Development,
1967). All subsequent statistics on Taiwan crop production
and overall economic performance are from this source unless otherwise indicated.

3. The Republic of China's Fourth Four-Year Plan for
Economic Development of the Province of Taiwan, 1965-1968,
Agricultural Sector (Taipei: Agricultural Production Com-
mittee, Council for International Economic Cooperation and
Development, 1965), p. 117.

4. M. H. Kwoh, Farmer Associations and Their Contribution Toward Agricultural and Rural Development in
Taiwan (Bangkok: Food and Agriculture Organization, 1964).
All statistics regarding Taiwan farmer associations in this
chapter are taken from this source unless otherwise indicated.

5. G. Hung, Extension's Help to Low-income Farmers,
Farm Extension Circular No. I-2 (Taipei: Joint Committee
on Rural Reconstruction, 1965, Mimeo).

6.   H. Jacoby, U. S. Aid to Taiwan (New York: Praeger, 1965).

7.   W. M. Ho, Planning and Programming for Agri-cultural Development in Taiwan, reprinted from Industry of Free China (Taipei: October, 1965), p. 2.

8.   Ibid., pp. 21-29.

CHAPTER 7 MALAYSIA

In 1956 the author first visited the Federation of Malaya (later Malaysia). It was the eve of Merdeka (independence) and he heard many people predicting administrative disintegration. He revisited the Federation in 1964, and again in 1967, and found that the rural development program was operated from top to bottom with a degree of competence, discipline, hardheadedness, and vigor that many a major American or European corporation could envy. The leadership of the Federation had created some ingenious working method which solved not only many of the administrative problems peculiar to developing nations but also many of the problems of bureaucratic arteriosclerosis found everywhere. Indeed, the author's wife remarked upon visiting a commune-level operations room, "That is the way we should run our household."

In contrast to Taiwan, however, Malaysia is not a finished product. Comprehensive agricultural services are still in the line phase. One might, indeed, criticize the Government of Malaysia for not getting a comprehensive pattern of agricultural services through the "line" phase a few years earlier. One must recognize, however, that the leadership of the Federation analyzed its problems carefully and set other priorities. Having set its priorities, the Government then applied a unique working method to achieve them. In contrast to Taiwan, the interest in Malaysia lies not so much in what has been achieved as in the working method that has been applied to achieve it.

ECONOMIC CONDITIONS

The population of the Federation in 1957 was 6,280,000 (49% Malay, 37% Chinese, and 11% Indian). The rural population was 3,611,000, including 2,521,000 Malays.[1] The rural sector is a dual one, a modern plantation and mining sector, which is the basis of Malaysia's wealth, and a traditional subsistence sector. The non-Malay rural population is employed largely on the plantations, although there are many Chinese rubber smallholders and truckfarmers. The subsistence sector is almost completely Malay, about 400,000 small farms; 70 percent are less than 2 hectares in size and 50 percent less than 1 hectare.[2]

The Malay farm systems vary greatly. In the northwest coastlands of Kedah and Perak one finds a rice monoculture like that of other South Asian rice basins. Here one finds serious land tenure problems, heavy crop-share rentals, and severe land hunger. In the rest of Malaysia one finds different combinations of rice-growing, perennials, and tree crops. The main perennial is rubber, but coconuts, oil palm, and fruit trees are also important. On the east coast there is substantial fishing. The predominance of perennials makes technical change difficult. Most of the technology goes into the seedling; improving production requires cutting down producing trees and waiting several years for the replantings to produce.

Malaysia is perhaps the richest of tropical nations. It is the world's leading exporter of rubber and tin. Its gross national product was $640 per adult male in 1957.[3] Yet within this relatively affluent society, the original Malay population in 1957 lived in a state of poverty and stagnation typical of South Asia. Population increases in the fifties were outpacing the modest increases in productivity achieved; per capita income was probably declining.[4] Forty thousand new families a year were seeking livelihoods; only 20,000 to 30,000 could be absorbed by the growing modern sector.[5]

The problem of rural development was thus largely that of the Malay peasant. The strategy and program could be conceived in terms of the Malay. Many Chinese smallholders found themselves in the same condition, however, and the program was careful to offer them something too.

ADMINISTRATION AND POLITICS

The basic structure of territorial units is similar to the typical structure described in Chapter 4. At the bottom is the kampong, a village of about 100 families. Typically, 10 such kampong make up a mukim (commune), often presided over by a hereditary "penghulu." A district will typically have about 10 mukim, some 10,000 farms and a rural population of some 50,000 to 60,000. There are some wide variations, however. Some districts cover vast jungle areas and other are almost exclusively large estates.

The Federation (as of 1957-60) was divided into 11 states and 70 districts, corresponding to provinces in the standard terminology of this book. They are quite different from the provinces of most countries, however; they have perhaps more autonomy than the U.S. States. As a whole they have strong parliamentary institutions and are presided over by hereditary rulers. Their autonomy is particularly strong on land matters, and this has considerably complicated rural development.

Save for certain important skill shortages, the country is well endowed with educated manpower. The average district probably has more cadre with university educations than the average province of most developing nations.

Malaysia has maintained vigorous parliamentary democracy since independence. A tri-ethnic Alliance Party has run the government with some strong opposition, particularly from a right-wing Malay party which has control in some states.

Independence evolved out of the 10-year "Emergency," the long, hard-fought Communist insurrection. This basic formative experience of the Federation had two main results:

1.   It left a serious imbalance in infrastructure spending. The key to victory in the Emergency was the resettlement of some 500,000 Chinese squatters from jungle clearings into some 500 new villages. Each new village was provided with a complete infrastructure, a location on a main road, and adequate schools, water, and clinics. Budget constraints of

the Emergency denied these amenities to loyal Malay kampong,
leading one Malay legislative leader to deliver an impassioned
protest ending in the words "What price loyalty?"[6] In the
first elections after Merdeka, in 1959, the Alliance Party lost
a large part of the Malay vote to right-wing Malay parties.
It was urgent, in order to maintain the tri-ethnic unity that
was the basis of Malaysian democracy, that the Alliance
government show the Malay rural population an immediate
and very effective concern for their needs. It had to produce
results rapidly and dramatically.

2.   The Emergency had provided an education in high-
pressure administration. The insurgency was defeated
through high-power planning and coordination. Within the
framework of the guidance provided by a comprehensive
"Anti-Terrorist Operations Manual," substantial authority
in each district was delegated to a district war executive
committee, composed of the civil, military, and police officers
of the district, who met almost daily in the operations room
for "morning prayers" to formulate ongoing operations and
coordinate activities.

The Alliance Government, faced with the urgent necessity of getting results fast, had the legacy it needed: a legacy
of know-how on effective delegation of authority, effective
guidance to local administrators, and effective committee-
work.

STRATEGY AND PROGRAM CONTENT

The Government saw its long-term strategy as a four-
phase progression. The first phase had the Government
shouldering its responsibilities to do something for the people.
Emphasis would be on "providing amenities" and building
physical infrastructure. The second phase would call for the
people to take full part in development, with emphasis on
kampong development committees, adult education, and
"gotong royong," the Malay tradition of community self-help
activity. The third phase would emphasize rural marketing
and credit. The fourth phase would attempt to rectify the
rural-urban imbalance with more rural industry and other
enterprise.[7]

Phase I was launched in 1960, phase II in September 1962. Phase III was nominally launched in 1964 but is still in the line phase.

Parallel to this four-step progression moves an expanding land program. Malaya is a peninsula of vast tracts of arable land, which require considerable financial and technical assistance to open to peasant exploitation.

Infrastructure

The best way for the government to show its immediate concern for the rural population was to build things fast-- roads, schools, clinics. This it did, as Table 7.1 shows. [8]

TABLE 7.1

Increase in Infrastructure, Federation of Malaya, 1956-63

Malaya	Increase 1956-1960 (5 years)	Increase Jan. 1961-June 1963 (2-1/2 years)
Roads (miles constructed)		
Bitumen surface	147	165
Nonbitumen surface	325	1,300
Irrigation (acres)	61,633	61,476
Rural health		
Clinics and subcenters	16	105
Midwife clinics	26	396
Rural classrooms		
Primary	6,233	2,803
Secondary and other	65	289

Construction of primary education classrooms slowed up
as basic needs were satisfied, but all other activities accelerated considerably. The percentage of allocated funds actually
spent also rose considerably in the early sixties.

Land

Alienation (transfer from public domain to private title)
of land had been almost at a standstill throughout World War II
and during the 10-year Emergency. Land hunger was perhaps the most serious problem of the Malay peasantry. The
Alliance Government immediately made a major effort to
relieve this need through four programs. First, it pressed
local officials to accelerate the processing of land applications
in the districts. Second, the States undertook Fringe Alienation schemes (preparation of blocks of land near existing
villages for transfer in parcels of three to five acres to
villagers with uneconomic smallholdings). A major effort
was also made in resettlement, by State Group Settlement
schemes and finally by the Federal Land Development
Authority (FLDA).

Land under the Fringe Alienation, Group Settlement, and
FLDA schemes are planted largely in rubber. They are operated initially as estates. The future smallholder proprietors
initially work much like estate laborers under block supervisors. As they gain experience and prove their competence,
parcels of land are gradually turned over for individual
management.

Lands suited to individual alienation, block Fringe Alienation, and the relatively small Group Settlement schemes were
limited, but by pushing into the jungle, vast tracts of land
became suitable for FLDA schemes. It was potentially the
most significant of the land development programs, since it
provided settlement on a scale large enough to warrant large
infrastructure expenditures. The typical settlement was some
400 families on 5,000 acres.

FLDA was set up as an autonomous corporation and placed
under the supervision of the Ministry of National and Rural
Development in 1960. Its first project was initiated in 1957;

for the next three years it averaged five new projects a year.
The new rural development program pushed the pace up to
about 12 projects a year in the midsixties. The projects are
expensive, costing over $5,000 per family. The main con-
straint has not been money, however, but the lack of competent settlement managers and supervisors.[9] Even in a
country as relatively rich in educated manpower as Malaysia,
cadre appears to be the binding constraint, just as in far less
developed countries.

Before anything can be done to relieve existing overcrowding, at least 10,000 families a year must be settled
just to match the population increase and to provide for new
families not drawn off by other sectors. This rate of resettlement was not achieved until the midsixties; only then did the
government really begin to reduce overcrowding. It has been
argued that the FLDA should have tried to settle twice as
many families on the 5,000-acre settlements, rather than
aim for an income four times that of the previous average,
which is what the 12-acre plots were designed to provide.
The main reason was that only rubber and, later, oil palms
appeared to provide enough income to be able to pay off the
heavy long-term debt each settler was undertaking. Since
world prices of rubber are steadily dropping, a substantial
extra margin of income seemed necessary to assure future
repayment.

Another important land measure that, in effect, relieves
some of the population pressure on land is irrigation, which
permits double-cropping and expands crop acreage corres-
pondingly. Irrigation schemes during the 1961-65 period
rendered 155,000 acres of land suitable for double-cropping.
Much of the benefits of double-cropping in the densely populated rice basins accrue to the landlords, but the 5-year
program provided adequate land to some 30,000 to 40,000
families.[10]

During the present First Malaysia Plan, 1966-70, large-
scale resettlement and irrigation schemes are accelerating
the pace of land development, thus permitting the Federation
not only to keep pace with its population growth but to actually
reduce the pressure on land. Work was scheduled to begin
in 1968 on the 150,000-acre Jengka Triangle Project in
Pahang, providing homesteads for some 12,000 families in

what is now deep jungle. This is in addition to an increasing
number of new 5,000-acre resettlement schemes. Under two
major projects (the Muda River scheme on the northwest
coast and the smaller Kemubu project near the northeast
coast) 186,000 acres of paddy basin are to be doublecropped.
In addition, some 180,000 acres are to be double-cropped
under smaller projects. [11]

World Bank assistance has been requested for the large
projects; the Federation now knows how to put together large
bankable projects in land development. One may consider
that it has built up this know-how gradually from its experience with small projects. Its years of experience with irrigation and resettlement small projects are thus the foundation
for the large capital projects that are enabling it to start reducing land pressure.

Agricultural Productivity

The Federation has an agricultural officer with one to
three assistants in each district. Since 1960 they have been
organizing kampong-level farmer associations. The impact
of extension and also of institutional credit and marketing has
been limited by lack of coverage, but some accomplishments
have been achieved. Although less than 20 percent of the
farmers were probably involved directly in institutional activities, some yields did rise. The approach was group project
subsidization rather than demonstration. An agricultural
officer would get a group of 10 to 20 farmers in a kampong to
undertake a new crop or package of cultural practices by
subsidizing them, assisting them with free plowing, or using
some other inducement. Because of the predominance of
perennials, replanting subsidies are particularly important
for achieving technological advances.

Rubber, the main crop, product, and export of the Federation, has a smallholder replanting grant program operated by
the Rubber Research Institute (RRI). Smallholders who re-
plant their rubber lands following the required practices are
granted $250 per acre, one-third at replanting and the rest in
successively smaller payments over five years (rubber trees
mature in seven years). RRI has a cadre of about 250 assistant

rubber instructors working with smallholders and supervising the program.

The program was started in 1952 and built up gradually in the 1950's. A lot of educational work was required to convince small growers that it would pay them to cut down existing low-productivity trees and wait seven years for high-productivity trees to start yielding. In the early 1960's the psychological barriers were finally overcome and the rate of replanting reached 80,000 acres a year. Over 50 percent of the smallholdings have now been replanted; the entire job should be complete by the midseventies.

About 1965 the Federation began preparing for comprehensive agricultural services by inviting experts from the Sino-American Joint Commission on Rural Reconstruction on Taiwan to make their recommendations on a suitable structure of services for Malaysia. Following these recommendations, legislation, regulations, and pilot operations were prepared for setting up comprehensive Taiwan-type farmers associations (FA's) at the mukim level. Eleven pilot FA's, one in each State of the peninsula were established in 1967, each with five agricultural assistants assigned as their initial staff. Each of these FA's had a distinct comprehensive program based on a rather thorough survey of farming in that mukim. The highly varied nature of Malaysian agriculture probably necessitated this type of locally tailored programming and dense staffing.

The so-called Green Revolution of the 1960's is particularly significant to a rice-importing nation with good cadre resources such as Malaysia. Some of the pilot FA's have achieved impressive production gains with the IRRI-8 rice variety; this innovation plus the replanting innovations provide a good base for comprehensive institutional development over the next several years.

PLANNING TECHNIQUE: THE REDBOOK

Shortly after the elections of 1959 the Deputy Prime Minister Tun Abdul Razak took effective command of the rural development program with the newly established portfolio of

Minister of Rural Development (later Minister of National and Rural Development). The first priority, as pointed out above, was accelerating the construction of infrastructure. The main obstacles, as summed up in the following "Seven Deadly Sins, " were bureaucratic:

    1. Interdepartmental jealousy in the course of day-to-day execution of Government functions, as well as conflicting departmental policies on the ground.

    2. Lack of co-ordination between Departments in what they are trying to do.

    3. Lack of complete day-to-day co-operation between Government officers on the ground, mostly due to a lack of understanding of each other's task.

    4. Every department thinking their function is the most important. In other words, too many priorities all pulling at cross purposes and leading no-where.

    5. Lack of proper planning in the departments aimed to fit into a Master Plan for the whole country.

    6. Lack of a Master Plan at all levels for the purpose of achieving the maximum development of the country.

    7. Lack of sufficient directive control at the top to ensure that the machinery of government at all levels functions as an efficient machine manned by a purposeful, single-minded team, and driven towards one goal only, that of National and Rural Development. [12]

    Tun Abdul Razak undertook to fight these problems with a minimum of staff and cadre (only one development officer per state and district) and a maximum of required working method.

    The basic working method was spelled out in a series of directives (in English), issued from March to May 1960, requiring each district to compile its proposed development projects on map tracings and standardized listings. To standardize and also to dramatize the planning procedure, the basic instructions and also the project listings and map tracings

were mounted on looseleaf folio sheets in a 2-foot-square red
binder which came to be called the Redbook.   The dramati-
zation worked; in Malaysia the district Redbook symbolizes
the business of rural development planning.

Part of a Redbook is reproduced in Appendix D, including
the general introductory sheets, some of the key specific
activity sheets, and some of its key appendix sheets.   The
Redbook speaks for itself; in lean, brisk, vigorous prose, it
spells out the planning procedure and salient policies to be
followed by each district.

In addition to spelling out the procedures clearly in the
Redbooks, Tun Abdul Razak toured the districts to explain
policy and procedures personally.   These visits also served
to impress upon the District Rural Development Committees
(composed of district-level departmental officers and elected
legislative representatives) the urgency and priority of the job.

Compilation of the Redbooks was handled in various ways.
In some districts the committees visited each kampong to
discuss projects.   In others the kampong and mukim leaders
gathered at the district headquarters to work out the program
with the committee.   In others the elected representatives on
the committee took it upon themselves to speak for the villagers,
and the popular consultation was very limited.   The deadline
for completion of the Redbooks was July 1960; nearly all 70
districts made the deadline.   In some cases the committees
worked round the clock the final week.   Tun Abdul Razak
visited many of the districts for special ceremonial submissions
of the Redbooks.   To the maximum extent possible, he tried
to make it an effort of mass witness, if not mass participation.[13]

The Redbook system has a very distinctive budgeting procedure.   There is no request for any specific amount of money
for any particular year.   The submission is simply a list of
projects in priority order, each with a cost figure.   State and
Federal authorities then decide how much they can afford to
finance the first year and draw a line under the last project
within that budget amount.   The rest of the projects on the
list are scheduled in a similar manner for subsequent years.
In the appendix to the Redbook there is a statement of financial
policy that partially explains this procedure.

The Redbook financial procedure avoids the "budget game" (described in Chapter 5) and overconcentration on finances. Lower echelons spend their time worrying about what will be accomplished rather than trying to guess how much money they can get out of higher authorities. At the same time the people in the district are forced to make politically difficult decisions on priorities. They must decide among themselves which kampong gets its facilities first and take responsibility for that decision.

For the First Malaysia Plan 1966-70, the process was repeated. New Redbooks were drawn up, this time with greater participation by kampong development committees.

PLANNING TECHNIQUE:
THE STANDARD REPORTING SYSTEM

Subannual planning and control is maintained at each district (with copies to State and national operations rooms) by means of progress charts for each category of project, with matching-format monthly reports. At the first of the year district offices fill out a progress chart for each category of project, listing the schemes approved for the district in priority order. To the right is a column for each month, in which the code for the expected stage of progress is entered for each item. Each month a report is issued for each category of project with the projects in the same order and on the same lines as in the progress chart. The report shows simply the stage achieved and gives a terse explanation for any delays.

The explanation of the coding system in one Malaysian document is reproduced as Figure 7.1.

In somewhat compacted form, without benefit of color, a district progress chart at the end of May for school construction might look like Figure 7.2.   The projects in Kampong A and E fell behind in March and have been gradually catching up. In May the Kampong Y project fell behind.

All progress charts of a district are kept in one binder. The author has thumbed through such a binder for only a few

PROGRESS CHART

The main five stages which any project will go through before completion: A, B, C, D, E, F.

A	B	C	D	E	F
Preliminary action and planning - Includes obtaining site or land for the project.	Detailed planning - Includes any detailed surveys, designing works, detailed plans and specifications or other form of detailed planning or action before commencement of works.	Purchase of Equipment - Where plant and machinery and other equipment are a necessary part of the project and are to be purchased from the vote of the project.	Tenders and Award of Contract for works.	Project under construction, installation or implementation.	Project completed.

CHART FOR EVERY PROJECT UNDER IMPLEMENTATION

| January | February | March | April | May | June | July | August | September | October | November | December |

Project behind Schedule (shown in "Red").

Project ahead of Schedule (shown in "Green").

KEY

Top triangles filled in at Planning stage by Officer responsible for project, i.e. on pre-assessment (in advance) of the stages A, B, C, D, E, F throughout the year.

Bottom triangles; empty at beginning of year but filled in each month giving actual stage reached -- from inspection report on the ground.

Note:
1. If stage A, B, C, D, E, F, in top triangle coincides with actual stage than both colours are the same.
2. If stage A, B, C, D, E, F, in bottom triangle is behind Schedule than it is shown in Red.
3. If stage A, B, C, D, E, F, in bottom triangle is ahead of Schedule than it is shown in Green.

FIGURE 7.1. Explanation of Coding System Used in Malaysian Progress Chart

minutes and was able to get a fairly clear impression of the problems of the development program in that district. Sometimes one finds every activity falling behind at one particular stage; this indicate that the stage is probably not being managed properly. In some cases it is the lower-priority projects that are falling behind; this is not as serious as delays at the top of the sheets. At times one finds many delays on only one of the progress charts of a district; this indicates a weak officer. At the national operations room one can get a feel for the performance of one district compared to others or one department compared to others by thumbing quickly through their progress charts.

In brief, this reporting system enables one to spot the main operating problems of a district or a department in a matter of minutes.

SUB-HEAD	ITEM NO.	SCHEME OR PROJECT	FINANCIAL PROVISION	STAGES OF PROGRESS						DEC
				JAN	FEB	MAR	APR	MAY		
7	21	Kpg. A, 6 classrms.	10,000	D	D / D	E / D	15 / 5	30 / 20	80 / 50	
7	23	Kpg. E, 8 classrms.	12,000	D	D / D	E / E	15 / 15	30 / 10	60 / 40	
7	24	Kpg. C, 4 classrms.	7,000	A	B / A	B / B	C / B	D / C	D	
7	25	Kpg. Y, 3 rm addit'n	3,000		A	B / A	B / B	B / B	C / B	80
7	27	Kpg. T, 6 classrms.	11,000				A / A	B / A	B / B	
		etc.								

FIGURE 7.2. Progress Chart for School Construction, Malaysia

PLANNING TECHNIQUE: THE OPERATIONS ROOM

A good planning system involves just the right interplay of man and paper, of decision-makers and documents. The Malaysian leadership had learned from the Emergency the importance of a proper setting to get this interplay to work.

The Setting

During the 10-year Emergency each of the district war executive committees met in an operations room where all data relevant to decisions were displayed as prominantly and conveniently as possible, as in the war room of a major headquarters. The "morning prayers" meetings were conducted according to rules designed to insure well-considered, clear, and prompt decisions.

Tun Abdul Razak applied the operations-room concept to rural development. He did this principally both for its intrinsic practical value and its symbolic value, and also to dramatize the need for wartime urgency. At district, state, and national levels, and later at kampong levels, operations rooms were established. (The district is the key level in the author's opinion)

The distinctive feature of a district operations room, as one enters it for the first time, is the map case at one end. Long tables arranged in a V face a large box with maps affixed to sliding panels. One can pull out a map of the district for each type of activity in the Redbook. Along the side or the bottom of each map is a list of projects under that activity in the order they appear in the Redbook listing, with the cost and a few other pertinent data by each item. Each is connected by a colored string to a pin at its location on a map. The color of the string and the pin generally indicate the year under which the project was funded. Other graphic devices are used to show the state of progress.

In addition to the maps, various charts and graphs around the room give salient statistics. Copies of all the standard reports, minutes of meetings, and project backup data are kept in the room for quick reference.

What all this adds up to is that the plan, instead of being filed in a cabinet, stares down at those responsible for its execution from the four walls of the operations room.

Uses of the Operations Room

Appendix A of the Redbook gives the basic procedure of a district rural development committee meeting. The committee is responsible for formulating and updating the five-year plan of the district. It also has a measure of problem-solving responsibility. The elected representatives on the committee quiz the officers on problems and performance regularly. In between full committee meetings, the officers of the district gather several times a week for morning prayers. At these meetings the focus is on delays and inter-departmental coordination. The district officer tries to find the point of origin of any current delay and to get commitments from the various officers to take the steps necessary to restore momentum on a project.

The physical presentation becomes particularly important during a visit by a team headed by Tun Abdul Razak or a lesser VIP. Ministers, state and national, always tour the district with a team of staff officers from various departments. With such teams, problems of coordination with higher echelons can be resolved on the spot. The meetings open with briefings by the district officer and various departmental officers on progress and problems. The officers talk from the maps, which are expressly designed to support briefings. The head of the team generally inspects the latest reports and progress charts before the meeting and he then asks some questions about the main problems he has noted on the standard forms. After the briefing, the team leader selects a few project sites to visit.

These visits, always impromptu, serve to keep everyone constantly on their toes. Everything in the operations room must be up to date and reflect reality; errors will all too likely be painfully exposed. Tun Abdul Razak gets to almost every district in the course of some 18 months; some districts may be visited several times during that period. His visits and those of other personalities maintain working discipline

dramatically. An officer whose poor performance has been
exposed by Tun Abdul Razak soon finds himself transferred
to a lesser post.

These impromptu visits have positive as well as negative
disciplinary aspects for district-level officers. They expose
lack of proper support from above as quickly as they expose
lack of performance below. Procrastination in State and
national offices can be a frequent cause of delays at the local
level. When team visits look at delays and find that upper-
echelon procrastination is the cause, the district officials
are able to get an immediate commitment to action from the
high-level team.

Finally, the operations rooms are used for explaining
the program to visiting groups of villagers. The purpose is
educational and also political--to gain support for the Government by showing the people what the Government is doing for
them and how earnestly the Government is going about serving
the people.

National and Other Echelons

The Ministry of National and Rural Development maintains a handsomely appointed National Operations Room on
its premises, a chamber some 70 by 30 feet with red leather
chairs facing the map panels in the shape of a broad C. The
maps cover most of the acitivites displayed in the district
offices, except village roads, minor irrigation projects, and
community centers and adult education classes. They show
in addition industrial parks, major roads, major health and
educational institutions, aborigine projects, police installations, and radio and telecommunication centers. On one side
of the central map case is a case on rollers with maps of all
the districts. On the other side is another case on rollers
with data on post offices, major welfare institutions, agricultural, cooperative, and Rural Industrial Development
Authority loans, and other government activities less directly
related to rural development. Another display exhibits
blow-ups of the regular and development budgets.

Along the back of the room are the Redbooks of all the districts. Also bound in red and stamped in gold are the books with the progress reports from each State, the minutes of the district committee meetings, and the tour notes of the Minister. Around the room are models of standard houses and clinics, photo displays, and posters.

Each of the departments responsible for maintenance of the maps and charts tries its best to use vivid graphic techniques to show discrepancies between planned and actual progress.

Traffic in the National Operations Room is heavy; the room is used for a variety of purposes. The Cabinet meets there at times. The National Development Planning Committee meets there, as do many subcommittees and working groups. Perhaps the most dramatic meetings are Tun Abdul Razak's monthly sessions of the National Rural Development Committee, consisting of all department and agency chiefs directly involved in the program. Tun Abdul Razak selects one department or agency to give the major briefing at each meeting, but he does not announce his selection until the meeting. Everyone, therefore, comes prepared to present and discuss his entire program. The selection is often based on some policy problem the Minister has in mind. Questioning and discussion focus on this problem.

At the national level as well as the local level, the plan thus stays under continual floodlight. Everyone is continually ready to go on stage and discuss the portion of the plan for which he is responsible.

VIP's have come from developing nations half a world away to see how the Malaysian rural development program works. Their observation tours start at the National Operations Room, which is obviously well set up for general briefings of the total program. Many neighboring countries have attempted to adapt some of the Malaysian techniques, with varying success. The operations room has become something of a status symbol for ministries in some countries. Unfortunately, they are frequently installed without the essential complementary techniques: the hardheaded reporting system and team tours. The result is show without content.

Villagers are given the VIP treatment at the National Operations Room, when busloads of village leaders are brought to the capitol for briefings.

Each State maintains an operations room, basically a smaller version of the National Operations Room, handsomely appointed with a variety of displays as well as maps. The State is the main echelon of operations room briefings for villagers. Busloads come daily in many States. The political uses of these tours is obvious; the educational uses are equally important. The state development officers emphasize to the visitors the importance of their contribution to development, particularly the importance of their traditional gotong royong community activity.

More and more of the kampong have established a sort of operations room by putting up bulletin boards in their meeting halls with maps, charts, and graphs, showing village development activities. Malaysia offers lessons to developed as well as developing nations on how to overcome some of the inherent problems of modern bureaucracy. Perhaps these lessons can best be summed up in Tun Abdul Razak's acrostic formula, prominently displayed in the middle of the National Operations Room:

R-- Resist changing policies and staff once policies have been finalized.

E-- Ensure coordination of all departments from the planning stage to the completion of projects.

S-- Stop paper arguments and departmental disagreements.

U-- Use standard plans and technical capacity correctly.

L-- Land to be acquired quickly; sites decided without delay.

T-- Teams to tour: a development team to be appointed and tour the country from time to time to deal with delays in development.

S-- Spotlighting progress from month to month in order to diagnose and remedy delays.

RESULTS ARE WHAT WE WANT

NOTES

1.   T. H. Silcock and E. K. Fisk, eds., The Political Economy of Independent Malaya (Berkeley: University of California Press, 1964), p. 164.

2.   Ibid., p. 169.

3.   Ibid., p. 3.

4.   Ibid., p. 167.

5.   Ibid., p. 169.

6.   G. D. Ness, Bureaucracy and Rural Development in Malaysia (Berkeley: University of California Press, 1967), p. 99.

7.   Rozhan bin haji Kuntom, "Techniques of Implementation, the Malaysian Experience," in Report on 1st Seminar on Development (Kuala Lumpur: Malaysian Center for Development Studies, 1966), p. 79.

8.   Ness, op. cit., p. 154.

9.   First Malaysia Plan, 1966-70, (Kuala Lumpur: Jabatan Chetak Kerajaan, 1965), p. 106.

10.   Ibid., pp. 117-18.

11.   Ibid., p. 118.

12.   Rozhan, op. cit., p. 72.

13.   Ness, op. cit., pp. 142-49.

CHAPTER **8** EAST PAKISTAN

The demographic time bomb ticks loudly in East Pakistan.
Over 70 million people are packed in some 55,000 square
miles, an area smaller than Iowa or Wisconsin. The cultivated land per capita has been declining steadily for decades;
up to 40 percent of families may be virtually landless. The
6.2 million farms of the region average about 3-1/2 acres.
Urbanization is negligible, and literacy is less than 30 percent. Few countries are as rural in population as East
Pakistan, yet it does not feed itself. It relies on its exports
of jute to pay for cereal grain imports.

This is not just a subsistence economy; the word subsistence is not adequate to convey the poverty of East Pakistan.
It is an economy which hovers on the margin of disaster. A
sense of urgency blankets the country. An unseen motto is
inscribed on the wall of every office in East Pakistan: "We
plan thoroughly today so that we can eat tomorrow."

This sense of urgency, however, is coupled today with
some reasonably sound optimism. East Pakistan is rapidly
approaching self-sufficiency in food production. It has a vigorous birth control program which promises to moderate the
demographic tide in the next few years. It has established a
rural institutional structure which not only reaches into all of
its 62,000 villages but actively involves hundreds of thousands
of farmers in the actual management of development.

East Pakistan is not a finished product like Taiwan. One
can say that it has reached stage IIIa of rural development,
but not without some important qualifications. Its method
lacks the political showmanship and highly efficient troubleshooting and follow-through of Malaysia. Its significance lies
first in its success in coping with extreme poverty and demographic pressure and second in its actually involving the
people in the planning and management of development.

143

Unlike the other case studies in this book, East Pakistan is not a sovereign state. It is properly speaking a province, one of two wings of the far-flung Islamic Republic of Pakistan. The province has a great deal of autonomy in Pakistan's federal structure, but its rural development program is in large measure a reflection of the policies of the central Government of the Republic. As West Pakistan has been the more advanced of the two wings in industrialization and urban development, so East Pakistan has been the more advanced of the two wings in rural development. The conditions for rural development were better and the urgency was greater in East Pakistan, so it has lead the way. It is therefore feasible and considerably simpler to examine rural development planning in Pakistan in terms of the east wing alone.

PRESENT CONDITIONS AND CIRCUMSTANCES

The present program and planning structure in East Pakistan is based on a strategy and on circumstances which evolved in the late 1950's and were still evident in the early 1960's. The data below are for 1963 unless otherwise noted.

Farming

The 6.2 million farms (average 3.5 acres) are divided into an average of six fragments each. Of the 3.5 acres, 3.1 are cultivated; the cropping ratio is 1.48 crops per field, giving an average net cropped area of 4.6 acres.[1] Tenancy is negligible.

The basic crop is rice, cultivated on almost all farms. Three crops are distinguished. The Amon is grown in almost all corners of the province, planted as early as July and harvested as late as January. On the better watered fields of the central districts a second crop, the Aus, is planted as early as February and harvested as late as September. In the Northeast a third crop, the Boro, is planted as early as November and harvested in April. The average yield in 1963/64 was 1,040 pounds per acre, up from 970 pounds

in 1959/60.   The acreage and production in that year was as
follows:

	Acres	Tons
Amon	14,604,000	7,290,000
Aus	6,586,000	2,659,000
Boro	1,069,000	509,000
	22,259,000	10,466,000[2]

The next most important crop is jute, grown on some
1.7 million acres in 0.3-acre plots on some 4,000,000 farms
down the center of the country.   Acreage has varied considerably from year to year.   Production was 6 million bales
in 1963/64.   Jute is the principle export and foreign exchange
resource of Pakistan and the main cash crop of most farms
in the province.

The central districts of the province are thus dominated
by a rice-jute farm system, which fades out into more
diversified farming in the western and northern border districts.   To the west one finds most of the sugar, oilseed,
pulse, and fruit-tree cultivation.   Tobacco is grown in the
far northwest, and tea plantations are found in the northeast.
The acreage of the main secondary cultivations is as follows:

	Thousands of Acres
Cereals (other than rice)	202
Pulses	689
Oilseeds	713
Fruits	272
Vegetables	1,088
Sugar	366
Betel nut	196
Tobacco	101
Tea	84[3]

The average farm has about three head of cattle, mostly
oxen and mostly inadequately nourished.   Farms usually
have a few chickens or ducks, but the main source of protein
is fish.   Some 600,000 tons of fish are caught annually in the

innumerable inland streams and in the tanks of the irrigation
reservoirs. The average village has some four or five tanks
averaging two acres in size, producing some four to six tons
of fish. Many of the tanks are derelict and only a fraction
of the tank fish production potential is realized. The protein
and vitamin content of the diet of the province is grossly inadequate.

Literacy estimates vary widely, but the 1961 census indicated that roughly a third of adult males are literate.
Perhaps a third of those have some secondary school education.[4] In the rural areas this must be discounted by another
third.

Administration

Rural East Pakistan comprises the following economic
and administrative units:

	Per Village	Per Union	Per Thana	Per Subdivision	Per District
6,200,000 Farms	100	1,500	15,000	105,000	345,000
62,000 Villages		15	150	1,050	3,450
4,100 Unions			10	70	230
410 Thanas				7	23
59 Subdivisions					3.3
18 Districts					

Note how these compare to the standard administrative terminology used in this book. The village is the same size in
terms of numbers of farms, but an East Pakistani village has
about 50 percent more families than farms (10 million families
and 6.2 million farms in the rural areas). The union, with 15
villages, corresponds to a commune but has 50 percent more
farms. In area it is very compact, averaging 12.5 square
miles exclusive of hill tracts. The thana corresponds roughly
to the district and the subdivision to the province in the standard terminology of this book.

Local units are well staffed in terms of numbers of professional cadre, although their education is often limited.

At the union there is a union agricultural assistant; until recent years the assistant had only some secondary school education and a smattering of agricultural training. They are gradually being replaced or recycled for two years of extension training. The thanas are gradually being staffed by thana agricultural officers with university degrees in agriculture.

The Government of East Pakistan has responsibility and administrative structure for rural development planning almost as complete as those of a sovereign state. The main units concerned with rural development are shown in Figure 8.1.

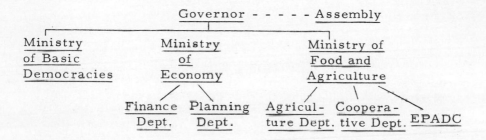

FIGURE 8.1. East Pakistan Rural Development Planning Structure

The East Pakistan Agricultural Development Corporation (EPADC) is a government-owned corporation with full commercial autonomy of operation; it provides most of the supply services in the province, agricultural chemicals, seed, and also small irrigation equipment. It distributes agricultural chemicals through small merchants in the villages, and importers have recently begun importing and distributing fractional "cu-sec" pumps, so called because they have a capacity of less than one cubic foot per second. The East Pakistan Water and Power Development Authority handles large irrigation projects. The private sector also has a role in the supply function.

Political Factors

Rural development in East Pakistan has been conditioned
by three political factors:

1.   The Unity Problem--East Pakistan has most of the
population and foreign exchange resources of the Republic,
yet during the first decade and a half after independence the
Federal Government was largely dominated by West Pakistan
and most of the development investment went into the west
wing. This was due more to lack of talent and suitable projects in the east wing than to deliberate discrimination.
Pakistan illustrated vividly the dominance of the learning
constraint over financial resource constraints in economic
development.

A national policy of favoring investment in East Pakistan
in order to bring income and growth up to that of West Pakistan began to be realized in the middle 1960's, as the creative
efforts of East Pakistani rural development planners began to
bear fruit, making it possible to funnel more resources into
rural programs in the east than in the west. This was also
the case in the late 1960's.

2.   Evolution of Democracy--Traditional parliamentary
institutions broke down in the middle 1950's, and General Ayub
Khan took over in October 1958, proclaiming martial law.
A program of systematic reconstruction of representative
institutions was undertaken by the military regime which has
largely, but by no means completely, restored full democracy.

The key to the program was the Basic Democracies, a
structure of local councils built from the bottom up. At the
bottom are the union councils, with one member elected to
a five-year term from each ward (1,000 to 1,500 population).
Union councils send representatives to thana councils, on
which some officials also sit. Thana councils send representatives to district councils. Union and district are the
most active layers of the structure, with a wide variety of
administrative and development functions. The Basic Demo-
crats, the 80,000 members of the union councils across the
Republic, elect the President.

The objectives of the Basic Democracies program were
twofold. First, it was to broaden the base of democratic
participation beyond the small urban middle class which had
monopolized political activity. Second, it was to make politics development-oriented, turning it away from demagoguery.
This concern for mass participation in development-oriented
political activity pervades rural development in Pakistan.

3.   Ideological Flexibility--Pakistan has been singularly
lacking in ideological dogmatism. The enormous economic
dislocations of the first years of independence left a legacy
of multifaceted economic controls which have been gradually
relaxed. Public corporations have filled the gap in fields
where private effort was not forthcoming, as in agricultural
supplies. This publicly owned distribution system has used
village merchants as retailers, and private importers have
been encouraged to get into the agricultural supply business
with fractional cu-sec pumps.

STRATEGY

There are three phases to the institutional side of rural
development since 1960: rural works, program-building, and
intensive thana development. The production side has aimed
at achieving food self-sufficiency, increasing yields, and
double-cropping rice and minor food crops.

Local institutional development has followed the logical
sequence outlined in Chapter 4. Rural works (physical infrastructure projects) has been followed by program-building
(as local planning and management of extension is called in
laboratory), to be followed by a comprehensive institutional
structure. The three programs were piloted about the same
time (1961-63), and the author has found nothing to indicate
that their sequence was explicit in East Pakistani planning.
The logic of the sequence is demonstrated by the fact that
rural works was able to establish province-wide effective
coverage first, and it has provided a firm foundation for
subsequent programs.

In evolving its institutional programs, East Pakistan did
explicitly and carefully observe point-line-network project
discipline. In 1959 the Pakistan Academy of Rural Development was established to execute the point phases and provide
training for the line phases of new rural institutions. It was
located at Comilla, the center of one of the poorest districts
in the country, with a permanent staff of varied first-rate
talents. The neighboring Comilla Kotwali Thana has been the
point locale for the rural works and intensive thana development programs. Other Comilla thanas and selected thanas
in other districts have been used for the line phases. In a
similar manner thanas around the East Pakistan Agricultural
University at Mymensingh were used for the point and line
phases of program building.

Rural Works

A massive mobilization of unemployed labor to build
physical infrastucture has arisen out of four circumstances:

1.   There was an urgent need to provide off-season employment for increasing numbers of landless laborers.

2.   In the flat deltaic terrain of East Pakistan, extensive
road links and water control works can be achieved with
simple earthwork, involving very little professional planning
and supervision or equipment.

3.   Development activities of the Basic Democracy
programs had been severely handicapped by lack of financial
resources.

4.   The U.S. was willing to contribute Public Law 480
commodities for direct payment of participating laborers.

The planning and management arrangements of the rural
works program will be described in detail later. Union, thana,
and district councils undertook sizable public works programs.
The union level is perhaps the most interesting because it is
managed directly by the farmers. At first it included little
besides earthworks. As the union councils developed pro-
ficiency and experience, buildings, bridges, and other

structures were added. In recent years, faced with an eventual termination of the Public Law 480 commodity distribution for paying labor, the Government has emphasized direct income-producing activities, particularly restoration of derelict tanks and stocking tanks with fishes for communal production.

The first experiment was conducted at Comilla Kotwali Thana in 1961/62. The program was extended to 54 thanas in 1962/63 and to all thanas in 1963/64. Since then the budget for the total rural works program has ranged from $20 to $40 million. In the current Five-Year Plan it is averaging $30 million a year.

Results have been impressive. By 1966 it was estimated that the new rural roads were reducing transport costs so as to increase real income of the villagers by 10 to 20 percent, and 15 percent of the cultivated land had been improved by water control works.[5] In 1966/67 182 million man-days of labor was provided by the program.[6] This amounted to about 45 days per landless family. Considering that the average landless laborer works from 100 to 150 days a year, this represented an increase in employment for each head of a landless family of 25 to 50 percent. It did not represent a corresponding increase in income, since the cash-plus-food wage rate paid on the rural works projects was lower than normal on-season wages, but it did represent a significant alleviation of the misery of the poorest of the East Pakistanis.

Food Self-Sufficiency

In 1966 the average yield on rice was 1230 pounds per acre.[7] Over 160,000 on-farm demonstrations during the previous five years had averaged 3,280 pounds.[8] If all farms were to achieve the results of the average of the demonstrations (and those demonstrations were prior to the introduction of the "miracle rice" varieties), East Pakistan could feed over 100 million people at current levels of nutrition. Self-sufficiency can be achieved at the projected 1970 population level if some 25 to 30 percent of the farms adopt all the practices which have been successfully demonstrated and if the fields irrigable by low-lift pumps are double-cropped.

Comprehensive food-self-sufficiency plans have been
adopted and updated regularly. A recent goal for 1969/70 was
13.5 million tons production, up from 10.24 million in 1964/
65.[9] In 1967/68 production fell about 400,000 tons short of
the target for that year of 11.44 million tons,[10] largely because
fertilizer utilization has been running about a year behind
schedule. Initial projections of fertilizer utilization were
excessively optimistic.

Nevertheless, there is some hope that self-sufficiency
can be achieved by 1970. Fertilizer utilization has been increasing by over 40 percent each year. Seed and low-lift
pump distribution have been running a bit ahead of schedule.
The new "miracle rice," the IRRI-8 has been performing
even better than hoped. This last element promises to compensate somewhat for the lag in fertilizer distribution and
bring the program up to target.

Though rice is the primary nutrition source, minor food
sources are scheduled for substantial increases. Potatoes
in particular have been rising rapidly from a small base of
100,000 acres early in the decade to almost 200,000 in the
late sixties. New potato varieties give yields 800 percent
over the old varieties.[11] The main hope for adequate protein
production lies in inland fish culture, particularly in tanks.
This is now a main effort of the rural works program.

Present Agricultural Services Strategy

The extension program is built largely around program-
building. Specific procedures will be discussed below. Suffice
it to say at this point that the crops subcommittee of the agricultural committee of the union council is generally responsible
for managing demonstrations. Recently large block demonstrations have been introduced to supplement and reinforce individual plot demonstrations.

Supply is a service provided almost entirely by the East
Pakistan Agricultural Development Corporation (EPADC).
Agricultural chemicals and seed are retailed through EPADC's
9,000 authorized village dealers, from the EPADC offices
and warehouses at thana level. EPADC has its own seed farms.

Supplies are allocated to thanas on the basis of indents (requirements projections) drawn up by the agricultural committees of the union councils. The indents are based on the
requests of individual farmers. Those active in program-
building thus act directly as the sales force of EPADC. Low-
lift pumps with a capacity of about two cubic feet per second
are also distributed by EPADC, which leases them to groups
of 30 to 100 farmers on a flat fee per acre. EPADC provides
maintenance and pump operators. Recently private importers
have become active distributing fractional cu-sec pumps.

    Marketing is not as yet a service with significant prob-
lems. Rice is generally grown for on-farm consumption.
Jute, which moves satisfactorally through traditional channels,
is the main cash crop.

    Credit has an ambiguous role in the current strategy.
Only about 10 percent of the farmers are getting any institutional credit, and various plan documents have stated that
credit of up to $16 per acre for half the acreage is needed to
achieve plan targets.[12] Yet two measures appear to have
avoided heavy institutional credit requirements. First, fertilizer is subsidized at from 45 to 55 percent, so that $1 in-
vested in fertilizer generally yields $6-$8 worth of increased
production. Such a return makes it worthwhile to borrow from
traditional credit sources at rates as high as 10 percent a
month to buy fertilizer, the most expensive current input.
Second, the leasing of low-lift pumps at a fee of about $7 per
acre, collected at harvest, eliminates what would otherwise
be the major item of medium-term credit required to achieve
plan targets.

Preparation for Comprehensive Agricultural Services

    Looking beyond 1970, modern marketing and credit ser-
vices will be essential to further progress. The institutions
to provide these services have been under careful experimentation for a number of years. In 1962 the Pakistan Academy
of Rural Development started a thana cooperative credit
association (TCCA) in Comilla Kotwali, to complement the
Basic Democracies institutions at the union level with strong
farmer-owned comprehensive service institutions at thana

and village level. In 1963, TCCA's were established in three
thanas in other districts. In 1965, TCCA's were established
in seven other Comilla thanas, and in 1968 they were established in the remaining 14 Comilla thanas. [13] This should
complete the line phase.

The TCCA provides comprehensive supervised credit,
extension support, and marketing. It is based in a highly
disciplined organizational routine at the village level. To be
eligible for credit a farmer must attend fortnightly meetings
of the village cooperative regularly, bringing a couple of
anna to deposit as savings at every meeting. Two percent is
paid on these deposits, and a farmer can borrow only 10
times the amount he has saved. The village cooperative discusses the merits of each individual loan and cosigns it.

The TCCA supervises the loans closely, with a staff of
eight professionals including six loan inspectors. The repayment record has been excellent. The TCCA charges 15
percent on loans, including a 3 percent commission to the
village group, which provides enough gross margin to cover
supervision expenses.

In addition, the TCCA's have engaged in a variety of marketing activities and extension support, particularly in the
form of training. Physical facilities of the TCCA generally
include warehouses, a training center, built around demonstration plots, and a tank. Extension support is in the form
of frequent farmer training sessions. The TCCA thus completes the structure of rural services, with the one possible
limitation that too few of the village groups so far have secured
the active participation of over 50 percent of the farmers of
the village. Broader participation may come with time, or
it may require some restructuring of the institution. The
TCCA as it now stands will be ready for network phase expansion of coverage in the early seventies.

Some other worthwhile institutional experiments are
being made. EPADC has established a few truckfarming
blocks, groups of contiguous farmers who produce a variety
of vegetables under closely supervised contract, following
a block plan that assures a year-round supply of produce for
nearby urban markets. The Agricultural Development Bank
will provide $37 per acre credit for the coming boro crop in

selected areas through EPADC, secured by a crop lien.
Government crop marketing warehouses purchasing on grade
are being tried out. East Pakistan should be able to move on
to stage IIIb in the seventies.

Family-Planning

Unless the birthrate is curbed, present and projected
agricultural development will do little more than stop the
decline in per capita income. East Pakistan has a goal of
reducing the crude birthrate from 50 per 1,000 to 40 per
1,000 by 1970, thus reducing the rate of population growth
from 3 to 2.5 percent per annum. To do this it must secure
the participation of approximately 3 million couples, about
25 percent of those of childbearing age. [14]

An autonomous East Pakistan Family-Planning Board
headed by the provincial Minister of Health operates the
program on a budget of about $5 million a year. [15] In addition
to higher-level staff, 400 thana officers, 1,200 full time
assistants, and 30,000 village-level agents, midwives, and
others working on referral fees, are employed. Mobile and
part-time clinics dispense family planning advice and intrauterine device (IUD) insertions. Condoms are distributed at
subsidized prices by village retailers.

The target for late 1967 was 105,000 couple-years of
protection per month, including 23,000 IUD insertions. The
program was roughly on target.

CENTRAL PLANNING

Pakistan takes planning seriously. The President of the
Republic and one out of every 15 East Pakistani farmers are
active members of planning committees. This section deals
with planning in the national and provincial capitals; the next
section will deal with local planning.

Five-Year Plans

These overall documents are prepared largely by the national Planning Commission, chaired by the President. The Third Plan, 1965-70, was prepared within the framework of the 1965-85 Perspective Plan.

Some thorough econometric studies went into the preparation of the plan. Aided by the Harvard Advisory Group, the Planning Commission staff used a variety of mathematical models, including linear programming, input-output, and national accounts projections, to test alternatives of strategy and policy. [16] The long-range plan chosen appeared to be the optimum for achieving the following 1985 objectives:

Increase in GNP from $8.8 to $29 billion.

Full employment.

Parity in per capita income between East and West Pakistan.

Universal literacy.

Elimination of dependency on foreign aid. [17]

The optimum growth path chosen also provided the breakthrough to self-sustained growth in the shortest possible time.

The Third Plan document provides a sector-by-sector description of types of activities and subsectoral allocations. It also has targets for a variety of outputs and for some inputs, such as fertilizer.

Projects

Provincial governments have almost complete responsibility for project planning. They are authorized to approve projects of up to $1 million with no reference to the central government. The Planning Department has an agricultural planning staff consisting of a Deputy Chief for Agriculture, two assistant chiefs, and two researchers, all with MA

degrees. The agriculture Department also has a full-time
planning cell.

The East Pakistan development program is divided into
11 sectors, of which 2, the agriculture and rural works sectors, cover what in this book is labeled rural development.
Agriculture consists of 15 subsectors, and 166 projects, for
which about $485 million is allocated for the 5-year period.
Subsectors are defined principally along agency lines. The
main ones are listed in Table 8.1. The Pakistan planning
system uses five basic documents: PC-I, the project proposal,
PC-II, the Feasibility Study, PC-III, the Quarterly Report,
PC-IV, the Completion Report, and PC-V, the Evaluation.
For rural development the PC-I is the main decision document. It consists of a cover sheet of basic statistics
followed by a narrative. It is theoretically a multiyear
document. It is revised, however, whenever a change of
over 10 percent in the budget is contemplated. In practice,
documents on major projects are rewritten annually. PC-I's
are generally drafted by project managers assisted by the
planning cells of their departments. At times the agricultural staff of the Planning Department participates in the
drafting.

Projects are reviewed by the Planning Department, then
by the Planning Authority, a senior committee with members
drawn from concerned agencies and also from outside the
administration. At both levels the PC-I may be sent back
repeatedly for rewriting if inadequate. Repeated rewriting
is generally required, however, only of major projects.
The result is that the major projects are reconsidered each
year over a period of many weeks.

The Projects Division of the Planning Department closely
reviews the PC-III's, the Quarterly Reports, of the major
projects. A quarterly meeting goes over the 10 or 15 major
agriculture projects. This may be supplemented by monthly
meetings on certain key projects. In general East Pakistan
has found the main causes of delay on development projects
to be slow fund releases, land acquisition, and design and
contracting bottlenecks. After these meetings the Project
Division frequently writes letters to responsible agencies,
signaling the action that must be taken to get projects back
on schedule or to prevent further delays.

TABLE 8.1

Principal Subsectors and Projects, East Pakistan
Five-Year Plan, 1965-70

Subsector	No. of Projects	Five-Year Allotment (millions of US$)
EPADC	14	$227*
Agricultural Dept.	28	39
Pakistan Academy of Rural Development Comilla	2	13
Marketing	6	2
Cooperatives	8	30
Livestock	18	20
Fisheries	13	8
Total	89	$339

*Includes $100 million for the fertilizer subsidy.

Source: Approved Annual Development Programme of
Government of East Pakistan (Planning Department,
1967).

The Food Self-Sufficiency Plan

Projects are generally institutionally oriented. They do
contain many tables relating inputs to outputs, but the main
document relating all efforts in agriculture to production is
the annual updating of the Food Self-Sufficiency Plan. This
document of some 60 pages projects food production targets
and the inputs and actions necessary to achieve them for
three or four years.

In the updating of early 1967 a table (Table 8.2) appeared,
giving the increased rice production anticipated from each

TABLE 8.2

Anticipated Increase in East Pakistan Rice Production

(in thousands of tons)

Source of Increase	1967/68	1968/69	1969/70	Conversion Factor*
Fertilizer	428	745	1,313	6.6/ton nutrient
Low-lift pumps	156	303	589	.6/acre irrigated
Large irrigation projects	74	111	44	.6/acre irrigated
Coast embankments	90	124	178	.15/acre protected
Private pumps and wells	8	29	60	.6/acre irrigated
Plant protection	89	143	173	.07/acre protected
Local seed factor	44	88	146	.07/acre sown
IRRI-8 seed factor	59	112	190	.19/acre sown
Other	258	300	455	
Total increase	1,200	1,960	3,260	
Plus 1964/65 production	10,240	10,240	10,240	
	11,440	12,200	13,500	

*Increased tons per unit of input, the seed factors being net of fertilizer and other inputs.

Source: East Pakistan Food Self-Sufficiency Program 1968 (Government of East Pakistan, 1967), p. 12.

source each year, which was to achieve food self-sufficiency
targets. For each of the items in the table the document has
a section which shows the physical quantities of inputs necessary to reach the targets, the costs, and the institutional
support necessary. These sections discuss the cadre and
training requirements and some of the problems and uncertainties to be faced. The plan has a section for each of the
minor food crops, setting targets and discussing the inputs
and actions necessary to achieve the targets.

Some of this detail is repeated in the project plans, but
it is in the Food Self-Sufficiency Plan that the East Pakistani
planners regularly though informally optimize their program.
They know roughly how various sources of increase can produce more rice by policy measures or by incremental expenditures of rupees or foreign exchange. In recent years foreign
exchange, from export earnings and foreign aid, has been the
binding constraint. The Food Self-Sufficiency Plan, in effect,
maximizes the increase in food production from the available
foreign exchange.

Project allotments are then adjusted to be consistent with
the latest food plan. This 60-page document thus relates all
the projects which immediately affect production to the updated
physical production targets of the plan.

The Agricultural Policy Committee

Since November 1966 a top-level Agricultural Policy Committee has met regularly each quarter. Membership includes
the central Government Minister of Finance, Minister of
Agriculture, Secretary of Finance and Secretary of Agriculture,
and the East Pakistan Chief Secretary and Additional Chief
Secretaries, (who are the heads of the relevant provincial
ministries) with the Governor presiding. The secretariat is
provided by the Planning Department agricultural staff and the
Agriculture Department planning cell.

Meetings generally have from 10 to 15 agenda items. The
Food Self-Sufficiency Plan is usually prominent; other common topics have included the new block demonstrations, annual
food campaign themes, foreign exchange allotments for private

import of fractional cu-sec pumps, and the fertilizer subsidy
rate. Heads of concerned departments and agencies stand by
to second the Additional Chief Secretaries and provide supplementary detail over the working papers presented at the
meetings. They often meet monthly with subordinates to update working papers between meetings of the Policy Committee.

Rural development in many countries frequently suffers
from lack of high-level attention. Rural development problems
do not tend to articulate themselves as issues on which cabinet-
level decision is necessary. Agricultural problems can go
unsolved for years with no administrative repercussions.
Foreign exchange allotments can be made without considering
agricultural project requirements without administrative repercussions. Such is the nature of noncapital-project development activity. The high-level policy committee device ensures
that these activities and problems get the top-level attention
they need.

LOCAL PLANNING

As in Malaysia, planning is decentralized to the maximum.
East Pakistan has gone a step further, however; it has placed
all possible responsibility for project planning and management on the villagers themselves. It has started them with
simple earthworks projects and gradually given them more
complex activities to plan and manage.

Rural Works

This is a public works program carefully adapted to the
limitations of amateur management.

The initial planning works from the very bottom up. Each
union council member holds a meeting in his ward to consider
what projects they could use. The union council consolidates
these proposals into a multiyear plan for the union (now a
five-year plan, originally they made one- and three-year
plans), with all projects listed in a single series in order of

priority. As in Malaysia, the hard decisions on priorities
must be made locally. The union council also advances proposals for projects beyond the scope of one union to the thana
council. Here the same consolidation process takes place
and proposals are advanced to the district council.

At each level multiyear plan books similar to the Malaysian
Redbooks described in Chapter 7 are compiled. The district
Redbook has the same format. There are two sections: water
control and roads. Each section has six sheets with accompanying map overlays, a sheet for 1964/65 and a sheet for
each year of the Third Plan. The thana and union plan books
are somewhat simpler, with provisions for other types of
projects as well.

The plan books form a basic catalog of projects, but each
year the councils submit proposals for the coming year. The
government requires that first priority be given to rehabilitation of defective old projects (the unions are required to provide adequate general maintenance from union revenues) and
completion of projects started in previous years. The Government of East Pakistan also gives the councils some indication
of how much of an increase over the previous year's grants
can be expected.

Projects are managed by volunteer committees, one in
each ward of the union, which handles all small projects in
the ward, and one for each of the multiward projects. The
secretary of the committee is compensated. Work crews are
drawn from the union lists of landless or almost landless
farmers. Committee secretaries draw advances at weekly
meetings and are authorized at the thana to pay crews on the
basis of the volume of work completed. The thana has a
supervisor, an overseer, and an accountant assigned to the
works program, who do a good deal of spot-checking.

Obviously a program involving vast numbers of amateur
managers requires a very thorough system of training,
scheduling, and reporting. The thana level officers are
trained for a month at Comilla. Each year they attend a four-
day training conference where they are introduced to changes
in procedures and new types of schemes. For example,
communal fish culture was introduced a few years ago. Union
councilmen also attend annual training conferences on the

works program and other aspects of the Basic Democracy
Program. Project committees are given a week's training
at the thana headquarters. These training sessions teach the
supervisory, scheduling, and bookkeeping procedures required
and stress particularly proper estimating and measurement
of work volume. Proper maps and drawings are required.
Estimating and measurement was somewhat haphazard at first
but has steadily been improved.

The union councils are held to a tight annual cycle; the
calendars hanging in their meeting rooms show different document submission deadlines every two weeks or so. Project
planning is scheduled over July, August, and September. In
October and November, thana and higher echelons review and
approve programs. Committeemen are trained in August,
and, as projects are approved in October and November,
materials are ordered and work teams mobilized. Work is
performed from December through April. In May and June
projects are completed, the books are closed, and final reports are submitted.

A scheduling/reporting format is used which is similar
to the Malaysian format but more specifically adapted to the
types of projects executed. Figure 8.2 reproduces instructions for planning and reporting road work. Figure 8.3 is
the progress report form. Figure 8.4 is the corresponding
form for building construction. As can be seen, the format
forces the project committees to think through their scheduling
carefully. It covers not only the physical work but the
preparatory steps and the order and receipt of material.
The formats are too varied and too detailed to provide a ranking official with the quick visual impression of the problems
of a locale, which one can get from the Malaysian system,
but they are an obvious boon to the amateur planner. They
break large scheduling jobs down into more manageable small
scheduling decisions and take the amateur planner step-by-step
through the project.

In addition to the physical accomplishments of the program
and its economic benefits, there is a most important human by-
product. This by-product has been summed up by Akhter
Hameed Khan and A. K. M. Mohsen, the guiding lights of the
pilot project at Comilla: "These projects have created a numerous body of managers in the nooks and corners of Comilla
Thana who are now ready to undertake bigger tasks."[18]

Plan of Execution and Physical Progress Report--Roads.

1.   After you have made a project estimate, fill in the blanks in Column 2 showing the total amount of each item to be accomplished to complete the road. It is likely that many projects will take more than one year to complete. Column 2 will show the total amount for the whole project. Column 15 will show the total amount to be completed during this financial year.

2.   Next decide how much of each type of work is to be accomplished during each month. Place this information in the upper left corner of the appropriate block. For example earthwork might be shown as follows:

Jan   Feb

| 10,000 | 50,000 |

3.   Do not use the lower corner of each block yet. In filling in the upper corner, use the same units as shown in column 2. Earthwork will be in cft., bricks in lakhs, box cutting in rft., etc. In some cases, such as the dressing of a road embankment, the item to be noted is the start of work and the completion of work. These two might come in the same month or in different months. The entry would appear as follows if the work was to be accomplished during May on this particular road:

May   June   May

| start | complete | or | start compl-ete |

The purchase of cement might appear as follows:

Aug.   Sept.   Oct.   Jan

| Tender | | Order | | 5000 |

4.   It is not necessary that there be entries for all items. For example, if a road is not to be surfaced, it is not necessary to fill in the items for Box Cutting, Soling, Herring Bone Bond, Khoa Consolidation, and Carpettings.

5.   The item for Bridges and Culverts to complete this road must be filled in. In addition, a separate proforma of a type similar to this proforma will be completed for each bridge. The culverts for one road may be grouped together on one of these proformas.

6.   Within five days after the end of the month, lower corners of the blocks will be coloured to show whether the month's target was achieved. If the target was achieved, the lower corner will be coloured green. If the target was not achieved, the lower corner will be coloured red. If some work was done, but the target was not achieved, the lower corner will be coloured red and the amount achieved will be entered. If the target is exceeded, the lower corner will be coloured green and the amount achieved will be entered.

FIGURE 8.2.   Instructions for Planning and Reporting Roadwork

Plan of Execution and Physical Progress Report - Roads.

Year.......... Subdivision/District

Road from..........to.......... Length.......... Sponsored by.......... Council/Committee..........

Item 1	Total to be Accomplished 2	July 3	Aug. 4	Sept. 5	Oct. 6	Nov. 7	Dec. 8	Jan. 9	Feb. 10	Mar. 11	Apr. 12	May 13	June 14	Total this year 15
Earthwork ...	cft.													
Dressing ...	(Start) (Complete)													
Purchase of Coal; Indent Placed ... Deposit of Money ... Receipt of Coal ...	(Indent) (Deposit) tons													
Burning of Bricks; Land Secured ... Bricks Burned ...	(Land) Lakh													
Purchase of Bricks; Calling of tender ... Placement of Order ... Receipt of Bricks ...	(Tender) (Order) Lakh													
Purchase Cement/Bitumen; Call tender/Indent Order/ Deposit Money Receipt	(Tender) (Indent) (Order) (Deposit) Bags/Drums													
Box Cutting ...	.... rft.													
Fitting–Breadth ...	.... rft.													
Herring Bone Bond ...	.... rft.													
Khoa Consolidation Depth ...	.... rft.													
Bitumen Carpetting of R.C.C. Pavement Depth........in.	.... rft.													
Bridges and Culverts to complete road	Number......													

FIGURE 8.3. Road Work Progress Report

PLAN OF EXECUTION AND PHYSICAL PROGRESS REPORT--BUILDINGS

Year _____

Name of Building (or purpose)————, Sponsored by————Council/Committee ————

Subdivision————— District —————

Item.	Total to be Accomplished	July.	August.
1	2	3	4
Plan and Estimate	(Complete)		
Purchase of Coal Indent Placed Deposit of Money Receipt of Coal	(Indent) (Deposit) ....tons.		
Burning of Bricks Land Secured Bricks Burned	(Land) ....Lakhs.		
Purchase of Bricks Calling of tender Placement of Order Receipt of Bricks	(Tender) (Order) ....Lakhs.		
Purchase of Cement Calling of tender Placement of Order Receipt of Cement	(Tender) (Order) ....Bags.		
Purchase of M. S. Rods Calling of tender Placement of Order Receipt of rods	(Tender) (Order) ....tons.		
Earthwork	........cft.		
Construction to plinth level	(Start, Complete)		
Floors	(Start, Complete)		
Walls	(Start, Complete)		
Roof	(Start, Complete)		
Plastering	(Start, Complete)		
Plumbing	(Start, Complete)		
Wiring	(Start, Complete)		
Doors and Windows	(Start, Complete)		
Painting	(Start, Complete)		

FIGURE 8.4. Building Construction Report

Program Building

Extension planning is done in such a way as to take the
farmers themselves through the entire analytical process of
development planning. This extension planning method is
called program building.

It starts with a survey of the present conditions and
problems of the union. As a first step the union council sets
up an agriculture committee and authorizes a house-to-house
survey by ward councilmen and leading farmers, assisted by
the union agricultural assistant. The results are recapped
on a summary sheet and discussed at a meeting. The sheet
shows land per family, crop yields, cash resources and
needs, water availability and problems, losses to crop and
livestock pests, and transportation facilities and deficiencies,
among other things.

The discussion of the survey recap revolves around the
same basic question that is demanded of the union council in
the rural works planning process: what are the priorities?
Again, the committee at the union level must list its needs
in priority order. The farmers are thus called upon to do
the complete analysis of development planning. They determine needs and potentials and decide what to do first, second,
and third. The analysis is obviously far less sophisticated
than that undertaken by national development planning staffs,
but it requires a long view and some hard decisions.

The next step is to establish subcommittees to develop
and manage action programs. These subcommittees are
supposed to be oriented on the problems which have been
identified; in actuality they are set up along standard functional
lines. About 80 percent of the unions now have crops subcommittees. Smaller numbers of fisheries, livestock, irrigation, horticulture, education, health, and other subcommittees
have been established.

Program building covers more than agriculture. The subcommittees become an extension of the total development program of the union council. They are a combination of advisory
committees and special executive agencies of the union council.
In those thanas where program building has been operative for
two or more years, more than 1 out of every 15 farmers is
active on a subcommittee.

NOTES

1.   Haroun Er Rashid, East Pakistan, a Systematic Regional Geography (Lahore: Sh. Ghulam Ali & Sons, 1965), p. 117.

2.   Ibid., p. 145.

3.   Ibid., pp. 381-83.

4.   Ibid., pp. 361-62.

5.   E. Owen, Democratic Development in East Pakistan
(Washington, D. C.: Embassy of Pakistan, 1966), p. 2.

6.   1968/69 Annual Plan (Government of Pakistan, 1968),
p. 10.

7.   East Pakistan Food Self-Sufficiency Program 1968
(Government of East Pakistan, 1967, Mimeo.).

8.   Rural Development in East Pakistan (The Rice Goal
Plan) (Dacca: U.S. AID Agriculture Division, 1966), p. 18
(Mimeo.).

9.   East Pakistan.

10.   1968/69 Annual Plan, p. 4.

11.   Ibid., p. 7.

12.   East Pakistan.

13.   1968/69 Annual Plan, p. 9.

14.   Manual of Reporting Procedures, Tech. Instruction
4/68 (Pakistan Family Planning Council, 1967), p. 2.

15.   Ibid., p. 4.

16. For a description of the principal model used, see W. Tims, A Medium Term Planning Model for Pakistan and its Application, Economic Development Report No. 43 (Cambridge, Mass.: Development Advisory Service, Harvard University, 1966, Mimeo.).

17. Outline of the Third Five-Year Plan: 1965-70 (Government of Pakistan, 1964), p. 7.

18. A. H. Khan and A. K. M. Mohsen, "Mobilizing Village Leadership," International Development Review (September, 1962), p. 7.

CHAPTER 9 SENEGAL

The milieu of this final case study is radically different
from those of the three preceding studies. From the densely
populated rice basins of the Far East, we now turn to the
sparsely populated fringes of the Sahara. The milieu is much
more primitive. Literacy is well under 10 percent in the
villages. The supply of cadre is far poorer. Cultivation is
often dominated by the hoe. Yet here in West Africa is a
small country whose main region has gone from stage I to
stage IIIb of rural development in less than a decade, on the
basis of innovations requiring a substantial technical advance
over traditional practices.

Senegal offers two types of lessons in rural development.
It shows how rapid change can take place despite a severe
lack of educated human resources. In addition, it demonstrates
excellent working method for building institutions on the basis
of specific innovations.

Senegal has two rural sectors: a food-producing subsistence sector and an export-oriented "peanut basin," with
which this case study is concerned. The so-called peanut
basin, with a population of 1 million covers the central
districts of the country and contains over 40 percent of the
rural population. Peanuts are the main export and the basis
of the economic life of Senegal.

The family structure is two-tiered. The nuclear family
of six farms an average of 7.4 hectares, roughly half in peanuts and half in millet or sorghum. [1] Half of these are organized in extended family exploitations called carrés, the
average carré having 1.5 nuclear families. The carré is
the main farm decision-making unit. The 109,000 carrés
of the basin average less than one traction animal each,

usually a horse or an ass.[2] As in the rest of Africa, much
of the land preparation is done by hoe.

Here is an unusual phenomenon: traditional cultivators
are very much into the cash economy. They must sell peanuts
to buy food. Senegal imports about half its food requirements,
mostly rice. Rice is the preferred cereal, but only a little
is grown and that outside the peanut basin. Farmers previously sold their peanuts to local merchants, whose fraud
and inefficiency grossly exploited the peasants. The farmers
went heavily into debt at exhorbitant rates in the months before
the harvest to buy food.

It had been recognized for some time that changes in
methods of cultivation were necessary for the survival of the
economy. Extension of peanut cultivation onto marginal land
was ruining the soil, and the world market for peanuts was
weak. France was supporting the Senegal economy by paying
a 15 percent premium over world prices for its peanuts.
French agronomists had been working intensively on adaptive
research for decades. The techniques for raising the yields
and maintaining fertility of the soil had been known to them
for some time.

The population of the peanut basin is scattered. The
average village has only 18 carrés, about 24 families. Ad-
ministratively the country is divided into six regions, subdivided in turn into 20 departments and then into 70 arrondissements. The peanut basin covers most of three regions and
about 42 arrondissements. In the standard terminology of
this book, the region corresponds to a province and the arrondissement to a district. The average arrondissement, however,
has only 4,000 families. There is no administrative structure
at the commune level.

FIRST STEPS IN RURAL DEVELOPMENT

Senegal was granted independence by France on August
20, 1960. As a preliminary to development planning, several
study groups were set up and two French consulting firms,
CINAM (Compagnie d'Industrialisation et d'Aménagement de

Territoire) and SERESA (Société d'Etudes et de Recherches
Economiques et Sociales en Agriculture) were contracted to
perform basic preplanning studies and make recommendations.[3] National and regional commissions then worked
from the voluminous documents submitted by the two firms.

The First Plan--1960-64

   The resulting plan was quite comprehensive. It defined
the stages of long-term evolution of the Senegal economy and
set forth, in accordance with the CINAM and SERESA recommendations, a comprehensive structure of new institutions,
a broad structural reform.

   The supporting studies contained a thorough analysis of
the cadre and organizational requirements of development.
As a first step in the structural reforms, the field operations
of all agencies were regrouped into a homogeneous structure,
whose main nodules were the region and the arrondissement.
Previously each agency had had a different set of boundaries
of field office territories. The power and coordinating
authority of the regional governors was augmented. Regional
agency officers and other notables were organized in a
regional development committee to coordinate activities and
consider the total development requirements of each region.
Each region was also endowed with an autonomous Compagnie
Regionale de l'Assistance pour le Développement (CRAD) to
handle supply and marketing services and other types of development support.

   At the arrondissement level, cadre of all rural service
agencies were assigned--at first largely on paper--to a
Centre d'Expansion Rurale (CER). The administrative officer
of the arrondissement was the head of the CER, advised by a
local development committee. Included in CER was a branch
office of CRAD, with several warehouses in each arrondissement. As the first commune-level institution, cooperatives
were established for groups of 10 villages, on the average.

   At the national level two important autonomous institutions were established, the Banque Sénégalaise pour la
Développement (BSD) and the Office de Commercialisation

Agricole (OCA), an agricultural marketing board. Both func-
tioned through CRAD. The BSD made loans exclusively to
cooperatives, whose books and finances were handled by the
local CRAD offices. The OCA centralized peanut exports,
with the crop collected by CRAD from the cooperatives. Thus
credit, supply, and marketing were conveniently linked in a
single structure of CRAD and commune-level cooperatives.
Loans of up to 25 percent of the expected peanut sales of each
carré were authorized (7 percent was authorized for consumption needs and 18 percent for production needs).

The production program of the First Plan was less well
defined. No action was planned on peanuts, but a target of
30 percent increase in rice and millet production was projected. The plan called for agricultural diversification. The
detail was to be worked out, however, by regional and local
planning.

Animation Rurale

A final important element of the new institutional structure
was a group-action stimulation program called Animation
Rurale.[4] This was a distinctive approach to community development initiated in 1959 by the Institut de Recherches et
de l'Application des Méthodes de Développement. Specially
adapted to the needs of more primitive societies, it sought to
stimulate group action and change by bringing potential young
leaders to loosely structured training programs in rural
centers. One such center was set up in each department, to
which each arrondissement sent a group of 35 trainees,
roughly two or three per village, each quarter.

In the training program simple lectures on rural technology and civics would be followed by discussion. Then the
group would go to a nearby village and make an inventory of
its resources and problems. The group would then discuss
the needs of that village and formulate a program for it. In
this way potential leaders for each village were introduced
to development-oriented thinking.

Animateurs, as the trainees were called, were encouraged
to follow up their training with a specific project in the village.
The centers offered some specific technical training to follow
up the general training and support projects. By 1965 some
7, 000 animateurs had been trained.

Results of the First Plan

The cooperatives achieved effective coverage faster than
in any other country with which the author is familiar. By
1964 some 1, 500 cooperatives were handling over 60 percent
of the peanut crop. This percentage rose in subsequent years.
Participation was completely voluntary, but circumstances
gave the farmers a compelling reason to join. They generally
needed consumption credit and could get it at reasonable rates
through a cooperative. The OCA/CRAD marketing structure
was overstaffed and inefficient, but it was more honest and
efficient than the traditional structure and gave the farmers
a better price.

The credit system worked well because needs were supplied in kind, thus assuring that the loan would be used for
its express purpose, and because supply and marketing were
handled by the same agency as credit. Repayment was assured
when the farmer came to market his crop. Rural nonpro-
ductive debt declined steadily. Thus what are usually the
most difficult problems of rural development, credit and marketing, were solved with surprising ease.

Other solutions proved more difficult. The difficulties
were frankly recognized by the government when it evaluated
progress after a major government reorganization in 1963. [5]
Local planning had proven illusory. Talent and method were
lacking. Extension work was very superficial, limited to a
few lectures and demonstrations at some of the general meetings of cooperatives. Yields were stagnant, little better than
in 1963. From a miniscule base the use of agricultural
chemicals had indeed tripled but was still less than 15 percent
of the optimum application in the peanut basin.

Supply and marketing still left much to be desired in
their operation. The cooperatives were dominated by the
marabouts, the traditional religious and political leaders,
who had previously worked closely with local merchants.

Because of the ignorance of the farmers, traditional short-weighting and other frauds continued. Supplies were ordered by CRAD on the basis of the indents furnished by the cooperatives. These indents were frequently prepared on the basis of guesswork by the cooperative president, without consulting the members.

Animation Rurale had undoubtedly made a great psychological impact, but its concrete accomplishments were very limited. A few villages produced spectacular projects, but generally there was little project activity or follow-up after the training. Subsequent events did show, however, that Animation Rurale had implanted a receptivity that was vital to subsequent rapid change.

ACCELERATED PEANUT PRODUCTIVITY PROGRAM

Events of the early 1960's forced a concentration on peanuts. The French price subsidy was scheduled for abolition under the European Common Market. Experience had shown the need for a trained and seasoned extension cadre at the arrondissement or lower level. Experience had also shown that it was too early to expect the regional and local bodies to plan their own programs. They must first be seasoned by carrying out a well-detailed national program. Senegal made a most explicit acknowledgment that institutional development must be based on specific productive innovations.

The SATEC Proposal

In 1959 Francis Bour, director general of the Institut des Recherches Agricoles Tropicaux founded the Société de l'Aide Technique et de la Coopération (SATEC). This public corporation was set up to apply Bour's concept of "action de masse," a composite of two ideas that have been often discussed but, to this writer's knowledge, not previously successfully applied. The first was individual optimum farm plans, applying the techniques of farm management that have been successful in the U.S. to peasant agriculture. The second

was "encadrement dense, " a dense network of one extension
agent per 200 to 400 families, which would be necessary to
apply individual farm planning. Such an intensive program
has often been considered necessary to bring about rapid
upgrading of peasant cultivation practices.

SATEC first tried to apply these concepts in Upper Volta,
but failed largely because of lack of adequate previous adaptive
research. [6] In Senegal the adaptive research on peanuts had
long been adequate. In 1964 SATEC set about testing its plan
of action in a few arrondissements of the peanut basin and
drawing up a proposal to the Republic of Senegal and the
European Economic Community, which would finance the program.

In September, 1964, a four-volume proposal was submitted,
on the basis of which a contract was signed. The first volume
was a "note de synthèse, " a summary of the proposed program
and the logic behind it. The second volume was a technical report by two collaborating research institutes--Institut des Recherches Agricoles Tropicaux and Institut des Recherches sur
les Huiles Oléagineux (Edible Oils Research Institute). The
third volume was a report on the general conditions and problems of agriculture in the peanut basin. The fourth volume
was an economic report.

The organization of the summary volume is worth noting.
The format is not recommended, since it does not show the
relationships of inputs to outputs in a few compact tables. It
does, however, convey the logic that the author would recommend.

It starts with a statement of both production and institutional objectives:

> The program of accelerated development of productivity
> aims, in a period of three years, to augment substantially
> peanut and millet yields. It should likewise result in the
> creation of a network of rural extension agents, destined
> to complete what has been accomplished since 1960 to
> provide the rural sector with appropriate developmental
> structures. [7]

Section I (of the first volume) locates the program in the
general agricultural policy of the Senegal. It first notes the

institutional progress to date and the increase, albeit a modest one, in production and the use of agricultural inputs. It then points out the gravest of the many problems of cultivation, the need for more fertilizer and better rotation, and the need for more weeding by animal traction. It points out the main institutional need, the lack of cadre in the CER. It then sets a target of 25 percent increase in yields. This target, by the way, was written into the contract.

Section II gives an analysis of the content of the program. First it summarizes the technical content, and ensemble of technical themes of which the main ones are:

Use of selected, disinfected seed

Sowing in line, with optimal density and space between lines

Proper application of fertilizer

Weeding with an animal-drawn hoe

The required equipment includes a seeder and the animal-drawn hoe. The recommended practices should produce a 45 percent greater yield, according to trials conducted by the two institutes preparing Volume Two. [8]

Section II then goes on to discuss the plan of action of the operation, the cadre and staff, the field routine, the training program, the organizational relationships, and the schedule.

Section III gives the economic evaluation of the program, the expected return on investment. [9] Assuming constant prices it would produce a total increase in net national income of $38.6 million a year, from total outlays, project budget, and a credit expansion, of $16 million. The farmers would gain an increased income of $24 million a year on their investment (their borrowing) of $5 million. The foreign exchange saving would be on the order of $34 million to $38 million. Removal of the French subsidy would lower this return on investment but leave it still clearly profitable.

Plan of Operation

Cadre--The staffing of the program had two distinctive
features. The first was the use of expatriates as district-
level line officers and the use of foreigners as field cadre
supervisors. SATEC hired 42 French and other European
technical assistants, one for each arrondissement. In status
and competence they were largely newly graduated agronomists, somewhat between Peace Corps volunteers and the
usual technical assistance experts. They were later replaced
by newly graduated Senegalese agronomists, to whom they
gave on-the-job training.

The second distinctive feature was the use of semiliterate
village-level cadre. SATEC eventually hired 850 monitors, 25
to 35 years of age, generally with four to five years of education and possessing a smattering of French but possessing
no illusions about the desk job in the big city awaiting them,
an illusion that plagues slightly younger and slightly better
educated Senegalese. Some 20 monitors per arrondissement
were each assigned about 150 carrés. The extension techniques were, as will be noted below, adapted to the limitations
of these village-level cadre.

An "encadrement dense" was thus achieved in spite of the
severe shortages of educated manpower. SATEC took what
was available in the villages and capped it with expatriates
temporarily. These were backed by a staff of four experts
at each region and at Dakar.

Routine--N. McKitterick has written: "Indeed, the
secrets of 'l'action de masse' are contained in the painstaking
detail of the routine of the operation, a routine which includes
census-taking, training, record-keeping, and demonstrations,
in the perfection of which all participated."[10]

The routine is organized first of all around a schedule
of seasonal themes. The schedule follows the cropping
season: disinfecting of seeds in March and April, planting
techniques in June, weeding techniques in July and August,
and harvesting techniques in September and October. The
monitor presents the rationale of each theme with various
dramatic devices, demonstrates the techniques, and then

works with the farmers in the field to assist them in getting
it right. Since the program requires the farmers to use new
tools and equipment, such on-the-job supervision is essential.

Secondly, the routine is organized around the farm management record system. The monitors keep spread sheets
with the basic data on each carré, the number of fields and
hectares, the number of laborers, the items of equipment,
and the seed and fertilizer from the previous year. From
this the technical assistant calculates an optimal plan for
the coming season after each harvest. From a table of standard coefficients he computes the additional equipment and
production supplies necessary to get optimum results. An
optimal plan sheet is then filled out for each farmer which,
if accepted by him, becomes the basis of his loan request for
the coming year. This becomes the basis for sound indents,
for a sound request to CRAD for supplies for the coming year,
and it serves as a check against fraud.

The monitor also keeps spread sheets recording which
themes each farmer has adopted. These are harder to verify
than purchases of equipment and supplies and must be spot
checked in the field by the technical assistants and others of
the SATEC staff.

Training--It would appear that long training would be
necessary to enable semiliterates to carry out such a routine.
Paradoxically, the longest training period they undergo is a
three-week preservice session. This is followed during the
season by four three-day sessions, supplemented by fortnightly review sessions at CER and a good deal of on-the-job
supervision. The training is geared to feed the monitors the
necessary knowledge and skills in small, well-digested portions which can easily be absorbed.

A striking feature of all training in Senegal is "étude de
milieu, " sessions of systematic observation of the village
economy. After a week of general preservice orientation at
regional centers the monitors spend a week in a village under
guidance conducting a census of agriculture, in effect, and
noting the practices. The technical assistants likewise, after
a week of orientation on peanut culture at Bambey, spend
three months just getting to know their arrondissement. The
"reléve des cadre, " the Senegalese agricultural school graduates

who replace them, likewise spend some weeks just getting to
know the arrondissement and reporting their systematic observations. The Animation Rurale training, as noted above,
also featured étude de milieu. For the monitors, étude de
milieu comes before specific technical training.

A second striking feature is the degree to which technical
manuals are simplified. The monitor is given a handbook in
which every point is explained with drawings and in the
simplest possible language. It is based on the comprehensive
manual on peanut and millet culture given to each technical
assistant.

A third feature is rehearsal. In the third week of preservice training the monitor learns the themes of the first
several weeks of operation. Once the themes have been explained and demonstrated, he is actually rehearsed in their
presentation and demonstration. A similar procedure is
followed in the four subsequent training sessions at the
regional center that come before each new phase in the crop
production cycle and present the balance of the themes.

A fourth striking feature is embodied in the fortnightly
review sessions in the arrondissement and close on-the-job
supervision. At the review sessions the themes are reviewed
and the experiences and problems of the past two weeks are
discussed by the technical assistant and all the monitors of
the arrondissement. This not only reinforces the training but
builds esprit de corps and confidence. Finally the technical
assistants work closely with their 20-odd monitors. Because
the monitor's literacy is limited, they generally fill in the
names and column headings for the monitors on their spread
sheets.[11] They supervise the monitors particularly closely
when they first fill in the spread sheet data. They also write
their monitors a weekly schedule of work. (The 1964 summary
report emphasized that "methodical working routine is important to training.")

The Senegalese replacements for the technical assistants
also need more training; they are not sufficiently seasoned
to take over immediately. After some weeks of étude de
milieu they are assigned a few monitors for supervision.
Gradually the technical assistants transfer all the monitors
over to the Senegalese officers, while giving them careful
on-the-job training.

Schedule--Table 9.1 gives the original plan's schedule of production increase, staffing, and budget.

TABLE 9.1

Accelerated Productivity Program, Senegal, 1965-67

	1965	1966	1967
Production (thousands of tons)			
Peanuts (979 in 1964)	1,046	1,127	1,222
Millet and sorghum (490 in 1964)	510	550	600
Staffing			
Monitors	560	850	850
Technical assistants	42	42	22
Senegalese replacements	20	42	42
Regional engineers			
French	9	9	9
Senegal	3	6	6
Budget (millions of US$)	$1.52	$1.97	$1.33

Source: Société de l'Aide Technique et de la Coopération (SATEC), Projet de programme de développement accéléré de la productivité d'arachide et de mil, dans les régions de Thies, de Kaolack, et de Diourbel (Rep. de Senegal, Min. de l'Economie Rurale et de la Coopération, 1964), I, 18.

Results

Setting annual production and income targets is essential to planning, yet in any one year production and income results will depend far more on weather and prices than on project activity. The peanut crop of Senegal went through some dry years with rapidly declining prices. Nevertheless, preliminary estimates for 1967 by the Food and Agriculture Organization show peanut production at 1,261,000 tons. [12]

Generally, the best available indicator of the success of this type of program is the actual, as compared to the planned, sale of production equipment and supplies. These were roughly on schedule. The worsening ratio of costs of inputs to price of output makes the technical success of the project (which apparently convinced the farmers they should purchase these inputs) all the more impressive.

The monitors' records of the adoption of cultural practices by each farm are spot-checked in the field to verify their veracity. These show that most practices have been adopted roughly on schedule, but some definitely have not. As of the end of 1967 roughly a third of the farmers of the peanut basin had adopted almost all the practices, and a third had adopted some of the practices. The next two years should see further increases in production.

Was the project a short-run economic success? The price of peanuts has dropped precipitously. Some years ago a kilo of peanuts could buy two kilos of rice; now it takes three kilos of peanuts to buy one kilo of rice. The increased production of millet and sorghum, which is difficult to estimate, since it is not marketed, has saved the farmer from severe economic distress, but his real income has decreased. He can no longer afford much rice, his preferred food. One must evaluate the results, however, by comparing the outcome with what it would have been without the project. The difference between farm income and foreign exchange earnings with and without the project may be half what it would have been had prices remained constant. Nonetheless, it still has provided a very rapid social payoff on the investment.

In terms of the long-run goals, the completion of the rural development institutions, the project has been a success. In late 1967 SATEC turned over to the Ministry of Rural Affairs a complete network of extension cadre. The monitors had proven their worth; although SATEC had full freedom to fire incompetents, the turnover had been light. In terms of service institutions, rural development stage IIIb had been reached. In terms of farmer participation and production diversification, stage IIIb was still some ways off.

Nevertheless, important symptoms of stage III are appearing. Development initiative is shifting from the national to the

local level. In some locales the farmers are beginning to
keep their own farm records. New production programs are
highly localized. In districts near urban areas the CER, now
staffed with competent Senegalese extension officers, are
planning diversification into vegetable production. In the more
fertile and, paradoxically, less populated southwestern districts SATEC is training cadre for promotion of cotton production and use of cattle-drawn equipment.

Senegal has thus demonstrated that complete coverage of
agricultural service institutions can be achieved rapidly if
(1) farmers are traditionally into the cash economy and (2) a
major innovation package has been adequately proven in adaptive
research.

MADAGASCAR POSTSCRIPT:
RICE PRODUCTIVITY OPERATION

Is "action de masse" applicable where farmers are not
into the cash economy? SATEC has initiated a project in
Madagascar to answer that question.

Madagascar, the Great Red Isle with its unique Afro-
Polynesian cultural heritage, has a central plateau which is
a replica of the rice basins of Southeast Asia. Here live at
least half the Malagasy rural population of over 5 million.
Farmers with one- or two-hectare farms sell their small
surplus over consumption needs to Indian and Chinese merchants, who are inefficient and often unscrupulous. The
demographic pressure is high and in the early 1960's there
was an increasing need to import rice.

Madagascar's situation in some respects resembles that
of Senegal. Its first development plan pinned excess hopes
on local planning and a variation on Animation Rurale called
"rasele sol" (scrape the earth). This grass-roots initiative,
while spectacular in some locales, did not make a significant
contribution to a solution of the growing economic problem.
Like Senegal, Madagascar was forced to concentrate on increasing productivity of its main crop to solve an immediate
economic problem and to build rural institutions.

Madagascar had some advantages over Senegal. The level
of education is somewhat higher; somewhat more cadre were
immediately available. The Malagasy have a reputation for
natural talent at paperwork. The country has a better administrative structure. Administrative units and their sizes are
quite similar to the standard structure used in this volume
and described in Chapter 4. There is a tradition of village
community discipline and a well-developed commune. Against
these advantages, however, is an offsetting total lack of
credit, supply, and marketing institutions such as Senegal
developed during its first plan period.

Plan of Action

SATEC made some small trials of action de masse with
a rice innovation package in 1965 and then in 1966 joined in a
trinational assistance consortium called Groupement pour
l'Opération Productivité Rizicole (Rice Productivity Operation
Group). Providing the technical assistance with SATEC were
two firms, Ifagraria of Italy and Agrar und Hydrotechnik of
West Germany. The innovation package included improved
seed, fertilizer, and pesticides, a variety of cultural practices,
and "microhydraulique," small irrigation works, largely
improvements on the existing network. On-farm trials showed
the innovation package could raise yields from the 3 tons per
hectare produced by traditional methods to 5.2 tons per hectare.

The organization and routine were based on those of Senegal, with certain differences. The most important was the
supply and credit organization that had to be set up parallel
to the extension organization. A trained extension network
had already been started, so some of the professional manpower was Malagasy from the start. Below the district level
(sous-préfecture as it is called in Madagascar) a fourth tier
was inserted in the structure at the commune, where a Malagasy extension officer supervised five to seven village-level
monitors. The supply and credit network also had a distribution point at the commune level.

The credit and farm record concepts are somewhat different from those in Senegal. The optimum plan is contained
in a rather elaborate individual farm record book with a

variety of stubs and tickets, printed in French and Malagasy.
The farmer becomes eligible for credit by signing an engage-
ment to follow the practices in the optimum plan, on a ticket
which is detached from the book. The book carries cultural
practice instructions, which some (but not most) farmers can
read. The monitor signs the record book certifying that cultural practices have been executed and detaches tickets on
those sheets for the records of the Operations Group. To be
eligible for midseason supplies on credit, the farmer's
record must have the certification that the cultural practices
have been carried out. The system is based on the principle
that the increased production from improved cultural practices
is the security behind the loan. The paperwork load is heavier
than in Senegal, but the Malagasy monitors are fortunately up
to the task.

Targets for participating farms were set at 2,000 for
1966/67, 20,000 for 1967/68, 48,500 for 1968/69 and 150,000
for 1970/71. [13] By 1971 the program should cover the best
half of the ricelands of the Great Red Isle, and the Malagasy
should be able to carry on with substantially reduced foreign
assistance.

Results

Another year is needed for a conclusive demonstration of
success, but results to date are encouraging. [14] About 80,000
farmers have signed engagements for 1968/69. In the first
year, however, farmers generally engaged less than half
their land, so supply and equipment sales were slightly below
target. The participants have generally gone ahead and engaged their full land in the program in their second year of
participation, so that it seems probable that targets will be
achieved. Loan repayment has been excellent.

Does this prove that action de masse is possible wherever
there is an adequately proven innovation package? The experience is strongly encouraging but not conclusive. More
time is needed to prove out the Malagasy experience, and
account must be taken of the special community solidarity
and talent for paperwork found on the Great Red Isle.

NOTES

1.   Société de l'Aide Technique et de la Coopération
(SATEC), Projet de programme de développement accéléré de
la productivité d'arachide et de mil, dans les régions de Thies,
de Kaolack, et de Diourbel (Rep. de Senegal, Min. de l'Economie Rurale et de la Coopération, 1964), II, 6.

2.   Ibid.

3.   P. Mersadier, Planning for a Balanced Social and
Development in Senegal, United Nations Document No.
E/CN. 5/346/Add. 13 (1964), p. 11.

4.   D. Hapgood, "Rural Animation in Senegal, " International Development Review (September, 1964), pp. 15-18.

5.   Planification en Afrique: Serie Rouge (Rep. Francaise, Min. de la Coopération, 1964), Dossier No. 3 (Senegal),
pp. 2-3.

6.   J. De Wilde, Agriculture in Tropical Africa (Baltimore: Johns Hopkins Press, 1967), I, 39.

7.   Société, op. cit., I, 1.

8.   Ibid., I, 3.

9.   Ibid., I, 8.

10.   N. McKitterick, "A Mass Attack on Low Productivity
in Peasant Agriculture, " International Development Review
(September, 1967), p. 3.

11.   Ibid., p. 4.

12.   Monthly Bulletin of Agricultural Economics and
Statistics, XVII, No. 4 (April, 1968), 17.

13.   Groupement pour l'Operation Productivité Rizicole:
Rapport de Campagne: 1966-67 (Rep. de Madagascar, Min.
d'Etat chargé de l'Agriculture, de l'Expansion Rurale, et du
Ravitaillement, 1967), p. 8.

14.   Ibid., p. 2.

CHAPTER **10** THE LESSONS OF THE
FOUR CASE STUDIES

The last four chapters have illustrated successful rural
development. They have illustrated different types and different ranges of advancement of the rural sector, progress a-
chieved in diverse economic, social, and political contexts.
They have illustrated different development strategies and
different planning techniques.

Following the overall model-building outlined in Chapter
1, this chapter will analyze the four case studies in terms of
systems concepts and models. We will first apply the model
of rural development as an activity (the concepts generated
in Chapters 2 through 4) to the four cases as a preliminary
test of their real-world validity and relevance. We will then
make a similar preliminary test of the planning model concepts of Chapter 5, applying the structural concepts and the
performance criteria of that chapter to the planning systems
in the four countries. Finally, we will make some general
observations on the techniques drawn from all four cases.

THE ACTIVITY MODEL

The four cases provide good illustrations of the staging
and phasing concepts developed in Chapter 3, as well as
choices among the strategic options discussed in Chapter 4.

The Stages of Rural Development

Taiwan first of all provides a good illustration of development activity within stage IIIb of rural development, as defined

in Chapter 4. Taiwan demonstrates that with comprehensive
rural development the farmers of a developing nation can
achieve a high degree of prosperity on one-hectare farms.
Stage IIIb proves on Taiwan to have some of the characteristics
predicted by the model. Initiative and responsibility for development is highly decentralized. Farming systems have
become highly diversified. Though sound and thorough project
planning continues, sectoral and multisectoral planning takes
on increasing importance. Financing problems on Taiwan
are now more important than problems of institutional strategy,
as predicted by the model.

Malaysia, by contrast, is still in stage IIa. The diversity
of its rural economy and the prosperity of its total economy
make it harder to launch comprehensive coverage of agricultural service institutions. Highly sophisticated and diversified
services are necessary for such an economy. Nevertheless,
Malaysia has done an exceptional job of laying foundations for
comprehensive rural development with its dramatically
efficient physical infrastructure program. It has originated
techniques that have attracted attention around the world.

East Pakistan illustrates movement from stage IIa to IIIa,
with planning and pilot-testing of institutions for stage IIIb.
Coverage of education and supply services, and possibly engineering services, is complete. Credit and marketing services are being pilot-tested; in another year or so they should
be ready to move into the network (or secondary) phase, defined in Chapter 3. As predicted by the model, sector planning
and financial problems are beginning to take precedence over
project planning and institutional problems. Because stage
IIIb has not yet been reached, diversification and the decentralization of initiative in agricultural development is just
beginning.

Senegal illustrates a rapid but somewhat defective movement from rural development stage IIa to IIIb. It is the most
primitive of the four countries examined in depth, yet it has
made the most rapid progress in terms of the model of this
book. Within the so-called peanut basin, coverage of education, supply, marketing, and credit institutions is complete.
Most of the farmers have participated in complex innovations
requiring new equipment and supplies. These innovations
have been limited to two crops, but they have built institutions

that can service a wide range of other innovations and enterprises.

Research in Senegal has not kept pace with this swift institutional development. Further suitable innovations are
not available to most of the districts of the peanut basin.
Senegal thus displays some, but not all, the characteristics
of stage IIIb. Initiative is localized in some districts, as
predicted by the model. Sector planning and comprehensive
financial resource allocation are not yet important, however,
because of lack of further innovations.

Senegal and Malaysia make a striking contrast that brings
out one of the basic paradoxes of rural development. In terms
of the bare model of rural development of this book, Malaysian
performance has fallen far short of that of Senegal, a much more
primitive country. Yet it is the very sophistication and diversification of the Malaysian economy that makes it more difficult to establish multipurpose institutions. The rubber
replanting scheme applied a cadre saturation approach similar
to that of the Société de l'Aide Technique et de la Coopération
(SATEC) in Senegal with equal success, but it did not build
permanent multipurpose institutions. Agriculture in Malaysia
is so diverse that the farmers association, the prototype
multipurpose institution, must be individually tailored to each
commune. One set of plans, by contrast, suited the entire
Senegal peanut basin.

The Phases of Project Evolution

By and large the four countries managed to avoid the
various types of project pathology discussed in Chapter 3.
Taiwan, of course, originated the point-line-network desig-
nation of project phasing used in this model. SATEC roughly
followed this phasing in both Senegal and Madagascar.
Pakistan established a special Academy of Rural Development
to execute the point and line phases. The Comilla academy,
with its on-the-spot, high-quality supervision and training
facilities in a typical rural district, is an institution other
countries might well emulate.

Malaysia did not use the point-line-network phasing on the Redbook project (see Chapter 7). Here is a rare example of a successful crash project. No new organizational patterns or cropping patterns were required for the Malaysian program of stepped-up and dramatized infrastructure development. Physical infrastructure alone generally does not need this careful phasing. Malaysia did use some of this phasing in its land resettlement program, building up gradually to a significant volume. Its farmers association program is now in the line phase.

STRATEGIC OPTIONS

Just how relevant are the main options, the strategy decisions listed in Chapter 4, and the strategy decisions regarding selection of innovations? The four cases indicate that serious attention to these specific options was the basis of the formulation of a strategy that successfully advanced the rural economy.

Basic Organizational Options

It was the Anderson Report of 1950 that led to the farmers associations reforms which enabled Taiwan to move from stage IIa to IIIb. From then on strategy was deliberately aimed at building the farmers associations and the peoples' irrigation societies as farmer-controlled sources of all agricultural services.

Pakistan studied its needs and took a different approach. Public corporations were established for the engineering and supply services, with local merchants handling the retail end of the supply business. Commune committees, together with commune-level extension cadre, provide the education service. Credit, as planned, will be provided by a district-level cooperative with professional cadre plus village-level groups.

Malaysia made a deliberate decision to concentrate first on infrastructure, land settlement, and selected agricultural enterprises such as rubber, postponing the development of comprehensive agricultural services. When the time did come to develop comprehensive agricultural services, a thorough study of organizational problems was made by a team from the Sino-American Joint Commission for Rural Reconstruction (JCRR).

One can see from the cases that different organizational options are successful in different countries. Taiwan's comprehensive farmer-owned service enterprise, Pakistan's combination of public corporations, commune committees, and village merchants, and Senegal's combination of public corporations, an extension service run by a foreign consulting firm, and village cooperatives--each is right for the given economic and social milieu.

Cadre Options*

All four case studies had cadre below the district level. Their cadre staffing was generally heavier than in most developing nations. Below the commune level two different strategies were used.

SATEC and the Malaysian rubber replanting scheme used what might be called a cadre saturation approach. A village-level monitor worked with some 100-250 producers. Pakistan uses a quite different approach. It has only one cadre at commune level, the union agricultural assistant. This is supplemented by village volunteers, a large farmer volunteer training program. Taiwan uses a combination; it has several credit and several extension and supply cadre in each commune, plus a large volunteer training program.

The discipline factor seems to determine whether the monitor or the volunteer is the better option. In the SATEC and Malaysian rubber programs the producer must conform to a certain discipline to be eligible for assistance. It is important that he follow specified practices closely. A government employee must enforce that discipline. Where

*See Chapter 4, pp. 74-76.

discipline is not important, village leaders can be trained to complement the commune-level cadre.

Can majority participation in innovations be achieved without cadre coverage at the commune level? In Thailand in 1959, Dr. F. Jamison Bell assisted the Ministry of Agriculture in successful demonstrations of four crops in all 900 villages of Udon Province, with no permanent cadre below the provincial level. The Udon program worked on the basis of training provided for farm leaders in the province center and of supervision by a few mobile teams of ministry personnel. It would appear that for some innovations cadre below the district level are unnecessary, though most countries have found staffing down to the district level only ineffective.

Geographic Expansion Options*

The author regrets that none of the cases followed his preference for the oilspot/vector option; political counter-pressures were too great. Senegal and Pakistan followed a combination of the even-spread and the greatest-payoff-first options, spreading activities to all feasible provinces as soon as possible but putting more effort into districts with a greater potential. Taiwan took the highest-bidder option as most appropriate to stage III, assisting first those farmers associations offering the highest local contribution to projects.

Interproject Structure Options**

The four cases demonstrate the principle that group action for physical infrastructure precedes group action for agricultural development. The former is easier to achieve than the latter, and it makes a firm foundation for the latter. Where group action on infrastructure is broadly successful, as in East Pakistan and Malaysia, it provides an adequate foundation for program building. Where it is only sporadically successful,

*See Chapter 4, pp. 76-78.

**See Chapter 4, pp. 78-80.

as in Senegal, it nevertheless provides the receptivity to new
ideas needed for "action de masse."

Turning to the basic options, one sees that SATEC has
followed rigorously the tight-simple structural option,
rigorously scheduling all services to two innovation packages,
peanuts and millet. Pakistan has followed a loose-simple
structure. It has established no hard rules of interproject
structure, but it has generally launched its program on the
basis of a minimum of innovation packages in any given commune. Malaysia has followed the tight-comprehensive option
on its farmers association program. In Taiwan, stage IIIb
having been reached, these options are no longer relevant.

THE PLANNING MODEL

Chapter 5 provides some concepts about the planning
process which are useful in analyzing and comparing the actual
planning systems of the four cases.

Levels of Aggregation

The planning systems of all four cases were noteworthy
in that they made projects the heart of the process, as suggested by the model. Taiwan was perfecting its project planning structure long before it got deeply into sector planning.
The SATEC approach concentrates exclusively on the development of one project. Pakistan does very thorough sector
planning, but it gives much heavier review to project plans.
Malaysia, of course, has concentrated on individual infrastructure project planning techniques.

The local module is an explicit element of the planning
system to a somewhat lesser extent. SATEC built up its
plans explicitly from a model of a typical district. Pakistan
through the use of a model commune and a model district,
has explicitly based its plans on a module. This approach has
not been as relevant in Taiwan and Malaysia because of their
diversity; they have no "typical" communes or districts.

Taiwan and Senegal have explicit regional planning. The
SATEC plan was limited to one agricultural region. Taiwan
analyzes its requirements on the basis of over 20 regions.
East Pakistan, however, is sufficiently homogeneous to be
planned as one region, and Malaysia is so diverse that regional
planning is futile.

Criteria of the System

In terms of the criteria of a good planning system, listed
in Chapter 5, the systems of the four countries might be rated
as in Table 10.1. The four cases fall particularly short on
two criteria, compactness and input-output functional relationship. Chapter 5 emphasized the particular importance of
compactness, yet only on the Redbook formats in Malaysia
and Pakistan is the principle fully applied. Pakistan boils a
great many decisions down to a few tables of the food production plan, but Taiwan and Senegal make no attempt at compactness. If this feature is so important to a good system,
how then do Taiwan and Senegal do without it?

In both cases a great deal of authority was delegated to
the planning staff. The staffs of JCRR and SATEC have a
great deal of decision-making authority on specific projects.
Thus those who have the authority also have the capacity for
a great deal of detail. It is generally politically impossible to
delegate that much authority. Therefore, compactness is
necessary to enable those above and below the planning staff
to participate properly in the process.

The weakness of all four cases on the input-output relationship criterion is partly a matter of need and partly a matter of
planning state-of-the-art. Malaysia is not ready for quantified
techniques of optimum resource allocation because its comprehensive agricultural development program is still in the
line phase; its problems are institutional rather than those of
allocation of scarce resources. Taiwan has achieved a degree
of decentralization in which projects no longer have a major
effect on this year's or next year's food outputs.

Pakistan probably makes the most serious attempt at
systematic optimum allocation of scarce resources in its annual

TABLE 10.1

Rating of Planning Systems

	Taiwan	Malaysia	Pakistan	Senegal
Are all plans and objectives stated concretely?	A	A	A	A
Are alternatives considered explicitly in the planning process?	B	A	A	B
Are key planning documents designed for maximum compactness?		A	B	
Does the documentation identify the main issues?	B	B	A	A
Is there broad participation at all levels in the planning process?	A	A	A	
Do the planning formats provide easy evaluation?	B		A	A
Do the documents exhibit an input-output functional relationship?			B	B
Is the system complete, with all financial and technical reviews integrated fully?	A	B	A	B
Are plans easily revisable?	B	A	A	B
Is progress against objectives easily reportable?	B	A	A	A
Is the system teachable to participants at lower echelons?	A	A	A	
Is the system enforceable?	A	A	A	A

A = criterion is fully met; B = criterion is only somewhat met.

food production plan. Its development is at that stage at which
allocations to projects do determine food outputs. The main
project documents in Pakistan, however, do not generally
exhibit this input-output functional relationship. It is this
shortcoming in the state-of-the-art which this book attempts
to remedy in Part III.

The four cases thus generally meet the criteria specified
in Chapter 5. It is interesting to note that they do so with a
wide variety of planning organizational structures. Taiwan
has its highly autonomous JCRR wearing many hats and writing
projects with many types of administrative entities; Malaysia
has a Deputy Premier and his Ministry with its small central
staff controlling rural development; East Pakistan has a Planning Department and a structure of interagency committees
and agency planning cells that exemplify what most textbooks
on development planning would recommend; the poet-President
of the Republic of Senegal has called on a variety of French
public corporations to detail and implement the concepts of
"socialisme Africain", which he has eloquently articulated.

Methods of Local Planning Guidance

Some of the most useful lessons from these cases are the
techniques used to stimulate and guide local planning. Much
of the discussion of rural development seems to assume that
local planning is a great dynamic force that needs only to be
unleashed and that if only the power-hungry central bureaucrats
would loosen the reins, local authorities and local farm leaders
would move forward with broad, vigorous development programs. The four cases show that local action requires persistent and highly sophisticated guidance and stimulation from
the center.

Etude de milieu (systematic survey of local conditions)
seems to be a good starting point. Senegal uses it as a basis
of training both cadre and farm leaders. Pakistan uses it as
the basis of program building. Malaysia uses it also as the
starting point for mukim farmer association program formulation. In addition to collecting data necessary for sound decisions, it is a very useful training device for local planners.

Simple initial programs is another useful training device.
Pakistan trained farmers as development project managers
by starting them on projects limited to simple earthworks.
SATEC trains cadre by starting them on one- or two-crop
programs.

The Redbook, an unbudgeted priority-sequenced catalog
of local projects, is a useful training as well as a planning
device. First, by avoiding the "budget game", by removing
the worry over what can be done with the funds available this
year or next, it stimulates local leaders to consider all the
infrastructure needs of their locale. Second, by forcing them
to agree on the order in which projects for a number of different villages will be executed, it teaches them to make hard
decisions.

In each of the cases forms and formats have been prescribed which guide the local leaders step-by-step through the
planning process. Taiwan has a standardized and painstakingly
detailed annual plan which each farmers association must submit. Malaysia and Pakistan prescribe scheduling/reporting
formats that guide local planning. SATEC provides formats
and standard planning factors that enable poorly educated
cadre to apply simplified farm management.

Of special note are the techniques that SATEC uses to
train semiliterate cadre. These include short training sessions covering only the routines for the next couple of months,
ultrasimplified technical manuals, rehearsal of demonstration
routines, and written weekly work schedules.

The standard operating procedures of the U.S. Navy have
been described (with some hyperbole) as "a system designed
by geniuses to be run by idiots." It would appear that naval
operations and successful rural development have something
in common.

SOME GENERAL LESSONS

The four cases, taken together, offer lessons of hope and
hard work. Taiwan demonstrates what can be done with one
hectare and what rising standards can be achieved. It also

demonstrates that farmers can successfully take full responsibility for the local management of development. Malaysia shows how to focus the eyes of the nation on the planned vs. the actual, how to instill development discipline from top to bottom. Pakistan shows that a nation can respond successfully to the ultimate, most frightening conditions of poverty and population pressure. Senegal demonstrates that the profoundest human resource gaps can be surmounted.

None of these examples, however, provide simple answers or magic formulas. Each country has thought through its planning problems very carefully and subjected its planning staff, its cadre, and even its farm leaders to a rigorous working method. These working methods are particularly effective at the lower echelons. Their weaknesses are in the basic central staff planning.

It is to this basic strategy and project planning that subsequent chapters of this book will apply the tools of systems analysis.

PART III: AN AGRICULTURAL
DEVELOPMENT PLANNING SYSTEM

CHAPTER **11** AN OVERVIEW OF
THE SYSTEM

We turn now to the central business of this book. Part III
takes up, first, a specific system for individual project planning, then a system for planning regional agricultural development programs. The project planning system is applicable
to a wide range of development activities, including many
which do not come under the category of rural development.
The regional agricultural development planning system is
applicable to regions in stage II of rural development (as defined in Chapter 4), for which there are adequate proven innovations on which to build the institutions that will move the
country on to stage III.

The explanation of both project and regional systems in
subsequent chapters is built around a mythical "Southern
Region" and its program. The features of this region and its
program are taken from a number of South and Southeast
Asian countries. It must be emphasized that these features
have been selected to illustrate particular planning problems,
not to illustrate any recommendations or prejudices of the
author on how agricultural development should be organized
or run. The subject matter is planning procedures, not program content.

FORMULATION OF INDIVIDUAL PROJECTS

In the section below we assume that planners and project
managers start with a vague general notion of a project. They
know its routines, the results it seeks, the parties involved,
and the kinds of inputs required. The procedure below then
starts from this vague, general knowledge and analyses the

project as a system. This method first defines the elements
of the project and their interrelationships concretely and then
determines a) how fast the activity can move toward its objectives, given the bottlenecks and constraints, and b) what
the activity will cost, in money and manpower.

This method, incidentally, can be applied to a wide variety
of regional or national level projects. In addition to rural development projects, it has been applied to the planning of
major educational institutions, public administration improvement activities, development of medical services, and a
variety of other institutions and activities.

A word should be said first about project delineation.
Avoid mixing megaprojects and microprojects in order to keep
project objectives and goals clear. First of all, a project
should not cross agency boundaries. It should be confined to
one governmental unit with an allotment in the regular national
budget. Second, any rural development activity that functions
out in the villages and has a field operation should be aggregated at the regional level. This is a departure from general
practice; major service projects such as extension, agricultural credit, and cooperatives, are usually aggregated at the
national level. Such projects, however, tend to become megaprojects. Breaking them down into regional projects makes
them more manageable and has a number of other advantages,
which will become obvious as the system unfolds.

Finally, institution-building projects and crop promotion
projects should, in general, be kept separate. Most essential
service institutions are developed to serve a variety of crops.
Most crops need the services of a variety of institutions.
Crop promotion activities are frequently carried as part of
extension projects. Keeping them separate helps to clarify
objectives.

The basic rules of one-sheet project formulation are discussed in detail in the following subsections.

List the Relevant Variables

The first step is probably the one which requires the
most imagination and judgment of the entire project planning

process. From all the various events, factors, activities, and cost elements entering into the work of a project, the planner must extract a maximum of 40 items that will give a clear picture of the realities of the activity and will provide the data essential to major decision-making. A lawyer has been defined as one whose profession is expertise in relevancy. At this point the planner has to exercise the same professional competence as a lawyer.

What criteria can one use to determine what is relevant? For a start, one can take the three criteria offered by Melvin Anshen:

1. Aggregation of information in totals that illuminate meaningful decision alternatives and aid rational comparisons;

2. Identification and summation of all pertinent inputs;

3. Organization of information to facilitate measures of inputs to outputs. [1]

To this one might add a few comments. Timing as well as the value of relationships of inputs to outputs is important; one should identify possible delay factors. Authorities should be able to judge quickly the overall feasibility and soundness of projects. One might sum up by saying that the choice of items should provide the authorities with answers to the questions: What is it? What does it cost? What is it worth? What are the problems? What are the chances of on-time and on-cost completion?

Why a limit of 40 variables? This is about the maximum number of items that can be kept on one oversized master for a stencil or spirit duplicator. Then why not go to two pages? First, that would break paperwork discipline; documentation would no longer be kept to a minimum. Second, it would separate inputs and outputs, making the evaluation much more cumbersome.

If one has compiled a list of more than 40 items, there are two possible remedies. The first is to combine or eliminate. One can usually find some items which can be eliminated without impairing any significant planning decisions. The second is to divide the project into two projects. In particular, central staff work or construction of facilities may be treated as projects separate from work in the villages.

Table 11.1 provides a handy checklist of most types of relevant variables. The general sequence in which variables should be listed is from outputs to inputs, from field work to central work and resources. Keeping to this consistent pattern facilitates review and evaluation, since the authorities will always know where to look for information on the single-sheet forms.

Time periods should be indicated as column headings. Generally these are one-year periods; for some activities there may be a reason for using quarter-year periods. The first column should show previous activity or work to date.

Determine the Coefficients

The next step is to establish what factors determine the values of each item for each time period, particularly the relationships between inputs and outputs. For example, a physical output (say increased production) may be a function of participation,* which is in turn a function of cadre coverage, which is in turn a function of recruitment and training in the previous period. Budget items should also be based on standard formulas and coefficients insofar as possible; the next chapter will elaborate the technique of doing this.

For some items no coefficients or formulas can be established. General overhead, for example, must be set down on the basis of pure judgment. Where possible, however, it is better to use a figure based on a coefficient or formula, rather than a figure based on pure judgment. Paradoxically, this renders planning more flexible. Three months later, when plans must be revised to accommodate unforeseen problems and opportunities, no one will know exactly what to do with figures based on judgment, but figures based on a specific formula are understandable and can be revised as conditions change.

---

*See Chapter 2, p. 41 for the important concepts of participation and coverage.

Where possible, these coefficients should be made explicit and listed in the comments column to the right of the form. Often there is not enough room to explain them, but the figures themselves reveal the implicit formula behind them.

Plot Delay Factors

Frequently major elements delay the start of field operations. These may include seasonal factors; more often they are the lead times necessary for planning, procurement, training, or authorization of funds and personnel. A good look at such factors often reveals that activities considered for the current year cannot possibly start until the following year. Obviously one can avoid a lot of rewriting by looking at these factors before rather than after the other constraints are examined.

Delay factors can be denoted on the plan sheet by bar graphs or alpha coding; the next chapter will explain the latter. If columns for each year are 12 spaces wide, 1 space will represent one month; if only 8 spaces can be allowed per column, 2 spaces will represent one quarter. On a multiyear plan, detail to the nearest quarter will generally be adequate to indicate what can and cannot be done.

We see that the planner must do some of the worrying ordinarily delegated to his typist. He must consider the number of lines and the number of spaces available on a page. Indeed, if planning compactness and all its contingent benefits are to be realized, the maximum size of the duplicator master must be added to the long list of constraints the planner must consider. Typewriter spacing, normally 6 lines and 12 spaces to the inch, become coefficients that must be remembered.

Plot Bottleneck Factors

The next step is to find the binding constraint that will limit the scale of field operations and the volume of the output of the project. In the early stages the bottleneck will generally be something other than money. First, there are the limitations

TABLE 11.1

Checklist of Relevant Variables

PHYSICAL OUTPUTS	Acres, tons, or dollars of production or marketing, square meters or miles of construction, etc.
PARTICIPATION	Number of families or people involved, by phases as appropriate.
COVERAGE	Number of villages, communes, or districts covered by the project, by phases as appropriate.
FIELD CADRE or FIELD SUPPORT UNITS	Number of agents and supervisors on the job, by type. Number of field or branch offices.
LOGISTIC SUPPORT UNITS	Provincial or regional support units.
TRAINING: VILLAGERS CADRE	Number of trainees or graduates each year. Indicate length of course and cost.
INVENTORY or SUPPLY or LOAN FUND	List by type, showing average or peak volume in units, tons, or dollar value.
SMALL CONSTRUCTION	By type; show number of units started, in construction, and finished.
MAJOR CONSTRUCTION	List major facilities and show stages by bar graph and abbreviations for main progress milestones.
PREPARATORY STEPS	List main preparatory steps such as issuance of standard plans and manuals, decrees, agreements, and legislation, showing progress by bar graph or milestones.
CENTRAL STAFF	List major positions or classes of personnel; show numbers of men and cost.

VARIABLE EXPENSES	By stage as appropriate:
Per participant	per farmer or villager trainee;
Per village/commune	per village or commune covered;
Per cadre	salary plus any other costs varying directly with the number of cadre, including equipment;
Per district/branch	include investments and fund or inventory increases.
TOTAL	Total variable cost per district or per branch.
SEMIFIXED COSTS	
Training	Fixed element plus so much per trainee.
Support units	Provincial or regional level facilities; distinguish initial investment and operating expenses.
Small construction	Include equipment costs.
Regional supervisors	All costs relating to regional personnel, varying with overall volume or coverage.
FIXED COSTS	
Central staff	Include in cost all fringe benefits and other supporting expenses.
Major construction	Include equipment.
Miscellaneous overhead	
TOTAL COST	Total project cost, sum of above items.
CREDIT EXPANSION	Change in total credit outstanding, as a result of the project.
FOREIGN AID/EXCHANGE	List foreign aid or exchange requirements by type, as appropriate.

of the "point-line" phases (as defined in Chapter 4). Cadre
shortages and possibly materiel shortages will then limit
operations. Engineering and supervision may also be bottlenecks.

One must use judgment and pick the constraint that will be
binding. If one's judgment is good, and if money is not the binding constraint, one will be able to complete the drafting of the
project with no backtracking. If the constraint that one has
picked as a pacing factor proves to be less binding than another
constraint, the detail will have to be reworked. A large
eraser should be kept handy.

Project Other Activity Variables

Once the value of the pacing factor has been computed for
a period or two (it is probably safest to compute the plan
period by period), other line items showing volume of activity
should be computed on the basis of it. One should generally
work up the table and then down. Look at Table 11.1: if the
bottleneck is cadre training, one should compute from that
pacing factor the number of field cadre available. From that
variable one then might compute coverage, participation, and
output based on participation. Working down, one would then
figure the required logistic support units, inventories,
etc.

Compute Costs and Consider Budget Constraints

Once the above has been completed, computation of the
budget is fairly straightforward. Budgeting techniques will
be discussed in the next chapter. The resulting budget total
tells us what the activity will cost if it is carried forward at
its maximum pace, subject to nonfinancial restraints.

If costs are within a reasonable range, the project as it
is should then be presented to the authorities responsible for
allocations between projects. If costs are way out of line
relative to the entire development budget and the importance
of this particular activity--out of line in a manner that is
obvious to everyone--the project should be scaled down somewhat.

Apply Above Steps to a Local Modular and
then to a Regional Project

If the project involves extensive field operation and participation, (most rural development projects do or should) the
sheet giving the total project summary should be backed up by
a sheet showing the project as it will evolve in the average
district or commune.   The local modular sheet will be drafted
following the same general principles as the sheet for a regional project.   There are a few important differences.   On
the local modular the time periods are standard stages.   On
the regional project sheet coverage of districts or communes
should be specified by stage.

The following example illustrates the coverage of a project in annual stages.   Assume a project to cover 27 new
districts; each district operation is built up in four annual
stages; an additional cadre is assigned at each stage, each of
whom secures 300 new participants a year.   The district
plan then is:

Stages:	A	B	C	D
Participants				
New	300	600	900	1,200 (300 per cadre)
Cumulative	300	900	1,800	3,000
Cadre	1	2	3	4
Budget	$1,600	$3,200	$4,800	$6,400 ($2 per new participant + $1,000 per cadre)

The regional plan is then based on the above coefficients per
stage plus the following assumptions: (1) that only two districts
can be launched in the "point" stage and only five in the "line"
stage; (2) that the budget cannot be increased by more than
200 percent or $45,000 in any one year, whichever is less.
The resulting project plan for the region would look as follows:

Year	1	2	3	4	5
Participants	600	3,300	11,100	27,000	48,000
Coverage					
Stage A	2	5	10	10	
B		2	5	10	10
C			2	5	10
D				2	7
Cadre	2	9	26	53	78
Budget	$3,200	$14,400	$41,600	$84,400	$124,800

In the center of the plan one sees a pattern of numbers of districts cascading diagonally into the next stage in the next year. This cascade into higher stages will be the main motif of most projects in this book; they can be conceived as a game whose object is to get all possible districts in the final stage in as few years as possible. All other figures are derived by by multiplying the coverage matrix by the coefficients of the district plan, the local module. Thus in year 2, the number of participants = (5 X 300) + (2 X 900) = 3,300; the number of cadre = (5 X 1) + (2 X 2) = 9; and the budget = (5 X $1,600) + (2 X $3,200) = $14,400.

Individual project planning procedure is summed up in very brief terms in Figure 11.1.

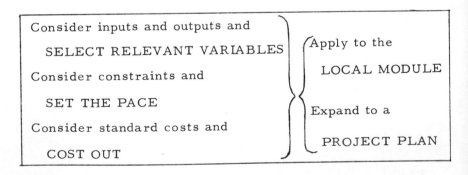

Consider inputs and outputs and	Apply to the
SELECT RELEVANT VARIABLES	LOCAL MODULE
Consider constraints and	
SET THE PACE	
Consider standard costs and	Expand to a
COST OUT	PROJECT PLAN

FIGURE 11.1.   Individual project planning procedure in brief.

REGIONAL AGRICULTURAL DEVELOPMENT
PROGRAM FORMULATION

Appendix A presents the document form of the system, as applied to the so-called Southern Region. A cursory glance at them at this point might prove profitable, although some of them might not be completely understandable until subsequent chapters are read.

Figures 11.2 and 11.3 give a picture of the overall structure of the systems. Figure 11.2 shows the sequence and interrelationships of the various documents of the system. Figure 11.3 gives a rough picture of the participants in the planning process and their main functions and interrelationships. Though the designations of the planning groups would vary widely from country to country, a roughly equivalent organizational structure would fit into a wide variety of governments.

Preproject Planning

Single-project formulation starts with at least a vague understanding of the activity content and delineation of a project. The system of regional program planning described in this section, by contrast, starts with no preconceptions of project content and delineation. It analyzes conditions, problems, and technical possibilities, and then defines project structure.

The Farm System--The system starts at the bottom with a look at an individual farmer. All relevant data on farm conditions in the region are summarized on Form A-1, the Farm System Analysis, in terms of one modular farm, an average of all the farms of the region following the same basic system.

Innovations--Form A-5, the Summary of Feasible Innovations, summarizes the basic data on potential innovations for the region in terms of the modular farm. This form yields an estimate of the potential income increase for the average farm and for the region, on the basis of present

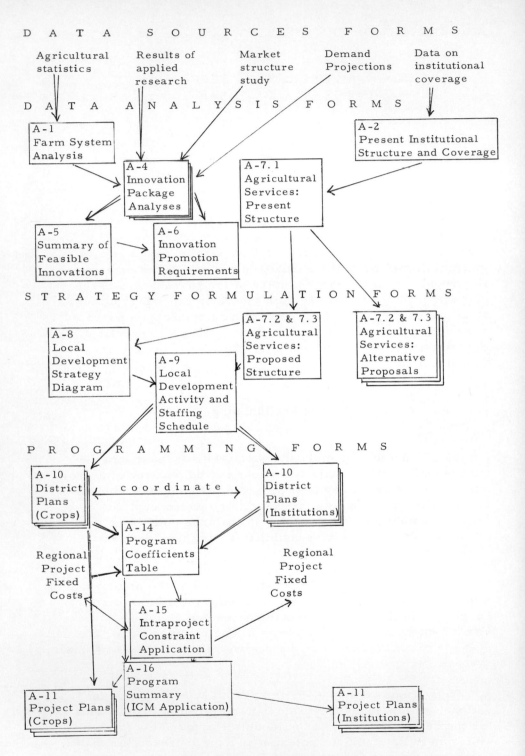

DATA SOURCES FORMS

Agricultural statistics | Results of applied research | Market structure study | Demand Projections | Data on institutional coverage

DATA ANALYSIS FORMS

A-1 Farm System Analysis

A-2 Present Institutional Structure and Coverage

A-4 Innovation Package Analyses

A-7.1 Agricultural Services: Present Structure

A-5 Summary of Feasible Innovations

A-6 Innovation Promotion Requirements

STRATEGY FORMULATION FORMS

A-8 Local Development Strategy Diagram

A-9 Local Development Activity and Staffing Schedule

A-7.2 & 7.3 Agricultural Services: Proposed Structure

A-7.2 & 7.3 Agricultural Services: Alternative Proposals

PROGRAMMING FORMS

A-10 District Plans (Crops)

coordinate

A-10 District Plans (Institutions)

Regional Project Fixed Costs

A-14 Program Coefficients Table

Regional Project Fixed Costs

A-15 Intraproject Constraint Application

A-11 Project Plans (Crops)

A-16 Program Summary (ICM Application)

A-11 Project Plans (Institutions)

FIGURE 11.2. Agricultural planning system: documentation

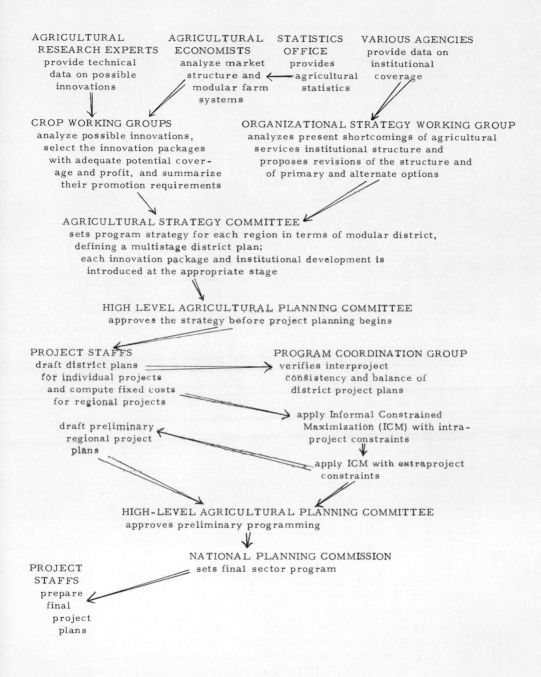

AGRICULTURAL   AGRICULTURAL   STATISTICS   VARIOUS AGENCIES
RESEARCH EXPERTS   ECONOMISTS   OFFICE   provide data on
  provide technical   analyze market   provides   institutional
  data on possible   structure and ←—agricultural   coverage
  innovations   modular farm   statistics
                        systems

CROP WORKING GROUPS   ORGANIZATIONAL STRATEGY WORKING GROUP
  analyze possible innovations,   analyzes present shortcomings of agricultural
  select the innovation packages   services institutional structure and
  with adequate potential cover-   proposes revisions of the structure and
  age and profit, and summarize   of primary and alternate options
  their promotion requirements

      AGRICULTURAL STRATEGY COMMITTEE
        sets program strategy for each region in terms of modular district,
        defining a multistage district plan;
          each innovation package and institutional development is
          introduced at the appropriate stage

          HIGH LEVEL AGRICULTURAL PLANNING COMMITTEE
          approves the strategy before project planning begins

PROJECT STAFFS   PROGRAM COORDINATION GROUP
  draft district plans ————————————→ verifies interproject
    for individual projects   consistency and balance of
    and compute fixed costs   district project plans
    for regional projects
                                     → apply Informal Constrained
      draft preliminary ←   Maximization (ICM) with intra-
      regional project   project constraints
      plans
                                     → apply ICM with extraproject
                                          constraints

          HIGH-LEVEL AGRICULTURAL PLANNING COMMITTEE
          approves preliminary programming

              NATIONAL PLANNING COMMISSION
PROJECT   ═ sets final sector program
STAFFS
  prepare
  final
    project
    plans

FIGURE 11.3. Agricultural planning system: organization
of work.

213

technology and economic conditions. This summary is backed
up by Form A-4, the Innovation Package Analysis, structured
in terms of Mosher's 10 factors (the 5 "essentials" and 5
"accelerators" described in Chapter 2). The promotion requirements of each innovation are analyzed and summarized
on Form A-6, Innovation Promotion Requirements (not shown
in Figure 11.2; see Appendix A).

    Institutional Structure and Coverage--Data on present
institutional structure and coverage are first summarized on
Form A-2, Present Institutional Structure and Coverage.
Planning of organizational change is worked out on Forms
A-7. 1, A-7.2 and A-7.3, Agricultural Services Structure
Analysis. Present structure is displayed on A-7. 1, which
highlights weaknesses and coverage gaps. Planners then
work out their ultimate organizational objective on A-7.2,
plotting the long-run structure they feel is best suited to the
region. They then work out a transitional structure for the
planning period on A-7.3, in light of the institutional needs of
the innovations to be carried out.

    Local Program Module--In the above steps, program and
project content have been determined. Knowing what crop and
institutional projects will make up the program for the planning
period, one must then decide their timing, their time interrelationships, and their tentative staffing. This is done on the
basis of a local module (average district or commune). The
logic of the time interrelationships (what must come first,
second, and third) is worked out on Form A-8, Local Development Strategy Diagram. The staging of activities and also the
tentative cadre staffing is then displayed on Form A-9, Local
Development Activity and Staffing Schedule. The preproject
structuring and coordination is now complete; planners can
now formulate projects.

    Local Project Modules--Form A-10, the District Plan,
presents the quantification of a project for an average district
(in many countries the commune might be a better module),
following the rules discussed above under individual project
formulation. Crop projects are prepared first, since these
will determine the activity level for the institution projects.
One then computes the total activity volume for each institution project, be it the number of demonstrations, the volume
of supply and market business, the number and volume of loans,
or the number and size of surveys.

At this point the complex of projects at the local level must be reviewed for balance. Is crop promotion activity adequate to sustain and justify the institutions? Is the tentative staffing of the institutions adequate to handle the volume of activity? Is activity excessively bunched at any season or stage, creating uneconomical peak requirements? On the basis of this review, a final structure and pacing of local project modules is determined.

The local module is the marginal unit of a project or a regional program. In program resource allocation, the option at the margin is whether to launch a project or program in an additional district this year or postpone it till next year. In actual program deliberations in many countries, discussion on resource allocation frequently revolves around the number of districts to be covered in the coming year. The marginal district is thus not merely a theoretical or ideal option; it is the very real subject matter of program decision in many countries. The local module gives the marginal costs and marginal revenue coefficients, which are summarized compactly on Form A-14, Program Coefficients Table.

In addition to providing guidance for planning the local module by hand, this book provides guidance for planning by computer simulation. The general procedure is described in Chapter 26; the basic equations are given in Appendix B.

Regional Level Programming

The final phase of the procedure is a mixture of project planning and regional programming. It can be done by linear programming on a computer, using the equations in Appendix B and the procedures in Chapter 26. Chapter 16 provides a simple method analogous to linear programming called Informal Constrained Maximization (ICM). Though the method does not yield precise, mathematically optimum solutions, it comes close, and it provides dual or shadow prices.

Simplifying the process somewhat, one might label it Coverage Maximization. Income resulting from the program is maximized by getting as many districts as possible into stages as advanced as possible as quickly as possible.

Subject to intraproject constraints and limited availability of
human and financial resources, the object is to launch as many
districts as possible each year into annual stage A and then
to move them without interruption through subsequent annual
stages.

Briefly, ICM proceeds as follows: First, maximize the
pace of launching districts subject to intraproject constraints,
such as training capacities, shortages of specialized personnel,
input production capacities, and point-line phase coverage
limitations. All these bottlenecks except the point-line phasing
can be solved with money, by higher fixed costs or higher unit
costs. This operation of intraproject coverage maximization
is carried out on two or more trial ranges of fixed costs or
unit costs for the relevant constraints. One then fills out all
the items of the project plans of format A-11, except for those
items dependent on coverage decisions.

Finally one computes the total regional program by ICM
on Form A-16 (Program Summary). Applying financial and
even personnel constraints to a program for one subsector is
a tricky matter; it implies guessing in advance the maximum
resource limits. As shall be seen in Chapter 16, the problems of this prejudging can be overcome, but one has to use
very loose constraints. Once one has determined, for purposes
of the regional program submission to the central planning
authorities, the number of districts to be launched each year,
one can complete the Project Plans on Form A-11.

Sectoral and Intersectoral Programming

The problem of allocating funds between projects of one
region and projects of another region of the agricultural sector, and between the agricultural sector and other sectors, is
exceedingly complex. Programming for development of the
total economy is outside the scope of this book, so we cannot
go into this massive subject very deeply. Since the planning
system for the region is obliged to furnish the data necessary
for all the considerations to be raised regarding sectoral
and intersectoral allocations, however, some assumptions
must be made on how these allocations may be decided.

A wide variety of considerations may come into play:
relative returns on investment and cost-benefit ratios,

intersectoral supply and market balance, special welfare
problems of lagging regions, foreign exchange problems,
preferences of aid donor agencies, allocations for research
whose payoff cannot be computed, allocations for welfare
services, etc. It is assumed that the total requirements of
the projects submitted will greatly exceed resources available.

Subsector programs will then be trimmed down, based on
the above considerations, until requirements match resources.
Subject to the other considerations, subsector programs with
higher returns on investment will be trimmed less than those
with lower returns and poorer cost-benefit ratios. The Program Coefficients Table (Form A-14) and the Program Summary (Form A-16) make it easy to calculate quickly the possibility of loss and the resulting loss of outputs of any cutback.

Project plans may then be rewritten on the basis of the
final authorized program.

PROBLEMS OF APPLICATION

Partial Application of the System

Rare indeed are those who are currently authorized to revise their country's entire rural development planning system.
While the system is adaptable in toto to countries as diverse
as Laos and Chile, it is also applicable in partu. Individual
formats neatly complement and fill gaps in existing systems.

The most broadly applicable formats are those used for
individual project formulation--Form A-10 and A-11. These
can be extremely useful as supplements to the usual project
submission forms or as forms for intradepartmental project
control. They can be profitably introduced at any point in the
planning process. They are obviously a good starting point
for project drafting and basic project conception. Their compactness also makes them useful control devices for project
implementation. Events and experiences frequently render
the original approved project document obsolete in a matter
of months. Forms A-10 and A-11 can be revised in an hour

to show the project manager how revised coefficients and performance to date affect future resource requirements or, conversely, what can be done with authorized resources in light
of changed conditions.

Other forms can be applied as issues and problems arise
which warrant them. A-1, A-3, A-4, and A-5 can be applied
to analyzing what innovations are feasible for a region and
what services they require. A-2 and A-7 can be applied to
analyzing organizational problems and formulating solutions.
A-8 and A-9 can be applied to problems of interproject coordination. A-14 can be used to compute the marginal revenue
and cost-benefits ratio of an agricultural development program.
If seat-of-the-pants judgment appears to be sufficient to solve
such problems to everyone's satisfaction, there is no need for
these formal analytical tools. If casual judgment does not
render an instant answer that is satisfactory to everyone, these
forms provide the planner with highly compact and efficient
analytical tools for tackling such problems.

Teachability

A planning staff which wishes to introduce these forms
must face the fact that their novelty will cause resistance on
the part of project staffs and authorities. Careful introduction
can overcome this resistance.

Step-by-step guidance is essential to introducing new
forms to project staffs. In place of a deadline some months
hence for submission of the entire plan, the planning staff
must break down the drafting process into a series of short
stages and closely spaced intermediate deadlines. Project
staff may find complete instructions for a new procedure
hard to digest, if not badly frightening. A series of lectures
on how to apply the new forms may leave staff members be-
wildered as to how to apply the formats to their own activities.
The planning staff must therefore feed instructions to the
project staffs in segments and personally show them how to
apply these instructions to their activities.

To illustrate, application of formats A-10 and A-11 might
be broken into seven steps, each with a two-week deadline.

Step 1 would be to list the relevant variables. In step 2 the project staffs would be asked to determine the relevant co-efficients. In step 3 they would select and project the pacing factors. In step 4 they would compute the activity and budget items for the first method. Then in step 5 they would complete the local modular. In steps 6 and 7 they would compute the regional-level project. During each step a member of the planning staff would meet with the project staff and see to it they got started properly on the work of that step. With such easy pacing of the plan drafting, the project staff can hardly complain, as they often do, of the inordinate paperwork burden imposed by a central planning staff.

The author has tried the above procedure in modified form and found that it worked. Project staffs get their plans into the central office for review quicker than before, yet they feel less overwhelmed by the burden of writing a long document. There is less procrastination. At first the project staffs resent a bit "being told how to plan their projects," but in the end they express their gratitude for a procedure which considerably deepens their understanding of their work and their needs.

Introducing these new forms to the authorities is somewhat easier. Instead of being presented with the long narratives they previously had to read about each project, the authorities should be given a briefing based on the new tables. An over-head projector is a useful device for this; the table can be flashed on a screen and the project officer can use a pointer to show the pacing factors and how the rest of the project evolves from them, and also to show the particular problem points. Authorities are normally amenable to any new procedures which reduce their document reading burden. An explanation of the proper briefing procedure will be given in Chapter 21.

Countervailing Oversimplifications; Murphy's Laws

One might object to some of the oversimplification, over-averaging, and implied overlinearity that characterize this system. For example, all districts are treated as equal in most procedures of the system. They all have the same unit costs and marginal revenue. In reality districts vary widely in their costs and potential; given a free hand, project managers will operate first in the districts with highest marginal revenue and work down the curve. Similarly, all farms in a district are considered equal; in reality the farms with the highest marginal revenue will probably be the first participants. Price and income coefficients are assumed to be constant for all years, yet one can assume that the increased production resulting from the program will cause prices to decline.

Obviously the use of constant coefficients makes the planning job easier. Does it not, however, grossly distort reality to assume linear relationships in a nonlinear world? Does not such distortion result in bad decisions and in misallocations?

One may contend that nonlinearities tend to offset each other, that the distortions caused by oversimplification planning process can be offset by countervailing oversimplifications. Basically, this means that a rising learning curve offsets a declining marginal revenue curve, permitting one to use coefficients that imply a horizontal marginal revenue curve, equal to average revenue.

More specifically, one may postulate that results of initial periods will be heavily determined by Murphy's Laws (precise origin unknown):

1.   Anything that can go wrong will go wrong.

2.   If there is a possibility of more than one thing going wrong, the thing that will go wrong will be the one that will do the most damage.

3.   Left to themselves, things always go from bad to worse.

4.   Nature always sides with the hidden flaw.

5.   If it appears that everything is going right, you are probably unaware of all that is happening.

Anyone who has gone through the growing pains of a project will recognize the validity of the above laws. Fortunately, as experience is gained, Murphy's Laws become less binding. They effectively offset the difference between marginal and average revenue to the left of the intersection of these two curves (Figure 11.4). Another countervailing oversimplification offsets the difference to the right of the intersection, where marginal revenue is less than the average revenue. The last districts and the last farmers to be reached will produce a marginal revenue less than the fixed coefficients would imply. This is offset by the fact that planning has been oversimplified by considering only those innovations promoted by specific crop projects. The institutions being built by the program will be serving other innovations as well. It is reasonable to assume that the activity volume and marginal revenue of these innovations will increase over time, offsetting the declining marginal revenue of the last participants.

Figure 11.4 illustrates these relationships. In the figure the curve BEC is marginal revenue; the line DEF is average revenue based on the fixed coefficient used in planning. The area OGH is the loss due to Murphy's Laws, which offsets the area DBE, the excess of marginal over average revenue to be expected in the early years, based on the economic potential of the districts. The area HLK represents the gain from innovations not calculated as part of the program. This offsets the area ECF, the excess of average revenue over marginal revenue on the basis of averages and fixed coefficients.

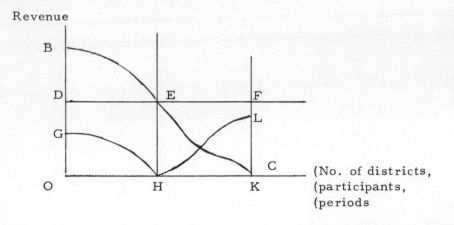

FIGURE 11.4.   Countervailing Oversimplifications.

The planning system described above may appear at first glance to make no provision for local initiative. On the contrary, it is designed to create the proper conditions for local initiative as rapidly as possible, and it counts on increasing local initiative, once the institutional foundations are laid. It does not count on local initiative before those foundations are laid.

To repeat, development is a learning process as well as an economic process. Paradoxically, this complicated double nature of development enables one to justify some important simplifications of the planning procedure.

NOTES

1.   M. Anshen, "The Federal Budget as an Instrument, " in D. Novick, ed., Program Budgeting (Cambridge, Mass.: Harvard University Press, 1965), p. 5.

CHAPTER **12** THE PROJECT PLAN

As emphasized in previous chapters, individual project planning is the most important phase of rural development planning. The underlying techniques of individual project planning are therefore particularly important. Some of these basic techniques might be labeled: Selection of Relevant Variables, Budgeting for Decision, Modular Pace Setting, and Coverage Matrix. After presenting some basic principles of budgeting, this chapter will demonstrate and discuss these underlying techniques. It will apply them to a hypothetical project in order to illustrate the procedures and the basic reasoning used in project formulation.

BUDGETING FOR DECISION

The rapid estimation and compact assembly of cost figures in a manner that facilitates decisions is something of an art. Like the selection of the basic items of a plan, it is an exercise in relevancy. The planner must rely heavily on his intuitive feel for what will and will not be relevant to a decision. Some notions of what to avoid and a few general principles will provide basic guidance to the budgeteer in the practice of his art.

What Not to Do

The following hypothetical estimate illustrates the mélange of excessive and inadequate detail that is typical of much budgeting:

Salaries

14 class-5 officers	$21,382.45
7 class-4 officers	14,287.37
2 class-3 officers	6,421.38
	42,091.10

Retirement	3,017.56
Health insurance	1,056.75
Housing allowances	4,325.00
Travel allowances	10,000.00
Per diem	25,000.00
Communications	375.00
Office supplies	288.00
Materials	200,000.00
Contract services	50,000.00

Equipment

1 Truck, 2-1/2 ton, 4-wheel drive	4,878.00
1 Passenger vehicle, 5 persons, 4-wheel drive	2,850.00
1 Typewriter, 14" keyboard	375.00
	8,103.00

Total	$319,256.41

Some items have been calculated to the last penny, others to the nearest $100,000. The drafter of this hypothetical budget appears to have spent some time on personnel-related expenses for which he knew the formula, working them out to the last penny. He apparently had no formula for materials, contract services, and per diem, which constitute 86 percent of this budget. In estimating these items he made the wildest guesses. Such budgets are all too typical.

In a budget of over $300,000 (or $100,000 for that matter), any item less than $1,000 is not going to affect a planning decision. If certain items can be approximated only to the nearest $10,000, what is the point of figuring other items to

the nearest $10 ? One must make an effort to bring all items
to about the same level of detail.

Another error illustrated in the above budget is premature
detail.   The truck and passenger vehicle items specify 4-wheel
drive.   This is important in the actual procurement documents;
it adds nothing to a budget.   In spite of all the detail in the
estimate, it is impossible to tell what volume of operation it
relates to or how a cut or an increase in the budget would
affect operations.

Compare the following budget with the budget above:

<u>Personnel</u>

14 Branch assistants	@	$3,400	$47,500
7 Branch managers	@	3,800	26,600
2 Service engineers	@	4,200	8,400
			$82,500*

*Includes salaries plus retirement (7%), health & housing
(12%), per diem (50%), and travel (80 days each).

With fewer items one can now see how a budget change
will change the number of branches that are supported.   The
way expenditures are classified makes a big difference in
their decision-making usefulness.

Some Rules of Budgeting for Decision

A few terse rules of budgeting are

List the big ones.

Lump the small ones.

Link all inputs to outputs.

To be more specific:

Group all costs attributable to one input or output element.
Compute costs per agent, per trainee, per client, per demonstration, per new office, or per village. The cost per agent,
for example, may include salary, retirement and health benefits, housing and travel allowances, and per diem. A cost per
demonstration may include supplies, brochures, and per diem
for field day participants. Costs, in brief, should be grouped
by purpose or by performing element, rather than by object.
These standard basic costs become modular building blocks,
with which to construct the next highest module, the District
Plan.

Average out variations which will not affect total accuracy.
One category of personnel may have salaries ranging from
$75 to $110 per month. A rough average of, say, $90 should
be used as the salary element of a personnel standard cost
factor. One may protest that this will be inaccurate, that a
careful computation on the basis of the actual number of people
in each salary step will give a result that is different from a
rough average. One must counter by asking if this difference
would affect the total accuracy of a project budget which includes some items estimated to the nearest $10,000. One may
also ask how well anyone can know in advance the number of
people in each salary step, considering the uncertainties of
recruiting. Overly detailed guesses may give an air of false
accuracy.

Round off budget summary element figures. Totals on
District Plans and all elements of Project Plans should be to
the nearest $1,000. This will speed up handling of figures
and make presentation much more compact without sacrificing
overall accuracy, considering that some items must be estimated to the nearest $10,000. Cost elements within district
project estimates should never be carried further than the
nearest $100.

Lump small items not dependent on other project variables
into miscellaneous overhead. Utility bills, office supplies,
repairs, postage, and many other items cannot be estimated
on the basis of number of agents, trainees, or clients. They
should be kept to a minimum by cost-conscious managers,
but there is no way of relating them to initial project decisions.
They should, therefore, be considered as part of the fixed overhead of the project, an item which may or may not be high
overall, relative to the total cost of the project.

A HYPOTHETICAL PROJECT

The following narrative description illustrates the kind of data from which individual project formulation starts. We begin with a general knowledge of objectives, routines, standards of action, and sequences of action. The project is one of the components of the hypothetical Southern Region agricultural development program presented in Appendix A. This particular project has the advantage of being computable and quantifiable independently of the other projects of the program. Since it comes first in the development sequence, its pace is not necessarily dependent on other projects. One should keep in mind that the so-called Southern Region consists of 10 provinces, 50 districts, 500 communes, 5,000 villages, and 500,000 farms. The description below is in the form specified in Chapter 21 (Form A-12 in Appendix A).

PROJECT DESCRIPTION: COMMUNITY DEVELOPMENT
                                    #11-S-120
      Min. Ag., Community Development Dept.,   Aug. 67
                  Southern Region

1.   Objectives

         This project organizes and trains local leaders in order to:

      a.   Stimulate village leadership for development activities;

      b.   Organize commune development councils which can gradually assume responsibility for the planning and execution of rural development;

      c.   Prepare villagers for participation in other projects of the program;

      d.   Stimulate maximum village contribution in labor and cash to community and individual development activities.

2.   Local Operation

      a.   Deploy cadre--A district is assigned a supervisor with a minimum of 12 years education and, starting in 1967, at least 3 years community development (CD) experience. In addition to basic CD training supervisors

are given 2 months supervisory training in the capital.
For transportation they are given loans to buy jeeps.
Supervisors are eligible for promotion to provincial
officer.

Under the supervisors are 1 commune-level
worker (CLW) for each commune. CLW's are recruited within the region, preferably within the province or district. A minimum 10-year education is
required. Twelve-year education is preferred for
those without experience. Many are seasoned schoolteachers. The CD Department gives them 4 months
preservice training at the CD Institute (near the capital), interspersed with five months field training in
pilot districts. For transportation they are given
loans to purchase motorbikes, which they must maintain out of their travel allowance.

b.   Train Village Leaders--CLW's organize meetings in
      the villages to explain the program. Each hamlet is
      asked to name two leaders for initial training.
      Generally, a CLW can only work intensively with half
      the villages of a commune the first year; it takes two
      years to train leaders from all the commune. One-
      week sessions are conducted in the district by the
      supervisor and the CLW's, largely nondirective in
      structure. They stress identification of village
      problems and analysis of what can be done. Partici-
      pants are also given some lectures on government
      services available and on agricultural practices.
      After the training sessions, the village leaders, with
      assistance of other volunteers in the community, con-
      duct a house-to-house survey of the resources and
      problems of the village, under CLW guidance.

c.   Execute Self-Help Projects--Once the village survey
      is completed, a village is eligible for funds for one
      or two self-help projects. Leaders hold general
      village meetings to discuss needs and select a project.
      Each CLW has a manual of standard data and designs
      for each type of project, and he helps the village
      leaders prepare project applications. Province en-
      gineers may be called upon to assist if necessary.
      Upon approval by the supervisor and district chief,

funds are released.   Note that a village labor contribution is required for each project.

d.   Institute Commune Budgeting--Once five or more villages of a commune have successfully completed self-
help projects, a commune development council (CDC)
may be organized, with the CLW as its secretary.
Each CDC member (approximately 1 per 100 families)
is given 2 weeks training in CDC budgeting and other
procedures.   The CDC prepares an annual budget for
development projects and maintenance of community
facilities in the commune.   The budget includes a
general subsidy, commune taxes, and specific subsidies and labor contributions to each project.   Individual projects and the total program are subject to
district and provincial approval.

e.   Institute Commune Development Programs--The third
and final phase of CDC development is the comprehensive commune development plan, a multiyear plan that
covers not only physical infrastructure but also agricultural production and marketing.   This must follow
a few years of successful CDC performance and also
some years of extension and farmer association work
at the commune level.   Again, CDC members and
CDC subcommittee members receive two weeks training in planning techniques.   Upon approval of a commune five-year plan book, the CDC is eligible for an
increased budget for infrastructure projects and a
commune budget for extension.

3.   Project Evolution

1962--Twelve CLW's and 3 supervisors were deployed in
three pilot districts of the Southern Region.   Various
self-help projects were undertaken.

1963--Three more districts were added to the project plus
30 new CLW's, bringing coverage to six districts and
42 communes.

1964--The first village leader training courses were held;
6 districts and 35 CLW's were added, bringing the
total (after some attrition) to 12 districts and 70
communes.

1965--The first manual of projects was issued. The first
province CD Officers were assigned to 3 provinces.
With 60 new CLW's trained, the number of communes
was raised to 130, and 8 new districts were launched
bringing the total to 20. Two CDC's were organized
in pilot communes and given special budgets.

1966--Ten new districts and 50 new communes were added,
bringing coverage to 30 districts and 180 communes.
Under a special ministerial decree CDC's were organized in all communes of 3 districts. CDC training
material was prepared and a comprehensive project
guide issued. Provincial CD officers were appointed
in 3 more provinces.

1967--CDC's have been organized in half the communes of
15 districts. Coverage has been raised to 225 communes. Permanent regulations covering CDC's have
been proposed to the Council of Ministers.

1968--Once CDC's have been given permanent status and
regular annual budgets by decree of the Council of
Ministers, work will begin on phase III, commune
development plans. Concepts will be tested in three
communes and legislation will be drafted. Materials
will be prepared for the first CLW inservice training,
to prepare CLW's for phase III. The CD institute
will be enlarged to accommodate inservice trainees.

1969--Commune development plans will be prepared for
a number of communes in the pilot districts. Standard village leader training programs for phase III
will be issued. Permanent legislation will authorize
the transfer of extension and other service budgets
to the communes.

1970--All phases will be expanded as fast as possible and
the first districts will achieve 100 percent phase III
coverage.

The above description gives all the qualitative information
needed for planning, but it tells almost nothing about the
quantitative aspects of the project. This is actually something
of an advantage in that this description will survive a number of
revisions of the quantitative planning without becoming obsolete.

THE LOCAL MODULE

With the above project description in mind, one can now proceed to plan the local module and quantify activity at the local level.

The Choice of Relevant Variables

This first step requires the greatest exercise of planning artistry and craftmanship as well as rigorous discipline to avoid paperwork sprawl. The list of relevant variables for the local module and the Project Plan should each fit on a single page. With these admonitions in mind, one may turn to Table 11.1 and select the relevant variables.

Output Elements--The categories at the top of the page should be the output units, those elements of the project which constitute, or at least indicate, its actual impact on people. This is particularly difficult to identify in a community development project. Project activities will result in more roads, schools, etc., and also in more farm income, yet these outputs can be much better planned and reported under the specific projects concerning them.

Having eliminated physical output units as unsuitable, one may now consider participation, which is indeed one of the outputs of the project. How may one define participation in a way that can be reported meaningfully and consistently? If we merely cite the number of people contributing to self-help projects, the number will vary so greatly with the type of specific project as to make such a reported statistic meaningless, relative to what is reported in other districts and other periods.

One might settle on the number of participants in training courses as the relevant output variable. The essence of the project's activity is, in a sense, education. One can set targets for the number of trainees of various categories for each commune in each stage. The District Plan, which is our local module, starts then with the following items (each item should have a number, for easy reference):

Leader Training
1. Initial
2. Program building
3. Special

The last of the output elements and, in this project, the most important, is the coverage of communes, which also indicates the progress of the phasing. The object of the project can, indeed, be defined in simplest terms as getting every commune into comprehensive development planning. Coverage is listed in the following manner:

Coverage of Communes
4. Phase 1: Self-help projects
5. Phase 2: Works budget
6. Phase 3: Total development program

Should coverage by village also be listed? The narrative points out that one CLW can only work intensively in five villages, so that five villages of a commune will always lag a year in development behind the others. This, as shall be seen, will be reflected in the number of trainees, so items for village coverage can be saved. It is important to save items wherever possible, to keep the number down to the minimum to avoid paperwork sprawl.

Input Items--One should start with the inputs closest to the village. In this case it would be the subsidies to the commune budget, albeit they are not charged to the project:

Subsidies
7. Phase 1
8. Phase 2
9. Phase 3

There are no other materiel elements being contributed within the project to the commune. The next and probably the most important input is the cadre. Two types are relevant:

District Staff
10. Commune-level workers
11. Supervisor

For these items, the number of personnel and budget for each stage will be listed.

Going down the checklist on Figure 11.1, the next relevant item is equipment. How detailed should a plan listing be? This is largely a matter of budget simplification. The basic rule is: List the big items; lump the small ones. Following this rule, one would list:

Equipment Purchases
12. Motorbikes
13. Jeep
14. Audiovisual and miscellaneous

The final items of input detail should be the financing, the main budget items. In this case one should distinguish the subsidies from the operating budget, since they are not financed under this project. Three items of expenditure can be computed on the basis of the items listed above: training, staff, and equipment. Since no other items amount to more than $2,000 per district, the rest can be lumped into a miscellaneous category:

Operating Budget
15. Training
16. Staff
17. Equipment
18. Miscellaneous
19.   Total

20. Commune Budget Subsidy

Have any important items been missed? A reader with some experience in CD work might well look over the checklist in 11.1 and find some items he considers highly relevant that is not in the 20 items listed above. This is one of several good reasons why those most directly involved must participate in the planning, from the moment the first relevant item is written on the left-hand column of a large-spread sheet. The job can best be done by a member of the central planning staff in consultation with several staff officers and officers of the operating agency.

FIGURE 12.2 (Form A-11)

Project Plan: Community Development

Project #11-S-120

Southern Region

Community Development Department

ELEMENTS	'67	'68	'69	'70	'71	'72	'73	End Yr. 1976	ADDITIONAL COMMENTS & EXPLANATIONS
1 Leader Training (000s)	8	9	12	16	21	22	19		Note: The pace of moving additional districts into stages A and B is limited by line 9, which in turn is limited by line 14, the maximum rate of CLW recruitment & training.
2 Coverage — A	15	20	10	5					
3 of — B	15	10	10	10	10				
4 Districts — C		5	10	10	10	10			
5 by — D			5	10	10	10	10		
6 Stage — E				5	10	10	10		
7 — F+					5	5	15		
8								50	
9 Staff: Commune Level Workers	225	250	300	375	450	500	500	500	-indicates coverage of Communes
10 Dist. Supervisors	30	30	35	40	50	50	50	50	-indicates coverage of Districts
11 Province Officers	6	6	7	9	10	10	10	10	-indicates coverage of Provinces...@$3,000/yr.
12 Staff Specialists	10	12	14	16	18	20	22	25	-@ $3,000/yr.
13 Others	20	25	30	35	40	45	50	50	-@ $1,000/yr.
Staff Training									
14 CLW Preservice (@$1000)	30	60	85	85	60	30	30		-following yr. need incl. attrition
15 CLW Inservice (@ $200)		50	100	100	100	100	50		-all stage D CLW
Program Development									
16 Commune Budget Regulation	D	M	C						-D=Drafted, M=Ministry Approval, C=Cabinet Approval.
17 Comm. Dev. Plan Regulation		D	M	C					
Project Costs	$000	$000	$000	$000	$000	$000	$000	All yrs. $000	
18 District Operation Costs	915	1025	1165	1425	1780	1795	1435	11,660	-includes $2,120,000 in '74-6
19 Staff Training Cost	50	80	115	125	100	70	60	600	-lines 14 & 15 + $20,000/yr. fixed cost
20 Prov. & Region Staff Cost	68	79	93	110	124	135	146	756	-lines 11-13
21 Miscellaneous Overhead	50	60	70	80	90	100	110	560	-lines 19-21 transferred to Admin Bgt in '74
22 total	1083	1239	1433	1725	2074	2075	1721	13,754	
23 Commune Subsidies	600	700	700	1400	1850	2300	2600	3,000*	*annually after 1976
24 Foreign Exchange	80	100	100	100	70	50	50	550	-equipment for districts and regional staff

Setting the Pace (see Figure 12. 1)

The next step makes what are perhaps the most critical of all operating decisions: How fast is the project to move in one district? How fast is coverage and participation to be advanced?

To set the pace, one must first identify the nonfinancial constraints. The first to consider are the delay factors, the elements in which time itself is the bottleneck. In this project it is obvious that a commune cannot move all the way into Phase III in two years. * The farmers and their leaders must gain experience; this takes time. The best experts on the subject must therefore make a judgment as to how many years a commune must remain in phase I and phase II, before going on to phase III. This type of decision should be made at the top level of the technical agency responsible for the project. Assume that the director of the Community Development Department has decided that a commune must remain in phase I at least one year and in phase II at least three years. This makes it a five stage operation: (each stage is one year):

Stage:	A	B	C	D	E
Phase I	X				
Phase II		X	X	X	
Phase III					X

The next question is whether all communes of a district can move through the stages simultaneously or whether their development must be staggered, adding a stage or two to the process. The only relevant constrained input variable would appear to be cadre. With enough cadre all villages and communes could be moved simultaneously. This would require, however, additional CLW's per district for a few years.

Two considerations lead to a decision to stagger village and commune development. First, there is the question of whether one supervisor can cover 10 communes simultaneously, if additional cadre are available. Second, there is the question

*In the Project Description (Chapter 12, p. 229) phases II and III are explained, respectively, in paragraphs 2d and 2e.

of whether new districts are to be launched in the next few
years. It should be noticed that not all the communes of the
30 districts launched previously have been covered. A decision to launch all villages and communes simultaneously
would probably require that all the available increment of
some 60 cadre each year be thrown into the old districts for
several years. This is the type of programming consideration
that affects structural judgments. On the basis of lack of
cadre and on the basis of supervisory difficulties, it is decided
to launch stage A in only five communes per district a year.
This gives the following pattern (the figures represent number
of communes):

Stage:	A	B	C	D	E	F
Phase I	5	5				
Phase II		5	10	10	5	
Phase III					5	10

Considering now the pacing of villages, it might be wiser
to stagger their development, but this staggering is impossible
as one moves into phases with commune-scale planning.
Therefore leaders from all 10 villages of a commune get the
same training each year. The following schedule of the number of leaders trained per village, by phase, has been approved
by the director of the department:

Training Program	Phase:	1	2a	2b	2c	3a	3b
Initial		3					
Phase II	Budgeting		4				
Phase II	special problems			5	5		
Phase III	planning					4	
Phase III	special problems						10

A glance at items 1-6 and 10 of Figure 12.1 shows the consequences of these pacing decisions. The first three items
(the number of leaders trained) are simply a product of the
two matrices above, with an additional factor of 10 villages
per commune. The leader training and also the total subsidy
per district (items 7-9 and 20) are simply products of the
standard factors per phase and the commune coverage by stage.

Costing Out

The next step is the application of budgeting for decision.
The first operating budget is training. In item 15 (Figure
12. 1), one notes that this has been evaluated at $25 per man
per week. This may be derived from:

Per diem @ $2 per day X 7	$14.00
Travel to and from district town	7.00
Training materials	2.00
Miscellaneous	2.00
	$25.00

Fixed costs of training sessions come under item 18 (miscellaneous).

The next consideration is staff salary and expenses. Item
10 shows a cost for one CLW of $1,500 a year, derived as
follows:

Salary @ $70 per month	$ 800
Fringe benefits @ 15% of salary	126
Vehicle operation and maintenance @ $20/month	240
Per diem, 200 days @ $1.50	300
2 trips to capital @ $50	100
	$1,506

Supervisor costs (item 11) have been estimated in the
same manner, with provision for raises in stage D. Equipment purchases (items 12-14) are estimated on the basis of
$500 per motorbike and $2,500 per jeep, with provision for
replacing 20 percent of the project fleet in each year after
stage C. These costs are summarized in items 15-19,
rounded out to the nearest $1,000.

Some of the simplifications have provided a built-in con-
tingency fund to cover unanticipated expenses. For example,
the training cost for the two-week training in item 2 is over-
estimated; provision for travel to and from training sessions
have been double-counted on the basis of a $25 per week cost.
Thus stages B, C, E, and F have water in them amounting to
$7 (travel cost) X 200 trainees = $1,400. As long as the

project manager and the junior budget examiner are aware of
this, there is no problem. When unforeseen expenses arise,
and they always do, one knows exactly where to find money
within the project. As long as the planners know what the
oversimplifications in the cost factors are and where costs
have been overaveraged, they can find money for contingencies
later.

A more common technique of providing for contingencies
is padding, adding 10 percent here and 20 percent there to
various unit costs and line items. Budget reviews then de-
generate into a game of hide-and-seek. In trying to fool the
reviewers, the project managers often end up fooling themselves. They are later often unable to remember where they
hid the water. Simplification is a legitimate, indeed an essential, budgeting device. It is honest and legitimate. Padding
is not only dishonest, it is often self-defeating.

Items 19 and 20 sum up two budget totals, the operating
budget and the commune subsidy budget, thus completing the
District Plan. These totals are kept separate because they
are charged to different sectors of the total development program. The commune subsidy is for infrastructure, which is
not part of the agriculture program, but it is shown for information purposes.

All explanations that can fit in the space available go into
the right-hand column. Ideally, the table should be totally
self-explanatory. Practically, this is impossible. One tries
to explain whatever can fit in, leaving the less difficult points
to be explained by the project description by the project
manager in a short briefing or by common sense.

One should try to make the interrelationships of the lines
explicit where possible. Many of the cost functions and pacing
functions are implicit. A brief comparison of the schedule
of leader training and the coverage of communes by phase
(items 1-3 and 4-6) show what training per phase is implicit.
If we analyze the figures along item 11, we can see that the
supervisor gets a raise in stage D, where the cost of one
man rises from \$2, 500 to \$3, 000. It is easy to analyze the
cost per vehicle in items 12 and 13. As long as cost and pacing relationships show a consistent pattern (they may be constant or may increase), they can be left implicit and unex-
plained on the sheet.

THE PROJECT PLAN

Having prepared the module, most of the work is done. Except for some heavy cumulative multiplication chores, the Project Plan (Figure 12.2) is a somewhat easier job than the District Plan, because so many decisions have already been made.

Selecting the Variables

The lineup of variables follows the same basic pattern as the District Plan, with some groups of items consolidated and other items added. One starts with an item showing the measure of output selected. Here, the three types of leader training are consolidated into one. This will constitute something of a performance measure for the project. The next set of items should be a feature of all rural development projects which are part of a coordinated complex, namely the coverage of districts by stage, from stage A to stage post-F (written F+).

The next two sets of items cover cadre elements: staff and staff training. The number of CLW's and district supervisors depend on coverage of districts by stage. The number of province officers indicates the number of provinces covered. When it comes to the next two items, staff specialists (in this case the regional CD staff) and others, one must decide how much detail is relevant, since there may be a variety of positions that might take pages to list individually. How many categories, that is, how many items, should one list for the regional staff?

To answer this or any other question regarding the selection of variables, one must try to visualize the review process, the questions that may be raised, the options to be considered, and the decisions to be made. One must also consider what categories might prove critical to the pace or the cost of the project. If, for example, trained audiovisual staff were scarce and there was a large audiovisual equipment component to the project, one would want to show such personnel as a separate category. One may assume here that the CD staff professionals,

FIGURE 12.1 (Form A-10)

Project #11-S-120

District Plan: Community Development

Community Development Department

Southern Region

Element	A	B	C	D	E	F	Additional Explanations
Leader Training (no. trainees)							**Subject of Training Sessions**
1 Initial 1 week	150	150					
2 Program Bldg. 2 weeks	200	200	200	500	200	200	-formulation of village needs
3 Special 1 week			250		250	500	-budgeting for phases 2 & 3
							-special interests of villagers
Coverage of Communes (No.)							explanation of phases
4 Phase 1: Self-help Projects	5	5	10	10	5		-hamlets do individual projects
5 Phase 2: Works Budget		5			5	10	-Commune Dev. Councils works budget
6 Phase 3: Total Dev. Program							-CDC has complete dev. program including extension budget
Subsidies ($000) per Commune							
7 Phase 1 $2,000	10	10	40	40	20		) preliminary estimate only
8 Phase 2-3 4,000		20			30	60	)-will vary from year to year
9 Phase 3 6,000							) depending on budget availability
District Staff (No. / $000)							qualifications & training
10 Commune Level Workers (CLW)	5 / 7.5	10 / 15	10 / 15	10 / 15	10 / 15	10 / 15	10 yr. grads., 1 yr. training
11 Supervisor	1 / 2.5	1 / 3	1 / 3	1 / 3	1 / 3	1 / 3	12 yr. grads., min. 3 yrs. CLW
Equipment Purchases (No. / $000)							
12 Motorbikes	5 / 2.5	5 / 2.5	2 / 1	2 / 1	2 / 1	1 / .5	
13 Jeep	1 / 2.5		.5	.5	.5	.3	
14 Audiovisual & Misc.	1.0	.5	.3	.3	.3	.3	
Operating Budget ($000)							
15 Training	14	14	14	10	16	22	- @ $25 per man/week
16 Staff Salary & Expenses	10	18	18	18	18	18	
17 Equipment	6	3	2	2	2	2	
18 Miscellaneous Expenses	2	4	5	5	5	5	note: expenses all transferred to admin. budget after stage F
19 total	32	39	39	35	41	47	
20 Commune Budget Subsidy	10	30	40	40	50	60	charged to infrastructure sector of Dev. Budget

though carrying out specialized tasks, have unspecialized backgrounds and are somewhat interchangeable. One then merely
distinguishes two categories of personnel at the regional level,
professional and other. The inevitable argument over whether
all those staff positions are really necessary can best be
handled by a review of individual positions after the project
review.

The next set of items covers the delay factors, a part of
the Project Plan which is quite distinctive from the District
Plan. Many of the greatest bottlenecks in the development of
the rural economy are found in the air-conditioned offices,
conference rooms, and assembly halls of the capital, where
planning documents, operations manuals, regulations, and
legislative documents lie waiting in in-boxes or are listed on
agendas. Chapter 2 distinguished three major elements of
institutional development: field service units, staff, and
program development. The delay factor items in the Project
Plan, in effect, cover program development.

One must now ask what major pieces of paper are critical
for keeping the project on schedule. In this project, it is
assumed that two regulations will be essential to enable the
project to move on to more advanced stages: the regulation
authorizing phase 2 commune subsidies and the regulation
authorizing phase 3 subsidies. These regulations would also
provide operating guidance; an operations manual would have
to go with them. These are listed as items 16 and 17.

At the bottom of the form are the budget summaries. The
first item of the project operating costs should be a summary
of the District Plan budgets. This, so to speak, is the variable cost component of the project, varying with the number
and the stage of districts covered. Then come the semifixed
and fixed cost items: central training, provincial and regional
staff, and miscellaneous overhead. As on the District Plan,
there is a project budget total and a separate commune subsidy
total, the latter not charged to the project or sector. Finally
one must show how much of the project costs are for imported
products which need foreign exchange. Foreign exchange requirements of each project are needed to provide a basis of
foreign aid requests and to compute the foreign exchange
budget.

Setting the Pace

Planning of this project is complicated by the usual problem
of incomplete previous activity. Rural development projects
rarely can be planned neatly from a scratch on a tabula rasa.
Rather, they generally build on the accomplishments and the
errors of previous activity. In building on accomplishments
and learning from errors, the planner finds his work advanced
by previous activity. He also finds his planning job more complicated.

This project starts with 15 districts already in stage A
and 15 districts in stage B. (This is actually a continuing
project but, being part of a new program, it can be considered
as starting at the point of planning.) This leaves a much
wider range of pacing options than if it were starting from
zero. Setting the pace means deciding how many new districts
a year are to be launched in stage A and how many are to be
advanced each year into further stages. The factors one
would generally consider in making this vital decision are:

> Relations with other projects
> Manpower constraints
> The point-line-network pattern (described in Chapter 4)
> Financial constraints

One may set aside the first and last considerations for
the moment. Other projects, as will be noted later, present
no significant constraints, and financial constraints are best
considered in the review of the entire program. Regarding
manpower constraints, the director of the department has
estimated that he can recruit 60 in the coming year and 85 the
following year. Deducting something for attrition, this will
give the following cadre increase over the next few years:

	1967	1968	1969	1970	1971
Recruited and trained	30	60	85	85	
On Duty	225	250	300	375	450

The net increase of 25 CLW in the coming year can either
open five new districts or advance five districts from stage A

to stage B. No matter what is done with additional manpower, either all or some of the districts can be advanced from stage B to stage C. To move all of them, however, would be to violate the point-line-network principle. It would mean 15 completely new operations to be supervised by personnel without previous experience. Therefore, one should start by moving five districts from stage B to stage C, and add five districts to stage A. Then the following year one can step up the rate of advance from stage B and also from stage A to 10 districts. This will give the following pattern:

Stage	CLW/Dist	1967 Dist	1967 CLW	1968 Dist	1968 CLW	1969 Dist	1969 CLW	1970 Dist	1970 CLW
A	5	15	75	20	100	10	50	5	25
B	10	15	150	10	100	10	100	10	100
C	10			5	50	10	100	10	100
D	10					5	50	10	100
E	10							5	50
F									
Total		30	225	35	250	35	300	40	375

The pattern one sees above on the districts, the advance by the right phalanx across the years and down to the final stage, is the motif of almost all rural development projects (see Chapter 11, p. 209). Along with this on every individual project or project complex should go an exercise such as the above matrix multiplication of the coefficients by stage (CLW/district here) by the number of districts in each stage in each year. This exercise should be carried out first on the particular input expected to be the binding constraint, so as to test out a trial pattern of coverage expansion. In the example above the trial pattern passes the test, since the CLW requirement does not exceed the CLW availability in any year. In this manner one determines the maximum advance of coverage possible, subject to the binding constraint.

One then computes the output elements, in this case the participation, with a similar matrix multiplication of coefficients by coverage:

	Stage:	A	B	C	D	
Standard No. of Trainees:		150	350	450	500	Total
1968	Districts	20	10	5		
	Trainees	3,000	3,500	2,250		8,750
1969	Districts	10	10	10	5	
	Trainees	1,500	3,500	4,500	2,500	12,000

And so on. In this manner the figures for leader training (item 1 on the Project Plan) are derived.

Now come two items radically different from the others: the program development variables. Here one must show approximate deadlines rather than quantities of input or output. Like everything else in the plan, these items are quantified, but it is time within the year that one is measuring and thus quantifying. One can do this by using a one-letter symbol for each major stage or milestone of that item and putting that letter at a point in the column which will approximate the quarter of the year in which the action must take place. For regulations, one can use three stages and symbols: D=drafted, M=Ministry approval, C=Cabinet approval. If the commune budget regulation is not approved on time, five districts cannot go into stage C in 1968. If the commune development plan regulation is not approved on time, five districts cannot go into stage E in 1970.

Costing Out

Before going into the details of the budgeting procedure, a word should be said about the life span of the project. One can take it as starting during the year in which pilot work is being done on advanced stages with funds approved under a previous project scope. The project ends when all 50 districts have gone through stage F. The last year would thus be 1976. It is advisable, however, to transfer the overhead elements out of the project before then; 1971 is actually the last year in which new developments will occur in the project. In that year the last 10 districts will be launched, and the first districts will go through stage F. About that time the regional staff will probably start devoting itself to other innovative development activities.

For this reason one may set 1973 as the last year in which training, higher staff, and general overhead will be charged to the project.

The first budget item, district operation costs, is derived by the same kind of matrix product summation as was leadership training. To get the figure for 1968, for example, one might compute:

Stage A	20 districts @ $22,000	$ 440,000
Stage B	10 districts @ $39,000	390,000
Stage C	5 districts @ $39,000	195,000
		$1,025,000

These standard costs per district are, of course, taken from item 19 of the District Plan.

The next item, staff training cost, is a mixture of fixed and variable costs. There is a variable factor of $1,000 for each CLW preservice trainee and $200 for each CLW in-service trainee. Multiply these factors by the number of trainees each year to get the variable element. To this, one adds a fixed cost of $20,000.

The last two items of the budget present some difficult problems of judgment. The regional staff and general overhead requirements are not tied to any other variables of the project. It is exceedingly difficult to predict them. The one consistent approach might be labeled Parkinsonian Realism. Whether one approves of the phenomenon or not, one should be realistic and assume that Parkinson's Law will operate: overhead will climb steadily in a manner independent of total coverage or output. One may fight this tendency later, but should be conservative in estimating costs and assume losses against Parkinson's Law. On this basis, the overhead staff (items 12 and 13) increases steadily. This is reflected in item 20, along with steady increases in 21 (miscellaneous overhead).

After the total project cost is added up (item 22) there are two final lines computed as matrix products of coverage by stage and district plan cost factors by stage. The commune subsidies are computed from the factors in item 20 of the District Plan. The foreign exchange requirement is computed

from equipment purchases (item 17 of the District Plan) with
some modifications. The first 30 districts already have
some equipment. In the first years of the project, however,
the central staff will also need some equipment. A rough
estimate of annual needs is made on the basis of these factors.

THE USES OF THE PROJECT DOCUMENTS

Figures 12.1 and 12.2 represent the main documents,
possibly all the documents, to be submitted to authorities for
approval and then to be used as the definitive multiyear
authorization of the project. They should contain within them
all necessary computations to facilitate rapid judgments.

The forms discussed here should be successful in focusing
the attention of the authorities on issues which require their
judgment. First, regarding the feasibility of the whole program, the forms should induce the reviewing authorities to
ask some questions that cannot be answered by the forms: Is
the training of local leaders adequate to enable them to carry
out their new responsibilities in phase II and phase III* communes? Is the cadre and supervision per district adequate
to the job? Can the necessary regulations (items 16 and 17
of the Project Plan) be approved on time? Paradoxically,
good planning documents should lead to questions that cannot
be answered by good planning documents. The authorities
must venture some risky judgments at that point, judgments
which can be verified only by point-line stage operations.

Pacing alternatives can be considered with these forms.
If pacing assumptions are changed, an officer and a secretary
can revise the two sheets and distribute revised copies within
24 hours. Some fast computations can be made from the
sheets right at the meeting. Suppose some reviewing authority
were to ask, for example, if it would be possible to complete
the evolution of a district by stage D, eliminating two stages
of developmental work, by transferring officers from other

_____

*In the "Project Description" earlier in this chapter, para-
graph 2d explains phase II and 2e explains phase III.

agencies temporarily into the program.   One cannot judge the
qualitative aspects of the feasibility of this proposal from the
forms, but one can judge the cost consequences.   It would
double the cost of stages B through D and eliminate most of
the costs of E and F.   This would add about $800,000 to
project costs in 1969 and 1970, while reducing costs in subsequent years.   By considering some alternatives in this
manner, one can judge the cost effectiveness of the proposal,
relative to the project's specific goal of getting all communes
into phase III as quickly as possible.

As mentioned above, the forms take only a few hours to
revise.   They also provide specific output benchmarks by
which progress can be judged.   Because of their many advantages over conventional narrative project documents,
these forms make a good starting point of a general systems
revision, a cheap and highly useful supplement to existing
systems of documentation.

CHAPTER 13   BASIC PLANNING DATA

Having designed the procedure for planning individual projects, which is the core of the planning system, the next step is to design the steps leading up to the core procedures.

The first step in this and in most planning procedures is data collection. This may, indeed, be the most arduous and difficult part of the work. Stage II economies (as defined in Chapter 3) are notoriously short on reliable statistics. A peasant economy compensates, however, for the lack of available statistics by being homogeneous. Fortunately, homogeneity and lack of statistics tend to go hand in hand. The more primitive the economy, the less the diversification and the more valid a small sampling or survey. In a primitive economy, farmers in a region with no radical soil and water variations and no ethnic variations will almost all tend to raise the same basic cereal crop and side crops, with the same techniques and scale of operation.

In collecting and presenting basic data, as in formulating plans, paperwork discipline is important. Data should be limited to those necessary to decision, compiled in a way that facilitates decision. Many texts recommend the collection of long lists of statistics, which might be helpful, but collecting data without knowing exactly how it is to be used is like swirling a butterfly net in the night air. There is no end to the data which might be useful. This is, perhaps, one of the main reasons for structuring the planning procedure very carefully before the planning work commences.

This system, therefore, limits carefully the amount of data it submits to the planners for consideration. It assumes however, that the decision-makers are knowledgeable men, broadly conversant with the history, economy, and sociology of their country and of each of its regions. This reservoir

of general knowledge is relevant to decision but does not have
to be included in the documentation.

DELINEATION OF PROGRAM SCOPE

Size of the Region

Before undertaking regional planning, one must decide
how the map of the country is to be carved into regions. Should
the regions be large or small? In Israel the regional planning
is done on the basis of units consisting of less than 30 villages. [1]
In other countries a planning unit may include millions of farms.

Delineation of planning regions will be subject to considerations of political pressures and availability of planning staff
and also to considerations inherent in the logic of the planning.
It should be noted, first of all, that in consolidating regional
programs into a national program, four to six regions are
easy to handle; beyond that the paperwork of consolidation gets
cumbersome. Secondly, the more primitive the economy, the
fewer the regional variations. As the economy develops and
diversifies, it will be advisable to subdivide regions for planning purposes.

The basic rule of the system is: one region, one strategy.
Two adjoining areas with different primary farm systems can
be treated as one region if the same strategy applies to both.
But if conditions in one region call for irrigation as the lead
innovation and conditions in another region call for corn-
growing as the lead innovation, they cannot be handled as one
regional program.

It is best to start with as few regions as possible and then
to subdivide them as progress in farm diversification and development program diversification proceeds.

Delineation of Farm Systems

Planning work must be based on specific farm system models, that is, on assumptions regarding individual farms. The easiest approach is to have only one farm system model of a given combination of enterprises per region with a given set of enterprise inputs and outputs.[2] One then assumes a normal distribution of these values around the averages used in the model.

Such homogeneity may not exist. One may assume, for example, that in our hypothetical Southern Region there are (in addition to 420,000 rice-growers) 40,000 riverbank intensive vegetable-growers, 20,000 upland crop farmers, 10,000 orchard-growers, and 10,000 cattle-herders. One may, however, assume homogeneity for planning purposes. In stage II a planner can generally ignore the secondary systems of a region. Although 20 percent of the farmers of a region may be something other than rice-growers, during the planning period it may well prove a herculean task to extend adequate services to even 60 percent of the rice-growers. Under such typical circumstances, planners are well advised to concentrate all available resources on a program for the primary system.

Unusual circumstances, however, often warrant very special attention to a small minority of farmers. The operators of a secondary system may offer a particular potential for dramatic increases in food production or export crop production which the country may desperately need. Or the operators of such a secondary system may live in misery, which provides fertile ground for insurgency; the minifundia coffee-growers in Latin America are an example. Under such circumstances, planners would be well advised to make special provision for secondary farming systems in the regional plan.

DATA ON CURRENT CONDITIONS

Before one can decide in which direction to go, one must know for certain one's present location. This means taking stock of the present natural resources of the region, the present farming systems, and the present agricultural services.

There is one other very vital type of information the planners need to know. They must know what farmers, and also businessmen, are thinking. This means getting out and listening to--not talking to but listening to--farmers. Experts and officials often have an unfortunate propensity to lecture farmers when they visit villages; they feel they have a duty to educate. One should recall that development is a process of education not only for the simple minds but for the master minds. It is important that officials and experts ask questions and listen when they visit the villages. The farmers should do the talking.

There is no set documentary format for information on what and how the farmers are thinking. This is a type of data which should be not on paper but in the back of the mind of all those involved in the planning process. Adequate time must be spent in the villages to get a feel for what interests the farmer, what concerns him, what worries him, what he can readily understand, and what will go against his way of thinking.

Natural Resources Data

All available soil data and rainfall data should be assembled on maps; 1:100,000 soil-type maps are probably adequate for strategy decisions. Certain crops may later require 1:10,000 or 1:5,000 soil-mapping, village by village.

At this point the interpretation of the soil data is more important than the degree of detail. For planning purposes, available land resources should be expressed in terms of capacity. Soils should be classified in terms of their capability to grow crops requiring certain levels of soil quality.

The data should be presented on maps and possibly on tables, district by district. They should list, for each district, the available land, cultivated and uncultivated, by soil capacity category. Fairly rough estimates will do at this point. The consumers of this data are those who will draft innovation studies and determine where specific new crops can be grown.

For the purposes of this volume, the so-called Southern
Region is, in very rough terms, an area of small valleys and
rolling hills, with the following land capability and present
land use (expressed in hectares):

Land Capability		Present Agricultural Land Use	
Double crop	400,000	Double crop	180,000
Single crop, wet	1,300,000	Single crop	1,140,000
Single crop, dry	800,000	Tree crop	40,000
Pasture only	1,200,000	Pasture/fallow	160,000
Nonagricultural	1,800,000	Woodland	80,000
	5,500,000 ha		1,600,000 ha

Present Farm Systems

The most important type of basic data is concerned with
what the farmers are doing now. One needs to know the
structure of their farm system. This includes: land and
labor devoted to each enterprise, by month; cultural practices;
purchased inputs and their costs; production consumed at
home; marketing channels; prices received; and number of
farms engaged in each enterprise.

Form A-1 (Farm System Analysis) in Appendix A is an
example of the type of summary of a farm system that is
needed. Looking down the list to the corn enterprise, for
example, one sees that the average corn-growing farmer
plants one hectare, gets a yield of 1,800 kg, consumes 300
kg and sells 1,500 kg; he gets a price of $50 a ton and thus
nets $75 (no purchased inputs used). Since only 15 percent
of the rice-growers also grow corn, this contributes only
$11 to the income of the average rice-grower.

Some overaveraging has gone into this Form A-1. No
farmer would grow kenaf, corn, and sugar as main side
crops; they would grow only one of the three. Nevertheless,
the form gives some basic data that can be used in judging
whether a new innovation package is likely to fit in with the
present farm system. Conclusive proof of feasibility of innovations comes not from more detailed data on present conditions but from actual field trials.

One can see from Form A-1 that farmers derive about a
third of their cash income from rice sales and the rest from
a wide variety of sources.   Substantial surplus labor is available from January through April and in July, September, and
October.

The main source of such information is farm management
surveys.   These surveys need not be elaborate or costly,
however.   Jacques Delvert, while a professor at the Royal
School of Administration in Cambodia, compiled a masterful
description of the farming systems of that country with the
aid of his students, who conducted field surveys during their
vacations. [3] Again the principle applies that the more primitive the agriculture of the country, the smaller the sample
needed.

The results of a survey should be confirmed by statistics
and observations.   Conclusions on production, based on a
survey of sample farms, should tally with the latest regionwide agricultural statistics.   Conclusions on inputs and cultural practices should agree with observations of the extension
staff who have been working with the farmers.

In addition to data on farm enterprises, it is important
to get information on nonagricultural employment.   This important aspect of farming is sometimes neglected, so that
one comes to erroneous conclusions about labor available
in the villages and may promote enterprises for which the
farmers have no time.   One is then liable to jump to the conclusion that farmers have not adopted a new innovation because they are too custom-bound, too inadequately motivated,
and too resistant to change.   Such explanations merely serve
to cover up inadequate planning.

Present Government Services

Form A-2 in Appendix A (Present Institutional Structure
and Coverage) gives a one-page summary of present governmental services in the region.   It lists the institutions, their
roles, the cadre, farmer participation, and coverage.   The
first column lists the national or regional institution and its
local group action affiliate.   The second column lists the main

functions of the institution. The third column states the lowest
echelon at which cadre are assigned. The fourth column indicates the grade of the cadre at that echelon (1-2 means
"one cadre at grade 2"). In the lower left-hand corner is an
explanation of the cadre-grading system used in that country,
the grade attained by people with certain levels of education
after 0, 5, and 15 years of service. Under coverage is listed
the number of provinces and districts with cadre assigned
from each institution and the number of communes or villages
with client organizations. (One should keep in mind that our
hypothetical region has 10 provinces, 50 districts, 500 communes, 5,000 villages, and 500,000 farms.) The last column,
Participation, gives the number of active clients or members
of client organizations of each institution.

     Information on coverage and participation is often sur-
prisingly hard to get, even from the files of the relevant
agencies. Service agencies tend to state their operations in
terms that would imply 100 percent coverage and participation.
It is surprising how many studies of specific development
programs neglect to give the vital statistics on how many
villages and how many farmers are actually reached by programs. Present institutional roles, staffing, coverage, and
participation are essential for strategy decisions.

     Form A-2 gives a picture that is typical for stage II de-
veloping countries. The Kenat Marketing Board, which services a common cash crop, has comprehensive coverage and
participation. Other institutions are reaching less than 20
percent of the farmers.

MARKET DEMAND

     Turning from data regarding the present to data on the
future, the next major input data are the estimates of market
demand for various crops.

     A good deal of excellent material has been written on
techniques of projecting market demand. Gittinger's study
of planning in Iran gives a particularly good description of the
procedures that should be followed. [4]   At this point, however,

one should note a major difference between the planning approach of this book and many other texts. During the strategy
planning phase no targets are to be set. This point will be
discussed further in the next chapter. The demand projections
at this point are statements of the maximum capacity of the
market, foreign and domestic, to absorb potential increases
in production. Without going into the techniques to the depth
that Gittinger has presented them, it is worthwhile at this
point to cite some of the main considerations and assumptions
that should go into demand projections.

Domestic Consumption

The projection of domestic demand over a 10-20 year
period is based essentially on three elements. First, it is
based on a projection of population growth. This is an essential element of planning for any sector; there is no need to
discuss the technique here. Planning for agriculture should
certainly be based on the same long-term population assumptions as plans for other sectors.

Secondly, demand projection must be based on assumptions
about changing income and the resulting changes in diet patterns. One must make some assumptions about the income
elasticity of various types of food. In particular, one can
safely predict that consumption of protein and meat products
will rise rapidly, once diet preferences for basic cereals
have been satisfied. Consumption of fruit and vegetables will
also rise with rising income.

Finally, the nutrition needs of the nation should be
examined, and demand projections should be adjusted to provide for filling in specific deficiencies in the nation's diet.

Export Markets

Projections of export potential are somewhat more difficult than projections of domestic demand, since they involve
evaluation of worldwide demand and of the production potential
of competing nations. A few general assumptions can be

made, however, on worldwide trends. First, over a 10-20
year period the present efforts of many cereal importing
nations to achieve self-sufficiency will achieve some success,
so export markets for cereals will drop. Second, there will
be a steadily increasing export market for meat and feed
grains. Third, there will be a steady rise in international
demand for fresh fruits and off-season vegetables. Finally,
there will be a declining world market for fiber crops, as
more countries achieve self-sufficiency.

Prices

Long-term price trends as well as current price trends
must be considered in planning innovations. If there is reason
to believe that the long-term price will be lower than the
current price, the lower price should be used in evaluating
an innovation.

Form A-3 of Appendix A (Market Demand Projection)
gives a partial listing of the demand projection for the
Southern Region, covering crops under consideration for
promotion.

INNOVATION STUDIES AND SUMMARIES

Each enterprise which now plays a major role in the
farm system, or on which successful adaptive research has
been carried out, should be analyzed to determine whether a
feasible and profitable innovation package exists. Such packages are essential modules, key building blocks of a program.
Again, we are looking into the future, to see what can be done.

Organization of the Work

The necessary data and analysis should be set forth on
two types of documents. The first is a study, as detailed as
possible, with full technical and economic documentation.

The purpose of the study is to demonstrate the feasibility of a
particular innovation package, to spell out the contents of the
innovation, and to show how it will make money and for whom.
The second type of document is a brief summary, giving the
facts relevant to strategy decisions in as few words as possible.

For study and summary, there are no magic formats.
However, the Mosher factors (the essentials and accelerators
described in Chapter 2) make a useful and comprehensive
checklist for individual packages. It is also useful to have a
single-sheet summary of the basic figures of all the principal
innovation packages being considered, so that they can be
easily compared.

In spite of the many drawbacks of committee authorship
(the giraffe was supposedly designed by a committee), the
studies and summaries can best be done by working groups.
These working groups, one for each crop, should be composed
of the specialists in various agencies and agribusiness firms
who are most concerned with that particular crop. Regional
and central units of the extension service, the agricultural
research establishment, agricultural faculties, cooperative
services, and private firms may also want to participate.
Organizing the staff work of planning along crop lines is a
major step forward in achieving coordination between a variety
of agencies and disciplines and also a means of securing
broad participation.

Different working groups should operate with a common
set of assumptions regarding present conditions. They should
be furnished with a common set of soil and water data and
with models of the farm systems of the region, as prepared
on Form A-1. Population and domestic food consumption
projections should also be furnished to the working groups.

A complete study, with the full content as specified below,
takes time. Planning deadlines may not permit complete
studies. The summary type documentation illustrated in
Forms A-4 and A-5 of Appendix A can be prepared by working groups in short order. Efforts should be made to do a
complete study of the basic crop of the region in time for
strategy formulation. Such a study, even in preliminary form,
is essential for the data it provides on market structure.

   This work need not be completely regionalized. One
working group can produce a crop study for the entire nation
that will be usable in this planning system, provided regional
differences are noted and regional summaries are prepared.

                     The Innovations Summary

   Form A-5 is worth noting carefully, since it provides
the basic computation of the feasibility of an innovation package.   Line 1 gives the expected average enterprise scale,
either in hectares or, if a livestock enterprise, in head of
breedstock (sows, hens, etc.).   Line 2 gives the yield per
hectare or, for livestock, per breedstock head.   Line 3 is
line 1 times line 2, or total production.   This, less the
amount consumed on the farm, gives the production sold,
line 4, which, times the expected long-term price, line 5,
gives the gross cash income, line 6.

   Lines 7 through 18 give the costs (per average enterprise).
Fixed investments are listed on lines 7 through 9 and annual
production supplies per enterprise on lines 10 through 13.
Line 14 gives the amortization of the fixed investment and
line 18 the total annual cost.   On these innovations it is
assumed that no hired labor is required, only family labor,
which is, in effect, a fixed asset of the farm.   Labor expenses
could be added to this form, however.   Line 19 gives the net
income per average enterprise.

   Line 20 is figured on a somewhat different basis; it is the
increase in net income over the previous enterprise.   Rice 2
is assumed to be a more comprehensive innovation package,
following Rice 1 (it is possible to have two or three innovation
packages for one crop), and Small Irrigation is assumed to
follow Rice 2; its techniques are used on the second crop.
Line 20 is thus not to be compared to line 18, which gives
total rather than incremental cost.

   The kenaf innovations illustrate a common problem: an
important cash crop whose market is declining.   Action must
be taken simply to minimize the anticipated loss in income.

Line 21 shows the percentage of the 420,000 farms of the primary system of the region to which the innovation is applicable. Line 22 is line 20 times line 21, the resulting increased income for the average farm. Line 23 is the total potential increase in income for the rice-growers of the region, an encouraging $155. This can make a great deal of difference to the welfare of a family with an annual cash income of $209.

Line 24 through 26 give the measures of return on investment on which innovation packages should be primarily judged. The return per day of labor is based on a computation of incremental labor requirements, not shown on these forms. Line 25 shows the return on fixed investment, and line 26 shows the return on annual investment (line 18 less the cost of the previous enterprise divided into line 20). All three of these measures of return must be considered in evaluating an innovation package.

This listing of innovations and their payoffs constitutes, in effect, the technical horizon of agriculture in the region. It also gives a partial capital coefficient. For a total investment (short, medium, and long term) of $347 per farm, an annual return of $155 is produced, a return of about 45 percent a year. This is on-farm investment only, however, to which must be added all the investments in off-farm services. Once these other investments are calculated, a capital coefficient based solidly on current technical judgments rather than on historic coefficients will be available.

Form A-5 also gives some indications of the overall magnitude of a possible program. About $75 million in annual increased income can be produced with a credit expansion approaching $173 million. At this point it can be seen that the region clearly has a technical potential that warrants a good deal more planning work.

Innovation Package Analysis and Study

The Innovation Package Analyses illustrated on several Form A-4's in Appendix A are summaries of crop studies with the same general format. The contents, organized to follow the Mosher checklist of essentials and accelerators (see Chapter 2) are as follows:

Market--The summary, under the subheading "Structure," should indicate first what marketing network exists at present, and what additions and improvements are required. If marketing innovations will improve the price to the farmers over what they now receive, the improved price should be stated. Under the subheading "Demand," the summary should state briefly how much of the production of the region can be absorbed by the long-term target year and what the price trend is.

The study should analyze completely the structural requirements of marketing: minimum efficient lots, inspection and quality control requirements, handling requirements and costs, and gross margin requirements at village, district, region, and metropolitan echelons. The study of the basic crop of the region should also have a fairly complete description of current marketing conditions in the region through both commercial and cooperative channels. To the extent that other crops are handled by the same or similar channels, other studies will be able to refer back to the main one. The study of present conditions should be organized somewhat like the analysis of the optimum structure: present lot sizes, quality control practices, handling practices and costs, and gross margin at various echelons.

Under "Demand," the study should analyze the projection of the price and volume figures given in the summary.

Technology--Under "Adaptation" the study should state first how far the innovation has progressed to date. Have many farmers already adopted it? Has it been demonstrated? Have field trials been made? Or is it still confined to the experimental stations? Under "Compatibility" should be stated any problems of relationship to the present system and any limits on the number of farms to which it is suited. These limits would include soil and water limitations and labor limitations.

The study should list the essential technical requirements of the crop: minimum soil and water requirements, essential cultivation practices, and labor requirements by month. It might be advisable to have a map showing the potential land available for the crop, by district. It is particularly important to analyze the compatibility of the crop to the present system, particularly regarding labor requirements.

Supplies--The summary should state the kinds of inputs
required and the average cost per enterprise. Under "Problems," the limitations of the present supply distribution
system should be stated.

The study should give technical recommendations on fertilizer, pesticide, seeds, and special equipment. The study
of the major crop should also analyze the supplies-distribution
requirements and present condition, in somewhat the same
manner as the study handled production marketing: lot sizes,
quality requirements, handling costs, and gross margins at
various echelons.

Transport--This factor as a limit to innovations can best
be conceived in terms of access: How large a vehicle must
be able to get how close to the village how much of the year
in order to handle the crop? The survey of access conditions
is discussed in Chapter 18. Assume for a moment that such
a survey has been completed; one then has a listing, by district,
of the number of villages in each access category: year-round
truck access, dry-season truck access, year-round cart
access, dry-season cart access, etc.

The summary should state what percent of the villages and
what percent of the communes and districts have the minimum
access condition required for the crop.

The study should analyze what the minimum conditions
must be. It should also include a map which, in effect, combines the transport and technical conditions, showing what
areas have the minimum soil and water conditions and also
what areas have the minimum transport access conditions as
well. It should give transport costs in the region.

Incentive--This factor summarizes the others. The incentive to farmers to adopt an innovation must be in three
forms. First, the innovation must increase net cash income
by a sufficient amount to make the undertaking interesting to
the farmer. An innovation which nets the farmer only $5 a
year in increased income will not be worth the risk and
trouble, even if it does give a high return to capital and labor
invested. Moreover, the government services necessary for
such a minor innovation would not be worthwhile. It is for this
reason that innovations must be packaged (i.e., combined into
one project).

The other two aspects of incentive are the return to capital and labor.

One might adopt a rule of thumb that the return on production inputs, fertilizer, etc., must be 100 percent ($1 net income per $1 invested). On fixed capital investments it should be at least 20 percent. A high return is necessary to offset the risks inherent in agriculture. On labor the return per day should be equal to the customary day-labor wage rate. Even though farmers may have idle time, they will probably not be tempted to undertake something which has a lower return to their time. In our Southern Region, the daily rate is set at 50¢.

The summary should state the three relevant incentive figures and should provide a detailed analysis of costs and returns.

Education--The study should analyze what techniques are needed to teach farmers the innovation. In addition to demonstrations of results, what practice demonstrations are needed and what practices may require initial supervision? Is it necessary to put the innovating farmers through a training course? The summary should simply list the necessary educational activities.

The working group should keep in mind that education, like other accelerator activities, is a necessary evil, as pointed out in Chapter 2. It is easy to fall into the trap of assuming the more education the better; rather one should seek to get the innovation adopted with the least amount of education.

The study should simply look at what is needed in terms of the individual farmer, without any look at what cadre and organizational effort this implies. The quantitative implications will be worked out in the project drafting; one should not attempt premature project drafting at this point.

Credit--The summary should list the loans that will be necessary to the average enterprise for this innovation. The study should further analyze some of the administrative aspects of the loans: what information the lender needs to evaluate the loans, what security can be offered, and how the loans should be evaluated.

The study of the basic crop should also include an analysis and evaluation of present credit facilities, both institutional (cooperatives, etc.) and noninstitutional (traditional village moneylenders).

Land--The summary should give an enumeration of the special measures necessary to prepare and preserve the land for the innovation. These include preliminary surveys, engineering, land clearing, irrigation, and rotation. The study should give a full analysis of the measures necessary in terms of the average enterprise.

Group Action--Here again an effort must be made to avoid premature judgments. The strategy formulation will determine the structure of group action; here we need indicate only the scale--for marketing, for supply distribution, for extension, and for other government servicing. In terms of minimum efficient lot sizes and in terms of the average enterprise size and yield, how many farmers in a village and in a district are necessary to provide enough volume for efficient marketing? How many irrigation projects should there be in one district to make the services of an irrigation engineer or assistant worthwhile? The study should analyze these requirements; the summary should state them.

The Work Calendar--A table or graph showing the seasonal factors should be attached to each Innovation Package Summary. It should give the workload on the farm by month (a figure particularly important in judging compatibility with the current system), and the storage capacity and local supply and marketing inventory needed per 1,000 farms by month. These will be quite useful later in planning supply and marketing services.

Thus, the basic data for agricultural planning has largely been summarized and illustrated on five forms (Forms A-1 through A-5). To these must be added the maps showing soil and water conditions. Three more types of data inputs will be needed to complete the planning job: overall national policies, standard costs, and resource constraints. However, on the basis of the data on the forms described in this chapter, given some indication of overall policies, strategy planning can now commence.

NOTES

1. J. Ben David, ed., Agricultural Planning and
Village Community in Israel (UNESCO, 1964), pp. 36-37.

2. Ibid., pp. 33-34, a good example of the use of modular farms in planning.

3. J. Delvert, Le Paysan Cambodgien, (Paris: Mouton,
1961).

4. J. P. Gittinger, Planning for Agricultural Develop-
ment: the Iranian Experience (Washington, D. C.: National
Planning Association, 1965), pp. 30-52; see also Agricultural
Planning Course, 1963 (Rome: FAO, 1963), pp. 71-83.

CHAPTER **14** STRATEGY FORMULATION

This chapter formulates procedures for a series of decisions that might variously be labeled preproject planning, structural planning, or strategy planning--preproject planning in that all the planning decisions necessary before the procedures of Chapter 12 can be applied to a complex of interrelated projects are considered; structural planning in that program structure, choice and sequence of institutional and innovational projects, and choice among the organizational options described in Chapter 4 are determined; and strategy planning for the reasons discussed below.

The procedures are illustrated on Form A-6 through A-9 of Appendix A. First, however, let us consider some of the particular problems of this phase of the planning.

BASIC PROBLEMS AND BASIC SOLUTIONS

There are four distinctive problems in this phase: two tightly interrelated problems of high uncertainty and the parochial agency interests at stake, the difficult problem of efficient sequencing of the decision operations of this phase, and the problem of suitable documentation for the primarily judgemental decision operations of this phase.

Strategy Planning and Agency Interests

The term strategy is used in operations research to describe the establishment of decision rules applicable to problems under the following conditions:

1. Decisions must be made at successive moments in time.

2. Future circumstances are uncertain.

3. Uncertainty diminishes with time. [1]

The classic example of a strategy problem is a chess game. A good player decides on his next move and also on how he will respond to a variety of possible subsequent circumstances. Agricultural development is obviously not as neat a strategy problem as a chess game, but there are certain resemblances: (1) Subsequent decisions (annual reprogramming decisions) are going to be made during a multiyear development plan period. (2) Future circumstances are highly uncertain, not simply in regard to price, demand, and weather trends, but in regard to the actual feasibility of the program; the whole range of choices among the options in Chapter 4 may prove to be the wrong ones. (3) Diminishing uncertainty applies particularly to the medium-range agricultural development. Over a five-year period a great deal will be learned about what does and does not work. Development is a heuristic process; it improves steadily on the basis of what is learned in the process of development.

A chess match is characterized by long pauses before moves. The moves in agricultural development are made generally not by individuals but by committees; the game could thus be called chess-by-committee. The participants in such a "committee" (it may be an interagency working group, a council of ministers, a planning commission, or a legislature) are, moreover, generally representatives of agencies or parties with divergent interests.

Staff members of different agencies generally agree wholeheartedly on the need for interagency coordination and integration of services, but they find it hard to make concrete decisions. They are reluctant to be involved in decisions which will levy requirements and place constraints on other agencies, feeling they may be dangerously overstepping their authority. They are reluctant to share their own agency's responsibility in a particular field or to commit their agency to support of another agency's program. They do not feel they have the authority for the drafting of such project.

The problem is further complicated when one of the agencies involved has an "unburied fatality" (see Chapter 3), about which it is on the defensive. Such sensitivity will induce it to fight certain valid options to the last ditch. Because of the uncertainties of the problem, any option is easy to fight.

Chess-by-committee can go a long time between moves. In some developing nations, decisions regarding the options listed in Chapter 4 have been postponed for years. While agencies continue servicing only a small fraction of the farmers, arguments concerning the merits of various proposals for more effective coverage go on and on.

How can such delays be avoided? By recognizing the limits of rural development strategy decisions. By keeping the commitment to a particular strategy tentative until it has proven itself in the "point" and "line" phases. By agreeing to try some of the alternative strategies while sticking to the main choice strategy the first year in the point stage.[2] Some countries have a capability for trying several alternatives at once; most developing countries have only enough administrative capacity to undertake one new comprehensive rural development strategy at a time in the point stage. The following year, however, an alternative can be tried. This procedure of trying alternatives will be discussed in more detail at the end of Chapter 17. The point to be made here is that deliberations should be structured so that no party suffers a clear-cut defeat. The uncertainties are too great to warrant a do-this-rather-than-that type of decision; rather it should be a try-this-first-then-try-that type of decision.

Sequencing of Decisions

Preproject planning involves the consideration of a number of interrelated alternatives which can ideally be structured in a decision tree like that in Figure 14.1.

Ideally consideration should start at A, move to either B or C, then down one of the two branches to D or E, etc. The usual procedure, however, is somewhat different. A committee or working party meets under the chairmanship of a senior member. Various members express opinions

at the first meeting which might eliminate, say, options L,
N, and G. The staff of the committee then prepares a project
draft for consideration of the group that will incorporate one
of the final options not yet eliminated, say K2. The members
of the committee then argue over the proposal and possibly
propose modifications. At this stage, they are more or less
lost among the branches and have no clear view of the tree.

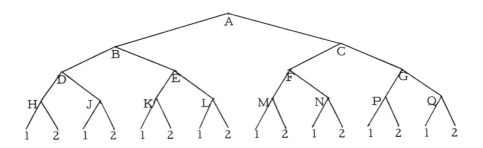

FIGURE 14.1. Decision tree.

Premature submission of full project proposals has that
effect on the decision-making mechanism. It causes the group
to wander among the branches rather than to proceed deliberately down one trunk line or another.

The decision-making should be sequenced so as to follow
the decision-tree pattern as much as possible. Some backtracking is inevitable, but an effort should be made to take
up first those options which are least likely to be affected by
subsequent options. The sequencing of the system in the balance
of this chapter follows roughly the pattern diagrammed in
Figure 14.2.

Suitable Documentation

The decision operations of the preproject phase are almost
entirely judgemental in nature. They require almost no computation or comparison of quantitative values. This means
that there is little work to be done by staff assistants with

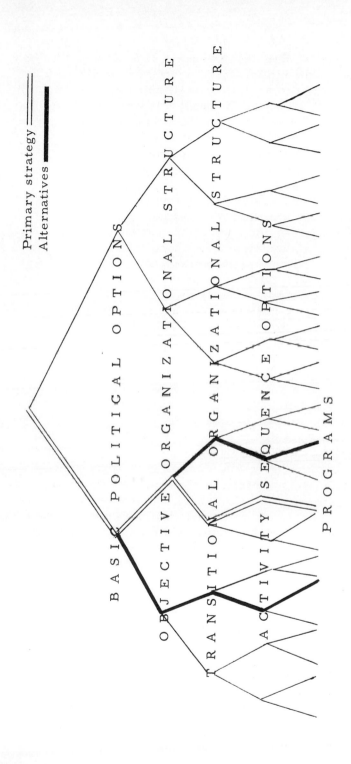

FIGURE 14.2. Sequence of the planning system.

spreadsheets and slide rules; the decision work must be done
largely at predocumentation-type meetings (see Chapter 5,
p. 91).   At times it is useful for staff assistants to prepare
working papers of a "scenario" type, illustrating possible
strategies (see Chapter 25).   Working papers for strategy
deliberation have drawbacks, however.   They tend to limit
the discussion to the pros and cons of one particular strategy
and one particular set of choices among options.

A strategy should evolve out of a working group consensus.
A special type of documentation is necessary to support this
type of deliberation--a documentation that can grow step by
step in a meeting as decisions are proposed and agreed on.
The necessary technique might be labeled Minimum Paperwork Maximum Deliberation (Minimax for short), but it would
then be analogous not to the minimax concept of game theory
but to the "Programme Minimax" concept of the French disk
jockey Le Président Rosko.*

The procedure boils down to substituting charts, tables,
and graphic aids for narrative documents, proposals, working
papers, and position papers, and then working out the decisions from whole cloth in committee deliberation.   This
means committee deliberation aided by special graphics techniques and requires a discussion leader skilled in the use of
the blackboard or the flipchart with acetate overlay.   It requires a discussion leader who plays a very active and at the
same time completely neutral role--a man on his feet, a man
with chalk or grease pencil in hand.   This procedure is a
considerable departure from the conventional committee deliberation, in which the chairman, who is a senior personality,
simply calls on each member to say his piece.

The discussion leader must be able to illustrate the participants' ideas graphically.   He should first brief the participants on the simple tables and charts on a blackboard or
acetate overlay.   As each speaker presents his ideas, the discussion leader should capture them in symbols and add them
to the charts.

---

*"Minimum de blah-blah, maximum de musique."

The results of the deliberation thus become visible, step
by step, rather than buried in the notes of the secretary.
Complex ideas of different participants can literally build on
each other, as the discussion leader displays their relationships. Different ideas and alternatives can also be displayed.
Unresolved differences can be left on the board, to be taken
up again later if the discussion fails to lead to a conclusion.

The ideal setting for such deliberations is a Malaysian-
type operations room like that described in Chapter 7, with a
full range of audiovisual devices and equipment. An overhead projector is particularly useful for displaying tables
and work sheets on a screen.

The timing of such strategy deliberations differs from
the usual program or project review meetings. Fewer but
longer sessions are needed. One all-day session should be
far more productive than two months of weekly two-hour
sessions. A weekend meeting at a get-away-from-it-all site
might be a useful alternative.

THE POLICY INPUT

The two types of inputs to the first operations of the preproject phase of planning are (1) data on current conditions
and technical and economic possibilities and (2) data on policies (the output of the policy decision system). In many
planning systems the overall policies come into play at final
review, when the highest authorities review the program. It
is more efficient to feed in policy at the beginning of the planning process. A lot of work can be avoided if it is understood
from the beginning, say, that between alternatives B and C,
C is ruled out for political reasons.

The application of political judgement is not always this
simple, unfortunately. It often involves politically sensitive
or even explosive issues which are best left dormant unless
it is absolutely necessary to reach some decision. If a
choice has to be made between working in area X or area Y,
for example, it is clearly better to rule out one area because
work there is unfeasible than to have to say no to the people

from that area for political reasons. Some issues, moreover, can only be defined and decided case-by-case; they may come alive only if there is a choice between two equally feasible and attractive options.

Nevertheless, the strategy planning working group should try to get all of the preliminary policy judgments out of the authorities that they can.

Program Objectives

The first essential policy judgment answers the question: What is to be maximized? The easiest answer is to maximize net cash income to farmers; therein the objective of the planners and the objectives of the farmers themselves, who are the ultimate decision-makers, will coincide.

The government may have some other objectives, which may or may not be consistent with maximum net cash income to farmers. It may want to improve nutrition; this may mean pushing crops less profitable to farmers. The government may urgently want to reduce food imports or increase agricultural exports; these objectives might require less profitable production options. The government may be more concerned with increasing median rather than mean net farmer cash income; it may be more concerned with lifting the standards of the poorest farmers than with maximizing total income. Finally, the government may be particularly concerned with building institutions for development in subsequent periods than with lifting income in the forthcoming period.

The government may have some relevant objectives on the input side. Which program costs does it want to minimize? Does it want to maximize or minimize foreign or domestic private investment, for example? Will the constraining financial input be government operating funds or credit expansion? In large measure these questions can best be answered when the whole program is submitted for evaluation. Some preliminary judgments may be useful, however.

Other Policy Questions

Geographic options, as listed in Chapter 4, may require difficult political judgments. For the planners, a combination of maximum payoff and "oilspot" options is the best. If planning is based on averages, the high initial returns from this geographic strategy will offset the operation of Murphy's Laws.* If the government wants a geographic strategy other than this, it should inform the planners from the start.

The organizational and field cadre options will involve some political issues. Any special government policy toward the use of public authorities and corporations, private agri-business firms, and farmer controlled services should, if possible, be known from the start.

For purposes of the planning illustrated in Appendix A, one may assume the following: The government wants private investment but prefers farmer controlled services. The hypothetical Southern Region has national geographic priority; within the region the maximum payoff/oilspot geographic strategy may be applied. The government is concerned with building solid institutions and does not want crash programs.

ANALYSIS OF INNOVATIONS

The crop working groups should, hopefully, present a number of brief Innovation Package Analyses (Form A-4's), which are summarized on a Form A-5 (Summary of Feasible Innovations). The first decision, then, is which innovation packages to select as core crop projects for the regional program.

For inclusion in the program, the projects should be (a) acceptable and profitable for the farmers, (b) capable of being extended during the planning period, (c) applicable in a substantial number of the districts of the region, and (d) applicable to a significant percentage of the farmers. There

*See Chapter 11, p. 241.

are, of course, other points of general feasibility to be considered, such as market demand, prospects for price stability,
compatibility with other important crops, etc.

The first point (a), acceptability to the farmer, can be
judged by applying certain minimum ratios to the returns
listed on lines 24 through 26 of Form A-5. One might assume,
for example, that framers will not be interested in any package offering less than 50¢ per day for labor, less than 25 percent return on annual investment, or less than 10 percent on
fixed investment (after payment of interest). For the second
point (b) one can also set a rule-of-thumb criterion: that an
innovation package must be ready for the point phase no later
than the third year of the plan period, for example.

The lower limits on the last two criteria depend on how
much increased income the most widely applicable crop projects afford and also on how many different crop projects the
planning and project staffs can handle. To illustrate, in
Senegal two crops, peanuts and millet, provided adequate
volume to justify a variety of services. Therefore the whole
program was built on these two crops. In Malaysia in many
regions it takes a wide variety of crops to warrant the services contemplated under the farmer association program,
but fortunately Malaysia has the staff to handle them. Whatever decision is made in a country on this particular point,
it can be expressed as a rule of thumb. One might require,
for example, that projects included in the program in stage
II be applicable to at least 25 percent of the districts of the
region and at least 10 percent of the farmers.

Having selected the crop projects to be included in the
program, the next step is to arrange the data on them in such
a way that one can spot quickly the relative priority of the
projects and their institutional requirements. Such an arrangement of data is found in Form A-6 (Innovation Promotion
Requirements) in Appendix A. The innovation packages chosen
for the program are ranged from left to right in order of the
year in which they are ready for the point stage and, within
each year, in order of the number of district to which they are
applicable. Thus the projects to the left are the ones that reach
the most farms the fastest. Form A-6 also shows at the top
the percentage of farms to which projects are suited and the increased income per farm (increased income to participating
farm times the percentage of potential participating farms).

The servicing requirements of each package are indicated below on the form. Ideally they should show a pattern of increasing requirements as one moves from left to right, so that the program can start with only a few services and add more as it grows. Fortunately, this is much the case in the illustration in Form A-6. The first innovation package, Rice 1, requires only one practice demonstration, supplies of fertilizer and pesticide, some improvements in the marketing, and short-term credit. Moving to the right, Sorghum requires, in addition to these, seed, equipment, marketing by grade, a land use survey, and medium-term credit. Such are the additional institutional features that must be added to support the Sorghum project.

At the bottom of the table are some figures which will be explained in Chapter 15.

ANALYSIS OF INSTITUTIONS

The next step is the difficult choice of institutional options, a step which particularly requires the minimax technique of group deliberation and graphic documentation. This should be broken into two steps. First, as institutional objective, a long-range preferred institutional structure should be selected that can provide almost all the farmers with all the services they need. Consideration of this objective structure should probably be in national rather than regional terms, although some regional variations may be warranted. The second step should be to decide on a transitional structure, based on the crop projects that have been selected, to providing farmers with the services they need.

Graphic Technique

The forms illustrating the making of these decisions are A-7.1, A-7.2 and A-7.3 in Appendix A (Agricultural Services Structure Analysis--Present, Objective, and Transitional Structures, respectively). To keep these forms compact, a variety of geometric symbols are used to indicate different types of organizational units. Abbreviations indicate services provided, and ciphers indicate the number and grade of cadre normally assigned to work in the field. Looking at A-7.1, which shows the present structure of services, one sees, for example, that the Community Development Department has stationed at the commune "1-4/5" (one cadre of grade 4 or 5 rank), whose function is "GA" (promotion of group action). Symbols on the line for community development indicate supervisory offices at region, province, and commune levels, and a farmer-owned institution at commune level (the Commune Development Council).

As a first step in the deliberation, the discussion leader would put table A-7.1 on the blackboard or acetate chart underlay. He would then brief the participants on the use of the symbols and abbreviations and the meaning of the tableau. One can see from the gaps in the table the paucity of organization and cadre at the commune and village level. One can see also that the cooperative, with supply, marketing, and credit functions, is located at a level where it cannot get enough volume to function efficiently. It should be noted that Form A-7.1 represents the ideal present structure, assuming complete coverage.

The participants in the meeting then propose changes or additions to the present structure. The result of the first phase of the deliberations is illustrated on Form A-7.2 (Objective Structure). One gets from Form A-7.2 a fast visual impression of the change, of services moved closer to the people and more tightly interrelated. Engineering functions have been moved from region to district and village level, with village irrigation societies. There are more cadre at district level. The Commune Development Council has more functions. The Farmers Association at district and commune level is staffed with cadre. The Agricultural Development Bank has cadre at district level. This is the picture presented to the meeting participants as their deliberations draw to a close.

There might also be a minority report version of this tableau. For example, the bank might channel all of its credit through the Farmers Association (FA), which might continue to have village units for credit purposes. The Kenaf Board might continue with an independent office at the district level. One can imagine a variety of such alternatives.

The next step of the deliberation is illustrated in Form
A-7.3 (Transitional Structure). Comparing A-7.2 and A-7.3,
one can see that the transitional structure features an extension cadre at commune level who is later replaced by the FA
commune agent. One may note also the absence of a commune-
level FA branch. The FA handles no credit. Again, one can
imagine many variations on this pattern and some emphatic
minority reports. One can imagine the discussion leader
putting symbols on the board and then erasing them, as members propose features which are not accepted by the group.

The graphics in final form would be submitted to a planning commission composed of higher-level authorities, together with a narrative report explaining the charts and the
reasoning behind them. Minority reports would also be submitted. Written explanations are not absolutely necessary;
it might be more efficient for the chairman of the working
group to present the graphics to the planning commission in
an oral briefing. Chapter 22 takes up the problem of written
vs. oral presentations.

Decision Criteria

The deliberation on institutional structure that goes into
the A-7 Forms is largely judgemental, as has been emphasized.
There are no quantitative tests of adequacy or rules of thumb
that can be applied. The following factors, however, generally
enter into making these judgments:

Effective Coverage--The objective is adequate institutional coverage to support a continuing volume of innovations.
This means putting adequate cadre close to the commune-
village level.

Economy--There must be an adequate payoff on investment in cadre. This means minimizing cadre costs, keeping
the number at commune-village level as few as possible and
as low in grade as possible.

Minimum Change--Existing organizational structures
should be preserved wherever possible. Organizational change
is time-consuming and expensive. It is particularly hard on
the nerves.

Farmer Participation--In the long run (not necessarily in the short run) the farmers themselves should be as involved as possible in the planning and management of agricultural services.

Private Incentive--Save in a few countries where it is precluded for ideological reasons, the government should seek to get the private sector to bear as much of the cost of development as possible. Chapter 24 will discuss this problem further.

Cadre Incentive and Discipline--The structure must provide cadre with rewards for good performance and penalties for poor performance, as well as providing them with general job satisfaction. For this reason, commercially organized services may be preferable in some countries to direct government services. Less-educated village-based cadre may be preferable to better trained men who previously deserted the village for academia. (The reasons for this preference have already been given in Chapter 4, pp. 71 and 74.)

Flexibility--The objective structure should be able to support a wide variety of innovations and service a variety of farm systems.

STRATEGIC PHASING

The third and final step of the preproject planning, once we have selected the innovations and made the institutional options, is to combine them all in a time frame. Even the transitional structure cannot be instituted in a locale all at once; it must be phased in over several years. The innovations likewise must be sequenced, supporting and building on the evolution of the supporting institutions.

All this sequencing is done in terms of the local module, the average district or commune, as it moves over several annual stages. Again, the minimax procedure, using graphics and special symbols, supports and expresses the deliberations.

Logic-Sequence Diagram

Form A-8 (Local Development Strategy Diagram) illustrates the use of networking to express a strategy of development. In appearance it resembles a PERT (Program
Evaluation and Review Technique) or CPM (Critical Path
Method) chart (see Chapter 22), but there is no critical path
involved. The arrows simply express what must come first,
second, and third. They express logical and temporal priority.

To understand the diagram, one must see that the activity
starts at two nodes, one of which is labeled

A
CD/FT
66

This means that in stage A, which went into the point
phase in 1966, community development (CD) farmer training
(FT) was initiated. The arrow leads to a node which indicates that stage B, initiated in 1967, featured CD organization
of a commune development council (CDC). This leads to a
number of nodes in stage C: supply, marketing, and credit
activities as well as first farmer production based on innovation packages (Pr/R1, or production under Rice 1, and
Pr/Knf, production under the improved Kenaf Project). A
one-way arrow means that the activity at the arrowhead must
occur in stage following that of the activity at the origin of
the arrow. A two-way arrow means that the connected
activities, while conditional on each other, may be initiated
in the same stage.

Again, the graphic evolves out of the deliberations of a
working group. The discussion leader starts by writing the
events code on the board and explaining the procedure. He
then starts it in motion by writing the starting event and
asking what should come next. The participants have before
them Forms A-6 and A-7.3. They propose sequences of developments and argue over how much can be done in one stage.

What unfolds in such deliberations is a development curriculum. The logic-sequence diagram depicts rural development par excellence as a learning process. The main

considerations are how many new developments can be absorbed
by the cadre and by the farmers in one year, and what lessons
must be learned first as a basis of further lessons. Thus,
for example, short-term credit (Cr/S) must be mastered before the district cadre and farmers can go on to medium-term
credit (Cr/M), which in turn must precede long-term credit
(Cr/L)--in the judgment of the working group which has presumably drafted the strategy illustrated in Form A-8 in Appendix A.

Table of Staffing and Activity

The final step in the preproject planning is a table which
serves as a guide to all individual project planners, a table
which can effectively coordinate the structuring of all the
projects of the program. Such a table is illustrated in Form
A-9 (Local Development Activity and Staffing Schedule) in
Appendix A. The numbers in each column of the table indicate the number of communes covered by component activities
or the number of cadre assigned to the district. The activities and staffing of the institutional projects are listed first,
followed by the crop projects. The "X's" indicate when certain new features of institutional programs are to begin, in
terms of staging in a modular district. Arrows after numbers indicate that those values continue indefinitely.

This table is based largely on the forms previously discussed in this chapter. The one new element is the phasing
in, by stage, of the number of communes covered and the
number of cadre on board.

This type of table has too much verbiage and detail to be
presented on a blackboard. Rather, blank forms might be
handed to all participants, and the discussion leader might
flash the form on a screen with an overhead projector. Each
agency representative might note on his own blank form the
phasing in of his agency's activity, based on the previous
forms and his judgment regarding the personnel and coverage
phase-in. The discussion leader would fill in the phase-in
of crop projects, the demonstration stage, and the farmer
production staging. Representatives of the various agencies
would then tell their plans for phase-in, and these would be

flashed on the screen. All participants would then discuss
how this fitted into their agencies' plans.

Form A-9 is finally presented to a commission of higher-
level authorities for approval. It is a statement of the
strategy on which programming will be based. The initial
coefficients of the agricultural development model have been
determined. Now cost figures and demonstration pacing
must be added, and programming can begin.

NOTES

1. H. Theil, J. C. G. Boot, and T. Kloek, Operations
Research and Quantitative Economics (New York: McGraw-
Hill, 1965), p. 135.

2. A. Mosher, "Administrative Experimentation as a
'Way of Life' for Development Projects," International
Development Review (June 1967), pp. 38-41; and R. Nelson
"Uncertainty, Learning, and the Economics of Parallel
R&D Efforts," Review of Economics and Statistics (November,
1961), pp. 351-64.

CHAPTER **15** LOCAL MODULE
FORMULATION

Both the individual projects and the regional agricultural
development program as a whole should have modules in the
planning system. This next phase of the planning system
deals with the formulation of these two types of modules.
The project modules are illustrated in Appendix A on
Forms A-10.1 through A-10.8. Since the program in
Appendix A uses the district as the module, these project
modules will be referred to as District Plans in the rest of
Part III. The strategy summary documents illustrated on
Forms A-8 and A-9 in the previous chapter were essentially
program modular documents. In this phase of the system
the program module will be summarized on Form A-13
(Local Cost Benefits Summary) and Form A-14 (Program
Coefficients Table).

GENERAL CHARACTERISTICS AND PROCEDURES

Characteristics of the Phase

This phase makes a gradual shift from structuring to
programming, from determining coefficients to determining
allocation of resources. As planning moves to higher levels
of aggregation, it becomes increasingly laborious and complicated to go back and readjust coefficients; resource
limits thus become more binding. In a sense programming
has already been given some consideration: in the strategy
formulation some consideration was given to economizing
scarce resources.

This phase does not, however, actually allocate specific limited resources. It is concerned with the planning of units of increment, not the total program. It does not undertake constrained maximization in the full sense. Rather, it seeks to balance the component projects against each other. It seeks to find a pace of expansion of activities that will neither grossly overcharge nor grossly underutilize any essential service institution at any stage. It seeks balanced institutional growth at the local level. The keynote is balance between projects at each stage.

Basically, this phase applies the procedures for modular planning specified in Chapter 12. The main departure from the procedures of that chapter is that projects will now be pacing and limiting each other. If these projects were drafted without a specific coordinating system, they might have to go through innumerable rewrites to get into balance with each other. This and the next chapter seek to define procedures that can keep project redrafting to a minimum.

General Procedure

Briefly, this phase executes the following planning steps:

Step 1--Compute activity volume and requirements of crop projects. Set the pace of expansion of participation and from that derive production and inputs per stage.

Step 2--Compute the activity volume of each institutional project in order of the first stage in which they are launched. The activity volumes are determined by the servicing requirements of the crop projects.

Step 3--Compute the cadre and, possibly, special plant and equipment requirements of each institutional project, as a function of the volume of activity.

Step 4--Compare the derived cadre and special plant requirements with the coefficients on the Local Development Activity and Staffing Schedule (Form A-9). Does the derived activity volume require much more or much less cadre and equipment than most of the projects have planned? If so, then readjust step 1 and recompute. Does the expected activity volume overload or underload certain cadres or plants? If so, then readjust those inputs.

Step 5--Compute financial requirements and enter the increased income and the total cost per stage of each project on the Local Cost Benefits Summary (Form A-13). Compute the discounted net benefits.

Step 6--Enter project outputs and inputs per stage on the Program Coefficients Table (Form A-14).

Types of Projects

One may distinguish three basic types of projects, in regard to relevant variables that make up the project structure. The first are crop projects, which have simplest structure. The second are noncommercial service projects, which have substantially more relevant variables. The third are commercial projects, public or private, that are expected to show a profit, and whose relevant variables are the major items of a profit and loss statement and balance sheet. The next three sections take up the formulation of these three project types in order of increasing complexity.

CROP PROJECTS

The agricultural development program of the southern region illustrated in Appendix A includes six crop projects. Project documents on three of them will be found in Appendix A: Rice 2 (Form A-10.6), Sorghum (Form A-10.7), and Hogs (Form A-10.8). These three have been selected because of the distinctive planning features and problems they illustrate. Rice 2 is an expansion on former enterprise, being a continuation of Rice 1, a previous project.

Sorghum and Hogs are new enterprises. Sorghum requires new land development and loans for land clearing; it cannot start until the Agricultural Engineering and Small Irrigation (A-10.5) Project has prepared a commune land use plan. Hogs illustrates the problems of a livestock project. (It should be remembered that "crop projects" in this volume refers to livestock projects as well as projects involving field crops.)

Relevant Variables

The general pattern of relevant variables for crop projects is illustrated on Form A-10.6, the District Plan for Rice 2. The output items lead off with farms participating, from which the other output variables are derived. The coefficients for the derivation of the other output variables are taken from Form A-5, Summary of Feasible Innovations. Under each stage there is a column for the increment of that stage and for the cumulative total.

Items 6 and 7 of Form A-10.6 give the pacing factor of the projects, the demonstrations. The lines below give the resource requirements and services requirements from various agencies, that is, the activity volume generated by this project for other projects. At the bottom is the marginal cost per district, composed of two elements. The first is the budget outlay (line 14), both the actual outlay in the district in each stage and the outlay outside the district in direct support of activity in the district. Line 16 is the incremental credit cost per district. This is the credit expansion required--development financial resources in any given year which could be used for other purposes but which must be put into this project in order to achieve the target outputs in one district.

The Sorghum Project on Form A-10.7, requires some additional line items to express the added complexities of a new enterprise with capital investments. It has a requirement for small tractors (see Form A-4.4) in addition to supplies for current production. It requires medium-term loans for land clearing. In the Hog Project on Form A-10.8, breed sows take the place of hectares as a determinant of enterprise scale, and replace seed as an input. The

quantity of breedstock (sows or cows or hens) determines
the scale of most livestock enterprises. Here it is assumed
that new breedstock are produced in provincial breeding
centers and sold to farmers on a basis that requires no
marginal investment in facilities per district.

Setting the Pace

Now comes one of the most important cause-and-effect
propositions of this book. The model makes one major
behavioral proposition. It postulates that, given an innovation that is suited and profitable to a substantial number of
farmers in a district, the number of farmers in that district
who adopt the innovation each year will be a compound
function of two variables: (1) a function of the number of new
demonstrations the previous year, since some farmers will
be sold on the innovation directly by demonstration; and (2) a
function of the number of farmers who have already adopted
the innovation the previous year, since other farmers will
be influenced by the success of their neighbors. A new
demonstration in a village, if successful, may induce some
10 to 40 farmers to adopt the innovation package, provided
the other essential services are present. In the following
year, some 0.5 to 3.5 farmers will be influenced by each
successful farmer to adopt the innovation.

This is what makes the whole program go. The demonstration of a profitable innovation sets in motion a chain of
activity. It has a multiplier effect, influencing a group of
farmers to improve and increase production and, in turn,
inducing other farmers to do the same--until all the farmers
in the locale to whom the innovation is suited and profitable
have adopted it. It thus paces the growth of demand for
other services--supply, marketing and credit activities.

One can state this relationship mathematically as
follows:

$$\Delta f_{ij} = d_{fi} f_{ij-1} + d_{di} \Delta d_{ij-1} \qquad f_{ij} \leq \bar{f}_i$$

where $\triangle f_{ij}$ is the increase in the number of farmers who
have adopted the innovation of project i in the j-th stage; d_{fi}
is the coefficient of new farmers adopting the i-th innovation
to farmers practicing the innovation in the previous stage
(f_{ij-1}); d_{di} is the coefficient of new farmers adopting the i-th
innovation in stage j to the increase in demonstrations of the
i-th innovation in the previous stage $(\triangle d_{ij-1})$; and $\overline{f}_i$ is the
maximum number of farms in the district to which the i-th
innovation is suited.

Take the Sorghum Project as an example. In this project,
$d_{fi} = 2$, $d_{di} = 35$, and $\overline{f}_i = 6,000$. The pace is then set as
follows.

j =	4	5	6	7
$\triangle d_{ij} =$	20	30	30	
$\triangle f_{ij} = d_{di} \triangle d_{ij-1} =$		1,700	1,050	1,050
$\triangle f_{ij} = d_{fi} f_{ij-1} =$			1,400	6,300
$\triangle f_{ij} =$		700	2,450	7,350
$f_{ij-1} + \triangle f_{ij} =$		700	3,150	10,500
				6,000=f$_i$

In general the demonstrations that count would be the
village demonstrations; in some cases they might be the
commune-level demonstrations. A crop promotion program
will frequently, if not generally, include both village and
commune level demonstration. One can then conceive the
commune demonstrations as a necessary support to the
village demonstrations.

This key relationship is essentially a sales relationship,
a typothesis regarding the impact of sales effort. The
farmer, again, is the ultimate decision-maker and must be
sold. The regional program is then a projection of a sales
and service effort. The output figures are sales targets.

How does one derive the key coefficients of the equation. One could use regression analysis on data for past comparable campaigns. Certainly project staffs should do a statistical analysis of the results of the first season under the plan and revise the coefficients on the basis of this analysis. It is often the case, however, that no adequate data are available on previous comparable campaigns. The coefficients will then have to be set on the basis of the seasoned judgment of the project manager, just as a sales manager of any private firm sets sales targets on the basis of judgment.

One may note that the Rice 2 Project moves rather quickly, since it takes over all the Rice 1 demonstrations at stage C. Sorghum is considered suitable for only eight communes in the average district in which the project operates. For those villages to which it is suited it has a high attractiveness, hence the high d_{di} coefficient of 35. Hogs is also somewhat localized to seven communes with a substantially more limited number of suitable farms, hence a low coefficient. The alpha coefficients will be found at the bottom of Form A-6.

Having determined the number of participating farms in each stage one can derive most of the other items with coefficients given on Form A-5. It is advisable to note those coefficients in the comments column of the District Plan, so that anyone reviewing the plan will have all the necessary values and relationships directly in front of him. Note that requirements of medium-term credit and equipment will be based on the number of new farmers.

A uniform phase-out rule should be set for projects, namely that the rule that the last year of funding of activity in the district on a crop project is the year in which the maximum number of farmers are to adopt the innovation. The demonstrations thus continue long enough for each farmer to be able to compare his results against those of the demonstration; they are then transferred out of the development budget. This rule thus limits development budget funding of field operation to that period in which the activity has a specific development target. Other rules may be appropriate in various countries; it is advisable to have a consistent phase-out rule in any case. Without a consistent phase-out rule, budgeteers will find themselves under pressure to continue activities in the development budget indefinitely.

The budget is basically much simpler than that of the Community Development Project, examined in Chapter 12, or than that of any institutional project. All variable costs are related to the number of demonstrations held. The "cost per demonstration" thus includes not only the on-site supplies and other expenses but also the per village or per commune cost of audiovisual materials and printed matter, farmer visits, and possibly some agent travel expenses over the fixed allowance.

The project cost per district also includes credit expansion. If medium- or long-term loans are required, this item continues beyond the phase-out point with negative values as loans are paid back.

SERVICE PROJECTS

As noted above, "service projects" is shorthand for government services of a noncommercial nature. There are three such projects in the Southern Region agricultural development program: Community Development (on Form A-10.1), which we have already examined, Agricultural Extension (Form A-10.2), and Agricultural Engineering and Small Irrigation (Form A-10.5).

Agricultural Extension

Demonstrations are, of course, the activity par excellence of an extension service, and the volume of demonstrations in the initial stages is determined by the crop projects. In the later stages it is assumed in the strategy that demonstrations of specific projects under the program will be augmented by commune-sponsored demonstrations, as the program decentralizes. For the first four stages, however, the activity volume is determined entirely by the specific crop projects.

The plan assumes that there will be no local initiative.
This is one of the basic conservative assumptions one can
make to cover the effects of Murphy's Laws. There will
undoubtedly be some intelligent local initiative in places, but
one should not count on this. If an institutional project cannot
be justified or sustained by planned innovations, it is probably
advisable to delay it until adequate innovations have been
tested out for the region.

Note that the number of demonstrations in some cases
differs from those shown on the crop project A-10 forms. On
the Extension Project the number of demonstrations for
specific crops is corrected for the average district of the
region. The Hog Project, for example, is applicable to 40
of the 50 districts. All activity figures for that project are
multiplied by .8, therefore, to relate them to an institutional
project covering all 50 districts. Similar adjustments are
made in relating other crop projects to institutional projects.

The items below the demonstrations on the A-10's give
the cadre staffing, as projected on Form A-9 (Local Development Activity and Staffing Schedule). At this point one com-
pares those tentative projections with the volume of activity
generated by the crop projects. Can the staffing handle the
volume? Is the volume sufficient to justify the staffing? This
can be determined partly by quantitative analysis and partly
by judgment. It might be worthwhile to draw up a monthly
schedule based on this volume of activity, to see if the staff
will be overburdened at some point, in an average district.
Even with a monthly schedule, however, a good deal of
judgment must be applied. Some activities will be complementary; others will make competing demands on the time of
the cadre. If severe imbalances are found, cadre may be
added or subtracted, or the pace of increase of demonstrations
may be changed.

In other respects, the relevant variables and budgeting
rules applying to the Community Development Project apply
to this project.

Agricultural Engineering and Small Irrigation

This project is a combination crop and institutional project. It is generally advisable to separate the two types of activities, but it is unavoidable in this case (as in many cases) because cadre attached to a particular institution work on one and only one innovation directly.

The service activity of this project is structured somewhat like that of Community Development: cadre efforts bring each commune through a series of stages. Each commune stage requires a given cadre staffing and a given amount of farmer training. The commune, rather than the individual farm, is the recipient of the services. What the commune receives, in effect, is advancement to a certain stage of development which is a prerequisite for certain types of innovations. Here, the land development plan (A-10.5,) line 5) is a prerequisite for projects requiring additional land, namely Sorghum and Cotton.

This and the Extension Project illustrate the two basic ways of relating crop and institution projects. The institutions may, as in the case of this project and Community Development, perform a service for the entire commune, which is a prerequisite for a crop project. Or, as in the case of Extension and the commercial projects described below, crop projects may determine the volume of activity of the service.

The budget structure of the service side of the Engineering Project is quite similar to that of the Community Development Project. On the innovation, the Irrigation, side of this project, some distinctive features should be noted. The current supply input requirements are not shown for lack of room; they are identical to Rice 2. The investments are long-term, to be paid back in 10 years. Investments are divided between earthworks and equipment in order to isolate the foreign exchange requirements of the latter. A heavy farmer training program rather than field demonstrations sets the pace.

COMMERCIAL PROJECTS

TABLE 15.1

Farmers Association Inventory Requirements
As Percentage of Total Annual Sales

	Jan	Feb	Mar	Apr	May	Jun	Jul	Aug	Sep	Oct	Nov	Dec
Rice	60	40	35	25	20	15	10	5				20
Kenaf									60	50	30	10
Sorghum								50	50	40	20	10
Cotton		20	40	20	10							

The Southern Region program has two projects which are commercial in structure: Farmers Associations (A-10.3) and the Agricultural Development Bank (A-10.4). Both earn a gross margin from services, both have a local-level profit and loss statement, and both are carried as projects only so long as a government subsidy is necessary to put them on their feet.

In many respects the Farmers Association Project is the most difficult project of the entire program to formulate within the limits of a single page. In addition to activity and expense structures relevant on most types of projects, this project has an asset and liability structure which is highly relevant to decision-making. Some drastic simplifications of normal commercial decision rules are necessary to boil it down to one page. The technique of radical simplification,* used here in planning the Farmers Association Project can be applied to projects for private commercial ventures as well, which often play a key role in the project structure of an agricultural development program. A regional program may well be a mix of public and private projects.

---

* The L3-5 series equations in Appendix B may provide a clearer picture of these computations.

The credit project on Form A-10.4 has a much simpler structure. The questions it raises can be answered by the explanations of the Farmers Association (FA) Project.

The lead items (the business volume) on Form A-10.3 are derived from the crop projects. The share of market the FA has on each crop is noted in the remarks column. From the sales volume total is computed the contribution to fixed costs (line 9), a fixed percentage of marketing and supply volumes exclusive of such directly variable items as bagging and packaging, handling, and shipping. In some circumstances it might be worthwhile to compute a different gross margin rate on each crop.

Next come the difficult problems of estimating staff, working capital, and building space requirements. One must first find the peak requirements by a seasonal analysis of the business. This can be considerably simplified by looking first at the marketing inventory pattern, since marketing has much greater space and capital requirements than the supply business.

Rice is, of course, the dominant business. Rice plus cotton keep business at peak level from January through March. There is another peak in marketing business in August and September, and the supply business is strong from April through June. One can thus estimate the peak need on the basis of January rice marketing. One can therefore set working capital requirements at 50 percent of rice marketing volume and space requirements at 1.2 square meters per farmer member (which equals the requirements of the Rice 1 participants), sufficient for the 70 percent share of the Market of the 4.6 tons of rice the average farmer will come to market.

Regarding the adequacy of staff, there is no formula one can apply; again one must use judgment. In some cases a formula based on so many clients or dollars, or tons of volume per cadre may be useful as a starting point for this judgment. On the Farmers Association Project, (Form A-10.3,) it would appear that the number of managers, assistant managers, and commune agents, when compared with peak monthly volume and total clientele, is adequate in all stages.

Line 21 on A-10.3 uses a very simple formula for equipment, starting with $10,000 and increasing it by $5,000 a year.

One might figure equipment on the basis of so much per cadre
and so much per $10,000 of volume. This completes the asset
side of the balance sheet, in grossly simplified form. One can
now compute the last expense items. Interest is computed, for
simplicity of calculation, on last year's debt. Amortization
is figured on the basis of a standard writeoff for equipment and
a standard writeoff for buildings. One can now close the profit
and loss statement, totaling expenses and subtracting them
from contribution to fixed cost to get net profit and the change
in earned surplus.

Computing the liabilities structure is the most complicated
part of the whole calculation. One first computes the debt on
the basis of some standard financial maximum ratios. One
can set short-term debt at 70 percent of net working capital
and long-term debt at 80 percent of fixed assets. One can
delay the long-term debt till the third year, however, so that
the added subsidy can give a debt/equity ratio that stays under
2:1. Membership capital stock purchases are set at $1 per new
member and $2 per old member each year. One can now com-
pute the required subsidy as total assets less long- and short-
term debt, membership capital, and earned surplus.

Thus on a single page one can show the complete derivation of the financing of a commercial operation. This can
apply to private as well as cooperative or publicly owned
ventures.

The Agricultural Development Bank

The business volume and district contribution to profits
of the bank as a whole are derived in much the same manner
as for the Farmers Associations. The subsidy need only
cover initial losses, however. It does not have to contribute
to an asset structure. The local assets held by the bank, other
than the loans themselves, are insignificant. One may note
that the gross margin is the difference between the rate at
which the bank borrows the money or pays the depositors and
the rate it charges farmers. One can assume here that the
bank has a special government-subsidized money source at
5 percent for long-term loans.

The staffing illustrates how strategy must sometimes be changed in light of quantitative analysis of local activity volume. One should set a standard of service. For example, in this case assume that one loan officer can handle a maximum of 1,200 new loans or 400 medium- or long-term loans. The cadre strategy as expressed on line 17 of Form A-9 called for gradually increasing the number of loan officers. It now appears, on Form A-10.4, that more officers than had been planned will be necessary to service the rapid increase in new credit clients in stages D and E. The strategy, as expressed on Form A-7.3, calls for these loan officers to be at grade 4 and to possess 12 years education or 10 years plus substantial experience. One may assume that only limited numbers of suitable candidates could be recruited in the Southern Region.

To require enough such loan officers in stage D to service the anticipated business volume would be to place a requirement on the program that would severely limit the number of new districts a year that could be moved into stage D.

One can eliminate this programming bottleneck by re-adjusting the organizational structure, by planning for assistant loan officers with less education but with other qualifications to work with the senior loan officers. Suitable candidates for assistant loan officers may be assumed to be in more ample supply in the region. This is what has been done on Form A-10.4 on lines 19 and 20. The strategy, the choice of cadre options, has been modified as the planning moves into programming. This type of recycling, by modifying of previous steps in light of more advanced steps, is typical of the unavoidable spiral motion of the planning process, although a good planning system can keep this spiraling to a minimum.

SUMMATION OF COEFFICIENTS

Ultimately in the system, resources will be allocated to the total regional program rather than to individual projects, with the district as the incremental, marginal unit of allocation. The figures for all the individual projects must therefore be pulled together in such a way as to facilitate programming for the entire project complex. This is illustrated in Appendix

A on Form A-13 (Local Cost Benefits Summary) and Form A-14
(Program Coefficients Table). The latter will be a basic
source of data for subsequent programming operations.

Local Cost Benefits Summary

Since the main consideration in overall multisector programming is maximization of net benefits, it is important to
know the net benefits of the marginal unit, or local module.
Benefits are defined in this system as the increase in net cash
income to farm households as a direct result of project activity.
This is a bare-bones definition. It ignores all secondary income benefits, such as increased factor income to handlers
and processors of the increased production. It also ignores
increased real income to farmers in the form of increased
home consumption; in some countries it may be essential to
consider this an inportant part of the benefits of a project.
This definition has the advantage of being conservative, re-
portable, and subsequently relatable to actual market volume
and prices.

The cost side is somewhat more complicated. Basically,
the cost of a program is the sum of the outlays which have a
positive opportunity cost and which could be used alternatively
for other investment. This includes, first of all, government
budget outlays. It also includes credit expansion, the annual
net change in institutional credit outstanding caused directly
by project activity. As project medium-term loans are repaid
and as the program, in effect, makes investment resources
available for other programs, this credit expansion may become negative. It is assumed that the opportunity cost of on-
farm labor is zero, that an unlimited supply is available during
the off-season, within the relevant range, and that during the
peak seasons no labor is available for innovations. These
assumptions may be somewhat more rigid than conditions in
the real world warrant. They considerably simplify cost
computations, however, and they roughly approximate typical
conditions in stage II of agricultural development.

The relevant net benefits figure is the present value of a
discounted future stream of increased income, less costs.
The formula is

$$N = \sum_{j=1}^{x} \frac{n_j}{(1+R)^j} \qquad \text{where } n_j = \sum_{i=1}^{n} y_{ij} - (b_{ij} + \triangle k_{ij})$$

and where N is the present value of the stream of net benefits, n_j is the net benefits of the j-th annual stage, R is the discount rate, y_{ij} is the net income to farmers resulting from the i-th project (the program is composed of projects i=1..n) in the j-th stage, b_{ij} is the budget outlay for project i in the j-th stage, and $\triangle k_{ij}$ is the change in credit outstanding in the j-th stage as a result of the i-th project.

A suitable rate of discount and a suitable time horizon (x) must be chosen. There has been some controversy among economists regarding the choice of a rate of discount for evaluating government investments. The problem is outside the scope of this book, since it is the same applied to rural development as it is for other government investments. Suffice it to say that one should apply the same discount rate to rural development that one decides to apply to other sectors. On Form A-13 a rate of 6 percent is used.

Regarding the choice of a time horizon, one may assume that agricultural innovations will become obsolete. Many countries are facing serious economic difficulties because the cash crops their peasant cultivators got into some decades ago now face ruinous competition. After a few decades, further innovation is essential to retain a competitive position. The time horizon used in the calculations for the Local Cost Benefits Summary on Form A-13 is 30 years. Between discount rates of 5 and 10 percent the system is not significantly sensitive to changes in the time horizon between 25 and 40 years.

Form A-13 executes the above formula on the program for a modular district of the Southern Region. The value for N is found at the bottom of the last column (roughly $15 million). At this point one can make a preliminary test of the economic feasibility of the program by comparing N with the maximum cost outlay, the total of the negative figures at the top of the discounted net benefits column. The total, $527,000, is the present value of the maximum cumulative social outlay. This gives a cost benefits ratio of about 1:28. This does not include the multidistrict fixed costs of the program; it is only for the incremental unit. Had it been less than, say, 1:5 the value of

further planning based on the agreed stategy would have been
dubious.   This preliminary test shows that the program is
clearly economically viable.

Although the district is the marginal unit, $15 million is
not the marginal revenue product.   In the investment programming decision the question will not be whether to do the marginal district now or never but whether to launch the program
in the marginal district this year or next year.   The investment
decision will be a decision to launch a certain number of districts in the program each year (the structure of this decision
will be examined more closely in the next chapter).

Therefore, the marginal revenue product of the investment is the increased net benefits derived by launching
the district this year rather than next year.   Using the subscript t to denote years, and $\hat{M_t}$ as the marginal revenue,

$$M_t = N_t - N_{t+1}$$

The value of N_{t+1} is less than the value of N_t for two reasons.
First each element of the income stream, n_j, has a larger
denominator, $(1+R)^j$.   Second, since it is projected out to the
end of a fixed 30-year time horizon, the income stream for
N_{t+1} loses the last year.   At the bottom of Form A-13 is the
net benefits and marginal revenue for each starting year.

A word should be said about the adjustments necessary
for crop project figures.   A crop project may be applicable
to only part of the districts of the region, say, 30 out of 50.
Its costs and benefits in the average district of the region
must then be derived by multiplying the figures on the District
Plan (Form A-10) by a factor of 30/50, or .6.   This will
apply to all coefficients on the A-14 format discussed below.

From the Local Cost Benefits Summary (Form A-13) one
can see that it is not only possible to calculate the return on
such service activities as community development and extension, but that one can expect a handsome return on investments
in such activities when they are properly coordinated with
complementary activities.   The figures in Appendix A have
not been taken from any one specific case but are based on
actual costs and returns in a number of rice-growing countries
on roughly the same economic plane.   The resulting program

shows a high return (1:28 cost benefits ratio) on the incremental
unit and for good reason: the program assumes the utilization
of presently unused labor and land. It assumes a large "sweat
equity" invested by peasant proprietors. As pointed out in
Chapter 1, rural development can be a very attractive social
investment.

Program Coefficients Summary

On Form A-14 all the data needed for programming except
the constraint values are summarized on a single sheet. The
data are derived from Forms A-10 and A-13 except the project
fixed costs in the bottom left, which will be discussed in the
next chapter.

In the three blocks across the top are the three types of
financial inputs relevant to programming. Project budgets
are distinguished from credit expansion because they are
likely to be subject to different constraints. It may be necessary
to distinguish two types of credit expansion if short-term credit
must be derived from domestic savings or inflation and medium -
term credit can be obtained from an aid donor abroad. Foreign
exchange requirements actually are financed by budget or
credit expansion, but again they are subject to different constraints.

The middle row of blocks gives the coefficients for nonfinancial constrained inputs. The treatment of crop marketing
as a constrained input requires some explanation. In order to
keep the model of the program workable and manageable,
prices are assumed to be fixed, and fixed price coefficients
are used. Converting the normally nonlinear price-supply-
demand relationships into fixed price coefficients requires
some narrow assumptions about demand elasticity. This
planning system postulates the price-supply-demand relationships shown in Figure 15.1.

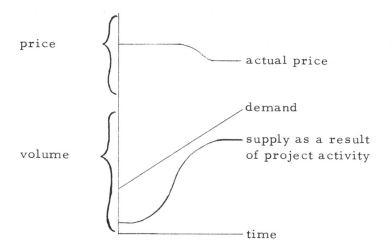

FIGURE 15.1. Price-Supply-Demand Relationships

The end price level--the lower price lever--is used as the
basis of the price coefficients. The model assumes that project activity will have little impact on price until accelerating
coverage and participation begins to approach saturation and
supply approaches demand. At that point one can anticipate a
resulting drop in price. If, however, supply should exceed
demand, the price coefficient is no longer valid. Thus, the
program breaks down if supply exceeds projected demand at
any period. In this respect demand is a constraint.

Review of the Modular Documents

One can, paradoxically, learn a great deal about a development program without having looked at a document that is
concerned with more than one district. The strategy exhibits,
Forms A-8 and A-9, explain how activities are sequenced and
interrelated in terms of a single district. Each of the A-10's
(District Plans) presents at a glance a picture of a specific
activity. One should be able to look Form A-10's over quickly
and get an instant impression of what is going on, how values
are interrelated, and what is quantitatively significant.

One should also be able to spot defects and anomalies in
the program by looking over the District Plans. Are relevant
variables well chosen? Are they listed in a meaningful order?

Have any important variables regarding the local program been left out? Is the pace of increase in inputs in line with the increase in outputs, stage by stage? These are the kinds of questions the planning staff and the reviewing authorities should ask.

Finally the Program Coefficients Table (Form A-14) gives some indication of the problems that will be encountered in programming. Stage D seems to be the bottleneck stage for the budget constraint; it will take a particularly high regional budget to move many districts through stage D in one year. Credit and foreign exchange should not cause any bottlenecks until a substantial number of districts move into stage E. Stages B and C seem to be the bottleneck stages for personnel.

From the Local Cost Benefits Summary on Form A-13 one can see that net benefits do not become positive until stage F. It is therefore a money-losing proposition to keep a district in any stage before stage F for more than one year. One should not program the launching of more districts than can be advanced one stage each year with expected available resources. The programming problem for the Southern Region program at this point can best be presented as a question: What is the maximum number of districts that can be launched each year without generating in subsequent years more personnel requirements in stages B and C than can be met, more budget requirement in stage D than can be met, and more credit and foreign exchange requirements in stage E and later stages than can be met?

Such questions can be answered effectively only if we have the kind of understanding of a program that comes from modular planning from the bottom up.

CHAPTER **16** PROGRAMMING BY
INFORMAL CONSTRAINED
MAXIMIZATION

This chapter deals with the actual resource allocation
operations of the planning system. To many this is the heart
of development planning and many texts do look upon such
planning as primarily a programming procedure. There is
a tendency for all those involved in the planning process to
eagerly take up the question of "How much money do we get?"

In this particular planning system, in contrast to most
conventional procedures, the question of resource allocation
is postponed to the end of the process. One may, however,
consider the decisions made in this system at the modular
level as substantially more important than the final resource
allocation decision. Certainly the success or failure of the
program will depend far more on the quality of the local modular decisions than on the overall resource allocation. What
is done in the average district determines success or failure.
Unfortunately, in many conventional planning systems such
strategic decision-making is neglected in favor of concentrating
on the budget game--the question of who gets how much of the
budget.

This system has one additional major difference from conventional planning systems: allocation is made to the regional
program rather than to the project. The relative allocations
to projects has already largely been determined at the local
module on the basis of the strategy and the proper quantitative
balance between projects at the local level. Final programming will use total program coefficients rather than
individual project coefficients.

The procedure for this final phase of the planning system will continue to oscillate between the general and the particular. Five major operations can be distinguished:

Intraproject Constraint Evaluation--Levels are set for the intraproject fixed resources by ICM* on Form A-15 of Appendix A (Intraproject Constraint Application).

Partial Project Documentation--Project Plans (Form A-11) are laid out, and fixed costs and other items not affected by the pace of coverage are filled in.

Regional Programming--A maximum pace of coverage expansion subject to preliminary constraints is computed on the regional Program Summary (Form A-16).

Complete Project Documentation--The Project Plans (Form A-11) are completed on the basis of the coverage by annual stages from the Program Summary (Form A-16).

Intersectoral Final Allocation--All documents are submitted to authorities responsible for intersectoral allocations. These authorities may then trim back the program on the basis of various considerations. Program and project documents are revised to reflect these changes.

INTRAPROJECT CONSTRAINTS

The first step is to determine the impact on the program of constraints that are peculiar to individual projects. This is done on the Intraproject Constraint Application Form A-15.

Selection of Constraints

Constraints peculiar to an individual project fall into four categories: (1) "point-line" phase restrictions, (2) training capacity, (3) specialized personnel, and (4) input production capacity. All but the first can be circumvented with money.

---

*See Chapter 11, pp. 215-16.

The point-line constraint is the simplest to apply. From
the diagram on Form A-8 in Appendix A one can see that each
project will be ready to launch into the point phase in the year
that it first is needed in the point district. In 1968 one may
assume that the first district is ready to go into stage C. The
maximum number of districts for the point stage may be from
one to three, depending on the capacity of middle- and upper-
level staff to supervise highly experimental programs. One
may assume that the capacity of such staff for the Southern
Region program is quite limited, so that the point stage must
be limited to one district and the line stage to five districts.

Training capacity and input production capacity have a
step-function relationship to activity volume. One may be
able, for example, to design a regional training facility on
such a scale that it can handle 100, 150, or 200 trainees. To
accommodate between 100 and 150 trainees, the 150 trainee
scale investment is needed. Seed farms and other input
production facilities likewise are designed for a particular
maximum capacity and have similar step-function relationships. The fixed cost of these facilities is determined by
the maximum scale of coverage one is contemplating.

In our hypothetical Southern Region it is assumed that the
community development village-level workers and the agricultural extension commune agents are trained at fixed capacity
facilities. Other training requirements are not so limited.
It is assumed that rice seed and cotton seed are grown on
farms with fixed capacity. All agricultural chemicals are
assumed to be imported, and other seeds are assumed to have
no significant fixed cost.

The final type of constraint to be considered in this exercise is specialized personnel, whose training and experience
is adapted to one project alone. In the Southern Region program agricultural engineers fall into that category. It is
assumed that there are only a limited number of qualified engineers now in the country or due to be graduated during the
planning period. For simplicity of presentation, it is assumed
further that they cannot be shifted between regions, because
of language barriers or for other reasons. The training
period of an agricultural engineer is so long that it is not
feasible to increase the supply in-country during the plan
period. It is possible, however, to import foreign engineers

at a higher unit cost, if the shadow price warrants it.   This
possibility will be examined later.

Intraproject constraints thus behave in three different
ways.   The point-line constraints are absolutely binding,
being based on a degree of uncertainty in planning which only
experience can overcome.   The input production constraints,
be they physical inputs or human inputs from training facilities, can be circumvented by higher fixed costs and by building and operating larger facilities.   Specialized personnel
constraints can be circumvented by higher unit costs.

Format Layout and ICM Procedure

One sees on Form A-15 the familiar pattern: outputs at the
top, inputs below.   The outputs in this case are the districts
to be covered in each stage each year.   This is the district
coverage matrix discussed in Chapter 12.   For each input
item of relevance, however, there are two lines.   The upper
line shows the amount actually needed to achieve the district
coverage.   The lower line shows the constraint value, that
is, the amount expected to be available.   There are two sets
of columns, one for a lower level of program operation and
lower fixed and special unit costs, and the other for a higher
level.   A third set of columns and a third level of operation
could be added if required.

The application of Informal Constrained Maximization
(ICM) on this operation then proceeds as follows:

Write in the constraint values.   Some judgment is necessary to set capacities of individual constrained inputs at each
level which are consistent with each other and which will not
waste fixed costs on underutilized facilities at each level.

Apply point-line constraints.   On Form A-15 one sees
the point coverage and line coverage (i.e., the numbers 1
and 5) cascading from C and B in 1968 down to F and G in 1972.

Start computing maximum requirements in the end year
on the input most likely to be binding.   This rule has a close
analogy to the rule on the choice of a pivot line in the Simplex

solution to a linear program. [1] Since input requirements rise
at an accelerating rate as districts pour into advanced stages
of operation, bottlenecks are more likely to be encountered
on fixed inputs in later years. In the Simplex method the rule
is to pick the line of the pivot column which has the largest
input coefficient relative to the constraint value and find the
input which will be used up fastest. In ICM likewise the
process starts at the input most likely to be exhausted first.
On Form A-15 the process starts with extension agent training in 1972.

Test a pattern of level district launchings. One must
now play around a bit with some figures. ICM is not as powerful a tool as linear programming; it does not lead monotoni-
cally to an optimum solution. It can lead down some false
paths, though fortunately only briefly. One might try launching districts after the line stage at a rate of 12 a year, as in
the following table, and see whether the program will have to
train more than the maximum of 100 agricultural extension
agents a year.

Stage	Agents per District to Be Added	Districts in Stage (in 1972)	Total Needed
A	0	8	0
B	5	12	60
C	5	12	60
D	1	12	12
E	-4	5	-20
F	-5	1	-5
		50	107

The total needed is greater than the limit. In some earlier periods, when there are no districts in stages E and F,
the excess will be even greater. Moreover, the requirement
for rice seed in the Rice 2 Project is even greater than the
capacity limit.

Trim back the number of districts launched until no constraints are exceeded. First, the above pattern of 1, 5, 12, 12,
12, 8 districts launched per year (1 in 1966, 5 in 1967, etc.)
should be applied to all the inputs of the last two years, to
see where the greatest excesses are. Then successive small

reductions should be checked against the most binding inputs
to find a pattern which will advance the districts as quickly
as possible and not exceed any constraints.

The above operations are, of course, repeated for the
higher level of constraints. The author found that this exercise required about three hours with an ordinary rotary desk
calculator. The essential results are to be read from the top
line. At the lower level one can launch 8 districts into stage
A in 1968 and 1969, 11 in 1970, 9 in 1971, and 8 in 1972, to
complete the 50 districts of the Southern Region. At the
higher level the pattern runs 12, 16, 16. One can see that in
1970 and 1971 the program uses training capacity fairly
efficiently.

PARTIAL PROJECT DRAFTING

The next step is to lay out and fill out the Project Plans
Form A-11's as far as one can go without specifying district
coverage and the values of items dependent on district coverage.
This means listing the relevant variables, plotting the delay
factors, and computing the fixed costs. The rules and admonitions of Chapter 12 apply.

The Relevant Variables

At the top, of course, one lists output elements. The
Agricultural Engineering and the crop projects are the same
as on the District Plan. On the Extension Project the lead
output is participation, which is the same as on Rice 1 but
advanced one year. This assumes that those who adopt the
first innovation in stage C are those who participated
actively in extension activity in stage B. For Farmers Associations and the Agricultural Development Bank the relevant
output is business volume. Moving down the A-11 form, one
sees next a listing of coverage of districts by stage, the same
layout on all projects as on the Community Development
Project.

Looking down the left-hand columns of the various A-11's, the first input elements for institutional projects are cadre and training, the same as in Chapter 12. The crop projects show instead the supply requirements, the seed production requirements, hectarage and investment per year, or the breedstock requirements. The hog project envisions a breeding center in each province. The province is an echelon which has been little mentioned in connection with the so-called Southern Region program, but it is often an important level of logistic support.

Next come the program development deadlines--delay factors. The technique is that of Chapter 12. In some cases the delay factors are legislation, in other cases they are issuance of instructions and manuals. Agricultural Extension also has some construction activity which may delay training. From a glance at the A-11 forms, one can see that there are a number of ways of using letter codes to denote stages and progress.

One then comes to the central staffing. The older national institutions have none committed to this regional program. They presumably are supervising the regional project with a variety of central personnel on a part-time basis. The Farmers Associations are a new institution and thus have a variety of specialists committed full time to the regional project. The crop projects likewise are assumed to have full-time staffs of specialists. Their costs, like those of cadre, include all personnel-related expenses.

Finally one comes to the project budgets and other financial data. Here there are two columns under each year for fixed and variable costs. The phase-out year for the fixed costs of these projects is set at either 1972 or the year in which the point district enters the last stage of budget support.

The Agricultural Development Bank Project has some items illustrating the handling of a regional project as part of a nationwide commercial institution. The real cost of the project is the cumulative negative contribution to profit at the bottom. This is the outlay on operating costs which will actually have to be made.

Staffing

Up to this point this book has said nothing about foreign aid in spite of its obvious importance to development. This has been for two reasons: first, this book is written from the viewpoint of the central planning or project planning staff, not the outside expert. Second, this planning-from-the-bottom-up system is only beginning to consolidate requirements to the point where it can define a foreign aid requirement.

But now it faces a clear need for foreign technical assistance. The Farmers Association Project and the crop projects need a variety of seasoned specialists on their staffs. This is precisely the human resource most lacking in developing nations. It is generally difficult for foreigners to function as cadre or as project managers, although there have been notable exceptions--in Senegal, for instance. They can generally function easily as project staff, seed specialists, marketing specialists, and even at times as training specialists.

With documents such as those prepared by the Southern Region in Appendix A, an adequate case can be made to any one of a number of donor agencies for providing the dozen or so missing specialists necessary to prevent delay of a program which will earn the farmers $85 million a year at its peak. There may be additional local currency expenses, however, even for foreign personnel whose salaries are paid by the donor agency. This accounts for the high unit cost of the supply and marketing specialists on the Farmers Association Project. It might prove worthwhile for the government to pay the full cost of foreign technicians to break these key bottlenecks, but it is generally impossible for a government to do the offshore recruiting that would be required; it must rely on a donor agency to recruit such talent.

Once the staff requirements have been projected, they should be costed in the manner as outlined in Chapter 12. Following the procedure of that chapter, fixed costs should be totaled and entered in the bottom block of the Program Coefficients Table (Form A-14) for easy reference.

CONSTRAINTS AND HYPERBUDGETING

At this point, all the data necessary for optimal programming is ready except the values of the extraproject constraints. This presents something of a problem. The
constraints to be considered are largely multisectoral in
application. Certainly the financial constraints represent
fixed quantities of resources that can be applied to any development activities in any sector. The other main type of constraint to be considered is personnel, represented by fixed
quantities of human resources with given levels of training
and competence. These also have varying degrees of mobility
between regions and sectors.

Ideally these two fixed resources, money and people,
should be allocated over the entire national development program in one grand optimization exercise, and the entire
multisectoral programming operation for the national development plan should be executed in one linear program. But this
is not possible within the current state-of-the-art for reasons
that are beyond the scope of this book.

The programming process must therefore work upward
from subsectoral to sectoral optimization and then to multisectoral optimization. This means that some kind of preliminary allocation of constrained resources must be made, for
the suboptimization exercises. Is this not premature? This
means an allocation decision that is not based on optimization.
How can this be done without distorting the subsequent optimization operations?

The distortion can be minimized by "hyperbudgeting," a
technique of systematically overallocating resources to suboptimization exercises.

Principles of Hyperbudgeting

The procedure can best be illustrated by an oversimplified example. Suppose a development program consists of
four sectors, A, B, C, D, and two scarce inputs, U_1 and U_2,

each with 100 units available. The optimization allocation
procedure is then as follows:

Step 1: Hyperbudget the available resources. First increase the amounts to be allocated by 20 to 30 percent. The
more complex the consideration and the more likely the final
activity allocations are likely to diverge from some simple
formula, the higher this overallocation should be. For simplicity, both are increased by 20 percent so that U_1 = 120 and
U_2 = 120. They then are distributed between sectors by some
oversimplified formula, say, 30 percent over previous allocations. Between regions they might be allocated according
to population. The result might be:

Sector:	A		B		C		D
U_1 = 120 =	25	+	35	+	40	+	20
U_2 = 120 =	25	+	35	+	40	+	20

Step 2: Suboptimize within each sector by ICM. Within
A, B, C, and D, determine the maximum net benefits that
can be realized with the alloted inputs and the maximim
amount of each input each sector can use, given the intra-
sectoral and other constraints. The result might look as
follows:

	A		B		C		D
U_1 = 112 =	22	+	25	+	40	+	15
U_2 = 99 =	20	+	25	+	35	+	19

In the example above all but one sector, D, ran into other
bottlenecks before they could use all the hyperallotment of
resources. The maximum amount of resource U_2 that can be
used is one unit less than the amount actually available. This
commonly occurs in development; the ability to absorb is less
than the resources available.

Step 3: Trim back the Program to Match Actual Constraints. The four sectors in the above example must be reduced by 12 units of U_1. The basic rule of this operation is
maximization of net benefits to reduce the activity that has

the lowest marginal revenue product and the lowest ratio of
net benefits per activity unit to constrained input required per
activity unit. Other rules, to be discussed later in this chapter, guide the trim-back decision. The final program might
look as follows:

$$
\begin{array}{cccccccc}
 & & & A & B & C & D \\
U_1 & = & 100 = & 22 & + & 17 & + & 36 & + & 15 \\
U_2 & = & 91 = & 20 & + & 20 & + & 32 & + & 19
\end{array}
$$

Conceivably an activity which uses more of U_2 and less of U_1
might be increased in the above example to achieve greater
total net benefits. Because the suboptimization operations
based on hyperbudgets have identified the bottlenecks and
narrowed the range of final solutions, a rough approximation
to a final optimum solution can be made by crude arithmetical
techniques.

Financial Constraints

Economists generally focus attention on two main constraints on development: investment and foreign exchange
resources. One of the first operations of most national development planning procedures is a projection of these available resources, adding to both the anticipated foreign aid.

Investment, however, has within it categories of resources
subject to different rules and restraints. In the computations
in the balance of this chapter government budget outlays are
distinguished from credit expansion, which is net lending for
development. Government expenditures would be limited by
anticipated tax collections, foreign grant assistance, and a
policy setting a maximum budget deficit. Credit expansion
is limited by monetary policies and expected foreign loans.

In establishing a hyperbudget for agriculture, one might
start with a figure that would leave nothing for the education
or transport sectors. This would then be divided among the
regions on the basis of rural population, with somewhat more
budget outlay per capita for regions in stage II and substantially

more credit per capita for regions in stage III of agricultural development (see Chapter 3, pp. 54-55).

Personnel Constraints

The first task in setting personnel constraint values is distinguishing economy-wide, sector-wide, and region-wide personnel constraints. Generally one can say that the more advanced and specialized the education, the fewer the geographic limitations but the more the sectoral limitations, the more difficult it is to switch personnel between sectors. One may assume, for example, that in the Southern Region program, grade-5 personnel will stick to their region for ethnic and other reasons. Grade-4 personnel will generally stick to their region, but some movement can occur between regions. Grade-3 personnel can be allocated by their agencies to any region.

The next problem is that of personnel attrition. This can and sometimes should be handled on the individual project plans, but it was not included in the calculation of the Form A-11 tables in Appendix A for the sake of simplicity of presentation.

There are three types of attrition to be considered. First, there is the loss of personnel on the job due to persons fired or resigning each year. This is liable to be heavy on new projects. Second, some are washed out in training. One can easily calculate these losses on individual project plans and add, for example, 5-10 percent of last year's cadre and 10-20 percent of the number of trainees to the total recruitment requirement.

The third and most difficult type of attrition is that which takes place in the recruitment process. It is not enough to have one candidate for every opening--for example, 100 secondary agricultural school graduates for 100 trainee openings. Many will find more attractive opportunities in agribusiness firms or in employment outside the sector. Many will not have the motivation and other personality characteristics needed to perform on the job. One may have to figure on 50 to 100 percent extra nominally qualified candidates for every position to cover this kind of attrition.

The simplest way to do this is to keep the constraint values net of such recruitment attrition. The extra margin on a single-subsector exercise is kept implicit rather than explicit. For example, if 600 men are available for a certain category in a given year but the attrition rate is 50 percent, the constraint is written as 450.

This may seem a bit alarming. After all the long strategy exercises and computations aimed at generating tight personnel coefficients, it might appear that the system is throwing in such wild allowances for error that the values of the coefficients are not significant. These attrition factors may appear to be so loose that they make the previous work of establishing personnel coefficients something of a game. Attrition factors, however, are actually easier to establish on the basis of experience than are cadre coefficients for new activities. Most government agencies in stage II already have some record of having interviewed x candidates to get y trainees and then netted z cadre from the training. Without any sophisticated statistical analysis of the data, administrators frequently, perhaps usually, have a good feel for these factors.

THE REGIONAL PROGRAM SUMMARY

Form A-16 of Appendix A, the regional Program Summary, illustrates the format of the summary document of the whole program. It is the document on which the final allocation of resources is computed and presented and the coverage of the program is decided. Once again one sees the familiar arrangement: outputs at the top, inputs at the bottom. The format strongly resembles the A-11 Project Plans, but there are two major differences: (1) this format shows only the constrained inputs on the lower part of the sheet; (2) next to each constrained figure is shown the explicit value of the constraint to the right.

The Relevant Variables

The output elements of Form A-16 are listed in the first seven lines. At the top is the primary maximand, the present value of net benefits from the program. This is derived, of course, from the coverage in the middle of the sheet, times the coefficients on Form A-14 (Program Coefficients Table). Indeed, all values on the sheet except the limits are based on the achieved coverage times the corresponding coefficients on Form A-14. In addition to the net benefits, the top lines show other outputs of interest to those making final allocation decisions: increased farm income, increased production, and farmers participating.

In the center is a familiar district coverage matrix. To the right in each column, however, is the coverage taken from the high-volume column of Form A-15. These maximum coverage limits represent the fixed cost and other intraproject constraints on the regional program.

Below are the constrained inputs. On A-16 are shown three categories of personnel and three types of financial constraints. Both the total annual and the cumulative figures are shown for budget and credit, on the assumption that resources of these types not used in one year may be carried over and used the following year. The item on line 24, the residual, is a cost based on previous strategy that must nevertheless be charged to this program. The community development project in the first year covers unnecessary extra districts opened in previous years, which must nevertheless continue to be supported. Programs never start on tabula rasa.

Technique of Computation

ICM is applied in a procedure similar to that described earlier in the chapter for intraproject constraints. The first step is to write in the constraints on the form, and also the fixed and residual costs.

The choice of an initial trial solution is a bit more complicated. One can see on the Program Coefficients Table
(Form A-14) that for the Southern Region stages A, B, and
C have the heaviest personnel requirements, C, D, and E
have the heaviest budget requirements, and E, F, and G
have the heaviest credit and foreign exchange requirements.
Therefore, instead of starting with the end year, one would
start with the end year for constraints on later grades and
with earlier years for peak needs in earlier grades. Table
16.1 is a sample initial trial (using the A-15 high volume
coverage).

The trial goes over the limit on personnel in 1970 and on
credit in 1971 and 1972. It would appear, then, that if the
district coverage is trimmed down in 1972 enough to stay
within the credit constraint, it should be able to keep previous
year peak needs within the most binding constraints. Thus,
the first trial solution indicates which constraints will be
binding.

On Form A-16 one can see that the final solution involves
the launching of 10 districts in 1968, 12 in 1969, 14 in 1970,
and 8 in 1971. The limit on credit in 1972 is exceeded a bit
in 1972, but that overage is covered by an underutilization of
of budget available. The outputs and inputs (save for personnel) grow on an accelerating curve, as might be expected.

Is the solution optimal? The test is whether any change
could increase net benefits and stay within the constraints.
One might test the program on A-16 by seeing what would
happen if one district were shifted from D to E in 1972. From
Form A-14 one can see that net benefits would be increased by
over $1 million. The budget would be decreased by $200,000,
but credit would be increased by $569,000, a net increase for
budget and credit combined of $369,000. This would be that
amount over the combined constraint and therefore is not
feasible. A few other trials on the example illustrated would
demonstrate that there is no change which would keep within
the constraints and increase net benefits.

TABLE 16.1

First Trial Solution

Stage	1970 Personnel			1971 Budget			Credit		1972 Credit		
	Dst Cvg	PRD	Need	Dst Cvg	BPD	Need	CEPD	Needed	Dst Cvg	CEPD	Needed
A	16	5	80	16	112	1790					
B	16	12	192	16	219	3500					
C	12	6	72	12	420	5050	72	1,150	16	72	1,150
D	5	1	5	5	220	1100	248	2,980	16	248	3,960
E	1	-4	-4	1	175	175	817	4,080	12	817	9,820
F							1030	1,030	5	1030	5,150
G									1	1370	1,370
Required			345			11,620		9,240			21,450
Constraint			300			12,000		7,500			18,000

Dst Cvg = district coverage
PRD = personnel required per district
BPD = budget per district
CEPD = credit expansion per district

317

Shadow Prices

ICM, like linear programming, indicates the shadow
prices, that is, the opportunity cost, of inputs. The scarce
resource does, indeed, have a very high opportunity cost.
Taking credit in 1972 as the scarce resource, one can see on
A-16 that more or less credit, in increments of $817,000
(the stage E requirements on Form A-14), will yield additional
or fewer high-payoff districts in stage E. The additional net
benefits of each district in stage E is $19,139,000.

The shadow prices in this exercise are somewhat fuzzed
by that fact that hyperbudget constraints rather than real
constraints have been used. This means that the differences
between quantities of inputs used in this program and the
limits on these resources are not pure slacks, as in normal
linear programming. These slacks do not indicate resources
standing idle, since the same resources have been hyperbudgeted to other programs. From the point of view of the
final allocation exercise, an additional district in Stage E in
1972 requires $1,035,000 in additional budget outlays over
the five years and a cumulative expansion of credit amounting
to $1,137,000. A $19 million gain or loss from a shift of
$2.3 million in financial resources is still a high opportunity
cost.

Sometimes shadow prices indicate where changes should
be made in the program structure. Suppose that the number
of grade-3 personnel available in 1970-71 was 40 rather than
50. This would have required a reduction in the number of
districts in stages B and C in those years, since B and C each
requires inputs of two men in grade 3. From the bottom of
A-14 one can see that a postponed launching costs over
$300,000. Should $300,000 in net benefits be foregone because
two grade-3 men qualified to be senior loan officers or community development supervisors are not available? If this is
the binding constraint, a highly costly rearrangement of
personnel or use of foreign personnel will clearly be profitable.

PROJECT COMPLETION
AND PROGRAM SUBMISSION

The program at this point has essentially been computed.
Once the project plans illustrated on the A-11's have been completed, it can be submitted to the top planning authorities.

Completion of Project Documents

The first step is to fill in the district coverage matrix on
each Project Plan. The crop projects will have to be adjusted
for their share of the suitable districts. Thus the Sorghum
Project, covering only 50 percent of the districts, would have
a launch pattern of 1-3-5-6-6-4 districts rather than 1-5-10-
12-14-8 for the projects covering all 50 districts. All the
items which have not been completed on the A-11 forms can
then be filled in by the familiar computation of multiplying the
districts per stage by the coefficients for those stages found
on the Form A-10 District Plans.

In addition to the A-16 Program Summary and its two
backup documents (A-14 and A-15), a dossier on each project
would be presented to the planning authorities. The project
dossier consists of the A-11 Project Plan backed up by the
A-10 District Plan. The planning authorities may require a
narrative document like that illustrated on Form A-13 in
Appendix A, which will be explained in Chapter 21. Crop
projects should also have the Form A-4 Innovation Package
Analysis in their dossiers.

Project Review

It is presumed that the central planning staff and then the
authorities review the individual projects. They are concerned
with the realism and consistency of the cost factors, of the
coefficients relating various items to pacing factors, and of
the delay and bottleneck factors. The lower-level examiners
ask for some of the cost factor details that have been left off
the project documents in this system because they would not

concern the reviewing authorities--unless the junior examiners
of the central planning secretariat take strong exception to
certain cost items. The cost factor details can best be presented orally in the bottom-level preliminary review, and
there laid to rest if no objections are made.

    This whole system tries to be an efficient combination of
written and oral presentation. It is often much more efficient
to present plans or analyses orally than in writing. Chapter
14 provides for working groups which evolve a strategy without requiring narrative type staff papers. At this point a
project review can be executed without full written details of
unit costs and without narrative documents. There are some
cases in chich narrative documents are essential (these cases
will be discussed in Chapter 21), but in this planning system
they are not necessary.

    One may envision a procedure in which project managers
brief the reviewing authorities on the A-10's and A-11's.
Ideally the briefing will take place in an operations room with
an overhead projector. The briefing procedure will be described in Chapter 21. Such a presentation leads the audience
through the pacing factors to the outputs and inputs, presenting
in 10 minutes what might be difficult to grasp in 30 minutes of
reading.

        Final Allocation--Intersectoral Programming

    Once the authorities are convinced that the projects are
sound and efficient, they are ready to consider programming
options. They should have before them a subsectoral program
for each agricultural region. Ideally data for other sectors
should be arranged in subsectoral program packages, with the
constraints, outputs, and marginal inputs and outputs properly
indicated. The structuring of other sectoral programs is outside the scope of this book, however, save for rural service
sectors to be discussed in the next chapter.

    The authorities may or may not receive the programs of
all sectors with such a highly useful arrangement of data.
Generally, however, planning authorities do receive sector
programs which, as in the hyperbudget procedure, add up to

a resource requirement substantially over what will be available. In some manner or other, the final programming exercise of the top authorities is an exercise in trimming back sector programs.

One of the purposes of this whole planning system has been to provide the relevant data for that final operation in the clearest and most efficient form. The top authorities may consider a number of factors in the final allocation decision. Since a development program is an investment program, the basic (though not necessarily the most important) consideration is maximizing return on investment and net benefits. Forms A-16 and A-14 are designed to provide the data on which the effects of tradeoffs between subsectors on net benefits can be seen.

There are a number of other important considerations. Development programs generally aim at an end-of-period income target. Form A-16 therefore has an income figure on line 2. Planners may be interested in raising median income in backward rural regions, so they will glance at the number of participating farmers on line 7. They may be particularly concerned with increasing food production for a growing urban sector or with production of export crops, so they will look mainly at the crop production figures. They may be concerned with intersectoral consistency, the consistency between rural and urban plans. They are concerned that the national program produce enough food for urban needs and enough rural income to buy products of new industries. For this they may need intersectoral input-output analysis. Needed coefficients can be derived for an input-output matrix from A-14 and A-16.

When the authorities make their final allocations, the A-11 Project Plans and the A-16 Program Summary will have to be rewritten to reflect any change from the proposed program. Fortunately only these singlesheet documents have to be rewritten. All the other documents are unaffected by final programming changes. Rewriting has been kept to a minimum.

OTHER SPANS, OTHER PATHS

The core planning procedures of a rural development planning system have now been elaborated. The procedures still to be explained in this book are complementary only.

The explanation of this core system has been in terms of a hypothetical program which, in one program, carries a region with diverse possibilities from stage IIa of agricultural development (see Chapter 3, pp. 47-49) to stage IIIb. The Southern Region has some distinctive and unusual features. One must therefore ask whether the planning system will work under other circumstances. Fortunately, the hypothetical Southern Region has a more complex program than that undertaken in most countries. Rarely does a region have such a range of proven innovations combined with such a paucity of existing institutions. The system has been tested on a hypothetical case, but it is a tough one.

Other Spans

Generally a country does not have enough proven innovations to carry even a pilot district from stage IIa to IIIb in one planning period. From IIa to IIIa two patterns of development are common. One is the promotion of agricultural production supplies by multipurpose services. The other is promotion of a broad innovation package requiring all basic services for a single cash crop.

India and Pakistan are good examples of the first pattern. Each has concentrated on promoting seed, fertilizer, and pesticides primarily for the main cereal crop, as well as for secondary crops in selected locales. On this they have built institutions for group action, extension, supply, and some short-term credit. There is no significant engineering or medium-term credit or marketing institution-building in these programs.

It is easy to apply this planning system to such programs. In the local module fewer relevant stages are required. Fewer institutional projects are required. There may be one crop project that covers all locales and a number of secondary crop projects reaching only a fraction of the locales.

The second pattern, full institutional development based on a single crop, may take one of two forms. Ideally, as in Senegal, it develops a complex of potentially multipurpose institutions, including medium-term credit and marketing. Most such programs, however, do not develop multicrop institutions. It may be possible to plan such programs as one project, when one crop-oriented agency such as a marketing board undertakes all services.

The next span, from stage IIIa to IIIb, generally adds engineering and medium-term credit to existing institutions. A good example is the Mexican medium-term credit program started in the early sixties. The planning forms of this book apply to such a program, but there would be more crop projects, since this span requires greater diversification.

Once into stage IIIb the planning system no longer applies. By then initiative should be decentralized to the point where direct government activity is no longer the motive force and regional projects no longer apply.

Agricultural Development
Tied to Other Activities

Agricultural Development is often tied to particular capital projects or reforms.

The relationship between major transportation, electric power, and irrigation projects and agricultural development might be characterized as arterial, since these projects reach out into the rural areas through main and subsidiary arteries. They have been called octopoidal services because they gradually extend their tentacles out from the center. Such projects are planned by well-established capital project procedures. Their coordination with agricultural development, however, has not been well established.

Perhaps the best way to coordinate such major capital projects of an arterial nature with the agricultural developments that take place over a multitude of villages is to estimate the number of additional communes they will reach each year. This then becomes an additional type of pacing factor for the types of projects considered in this book. A good example is the Indian rural electrification program, primarily designed to support low-lift pump irrigation. This is scheduled to extend a certain number of kilometers in each applicable subdivision (the Indian equivalent of a province in our terminology). From this the annual increment in communes and villages serviced can be estimated. This sets the pace for an irrigation innovation package, as does soil and water surveying in the project illustrated on Forms A-10.5 and A-11.5 in Appendix A.

Another important rural development activity not yet discussed is land reform. This takes three basic forms: sharecropper titling, plantation subdivision, and resettlement. Transfer of ownership to sharecroppers involve project planning similar to the Agricultural Engineering Project of the Southern Region. Different cadres perform a series of surveys, commune by commune or village by village. One may plan this in terms of three or four annual stages per commune, on Form A-10, the local module.

Plantation subdivision and resettlement involve a very broad complex of managerial services, extending over a number of years, right down at the village level. The village must be the local module. These are expensive activities requiring village-level cadre teams.

The procedures that have been applied to one hypothetical region can thus be applied to other types of programs generally found in stage II and stage III. Indeed, the application of these forms to most regional programs should be easier than in our hypothetical case, which was chosen because of the broad range of difficulties it provides for testing the procedure.

NOTES

1. W. J. Baumol, Economic Theory and Operations Analysis (Englewood Cliffs, N. J. : Prentice-Hall, 1965) pp. 82-97.

CHAPTER **17** IMPLEMENTATION
AND FEEDBACK

In one sense the procedures of the previous chapter
finished the planning process. Plans were laid and
resources allocated. In a broader sense, however, planning is a continuing process, a closed loop which includes
feedback and revision.

This chapter provides the procedures for closing the
loop. First, there are a few additional steps in the
allocation of resources. Resources must be allocated to
districts within a region and to periods within the year.
Further details are needed before funds can be released
and activities can commence. Once activities and plan
implementation is under way, systematic feedback is
necessary to close the loop. Reports provide the basis
for troubleshooting and for taking the corrective actions
necessary to achieve plan targets. They also provide the
basis for plan revisions, particularly for determining
realistic planning coefficients based on experience.

Rural development plans are often built on unproved
assumptions rather than knowledge. The best example is
the key behavioral equation of chapter 15 (page 296). Of
necessity, these coefficients are initially based on guesswork. Properly structured reporting, however, can considerably improve the realism of such estimates each year.
There are certain things one can learn only by doing -- first
by making assumptions and basing a project on them, then
by observing the results. The major allocations come after
the point and line stages, after a couple of cycles of planning, feedback, and revision. This feedback must thus be
considered an integral part of the basic data collection that
goes into final resource allocation decisions. Reporting
provides the data.

ALLOCATIONS TO DISTRICTS

As discussed in Chapter 4, there are many ways to
select the districts in which projects will be launched each
year.   There are many possible strategies and many
possible sets of decision rules that can be applied.   The
author can propose no suitable tabular format for such a
decision.   A map is an obvious first choice.   Maps giving
economic and other pertinent data can help the decision-
makers to express the decision clearly.

Characteristics of individual districts will vary considerably from those of the modular district.   In the early
stages this will not make much difference.   At that time,
when an activity only involves some 2,000 farmers or
20 percent of the average district, the standard input of
resources can reach 40 percent of those a half-size
district or 10 percent of those a double-size district.   The
resources needed to complete activities in different districts, however, will vary.   When the first 10 districts
enter later stages, overall project requirements may vary
considerably from the original plan, depending on whether
those first districts are larger or smaller than average.
Over several years these differences will balance out, but
in a given year adjustments of resources between projects
may be necessary.

It should be noted that many of the problems of inter-
district allocations are faced in intradistrict allocation
decisions.   Concentration in a few communes at the start
may be more efficient and effective, but district level
officers are under political pressure to spread activities
evenly among communes and villages.   Even in a completely centralized administration, local officials are somewhat dependent on the continuing good will of the villagers
for the cooperation they need for successful performance.

One way of avoiding political obstacles to efficient
geographic concentration of programs is to leapfrog location
decisions.   Instead of asking a province chief to make the
unpopular decision of selecting two out of seven districts in
which to concentrate a program, that decision should be

made centrally. The province chief, in turn, should select
the communes, rather than force the district chief to
choose among those directly under him. Finally, the
district chief, rather than the commune chief, should select
the villages. In that way face-to-face relationships are not
poisoned by unpopular decisions.

SUBANNUAL DOCUMENTATION
FUNCTIONS AND PATHOLOGY

All documents considered up to this point have been
multiannual documents. In actuality, funds are generally
released for a subannual period of 2, 3, 4, or 6 months.
The typical and probably most suitable fund release period
is the quarter, although in some countries the seasonal
pattern lends itself to a four-month period. For reasons
which will be indicated later, reports should be for similar
periods. Release and report documents are closely interrelated.

Functions of Subannual Documents

Release Justification--Once a plan and an annual budget
has been approved, a standard form or set of forms is
generally required for release of funds to the agency or for
spending authority. These forms generally include a listing
of financial detail that is standard for all government
activities, regardless of sector. It is futile to propose
special forms for the agricultural sector.

It is useful, however, to have a special form to justify
the period-by-period financial release being requested and
to relate it to the plan. In some cases it is useful to submit
such a form to the budgeting agency as additional justification. In other cases it is useful just to have such a document
within the action agency, to clarify the thinking and computation of the project managers regarding their financial
requirements.

Activity Scheduling--In Malaysia and Pakistan special forms are used to schedule physical infrastructure projects month by month. Quarter-by-quarter scheduling is likewise important to agricultural projects, to determine when action is required and to evaluate quarterly results. Some of this scheduling is accomplished by the forms proposed later in this chapter; more complex scheduling is accomplished by the Critical Path Method (CPM), as explained in Chapter 22.

Troubleshooting Guidance--The most immediate function of reports is to guide necessary corrective action. They show where activities are not going according to plan, and where changes of resource inputs and changes of project routine are in order. Reports should be the basis for management-by-exception. They should draw project management attention to the most serious divergences of actual results from the plan.

Plan Revision--Reports should be so structured and so summarized that they show what the actual coefficients were for the assumed relationships on which the plan was based. They should guide improved planning and revision of previous plans.

Fund Release Pathology

Rejustification--As mentioned above, the fund release procedures are generally standardized for the whole government. The ministry of finance or the budget office requires the same documents and approvals for all releases of funds or spending authority, be they for rural or urban, development or for administrative activities. These standard procedures sometimes include a full justification and review of funding requests. This may mean a repetition of the justification and review that has already taken place in the development planning procedure.

Approval under the development planning procedure should constitute basic justification of project funding requests. The budgeting agency should limit its review to the timing of the need for funds and to the question of whether the activities planned for the next fund release period really require the funds requested. The need for those activities should not require a rejustification.

It is for this reason that broad participation is important to the planning process. Representatives of the budgeting agency should take an active role in the development planning process, so that they are fully aware of the extent to which the activity has been reviewed and justified.

Input-Only Documentation--The documentation required for fund releases often must have exhaustive details of projected expenditures by object code--so much for salaries, so much for housing allowances, so much for postage, etc. This information is useful for subsequent checking against misuse of public funds. However, it provides no basis for planning decisions since it tells nothing of the outputs, activities, or results to be obtained with those funds. Some supplementary documentation is needed to show how a planned activity is broken down by spending periods and the funds per period that this activity will need.

Lost Water--Project will have funds for certain purposes left unspent at the end of the period, due to unforeseen delays or operational failures in some locales. Fund releases are generally requested on the assumption that everything will move at maximum speed everywhere; this never happens. There is bound to be "water" in every spending request, but this water has a legitimate role to play. Along with delays preventing expenditures, there will also be unforeseen contingencies requiring additional funds. These should be covered by the water--the unspent balances in other funding categories under the project.

If the documentation is not properly structured, however, that water can get lost. Input-only subannual documents leave no way of judging at midperiod whether funds in any category will be used or not. For example, recruitment may be only 80 percent of target. If the documents have not explicitly related personnel expenditures for the period to a specific recruitment target, there is no way of knowing that 20 percent of the period's budget for salaries and personnel support can be transferred to another category. It often happens, of course, that someone

in the office remembers the assumptions on which the fund
release was based. It also often happens that no one in the
office remembers those assumptions, and the water is lost.

Delays--Developing nations are strewn with the debris
of projects wrecked by late fund releases. Many governments have made great strides in the past 10 years in
speeding up the release procedure, but delayed releases are
still an ever-present danger for development projects. When
delays occur, there is often finger-pointing. The budgeting
agency accuses the operating agency of late or inadequate
submissions, and the operating agency accuses the budgeting
agency of dilatory processing.

The causes of fund release delays are complex and
manifold. They may be completely out of the control of
those responsible for rural development planning. Bringing
budgeteers carefully into the development planning process
so as to avoid rejustification delays may help. Relating
inputs to outputs in supporting documents so as to provide
a more solid justification of the requested timing of funds
may help. Beyond that, one must be realistic about possible
delays and provide adequate leadtimes. The CPM techniques
explained in Chapter 22 are useful for this purpose.

Reporting Pathology

Hyperfrequency--Field officers complain loudly of the
burden of report writing. In country after country one hears
the complaint that the field officers are "tied to their desks"
and so burdened with paperwork they have no time to get out
in the villages. The author has observed that this is often
an alibi, even though the monthly report requirements of
many agencies are excessive. The monthly interval is too
short for corrective action. By the time the top authorities
in an agency have fully digested the reports, a month has
gone by.

There are times of the year when frequent reports are
justified. At key stages of a field campaign, when participants
are being signed up or materiel is being distributed or

collected, central offices may need weekly or even daily
reports on a few key statistics for a period of a few weeks.
One should not try to accomplish this kind of information-
gathering with a year-round reporting system. The author
believes that the general reporting system for agriculture
projects should be bimonthly or quarterly. On physical
infrastructure, as will be noted in Chapter 20, there is some
justification for monthly reports.

Isolation from Plan--The reporting format is often
loosely specified. Certain statistics are required, plus a
narrative covering certain topics. Such a format in no way
generally matches the format of the original plan. It therefore takes laborious analysis to determine from the reports
the degree to which the plan is being executed. Since divergences from the plan are not explicit in the reports, management by exception is impossible. They make a poor guide
for troubleshooting or for plan revision.

Ever-victorious Prose--When the format is loosely
specified, it is easy to look ever triumphant. Let us suppose,
for example, that action is moving as planned in only one out
of 10 villages. If the format is loosely specified, one can
write about the success in the one village in great detail and
then briefly but frankly admit that problems are being
encountered in other villages. In spite of 90 percent failure,
the report will have a ring of success about it.

Indeed, when reporting formats are loosely specified
and not tied closely to plan, it is difficult to report honestly.
Honest reporting in such a case embarasses one's immediate
superior and puts one at an unfair disadvantage, vis-à-vis
those who are sending in reports in ever-victorious prose.

Indigestion--Reports often lie in the agency's gullet
without being digested into the decision-making process.
They are not used as a basis of troubleshooting or plan
revision. This may be due to the poor quality of the reports
or to the lack of systematic review and follow-up.

Principles of Subannual Documentation

Certain recommendations, based on the above considerations, can be made regarding the formats and the handling of subannual documents.

Link inputs to outputs and planned inputs and outputs to actual inputs and outputs.

The basic principle of previous project documents, that outputs are never shown without the inputs required for them and vice versa, is continued. The schedule of expected results and expected activity is the justification of the expected fund releases. One explains the other. For similar reasons actual inputs and outputs should always be displayed alongside planned inputs and outputs. Results are meaningful only in relation to the plan.

Use the same period for reports and fund releases.

Only by using matching periods can expenditures be related to fund releases. In examples and discussions below, the quarter is used as the release and reporting period. In rare situations where releases are for a six-month period, quarterly reports may be in order, but the two quarters should coincide in dates with the six-month fund release period.

Combine the release justification and the report summary forms.

The Malaysian and Pakistani schedule/report formats do this for physical infrastructure projects. This same principle can be applied to agriculture projects. The general form, then, would be:

	1st Quarter		2nd Quarter		4th Quarter		Total Year	
	Plan	Actual	Plan	Actual	Plan	Actual	Plan	Actual
Outputs	xxx	xxx	xxx	xxx	xxx	xxx	xxxx	xxxx
	xxx	xxx	xxx	xxx	xxx	xxx	xxxx	xxxx
Inputs	xxx	xxx	xxx	xxx	xxx	xxx	xxxx	xxxx
	xxx	xxx	xxx	xxx	xxx	xxx	xxxx	xxxx

Thus, the data from reports are posted to the original schedule to provide a running record of progress through the year. Though the figures are not cumulative, they present a clear picture of cumulative progress and also indicate how plans for subsequent periods should be modified. It may be useful to provide an additional column for readjustments of the plan through the year, with the following column headings:

First Quarter	Second Quarter	
Plan Report	Plan Report	etc.
Orig. Final Actual	Orig. Final Actual	

With this expanded format it is possible to submit a revised justification for releases each quarter. It is also possible to evaluate performance better, since a new measure of performance is thus prepared before each quarter. The revised form, however, may require more than one sheet. Generally, it should be possible to put this basic form on stencils and add a column to the original stencil each period for the updated version, thus saving retyping. Two stencils may be necessary, but it may be worth it. The two sheets could be glued together for presentation as one large spread sheet to the authorities.

Expand the list of relevant variables.

The listings of relevant variables of subannual project documents should be derived from the relevant variables of the multiyear project documents, so that they can be easily compared. Three types of items should be added, however, to provide a better guide for management-by-exception:

Intermediate Benchmarks--Schedules and reports should indicate progress per quarter. If construction is required, the form should show the projected percentage of completion per quarter. If provision of supplies is involved, the forms should show inventory accumulation and possibly ordering per period. If demonstration is involved, the forms might show the number of plots committed, planted, and displayed on field days. Subannual documents and feedback should signal when action is not getting started, not just what has been completed.

Releases vs. Expenditures--In both planning and reporting it is important to distinguish releases and expenditures.
It is important to see both what was spent and what was expected to be spent, as a guide to progress and an indicator
of budget water. Spending expectations for a period and
planned releases, however, will not always coincide. Funds
may be released or spending authority may be granted in one
period for a contract to be executed over several periods.
For this reason it is important to show planned expenditures
as well as planned releases.

Additional Activity and Financial Detail--Large stencils
have room for about 60 one-line items. If the items on the
local Project Plan (Form A-10) plus the "Intermediate
Benchmark" and "Releases vs. Expenditure" items above
add up to 40 lines or less, then the form has room for more
detail. One can break down personnel expenditures into
several object categories, to correspond more closely with
the detail required on government-wide budget documents.
One can show some of the important coefficients of the outputs, such as yields and prices.

All depends on the amount of room available. Each
activity has its own set of most relevant variables for
quarterly planning and reporting. One should try to get
as much relevant detail on the format as possible without
sacrificing the principle that inputs and outputs must be on
the same sheet.

On quarterly reports show planned vs. actual and the explanation of the major divergences.

The Malaysian report format can apply to agricultural
projects. A word of explanation signals those items off
schedule and thus facilitates management-by-exception.
One can glance over a number of reports from districts and
spot quickly which items are giving the most problems and
what kind of problems they are giving.

Comments should be limited, however, to those items
whose divergences are not caused by other items. If recruitment falls short, for example, training will fall short and
expenses and coverage will be lower. Any explanation should
be put beside the recruitment item only.

Summarize district operations by stage group.

A great deal can be learned quickly by glancing over
the reports from individual districts. Multidistrict summaries
of the whole project are needed, however, at least a summary
of the quarterly breakdown of the financial requirements.
Yet, lumping together or averaging out the output items for
districts of different stages is meaningless. The nature of
projects changes rapidly from stage to stage.

There are two ways of summarizing the quarterly operations of a total project. If the number of key items at the
district level can be kept to 10 or less, it may be possible
to summarize the entire project on one sheet in the following
manner:

Plan Actual

Stage B   Key outputs
12   Key inputs
dists.   Released
             Spent

Stage C   Key outputs
6   Key inputs
dists.   Released
             Spent

Stage D   Key outputs
2   Key inputs
dists.   Released
             Spent

Key cadre: Recruited
             Trained

Central staff
Central expenses

Total: released
        spent

In the above rough schema some selected key inputs and
outputs plus total releases and expenditures are aggregated
by stage group, a stage group being all the districts launched
in the same year and now in the same stage. Below that the
key central variables are listed. Below that should be listed
the key items which are, in effect, procured centrally for
the districts; they might include cadre, supplies, or credit.
Finally the main categories of central staff money-using
items are listed: personnel and possibly some equipment or
central investment in facilities. At the bottom the project
releases and expenditures are summarized.

The other approach is to have a schedule/report summary
sheet for each stage group that matches exactly the district
report form. This could be topped with a sheet giving the
principle items. Thus, if the project cannot be summarized
on one sheet, it can be summarized on two to five sheets,
depending on the number of years since the first district was
launched in the project.

Schedule systematic review and followup.

The central office of the operating agency and possibly
the central or interagency planning agency should schedule
a regular meeting each period to consider the reports.
These meetings should reach decisions on necessary corrective action and possibly on revision of funds required for the
next period. At the end of the year or just before the plan
for the following year is submitted, a meeting should be
held to consider how the coefficients should be revised on
the basis of the experience shown in the reports. In brief,
a formal schedule should be set for executing the functions
of the feedback phase of the planning system.

The reports should also be the basis for troubleshooting
in the field. The regional supervisor of the project should
discuss the reports with provincial officers and with as many
district officers as possible. In particular he should followup
with visits to those districts showing the most difficult
problems on the reports. Reports worth making are worth
systematic follow-up review and action.

<u>Supplement periodic reports with ad hoc reports.</u>

As mentioned above, there are certain critical seasons
for most projects during which daily or weekly reports are
in order. It may even be worth while to phone in daily results during a few critical weeks when important materiel
is being moved. It may also be advisable at times to require
special midperiod reports. If the following year budget submission is due in the middle of a reporting period, it may be
worthwhile to get up-to-the-minute data on the major indicators of activity and the major budget items. These ad hoc
reports, however, should be kept to a minimum, both in
number and size.

SUBANNUAL DOCUMENT FORMS

The two forms recommended are shown in Appendix A.
They are A-17, the operation sheet (Project Annual Plan),
which corresponds to the Malaysian and Pakistani
schedule/report forms, and A-18 (the Quarterly Report).
The examples given are for the Farmers Association project of the hypothetical Southern Region program, since this
is the most complex and difficult to present in a one-page
format. Following an explanation of the examples given, the
relevant additional items for other projects will be discussed.

The Farmers Association Project Subannual Documents

The Annual Plan--The items on Form A-17 are based on
those on Form A-10 (the District Plan), with the Actual
column (under Total Year) blank. The additional items are
32 through 39, the inventory breakdown, warehouse space,
and construction space and expenditure all necessary to
determine the financial scheduling, long- and short-term
debt, and subsidy releases.

The first step is to fill in the Plan columns of A-17.
Under Total Year one puts the figures from the District
Plan for stage E, modified as necessary for that particular
district. One then distributes the business figures, Crop
Marketing and Supply Sales, items 2-17, over the four

quarters, according to the cropping calendars. Rice
Marketing (line 2) is the sales from the previous year's
harvest during the first three quarters and the new harvest
during the last quarter. Then one schedules the increase in
membership and Warehouse Space over the year. In Scheduling warehouse space buildup, one should keep in mind the
peak need deadline of the fourth quarter. It is assumed here
that new personnel and equipment are acquired in the first
and second quarter; note lines 20 and 41.

Then one derives the planned schedule of finances.
Expenses in lines 23-30 are distributed over the year. From
this, Profits (line 31) and Earned Surplus (line 46) are
derived. Net Working Capital (line 40) is then computed,
inventory and cash on hand (assume $5,000) less accounts
payable. Note that the accounts payable would be particularly
high during the second quarter, when most of the supplies
are sold, so that Net Working Capital is less than half of
total inventory.

Note that one item of expenses (Interest) is distributed
across the four quarters according to the debt outstanding in
each quarter, long- and short-term. This may require some
small final readjustments.

It is assumed that the subsidy is released on the basis of
expected expenditure on new buildings, during the quarter.
On this basis the subsidy releases (line 50) resulting in
increases in line 48, are set for the second and the third
quarters. The long term debt (line 45) starts in the third
quarter, when all construction is completed and a mortgage
can be granted on all the buildings. Short-term debt is then
distributed over the quarters (line 44) to balance liabilities
to assets, subject to the limitation that it can be no more
than 70 percent of inventory.

This completes the Project Annual Plan (form A-17)
as an operating plan for the year. It is a sales plan and a
financial plan for a district-level enterprise. The Forms
A-17 for noncommercial projects should also represent
total business plans. In a formal sense, it is the total
business plan which justifies the funds release and launches
implementation.

The Quarterly Report--Feedback comes on Form A-18,
the Quarterly Report. Note that some lines have only
numbers in the explanation column (#1, #9, etc.), which
refer to other lines which have caused their divergence from
plan. They are, so to speak, dependent divergences.
Line 42, the value of the buildings, is short of its target
because of line 39. There are six lines with what might be
called originating divergences, which have comments in the
explanation column.

One can see quickly that business was off because one
commune had a flood disaster the previous season and that
this season the rains came late. Also the Sorghum Project
the previous year had failed to gain the anticipated number
of participants, though this was partly offset by a special
tomato marketing program in the district. As a result of
the setback in one commune, the establishment of a commune
warehouse is being delayed a year. Is corrective action
indicated by this report? Lost construction time must be
made up. One learns also that there is water in the subsidy budget for this district and that a few thousand dollars
can be shifted next quarter to unforeseen needs in other
districts.

This, then, is management-by-exception. It is not
necessary to examine all 51 lines of the report. One need
only look at the five or six lines, where significant divergences are explained. It is possible, then, to thumb
through a few dozen of the district's Quarterly Reports and
get a quick impression of what kinds of problems are coming
up most frequently. If construction is late in many districts,
corrective action may be called for at the central echelon to
speed up basic procedures. If this problem has occurred
only in this district, the fault would appear to be with the
individuals responsible. If business is off due to flood
damage in several districts, the whole project has budget
water which can be used to cover unforeseen contingencies
in other projects.

The actual results from the Quarterly Report are then
posted on the operations sheet (Form A-17, Project Annual
Plan), and the feedback documentation is complete. This
can be done by having the district office type the Actual
column for the second quarter on the old stencil and run

copies for distribution to all concerned, stamping the date
in the upper right hand corner. The updated record thus
arrives at the central office together with the Quarterly
Report, with little additional typing.

The final step in the feedback is the analysis of the
actual coefficients to determine how plans should be revised for next year or, if gross divergences are appearing,
for next quarter. What is the actual ratio of inventory to
business volume and to warehouse space? What is the actual
realized gross margin? From this report it appears that
the original coefficients are correct and that no revisions
are in order. Other coefficients must be evaluated by field
inspection. Is the staffing of the farmers association
adequate to handle the job? Are there too few or too many
employees? Are the vehicles sufficient? These questions
must be answered on the spot, in the field, before Project
Annual Plans are prepared for the following year. The
annual plans for the following year thus close the loop of the
planning process or, more correctly, advance the spiral
one more cycle.

The example given illustrates one important feature
of feedback in agriculture: in any given year weather and
prices will affect results much more than project activity.
On Form A-18 the results are below expectations, yet the
business is generally being run properly. It is only over
a period of several years, or in that rare year when
weather conditions are close to average, that the full impact
of agricultural development projects on production and income can be judged.

One can be reasonably sure that actual figures will vary
widely from planned figures even if the project is successful,
for a variety of reasons. A military analogy, an analogy
between development projects and military campaigns, is
useful:

In war, mistakes are normal: errors are usual; information is seldom complete, often inaccurate, and frequently
misleading. Success is won, not by personnel and materiel in prime condition, but by the debris of an organization
worn by the strain of campaign and shaken by the shock
of battle. [1]

Victory in rural development is won by projects whose heads are bloody but unbowed, by projects which, because of thorough initial planning, have been able to withstand the buffeting of a thousand unforeseen misfortunes.

Other Projects

Other projects have considerably fewer items and complex interrelationships between items than a commercial supply and marketing project.

Crop Projects--These projects are distinguished by the fact that action on any item generally occurs completely or almost completely in one quarter. Supply sales will occur in one quarter, marketing in another, land clearing in another, with a small overlap into preceding or following quarters. There are often, however, significant commitments on these activities made the period before the action. Loans and supply sales are preceded by organizing and promotional activities which result in applications or indents, village- or commune-level estimates of seasonal requirements. These commitments are not conclusive, but it is important to know what they are. They can be indicated on the forms as separate items or as nonadditive elements of the same item. Taking the Sorghum Project as an example, line 9 of District Plan A-10.7 gives the expected volume of fertilizer sales (about 43 tons in stage E). This would all be sold in the second or third quarter, but there might be a farmer indent in the first quarter. This would go along with loan applications (line 12 on Form A-10. These might be shown as nonadditive items on the same line of the Project Annual Plan in parentheses:

Stage E	First Quarter Plan	Actual	2nd Quarter Plan	Actual	3rd Quarter Plan	Actual
Fertilizer(tons)	(43)	(40)	35	29	8	
Credit ($000)						
Short-term	(26.6)	(23.2)	26.6	21.5		

Likewise, on demonstrations one can show commitments of
villages in the first quarter, prior to actual planting. One
thus gets signals of divergences one or two quarters earlier
than the final events, and in some cases one can take corrective
action that would not be possible later. This is particularly
important, by the way, when the indents and commitments are
substantially over the planned volume of activity. This can
happen and does happen, and timely action can sometimes get
the added supplies and personnel to do the job.

In other cases separate items may be needed because the
quarters in which the supplies are sold or other action takes
place may lap over into the quarter the indents or applications
are placed. The above line items would then be listed:

Plan Actual

Supply Sales
   Fertilizer: indented
              sold

Credit
Short-term: applications
            contracts

On the total project summary sheet for crop projects, it
may be useful to have a recap of the indents, sales, and central
ordering or production of key supply items/e.g.

Plan Actual

Certified Seed
Ha. planted
Production
Inventory
Orders from districts
Shipments to districts

What other additional items are needed for crop projects,
in addition to those found on Form A-10, the District Plan?
The Sorghum Project, again, is a good illustration because of
the variety of its inputs and investments. Under Outputs might
be added items for hectares newly cleared, hectares newly
planted, and total hectares planted. In addition, under that
heading might come lines for the yield per hectare, sales (as
distinguished from production), and price. Under Demonstrations one might add the number of field day events, the number

of farmers in attendance, and perhaps the average yields on
the demonstration plots. Under Contract Plowing Units one
might distinguish the number ordered and delivered and show
the number of hectares plowed. Under Credit there should be
separate lines for new and total outstanding loans of each
category, since it is not possible to have separate columns
for New and Outstanding on subannual documents. Finally,
under demonstration budget one might distinguish demonstration plot expenses and field day and training expenses and
releases.

The Work Involved

The implementation-feedback phase of the total planning
system thus requires two types of forms:

> District (or other local-level) Project Annual Plan
> District Quarterly Report

To some this may look like a lot of work, compared to the
usual input-only annual financial plans and narrative reports
required in most countries.

The bulk of the documentation should be a good deal less
than the monthly narratives usually required, yet in one sense
it is more work: it requires more thinking. But system also
aids thinking. It guides thinking step-by-step, and unlike
looser systems of planning and reporting makes thinking in-
escapable. Input expenses for example, must be logically
deduced from the volume of activity. They cannot be guessed.
Accuracy beyond the nearest hundred dollars is not necessary,
but logic rather than guesswork is. On the reports, likewise,
round numbers are permitted, but the figures must be there
and must tie out.

REVISION OF PLANS

The final phase of the entire planning system is the set
of operations which use the feedback to revise plans. Planning is a spiral process, gradually moving forward while

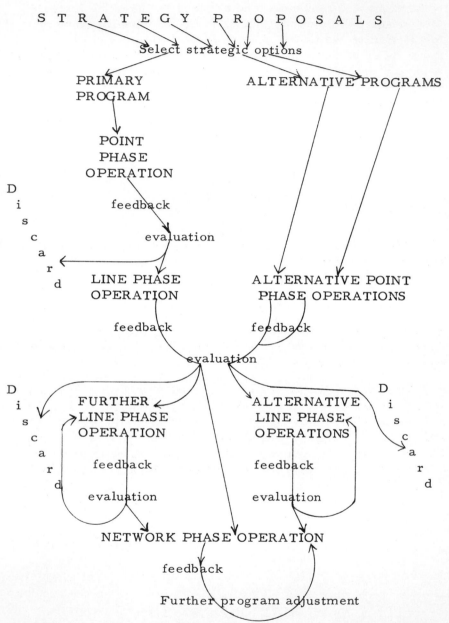

FIGURE 17.1 The planning-implementation-feedback system. Bifurcations indicate choices. Alternative point phase operations are carried out simultaneously with primary line phase operation, but, following that, a choice should be made between the primary or an alternative strategy.

cycling around planning, implementation, and feedback. It has a circular forward motion. The use of feedback to revise plans sets another cycle in motion.

It was pointed out in Chapter 14 that planners must not only consider but also try out alternatives. Experimentation is an integral part of planning itself. Rural Development is so full of uncertainties and imponderables that planners must maintain a healthy humility regarding their preferred strategy and an open mind about alternatives. This open-mindedness must not result in indecision; work must go forward. The experimental nature of the point and line stages, however, should be clearly recognized, and alternative experiments should be undertaken.

Figure 17.1 illustrates the general schema of experimentation, feedback, and evaluation to evolve a final strategy. The planning steps elaborated in Chapter 14 produced not only the primary program illustrated in Appendix A but also, presumably, alternative proposals. Chapters 15 and 16 outlined the procedure for formulating and programming a primary program. After one season of point phase operation of the primary program, action should start on the point phase of alternate strategies.

Experimentation thus proceeds along parallel lines, with the alternative strategies lagging a phase behind the primary choice of the planners and authorities. When the primary strategy goes into the line phase the alternative strategies should be tried in the point phase. For example, if there is one alternate strategy, then instead of five districts in the line phase of the primary program there might be four districts in the line phase and one district given over to the alternative.

After the second evaluation there are several possible alternative paths. Alternatives or the primary strategy may be discarded as clearly unfeasible or inferior. If the primary strategy has proven itself adequately, it might then go into the network phase. Or, it might continue in the line phase. The alternative might be advanced to the line phase, if the primary strategy has been discarded. On the subsequent evaluation one of these alternatives may be advanced to the network stage or continued in the line stage.

In this way the system learns by doing.

NOTES

1.   Sound Military Decision (U.S. Naval War College, 1942) p. 198.

PART IV: COMPLEMENTARY SECTORS AND ECHELONS

CHAPTER **18** COMPLEMENTARY
SECTORS

Agriculture is the heart but not the whole of rural development. The welfare and progress of the village is largely but not entirely dependent on agricultural development. Other sectors, other types of development activity, are also vital to the welfare and progress of the village.

Education and health, the two major welfare services-- as they might be characterized--are in some measure an important part of actual rural income and in some measure an important investment in future income. By nature they are partly investment and partly consumption; it is difficult to distinguish between or measure these two aspects of these services. This book is concerned only with those education and health activities which have special planning problems because they are rural. By and large this includes only those activities which operate at the district level and below and excludes secondary and higher education. In health, attention is confined to those activities generally labeled rural health. This would exclude provincial hospitals or the training and deployment of MD's.

Family planning, because of its importance, is treated as a separate sector.

The next major complementary sector considered is transport. The absence of transport is often a greater constraint to growth of rural income than lack of agricultural development activities. Provision of transport lines alone, without complementary agricultural promotion activities, has in some regions been sufficient to get agriculture moving. There have also been notable failures of expensive transport links to produce results because of lack of an agricultural development program.

One must distinguish two levels of transport development: the major connecting rail and highway links from the main cities to the provincial and district centers, and the village access links. The former are capital projects, easily handled by capital project planning activities and are therefore outside the scope of this book. It should be noted, however, that major transportation links are expensive. The provision of a basic transportation network to a sparsely or moderately populated region can require an investment much greater than the pure budget outlays for an agricultural development program of the type described in Part III of this book. This book is concerned, however, with the planning of local access roads, (farm-to-market) roads, links too small to be handled by capital project planning at the national level.

While all these activities are important, it is necessary to keep them in proper perspective. It is a common fallacy to say that rural development consists of "Education, health, transportation, agriculture, and community development," implying that all these components carry equal weight. Such thinking has sometimes led to serious underallocations to agriculture. Except for regions desperately short of transport, one can maintain better perspective by thinking of rural development as consisting of "agriculture plus complementary sectors."

The activities of these complementary sectors that fall within the scope of the book have two features which distinguish them from most agricultural development activities. First, the participants are not generally individuals but whole communities, and these activities result in community facilities, largely Infrastructure, as the term was defined and described in Chapter 2.

The second feature is a relative planning independence; these activities generally do not require the tight coordination that is required for the component activities of agricultural development proper. There are notable exceptions; road-building, for instance, must often be tightly coordinated with agricultural development. But by and large, it does not matter if a village gets a school or a dispensary first. It does not matter which commune in the district gets the first new road.

These features make it possible to transfer much of the burden of choice, decision, and project management to the local community much faster than in the case of agricultural development. As pointed out in Chapter 3, the local community must build its solidarity and competence on infrastructure activities before taking on responsibility for agricultural development. A community must be able to build and run a school before it can operate a cooperative. A community can prepare for the responsibility of setting agricultural development priorities by deciding on infrastructure priorities. Conceiving development as a learning process, the activities of the complementary sectors are thus essential curriculum prerequisites to some of the more advanced courses in agricultural development.

This chapter examines the complementary sectors one by one, looking at their general role and contribution to rural development, their structural options, and their overall programming by means of the Project Plan form. The next chapter will consider planning of infrastructure in toto, and the preparation of local planning guidance, and the concluding chapter of Part IV will outline a procedure for local program building, decentralized programming, and project management, both in these complementary sectors and in agriculture.

EDUCATION

This chapter is concerned with planning of the primary level only. One might consider first, however, the total educational requirements of agricultural development, the total educational planning implications of discussions of previous chapters on agricultural development.

The Role of Education in Rural Development

The agricultural development program set forth in Appendix A requires about 30 cadre per district of 10, 000 farms, plus another 20 clerks or so with about an eighth grade education. Other innovations in other circumstances might

require three times as many cadre or half as many; in any
event the educational requirements of the cadre complement
alone for agricultural development are modest. The Senegal
program manages with almost no secondary school graduates.
It is a one-and-a-half crop program, however; a more diversified program requires more of an educational input. A
requirement of 30 cadre with specialized agricultural training
per 10,000 farms, moreover, might be a formidable requirement for many lands.

The formal training requirements of the cadre positions,
however, are only the beginning of the educational requirements of agriculture. First of all, the educational system
must produce at least two formally qualified candidates for
each position. At most half of those with the formal educational qualifications for cadre jobs will have the motivation
and other necessary emotional qualifications. A surplus of
qualified candidates is also necessary to maintain job discipline.

The farmers also need some education. How much?
Senegal is not the only example of significant agricultural
development among illiterates. If the innovations are simple
and the incentives exciting, or if the cadre network is dense,
any obstacles due to illiteracy can be overcome.

To build a structure of rural institutions and local initiative and then move on to broadening diversification, however,
requires an increasing level of education in the village. The
program for the so-called Southern Region, outlined in Appendix A, involves a great many farmer organizations, committees, loan groups, etc. Each group or committee needs a
few members who can read and at least one who can organize
thoughts on paper. In the absence of a dense encadrement such
as that of the Senegal, it is important to have a few farmers
with some secondary education in the village, whose aspirations and whose ability to learn from radio and the printed
page will lead them to pioneer innovations in their communities.

What is needed, it would seem, is not so much a minimum
standard of education in the village as a structure of education--
not a floor but a pyramid; a well-structured hierarchy of educational attainment. This means a couple of villagers with
four years of secondary school, some with one or two years

of secondary school, some who have completed primary
school, and others with only some primary education.

The dropout has an important role to play. In contrast
to his role in the modern city, he is an important asset to the
village. The diploma is looked upon in too many developing
nations as a one-way ticket to a high-status desk job in the
city, but rising educational requirements for desk jobs come
with an increasing flow of graduates. The man with a diploma
expects to get the job his diploma would have gotten several
years ago when graduates were scarce; now thousands may
have that diploma, and this "overexpectation" often compli-
cates cadre recruitment; cadre with diplomas are demoralized
when sent back to the village.

The dropout, by contrast, has no overexpectations. He
knows he is stuck back in the village. Still, he does have a
residuum of aspirations, a drive to do better economically
and socially than the average farmer of his village, as well
as some extra reading and writing ability. The men with one,
two, and three years of secondary education are the reservoir
of development leadership in the village.

With some risk one might venture a few tentative quanti-
fications of the educational requirements of agricultural development. To move up to stage IIIa of rural development,
from 2 to 5 percent of a district's male population over the
age of 15 should have some secondary education, and about
20 percent some primary education or at least functional
literacy. This is a nucleus that can learn from the cadre
and that the others can imitate. The larger the literate core
in the village at this stage, the greater the value of d_d, the
ratio of initial adoption to initial demonstration in the key
equation in Chapter 15.

To move into stage IIIb or stage IV, at least 80 percent
male functional literacy is important. Individual diversification and mechanization requires the ability to refer to written instructions. As long as all farmers are following the
same system, a core of literates in the village is sufficient
for development. When development becomes individual,
literacy must be almost universal.

Planning Primary Education

In some countries schools are all locally financed. School construction planning and management can be left largely to the village or the commune, with varying subsidies. Education need not be tied to the pace and location of agricultural development; its payoff in terms of any agricultural development will not come for another seven years.

Some central planning is, nevertheless, necessary. The central government must provide teachers and teacher training, subsidies, and educational supplies. These inputs have structural and allocation problems which the central government must resolve through its planning process.

Structural Options--The village generally presents a homogeneity that contrasts sharply with the diversities and complexities of a developed society. The primary educational structure of a developing nation, however, is generally a colorful kaleidoscope compared to the bland uniformity of the primary educational system of a developed nation. In a developed country all the children start school at about the same age, attend primary school the same number of years, are taught by teachers with roughly the same training, and use the same books.

What a contrast to a developing nation! One village has a six-year school; the next village has a three-year school that is in its second year of operation and has only two grades. In one village children may be starting at five; another village with a brand new school may have a first grade crammed with 10-year-olds getting their first look at the alphabet. Occasionally one may find a school where children have individual textbooks. More often the teacher has the only textbook and writes the lessons on a rough blackboard; children are lucky if they have their own slates. Teachers in the same school may have from 7 to 13 years of total education, some with four years at a normal school, some with none.

All this leaves a variety of structural options and trade-offs to the planners. One may look at some of them in terms of our hypothetical but familiar Southern Region. There one may assume that the primary system is divided into two three year cycles; the first cycle is given at small village schools, the second at larger commune-level institutions. Many countries have structures which formally or informally parallel this. Teachers fall into three categories: (1) temporary, with some secondary education plus a six-week pre-service course; (2) two-year normal school graduates; and (3) four-year normal school graduates. A look at the column for 1967 of Table 18.1 reveals the situation at the beginning of the planning period.

TABLE 18.1

Primary Education In The Southern Region, 1967-1972

	1967	1968	1969	1970
First Cycle				
1 Pupils	300,000	322,000	364,000	406,000
2 Classrooms	8,000	9,200	10,400	11,600
3 Schools	2,400	2,800	3,200	3,600
4 Teachers	8,000	9,200	10,400	11,600
5 Temporary	2,000	2,550	3,100	3,400
6 2-yr grads	5,800	6,400	7,000	7,800
7 4-yr grads	200	250	300	400
Second Cycle				
8 Pupils	88,000	99,000	109,000	126,000
9 Classrooms	2,100	2,350	2,600	3,000
10 Schools	150	170	190	210
11 Teachers	2,100	2,350	2,600	3,000
12 2-yr grads	800	800	800	600
13 4-yr grads	1,300	1,550	1,800	2,400
14 Teachers Graduating				
15 2-yrs	600	600	600	800
16 4-yrs	300	300	300	500
Construction				
First cycle				
17 Schools	400	400	400	400
18 Classrooms	1,200	1,200	1,200	1,400
Second cycle				
19 Schools	20	20	20	30
20 Classrooms	250	250	400	400
21 Development Budget *	733	733	800	890
22 First cycle	600	600	600	680
23 Second cycle	133	133	200	210
24 Regular Budget *	8,920	10,180	11,520	12,860
25 First cycle	6,400	7,360	8,400	9,260
26 Second cycle	2,520	2,820	3,120	3,600

* In thousands of dollars.

1971	1972	5-yr. Total	
			Grades 1-3
455,000	501,000		Aver. 35 per classroom
13,000	14,500		Min. 3 per school
4,000	4,500		Target 90% coverage of 5,000 villages
13,000	14,400		All min. 9 yrs. education
3,900	4,300		Min. 9 yrs. education (max. 30% of total
8,600	9,500		teaching staff)
500	600		Eventual goal 1 per school
			Grades 4-6
143,000	160,000		Aver. 42 per classroom
3,400	3,800		Min. 12 per school
240	270		Eventual goal 1 per commune (500 in region)
3,400	3,800		
600	500		
2,800	3,300		
800	800		9 yrs. education + 2 yrs. normal school
500	500		
500	500	2,100	
1,500	1,500	6,300	
30	30	120	
400	400	2,000	
960	960	4,263	
750	750	3,300	@ $ 300 per new school + $400 per new classroom
210	210	963	@ $1,000 per new school + $450 per new classroom
14,480	16,000		@ $ 800 per classroom
10,400	11,440		@ $1,200 per classroom
4,080	4,560		

Teacher production is a lumpy operation, taking place in large infrequent steps, some two to four years after particular teacher-training institutions have been expanded. One can realistically assume teacher production to be fixed for the coming planning period, with the exception of one or two scheduled stepups. Use of temporary teachers is more flexible, but their use dilutes the quality of the education seriously. It is particularly dangerous to use untrained teachers at the first-grade level.

Some of the options or tradeoffs for the Southern Region are: (1) to maximize the number of schools or to stress expanding capacity of existing schools, which would be cheaper but cover fewer villages; (2) to maximize coverage by using large numbers of temporary teachers or to upgrade the level of quality of teachers; (3) to give priority to expansion of first-cycle or second-cycle schools; and (4) to maintain, raise, or reduce the average number of students per class, which in most developing nations is too high.

Political and pedagogical considerations will determine the choice among these options. Such considerations are outside the scope of this book and generally outside the competence of the central planning staff. It is important, however, that the central planning staff see to it that the Ministry of Education and political authorities make explicit decisions on these options.

Planning Procedure--Table 18.1 is the familiar one-sheet Project Plan (Form A-11 of Appendix A) with outputs at the top, pacing factors in the center, and inputs at the bottom. The figures for the base period, 1967, are written in the first column, and some of the coefficients are provided in the remarks column to the right. Then the five years of the plan period are filled out on the basis of the following:

The tentative primary goal is 4,500 first-cycle schools in 1972; the government is stressing coverage of villages.

A minimum of 20 new second-cycle schools are to be built
each year.

Teachers graduating (lines 15-16) determine lines 6, 7, 12,
and 13.

The number of temporary teachers can be expanded but cannot exceed 30 percent of the total in the first cycle.

The regular budget may not be increased by more than 15
percent in any one year.

Fifty and then 100 four-year graduates are to be assigned to
first-cycle schools each year; eventually every first-cycle
school is to have one.

The development budget must not exceed $1 million in any year.

If possible, the number of temporary teachers and two-year
graduates in second-cycle schools should be reduced.

Such are the typical kinds of constraints under which
education in a developing nation must be planned. The objectives and constraints may be complex. A procedure for
working out a project plan that will satisfy these objectives
and constraints is as follows:

1.   Fill in lines 6, 7, 12, 13, 15, 16, the new teachers
and total trained teaching staff through 1972.

2.   Project new school construction for the first cycle,
at a level or rising pace that will reach the 1972 target, on
lines 17, 18 (3 per school), and then the cumulative total
(line 3).

3.   Increase temporary teachers (line 5) to the maximum
allowable under the fourth rule above. See if this gives a sufficient total annual increase in teachers to fill all the new
classrooms on line 18.

4.   If not, transfer two-year graduates from second-
cycle schools in line 12 (as it turned out, this move was necessary to fill out the required expansion of first-cycle classrooms).

5.   Increase second-cycle classrooms (lines 9 and 20)
by the net increase in second-cycle total teachers in line 11,
and increase second-cycle schools by a uniform number as
permitted by line 18.

6.   Compute development and regular budgets and see if
they are within the limits of the fifth and sixth rules above.
7.   If so, fill in remaining lines.

Again, the reviewer will look critically at the project
plan.   Is the relevant data there?   Is the payoff on investment
evident?   Is the plan consistent?   Are the figures realistic?
(More data will be given on the basis of the cost data in the
next chapter.)   Note that one space-saving technique has been
used here for the first time: totals on lines 4, 11, 21, and
24 are given with the category heading.   This technique is
possible when column subheadings are not used.   Again, compactness of documentation is of the essense.

Other Education Activities

The major development expenses in education are the
construction of new schools and the training of new teachers.
In the above project the number of teachers graduating is
exogenous.   Normally there is a separate project for expansion of normal schools; frequently each normal school and
each specialized secondary or higher educational institution,
is a separate project.   Institutions which stand as discrete
physical installations are outside the scope of this book.
Major schools and research installations may not, technically
speaking, be capital projects, but they can be planned by capital project techniques.

To avoid a megaproject (as defined in Chapter 5) it might
be advisable to break primary education expansion into regional
projects, such as the one above.   It is then possible to offset
the political consequences of favoring one or two regions most
ready for concentrated agricultural institution-building by
spending more on schools in other regions.

A number of projects raising the quality of primary education may be operating at different rates.   For example,
textbook distribution might be undertaken.   The delay factors
then are the editing and publication deadlines for each book or
set of books.   The pacing factors are the funds available for
printing and distribution and the capacity for training the
teachers in their use.   Other in-service training programs
may be carried as separate projects.

RURAL HEALTH

Available health services are obviously an important element in welfare and the ability to work, but attempts to evaluate government health services quantitatively as an element of income or investment have not been encouraging. The one exception is malaria control; this activity has had an enormous direct economic payoff in certain regions where areas previously uncultivated were thus opened up. Although not subject to evaluation as an income item, rural health is a sector of development activity in which, for the reasons discussed below, a little money properly spent can have a major impact on people's lives.

There is one problem which the developing nations share in kind, though perhaps not in degree, with the most developed nations: the lack of doctors in the countryside. The causes of concentration of medical talent in the cities is somewhat the same in both cases, but the results are much more acute in developing nations. The literature of development contains many a shocked reaction, many an "Isn't that terrible!" to the statistics on doctors per 100,000 population in developing nations. They may be 2, 4, 10 doctors per 100,000, and this statistic is cited as the main indicator of shockingly poor medical services. Yet these statistics exaggerate the medical services actually available to most of the population, since the few doctors available are mostly located in the major cities. The countryside generally has only one public health officer and one qualified doctor per province--or, at best, per district. The real ratio then is one doctor per 350,000-- or per 60,000 at best.

Expenditures to increase the number of physicians seem to have a poor payoff in terms of rural coverage. The new doctor stays in the city or, if trained abroad, stays abroad. The world is the doctor's job market.

The main line of rural health improvement, therefore, is subprofessional cadre. A man with two months training and a satchel of antibiotics can handle many ailments and illnesses that the finest physicians had trouble with 30 years ago. When a mother brings in a child with a swollen belly in a tropical village, it requires no expert diagnostician to reach

for the worm medicine. The subprofessional will make mistakes and bury some clients a physician would not but, at the
price, he is highly cost-effective when it comes to saving
lives.

One may therefore consider rural health in terms of a
structure of clinics and dispensaries, staffed by subprofes-
sionals at the district level and below, backed by a hospital
at the provincial level, and supplemented by some other activities.

The Options

The cadre options are essentially those of Chapter 4.
Between the district, commune, and village echelons, one
can trade off, for accessibility, quality and versatility of
treatment at higher echelons and denser coverage below.
Assuming it is not possible to put physicians at the district
level, one might concentrate on good clinics at the district
level staffed by clinicians with a few years of university-level
medical training, like the "people's physicians" of Eastern
Europe. Or one might put the same resources into an effort
at the commune level, using upgraded midwives and techni-
cians with a few years specialized secondary-level medical
training. With some of those resources one might have dispensaries at the village level, using cadre with primary educations and two to six months training.

The optimum choice will depend on a number of factors.
First, the general level of education of the population will
determine what level of cadre can be recruited. Population
density will determine the effective coverage of district or
commune clinics and the need for a village facility. The level
of income of a country is a major determinant of how much
medical care it can afford. The types of ailments and diseases
most prevalent will influence what kinds of health cadre are
needed. If a lowly village health worker with two broad-
spectrum antibiotics and a dozen other medicaments can cope
with the most common ailments, this may be the echelon at
which to concentrate effort.

Some other options are relevant. Cadre outside the health organization may play a role. Community development workers or schoolteachers may be able to handle some health treatment. Teachers can be trained in a few hours, for example, to treat children for trachoma, at a cost of less than 50¢ per child. Monks or traditional healers can be trained for some simple modern medical treatments. Traditional midwives can be upgraded. A maternal and child-care program can be handled through the same project and facilities as the general rural health program, or it can be handled separately. Emphasis and resources can be put into health education and village sanitation rather than health treatment. Sanitation can be handled by separate cadre as a separate project or as a function of the same project.

What will work? What combination of options will prove most cost-effective, in terms of reducing suffering and mortality? Careful pilot testing of seemingly feasible and economical alternatives is the only way to tell. Health, like agriculture activities, must go through "point" and "line" stages before expansion into the "network" stage. One point must be emphasized about the use of low level cadre: the lower their education and training, the more supervision they need. Health services require expensive supply inventories which are difficult to control. Only pilot testing will determine what system of health services will best stand up under the subtle, complex social pressures which determine work discipline and health practices.

Planning Procedure

As mentioned above, a rural health program may be carried out by a complex of projects: village dispensaries, commune clinics, commune maternity centers, district clinics, village sanitation programs, trachoma eradication, malaria control, smallpox eradication, etc. Each may have its own pacing factors, coverage goals, and project management. Except for some supervisory relationships between higher and lower echelon units, however, these activities do not need tight coordination in the manner of an agriculture program. Stage-by-stage logic-sequence diagrams, such as Form A-8 of Appendix A and activity and staffing schedules, such as

TABLE 18.2

Layout of a Project Plan for Commune Health and Maternity
Centers

	1967		1968		1969	
	No.	Cost	No.	Cost	No.	Cost
1 CHMC's operating						
2 Cadre						
3 Commune health workers						
4 Midwives: trained						
5 untrained						
6 Asst. midwives						
7 Training						
8 Commune health workers						
9 Midwives						
10 Asst. midwives						
11 Procurement						
12 Initial inventory						
13 Vehicles						
14 Equipment						
15 Construction						
16 CHMC's						
17 Regional training center						
18 Development Budget						
19 Training						
20 Procurement						
21 Construction						
22 Regular Budget						

Form A-9, are not necessary. What may be necessary is a
services structure analysis, such as Form A-7. Those responsible for health services planning may want to think out
the relative staffing and roles by the minimum paperwork
maximum deliberation technique described in Chapter 4.

To illustrate the general structure of the planning procedure, one may take the familiar Southern Region, although
regional strategies are rarely necessary in health. One may
assume that it already has district clinics in varying degrees
of working order. During the next planning period the emphasis might be placed on establishing commune health and
maternity centers (CHMC), while upgrading the district health
officer position to a supervisory role. The CHMC, then, is
a separate project, perhaps the core institutional project of
the health program. Other projects of the program might
include the upgrading, retraining, and reequiping of the district
health officers, village-level health education and sanitation
campaigns, and campaigns against specific diseases.

On the CHMC project, the commune is probably the most
useful module. One might imagine, for example, a standard
unit with five beds, staffed by a midwife and a commune health
worker (CHW). The CHW has 10-12 years of education plus
one year of training and one year of "internship." After a
few years a second stage of modular development would add
another 10 beds plus assistant CHW's and midwives, the assistants possibly being interns. The modular plan would
specify the standard design and construction cost of the structure, the standard equipment and standard inventory, anticipated use of medicines and medicaments, and the cadre qualifications, training, and annual cost. On the modular plan one
might also project the main outputs, the number of consultations, bed-days occupied, and deliveries.

With the module properly prepared, the next step is the
layout of the project plan and the selection of relevant variables. Since this service is made available to all the people
in a commune, the one relevant output item for a project plan
is the number of communes covered. The possible layout of
the project plan is shown in Table 18.2 below. Among the
pacing factors are recruitment, training capacity, development budget, and the increase in the regular budget for clinic
operation (one may assume that the commune council provides

maintenance personnel and makes some other contributions). Among the delay factors would be the point and line phase limitations and the construction of training facilities.

The computation is simple. Each new CHMC has input coefficients for the other items. One might conceivably break development into annual stages, with the training of the mid-wife and the assistant midwife plus some add-ons of equipment and supplies in the second year. This would not greatly complicate the matter, however.

This, then, is the pattern of a health institution project. The other basic type of health project is an eradication or control campaign. These are frequently, if not generally, carried out by mobile inoculation or spray teams. One unit can cover a given number of villages or communes a year. In the case of malaria control, different stages are defined, with different spraying frequencies. On a multiyear basis, the frequency of the disease can be used as the main output item, the object, of course, being to minimize the frequency. It should be noted, however, that the first year of a campaign may see a rise in disease incidence statistics, as reporting improves as a result of the campaign.

The main targets of eradication and control campaigns can be expressed in terms of coverage of villages, communes, and districts, possibly by stages. The delay factors again are the point and line phase limitations. The subsequent pacing factors are cadre recruitment, training capacity and budget.

FAMILY PLANNING

So much has been written recently about the population crisis that there is little or nothing this book can add to the innumerable comments on the gravity of the problem. Indeed, one might classify family planning as a coequal rather than a complementary, sector to agriculture in many countries.

Assuming a successful resolution of the now uncertain problem of device retention (more on this below), the return on investment in terms of income per capita in family planning may be far higher than in agriculture or industrial development.[1]

Family planning in developing nations on a serious scale is very new. Only since the middle sixties have family planning campaigns in these countries been carried out or even planned on a mass scale. Korea and Taiwan appear to have made the first breakthrough, realizing a genuine reduction of the birthrate as a result of such campaigns.[2] In a few other countries such as Pakistan, operations in the network phase are moving on schedule. The handful of large-scale programs under way, however, are still so new that it is still too early to make a conclusive evaluation of their techniques.

The state-of-the-art of family planning is evolving rapidly, probably far more rapidly than any other development activity. A number of contraceptive devices and practices are being promoted at present. The most common are the intrauterine device (IUD), the "pill," and the condom. Each has its major advantages and disadvantages; each is suited to different couples. The major national programs are currently placing main reliance on the IUD, with the pill and the condom reserved for couples to whom the IUD is not suited for physical or psychological reasons. With the rapid evolution of the state-of-the-art, the relative emphasis on these devices could change in the next few years.

A Conceptual Framework

The objective of a family planning program can be defined relatively simply: to get a given substantial percentage of the couples of childbearing age to adopt and continue to use some effective contraceptive practice or device in the shortest possible time, given the delay factors and resource constraints. For some of the decisions of the total planning process one

should look at the other side of this object: to minimize the
cost per family of the total family planning operation. In
light of the first, the main objective, the cost-effectiveness
of various alternatives can be evaluated. Even with the present highly imperfect state-of-the-art, the cost-effectiveness
of family planning for increasing per capita income may well
be far higher than any other development activity.

Each practice or device can be conceived somewhat in the
manner of an agricultural innovation package. The feasibility
and the promotional and service requirements of each must be
tested and proven out in-country. The overall goal is achieved
by getting a target number of families to adopt each practice.
These family planning innovations differ from agricultural innovations in two important respects. First, regional differences within a country have little or no planning significance,
compared to agriculture. The promotional and treatment
needs of a practice are likely to be the same in all regions,
unless there are large educational or ethnic differences between regions. Second, there is a good deal of slippage of
coverage and participation in the present state-of-the-art. A
substantial portion of the couples covered discontinue their
practice each year and must be resold. Some of this slippage
is due to physical causes, some to lack of personal discipline.

Within an overall family planning program one can distinguish three basic services: education, supply, and treatment. Family planning programs require, first of all, massive
motivational and educational campaigns. The IUD, the pill,
and some other devices require a medical or paramedical
consultation; the IUD and some other techniques require in-
sertion or other treatment. The pill, the condom, and other
devices require a comprehensive supply network, which may
move through a variety of channels.

Options

The first decision is what practices and devices are to be
promoted. This requires analysis similar to that applied to
agricultural innovations. One must examine the relative tech-

nical effectiveness of each device, the promotional requirements and cost, and the overall cost-effectiveness of each.
Sequence of introduction is not a problem, but there are
decisions of relative emphasis to be made.

There is some range of organizational options. At one
extreme, all three services can be handled by the regular rural
health organization. At the other extreme the three services
can be handled by different organizations outside the ministry
of health. The former option may utilize more efficiently
existing institutional capability, but the ministry of health may
not be psychologically or organizationally suited to a massive
promotional campaign. There are a number of organizational
solutions in between these two extremes. Many devices can
be supplied through commercial channels. Education can be
handled by a special agency, while treatment is provided by
regular health officers.

Cadre options are varied, depending heavily on the existing structure of health cadre. A special cadre may be established to handle education and possibly supply. It may have to be
a female cadre, since the subject matter is fairly delicate
and personal. Or, the regular midwives can be trained and
paid a supplement to promote family planning. Treatment
may be provided at regular district or commune health clinics,
by regular health officers or by special medical or paramedical
officers. In many countries the treatment must be handled by
a female.

Cadre are frequently paid per case or per referral. A
variety of combinations of salary and incentive pay schemes
are possible. Volunteers in the villages may be paid a premium for each case they refer to a clinic. Women can be
paid a premium for coming for consultation. The premium
can be split several ways.

Other organizations and cadre may play a role. Meetings
and other publicity and promotion can be provided by village
farmer and other clubs and committees. General community
support is essential; participating couples must feel social
approval.

There is a variety of possible project structures. One
might recommend that family planning be treated in the overall development plan as a sector or at least subsector. The
central operation will involve a good deal of research and
evaluative activities that should be accounted separately from
the field operations in order not to confuse the actual cost of
current family coverage. Education, treatment, and supply
may be handled as separate projects if handled by separate
organizations. If all three services are handled by one organization, it may be advisable to divide field operations into
regional projects to avoid a megaproject.

Project Planning Procedure

To illustrate procedure and problems by a hypothetical
case, Table 18.3 presents another project in terms of the
familiar Southern Region. The eventual goal is participation
by 275,000 couples of childbearing age with two or more children. The strategy is to train supplementary midwives, one
per commune, as the main educational cadre. They will be
supervised by an agent in each district, who will also be responsible for distribution of pills and condoms through village
shops. A female paramedical family planning clinician will
be trained to handle consultations and IUD insertions. Midwives will be paid salary plus commission, with part of the
premium going to the couple. The program enters the line
phase in 1968, after two years of testing in two selected communes. Coefficients of cost and other operating factors have
been taken from a variety of actual national programs.

The main constraint in this case is training. The annual
number of trainees is limited by the fact that each trainee
must work for a time on-the-job under an experienced officer.
It thus takes three years to train cadre for all districts and
communes. The number of midwives determines the number
of referrals. As the cadre gain in experience and competence,
and as the cumulative effect of the publicity of the program and
and its acceptance by increasing numbers comes to bear, the
number of referrals per midwife increase from 100 to 200 per
year. It is expected that 80 percent of the women or couples
who come for a consultation will adopt a contraceptive prac-

tice. This determines the number of families covered. Only
75 percent of those covered, however, are expected to stick
with the practice over a year. The procedure thus works up
the table from line 7, the pacing factor, to line 1, the target
output.

Publicity, supplies, and equipment are needed to support
the program in addition to training. Under "procurement" there
is a presentation device that helps clarify interrelationships
of inputs and outputs. The pills and condoms are counted in
units of one couple's annual supply. Lines 21 and 22 thus relate directly and clearly to lines 2 and 3.

TABLE 18.3

Illustrative Family Planning Project   No. 45-8-103
                                              6 Sep 67
PROJECT: FAMILY PLANNING   agency: FAMILY PLANNING DEPT.

(All figures in "no." columns in thousands except lines 6-13; all cost figures in $000.)

		1968		1969		1970	
		no.	Cost	no.	Cost	no.	Cost
1	Families Covered	.8		10.3		40	
2	by IUD 65% a/	.5		6.7		26	
3	by Pill 15%	.1		1.5		6	
4	by Condom 20%	.2		2.1		8	
5	Referrals	1	1.5	12	18	40	60
6	Cadre Operating		23		264		640
7	Midwives b/	10	13	100	130	300	390
8	District agents c/	2	5	25	67	50	125
9	FP clinicians c/	2	5	25	67	50	125
10	Cadre Training		157		234		172
11	Midwives	110	77	220	154	220	154
12	District agents	25	30	25	30	5	6
13	FP clinicians	25	50	25	50	5	12
14	Publicity		4.2		14		33
15	Meetings	.5	.2	5	2	15	6
16	Posters	.2	.4	2	2	6	6
17	Pamphlets	8.0	1.6	48	5	160	16
18	Other		2.0		5		5
19	Procurement		6.7		10.1		30
20	IUD's	.5	.2	6.2	.5	21	1
21	Pills	.1	.3	1.5	4.5	6	18
22	Condoms	.2	.2	2.1	2.1	8	8
23	Clinical eqpt.		1.0		1.0		1
24	Other		5.0		2.0		2
25	Budget d/		263		645		1,048
26	Premiums		2		18		60
27	Cadre		23		265		630
28	Training		157		234		172
29	Publicity		4		14		30
30	Procurement		7		10		46
31	Regional Staff	10	50	15	75	15	75
32	Miscellaneous		20		30		35
35	Cost per Referral d/		$256		$52		$26
36	Cost per Family d/		373		92		52

1971		1972		
no.	Cost	no.	Cost	
<u>93</u>		<u>148</u>		80% of new referrals + 75% of previous year
60		97		
15		21		)
18		30		)– sold at 50% subsidy
				)
75	113	100	150	100 increasing to 200 referrals per midwife
				@$1.50 per ref. premium incl. travel
	<u>900</u>		<u>900</u>	
500	650	500	650	@$1,300 (not incl. share of premium)
50	125	50	125	@$2,500
50	125	50	125	@$2,500
	<u>39</u>		<u>39</u>	Note extra trainees to cover attrition
30	21	30	21	@$700
5	6	5	6	@$1,200
5	12	5	12	@$2,000
	<u>56</u>		<u>66</u>	
20	6	20	6	
10	10	10	10	2 per village @$1.00
300	30	400	40	4 per village @$ .25
	10		10	
	<u>68</u>		<u>99</u>	
39	2	52	3	@$50 per 1,000 incl. inserters
15	45	21	63	@$3 per year) Unit is 1 yr. supply 1 fam.
18	18	30	30	@$1 per year) Cost is 50% subsidy
	1		1	@$40 per clinician trained + misc.
	2		2	
				All Years
	<u>1,291</u>		<u>1,369</u>	<u>4,617</u> a/ percent of total covered
	113		150	343 b/ one per commune
	900		900	2,718 c/ one per district
	39		39	641 d/ all cost figures in thousands
	56		66	170 of dollars
	68		99	230
15	75	15	75	350
	40		40	165
	$16		$13	= line 6 – line 32 + line 5
	35		27	= (cumul. budget – lines 21-2) + line 1

At the bottom of the table are two key measures of cost-effectiveness. The cost per referral is the total current year budget, excluding supplies, divided by the number of referrals. This is a measure of the economy of the promotion effort. The cost per family is a cumulative cost, equal to the cumulative budget to date, excluding consumed supplies, divided by the number of families now covered.

The project plan reveals some interesting features of the dynamics of family planning. Because of the 25 percent slippage, which is typical, a gradually increasing percentage of the referrals are recoveries of the previous year's couples who have discontinued practice. This serves to decelerate the growth of coverage, particularly after all cadre are deployed and the rate of referrals per cadre reaches a maximum. If in subsequent years, for example, the referrals per midwife stay at 200 a year, total coverage will grow as follows: 191,000 in 1973, 223,000 in 1974, 248,000 in 1975, 266,000 in 1976, and 280,000 in 1979. The original target of 275,000 is reached after 10 years, as the increments grow smaller and smaller. Had the rate of referrals been 150 per midwife rather than 200, the target would never be reached; the coverage would level off below the target level.

Given the present imperfect state-of-the-art, a family planning project which is to cover a significant portion of the population must have a lot of steam behind it. The steam is provided by deployment of adequate numbers of cadre, with the training and accompanying publicity support that can enable them to get the maximum number of referrals a year.

TRANSPORTATION

The main transportation arteries which join rural market centers to metropolitan centers are built by capital projects, which are outside the scope of this book. The next two chapters cover the procedures for planning the feeder roads linking villages to rural market centers. It is useful here, however, to consider the overall role of transportation in rural development and some of its more general planning considerations.

Role

The end product of a transportation project is basically improved access--a facility to be used by means of conveyance. Only a railroad project generally includes within its planning and financing the actual means of conveyance. Access can be defined for each village or commune and possibly for each district in terms of two factors. The first is the optimum mode of conveyance for the access--large truck, small truck, oxcart, or movement by foot. The second factor is the seasonality of that access, whether it is open all year round or only in the dry season. The effect of a transportation project is to move a certain number of localities up the scale of access quality.

Does it pay to move them up the scale? Taking an extreme case, one may consider a village which is highly self-sufficient, selling only silk (unlikely, since silk has an unusually low return to labor) and buying nothing bulky. No innovation packages have been adapted to the region which are suitable for this village. It has foot access only, and that only six months of the year. Yet, on the basis of the above assumptions, improved access would result in no innovation, no increased production, and no increased income.

If, however, the village was suited to a fertilizer innovation, then oxcart and perhaps truck access would have a payoff. A horticulture enterprise, with marketing by daily deliveries to the metropolis, would require main road access. The grade of access a village needs, or which can pay off for a village, depends on the innovations available.

Transportation is one of the "essentials" described in Chapter 2, but only for specific innovations. Almost every innovation requires a certain minimum grade of access. In terms of the procedures in Part III, transportation has the effect of expanding the potential participation of an innovation.

But transportation is also something of a consumption good. Like housing projects, transport projects produce a good that is consumed over many decades in the form of greater consumer goods purchasing power. East Pakistan found that small roads increased real income 10 percent to

20 percent without any innovation, by lowering prices currently paid on transport.[3]

To illustrate the quantification of this effect, suppose a village has 100 families, each marketing an average of $100 in crops and spending the money on bulky consumer goods. If lower transport costs from a road project reduce prices 10 percent each way, each family will earn $110 and be able to buy goods worth $121 at the old prices, an annual gain of $2,100 for the village. It should be noted, however, that this is a net increase in GNP (rather than a redistribution) only if it results in increased production of domestic manufactures. Transportation as a consumption good must therefore be considered as secondary in interest to transportation as a production investment.

There are also important tertiary benefits to consider. Improved access can have a powerful educational impact, creating new tastes and aspirations in the village. It can increase the effective range of coverage of cadre. It can make marketing more efficient by giving farmers direct access to higher echelon market centers and to more alternative buyers and suppliers.

Strategy

The above considerations permit two basic approaches to transportation programming. One is to require a specific justification for each project and program on the basis of maximizing net benefits with limited investment funds. The other is to consider transport of a certain access grade a necessary service which must be achieved as a basis of diversification in stage III of rural development, anticipating the innovations that will justify it. The second approach thus programs on the basis of long-range attainment of a minimum standard for each community, as one might for education and health facilities.

There are some other options to be considered. First, one may program transport where the payoff is greatest, where the need is greatest, or where lagging regions need some such stimulus. One may thus give first priority to stage IIa or IIb regions. The second type of option is arteries vs. feeder roads (the creation of new networks or the expansion of existing networks). The third option is hard vs. soft financing, i.e., to build roads with maximum self-help or to build roads on grants as a government investment in the countryside.

All these options may be summarized in three different types of programming objectives. The first is to get a maximum net return on the investment. The second is to elicit maximum self-help and maximum local investment of savings. The third is to minimize interregional disparities.

A differential strategy based on stage of evolution can harmonize these possibly conflicting objectives:

Stage IIa--Straight government budget outlays should build main arterial roads into such lagging regions, where it is impossible to justify financing on the basis of currently feasible innovations, and the people do not have the resources to make a meaningful self-help contribution. Such roads lay the foundation for stage IIb.

Stage IIb--Roads can now be justified by feasible innovations. Arterial roads should be built by loan financing. Feeder roads should require at least a token self-help contribution.

Stage III--With farmers now well organized and benefitting from previous government investments by earning increasing income, the cost of feeder roads should fall increasingly on the local community. By this stage the arterial network should be completed.

Payoff Computation

This means that the payoff calculations of capital projects for stage IIa regions must be based on very rough calculations of the payoff potential starting 10 years later. They must be based on the basic biological potential for lack of specific proven innovations. If planning in the agricultural sector is properly done, however, cost-benefits analysis for capital projects in more advanced stages can be based on much more solid calculations than are generally used today.

To illustrate with some calculations relating to Appendix
A, suppose that a main road plus a minimum network of feeder
roads costing $1 million over a three-year period will bring
the sorghum and hog projects to three additional districts.
Expenditures on the roads are $100,000 the first year,
$200,000 the second year, $400,000 the third year, and
$300,000 the fourth year. The first district goes into stage
D the first year, the second district the second year, and the
third district the third year. On the basis of that schedule,
one computes the benefits in increased income of the two
projects in three districts, which rises to a maximum of
$1,389,000 in the seventh year. The costs are combined by
year in the same manner for the two projects in staggered
districts plus the road. With a 25-year time horizon and a
6 percent discount rate, the total discounted costs are
$2,162,000 and the discounted benefits $12,835,000 (based
on the coefficients of Form A-13), a benefits-cost ratio of
about 6:1, not including secondary and tertiary benefits.

This type of calculation is important not only to justify
the expenditures on transport in areas where agricultural
development is progressing but also to keep in mind the expenses of projects which must be coordinated. The road
project in the example above has no payoff unless the outlays
for the sorghum and hog projects are executed with properly
coordinated timing. Transportation, like any agricultural
service, cannot be considered as an isolated investment. It
can be justified for regions which do not yet have active agricultural development programs, but only by keeping in mind
that the real payoff will not come until the agricultural development programs do become active.

INTERSECTORAL ALLOCATIONS

The above transport allocation strategy based on stage-
oriented interregional policy gives some guidance for interregional intersectoral allocation. Deciding how much to
spend on agriculture in region A as opposed to health in region A or region B is particularly difficult, but a stage-
differential policy gives some rational basis.

Form A-16 of Appendix A shows that the total budget outlay for the Southern Region over five years comes to $40 million, about $700,000 to $800,000 per district. Political pressures and general considerations of equity would demand equal or greater spending for lagging regions. Extra spending on research and infrastructure in lagging regions can balance that inequity without seriously distorting the economic rationale of the overall development program allocations--assuming the lagging regions have the basic biological potential (the minimum soil and water conditions) to warrant it. Conversely, there should be less direct government outlays for infrastructure in more advanced regions, which are better able to finance their needs locally.

NOTES

1. S. Enke, "The Economic Effects of Slowing Population Growth," Economic Journal, LXXVI, No. 301 (March, 1966), 44-56.

2. F. Notestein, "Approaches to Population Control," Development Digest, VI, No. 2 (April, 1968), 13-19.

3. E. Owens, "The Local Development Program of East Pakistan," International Development Review (March, 1967), p. 27.

CHAPTER **19** INFRASTRUCTURE

This and the following chapter deal with the planning of infrastructure, a term used in this book to mean rural public works, community projects of strictly local scale resulting in discrete physical installations. It should be noted again that this usage differs from another common application of the term to mean service institutions.

The subject has, in effect, already been treated in chapters 7 and 8 in the case studies of Malaysia and East Pakistan, and it will be difficult to say anything on the subject that would be more enlightening than a straight description of how these countries do their infrastructure planning. Their specific procedures, however, are specially adapted to their unique conditions. This and the following chapter will attempt to present the lessons and the techniques of those two successful operations in a generalized fashion that will facilitate their application to widely varying conditions.

INFRASTRUCTURE CATEGORIES

It must be emphasized again that standardization is vital to rural development. The vast number and small size of projects preclude professional individual design, review, and supervision. Standard design, costs, and allocation and authorization procedures are needed. It is therefore important to identify broad categories of work to which the same procedures can apply.

Types of Projects

With some overlap, projects will fall into one of the four categories: (1) transport, (2) water control, (3) water supply, and (4) community buildings. Each of these categories has common planning considerations. Within each subcategory one should distinguish new construction, rehabilitation of derelict installations) and maintenance activity. Maintenance should not be considered as a development project, but it should enter into local planning and be adequately provided for.

Transport--This generally means roads; in some cases it means canals and overlaps water control. One can subdivide this category into: connecting roads, which link market points, access roads linking villages to market points or to roads leading to market points, and spans) which includes bridges and culverts.

Water Control--Irrigation, drainage, and flood control are important elements of agricultural innovation packages, but they must frequently, if not generally, be executed as community projects. In the program for the Southern Region (Appendix A) irrigation (Form A-11.5) was treated as an innovation package similar to other crop promotion projects because small groups of farmers in the illustrative project joined together to build small water diversion and distribution works. The village or commune as a community did not take responsibility for such works. When the village, the commune, or the district takes the responsibility, infrastructure planning procedures apply.

Five types of works may be distinguished: dams, reservoirs, canals, lateral channels, and embankments. Irrigation installations are generally combinations of the above types of works.

Water Supply--These works are generally for provision of drinking water, but sometimes they may be part of irrigation projects. Ground water must be provided by wells, either dug or drilled. The latter require professional crews and modern equipment (the author learned the hard way that one must not let the tongue slip and refer to the well driller's

work as well digging). Reservoirs may also be sources
of drinking water. Drinking water from surface sources may
require purification units. Finally, potable water may be
distributed by piping.

Installations other than dug wells and reservoirs can be
expensive; they require professional design and supervision
and often a substantial investment in imported equipment
and materiel. Well drilling can be very risky in regions with
inadequate ground water surveys or irregular water tables.
Expensive potable water supply may be a poor allocation of
limited resources for primitive economies. For more advanced economies such as Malaysia, however, potable water
supply and distribution represents a sound distribution of the
benefits of the economy to the rural population.

Community Buildings--Schools, clinics, marketplaces,
and community centers are in this category. Schools and
clinics, it should be noted, may be easier to build than to
staff. Many countries have made the mistake of considering
them purely in terms of their structural investment and
found they could not staff all the schools and clinics that
were built.

Types of Work

One must first of all distinguish new projects, rehabilitation of derelict old installations, and repair work. The last
should not be considered a redevelopment activity, but it
should be considered fully in development planning. Maintenance costs should be considered in evaluating projects, and
a community should be required to show it is adequately
maintaining the facilities it has before it is given grants for
new facilities. Rehabilitation of unusable old roads, channels,
reservoirs, and buildings often can make a substantial contribution to the supply of infrastructure facilities. These
projects are not as easy to standardize as new projects, but
some standard factors and elements can be used in their
planning and design.

The work involved in an infrastructure project falls into
three broad categories: (1) earthwork, (2) buildings, and
(3) civil structures.

Earthwork--Dirt roads, embankments, channels, and
some reservoirs require little work other than earth-moving.
If the density of population and available labor is adequate
and if the terrain is flat and easy to work, earth moving can
be accomplished simply by mobilizing gangs of laborers with
simple tools. No equipment is needed. Large numbers of
laborers can be given employment at a minimum cost, providing productive relief to the poorest strata of the community.
Volunteer farm leaders can be trained to design and supervise the projects, provided the training teaches them how to
measure properly and provided they are adequately spot-
checked to prevent fraud.

If relief is one of the objectives, such earthworks provide
one of the most efficient means of providing it. Up to 90 percent of the money spent can go directly to the laborers. If
relief of landless laborers is not an objective, then such works
can be financed almost entirely by voluntary labor contributions, the "sweat equity" of the community. Or a compromise
can be achieved between the two objectives: laborers can be
paid, but at half the going wage. The other half becomes the
local contribution to the project. Such has been the procedure
in East Pakistan.

If the population density is low, however, or if the terrain
is difficult, local labor will not be sufficient to finish the job in
a reasonable time. Heavy imported earthmoving equipment
and skilled engineers and operators are then necessary to do
the job. Earthwork thus requires either the least or the most
scarce resources, depending on the density of population.

Laying gravel or other aggregate on roads is essentially
the same type of work. Male and female village labor in many
countries has traditionally found off-season employment by
breaking rocks into finer aggregate: "making little ones out
of big ones. "

Buildings--Community structures in some countries go
up with no central financing and no professional design or
supervision. Many a village one-room school has been built
with traditional bamboo and thatch or other light structural
material. Larger and more permanent structures, however,
require more expensive materials and professional design and
supervision.

Buildings are the easiest types of projects to standardize.
One design will work for a wide variety of sites. It is also
possible to train village leaders to manage and supervise
building construction, except perhaps for some finishing details, such as door and window fittings. Care must be taken
to prevent fraudulent overdilution of cement mixes.

Because of the possibility of standard design, it is relatively easy to control costs of building structures.

Civil Structures--Dams and other water flow control devices, some building foundations, and heavy duty roads are
among the types of infrastructure work which require custom
engineering design and supervision. Drilled wells and pumps
require imported materiel. This type of work requires the
most of scarce resources, human and financial.

Many projects require two or three of the above basic
types of infrastructure work.

CONSTRAINTS

Like agricultural development projects, infrastructure
projects are subject to a variety of financial and human resource constraints. Unlike agricultural development projects,
they are not subject to the "point-line" phasing constraints.
Most countries have sufficient experience with each type of
infrastructure project to issue standard designs or standard
specifications without further experimentation. The overall
organization of cadre and community -- the institutional aspects -- need careful experimentation and point-line phasing,
but the technical aspects do not.

Financial Resources

One must first distinguish central budget outlays and local
contributions to projects. The latter may come from taxes
levied by local bodies, voluntary fund-raising in the community,
voluntary contributions of labor, or labor performed for wages
substantially below the going wage.

The constraints on these two resources are determined very differently. Central budget outlays for infrastructure are limited by the tax base of the central government, first of all. The tax base of developing nations is limited to those levies which are easy to collect. To this is added government resources from borrowing and foreign aid, less the demands of other sectors. Local contributions, on the other hand, are determined by the amount of surplus labor in the village, by the cash earnings of the local farmers, and by the degree of community discipline. As the economy advances the local contribution changes in kind. Expansion and, particularly, diversification reduce the available off-season surplus labor, while local cash resources increase.

There is a third relevant financial constraint: foreign exchange. Foreign exchange earnings and the demands of other sectors limit the amount of foreign exchange available for infrastructure projects. The foreign exchange requirements for earth-moving equipment, pumps, piping, reinforcing bars, sheet steel, etc., are found largely in the categories of expenditure financed from the central budget, although some might come out of local contributions. If earth-moving must be done by equipment, these outlays of scarce foreign exchange can be substantial.

Staffing Bottlenecks

Scarce staff and cadre is likely to be the most binding constraint on infrastructure development, at least in the early stages of a large program. This bind is caused by the shortage of technically trained personnel and by inefficiencies in their use.

Engineering design can be a binding constraint. If a wide variety of individual designs must be prepared and approved, a growing backlog of jobs may pile up in the technical offices of the ministry of public works. This may be avoided or reduced in three ways. First, standard designs may eliminate the need for drafting and review of individual projects. Second, good standard specifications and design of components may make it possible to delegate approval of project engineering to local offices (elimination of higher-level review has relieved

engineering bottlenecks in many countries). Finally, foreign
technical assistance can relieve critical temporary shortages
of competent, seasoned engineers.

Where infrastructure is built by local contractors, the
contracting process can be a bottleneck. Invitations to bid
and acceptance of bids require painstakingly thorough documentation and often too many approvals. Again, standardization and delegation is the solution. Contracting is particularly
a bottleneck in periods of rising prices, when bids consistently
exceed original estimates and every contract has to go up for
top-level authorization. A special procedure is essential for
expediting top-level authorization or rejection of bids over
the estimates. A further problem arises when the work capacity of private contractors is limited. If the penalty for
delays is moderate, a contractor is tempted to accept far
more jobs than he can handle and get around to them at his
leisure.

The supervision and inspection capacity of public works
agencies can be a bottleneck. This obviously limits the amount
of work that can be done directly by government agency crews
rather than by contractor. It also limits the amount of work
that can be contracted and adequately inspected. Inadequate
inspection invites gross fraud. Again, simplification and
standardization of specifications and design make it possible
to use lower-level supervisory and inspection cadre.

Engineering and contracting present serious problems of
corruption, collusion, and kickbacks. The whole problem of
corruption in developing countries is a serious one, meriting
study. [1] Unfortunately such a study has not yet been written.
Suffice it to say that simplification and standardization can help
reduce the opportunities and temptation for corruption. In
some cases arbitrary oversimplification and overstandardiza-
tion are necessary to bring engineering and contracting and
inspection work in line with the administrative capacity of the
government.

The concatenation of the budget cycle and a limited work
season aggravates the above bottlenecks. If preparatory staff
work cannot start until expenditures are authorized, and the
new fiscal year begins well into the work season, contracts
may not be approved until almost the end of the work season.

This may cause a chronic one-year delay in project execution.
Fund releases should be timed to permit engineering and contracting to be done in advance of the work season.

Finally, a shortage of earth-moving equipment and operators may be a bottleneck. The latter may prove the more
binding constraint; it is easier to order large amounts of
equipment in one year than to recruit and train large numbers
of operators. Along with operators one must consider equipment maintenance personnel and facilities as necessary to
utilize the equipment spreads available.

All the above constraints can be estimated in the following
manner: First, one must define standard servicing units,
district engineers, provincial engineering offices, provincial
equipment spreads, etc. The next, and most difficult step, is
to define the monthly work capacity of each of these units (so
many building designs, so many kilometers of road, so many
bridges or small dams, etc.). In defining such work capacities, precision is fortunately, neither conceivable nor, important. On equipment and field supervision, one must then
consider the number of months of work actually available in
order to estimate annual capacity. Finally one must estimate
the staff available, the number of servicing units which have
now been fielded and which can be recruited and trained in the
next few years.

All of these figures are difficult to estimate, but even the
crudest estimate of the infrastructure project capacity of the
government staff and cadre is of significant value. Many a
rural infrastructure program has fallen several years behind
schedule because of failure to anticipate these needs. The
danger is not one of overloading the project capacity by 25 or
35 percent but of overloading it by 125 to 235 percent because
of failure to consider these constraints.

CENTRAL PLANNING PROCEDURES -
BASIC DATA COLLECTION

In all rural development planning targets are sales targets.
The principle that the farmer makes the ultimate decision and
the government can only "market" a development program has

already applied to agricultural development in Chapter 15.
Beyond stage II of agricultural development this should be increasingly true of infrastructure projects. Nothing should be
executed unless the community is willing to make some contribution, at least by investing some "sweat equity." The required community equity in projects should increase as the
government's activities move the community into more advanced stages of development.

This creates a planning paradox. On the one hand specific
regional and national physical targets for the main categories
of projects are essential to coordinate resources, to balance
projected manpower and financial inputs. In order to plan the
training and utilization of teachers rationally, some target has
to be set for school construction. In order to plan roadbuilding
equipment, procurement, and engineering staffing rationally,
some target has to be set for number of kilometers of road
constructed. On the other hand, local communities must be
given a wide latitude of choice of projects if they are to contribute some equity to them and plan responsibly.

The programming procedure in this and the following
chapter will attempt to reconcile these two conflicting objectives: rational central planning vs. complete local project
option. The reconciliation will be imperfect, but it will avoid
serious misallocation of resources, serious shortages or over-
supply of funds and manpower in particular projects, while at
the same time giving local communities serious alternatives
to consider in planning.

As in agricultural development, planning must start with
the collection of data relevant to decisions. These data fall
into three broad categories: government work units and their
cost and capacity; project standards and unit requirements;
and village needs. As in agricultural development, one must
start by defining, standardizing, and costing out the modules
that are the building blocks of planning.

Work Units

Engineering support to infrastructure projects is usually
deployed in teams. Standard combinations of men and

equipment are posted at the district, provincial, and regional
level, with increasing specialization of talents as one moves
up the hierarchy. At the district level one might find from
one to three all-purpose supervisors plus some small equipment for road maintenance. At the provincial level one might
find a team of engineers who can design small roads and buildings and water control embankments, plus a spread of small
to medium road building equipment. At the regional level one
might find more specialized designers and a variety of heavy
equipment.

It is best to conceive the constraint imposed by the work
capacity limit in terms of one level only, preferably a middle
level, and plan the other levels to match that level's capacity.
Working with multiple level constraints is too complicated for
ICM (Informal Constraint Maximization). If there is a manpower construction team and equipment at the provincial level,
one may focus planning on that level.

As the program builds up, more staff and equipment may
be added to the team. Some provinces will have more, some
less. One cannot, therefore, plan in terms of one standard
provincial level spread.

There are two alternative approaches to defining the
modules of engineering support: the individual or the team
approach. Combinations of the two approaches are also
feasible. Looking at the team approach first, a tabulation
should be made like that of Table 19.1.

One thus classifies the types of teams or spreads into two
to four size categories representing personnel and equipment
add-ons planned for subsequent years or for locales with higher
work loads. For each category of work unit one then has the
total manpower requirement, the total initial financial investment, and the total annual cost.

The other alternative is to list first all the key categories
of individual professional cadre whose number determines total
work capacity. These might include surveyors, design engineers, construction supervisors, etc. To each of these should
then be charged, for budgeting purposes, not only their personal salaries and expenses but also all other expenses, including supporting personnel and equipment, which would vary

TABLE 19.1

Modules of Engineering Support: The Team Approach

Type of Unit	Investment	Annual Cost
MINIMUM		
Prov. survey/design		
List members	Preservice Training costs	salaries + fringe benefits + misc. allowances
List equipment	Purchase and Installation	maintenance and operation and depreciation
List supplies		list quantities and costs
Prov. road construction		
List members	repeat above types of items & details	
etc.		
Dist. inspection and maintenance		
List members		
etc.		
MAXIMUM (or medium scale unit, with maximum scale units below)		
Prov. survey/design		
List members		
etc.		

directly with them.   Then would be listed the major pieces of
equipment which might determine the volume of work, for
example, bull-dozers, crushers, and rollers.   To these
would be charged the costs of the balance of the spread.

With either team or individual, type of module, it is
possible to draw some rough relationship of inputs to outputs.
The basic unit connecting work units to projects might be the
minimum-unit work week.   Let us assume that there are three
sizes of survey/design teams, and the smallest can do 40 weeks
of output a year.   For each type of project one can estimate
the number of weeks of survey/design work typically required.
The work capacity of the medium unit might then be defined as
60 work weeks, and the maximum unit 100 work weeks.

With such modules one can express engineering support
plans very compactly.   Table 19.2 below might be the pacing
factor section or the coverage matrix section of an engineering
support or feeder roadbuilding project plan (again, for the
Southern Region and its 10 provinces).   As most of the survey/
design units grow from minimum to maximum size in the table,
the total survey/design work capacity in the region rises from
320 weeks a year to 860.   Road construction and inspection and
maintenance work capacity is built up with an appropriate lag.
Note that one week of survey/design capacity is in no way
equivalent to a week of construction capacity.

A matrix like Table 19.2 would determine how many
kilometers of earthwork type projects could be done each year.
In turn, the projects might be constrained by the number of
engineers graduating or otherwise recruitable each year, or
by the foreign exchange available to buy equipment.

Project Units

The next step is to set project standard costs and project
standard modular work unit requirements.   It is important to
know not only how much money but how much work-unit time
a project needs.

Again, one must start by defining a few modular units.
Buildings are simple; there is probably a standard design for

TABLE 19.2

Engineering Support Project Plan, "Southern Region," 1967-72: Pacing Factor Section

Engineering Units and Work Capacities	Work Week Capacity	1967	1968	1969	1970	1971	1972
Survey/Design							
Maximum units	100			1	2	5	7
Medium units	60		2	4	6	4	2
Minimum units	40	8	8	5	2	1	1
Total capacity (work weeks):		320	440	540	640	780	860
Road Construction							
Maximum units	80				1	2	5
Medium units	50			2	4	6	4
Minimum units	30	8	10	8	5	2	1
Total capacity (work weeks):		240	300	340	430	520	630
Inspection/Maintenance							
Maximum units	80			2	10	25	35
Minimum units	40	45	50	48	40	25	15
Total capacity (work weeks):		1,800	2,000	2,060	2,400	3,000	3,400

a lower primary school, an upper primary school, a clinic,
and a commune marketplace. These then have standard costs
and standard construction supervisory time requirements.
Earthwork and civil structure type projects may be more difficult to standardize, though many countries have set classes
of roads, with standard widths and other specifications. Set
classes of bridges and embankments should be similarly defined. The following form of table provides for the essential
planning data of such projects:

Project type:	New Roads		Bridges		Rd. Rehab.		Embank-ment	
Standard width:	3 m.	5 m.	2 m.	4 m.	3 m.	5 m.	2 m.	4 m.

Cost (per 100 m.
      length)

Workloads (0.0
weeks per 100 m.)
Survey/Design
Construction
Inspection

Obviously the estimates will be only approximate. A variety
of local conditions and construction factors will affect costs
and workload coefficients. Location will also affect the requirements; six projects in one commune can be supervised
with less personnel than six projects in six communes. The
members of the teams are not homogeneous and the mix of
projects will also affect the number of jobs that can be handled
in a month. In addition to time on the projects, work units
must devote time to routine administrative chores, maintenance of equipment, in-service training, etc. Construction
units work time is limited by seasonal factors. For this
reason, the basic construction unit in Table 19.2 was limited
to 30 weeks and the survey/design unit was limited to 40 weeks.

All these limitations and qualifications mean that project
capacity estimates may be up to 40 percent in error. Nevertheless, these estimates are important in order to avoid 100
percent errors, which can easily occur in the absence of systematic planning. Local annual and subannual programming,
following the procedures described in the next chapter, can
reduce the error considerably.

An inventory of existing conditions is essential to any planning. On infrastructure, such an inventory would be a listing of the number of communes and villages with and without certain standard facilities. Data on the numbers of village schools and rural clinics can usually be obtained from ministry reports. Statistics on rural marketplaces and community centers will probably be found only in provincial records.

Proper data on transport is generally not readily available from standard reports or records. What is needed is a tally of the number of villages and communes by access category. Such a listing (listing the best access only) would be structured like Table 19.3. Such information is generally to be had only by a district-by-district survey. Experienced administrative officers at the district level, however, can provide such a tally very quickly; they know intimately the access limits of every community in the district. It has been the author's experience that a district officer can provide such a tally in 30 minutes. It should be noted that there is no easy way to tally water supply and water control needs of villages.

On the basis of such data a table can be set up showing the total cost of providing the basic facilities to every community. First, however, some additional decisions must be made. The first concerns the definition of basic facilities: What are the minimum standards? For this purpose the minimum standards must be considerably simpler than the project eligibility rules. One might, for example, state simply that the general objective is to provide every village with year-round light truck access and a lower primary school and to provide every commune with year-round heavy truck access, a higher primary school, a clinic, a meeting hall, and a marketplace.

The basic local contribution required must be decided next, so that one can deduce the overall net cost to the central government. To do this one must decide the priority the central government places on these facilities, since the percentage paid by the central government should be proportionate to the priority it places on the project. Once such decisions have been made, the basic infrastructure needs of the Southern Region can be tabulated (Table 19.4). The first line of the highly compacted table shows first of all that 3,000 villages are without minimum standard access, defined above as

TABLE 19.3
Southern Region Transport Access

	All-Year Access		Dry Season Only	
	Communes	Villages	Communes	Villages
Foot only		580		50
Ox-cart		1800		570
Light truck	130	800	55	350
Heavy truck	235	550		
Main highway	80	300		
	445	4030	55	970

TABLE 19.4
Basic Infrastructure Needs,
Southern Region

	Aver. Size	Villages or Communes		Pri-ori-ty	Cost *		Cost to Govt. *	
		With	W/out		Unit	Total	%	Total
Village Level								
Road (Min. std.)	4 km.	2,000	3,000	4	6	18,000	80	14,400
School	4.5 rm.	2,850	2,150	1	4	8,600	85	7,500
Commune Level								
Road(Min. std.)	10 km.	315	185	2	60	11,200	85	9,500
School	15 rm.	210	290	3	17	4,900	80	3,900
Clinic	15 bed	75	425	5	20	8,500	70	6,000
Marketplace		130	370	6	5	1,900	70	1,300
Community Center		45	455	7	4	1,800	50	900
						34,900		31,500

* In thousands of dollars.

year-round light truck access. For the average village, about
4 kilometers of road are needed at a cost of $6,000 ($1,500
per km.), a total cost for the region of $18 million. Sub-
tracting a basic local contribution of 20 percent, this comes
to $14.4 million for the central government. The total cost
of all these facilities to the central government will come to
about $31.5 million.

For particular villages, other infrastructure needs may be
more urgent, such as a dry-season drinking water source or a
flood control embankment. For some villages a community
fishpond or silk-raising shed may be far more productive than
a road. The above list includes only those requirements which
can be easily standardized. It does present, however, a compact picture of total common needs.

CENTRAL INFRASTRUCTURE PROGRAMMING

The programming process must proceed along two lines
if it is to cover the above range of activities and if the projects
require extensive engineering support. First, there must be
an overall allotment of development funds for infrastructure
to the region and then to the locales. This is an allotment
which, in effect, cuts across conventional sector lines.
Second, there must be programming along conventional sector
lines, education, health, transportation, etc. including project
plans such as the Primary Education Project discussed in the
previous chapter.

Overall Infrastructure Grants

The table of basic infrastructure needs (Table 19.4) showed
a total long-term budget requirement of $31.5 million. This
is, essentially, for about 80 percent of the communes and
villages of the region; roughly 20 percent of them already have
most of these needs satisfied. On the other hand this figure
does not include other needs, some of them urgent, and many
other good project possibilities. In the period that it would
take to achieve these standards, the government might

therefore spend a total of about $40 million on infrastructure
in the region. This would provide for the other needs and
give communities which are already equipped some activities
necessary to develop local planning capability.

Should this $40 million, an average of $80,000 per commune, be spread over 5, 10, or 25 years? The more immediate question would be how much of it should be expended in
the next five year plan. How much of the total national development plan investment should be devoted to infrastructure for
one region, considered as one sector or subsector? It is
impossible to compute the marginal revenue product of investment in this sector, so it is not possible to trade off with other
sectors at the margin so as to maximize the total return on
development investment.

Three types of considerations can determine the allotment decision. The first is the institutional development needs
of the region. The nature of the agricultural development
program being launched make it necessary that each commune
get significant grants for infrastructure projects, gradually
rising until the district is in stage D or E (see District Plan
for Community Development Project, Chapter 12). In stage
II of rural development, local infrastructure projects are important to the development education process.

The next consideration is the infrastructure needs of the
innovation projects. For our hypothetical Southern Region
they are not serious; the innovations are based on existing
levels of community education facilities and transport access.
In another case these might be serious. The agricultural
development program might require a great deal of feeder
road development. Or planned capital projects might need
concomitant development of local facilities.

Finally, as pointed out at the end of the previous chapter,
infrastructure is a means of compensating backward regions
for which there are not enough feasible purely economic investments. Regions in stage IIa should receive more generous
allotments of funds for research, main roads, and infrastructure than more advanced regions. On the other hand, regions
in stage IIIB or highly commercialized regions should be expected to finance infrastructure from local resources.

Applying these considerations to the Southern Region, one might assume that the country has three other regions, one highly commercialized with plantations and truck farms and two others in stage IIa. The latter two should get more infrastructure funds with lower requirements on minimum local contributions. The agricultural development program for the Southern Region represents roughly $40 million in budget outlays over five years. Let us set the infrastructure allotment for the region at about 40 percent of that figure ($16 million), assuming that this will allow sufficient infrastructure investment in other regions to equalize spending around the country. This will allow an average of about $32,000 per commune (about $6,000 a year). The basic needs of the average commune should thus be met in about 12 to 15 years, or approximately 10 years from the time it enters stage IIb.

NOTES

1. G. Myrdal, Asian Drama (New York: Twentieth Century Fund, 1968), pp. 937-58.

CHAPTER **20** DECENTRALIZED
PLANNING

This chapter deals with planning of infrastructure and
also of agricultural development by villagers, directly or
through their commune and district councils. After reviewing
the advantages and dangers of decentralized planning, the
chapter outlines an infrastructure planning procedure which
can reconcile local preferences with national constraints and
policies. It then surveys the techniques necessary to educate
and guide villagers in playing their full role in development
planning and management. Finally, this chapter considers
how to expand the villagers' responsibility from infrastructure
projects to overall agricultural development.

ADVANTAGES AND PROBLEMS

The importance and the varied functions of local planning
in rural development has been discussed in Chapters 3 and 4
and has been considered at length in Part II. To synthesize
these previous observations, the advantages of decentralizing
planning and of delegating the maximum choice of options to
the villagers are:

Response to Felt Needs--It should be noted that infrastructure projects are the easiest way for the government to
show all the villagers it is sincerely concerned with their
welfare. For political purposes capital projects reach too
few people. Agricultural development programs must sell
villagers on things they originally did not have in mind and
then impose a variety of credit and other disciplines. Pushing
villagers to adopt new techniques and accept new disciplines
does not produce short-run political gains. Schools, clinics,
roads, and embankments do. Relatively small overall outlays

399

can finance such projects in every village. Making these
projects a genuine response to felt needs by basing them on
the express decisions of the villagers builds political support
in two ways. It gives the villagers a feeling of having been
consulted, a feeling that the government respects their intelligence and judgment and values their opinions, and it gives
them the feeling that they are getting what they really want.

Maximum Local Contribution--The more the projects are
a genuine response to felt needs, the more the villagers are
willing to contribute time and money to them, because they have
a proprietary feeling that these are "their projects." Maximizing domestic savings (in the strict economics sense of
effective savings going into investment) is a vital aim of development planning. Getting villagers to raise local taxes or
contribute more voluntary money or labor increases savings
in the same manner as increased national tax rates and
collections.

Trained Local Leadership--As observed in Pakistan (see
Chapter 8), infrastructure projects develop leadership of a
special kind in every nook and cranny of the district. It is
not merely leadership in the political sense of personalities
whose judgment and initiative is accepted by their neighbors.
It is leadership with budding entrepreneurial talent, which
knows how to identify problems, needs, and opportunities,
knows how to get people to work, knows how to handle substantial sums of money, and knows how to tap modern technology. It is leadership that can take entrepreneurial initiative.

Development-Oriented Leadership--Local infrastructure
project management leads people to select leaders who show
project competence, or at least to reject those who do not.
It gives people a chance to judge leaders by performance.
The leadership emerging from such a crucible is likely to be
development-oriented and inclined to support national development-oriented leadership against demagogic opposition.

Broadening Community Cohesiveness--The process of
commune- and district-level popular planning builds up a
pattern of mutually satisfactory give-and-take among people
of different villages. They must agree among themselves
whose projects get done first and must work together on many
projects. They develop confidence in each other and a

willingness to respond to intitative of leaders from outside
their own village. This builds a vital basis for marketing and
other cooperative commercial ventures on a larger scale.

All the above advantages of decentralized planning are
widely accepted, sometimes too readily accepted. Enthusiastic
governments have often launched decentralized development
programs with inadequate preparation with the following
results:

Sham Participation--A district officer is sometimes ordered to get the villagers to plan and submit a development
program on very short notice, with little guidance and no
training of villagers. What is he to do? He and his staff
draw up a program, call in the commune leaders, and read
the proposed program. The commune officers agree to it.
What else can they do? Why should they argue with the district officer about his program? If it fails, they are not hurt.
It's not their program.

Conflicting Programming--As noted in the last chapter a
program dictated by local preferences is not, when consolidated with those of all other locales, going to coincide with
that drawn up by central project planning procedures. Explicit
procedures must be provided to resolve these differences.
When these problems are not anticipated and procedures are
not provided, no one has the authority to modify the ministry
program. This may turn local planning into a sham exercise.

Santa Claus Letters--Rural development is often painted
in utopian terms and presented to the villagers with inspiring
oratory. Villagers are encouraged to think big. Programming
problems and resource constraints are not discussed. The
villagers respond by thinking big and including everything they
can think of in the request for the coming year. The government has presented itself in the guise of Santa Claus and then
finds itself unable to answer the letters sent to #1 North Pole.
Unanswered letters to Santa Claus have been known to create
a credibility gap at the early age of six. Consequently villagers learn to let the words of government officials go in one
ear and out the other.

Competitive Budget Escalation--Local leaders are often
aware of budget constraints but are under the impression,

perhaps correct, that the government is scaling requests down
to available resources by cutting every request by the same
percentage. In other words, the more you ask for the more
you get; other locales are getting a lot by asking for outra-
geous programs. The size of the requests then escalate com-
petitively out of fear that everyone is doing it, and that those
whose requests are reasonable will be penalized.

Brick-and-Mortaritis--The advantages of decentralized
planning can lead to an overemphasis on infrastructure. Development becomes defined simply in terms of brick-and-
mortar projects, things that can be photographed. "See, we
now have a school, a well, etc." This becomes the standard
evaluation of development success. Brick-and-mortar projects of and by themselves may not increase production or
income by one cent. The real payoff comes when an infrastructure program is followed up by an agricultural development program. The latter is hard to plan and hard to staff.
A government must be careful not to succumb to the temptation to try to use success with highly visible brick-and-mortar
projects as a substitute for hard work on agrarian reforms
and agricultural development.

PROGRAMMING METHOD

This section attempts to chart the most efficient way of
reconciling the preferences and priorities of local communities with national policies and resource constraints, as
well as with constraints at the district and provincial level.
The programming system proposed might be called "systematic constraining of hyperbudgets." Briefly, all local units
at the bottom planning echelon submit annual hyperbudgets
(budgets a fixed percentage over what is allocated for infrastructure), and these are cut back at each successively
higher echelon on the basis of nonmonetary constraints at
those echelons.

The procedure is designed for a combination of Malaysian
and Pakistani conditions. As in East Pakistan, it assumes
planning at the commune level with no engineering design
capability or earth-moving equipment below the provincial

level. As in Malaysia, it assumes that many projects even
at the lowest echelon will require engineering design and
equipment support.

Plan Books

Planning should start with a document such as the Malaysian Redbook (described in Chapter 7 and reproduced, in part,
in Appendix D), a priority-sequenced listing and mapping of
projects by type with no annual budget figures (it is a multiyear proposal). The plan book should have a section for each
type of project; transport, water control, education, and
health is the minimum breakdown into categories. Later,
particularly at the district levels, there may be attitional
sections for crop promotion, livestock promotion, agricultural service institutions, and rural industries.

Each section contains a base map, an overlay, and a
project listing. The base map should show the size-category
of villages and current land use in rough terms with a minimum clutter of symbols. The overlay shows existing facilities
and proposed new facilities, with symbols to distinguish actual
vs. proposed and various subcategories of projects. The
listing is by priority and gives for each project, the identification, location, size, cost, and local contribution. This
listing may show a total planned budget for five years, but
there is no reason to break that down into amounts for each
year. That can wait for the annual programming cycle.

The Annual District Request

Once a year at a date sufficiently in advance of the work
season and the new fiscal year (which should be in advance of
the work season), districts and communes submit proposals
for annual programs in the following sequence:

Preliminary Hyperbudget Announcement--To start the
process, the government should authorize a hyperbudget
(maximum budget request) for each commune. Assuming
that the total infrastructure budget for the region for the

coming year is $4 million to be divided among 500 communes, final budgets will average $8,000 per commune, varying according to the size of the commune and the stage of the commune under the Community Development Project (see Chapter 2). A hyperbudget might then be set on the basis of an average of $10,000 per commune, or 25 percent over the expected final allotment. The more the nonmonetary factors are likely to limit expenditures, the higher the hyperbudget should be over the average final budget, thus providing for greater variations based on other factors.

This is often done unsystematically and informally, if only because of competitive budget escalation. Local units will pad budget requests to protect themselves from cuts. What is proposed here is that this process be systematized, that the padding be officially limited, and that the scaling down be based on constraints at various echelons.

Along with the hyperbudget allotment, the government should announce the required local contributions for the year. These will have to be adjusted from year to year to accomodate supply and demand for projects such as schools and clinics, which require a centrally fixed supply of teachers or cadre. If the demand for teachers or equipment proves too high in one year, the government should ration these scarce inputs by raising the prices on the projects that need them. In this way central planning and local choice of projects can adjust through a rough market mechanism.

The Commune Program Request--The commune selects $12,000 worth of projects (net of local contribution) from the top listings in its plan book for transport, water control, education, and health projects. The top projects on the list should be those started or engineered in the previous year. At the bottom of the list, after the $10,000 limit has been reached, there should be a listing of some projects that might be engineered late in the year for construction in the following year.

The result is a consolidation of the separate priority listings for different types of projects. It is a statement of the preferences and priorities of the people of the commune, their consensus of what types of projects should come first and which villages should benefit first. It is an expression of

popular demand, subject to the prices and the minimum local
contribution which the government has set on different types
of projects.

The District Consolidation--At the district level the projects submitted by the communes are consolidated with the
district-level projects in a single priority-sequenced preliminary listing. This should be done by the district officer
together with the district council, consisting of representatives of the commune councils, since it involves some new
priority decisions. This listing is then entered on a schedule
worksheet with a format like that of Figure 20.1, which is
basically similar to the Malaysian format and coding.

Schedule Worksheet   District Yakyak   Fiscal Year 1968

	Project Identification				Project Cost		Schedule			
No.	Commune	Village	Project Type	Size	Nat. Bgt.	Local	Oct.	Nov.	Dec.	Sept.
308	Abab	Caca	Road, 4 mtr.	3.6 k	4,500	900	10%	30%	30%	
511	Dada	Eded	School, Lower	3 rm	3,600	900	D	10%	25%	
295	Fafa		Road, 6 mtr.	5.8 k	3,100	400	D	10%	15%	
Totals										
(max. $110,000)		Total cost			130,000	18,700				
(max. 14/mo.)		Inspection time					5	7	17	3
(max. 10/mo.)		Eng. design time					12	12	9	7
(max. 5/mo.)		Equipment time					1	2	7	0

FIGURE 20.1. Format for a schedule worksheet of district projects.

Letters indicate stages prior to construction and percentages
indicate construction progress. Personnel and equipment
resource requirements are totaled at the bottom, in terms of
man-weeks or team-weeks per month. Preliminary limits
are set which are still hyperbudgeted except for inspection,
which is assumed here as a district-level function. That is,
the maximum inspector time available in the district, including overtime effort, is 14 man-weeks a month. Engineering and design time and equipment time are higher than
the average per district that the province can actually allot.
The maximum funding of $110,000 is also higher than the
$100,000 that would be, on the average, available for a dis-
trict this size (assume 10 communes plus district level
projects).

The District Program Request--The district must now
reduce its consolidated preliminary program to fit within the
preliminary constraints in the bottom left of the worksheet.
It thus makes a first partial approximation or approach to the
final program.

The first step is to reschedule some higher priority jobs
to bring personnel and equipment requirements in the early
months in line with the maximum limits which have been set.
It is the higher priority jobs which cause peak needs early in
the season, so these must be put off to later in the season.
Excess requirements later in the season are then reduced by
eliminating jobs from the program, starting at the bottom of
the list, with the lowest priority projects. Low priority
projects are scratched one by one, until the budget is reduced
to $110,000 and inspection, design, and equipment time is
within the limit for each month. The resulting program is
then sent to the province.

To facilitate this computation, a large spreadsheet might
be used for the schedule worksheet with two columns under
each month, headed "Pre." and "Fin." (for preliminary and
final). As schedule changes are made, the change is entered
in the final column. In this way the whole task of adjusting
the program to the preliminary constraints can be done on
one sheet (actually the total listing may go to two or more
sheets, but in this case it presents no problem).

Provincial Programming

At the provincial level the process is, in effect, continued, a process that combines programming and production
scheduling. This and the hyperbudget set from above are the
features which distinguish the system proposed in this chapter from what is conventionally done. It may seem like added
work to schedule while resources are being programmed, but
since it is a more realistic approach to programming, it saves
a lot of adjustments and frustrations later. The most binding
resources, personnel and equipment, are available in limited
quantities per month, and it is the scheduling that determines
how much is needed each month.

Preparation--Some calculations and allotments must be
made in advance of programming. As noted above, there
must be some notion of district and provincial budgets. The
government must make allotments to the provinces that are
close to final and add up to the total available in the budget.
This will be subject to some modification (see below). There
must also be an allotment of teachers and health cadre.
Finally, the work capacity of the provincial engineering and
construction services must be computed in terms of standard
planning factors (work weeks). It is on this that the engineering and construction hyperallotments to the districts are
based.

Consolidation of Requests--The district requests are put
together with a listing of province-level projects. The summary at the bottom follows the same pattern as the summary
on the district worksheet except that it has a few more items.
It also shows the total number of teachers and health cadre
(or any other personnel requirement of the projects). The
preliminary totals are certain to show a budget requirement
greater than the allotment and are likely to show cadre or
engineering support requirements for certain months greater
than that available.

Adjustment of the Program--The consolidated request is
adjusted to available resources in the same manner as at the
district level. Engineering and construction excess requirements in the early months are reduced to the available capacity by rescheduling work for later months. Excess engineering
and equipment requirements for later months and also excess
financial and cadre requirements are then eliminated by
scratching low-priority projects, working from the bottom up
on the lists.

It should be noted that only jobs with heavy engineering
requirements would be rescheduled at the provincial level.
The basic scheduling of all work, including much of the engineering support, is done at the district level in this system.
The district has planned its schedule on the basis of some
preliminary monthly engineering support outside limits. This
should eliminate the need for rescheduling of large numbers
of projects at the provincial level.

Central Review--As a final step, the central authorities review the results of the provincial programming. Some provinces may be using their financial allotment to the maximum in the proposed programs but may be underutilizing their engineering support capacity. Other provinces may have engineering bottlenecks preventing them from using all their budget allotment. Such minor imbalances can be ignored, but the central authorities can work certain tradeoffs to correct major resource imbalances. It may be possible to transfer engineers and equipment, part-time or full-time from provinces with financial bottlenecks to provinces with engineering bottlenecks. Or funds may be shifted from provinces with engineering bottlenecks to provinces with excess capacity.

Once these adjustments are made, revised final budgets and schedules are returned to the districts.

Feedback and Follow-through

At this point nothing can be said to improve on the reporting practices in Malaysia and Pakistan. For projects under commune control, the East Pakistani formats are best. For district-level schedule and reporting summaries, the Malaysian formats are best. A combination of the Pakistani individual project schedule forms and the Malaysian project-category schedule and reporting forms should provide effective feedback. Team tours, as in Malaysia, should provide effective troubleshooting and evaluation.

GUIDANCE

The programming system described above can avoid a great deal of confusion and frustration, but it must be supported by thorough guidance and training. The greater the number of participants in the planning process, the more staff work the central planners have to do preparing guidelines, instructions, standards, and training materials. Effective guidance must consist of well-written manuals, adequate training of cadre and farm leaders, and a well-planned "development curriculum," a sequence of introducing local planning that moves from the simple to the complex.

The Project Guidebook

The basic facts needed for local infrastructure planning should be presented in one easy-to-use reference manual. It should have a section on planning procedures in general and a section on projects, with a sheet for each type of project. It may be in loose-leaf form with updatings of individual pages as needed or in the form of a booklet, revised at the beginning of each budgeting cycle. The Malaysian Redbook is, in a sense, such a guide; its pages give details about special government policies and requirements on different types of projects. If farmers are to participate fully and lower-level cadre are to be involved, more detail is needed. It should be noted, however, that any guidebook put out is only a reference document, not a substitute for training. Thorough training, described below, must precede the use of such a book.

Figure 20.2 is an example of one such project sheet. The topic headings in the figure provide a good general outline for any project guidance:

Objective--The government policy on any type of project should include some type of minimum service standard, some level of service that it is trying to achieve.

Policies--The conditions of project eligibility not mentioned above and other special government policies toward a type of project should be explained, particularly the government approach to priorities.

Standard Design--Only the numbers of the government documents which contain the standard designs are needed. Details, such as overall size, which affects basic planning decisions should be included.

Standard Costs--Certain minimum details are needed for planning; they should be expressed in the simplest possible formulas: So much per square meter, so much per room,

PROJECT PLANNING GUIDE: LOWER PRIMARY SCHOOLS
MNE-MRD/68/502 1May68

Objective——1 lower primary school per village, minimum 3 classrooms
except villages with less than 40 school-age children or
villages within 1 kilometer of another village school.

Policies——Villages must provide free housing for teachers and adequate
maintenance and book replacement funds (see below).
Priority will be given to villages offering the greatest local
contribution over the minimum.

Standard——35 m.^{2} per classroom, minimum 100 m.^{2}
Design   see circulars MinEd/DC/63-281 & 66-340

Standard——Construction $25 per sq. mtr. = $2,500 + $700 per additional
Costs   classroom, excluding site & foundation (38% labor cost)
Furniture & Equipment $400 + 100 per added classroom
Textbooks $.40 per child

Minimum——Cleared site .4 hectare minimum and level foundation
Village   15% of construction cost, in cash or labor valued at $.40/day
Contri-   50% of furniture & equipment budget, including furniture made
bution   to MinEd specifications in the village.

Mainte-——See circular MinEd/DC/67-109
nance   Village must set up a fund of $20 per year per classroom
minimum for repair cash expenses and replacement of textbooks.

Admini-——Construction: an elected committee of at least 9 members must
stration   meet at least every 10 days and report to the district
Operation: an elected committee of at least 5 members must
meet at least once a month and report to the district

Application——6 months before the fiscal year for which construction is contemplated the Commune Council must send the following information to the Provincial Education Inspector, certified by
the District Chief:
a) name & location of the village
b) list of school-age children & educational status
c) map & drawing of the site
d) members of the construction or operation committee
If approved by the PEI, project can be included in the annual
district budget request.

Schedule   Order of Materiel: 9 weeks before construction starts
Factors   Foundation: 4 weeks or 90 mandays per classroom
Walls & Roof: 10 weeks or 300 mandays per classroom
Finishing: 6 weeks or 140 mandays per classroom

FIGURE 20.2. Sample project planning sheet for a local project guidebook.

so much per 100 meters of road length, etc. Total and labor
costs (possibly man-days), should also be noted.

It is very important to keep standard cost figures up to
date and to inform locales how far they can go over these costs
to cover local factors causing higher prices or expenses. In
a period of rising prices it may happen that all the bids or
estimates on jobs may be substantially over standard and require high-level special approval if standards are not revised
frequently. This can create a very serious bottleneck, as
local projects pile up on the desk of some director-general or
minister for approval of costs in excess of standard estimates.
Adequate and up-to-date guidance can ensure that responsibility for approving estimates is delegated to someone at the
province, or preferably the district, level.

Minimum Village Contribution--In addition to requiring
the villagers to provide a percentage or share of the overall
cost or labor requirement, it is advisable to assign them
some more specific responsibilities. Selection of sites should
be a village responsibility on village-level projects, including
roads, so as to avoid long-drawn-out haggling between individual owners and the central government over compensation.
Villagers among themselves can work out land compensations
much more easily. Clearly definable tasks that involve only
labor can also be left completely to the village, such as preparation of the foundation. Care must be taken, however, not
to set such a high minimum contribution that the projects are
priced out of the market.

Maintenance--Community performance should be spot-
checked and made the basis of further grants. If the local
community does not maintain its projects, the district can do
it directly or by contract and deduct the cost from the allotment for new infrastructure for that commune.

Administration--Project committees should be established
to construct projects and to operate or maintain them afterwards. In East Pakistan the construction committees meet
regularly at the district (thana) office to submit progress reports and pick up advances for wages. Regular meetings permit district officers and other cadre to schedule frequent
contacts with village leaders.

Application--The application cited here should be for
verifying the eligibility of a project; the final approval and
allotment comes through the programming process. In the
example given in Figure 20.2, information is required to
verify that there are sufficient eligible children, that there is
no other school within one kilometer, and that a site has been
committed.

It is important to define carefully the basis of project
eligibility and to leave the absolute minimum to the discretion
of provincial or local officers. Even at the expense of making
the standards excessively mechanical, eligibility of a project
should be automatic upon fulfillment of the written specified
conditions. A number of dangers can arise from giving officials broad discretion on project eligibility. They may be
open to corruption. Approval may be delayed while officials
agonize over choices which may earn them enemies in some
villages. Villagers may conclude that their own so-called
freedom of choice of projects is a sham.

Schedule Factors--Some basic timing factors are needed
for schedule planning. The main work phases here are given
standard times in terms of the absolute minimum time (4
weeks, etc.) or the amount of labor available (90 man-days
per classroom, etc.). The commune can thus make some
judgment about how much labor will be available to work on
the project and thus how fast it can be done.

Some other topics not relevant to this type of project may
be relevant on others. On water control and other projects
complementary facilities may be required. Some projects
may have other projects as essential prerequisites. A marketplace may need some minimum road connections, for
example.

Training

Both general orientation and specific project management
training is needed. The discussion below focuses on village
leader training, but it should be understood that cadre need
the same background and guidance.

General Orientation--Community development or "animation rurale" programs generally provide for general-purpose village leader training sessions of from three days to two weeks. The training covers three general subjects.

The first is the idea of development through self-help and through the government services available to the village. From this should come a general understanding that government help is available but that the village must organize properly for it.

The second is what the French call "étude de milieu," the ability to observe and evaluate accurately the economic and social conditions of one's own village. This may be imparted by a group visit to a village during the training session, as is done in Senegal, or by a survey of the villages after training, as in Pakistan. Ideally, a large number of villagers should participate by filling out survey forms on sections of their village, if illiteracy does not preclude this.

The third and most important aspect of the training might be labeled committee problem-oriented decision, or the ability of a committee to identify the problems of a community, to set priorities on such problems, and to formulate corrective action programs. This must be done by open-ended discussion in groups, with a moderate amount of guidance by a cadre trained in techniques of group discussion.

Problems and action programs do not fall into neat matching categories, and attempts to structure an action program along problem lines can be rather artificial. Farmers may first identify their problem as lack of income; subsequently they may break that problem down into low yields, poor water control, low prices, and poor cultural practices. The structure of action programs to correct these problems would be along these lines: flood control, which helps yields; roads, which help prices and use of production inputs; and demonstrations, which affect yields, cultural practices, and use of water. Nevertheless, it is important that planning start with problem identification so that village leaders understand fully why they want certain programs.

Committee Training--The members of a commune council must, in addition to general orientation, receive training

in council procedures, budgeting, reporting, parliamentary
rules, etc. The job of secretary to a multipurpose, multi-
village council is too difficult for an amateur; a commune
level cadre, such as a union assistant in East Pakistan, must
take that responsibility.

In addition, individual project committees must be
trained in making estimates, designs, costs, schedules, etc.,
in organizing and supervising work groups, in keeping cash
records, in computing work accomplished and pay due, and in
reporting progress. The secretaries of these committees
must receive extra training.

Here one may note another paradox of rural development.
Committees and reports are a necessary evil in general administration, to be kept to a minimum. Committee participation and report-writing by villagers is good in itself. In
addition to building community cohesiveness and teaching villagers to work and think together, it advances their general
education and forces them to use literacy skills, thus helping
prevent backsliding into the functional illiteracy which is
common in some countries. Decision-oriented argument
sharpens their ability to think logically. Report-writing
builds further literacy skills; indeed a few years of active
committee participation may be the equivalent of another year
of secondary education. The training imparted by participation in the projects may prove, in some cases, more beneficial than the actual project itself.

The Development Curriculum

Local planning should start as simply as possible and
then gradually become more and more complex. There are
many ways of doing this.

Planning can start at the village level and then move up
to the commune level. Conversely, it can start at the district level, with consultation of village leaders before program drafting, and then gradually be delegated to a commune
council. The commune is the level toward which development
planning should tend, but it requires village leader training
and experience.

Planning may start with a one- or two-year horizon and
then move on to a five-year or longer plan. It may start with
scattered projects to give the villagers some experience with
project management and then move on to problem-oriented
integrated thinking about village needs. It may start with a
simple listing of projects and then develop into a district and
commune plan book. It may start with consultation of traditional commune leaders and later include broader participation.

Planning and village responsibility may start with simple
earthwork projects and then move on to structures requiring
professional design. It is advisable to limit the number of
types of projects at the start but to add more types every year.
After a few years directly productive projects should be included in the program, as described in the next section.

LOCAL AGRICULTURAL
DEVELOPMENT PLANNING

After infrastructure planning, the next step in the development curriculum is agricultural development planning by the
farmers themselves.

Activities and Considerations

Certain preparations are necessary. First, there must
be a more sophisticated étude de milieu, a survey of actual
crop yields, acreage, and labor resources. At some point
a soil survey and engineered land use plan may be needed.
Second, there must be agricultural cadre permanently at the
commune level; further agricultural training of general-
purpose cadre may fill this gap. Third, there must be proven
innovations on a variety of crops for the region. Single- or
two-crop programs like those in Senegal and Madagascar (see
Chapter 9) do not provide meaningful options for local planning.

The easiest starting point is a farmer-planned demonstration program. Within the framework of a four-crop demonstration target for each village, farmers may exercise options

on what secondary crops they would prefer to try. From there the farmers can move on to planning new farm enterprises for the district or the commune. Any new farm enterprise in a locale requires a certain minimum number of initial producers to permit economic services, economic extension, supply, credit, and marketing servicing. Government support for such new enterprises should be conditional on a minimum number of farmers in each commune signing up to participate.

Exploitation of marginal lands should be planned by the farmers jointly. This may require engineering support, like the commune land use plans envisioned on line 26 of Form A-9 in Appendix A. It may require contract or custom tractor work. It may require soil conservation structures.

Community production enterprises (community fishponds, seed beds, certified seed production, livestock breeding, or silk raising) are difficult to organize and sustain but often important. In East Pakistan the breeding of fish in community tanks is probably the best potential source of increased protein production. In Malaysia village seed beds are considered to have important economies in the production of new high-yielding varieties. In Korea community silk cocoon breeding has been an important source of sideline income.

Yet community production has been a failure in many places because it is difficult to fix responsibility for year-round voluntary work contributions and difficult to maintain work quality when responsibility is widely spread. Where community enterprises require year-round operation (as con-trasted to a community rice seed bed), individuals should be paid by the community to operate them. Planning such enter-prises, however, is part of the total community planning effort.

Finally, multipurpose cooperatives require community planning once they are on their feet. Each new business line, each new supply product item or crop marketing line that the cooperative takes on requires a broad selling effort in the vil-lages. The best way to accomplish such broad selling is through the farmer planning process. Farmer meetings at district, commune, and village levels should discuss the various business options open to cooperatives. They should discuss the pros and cons of new products and new farm en-terprises. More will be said on this in Chapter 24. When the

farmers have sold themselves and each other on a new business line, it can expect a reasonably good volume.

Local Agricultural Planning Procedures

Local agricultural development activities are only partly
articulated in the form of discrete physical projects, as in
infrastructure. They take a variety of forms:

Budgeted activities--Demonstrations and training sessions.

Land Development Projects--Group clearing and conservation schemes based on community land use plans.

Crop Promotion Targets--Targets for new enterprise
participation or new higher yields on traditional crops based
on adoption of innovations.

Group Production Projects--Community-owned fishponds,
certified breedstock or seed production, etc.

Cooperative New Business Lines--New supply or marketing lines.

Planning can best be organized by permanent subcommittees for field crops, horticulture, livestock, irrigation,
land use, etc. These committees can then consider long-
range targets, long-range objectives for yields, crop acre-
ages, and the next year's activities. For some activities an
ad hoc committee may be advisable. In the hypothetical
Southern Region Program in Appendix A there are three principle new enterprises, sorghum, hogs, and cotton. A commune with such a new enterprise should have a sorghum or
hog committee while the program is getting under way, in
order to solicit participants, arrange meetings with extension
specialists, establish indents for production supplies, organize credit groups, schedule production deliveries, etc.

There are two approaches to the documentation of such
plans. One is the annual written plan. On Taiwan such a
plan is an integral part of the required annual farmers association program, with quantitative targets and a budget figure

attached to each subactivity. Another approach is to incorporate this planning into the plan book.

The plan book, in that case, has additional sections on
land development, field crops, horticulture, livestock, and
possibly fishponds. The land development map shows present
and projected irrigation, flood control embankments, and marginal land clearing schemes and lists proposed projects. The
field crop map has symbols to indicate present and targeted production and yields by villages, and proposed demonstrations.
This is accompanied by a listing, by village, of planned demonstrations, supply requirements, and cooperative marketing
volume. This section might be further subdivided into a primary and secondary crop section. Other sections of the book
are handled in the same manner.

As prices change and new technical developments are extended, the agriculture section of the plan book must be revised.

One of the important advantages of such group planning is
that the farmers look at themselves not just as individual businesses but as a consolidated business organization. They look
at, say, a potential tomato enterprise not just in terms of how
it fits in with their individual farm system but in terms of
regular truck deliveries from the commune or the district to
the metropolis, and in terms of cut rates on volume purchases
of pesticides. They look, in brief, at the entire business picture, because only on the commune or district level can the
entire business picture be organized.

Successful development must produce not only a rising
GNP but also a rising GNE (gross national entrepreneurship).
By getting large numbers of farmers involved meaningfully in
the total range of development and business decisions, a
rising GNE is generated. The accent, however, must be on
meaningful involvement and responsible decisions over meaningful options. This requires increasingly comprehensive
institutional coverage, an increasing variety of feasible infrastructure and innovation activities, and a carefully planned
development curriculum.

Decentralized development planning and management activities are the breeding ground for development-oriented
local political leadership. The democratically elected

members of the local boards acquire through their activities the two essentials of a political leadership group: loyalty and solidarity. By getting things done for their communities they individually acquire a loyal following. Out of their give-and-take on board activities and their mutual favors and understanding, the members acquire a group solidarity.

Any party or administration seeking the vote of these locales must appeal to the local development leaders. Since the position of these local leaders is based on democracy and development (particularly on development performance), demagogic appeals, ideology, and slogans are not what interest them. To maintain their position they need a national administration that can perform on development and sustain local performance. Barring serious ethnic conflicts or inaction on essential reforms, an administration which properly supports local development institutions can thus be assured of solid democratic support.

PART V: SPECIAL TECHNIQUES & PROBLEMS

CHAPTER 21   PLAN NARRATIVES

Perhaps the most distinctive feature of the planning system of this book is the sharp separation between plan quantification and scheduling and plan description and narration.
Part III presented a complete planning system that involved
no narrative documents. Not only the programming but the
strategy was documented in tabular-graphic form. The
closest form to a narrative was Form A-5, and that was not
a full narrative but only a bare-bones outline of the requirements and potential of an innovation package.

All this is rather unusual. Most, if not almost all, development planning documentation formats involve a combination of narrative, setting forth the objectives and activities
of the project, and tables that support the text.

This book has undertaken to develop a planning system
without narrative documents for several reasons. The main
reason is compactness, a striving for all-on-one-sheet documentation, which was stressed at the end of Chapter 5. Narrative documentation has other disadvantages in addition to
bulk. It cannot be followed up and enforced as can decisions
in tabular-graphic form. It can be used to avoid quantification;
tabular-graphic forms require complete quantification. Quantification does not give the whole story of development activity,
of course, and some narrative form is needed. Part III recommended the use of briefings and oral presentations for presenting the qualitative aspects of plans. This at times is
more efficient than narrative documentation.

Narrative documentation does, however, have its place
in planning. Its role, particularly vis-a-vis briefings, will
depend partly on the nature of the issues and problems of
programs and partly on the authorization procedure and the
personalities and working habits of the authorities. This

chapter first considers what narratives are expected to accomplish and then looks at some rules and guides for plan
narratives, oral and written.

THE FUNCTION OF NARRATIVE

In any planning system narrative supplements quantification. Decisions will focus on the figures. Even if the figures are scattered through a narrative, the authority will tend
to scan the document for figures, often skimming over the
rest. Frequently the figure work on the output side in a plan
document is meager--the object of the activity being expressed
as "to expand and improve the department of ... " In that case the
discussion tends to revolve almost completely around the input side, which has to be quantified. If there are organizational problems, the discussion may tend to focus on qualitative
problems, but generally the narrative supplements and fleshes
out the figure work.

There are some important aspects of plans that cannot be
communicated efficiently in tabular-graphic form. Presenting
these aspects is the essential function of narrative. There are
seven such aspects.

1. Cadre routines, the particular services the cadre perform and the way they go about their business--their standard
operation procedures.

2. Conditions of servicing, the policies defining the clientele, and the participants, and the rules and contingencies
under which they are to be serviced by the cadre.

3. Authority and responsibility, or who is in charge of
what, and who has delegated authority to decide what.

4. Qualitative outputs and inputs, the social and political
results anticipated from a project, and the social and political
conditions that are essential to its success.

5. Institutional changes and reforms, the organizational
changes and legislative measures which must be taken

(tabular-graphic forms can show the deadlines for these measures but not their contents).

     6. <u>Contingencies and probabilities</u>, i.e., identification of
those variables whose values are uncertain or highly dependent
on other uncertainties.

     7. <u>Points of emphasis and key relationships</u> in the figure
work.

     These aspects do not always have to be written down in
plan documents. They may be known to all if the authority has
been delegated to a small group closely involved in the program. They may be known from previous documents. Points
1 to 3 may have been made known by the manual of operations.

     Under certain conditions these aspects may be better
communicated by a briefing than by a written document.
Briefing is better if the relevant information on points 1
through 5 is simple and obvious. This information can best be
communicated by a document in some cases, but points 6 and
7 can best be presented in a briefing. If there have been very
few changes on points 1 through 5 since the last major plan review and document revision, it may be clearer to point out the
changes orally, rather than to prepare new descriptive documents. Briefings may also be preferable if the authorities
have an aversion to reading long documents.

     The written description is better if there is a great deal
of relevant new detail to be communicated about points 1
through 5. It is also better if the authorities are accustomed
to studying lengthy reports at leisure and are happy with this
form of presentation.

     When a written description is called for, however, one
may strongly recommend that it be done as a supplement to
the tabular-graphic forms in Appendix A and discussed in Part
III. Quantification is still the cutting edge of decision. Narrative is communication; it is not a good medium of decision.
With fully quantified tabular-graphic decision documents it is
easy to set up a management-by-exception, planned-vs.-actual
reporting system (as in Chapter 17). Such a feedback system
is enormously difficult, if not impossible, with conventional
narrative plan documents.

THE ART OF BRIEFING

Chapters 14 and 16 alluded briefly to the role of oral presentation of tabular-graphic forms in strategy planning. Most of the forms in Appendix A are designed for presentation in a briefing. As mentioned in previous chapters, a conference room equipped for decision-making should have an overhead projector and a screen. The room should be arranged so that discussion can focus on a table projected on a screen. The pointer then becomes a potent instrument of communication.

Forms A-1 to A-9 require mainly interpretive briefing, to make them clear to the conference participant encountering them for the first time and to point out the highlights. Form A-8, the Local Development Strategy Diagram, requires a good deal of interpretation, of course. Form A-7, the Agricultural Services Structure Analysis, also requires a good deal of interpretation. A moderator can use the A-7 forms to illustrate gaps in the present organizational structure and contemplated changes. The form shows quite graphically how gaps are to be filled in.

The programming documents A-10, A-11, and A-16 are particularly designed for presentation at briefings, although they are self-explanatory to anyone generally familiar with this type of format.

Planning is an abstraction of reality; the art of planning consists in part of giving as vivid an image of reality as possible with the least number of brush strokes. A procedure is given below for briefing a conference from the forms presented in Appendix A. Such a briefing should give the conferees a swift and efficient image of the realities of the activity and leave them with a visual sense of the dynamics of its development.

1. Start with the modular and then present the project plan and the program summary. If the whole program is being presented, Form A-9, the Local Development Activity and Staffing Table, is a good starting point. District-level activities can be understood without reference to regionwide totals; regionwide figures cannot be understood unless we know what happens down near the farmer.

2. <u>Identify the relevant variables</u> at the start, working
from the top of the form to the bottom. It may be necessary
to define the output variables carefully. Point out which are
the most important pacing factors. Finally point out the essential inputs and the structure of the budget.

3. <u>Point out the evolution of the pacing factors</u>, discussing their limits and some of the important factors that govern
their growth.

4. <u>Relate the pacing factors to the outputs</u>. Point out how
the outputs derive from the pacing factors. Discuss the relating coefficients and their derivation.

5. <u>Point out the growth of the outputs</u> and their relationship to total needs.

6. <u>Show the derivation of other inputs</u> and the key coefficients relating the outputs to the budget.

7. <u>Discuss the key elements making up the budget</u> and
their determinants.

8. <u>Point out the cost-benefit relationships</u>.

9. <u>Discuss the effect on outputs of increases or decreases</u>
in constrained inputs. Show what a budget or personnel cut
(or increase) will do.

Each of the above points can be executed with a few well-
chosen sentences. The pattern of the presentation and the
probable movement of the pointer is shown graphically in
Figure 21.1.

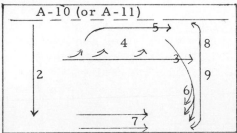

FIGURE 21.1. The pattern of a briefing on Forms A-10,
A-11, and A-16.

The numbers correspond to the above steps of the briefing
procedure. It is in this fashion that one covers the all-on-one-
sheet plan in such a way as to show its dynamics. If properly
done, the conferees will plunge immediately into a discussion
of the key issues. The project manager can judge the success
of his presentation by the cogency of the issues discussed.

THE ART OF PROJECT
DESCRIPTION DOCUMENTS

Some governments have a well-defined outline that all
project description documents must follow. Others allow for
wide variations in format and style. The following general
principles can be applied in toto if no rigid outline is specified, or in partu if an outline is specified. A central planning
staff seeking to guide project staffs in the preparation of
project descriptions might use this section as a starting point
for a guidance circular. Form A-12 of Appendix A is a sample
of the result that might be expected.*

Basic Principles

These techniques have two basic objectives: to communicate effectively and to relieve the tedium inherent in these
dull, dry, unavoidably abstract documents.

Consistent Pattern--If all project descriptions follow the
same outline, the reader will know where to look for what.

Short Paragraphs--Because planning documents in any
language are so dull and dry, they are hard to follow. Di-
viding the content into short paragraphs helps relieve the
tedium and make the document easier to follow.

---

*The Farmers Association Project was chosen as the
subject because it is the most complex project in the program
of the so-called Southern Region.

Frequent Headings--The document should consist of short numbered or lettered sections, with underlined headings or half-underlined lead-in phrases, such as:

1. Objectives
    a. To determine the land potential, etc.
    b. To guide farmers in best use of land, etc.

Frequent headings serve three purposes. (1) They give the close reader a good sense of direction; he always has some feeling of what a section of the document is driving at. (2) They make it possible for a hurried reader to skim through the document; all plan documents should be designed for skimming as well as close reading. (3) They make it possible for conferees to refer back to points in the document and find them easily.

Short Sentences--In any language unrelieved abstraction plus long sentences adds up to foggy writing that must be reread, sentence-for-sentence, several times to get the meaning. Planning documents cannot avoid unrelieved abstraction, but they can dissipate the fog by breaking up some sentences. Where a long sentence is unavoidable, it should be followed by a short sentence.

A related problem in English and some other languages, such as Hindi, is the use of big words. A sequence of polysyllables such as "systematized management capability for functional incremental logistical flexibility" can leave the reader in a total fog (even when the phrase means something, which the above example does not). Clusters of polysyllables should be avoided. Short words should be substituted for long words wherever possible. If long words cannot be avoided, the average sentence length should be reduced.

Identified Actors--A project description should identify clearly who does what. Instead of "trainees are selected," the narrative should read: "The Commune Council selects the trainees."

Absence of Nonstatements--Cover-the-waterfront statements often creep into project documents, such as "Emphasis will be placed on improvement of traditional crop cultivation practices, introduction of new crops, and introduction of new

livestock varieties." Or "Attention will be given to improved
training at district, commune, and village levels." Such
statements tell the reader nothing. Emphasis on everything
is emphasis on nothing. The writer is not obliged to tell the
reader of a plan document that he has forgotten no possibilities;
he is obliged to tell the reader what the main line of attack
will be.

No Quantification--Important as they are, numbers should
be left out of the project description. Figure work gets out of
date rapidly. Tables usually have to be revised several times
during the course of a project review; during project operation
they must be revised a few times a year if they are to continue to reflect reality. The nonquantitative aspects have more
durability. A project description which has avoided quantification can still be valid a year later. A description should be
considered as a supplement to the tabular documents.

It is not always possible to hold to this rule. Authorities
often insist on narratives with all the figures in them. The
result, however, is all too often disregarded documents, that
are old and obsolete five months later and that no one has the
time to bring up to date.

Local Operation Described First--The principle of from-
the-bottom-up exposition applies to written descriptions as it
does to oral presentation and for the same reasons.

A Suggested Project Description Outline

A sample of a narrative following this outline will be
found in Appendix A (Form A-12). The format applies to all
institutional projects, in agriculture and complementary sectors. It does not apply to crop promotion projects, for which
an amplification of Form A-4 is probably the best pattern for
a narrative.

Objectives--The purposes of a project can best be presented by a series of brief statements with half-underlined
lead-in phrases, preceded by a short description of the general nature of the project, as in the following:

1. Objectives
   This project establishes yakyak, in order to:
   a. Achieve yakyak, which . . .
   b. Promote yekyek, such as . . .
   c. Build yukyuk, by . . .

Local Operation--Now comes the most difficult and important part of the project description, the presentation of
what goes on. Anyone responsible for drafting a project
description faces a formidable task of arranging details of a
wide variety of component actions into a narrative that will
be clear and will properly reflect the interrelations of all
these actions. The chronological sequence may confuse
logical interrelationships; the logical sequence may confuse
the chronology. The following approach may simplify and
lighten the drafting process.

The narrative should be divided into a series of short
paragraphs, each describing one type of action. Each should
be headed by a verb followed by an object. For the Family
Planning Project description (Chapter 18), for example, the
list of topical headlines for the paragraphs might read:

   a. Recruit & Train District FP Staff
   b. Train Commune Midwife
   c. Equip District Clinic
   d. Organize Supply & Propaganda Distribution
   e. Organize Village Meetings
   f. Refer Couples for Consultation
   g. Follow up Participants

The actions are thus arranged in rough chronological order.
One can conceive of most rural development activities as
being composed of a limited number of types of actions. The
following checklist may be of use as a starting point for the
person doing the drafting:

   a. Survey * * *
   b. Plan * * *
   c. Recruit * * *
   d. Train * * *
   e. Organize * * *
   f. Build * * *
   g. Equip * * *

  h. <u>Distribute</u> * * *
  i. <u>Collect</u> * * *
  j. <u>Follow up</u> * * *

Only some of the points will be relevant. Some of the verbs
may have to be modified, of course.

  The following is a checklist covering the contents of each
paragraph. The first item is absolutely essential; the others
should be covered when relevant.

   Who does what?
   Why is the action important?
   Who has overall responsibility?
   What other projects and agencies are involved?
   How is the action financed and equipped (if not
    told elsewhere)?
   What aspects of the action are particularly
    critical?

  <u>Project Development</u>--Finally one writes a chronology of
the project, with one paragraph (more if necessary) for each
year of the life of the project. Essentially these paragraphs
tell what stages are in the point, line, and network phases
each year, and what is going on back at headquarters and back
in the capital. They describe the evolution of the planning, the
financing, the legislation, and the central staffing.

  Note that details need not be repeated. If certain types of
planning and financing take place each year, only the first
cycle need be mentioned. This section of the description should
tell of the new developments that take place each year.

OTHER WRITTEN DESCRIPTIONS

  At times a narrative description of a complete sector or
subsector program is required. For such a document the
outline for a briefing presented in the second section of this
chapter should serve as a guide to organization of the material.
One element should be added, however, at the beginning: the
magnitude of the problem. The document should start with a

brief discussion of the needs of the people or the overall development potential of the area or the sector, plus a few words
on the present coverage of services.

In rural development, a document describing any sector
or region should first present the needs and the program in
terms of one locale. This is a principle the author learned
the hard way. For a long time he was dissatisfied with the
lack of clarity in his own descriptive documents, until he dis-
covered this editing device.

The necessity for explaining activity in terms of one locale is a distinctive feature shared by all rural development
projects and programs, in whatever sector. In contrast to
other development activities, they must be described from
the bottom up.

CHAPTER **22** SCHEDULING BY
SIMPLIFIED PROGRAM
EVALUATION REVIEW
TECHNIQUE

It is strongly possible that more development plans fall short of hopes and expectations due to delays than due to lack of resources. Most national development plans do not spend all the money originally planned for them, in spite of cost rises. More often than not, projects start late and finish late. This is particularly true in the point and line phases.

The possible impact of delays can be clearly seen on Form A-16 in Appendix A, the regional Program Summary. Note what would happen if the point phase of stage C were postponed for a year. The income increase planned for 1971 would not be realized until 1972. For want of activity in one district in 1968 the final increase in income would be less than 50 percent of plan.

Problems of delay are also shared by developed nations, where projects vital to national interests often fall far behind schedule. Large engineering and research and development projects have all and more of the scheduling headaches of rural development projects in the point and line phases. In the late 1950's it became apparent that existing production scheduling techniques such as Gantt charts, were inadequate to cope with the complexities of these projects.

In 1957-58 two new techniques based on a network concept of activity relationships were developed simultaneously. The U.S. Navy, assisted by the firm of Booz, Allen, and Hamilton, developed PERT (Program Evaluation Review Technique) for management of the research and development of the Polaris weapons system. Du Pont, assisted by Sperry-Rand Corporation, developed CPM (Critical Path Method) for controlling plant construction. The logic of the two systems is basically the same. This chapter presents a simplified networking procedure that borrows (and also eliminates) concepts from both systems. The label PERT is used to identify the simplified procedure, since PERT, perhaps because of its catchy title, is much the better known of the two systems.

Use of the two techniques has spread rapidly. PERT is used heavily in research and development work, particularly in the development of large weapons systems and their components, where each element is characterized by a high degree of uncertainty. CPM is used largely in construction; its use has spread to large capital projects in developing nations. Many refinements and elaborations have been made on the two systems, particularly in the handling of cost considerations.

In 1966 the author made what apparently was the first application of PERT to rural development. Results were good. Application to rural development required, however, some simplification of usual PERT practice and also some innovations in the techniques of work packaging and PERT display.

RURAL DEVELOPMENT
SCHEDULING PROBLEMS

The Campaign

At the end of Chapter 2 it was noted that innovations and institutions must move forward together in well-coordinated campaigns. Institutions develop on the basis of innovation projects. These innovations have planting season and harvesting season deadlines which all the necessary institutional services must be carefully timed to meet. This is the nature of our "Southern Region" program. On Form A-8 of Appendix A, the Local Development Strategy Diagram, stages C, D, and E are complexes of interdependent institutional developments and new innovations.

Each of these three key stages of the program can thus be conceived as a set of campaigns. At stage C, for example,

there is a campaign necessary to provide farm supplies for
crop project Rice 1. It requires establishment of farmers
associations, deployment of loan cadre, and coordinated efforts of community development and extension cadre. There
is also a campaign to initiate demonstration of sorghum at
stage C. In stage D there is a complex campaign to initiate
sorghum production (involving the introduction of the commune
land use plan and contract land clearing and plowing) and the
first medium-term loans.

Each of these coordinated efforts involves careful scheduling of planning, staff recruitment, cadre recruitment, and
training, fund requests and releases, supply and equipment
procurement, farm leader training, canvassing of villagers,
and possibly major decrees or legislation. As these activities
move from the point to the line and network phases, new kinds
of staff efforts are required which involve scheduling substantially different from the previous phase. Thus each new
development requires three successive campaigns. After the
first season in the work phase, the campaign concept of scheduling no longer applies. Scheduling problems become more
routine; the problem becomes one of resource allocation rather
than time allocation.

Military and aerospace analogies are useful here. Like
a military campaign, a variety of different organizational
units must be coordinated. Each must receive battle orders
that will bring it on the objective at the right time. Like an
aerospace effort, all necessary rural services must be ready
to go when the innovation is launched. It is no wonder then,
that the type of network scheduling used in aerospace efforts
is applicable to rural development. It should be noted that
these techniques--and this concept of the campaign--apply not
only to agriculture in rural development but to infrastructure
and other sectors as well.

Scheduling Pathology

Having looked at the basic nature of the scheduling problem, one may now take a look at some of the things that can
and, indeed, do go wrong with the scheduling of rural development, largely due to lack of working method.

Unrealistic Lead Times--The most common error is totally inadequate lead time allowances for design, procurement, recruitment, canvassing, etc. Plans are set for activities in the next fiscal year which would require preparations which should have started months ago. The preparation for a campaign to end in April must generally start the previous June.

Neglected Steps--Planning often fails to take into account all the tasks that must be accomplished to reach a target. Particularly easy to forget are the many time-consuming bureaucratic clearances necessary for most development actions and the various echelons of approval necessary for designs, fund releases, personnel assignments, contracts, etc.

Uncoordinated Schedules--Rural development generally requires cooperation of diverse agencies. Frequently agencies agree whole-heartedly to cooperate on a campaign but do not examine the scheduling carefully. Then when the cadre of a particular agency are most needed on a campaign, they are tied up with other activities.

Ignored Deadlines--The main seasonal deadlines are generally obvious to everyone. There are other externally determined deadlines that a campaign schedule must observe, such as annual budget submissions, initial quarterly fund releases, and monthly or quarterly meetings of important bodies. If such deadlines are missed, only an extraordinary action of the council of ministers can get the activity back on schedule, since the agenda of the council of ministers is often booked long in advance.

Indecision--A great many deadlines are missed because of simple indecision. A plan is put before a committee and opposition is voiced. Instead of voting to accept the plan, reject the plan, or modify the plan, the committee postpones action till the meeting next month. By that time it is too late to launch a program for the coming season. Or the bids on a contract are all higher than the planning estimate. Should a bid be accepted or should new bids be asked? The provincial engineer is afraid to make a decision; he leaves the decision to his superior, who in turn leaves it to his superior, etc. All action comes to a halt while the decision wanders about, searching for a decision-maker.

<u>Lack of Critical Troubleshooting</u>--Most successful oper-
ations work out only because the responsible manager puts in
extra time, extra personnel, and extra-tough decisions when
things go wrong, as they always do. To do this the manager
must be aware of the critical points of the schedule. He needs
a scheduling working method.

PERT PRINCIPLES

Networking

A project or a campaign is conceived as a <u>network</u> of
<u>events</u> connected by <u>activities</u>. The reader is advised at this
point to examine Figure 22.1 (disregarding the numbers on it
for the moment), which represents a small project, the installation of a pilot commune maternity clinic. The circles
are events and the arrows are activities. The circles are
moments in time; the arrows are periods of time (weeks in
this case). This is a very important distinction to make if we
are not to be confused.

Events are usually starting points of activities ("contract
let" or "begin training" or "clinic functions") or end-points
("clinic designed" or "furniture arrived" or "structure completed"). Actually an event such as "contract let" is in the
nature of the end-point of one activity and the beginning point
of another. Events are often referred to as <u>milestones,</u> which
is more descriptive than "events."

The activities, represented by arrows, are not explicitly
labeled in the figure but they can easily be surmised. In some
cases they represent actual working time, as in DE (all activities are designated by the letters labeling their end-point)
the time required to lay the foundation and build the structure,
or LM, the time required to train the midwife--presumably
a traditional midwife who is to receive on-the-job training in
a modern hospital. In other cases the activities are a mixture of actual working time and inevitable bureaucratic delay.
BH is partly the time it takes to process the documents to
order equipment and partly the time those documents sit in

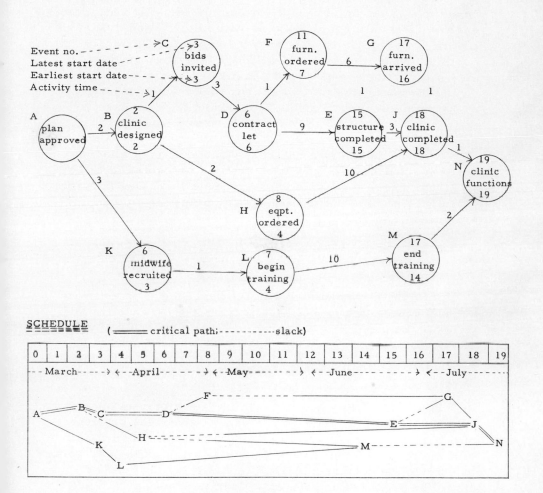

FIGURE 22.1. Application of a PERT network to a pilot commune maternity clinic. All time units (1-19) are in weeks.

in-boxes and out-boxes. The people involved in most of the
activities of this and other rural development projects are
involved in many projects; they devote only part of their time
to this one.

Note that one must be selective in identifying milestones.
One might have, for example, broken up DE with other events
such as "foundation laid," "walls completed," and "roof completed." One might have eliminated event L. Obviously one
needs an event wherever two or more activities start or end.
How many more events need be identified? This is a matter
of networking aesthetics and artisanship. Too many events
make the network impossible to read and too few make it
difficult to understand the nature of the activities.

Some of the arrows may represent what are called dummy
activities. EG simply indicates that the structure must be
complete before the furnishings are installed. One might have
given EG a time value of zero, as is often done on dummy
activities.

Activity Time Estimates

Once the network is drawn, the next step is to estimate
activity times: the expect time it takes to complete the activity or the expected time lapse between the events. The
activity times, in weeks, are indicated by the numbers on the
arrows on Figure 22.1. Obviously experience and judgment
are the basis of these estimates.

The author has found that in rural development operations
the week is the best time unit to use. Campaigns or projects
of a complexity which require PERT are generally a minimum
of three months in duration. The day, which is the unit commonly used in construction PERT charts, is too small a time
unit to be practical or relevant. It is impractical because a
chart several feet long would be required to display a typical
campaign (more on display problems below). It is irrelevant
because there is a bureaucratic slippage between events which
makes it exceedingly unlikely that two significant events that
must occur in sequence can be accomplished the same week.
Almost every significant event requires approval of persons
who may or may not be in their office or in town the day after
the preceding event takes place.

Some activity times require special computations to
evaluate. LM, the training period, for example, requires
an evaluation of what training is needed and how it can be
executed. DE, the construction period, requires an evaluation of the time required for the separate component elements of the job, the time for mobilization of a crew and
building materials, the foundation-laying time, etc. In some
cases it may be worthwhile to do a PERT subnetwork in days
to determine an activity time. Evaluating the uncertainties is
a difficult matter on which to give guidance; one can only say
that the planners should be conservative but not pessimistic.

Computation

The object of the computation is to find out how long it
will take to reach the final event and when each of the other
events must be completed in order to reach that event in the
shortest possible time.

Forward Pass--The first step is to compute the earliest
possible date for each event. One works from left to right on
the table, writing the earliest date computed under the label
in the circle for each event. Where only one arrow leads into
an event, the computation is simple, as in the case of event
K. Since event A is 0 and the activity time for AK is 3, the
earliest date for event K must be 3. Similarly, the earliest
date for event L is activity time KL (which is 1) plus the
earliest date for event K (which is 3); 3 + 1 = 4, which is
written in below the label of event L. Similarly, M equals
14, LM plus L (10 + 4).

Where two or more activities lead into an event, a com-
plication is added. G, for example, is preceded by EG, 15 +
1, and FG, 7 + 6. Where this occurs, one must always take
the highest combination of a preceding lead-in activity plus
event. FG is completed at 13, but one cannot proceed beyond
G until EG is finished at 16. Therefore the earliest event
time for G must be 16. Similarly, on J there is a choice of
GJ (16 + 1), HJ (10 + 4), or EJ (15 + 3). One cannot move
beyond J until EJ, the highest value, is finished at 18; the
earliest date for J, therefore, is 18.

As a result of the forward pass computation, it is determined that the earliest possible date for the final event N on Figure 22.1 is the 19th week.

Backward Pass--The next step is to work backwards and find the latest possible date at which each event can take place without upsetting the final completion date. On Figure 22.1 the latest date of each event is written above the label. The computation is the reverse of the forward pass in that the latest date for an event is the minimum of any of its activities leading out, subtracted from the connected events.

Again, this is simple if there is only one arrow leading out. M has a latest date of 17, N minus MN (19 - 2). H has a latest date of 8, HJ minus J (18 - 10). Note that on the backward pass one is always working with the numbers above the label of the event. Below are some of the events with more than one activity leading out:

Event Evaluated	Activity Leading Out	Terminal Event	Latest Start	Event's Latest Date
E	EG = 1	G = 17	16	
	EJ = 3	J = 18	15	E = 15
D	DE = 9	E = 15	6	
	DF = 1	F = 11	10	D = 6
B	BC = 1	C = 3	3	
	BH = 2	H = 8	8	B = 3

The logic again is simple: The latest date at which any event can take place must be early enough to give adequate time for completion of all connected subsequent events on time. If, for example, D is put off to 7, DE cannot be completed and E cannot occur until 16. This will in turn postpone J till 19 and N till 20.

Slack and the Critical Path--All the numbers are now in place. One notes that there are differences between many of the upper and lower numbers, between the earliest date and the latest date of many of the events. What does this mean?

It means that an event <u>can</u> occur as early as the lower date
but does not <u>have</u> to occur before the upper date. On event K
the midwife can be recruited as early as the third week, but
if she is not recruited until the sixth week, the whole operation
can still be completed on time.

This difference in time between the date when an event
can feasibly occur at the earliest and the latest date at which
it must occur is called <u>float</u> in CPM parlance and <u>slack</u> in
PERT parlance. The author prefers the term slack as being
more emotionally descriptive of the phenomenon. Where
there is slack, the manager can afford to relax his tight grip
on the operation until all the slack is taken in.

Note that the slack indicated on each event includes the
slack of the events ahead of it. K has a slack of 3 because L
has a slack of 3 and M has a slack of 3.

Some events have no slack. The top and bottom numbers
match. This means that the earliest date on which they can
occur is also the latest date. Their on-time completion is
critical; a delay in any of them will delay final completion.
Taken together in chain they form the <u>critical path</u>. In Figure
22.1 the critical path is ABCDEJN, a path easily spotted because the numbers top and bottom in each circle are the same.
The manager must give the utmost attention to the activities
along this path, because there is no slack. Absolutely no
allowance can be made for delay.

Scheduling and Slack Allotment

One can now do the actual scheduling, that is, put the
events on a time scale and set actual calendar dates for them.
Such a schedule appears at the bottom of Figure 22.1. To do
this, however, some further judgments and decisions are
necessary. It is obvious into which weeks the events on the
critical path will fall; they must be scheduled for the week
which is their latest and also their earliest date.

But how should one schedule the other events? Event M,
for instance, could be scheduled for week 14, 15, 16, or 17.
Note that if M is scheduled for 15, L can be scheduled only

for 4 or 5, and if L is scheduled for 4, K must be scheduled
for 3. Moving in the reverse direction, if one were to decide
to schedule K for 6, one would have to schedule L for 7 and
M for 17. There are three weeks of slack in that path but
one has to decide which activities to allot it. Scheduling involves slack allotment.

Along a given path, one should allot the slack to those
activities which have the greatest probability of needing more
time than their activity time estimate. The simplest example
is the path BHJ, procurement of equipment, which has 4 weeks
of slack. BH, the processing of the equipment order, is
fairly well under the project manager's control, but HJ, the
shipping of the equipment by the suppliers, is somewhat out
of his control. Therefore he wants to allot most of the slack
to HJ, as has been done in Figure 22.1.

The path AKLMN, recruitment and training, presents a
different type of problem. Here one may assume that the
midwife training course begins at the first of April, so there
is no choice but to put L at that date and allot all slack to MN.

The path DFGJ, procurement of furnishings, presents
some complicated problems of slack allotment. FG, production and shipment by the supplier, presents the most uncertainty. However, if the furniture arrives earlier than the
week after event E, structure completed, it will have to be
stored temporarily elsewhere. If it arrives more than a week
late, however, the whole operation will be delayed. One can,
therefore make a compromise, alloting most of the slack to
FG but some of it to DF.

The Uses of PERT

What has the procedure accomplished? Essentially it
has alloted time, and nothing else. It has solved a time
minimization problem. In the example it has worked toward
a single objective, the functioning of one clinic. One might
have set up a similar network for simultaneous construction
of a dozen clinics, but PERT would not tell us anything about
how many units (in this case, how many clinics) are or are
not completed.

This is essentially a method for planning single jobs, not for planning varying quantities of production. It adds nothing to the planning of repetitive jobs or high-quantity production. PERT is useful for planning research and development, major engineering works, major construction, pilot operations, and initial production runs.

STANDARD RURAL
DEVELOPMENT EVENTS CODE

In applying PERT to rural development two serious problems arise: the preparation of a meaningful and understandable display of a schedule and the proper choice of relevant events.

Display is always a difficult problem with PERT. If the labels are written out in plain English, at least 10 spaces and several lines are needed for each event to provide clearance from other events. Printed in normal 12-characters-to-the-inch type, a schedule of 40 weeks would be over a yard long and might be so cluttered that it would be difficult to read. It is not unusual to see a PERT schedule covering a whole wall. If the events are merely numbered, as is frequently done, the reader is obliged to consult a separate listing of events every time he uses the schedule. This is not a serious problem if there are only 13 events, as in Figure 22.1, but when the number of events reaches 30 or more, as is typical, it becomes impossible to keep in mind what all the numbers mean as one looks over a schedule. It becomes impossible to get a meaningful picture. A highly compact yet understandable means of labeling events is needed.

The choice of relevant events is obvious in industry and construction, which have well-defined operations for which there have always been cost estimates. Production scheduling has used standard breakdowns of processes into calculable operations for years. Rural development has no such traditional production scheduling behind it. The author had to start from a scratch in defining meaningful activities and events.

The Basic Technique

Both problems were solved with a technique of alpha-mnemonic coding and cataloguing. (Mnemonics is the technique of using memory aids) This is a technique which was developed around 1960 by a noted industrial engineering firm, Serge Birn and Co., to solve similar problems in the application of predetermined standard times to industrial piece rates and work bonuses.[1] The coding system made is possible for industrial engineers to keep in mind the meaning of hundreds of three-letter codes.

Basically it starts from a cataloguing of all possible events by major categories (the first letter), minor categories (the second letter), and steps within those categories (the third letter). The resulting catalogue of standard rural development events, which the author drew up, is found in Appendix E. At first one might think that there would be an enormous variety of possible events, but such is not the case.

Examining Appendix E, one finds 14 basic categories of rural development tasks, as designated by the first-letter codes. Each of these categories has a homogeneous sequence of events, as shown in their respective third-letter codes. The second-letter code is for specifying the task (or work package as it is commonly called in PERT parlance); it distinguishes, for example, one agreement from another on the same schedule. The second letter can be modified to specify the task more literally.

Suppose, for example, that one is scheduling one of the phases of a campaign involving the farmers associations and related projects. The first step would be to go down the catalogue of events, considering each category and jotting down the relevant tasks and their codes. Looking at A (Agreements), one would remember that agreements are required with the Agricultural Development Bank and with the Kenaf Board, two autonomous agencies. So one would jot down:

AB Agreement with Bank
AK Agreement with Kenaf Board

Looking at B (Building), one might note one task, warehouse construction, and jot down:

BW Build Warehouse

Under C (Commodity procurement), one might distinguish procurement of equipment and procurement of supplies, such as agricultural chemicals. One might have distinguished two or more types of equipment, for example vehicles and furnishings. Having limited category C to two categories, one jots down:

CE Commodity procurement, Equipment
CS Commodity procurement, Supplies

And so on down the list. Several categories would be skipped, such as D (Demonstration), L (Land improvement), and M (Major law or decree). Most of the categories should be self-explanatory except for the last two, V and X, which will be explained later.

Once the list of work packages is complete, the networking can start. One scans the list for the task that should come first. This would appear to be SE (Survey Evaluation of operations to date). One looks at the third-letter codes in Appendix E and selects those which are relevant, that is, those which come at least a week apart and are either a juncture point for some other activity or a significant milestone of progress. Since SEP = Survey Evaluation, personnel assigned, etc., one might then write the path:

SEP——SES——SEA

taking as milestones the points at which Personnel are assigned, a report is Submitted, and the report is Approved.

One then writes paths for tasks that lead out from this one. The project planning and agreements with the bank and the Kenaf Board will follow the survey, so one may write:

The reader will find the meaning of these codes in Appendix E.
One gradually extends the network until all tasks have been
covered and the end event is reached. The final network, on
a time scale, is shown in Figure 22.2.

In looking down the third-letter codes for the various
categories in Appendix E, one can see that they are a mixture
of work completion points and decision points, realizations of
various echelons of bureaucratic approval. Such is the nature
of rural development; decision-making and its preparatory
staff work may consume a good deal more time in a campaign
than the field work. The memorable breakthroughs of rural
development are as likely to occur in the air-conditioned conference rooms of the metropolis as in the muddy fields of the
villages.

Two final categories, V (Village canvass or campaign)
and X (eXternally given dates) require special explanation.
Most major rural development campaigns end with an operation in which cadre or teams work successively in a number
of villages in a locale, educating, selling, soliciting, surveying, and somehow servicing the villagers. One is faced,
then, with the problem of handling a repetitive, high-volume
routine in PERT, where it does not usually belong. The number of villages each cadre or team must handle in this case
makes a difference in the schedule.

One can handle it by scheduling the first and last village
handled in the average locale, by finding the average field
service complex, and then by determining the activities that
will most directly connect them. The third-letter codes of
category V in Appendix E provide a sequence of events which
apply to a wide variety of village-level cadre servicing activities. As an example, one might assume that the canvass
preparatory to the first agricultural chemical sales in the
Southern Region program is handled by teams of cadre and
volunteers, each team handling four villages. In the beginning
village-VB-they start by presenting the program to the villagers (VBP), and then surveying requirements (VBS). The
team can then move on to the next village and finally the
ending village (VE), repeating these steps:

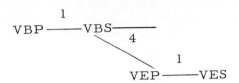

The requests for credit (VBR) are collected and approved
(VBA). Finally the fertilizer is delivered (VBD, VED) and
used (VEU). Collection and approval of the credit applications
of each village takes a week. Deliveries can be made to two
villages a week. The final subnetwork with times is:

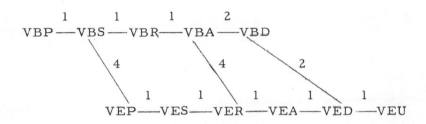

The times indicated on lines VBS-VEP, VBA-VER, and VBD-
VED indicate the times necessary to achieve the terminal
event of those activity lines in four successive villages. In
this manner one can schedule a repetitive activity by PERT,
but for one average or typical field unit only. Presumably
a number of field cadre or teams in various districts are
executing, or are supposed to execute, this same schedule
simultaneously.

The final category in the catalogue in Appendix E is X
(eXternally given dates). Almost every schedule will have
some events whose dates are set by factors outside the project or campaign. These factors might be the crop season,
planting and harvest times, the work season, the months
during which bad weather makes construction impossible, the
budget cycle, the dates for submitting budgets or releasing
funds, or the activities of other projects. Any of these factors may determine the earliest or latest or even the exact
date on which an event can take place. One can see in Figure
22.2 how these are handled.

A few networking drafting hints are in order. One needs
enough space around each event to write the earliest and
latest event times and to write activity times on the lines.
One problem plaguing the novice at networking is crisscrossing
lines, which can soon render a network incomprehensible.
This can be avoided by keeping the convergence nodes (the
events with two or more activities leading in or out) toward
the center. Simpler, less interrelated paths should be drawn
toward the top and bottom of the network.

A Realistic Application

One can find a schedule for a complete campaign in Figure
22.2. A briefing officer can expect that the audience will feel
a bit overwhelmed when it is first presented. The chart is not
meant to be immediately self-explanatory. It must be presented in a briefing or read alone very slowly, event by event.
One might recommend that the reader look over the events
code before starting to decipher the schedule; it will come
easier that way.

As the reader or the audience deciphers the codes, the
obstruseness of the schedule will wear off, but the impression
of formidable complexity will remain. These campaigns are,
indeed, formidably complex. Note that the action up to November is almost entirely paperwork and conferencing. There
is a network of decision that must be completed before the network of fieldwork can begin. This is typical of major rural
development undertakings. Long before one season's work is
completed, the project manager must start work on the next
cycle.

Note the way externally given dates have been handled.
In October there is XBE, the earliest date of budget approval;
in April there is XCL, the latest date for plowing. These are
connected by dummy activities to the events in the network
they control. This may seem to force the schedule artificially;
what would happen if the earliest date for VEU was later than
XCL? One would then have to go back and examine the assumptions behind activity time estimates on the critical path,
seeking some way to shorten it. At some point more money
would have to be put in or some feature would have to be for-
saken to shorten the critical path. In this way one adjusts
the schedule realistically and for a price to the fixed deadline.

In this schedule the critical path is largely along construction of the warehouse. What could be done if the construction
time pushed the end event past the deadline? Extra money
would have to be spent on temporary storage or on extra
crews for the construction job. Or perhaps some procedural
waivers and special allotments could be obtained to get the
bidding and contracting done earlier.

One might question how the slack has been alloted on this
schedule and consider what the effect would be of alloting it
in other ways. For example, the village canvass, starting at
VBP, could start two weeks earlier if all the slack in previous
operations were taken up. This would allow more slack within the main field operation. Would this be a good move? This
is the type of very real scheduling problem that can only be
handled by PERT.

UTILIZATION OF PERT

One hears stories of the difficulties family planning
workers have had convincing some villagers that it is not
enough to post a contraceptive device over the bedstead. One
also hears of difficulties in developed countries convincing
project managers that it is not enough to have a PERT schedule posted on the wall. It is not enough to have a device. One
must use it.

How to Use PERT

The network should first be drawn by a planning staff
member in conference with the project manager and his aides,
and possibly some of the staff of other agencies involved in
the campaign. After writing a list of the work packages on a
blackboard, the planner then draws the network, asking the
conferees which events must follow which. He then gets their
estimates of the activity times. Once he has done the computations, he draws the schedule, showing the slack allotment
options to the conferees and asking their opinions. The resulting schedule is thus the consensus of those with actual
experience and responsibility in the operation.

Coordinating committees and authorities within the ministry should be briefed from the schedule. The briefing technique is simple. Copies should first be distributed: if possible, the schedule should be projected on a screen by an
overhead projector. For a briefing to an individual or very
small group this may not be necessary. The project manager
starts the briefing by pointing out the objective and mentioning
who is involved. He runs over the critical path, explaining
each code. Then he goes back and explains the other events,
discussing the main slack allotment decisions. Each event
should be read off and explained carefully, even though an
explanation is written below the chart. On the basis of the
author's experience, a PERT schedule like that in Figure
22.2 can be explained in 15 minutes.

The PERT schedule is particularly useful in getting decisions made on time and in overcoming indecision. With it
one can show an authority exactly what will be the consequence
of putting off a decision and how the final event will be affected.
It is also obviously a good device for making sure that lead
times are realistic, that no deadlines are ignored, and that no
steps have been left out. It is a good cure-all for scheduling
pathology.

The next step in effective use is careful discussion with
all staff personnel involved. Each should be shown how his

tasks tie in with the rest of the operation and what time flexibility he has. Every staff member should have a copy of the
schedule. It should also be discussed with cooperating agencies to show them when their cadre will be needed in the
campaign and with what urgency.

Finally the schedule should be used as a basis for progress reporting and troubleshooting. A simple reporting
technique is to save the duplicating master and periodically
mark progress on it with crosshatching or parallel lines along
the paths, up to the point reached to date. Revised copies
then show progress to date, planned vs. actual. The schedule is also a good medium from which to brief authorities and
committees on progress to date. Where operations have
fallen behind schedule but slack remains in the path, delays
are not serious.

JUNE	JULY	AUGUST	SEPTEMBER	OCTOBER	NOVEMBER

(PERT network chart)

XBE
BWA — BWC
AKB
FBN
FBC — FBD — FBR
AKD
SEP=SES   ABD — ABB   SLS
SEA   PPC   SLA
PRO
PPD   SLP   OFC = OFE
RMP — RMA
PSD — PSO
TMP
TMB
RSR — RSP — RSA

Events Code

A	Agreements
B	with Bank
K	with Kenaf Board
D	Drafted
B	Bilateral Approval

BW	Build Warehouse
B	Bid Let
C	Contracted
F	Foundation laid
S	Structure completed
O	Occupied

C	Commodity Procurement
E	Equipment
S	Supplies (ag. chemicals)
S	Specifications written
O	Ordered
A	Arrived

FB	Finance from Budget
N	Needs determined
C	Commitment received
D	Documents submitted
R	Release funds

OF	Organize Farmer Accocia-tions
C	Call for first general meeting
E	Election of officers

P	Plans
P	Project
S	Standard routines
D	Drafted
O	Originating agency approval
C	Committee approval

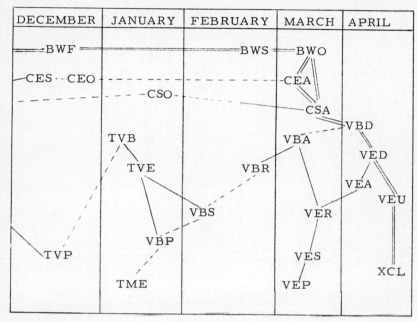

DECEMBER	JANUARY	FEBRUARY	MARCH	APRIL

Events Code

R	Recruit		V	Village canvass
S	Staff of FA Division		B	Beginning village
M	Managers of FAs		E	Ending village
P	Presentation of candidates		P	Presentation in village
A	Acceptance of candidates		S	Survey of applicants
			R	Requests of village received
S	Survey		A	Approval of Loans
E	Evaluation of past operations		D	Distribution of ag. chemicals
L	Location of new FAs		U	Use of ag. chemicals
P	Personnel assigned to survey			
S	Submission of report		X	eXternally given dates
A	Approval of report		BE	Budget approval Earliest date
			CL	Crop Planting latest date
T	Train			
M	Managers of FAs			
V	Volunteers for village canvass			
P	Preparations complete			
B	Begin course			
E	End course			

RURAL DEVELOPMENT PLANNING

Where the delay is on the critical path, or on a path that has become critical because all the slack has been used up, urgent troubleshooting is a must. Crash procedures are in order to make up the lost time or to get to the next event by another route. If in Figure 22.2, for example, it is August 15 and agreements have not been reached with the bank and the Kenaf Board, it is time for the minister to arrange a special high-level meeting with the heads of these agencies to get matters settled promptly. If it is mid-January and construction is falling behind, preparations must be made for temporary storage. In this way one uses a PERT schedule as a guide for troubleshooting.

When to Use Pert

PERT preparation takes a small amount of training and a degree of innate motivation and talent. Those who have the type of motivation and talent necessary should be able to grasp the technique after going over this chapter carefully. It is too much to ask that all project managers and staff be expected to learn PERT. Their talents and motivations may lie in other directions. But it is not too much to demand this competence of a planning staff. A planning staff member who does not have the motivation to learn this type of planning technique, which is far more simple than much of the economics which planners generally learn, is of questionable competence and his suitability for that type of work is in doubt.

The time of planning staffers is limited, however. They do not have time to apply PERT to every project. The technique must therefore be selectively applied to those campaigns which clearly need it. A simple test is to do the preliminary selection of work packages. If there are a number of tasks that will probably be running in parallel, PERT is in order. If the tasks can be done in sequence, one after another, PERT is not necessary to determine the schedule.

A good way of introducing PERT would be to try it on the project or campaign coming up next year that needs it the most, the one which causes the most concern in regard to timing. On his first PERT schedule, the planning staffer must devote extra time and effort to see that everyone is properly briefed. He must work particularly closely with the project manager. On later operations the project manager will follow up more on his own, once the schedule has been drawn up.

PERT, like any other planning tool, requires time, attention, and effort on the part of scarce talent. Is it worth it? When one considers the endless conferences that are often held to reassemble the pieces of schedules gone astray, it may even be considered economical of scarce talent. Without an adequate working method for scheduling, the planning and project staff must cope with problems rather than plan in advance and coping is almost always more expensive and more time-consuming than planning.

NOTES

1. Crossan, R. M. and H. W. Nance, <u>Master Standard Data</u>, (New York: McGraw Hill, 1962).

CHAPTER **23** AGRICULTURAL
CREDIT

A bit of fantasy may illustrate many of the problems of
agricultural credit in developing nations. Imagine an American small-town bank being informed that a certain poor
farmer desperately needs a $50 loan for production supplies.
He owns 7 acres, from which he feeds his family. He netted
$247 in cash last year. He is located 25 miles from town,
down a bad road that is impassable several months of the
year. He has three years of education, no telephone, no
social security number, no job record, no charge accounts.
Would any American banker touch such a client at any interest
rate?

The farmer described is, of course, a typical peasant in
a developing nation. Of all the services essential to agricultural development, credit is by far the most difficult to
provide. Traditional moneylenders in the village typically
charge between 5 and 10 percent per month, rates which rule
out credit for production purposes except in rare cases. Yet
the problems and risks are such that the village moneylender,
even at these exorbitant rates, accumulates no great fortune.

Governments of most developing nations have undertaken
projects to provide farmers with credit at reasonable rates.
The Third World is littered with debris of these projects,
with unpaid loans, inactive cooperatives, projects which
reached only a handful of large commercial farmers. The
author knows of no developing nation other than Taiwan in
which farmers can get all the credit they can legitimately
use for productive purposes. Medium-term credit comes
particularly late in the evolution of the rural economy.
Mexico, with its booming industrial economy, is only beginning to provide medium-term credit to small farmers.

   This chapter will first examine the problems and administrative complexities inherent in lending money to peasant cultivators.   Then some techniques and policies will be proposed
that may make it possible for the man with seven acres and an
annual income of less than $250 to get his loan.

PROBLEMS

Gross Margin

   Consider a typical short-term production loan for two
hectares: $50 borrowed for 8 months.   The government fre-
quently sets a maximum interest rate of 12 percent on such
loans; the bank has to pay at least 6 percent on its money.
This leaves a gross margin of 6 percent annually over 8/12
of the year, or 4 percent.   On a $50 loan, 4 percent is $2.   It
takes a lot of these loans to pay one day's expenses of a bank
branch.   Loan officer salaries are far more modest in developing nations than in the United States, to be sure, but
gasoline is frequently higher; the cost of the gasoline used to
drive a Land Rover out to a village to see a farmer might use
up all the $2 gross margin.   In any event, it is totally un-
economical to send a university graduate loan officer out in a
vehicle to look at one farm for a loan with a $2 potential gross
margin.

   The gross margin is somewhat better on a medium-term
loan.   A typical medium-term loan in a developing nation to a
farmer would be about $150 for three years.   The gross mar-
gin would be 18 percent or $27.   The administrative burden
of a medium-term loan, however, is considerably greater
than that of a short-term loan.   A bank can make a commercial loan earning several times the gross margin with about
the same administrative burden.

   Three moves can be made to improve earnings from agricultural credit.   First, the interest charged can be increased.
Second, the bank can be provided special low-cost money for
agricultural credit, to widen the gross margin spread.   Third,
administrative costs can be reduced.

Loan Selection

A great deal of the administrative burden and risk stems
from the problems of selecting sound credit risks among actual or potential farm borrowers.

A brief word should be said about potential borrowers.
Farmers in a traditional milieu do not like to think of themselves as potential borrowers. Credit, to them, is a last
resort in an emergency, a matter of desperation. They perceive productive credit requirements only in connection with
specific innovations. Surveys have shown that, when peasants
are asked the general question "Do you need credit?" they will
answer in the negative. At the same time, however, if asked
whether they plan to use fertilizer, they will counter with a
question: "Where would I get the credit?" A bank, like any
other business, needs a sales effort to get customers and
maintain a flow of prospective clients. Crop promotion projects are the sales effort of the bank; without them no agricultural lending service can get significant volume of customers.

Ability to say Yes and Ability to say No--The first problem of loan selection is the ability of the lending agent to
make an independent, businesslike evaluation of each prospect.
This ability is often seriously imparied by political and social
pressures. Cooperative officers or government civil servants,
for example, often find themselves in a position where they
can't say no. The officers of a village cooperative are close
friends and neighbors of all the applicants. Their relationships with the applicants have a long history of mutual favors
and obligations. It may be socially impossible for them to reject a loan application from a friend and neighbor.

The government official is somewhat more detached, but
he likewise has a continuing problem of maintaining rapport.
His success as a district chief or district extension officer
depends in large measure on the continuing good will of the
farmers. He is in no position to be a bad guy to a large number of ordinary farmers. His overall role precludes his
taking an unpopular stand on credit.

For these reasons a great many credit programs channeled through village cooperatives or government officials

develop into give-aways. Not always, however, for credit
discipline, like other aspects of social discipline, varies
widely among countries and regions at the same level of
economic development.

The ability to say yes can also be imparied by psychological pressures. At times government-owned banks have
gone into agricultural credit programs nominally committed
to providing credit to the broad mass of farmers but not committed to the changes in normal banking practice that this
would entail. Loan officers were nominally authorized to deal
with small farmers, but they feared they would be held personally responsible for the smallest loss from such loans.
They felt, in brief, that their superiors would not back them
up on taking such risks and that their superiors still felt that
small farmers were not reasonable credit risks.

Evaluation of the Borrower--Evaluation of a loan proposition involves a close look at the purpose of the loan, the investment to be made, and a close look at the recipient of the
loan. If the recipient has a credit record one need look no
further, but the peasant in stage II of rural development
rarely has a credit record, and evaluating the borrower means
taking a close look at his character and his assets.

How is the loan officer to judge the character of a farmer
in a village several hours from the bank? How is he to know
that this is a man who takes his business obligations seriously?
The loan officer must rely on the judgment of the applicant's
peers in the village. Simply asking their opinion is not
enough; villagers will invariably give a good report on any
neighbor to an outsider. Rather, the loan officer must get a
guarantee from the borrower's peers, carefully tailored to
cover the character of the borrower but not the character of
the investment. The latter is a matter the loan officer can
judge better than the villagers.

The second aspect of a borrower which must be examined
is his assets and income. A borrower must have sufficient
overall assets and income relative to the size of the loan to
be able to pay it off if something goes wrong with that specific
investment. The size of the loan, in other words, must be
scaled to his overall assets and income. It takes on-the-spot
verification by a properly trained agent to evaluate assets and

income--albeit simple procedures can be devised that will
permit a man with four years' education and one week of
training to make such an evaluation.

A farmer need not show sufficient assets to pay off a
loan in the event of a general crop failure. In America and
in any country with a properly functioning agricultural credit
system, a farmer hit by weather conditions causing a general
crop failure has his loans automatically extended one year--
with continuing interest charges of course.

One further aspect of a borrower to be examined is his
need for further credit. If a farmer must borrow from someone else before harvest to feed his family, for example, that
consumption loan may be paid off first and leave nothing to
pay the production loan. A lender must either provide a borrower with all his credit needs or have a clear understanding
with the other credit source regarding repayment priorities.

Evaluation of the Investment--The evaluation of a short-
term loan is relatively simple. These are generally for crop
production inputs. If the inputs are those generally recommended and the market for the crop is not in trouble, the investment should be sound. A crop production input package
that is sound for one grower in a locale will probably be sound
for the other growers. Exceptions need be made only for
farmers with soil presenting special problems.

Evaluation of a medium-term loan is more difficult.
These are frequently, if not usually, for new enterprises. It
takes a measure of expertise to evaluate the soundness of a
new enterprise for a particular farm. One must also use
judgment to determine a suitable repayment schedule. On
short-term loans the logical repayment is at harvest. Medium-
term loan repayments must be scheduled over several harvests; one must judge what the net return of the investment per
harvest will be, and what the farmer's overall cash flow will
be.

Long-term loans are generally for land improvements to
which some agency in providing competent technical guidance,
irrigation, well drilling, land clearing, or terracing. The
technical judgment of the guiding agency can often be relied
upon for evaluation of such investments.

Collateral--Adequate collateral can reduce or eliminate the risk of incorrect evaluation. For some types of loans farmers can easily offer liens on adequate collateral. If a farmer is acquiring supplemental land or buying a major piece of new equipment, he can afford to give a lien on the new asset because he can afford to lose it. If the investment goes bad he loses the land or equipment and is back where he started, minus the "sweat equity" he has invested. A farmer cannot afford, however, to give a lien on the basic family fields from which he feeds his family. No investment, no matter how attractive, can justify the risk of losing these fields.

It is therefore generally impossible to ask collateral on a production loan for a farmer's main crop. Only supplemental land and equipment can be asked as collateral.

Foreclosure may present serious problems. Legal costs of foreclosure on two hectares may amount to more than the value of the land. In some countries legal obstacles to foreclosure may be forbidding. Liens on equipment may present special problems. In any event the cost of taking action on nonpayment of a $150 loan will cost a good deal more than the $27 gross margin it might earn.

Collateral must be considered not as a substitute for sound evaluation and social credit discipline but, at best, as one element of a total system of credit discipline.

Cadre Requirement--The field cadre of a bank or other credit agency have a particularly heavy responsibility. They must make judgments involving much more money than any other cadre. Though their education requirement varies, they must be well trained, well motivated, and well paid.

Only a limited number of such cadre can be paid out of the narrow gross margin on these loans. This means their utilization must be highly efficient. Every trip to a village must generate enough loan volume to make dealing with that village worth while.

Loan Collection

There is an old saying that nothing is easier than extending loans nothing is harder than collecting them. Sound evaluation of borrowers and investments is the first step in assuring that cash will be available to pay off the loan. Further measures are necessary, however, to get that cash back to the lender.

Control over Utilization--A loan will not generate the cash for its repayment unless it is used for the purpose for which it was intended. A farmer may be strongly tempted to use the cash from the loan for other purposes. Providing the loan in kind rather than cash helps him resist such temptation. Some cadre follow-up is also necessary. It is not always possible to provide the loan in kind, so the lending agency must check promptly to see that the cash was used for the purpose intended.

Timely Collection--When the farmer realizes his cash at harvest, he is under many pressures to use the money for purposes other than bank loan repayment. Creditors in the village may get to him before the bank; careful provision of all his credit needs by the bank can avoid this. Beyond that, friends and family or local merchants may tempt him or pressure him into consumption expenditures with the cash that is due for loan repayment. The ideal arrangement is loan repayment by the merchant or cooperative that buys the crop. The crop buyer pays off the loan and gives the farmer the balance of cash due. Failing such an arrangement, the loan officer must see to it he contacts the farmer immediately after he sells the crop.

Workable Sanction--There must be a credible penalty for nonpayment. The lending agency must have the ability and the willingness to enforce a sanction. The problems of recovering collateral have already been mentioned. Persistent dunning is often sufficient to get a repayment from a delinquent debtor. Village cooperative officers and government officials, however, are often reluctant to press delinquent debtors for the same reasons they are reluctant to say no to an applicant. The role of credit policeman and tight-fisted banker conflicts with their other roles.

Credit Discipline Incentive

The above paragraphs may give a false impression of the peasant farmer as an unrepentant deadbeat. In some societies the traditional structure generates excellent credit discipline; peasants in some lands have been known to walk for days to pay off their first loan.

Credit discipline grows out of a complex of formal and informal social and legal pressures. In this it somewhat resembles tax discipline. Communities which are highly scrupulous in paying promptly most business and social obligations may indulge in mass evasion of certain taxes. These matters tend to be a matter not of individual but of group morality. People tend to do what they perceive everybody else to be doing.

For this reason it is important to have adequate policing and sanctions so that individuals who are playing new and unfamiliar roles as debtors to an extravillage institution get the impression that others are not attempting evasion. The policing and sanctions must create an atmosphere of compliance.

More important than the policing and the sanctions, however, is the positive incentive for credit discipline. If the farmers have an ongoing appetite for credit, they will be concerned with maintaining their credit rating. If they have ideas for using credit next year, they will see to it their credit rating stays solid. The work of the extension service and the general technical ambiance is important to credit discipline.

Credit discipline can evolve. A community might start down the path toward stage III of agricultural development, for example, with an initial code of scrupulously observing obligations within the village while evading outside obligations. The credit program might then feature heavy policing. After a few years the obligation of repayment will likely become accepted as a matter of community morality, and policing can be reduced.

SOLUTIONS

Some of the following policies and techniques can overcome the problems discussed in the previous section. These are not offered as a package that can be applied to all or any situations but as a grab bag. Credit policy and technique must be carefully adapted to the existing social structure with its strengths and weaknesses, and to the needs and features of the innovations being promoted.

Group Operation

Working with creditor groups is a must for maintaining adequate volume in any village to keep administrative costs per loan within reason. When a loan officer goes to a village, he should be able to deal with at least 10 clients at once in the initial stages of the program.

The lending institution can keep its administrative costs within reason by requiring that there be a minimum number of clients in one village or commune who are borrowing for the same purpose. One might, for example, require a minimum of 10 members per loan group and a minimum of three loan groups in a commune for consideration of applications. A loan officer would then be assured of a $1,500 loan volume (assuming $50 short-term loans) to be handled on each visit. It might take three to five visits to service and collect from a loan group, but three such groups close together would provide a minimum of $60 gross margin, which would cover the servicing expenses.

Note well that the key to economic feasibility of agricultural credit is the volume of business and gross margin that each loan officer can handle a year.

Group operation can also provide a very effective sanction. Each member of a loan group can be asked to cosign every other loan in the group as guarantor. If one member of the group does not repay his individual loan, the entire group can then be blacklisted for further credit. The other members may then find it worthwhile to repay the deadbeat's loan rather than lose their chance at further credit. This technique has worked very satisfactorily in Thailand; the groups apply intense social pressure on their members to pay on time. A group sanction can be far more effective security to a bank than hard-to-foreclose collateral.

Lender Autonomy

Although in Taiwan and in some other countries farmer-run organizations successfully administer credit, it may be advisable for government or private banks initially to deal directly with individual farmers, but in cosigner loan groups to be sure. A bank loan officer is not under the political and social pressures that might prevent him from rejecting unsound applicants or dunning delinquents. Unlike the village cooperative officer or civil servant, he has no other roles which would conflict with businesslike credit administration. He does not have to worry about how a rejected applicant's wife may treat his wife in the village.

Maximum Use of Other Cadre

If the loan officers play judge and policeman in the credit process, other cadre can do much of the rest of the work. Community development workers and extension officers can organize loan groups. They can help the farmers fill out loan applications, if the application forms are properly laid out and if the cadre have been properly trained. In Thailand, schoolteachers have been successfully used to help farmers fill out loan applications.

The loan application must be carefully structured if other cadre are to use it. A good application for a new borrower should spell out his net worth and his income, as well as the purposes and payoff on the loan. A well-educated and well-trained loan officer can use his judgment in filling in the elements of these calculations; other cadre must be given fairly clear-cut formulas for computing or estimating these elements. With the applications filled out in advance of his arrival, the

loan officer can spot-check the details on the application and
approve applications quickly. With such help from other
cadre, a loan officer can service 200 applications in a commune in the time it would take him to service 50 applicants
without such help.

Other cadre can also help with the follow-up. They can
visit villages at the right time to check the utilization of loans.
They can organize loan repayment. In follow-up activites,
however, the other cadre must carefully avoid a policing role.
If they find improper utilization of a loan, they should say
nothing but suggest that the loan officer visit the village. They
may take initiative to get the loan group to schedule a repayment meeting with the loan officer, but they should not pressure anyone to repay. Such a disciplinary role definitely
conflicts with other cadre roles.

Combining Credit with Supply/Marketing

In the long run, short-term production credit can be administered most cheaply by combining it with the supply and
marketing functions.

The most effective arrangement from the start is a contract farming system. The agency buying the crop contracts
with the farmers organized in loan groups to buy their crops
at a fixed or minimum price and to advance them the necessary production supplies and equipment. At harvest time the
buyer then deducts the credit advance from the price paid to
the farmers. The on-time collection problem is solved, and
the buyer has the additional sanction of refusing a contract
next year. This can only be done, however, on cash crops
handled by a limited number of agribusiness firms. Local
merchants will bid away each other's contractees when the
price starts rising; moreover, they lack the management and
resources for such arrangements.

A more common arrangement is supplier-administered
credit, in which the supplier sells the production inputs on
credit. This will work once the farmers have developed adequate discipline. A supplier is not in a position to do extensive policing and he cannot hold up the sanction of credit

blacklisting, as can a bank. Once a farmer has a credit rating, however, the supplier can, in effect, combine the sales trans- action with the credit transaction. He can get bank financing to carry his accounts receivable or he can hypothecate them. The additional administrative cost of a credit sale to a reliable customer is negligible.

It was stated above that, where credit policing is neces- sary, a bank could do a better job of credit administration than a farmer-run production and marketing cooperative. Once the policing phase of credit development is over, how- ever, short-term credit can more efficiently be handled by a cooperative as part of its supply sales operation. The co- operative then becomes the credit retailer for the bank.

Shifting to Lower Level Cadre

A new credit program will want well-educated, highly mobile loan officers. This may mean university graduates and the use of jeeps for several reasons. First, the program is still learning from experience; it needs field officers who can use judgment to reach decisions with very little guidance. Second, it is a new institution with an evolving discplinary structure that is responsible for large sums of money and needs men who can be trusted with substantial financial re- sponsibility. Third, it needs a core of well-educated men who can gain experience and furnish leadership to a growing program.

Once the lending institution has developed an adequate core of experience, routine, standard policy, and experienced leadership, it can staff out further expansion with much cheaper secondary school graduates mounted on motorcycles. As the program develops, the network of clients becomes denser and a man on a motorcycle can reach as many cus- tomers as a man on a jeep could previously. As operations become more routinized, they fall well within the capability of secondary school graduates.

Shifting to lower level cadre and transferring short-term credit to cooperatives considerably reduces the cost of admin- istration. The initial extra cost of using university graduates to check out and police the members of each loan group must thus be considered a long-term investment. The additional administrative expense needed to make credit work from its inception is a fixed investment that will pay off for many years to come.

Maximum Simplicity Inception

Some countries do not have university graduates to start a credit program. What then? One can use lower level cadre for credit administration provided one keeps the program very simple. Senegal is the model for such an operation. The loanable innovations and investments must be sharply limited. The cadre must be given forms which leave no room for judgment. They must be rehearsed and re-rehearsed in the filling out of these forms. They must be assigned a very limited number of clients. They must be closely supervised.

Maximum Interest Rates

There is a popular fallacy that it is important to get the interest rate to the farmer down to 6 percent. Such an interest rate leaves no margin for administration and makes it impossible to interest private savings investing in agriculture. A substantially higher interest rate will add very little to the cost or risk of a short-term investment for the farmer, but it will make a great difference to the lending institution.

How high should the rates be? One must consider this from the point of view of the farmer, the lending institution, and the sources of funds.

For the farmer, the rate must be low enough to make the investment attractive. Consider first a $50 loan for production needs, for eight months. The risks in crop production are such that the farmer should not go into debt unless he has a good prospect for a $100 gross return. At 12 percent his interest charge is $4. At 18 percent he must pay $6. Another $2 is not going to discourage him from a $50 investment in production inputs which can gross him $100. On medium-term loans the rate becomes a bit more significant. Certainly the 5 percent a month charged by traditional interest sources rules out most productive investments, but a charge under 2 percent a month does not.

On long-term loans the interest rate becomes more important; the interest charges can add up to more than the principle.

The lending institution is concerned with adequate gross margin. Ultimately it can get the administrative expense down to 2 to 5 percent, but initially it will need more gross margin to cover the heavy basic investment in checking out and policing new clients. Since this requirement is closely tied to the efforts of other cadre and the total educational and institutional job the government is doing in the countryside, this extra cost might well come out of the government budget, as a direct subsidy.

The sources of funds may be foreign or domestic. To the extent that credit is going for imported agricultural chemicals and machinery, the logical source of funds is foreign. The interest rate should then be enough to cover the cost of a foreign loan at 5 or 6 percent, plus 5 percent long-term gross margin, plus profit to the banking institution. Such would be the average rate; the short-term rate would be higher and the long-term rate would be considerably higher. If the investments are going for domestically produced inputs, then the rate should be high enough to provide adequate gross margin (including profit) and pay the going rate for domestic money. This is likely to be higher than the international borrowing rate.

Thus one can see that there are businesslike ways of getting the typical peasant farmer the credit he needs. One should remember that in Taiwan the credit section of the farmers association is generally the most profitable and supports some of the other association services. As emphasized in previous chapters, the peasant cultivator is not a charity case. He is an excellent potential business prospect if the proper investment is made in rural services. He will far more than match that investment with his own sweat equity.

At this point it may be worth while to present a variation
of the fantasy that led off this chapter. Suppose an American
small-town bank is informed of the following situation out in
the southwest corner of the county, where a piece of the underdeveloped world has been mysteriously transplanted: One
hundred farmers need loans averaging $50 for a particular
crop. The extension service has established the profitability
of this $50 investment on this crop in this area. It has as-
sisted these farmers in filling out loan applications. They
are organized in mutual-guarantee groups of 20 farmers each,
ready to meet with a bank officer as a group. They are organized so that the bank officer can meet with all of them and
spot-check their applications in one or two days. The bank
can make an 8 percent gross margin on these loans, or $400
on all 100 loans. Is it worth a two-day effort on the part of a
bank officer to gain a $400 gross margin--and 100 new clients?

CHAPTER 24 THE PRIVATE SECTOR

In Part III and Appendix A, this book explains a basic procedure for agricultural planning in terms of a hypothetical program for a "Southern Region," in which the private commercial sector has a very minor role. Yet, as Chapter 2 points out, every basic service can be performed by private firms. Indeed, such firms as CFDT (Compagnie Francaise pour le Developpement des Fibres Textiles) which promotes cotton production in West Africa, do provide all the necessary services: extension, supply, credit, marketing, and sometimes engineering.

A government should have an inherent interest in getting the private sector to play a maximum role in agriculture development as part of its inherent interest in maximizing effective domestic savings. Private savings in developing nations are often neutralized in unproductive land speculation or commodity speculation, or are placed abroad instead of going into domestic productive investment. The more this saving is effectively channeled into investment in agriculture in the basic productive sector of a developing nation, the more development can be realized with a given fixed amount of government resources.

There are other basic advantages to getting the private sector to play a maximum role. The entrepreneurial talent and managerial ability is there, in some countries, but the public sectors (the government agencies and public corporations) find it very difficult to sustain business discipline on supply and marketing operations. They find themselves unable to resist political and social pressures to swell their payrolls with unneeded and incompetent employees. In such countries only private firms can sustain efficient commercial operation.

473

Yet integrating the private sector in agricultural development is a difficult, complex matter, often strongly opposed within the government. This chapter will look first at the various types of private firms in agricultural development and then at the barriers to their playing a significant role. It will suggest some basic principles and useful techniques for bringing these firms in. Finally it will examine the particularly difficult problem of local merchants vs. cooperative channels.

TYPES OF PRIVATE FIRMS

Reviewing the Lewis model of the dual economy, described in Chapter 1, it should be noted that the subsistence or traditional sector contains not only peasants but small peddlers and other local merchants. One can thus distinguish two basic types of private firms, the traditional and the modern. The real world also exhibits some in-between cases. The traditional firms may be characterized as local merchants and the modern ones as agribusinesses. The in-between cases are generally trading companies.

Local Merchants

The traditional private mercantile enterprises are basically of two types. The first is the general-purpose merchant, who sells a wide variety of consumer goods and also may purchase crops and even handle some farm supplies. Such enterprises range in scale from itinerant peddlers to substantial general-goods stores. The other type is the specialized agricultural products merchant, generally a grain buyer or miller, usually specializing in one or two crops, and sometimes also selling farm supplies. The general-purpose merchant usually has traditional mercantile origins, often of an ethnic minority or caste that has a traditional monopoly of such occupations. The specialized merchants are often large farmers who have branched into commercial operations.

The commercial efficiency of these traditional local merchants generally leaves much to be desired, but it seems to
vary widely from country to country. The gross margins they
earn may be miserably narrow and provide a bare subsistence,
or they may be exorbitantly high.[1] They often serve a multiple
role, providing consumer goods and credit as well as a marketing outlet. Sometimes they are helpful and generous with
farmers; often they exploit the farmers ignorance, lack of
alternatives, lack of bargaining power, and state of indebtedness. They generally fail to distinguish quality or buy on
grade, and their handling and storage practices often lead to
substantial losses. The structure is generally overlayered;
the goods may pass through many layers of unnecessary
middlemen between the village and the metropolis.

They are not averse to handling new products on consign-
ment, but local merchants do not see profit maximization as
the product of business innovation. They conceive profit
maximization as a function of sound speculation, of buying
low and selling high, of good timing and competent haggling.

Can the traditional merchant play a positive role in agricultural development? Obviously the process of agricultural
development, insofar as it rationalizes marketing structures
to assemble and distribute carload lots as close to the village
as possible, will force a lot of middlemen and marginal village dealers out of supply and crop marketing. This should
cause no hardship for the general-purpose merchant, since
agricultural development results in greater purchasing power
for consumer goods in the village. Development is good for
retailing.

Specialized crop merchants are more directly affected.
Like the peasants they service, they need supporting institutions and a development curriculum to bring them into the
development process. They need a public agency or larger
organization to do the sales promotion among the farmers on
new supply or marketing lines. They need some education
and training. They may need some regulation, to prevent
unscrupulous operators from victimizing both farmers and
competitors. They may need some financial assistance to
install modern milling equipment, build additional storage
space, and hold crops longer while giving the farmer a better
postharvest price.

Agribusinesses

The term agribusiness is used in this book to designate a
large modern firm with ample financial and technical resources,
actively interested in promoting agricultural development. On
the supply side, agribusinesses include the agricultural chemical and equipment distributors. Due to lack of a proper distribution network and lack of other supporting services to the
village economy, they are often constricted to selling to plantations and large commercial farmers. However, the major
oil companies, perhaps the most international of all firms,
and some specialized agricultural chemical firms such as
International Minerals and Chemicals, are actively interested
in sales to the peasant sector.

On the marketing side, it has been observed that the
newer export crops are generally handled efficiently by agribusinesses.[1] With the growing international trade in feed
grains, such firms as Ralston Purina and Corn Products are
active in agribusiness in developing countries. Processing
firms, canneries, or textile mills, are often interested in
agribusiness.

Most agribusiness firms have agronomists on their marketing staff. Some, such as CFDT mentioned above, have a
complete extension network. In Thailand, Honda has mobile
teams demonstrating its two-wheel tractors and its pumps.
The international agribusiness firms are, in effect, supplying
foreign technical assistance to developing nations at no cost
to host governments or to aid donor governments.

Trading Companies

Exporting and interregional distribution of traditional
crops is largely in the hands of large firms which have modern
financial resources but a traditional speculative concept of
their business role. Unless they see their markets threatened
they are not motivated to business innovation, to improving the
structure of their marketing and distribution, or to promoting
agricultural innovation. Some agricultural supplies are

imported by traditional trading companies, which handle a wide variety of lines but which are technologically involved in none of them.

Individually the trading companies are probably not in a position to profit from investment in business innovation or in promotion of agricultural innovation. Through their trade associations, however, they might be able to cooperate with the government in improving the marketing structure.

BARRIERS TO PRIVATE
RURAL DEVELOPMENT

Governments have become heavily involved in the commercial side of agricultural development, in some cases because they wanted to and in other cases because a desired private response to agribusiness needs and opportunities was not forthcoming. The barriers to effective private participation in the rural development process are to be found both on the private side and on the government side.

On the Private Side

Private firms have been reluctant to innovate for a number of reasons:

Lack of Interest--As mentioned above, local merchants and trading companies do not consider innovation to be a normal ongoing function of a businessman.

More Lucrative Alternatives--Capital-short developing nations often present highly lucrative short-term speculative opportunities. The big fortunes are made in rural and urban real estate. The necessary good luck may be unevenly distributed, but the technique is known to all. Commercial banking policy may discourage innovation by insisting that all loans to businesses be secured by mortgageable property or by widely traded commodities.

Lack of Experience--Agribusiness are largely foreign firms, which have acquired the necessary know-how and experience in developed nations.

Atomized Markets--A firm seeking to distribute agricultural chemicals or promote a new crop in a region is faced with the task of building a network of agents or distributors from scratch to reach producers whose individual purchases or sales will be minute. Agricultural chemical distributors in some countries look in vain for an agent at district or commune level who will do anything more to sell fertilizer than to stack a few bags alongside the yard goods.

Missionary Sales Requirement--A great deal of basic education is necessary to sell farmers on new production supplies or new crop enterprises. These businesses require a heavy promotional investment.

Inadequate Overall Planning--If the government does its agricultural development planning superficially, fails to put together adequate innovation packages with all the "essentials" and enough of the "accelerators" (see Chapter 2), and fails to provide the necessary complementary services, then a prudent firm may be justifiably reluctant to venture into a new market in response to what the government sees as a need.

On the Government Side

Government officials have been inclined to make plans without active planning participation or an active operation role for the private sector, for the following reasons:

Ideology--Although some socialist governments have accorded a significant role to agribusinesses, private agribusiness projects are often opposed by governments on ideological grounds.

Ethnic Differences--Agribusinesses are usually foreign and local merchants, and trading companies are often manned largely by an ethnic minority, with a different outlook from the government and the peasantry. This is often behind ideological opposition to agribusinesses; it may also produce nonideological, purely nationalistic opposition to private participation in development. In large measure this may be based on the very worthy aim of bringing the ethnic majority more into the commercial life of the country. Blanket opposition to foreign or minority agribusiness projects can, however, reduce the overall funds going into productive investment, a result which is hardly compatible with sound nationalism.

Delicacy of Negotiation--Working with private firms on agricultural programs is not just planning, it is planning-cum-bargaining. The government should strive to get the greatest investment and risk posture from the private firm with the minimum government commitment. This puts the government official in a delicate, vulnerable position. Whatever the outcome, he may be accused of favoritism, collusion, corruption, or improper ideological tendancies.

Lack of Working Method--At some point in almost every description of development planning procedure there is a statement to the effect that "various agencies should submit projects." How are private firms to submit projects? Or how is a public agency to submit a project involving private participation, when it can accept no commitment from a firm because it cannot as yet give any commitment in return? The ministry of industry or an industrial finance corporation in the government has standard procedures for projecting activities with the private sector. Agencies involved in rural development usually do not.

APPROACHES TO
AGRIBUSINESS PLANNING

Some countries are richly endowed with entrepreneurial talent, foreign and domestic, central and local. Others have nothing but general-purpose local merchants and have yet to interest a foreign agribusiness firm. In some countries the development capability of agribusiness firms exceeds that of the government. In others they have nothing to offer at the present time. Obviously, the role of private firms in the planning process will depend on their potential contribution. Assuming that they do have something to offer, some general negotiating principles and some planning and project techniques can be suggested:

Principles

Three general principles can overcome the barriers listed above:

Consultation--Government officials should be talking with private firms or trade organizations at all stages of planning, either formally or informally. When general institutional strategy is being considered, trade organizations should be asked to state their views. Agribusinesses with plans for major projects should be asked to present them to interagency groups early in the planning process. Some of the techniques mentioned below elaborate on the consultation principle. It is important that government officials know what private firms have to offer and how private firms will react to government plans. Knowledge of government plans and participation in the planning process may induce private firms to play a bigger role.

Competition--Government officials can avoid ethnic complications and accusations of impropriety by structuring negotiations so as to maintain competition. Discussions on any project should always go forward with several firms, at least one of which should include some participation by the ethnic majority. If foreign agribusinesses are involved, it is advisable to deal with firms of more than one foreign nationality, both to avoid charges of favoritism and to learn from the ideas of firms with diverse backgrounds.

The program structure should protect the farmers against possible monopolistic exploitation. It may be necessary to work with one firm at the "point" stage, but at the "line" stage more firms should be brought in. If it is necessary to accord one firm a monopoly in a particular district to assure an economic volume, a strong farmer organization should be established to negotiate with it and to negotiate with other firms at a latter period.

In some cases a monopoly on a particular crop cannot be avoided. Then the farmers should be vigorously encouraged to diversify and to avoid excessive dependence on the price offered by one firm. This can avoid serious future social and political troubles.

Cheapest Inducements--Because of the lucrative alternatives and other barriers to private participation, the government must offer agribusinesses special inducements to venture
into servicing the peasant economy. Some inducements may
cost the government nothing; others may have costly side-
effects in addition to their actual budget outlays.

Essentially, all inducements must relate to the potential
profit and risk, which are determined by the prospective
prices, unit costs, and fixed outlays. Initial fixed outlays
have a particularly strong bearing on the risk of an operation.
Many normal government functions can reduce the initial fixed
outlays and also the unit costs.

First of all, the government's agricultural research and
economic surveys can reduce the firm's initial outlays. The
government can, in effect, do the feasibility study and market
survey for the firm. It can also do the missionary sales work
for the firm through its normal extension service. As pointed
out at the beginning of Chapter 4, extension can pay, and private firms often find it profitable to hire their own extension
workers. The multipurpose extension service of the government or of a Taiwan-type farmers association, however, can
be a much more economical sales force than the single-purpose
agents of a firm.

Indeed, the multipurpose cooperatives or farmers associations organized by the government can be the most effective
and economical local agents of an agribusiness firm, since
they concentrate on pushing agricultural innovation, yet their
overhead is spread over many lines. The traditional sector
is generally devoid of merchants interested in concentrating
on sales of production supplies.

Even where firms intend to use private local agents,
however, the government may be considerably more effective
in organizing farmer groups which can buy or produce an economical volume from the start. Government cadres circulate
regularly in the villages and can organize producer groups as
part of their regular routine. Where cadres are lacking, the
district officers can arrange through commune and village
chiefs to bring representatives of each village to meetings
with agents of agribusiness firms.

All these normal government services, if properly planned and coordinated with plans of the firm, can do much to reduce risk and increase potential profit. In addition, tax concessions, property concessions, and special financing may be necessary. Special concessions, however, may create dangerous precedents and long term financial problems for the government. Before they are considered in negotiations with private firms, the full value of the normal government services should be carefully evaluated and presented to the firms.

Project Techniques

Agribusinesses may reach farmers through three types of channels. They may have their own branches at district level, dealing preferably with commune-level farmer groups. They may use local merchants as agents. Or they may use district- or commune-level cooperatives or farmers associations as their agents.

The first contribution they can make to agricultural development is streamlining commercial channels by eliminating all possible middlemen and intermediate handling, storage, and moving of goods between the metropolis and the district (or commune, or even village) in direct truckload lots, if possible.

Beyond that, agribusinesses can cooperate in arranging and possibly financing integrated commercialization, as discussed in the preceding chapter. A marketing firm, or a supply distributor and a marketing firm working together, can provide the inputs and buy the crop through a local agent, providing the inputs on credit and deducting for repayment from the crop purchase price. This eliminates most of the administrative risks and burdens of production credit and uses local agents (branches, local merchants, or cooperatives) economically for three functions. From the government point of view, a contract farming arrangement gets the maximum contribution from the agribusiness firm. The firm, through its agent, signs with the farmer to provide his production needs and buy the crop at a fixed or minimum price. The firm thus provides all the financing and takes the full risk.

In addition, private firms may provide <u>extension spe-</u>
<u>cialists</u>, field agronomists who can work with local govern-
ment cadre or directly with farmer groups on local technical
problems. They should give some assistance at demonstrations.

Finally, the <u>nuclear plantation technique</u> should be mentioned, although it is basically a capital project arrangement
for getting private investment and management in land settlement. In this day and age large foreign-owned plantation concessions are no longer politically feasible, but Malaysia and
other countries have been considering concession of land to
plantation management firms on the condition that they use the
land as a core for a smallholder settlement. The core holding
contains cash crop plantings and a processing plant. The company first trains the settlers on its own land and then clears
holdings for them and assists them financially to settle on
circumferential lands.

Agribusiness initiative is largely in the hands of international firms. Where possible, however, domestic trading
companies should be brought in as partners to joint ventures
to eliminate problems of nationalism and to educate domestic
entrepreneurial talent.

Planning Techniques

<u>Crop Working Groups</u>--As mentioned in Chapter 12, per-
haps the best way to organize the planning of innovations is by
a separate working group for each crop. These groups should
include representatives of concerned agencies and also representatives of agribusinesses or trade organizations. Even if
no project immediately results from the deliberations, both
sides can gain from participation. The private firms can get
useful technical and economic data, and the government agencies can get valuable insight into marketing problems. In
some cases the private firms may make the greater net technical contribution.

Crop working group procedure has been discussed in
Chapter 13. The government should endeavor to get the private participants to make the maximum research contribution
to the procedings. This may be through their in-house

agronomists or through the marketing data they provide. Discussions must initially be structured to avoid questions of fair
commercial profit margins, or the private participants will be
motivated to exaggerate marketing costs for bargaining reasons.

The deliberation should move from an analysis of present
farming and marketing conditions and latest research results
to a summary of a feasible innovation package (like that on
Form A-5 of Appendix A), if a feasible package is indicated.

Pilot Projects--If the analysis of possible innovations is
favorable, the deliberation of the working group should lead
into a pilot program on the basis of existing or needed additional institutions. Arrangements, as mentioned above, should
certainly include streamlined commercial channels and possibly integrated commercialization. Participation in the point
phase should go to the firm willing to make the greatest financial contribution, assume the greatest risk, and (most impor-
tantly for that phase) contribute the greatest managerial effort
and talent.

Program Building--Once strong farmers associations or
local councils are established and engaged in agricultural
planning, representatives of private firms should be invited
to meet with them regularly. Marketing firms should present
to committee meetings and general meetings the advantages
of new crop production they are promoting. Supply and equipment distributors should arrange through these local groups
to demonstrate their products. General membership meetings
at village and commune level should then debate whether these
business lines should be included in the local program. Thus
the planning process becomes the sales process, with the
farmers themselves doing the selling.

In both pilot projects and, later, decentralized program
building, private firms should insist on a certain minimum
volume. The government or the local farmers association or
council must take responsibility for lining up the minimum
number of producers or customers. Local planning takes on
more meaning if the farmers understand that, unless a minimum of 80 producers in a commune are committed, say, the
firm does not come in once the innovation has been successfully demonstrated. This insures streamlined commercialization and serious farmer sales effort. It is selling through
planning.

COOPERATIVES VERSUS
LOCAL MERCHANTS

The planning of agricultural institutions at the local level may face some real problems of conflict basic social interests.

On the one hand, a Taiwan-type farmers association at the local level appears to be a sound long-range objective, particularly for stage III of rural development. Diversification in that stage requires a strong local enterprise that actively involves all the farmers and has a strong business incentive to push diversification of local production. Farmer participation is essential in order to achieve the economies of selling through planning and to keep the farmers themselves continually exploring new possibilities. It should provide a variety of services, so that it can make money several ways from diversification. It should have the participation of at least 80 percent of the farmers of a locale, in order to have enough volume to afford the best possible professional management.

Experience in Taiwan, and Senegal, and elsewhere would indicate that such a multipurpose cooperative must start out with some kind of monopoly in order to induce almost all the farmers to join and continue in active participation. Cooperatives which do not start out like this must build up membership from a subthreshold level of volume, too low to provide commercial efficiency. The odds are against their ever reaching threshold level.

On the other hand, a development program should always build on existing assets, and the local merchants may constitute substantial existing assets. If their livelihoods are threatened by new cooperatives, they may combine to undercut and destroy the cooperatives. If the government gives the cooperatives monopoly features that no merchant can aspire to, the new cooperative structure, behind this safe barrier to competition, is liable to become even more inefficient than the old commercial structure.

A number of measures can resolve this conflict. First, cooperative enterprises must be established on the basis of innovations, rising production, and income. Rising income means more business opportunities for every merchant, so that their livelihoods are not so critically affected. Second, these cooperatives should stay out of consumer goods, so that they do not threaten the general merchants. Third, their monopoly should be on something not previously provided by local merchants, such as reasonable credit and government subsidized fertilizer.

Finally, new cooperatives should work together with competent local grain merchants and crop buyers. With assured large volume and assured financing, the cooperatives are in a position to contract with merchants to use their storage, milling, or trucking facilities, giving them an economical volume spread out over many months.

The experience of Taiwan shows that an agricultural development program that includes strong monopoly features for farmers associations can nevertheless stimulate private enterprise and investment in agriculture. The possibility, however, of severe conflict must not be ignored. This is one of a number of very good reasons for reiterating that institutional development must be based on innovations. Developments that mean social change must take place in an atmosphere of expanding opportunity for all.

NOTES

1. J. Abbott, "The Development of Marketing," B. Johnston and H. Southworth, eds., Agricultural Development and Economic Growth (Ithaca, N.Y.: Cornell University Press, 1967), p. 372.

CHAPTER **25** COUNTER-
INSURGENCY

This chapter takes up the most difficult and agonizing of
all rural development problems--counterinsurgency. This is
indeed a rural development activity and a rural development
problem. As an activity, it has many of the same types of
strategic options and planning requirements as other rural
development activities. It exists as a problem, partly because
of the nature of the environment of stage II of rural development. The police, as the service of law and order, have the
same lack of effective coverage in most stage II countries as
the various agricultural service institutions. Indeed, a program for development of effective rural police coverage must
choose from among the same types of options as an agricultural development program, and rural police activities can be
planned on the same project forms.

The stage II environment, combined with the political and
military factors discussed below, can breed an insurgency
which must be met by an extraordinary combination of military and development activities.

The scope and applicability of this chapter must be carefully defined. First of all, it deals only with insurgencies in
countries or regions in stage II of agricultural development,
as defined in Chapter 3. Secondly, it tries to avoid discussion of the purely military or conventional military aspects of
counterinsurgency. This is somewhat difficult, since the security and developmental aspects of counterinsurgency are
tightly intertwined. With full awareness of the weakness of
any such line of demarkation, one might delimit the scope of
the following discussion in this manner: excluded are all military operations other than routine perimeter patrols and ambush missions, in platoon strength or on a smaller scale
(this excludes search and destroy missions and company or
larger-size engagements, all of which are important elements
of counterinsurgency).

BASIC CONCEPTS

The fundamental doctrine of counterinsurgency has been
laid down by David Galula, whose book Counterinsurgency
Warfare, Theory and Practice (Praeger, New York, 1964) is
must reading on the subject. The following basic concepts
are, by and large, a brief paraphrase of Galula. One must
consider first the nature of the insurgent operation and then
the nature of the counterinsurgent operations. They are often
erroneously confused by those who seek the solution to counterinsurgent problems in the writings of Mao, Giap, Guevara,
and Debray. Insurgency and counterinsurgency are highly
asymmetrical operations. They do have certain important
points in common, however. First, they both have control of
the population as their objective. Second, they both require
profound patience and sophistication.

The Insurgent Operation

A group intent on launching an insurgency requires (1) an
organization, (2) a main cause, and (3) a base area. The latter should be a rather inaccessible sanctuary adjoining a popu-
lous area, a trackless and preferably densely wooded swamp
or mountain range.

The main cause is generally based on a combination of
the following grievances: ethnic subjugation, oppressive land
tenure institutions, and bureaucratic corruption or arbitrari-
ness. The record of recent years would indicate that the pull
of these major grievances is in about the above order. The
cry is for independence and/or land reform and/or clean
government.

The lack of institutional coverage characteristic of stage
II has some important security consequences. It isolates the
villagers from the government psychologically. Their dealings
with the government more often concern regulatory matters
that irritate them than development matters that benefit them.
They therefore prefer to minimize their dealings with the
government. This lack of communication from the villages to

the government provides an effective screen for insurgent
activity, especially when the psychological isolation is reinforced by a viable main cause. The police at this stage are
rarely deployed below the district level. The insurgents can
thus move out of their base area and into adjoining villages
with a good deal of impunity.

Insurgencies develop with a fairly consistent pattern.
They start with scattered acts of violence and defiance on the
smallest scale. Small insurgent bands hold propaganda meetings in villages and assassinate progovernment village notables.
In time government officials fear to remain at night in the villages of the affected area. Out of sympathy with the main
cause or out of fear of insurgent terrorism, the villagers cooperate with the insurgents. They tell the government nothing
of insurgent movements. They contribute levies of money,
food, and men. Recruits are given careful political training.

Insurgent bands gradually expand, and insurgent control
gradually expands in area and in depth, outward from the villages adjoining the base area. Nighttime control is translated
into daytime control; there are areas into which the government ventures in substantial military force by day only. This
absence of government presence convinces those in sympathy
with the government that they have been abandoned, and they
cast their lot with the insurgents. In its rare sweeps through
the area in force, the government often "arrests hundreds of
suspects." Unjust arrests, combined with possibly brutal
treatment of suspects, convert passive supporters of the insurgency into active supporters.

In the areas in which the government presence comes and
goes with military sweeps, the insurgents assume many of the
functions of government. With broader areas under a degree
of secure control, the insurgency consolidates some of its
small armed bands into larger military units. The threat of
attack by larger units compels the government to use its
troops in larger units. This further reduces the government's
ability to deploy troops widely and to respond to small insurgent actions, and the government presence in the rural areas
is further reduced.

As the insurgency gains control of more and more of the
population, its recruiting base is expanded and the government

recruiting base is reduced. As the insurgent military forces
approach parity with those of the government, they form into
regimental and division-scale units equipped with heavy weapons. The government is forced back into its cities and overwhelmed.

Such, in brief, and greatly oversimplified, is the pattern
of a successful insurgency.

Counterinsurgent Operation

An insurgency can be reversed if the government recog-
nizes the scale of the problem and takes adequate measures
in time. The cost of turning back an insurgency increases at
an accelerating rate. Let us first look at the basic principles
of counterinsurgency, taken largely from Galula, and then at
the usual pattern of successful counterinsurgency action.

Some basic principles are:

The objective. The objective is "the destruction in a
given area of the insurgent's forces and his political organization...plus the permanent isolation of the insurgent from
the population, isolation not enforced upon the population but
maintained by and with the population" (Galula, p. 77). In
other words, when the boys from the village are running their
night ambush patrols on the village outer perimeter, the war
is won in that village, even though it may still be subject to
some terrorist attack.

Security comes first. The insurgent threat must be reduced in scale, so that village patrols are not suicide missions.
Above all, as Galula points out, "Even after the threat [of local
insurgents] has been lifted, the emergent counterinsurgent
supporters will not be able to rally the bulk of the population so
long as the population is not convinced that the counterinsurgent
has the will, the means, and the ability to win" (Galula, p. 78).

Development and reform must follow. The villagers
will not rally nor volunteer as guards nor volunteer intelligence until their psychological isolation from the government
is broken. This means that a high volume of development activity initiated in a short time is essential to change the quality

of the relationship between the people and the government
from negative, irritating regulation to positive beneficial development. This means that reforms are necessary to neutralize the main cause.

Development activity is also necessary to create a degree
of community solidarity, which is essential to a village guard
operation. Development must be oriented heavily to projects
which involve broad participation and interaction among all
the people of the village.

Intense efforts and vast means are needed. "The operations needed to relieve the population from the insurgent's
threat and to convince it that the counterinsurgent will ultimately win are necessarily of an intensive nature and of long
duration. They require a large concentration of efforts,
resources, and personnel. This means that the efforts cannot
be diluted all over the country but must be applied successively
area by area." (Galula, p. 79.)

Galula further points out why insurgency is cheap and
counterinsurgency costly:

> Promoting disorder is a legitimate objective for the in-
> surgent. It helps to disrupt the economy, hence to pro-
> duce discontent; it serves to undermine the strength and
> the authority of the counterinsurgent. Moreover, disorder--
> the normal state of nature--is cheap to create and very
> costly to prevent. The insurgent blows up a bridge, so
> every bridge has to be defended ... When the insurgent
> burns a farm, all the farmers clamor for protection; if
> they do not receive it, they may be tempted to deal pri-
> vately with the insurgent ... Because the counterinsurgent
> cannot escape the responsibility for maintaining order,
> the ratio of expenses between him and the insurgent is
> high. It may be ten or twenty to one, or higher. The
> figure varies greatly, of course, from case to case, and
> in each situation during the course of the revolutionary
> war. It seems to apply particularly when the insurgent
> reaches the initial stages of violence ... There is, it
> seems, an upper limit to this ratio. When the insurgent
> increases his terrorism or guerrilla activity by a factor
> of two, three, or five, he does not force the counter-
> insurgent to multiply his expenditures by the same factor.
> (Galula, p. 11.)

Such are the basic principles. The procedure is roughly as follows:

Patrolling--Over a given area, a commune or a cluster of villages, the army applies "quadrillage," more and more intensive patrolling with smaller and smaller units, making it impossible for the insurgent to function overtly. Covert insurgent agents remain in the village, but it is now possible for government agents to sleep there at night.

Pacification--A paramilitary team is stationed in the village. It may be an army detachment trained for civic action, a police unit, or a special type of pacification cadre. It generally has some patrolling responsibility. The team first takes a thorough census and registration of the population. It then engages the villagers in a variety of development activities, while assisting them in getting government action on their personal problems and grievances.

The objectives of these activities are varied and subtle. Obviously they are aimed at breaking down the psychological isolation of the villagers from the government, but one must beware of oversimplification in this matter. It is not simply a matter of doing nice things for the poeple so that they will like the government. Rather it is a matter of getting them intimately involved with the government, of getting them in the habit of going to government agencies for assistance on objectives they want. It is also a matter of getting them intimately involved with each other on projects and, more immediately, getting them intimately involved with the cadre. It is the increased level of social interaction, not the increased level of per capita income, that counts.

Another immediate objective is to get the people so closely involved with the cadre that the cadre get to know everyone's personality and his comings and goings. At first the people will fear terrorist reprisals if they have anything to do with the cadre. The cadre may have to give them an alibi when the insurgents' covert agents ask them why they participated. At this stage, insurgent agents are still in the village, watching. Everyone must be involved in frequent private conversations with the cadre, so that someone can volunteer information on the insurgents without being the obvious informer.

All this activity may or may not lead to identification of
the insurgent agents. If adequately handled and covered with
a modicum of security, it should lead to breaking the insurgent hold on the village. Contact between the village and insurgent bands will be effectively broken; people will see that
they can cooperate with the government to their advantage
and without fear of insurgent reprisal. Community leaders
will emerge in the course of the development activity.

Consolidation--When the time is ripe, village elections
should be held, if elected village leadership does not already
exist. A village militia or guard unit of some kind should be
recruited and trained to take over the patrolling responsibilities. The cadre, in effect, transfer their functions to the
people of the village. Pacification resources can now be
transferred out of the village; the war there is won. Subsequent police work may identify the insurgent agents, or the
agents may have fled.

A few more basic concepts of counterinsurgency should
be mentioned. Area concentration, which is very helpful to
rural economic development, is indispensable to counterinsurgency. Limited military resources must be used to protect the maximum population in the minimum perimeter.
Other basic principles will become apparent as one examines
the problems of planning, particularly the principle of simplicity of program content and the principle of broad latitude
to local officials.

PACIFICATION STRATEGY
DECISION-MAKING

The Options

Institutions and Cadre--There are a variety of services
necessary to a pacification effort, and the range of workable
institutional and cadre arrangements is broad. Soldiers can
perform specialized civil services, such as health treatment
and distribution of fertilizer and seeds; specialized civil
cadre can go armed and participate in patrolling. Police can

do small combat patrolling or, moving their function in the opposite direction, assist in development activities. More general-purpose pacification cadre can be trained and deployed, with paramilitary and police and development responsibilities.

Both troops and paramilitary and civil cadre can remain attached to conventional government agencies, or they can be assigned to a special pacification agency. Generally there must be a special pacification committee meeting regularly at the national level, coordinating efforts of all supporting agencies even when all cadre are assigned to one agency. Coordination at province and district level must be much tighter than that required for rural economic development. Program adjustments must come at much shorter intervals than in ordinary rural development, requiring an exceptional degree of financial flexibility and local decision-making authority, particularly regarding deployment of personnel.

Geographic Expansion--On this matter flexibility can be dangerous. National and local authorities will be under enormous political pressure to spread themselves too thin. The planning system itself must be structured to maintain discipline on this matter. Pacification must not be initiated where it cannot be sustained; abandonment of a village in which pacification is well advanced will gravely escalate the cost of a subsequent pacification attempt. The choice of a geographic pattern of expansion will be largely based on military considerations, but it will generally take on an oilspot or vector configuration.

Development Program Content--A wide variety of development activities will be proposed by concerned agencies and individuals as vital to winning the hearts and minds of the people. A few simple rules of thumb can identify those which are suitable and those which are not:

1. High community interaction. Projects which get the whole community working together are excellent.

2. Easy coverage. Projects must be applicable to hundreds of villages. They must require a minimum of engineering and a minimum of cadre talent and training.

3. Easy salability. Activities should respond to felt
needs. There is not enough time during the pacification
operation to educate the villagers in what is good for them.

4. Minimum outside regulation. One of the objectives of
pacification development activities is to change attitudes toward the government and to get the villagers to consider
government agents as helpers rather than regulators. Activities which require a great deal of policing to get loans repaid or to get equipment or material maintained should be
avoided if possible.

What kind of projects meet these criteria? The best
example, perhaps, is a pest control campaign. It is salable
because villagers are frequently quite aware of crop losses
to pests. To be successful the villagers must work in spray
teams and 100 percent of the villagers must cooperate. Community interaction is high. Coverage is easy. Cadre are
easily trained to manage the program, and spray team leaders
can be trained in a short time in the district towns. Activities
which require the villagers to visit the district town are useful in many ways to counterinsurgency.

The key to selecting development activities suited to pacification is simplicity. Substantial irrigation works and credit
requiring careful supervision may be unsuitable. It is important to understand the difference between development for
pacification and conventional development. What is important
here is not the institutional framework being built for the future but the immediate psychological impact. Development
activities may have to be carefully restructured. Free distribution of heavily subsidized sale of farm supplies may have
to replace sale on credit at normal commercial prices. Village health cadre with a limited variety of pills may have to
substitute for more highly qualified and better equipped health
officers, whose recruitment and training comes much more
slowly.

It takes a number of good development activities to achieve
the psychological impact needed for pacification. How many?
This is impossible to predict, and it is probably impossible to
evaluate afterwards whether a successful pacification operation included just enough or more than enough development activity. It is therefore advisable to include in the pacification

program all development activities which clearly meet the
above criteria and to exclude those which do not.

Reform Program Content--One now comes to the most
difficult part of a counterinsurgency program: the choice of
activities necessary to nullify or neutralize the main cause.
In contrast to security and development activities, which require tax resources but otherwise harm no one's personal
interests, reforms generally touch very deeply at the personal
interests and convictions of many people. They are thus con-
troversial and likely to be resisted in a variety of ways. They
generally require major legislation or prime ministerial decrees, and the drafting of such acts is likely to be dragged out
in long controversies.

Those responsible for reforms should therefore avoid
locking horns with their opponents but should first test out the
reforms on a small scale in those villages which are in the
point stage of the whole pacification program. Once they have
proved themselves in this manner, it will be easier to get the
necessary legislative endorsement to apply the program on a
broader scale.

It is also important to time the reforms carefully. They
do little good in the early stages of pacification in a particular
village when the terrorists still have a grip on the population.
Their payoff comes at the point where the population should
rally and give its active support to the government.

Strategy Planning Procedure

A word should be said about the circumstances under
which pacification planning takes place. An insurgency may
take some time to recognize. The first response to scattered
terrorist incidents in a region will be police and military
sweeps into the base area. The police and military in the region will then be reinforced to respond more quickly to insurgent incidents. The development program of the region will
be stepped up.

All this may prove adequate, particularly if the main
cause is weak; in some countries such measures have ended

insurgencies, but in some countries it has not proved adequate
and insurgent control has grown in spite of stepped up sweeps.
At this point the government may decide that nothing short of
the intensive pacification described by Galula will do. Hopefully, the government at that time will recognize that some
reforms will be necessary, although specific widely publicized
commitments can be put off till they have been tested in pilot
villages. At this point a special pacification agency or committee is generally established, and its staff begins drafting
plans. These plans may cover purely military operations as
well as pacification. The staff is often basically military or
police, but it will be concerned with many civilian matters
and will use civilians at least in consultative capacities.

In contrast to the economic development planning procedures described in previous chapters, pacification planning
will have to begin with narrative descriptions. The objective
is not an institutional structure that can perform a variety of
services while raising GNP, as in economic planning. Rather
the objective is a social and psychological transformation in
the village. The drama of the operation is thus a bit more important than its logic. A common device used to initiate planning is a staff paper, sometimes labeled a scenario, a straight
narrative description of who is to do what and how pacification
is to be accomplished in a typical village or commune. A number of different scenarios may be circulated among the staff,
if substantially different concepts are being advocated.

Once a particular scenario is selected as the starting
point of planning, the Minimum Paperwork Maximum Deliberation technique (see Chapter 14) can be used for working
group and committee review and modification. Following this
technique, a single-sheet tableau of key pacification stages is
distributed to the participants in the meeting and written on a
board. Figure 25.1 is an example. The stages that have been
defined in the scenario, at least the key stages, are listed
horizontally; cadre types and functional activity classifications
are listed vertically. The stages are given one- or two-word
labels, which are convenient for identifying them but will not
adequately describe them. From this tableau the author
briefs the meeting. Participants then suggest modifications
which the moderator writes on the board; the changes on the
board reflect an evolving consensus.

The reader is now invited to look at the strategy shown in
Figure 25.1 critically, as would a member of the working
group. Some of the circumstances and operational concepts
of the strategy need further explanation.

The example used in this chapter is a region of 10 districts and 1,000 villages, with an insurgency that controls
several hundred villages at least by night. The main cause is
based largely on land tenure problems. Under the interministerial pacification committee, a special agency has been established, responsible for training and deploying the special
pacification cadre. The agency has also been given a budget
for financing special activities of other ministries which are
incorporated into the pacification plan. It is assumed that,
when cadre are assigned to a cluster of villages, they will
have gone through at least six months of "quadrillage" (systematic small patrolling), but the villagers will still be afraid
to cooperate with government agents.

The cadre will first spend about two weeks doing a thorough job of interviewing each family, taking a thorough family
history and inventory, as well as investigating some individual
grievances. They will then do a report which will include a
preliminary village development plan. The strategy envisages
engaging the villagers in their free time in village projects and
committee activities, which will be compulsory but compensated, for the next month. A youth club, a farmers club, and
a women's club will be organized.

One should ask certain questions from the point of view of
a participant in a working group. First, is the plan consistent?
Are the activities consistent? Is the sequence right? The
example has features drawn from counterinsurgency programs
in a number of countries.

This strategy becomes the basis for programming of resource allocations. Particularly, it determines the programming coefficients; the numbers in the figure become, with
slight modifications, the input coefficients. The strategy
should be revised as experience is gained from actual operation, particularly after completion of the point and line phases.
Although the programming is written on a multiyear basis, the
strategy should be considered only a tentative multiyear plan,
as the programming will be revised at least as often as the

stages:	ENCADREMENT	CONSTRUCTION	RALLY
Security			
Troops patrolling	10 - - - - - - - - - - - - - - - - - - -	5 - - - - - - - - - - -	
Guards recruited		5	10 15
Guards trained			10 15
Police: no. assigned	1 - - - - - - - - - - - - - - - - - - -	4 - - - - - - - - - - -	5
Activities	Registration ID cards, Radio installed issued	Movement Control - - - - Resource Control - - - Recruit Guards	Train Guards
Pacification Cadre no:	15 - - - - - - - - - - - - - - - -	5 - - - - - - - - - - -	
Activities	Census & Fortification, grievance listing	Small Village Projects	Commune Projects
	Leader Club training organizing, Community Development	Organize Land Committee, Village Election	Commune Election
	Village requirement report	Temporary Village Council	Permanent Village Council
			Commune Council
Construction (where required)	School	Health Station, Village Road & Bridge	Commune Warehouse
Information Teams visits:	15/month	10/month	5/month
main propaganda themes	Government Power & Solidarity, Community Development	Reform Democracy	Responsibilities of Citizens
Health Workers no.	1 per village	1 per 2 villages	1 per 3 villages
Activities	inoculations, recruit assistant		
	daily sick call -		
Land Reform Team cover 4 villages at a time	on site - - - - - - survey - - - - - - - - - - -		Title Distribution

FIGURE 25.1. Pacification strategy, applied to one village.

499

strategy. The working group and authorizing committee should,
therefore, not delay implementation by haggling over the details of the strategy, which will still be tentative, even when
authorized. As in other types of rural development activity,
nothing is final until it has been proven it works in the point
and line phases.

PROGRAMMING

Once the strategy has been determined, one knows what
inputs are required for each stage for each village. On the
basis of this, the next step in planning is programming, for
optimum results of allocation of resources. The linear programming model for pacification below presents the concepts
of the programming in their full rigor. Informal Constrained
Maximization (ICM) will then be demonstrated as a more practical method of executing the programming. Figure 25.2, an
example of ICM applied to pacification, gives some notion of
the kinds of coefficients required.

The Linear Program

Notation--The following notation will be used:

Variables	Coefficients	Subscripts
v = number of villages	b = cost per unit	c = personnel class
P = personnel available	p = personnel per village	s = pacification stage
B = budget available	d = time discount rate	t = time period
$\overline{V}$ = total number of villages of the region	r = recruitees per village	
	s = phase limit of cadre expansion	
	w = stage payoff weighting factor	

The Objective Function--The object is to get all the villages through the stages leading up to Clear, as quickly as
possible. In each period we want to get as many villages as
far advanced as possible.

Maximize

$$\text{Maximize} \quad \sum_{t=1}^{n} \sum_{s=1}^{n} \frac{w_s v_{st}}{(1+d)^t} \quad\quad (1)$$

The higher the stage, the higher the value of w. For
stage 1 in the example it would equal zero. We might set
values as follows:

$$w = \begin{array}{l}
.2 \text{ for stage 2, Light Patrolling} \\
.4 \text{ for stage 3, Heavy Patrolling} \\
.7 \text{ for stage 4, Encadrement} \\
1.2 \text{ for stage 5, Construction} \\
2.0 \text{ for stage 6, Rally} \\
2.8 \text{ for stage 7, Consolidation} \\
3.6 \text{ for stage 8, Clear}
\end{array}$$

Initial stages have some value in that their activities interdict
insurgent activity. From the Rally stage on, the payoff increases sharply because the recruiting base of the government is enlarged and the pacification requirements drop off.

Basic Rules--Turning now to the "subject to" section of
the linear program, the next two equations are a matter of
basic definition.

Total
Villages

$$\sum_{s=1}^{n} v_{st} = \overline{V} \quad\quad (2)$$

In other words, for each time period the total number villages
in all stages must equal the total villages of the regions.

No Skipping
Stages

$$v_{st} = v_{(s-1)(t-1)} \quad\quad (3)$$

A given village cannot jump from, say, stage 2 to stage 4. It
can remain in a particular stage an extra period or two,

however, if resources are not available to advance it. The
rule expressed by the above equation might be violated if villages have been in a stage for extra periods. Then v_{st} might
include some of $v_{(s-1)(t-1)}$ and some of v_{st-1}.

Resource Constraints--The next two equations state formally the constraints of limited personnel and funds available.
Conceivably there might be materiel constraints, but those
would only be for a few periods, if funds are available to buy
them. One may therefore ignore them in the model.

Limited
Personnel
$$\sum_{s=1}^{n} p_{sc} v_{st} = P_{ct} = r_c \sum_{s=x}^{n} v_{st-2} \tag{4}$$

Training
Capacity
$$P_{ct} = T_c \tag{4a}$$

where x = stages secure enough to recruit. The above equations say that personnel available is limited by the population
base in secure villages (stages 7 and 8 in the example) in the
period before last. The coefficient r_c is the MRV in Figure
25.2, the maximum recruitable per village. The MTQ column
in Figure 25.2 gives values for T_c.

Now to look at the budget constraint:

Limited
Budget
$$\sum_{s=1}^{n} b_s v_{st} + \sum_{c=1}^{n} b_c P_{ct} = \bar{B}_t \tag{5}$$

The total pacification budget is thus defined as the sum of two
kinds of costs, those which vary with the number of villages
in various stages (b_s) plus those which vary with the number
of new personnel to be trained and equipped (b_c). The values
of b_s for the example are found on the bottom line of Figure
25.2. They are based on the values in the UCQ column (unit
cost per man per quarter) times P_{sc} (the personnel requirement), plus the construction and materiel budgets for each
stage. The second element coefficient b_c is found in the UCM
column, the unit cost of mobilization, including training and
various equipment, particularly vehicles.

This has somewhat oversimplified the resource limitation problem by considering only one level of aggregation, the village. Behind the men working in the villages in various stages must stand supporting men and equipment at the district level. Districts also go through distinct stages of pacification. As a matter of practice, these costs and requirements, forming something of a step function, are small enough to be ignored for purposes of this model. One should keep in mind, however, that there are fixed costs in addition to those accounted for in the model.

Point-Line-Network Constraints--During the first periods that a new cadre activity is being initiated, the point-line constraints discussed earlier in the book apply:

$$\underline{\text{Point}} \qquad p_{sc} v_{st} = s_{c1} \qquad p_{sc} v_{st-1} = 0 \qquad (6)$$
$$\underline{\text{Stage}}$$

$$\underline{\text{Line}} \qquad p_{sc} v_{st} = s_{c2} \qquad p_{sc} v_{st-2} = 0 \qquad (7)$$
$$\underline{\text{Stage}}$$

Beyond the line stage the training capacity limit will act as a brake preventing the expansion of activities beyond the administrative capacity to handle them. In the above equations, following the example in Figure 25.2 the pacification cadre s_{c1} value is 20, the s_{c2} value is 50.

Reform Constraint--Given the assumption that reform is essential to pacification, there are a number of ways of figuring in this constraint. One of the simplest is to designate a cadre function in connection with the reform, designating the reform cadre by the subscript c':

$$\underline{\text{Reform}}$$
$$\underline{\text{Cadre}} \qquad p_{sc'} v_{st} = 0 \qquad t \quad L \qquad (8)$$
$$\underline{\text{Limit}}$$

where L = the period in which the reform is first launched at point stage. What this is saying, in effect, is that no village can get up to stage s until t = L.

<u>Application of the Linear Program</u>--One should note that variables act as constraints in this linear program. This gives a large number of equations. Still, it might be feasible to solve each period in succession as a separate operation. The values of w are such that each period's solution yields values that are optimal considering all the periods as a whole. Bottlenecks in subsequent periods which prevent villages from automatically advancing one stage each period do not reduce the optimalization of a solution for a previous period, since something is gained by any one stage advance, even if it cannot be followed up by a further advance the next period.

In this regard one should remember that the payoff from pacification comes in two ways. The main payoff comes when a village goes into stage 6 and beyond, when all troops can move out to a widening perimeter and cadre can move on elsewhere, and when troops and cadre can be recruited from the village to swell the pacification resources available. There is a secondary payoff, however, whenever a village advances one stage, for each advance, from stage 1 on, reduces the insurgent hold and the insurgent base.

INFORMAL CONSTRAINED MAXIMIZATION

A rough approximation of the linear programming solution can be realized by informal constrained maximization (ICM). The solution is illustrated in Figure 25.2. It represents about one afternoon's work at a rotary calculator; the method is certainly efficient in terms of time expended relative to the magnitude of the problem and the quantity of data involved.

Basic Rules

1. The object is to get all villages into stage 8 in the fewest possible periods, having each village in as advanced a stage as possible in each period.

2. No village can skip a stage.

3. No village can be retreated to a previous stage; gains in higher stages cannot be made at the expense of villages in earlier stages.

4. Point-line phase constraints must be observed; in the application illustrated here the maximum for the point stage is 2 villages, for the line stage 8 villages.

5. Rounding off to the nearest 5 is permitted, also over-runs of up to 10 percent on minor cadre inputs.

Preparation

The coefficients must be determined first. These are illustrated at the bottom of Figure 25.2; the whole exercise is thus confined to one page. Cadre requirements by stage are derived largely from Figure 25.1. There is a line for each constrained input and a column for each stage. Following the stages are columns for other costs and planning factors:

UCQ = Unit Cost per Quarter per man, including all cost elements that vary directly with the number of men.

UCM = Unit Cost of Mobilization, all costs necessary to put one additional man into operation, charged to the first period of operation for simplicity of computation.

MTQ = Maximum Trainees per Quarter, the maximum number of men who can be trained with facilities planned for the relevant period.

MRV = Maximum Recruitees per Village, the number of men for each cadre who could probably be recruited in stages 7 and 8.

The MRV coefficient obviously represents a very wild guess, although judgment on this factor will improve with experience. Nevertheless, it is a very real constraint and a very important one, so judgment must be used in the planning.

Solution Procedure

The following rules should yield an optimum solution with a minimum of false computation and recomputation. One starts by writing in the current figures for the first quarter, then applying the rules to each successive period.

1. Start with the highest stage and try to advance as many villages as possible into it. An exception to this is the first five periods, in which the point and line stage villages are more important to advance than the stage 7 villages. One then advances as many villages as possible from successively lower stages.

2. Use up the bottleneck resource first. Some judgment is required to identify the bottleneck input. Basically it is the one with the highest coefficient at the highest stage into which a substantial number of villages are about to move, relative to the quantity available. One tests how many villages can be advanced without overrunning the constraint for that input.

3. Test the solution value of villages per stage for the bottleneck resource on the next tightest input. If the solution for the first bottleneck overruns the available quantity on the second bottleneck, reduce the number of villages advanced to stay within both bottlenecks. Repeat for successively less important or less binding input factors.

4. Where possible, use slacks to advance as many villages as possible from stage 1. In terms of the application illustrated, this means all troops for the patrolling stages, in which little use is made of other cadre inputs.

5. When all cadre inputs have been calculated, compute the budget and adjust the solution, if the budget is overrun.

6. Enter the constraint values for the next period and repeat the above steps.

AN APPLICATION OF ICM

It is revealing to examine in Figure 25.2 how ICM actually applies to an example. It should be noted again that, although the example is not drawn from any one country, the costs and other coefficients are realistic for a number of developing nations. One will note that different constraints become binding in different phases of the total operation, a very real characteristic of such struggles. The main binding constraint in each period is labeled A in Figure 25.2; secondary constraints that bind are labeled B.

2nd Quarter

In this, the first actual operational period, there is only a pilot group of 30 pacification cadre and a pilot group of 50 of the new rural police. Their coefficients limit the advance into stage 3 to two villages. Only 10 of the villages in stage 7 can be activated into the program due to a shortage of police.

3rd Quarter

As the pacification cadre and rural police are moved into the line phase of expansion, eight villages can be advanced into stage 3. Sufficient police are left over to activate 25 villages in stage 7, for advance into the next period. The pilot reform program is ready (the next section will explain why), so the first villages can move into stage 5. There is some flexibility in use of troops to advance more villages from stage 1 to 2 or fewer villages from stage 2 to 3. Something of a balance is struck between the two options.

4th Quarter

The main event here is the first real payoff; the pilot villages move into the Rally stage behind an expanding perimeter

of security. At this point, in actuality, the whole plan will be
redrawn on the basis of the pilot operation. In subsequent
periods some of the manpower constraint levels will begin to
rise, as the population base for recruitment begins to increase.

5th Quarter

The last of the 100 villages originally in stage 7 now move
into stage 8. Pacification cadre are no longer a binding constraint, but now the growth of the reform program is binding.
The budget limit is slightly overrun, largely because of heavy
mobilization costs in this period. An overrun due to peaking
of mobilization costs can be compensated by some of the budget slack from a previous period.

At this point there will be a sharp public reaction against
the conduct of the war. Newspaper correspondents will report
that the situation is stalemated and that pacification has accomplished nothing except in two showcase villages.

6th to 8th Quarters

At this point the program hits its stride; it is out of the
pilot phases. All cadre training is at maximum capacity.
Recruiting bottlenecks now become dominant and remain dominant until large numbers of villages reach stage 7. First the
military reach their recruiting bottleneck of 400 villages x 8 =
3200 troops. Then the pacification cadre reach the bottleneck
of 400 villages x 5 = 2000. Budget bottlenecks are passed as
recruitment slows up. In the 6th quarter the bottleneck is
pacification cadre training, which limits the increase to about
450. In the 7th quarter it is police training that binds. In the
8th quarter the constraint is health cadre recruitment.

Is this realistic? Would a matter as deadly serious as a
pacification program be slowed up because of lack of health
cadre? The 8th quarter is a long way off. One should complete this initial plan following the computational rules, mean-
while considering what structural adjustments can be made in
the next year to avoid this minor bottleneck.

9th to 12th Quarters

During these quarters there is something of a break-through, as recruiting limits rise rapidly. The step-up in the pace can be observed by looking across the line for the 5th stage, with rises from 45 villages in the 8th period to 100 in the 13th. Health cadre are continuing to have a recruitment bind, and in the 11th and 12th periods pacification cadre training in binding. The bottlenecks which have limited progress in later stages are largely eliminated, as can be seen by the fact that uniform figures are now cascaded down the diagonal out of stage 3. After stage 10 the military are in no way a binding constraint, as all villages are out of stage 1 and only a fraction are left in the patrolling stages.

13th to 17th Quarters

In these periods all bottlenecks are passed; the only limit is the number of villages in the previous stage. The declining budget, which reached a peak in the 10th quarter when recruitment limits were broken through, drops off rapidly as the scale of the effort dwindles away.

PLANNING BY
SIMPLIFIED PERT

One notes on the pacification strategy figure (Figure 25.1) that a land reform team is supposed to be on site in the last month of the encadrement stage. According to the program, the two pilot villages are supposed to be at that point in less than six months. Can the land reform team be ready in time?

This is a question that can only be answered by PERT, when a complex of plans and authorizations must precede action. PERT must thus become an integral part of pacification planning. Figure 25.3 gives a PERT charting of the reform operation. It starts with a survey of requirements, followed by planning of the point-line phase field operations, and then

Figure 25.2

WESTERN REGION PACIFICATION PROGRAM

STAGES — villages per stage

Quarters:	1	2	3	4	5	6	7	8	9	10	11	12	13	14	15	16	17
1. UNPATROLLED	470	440	415	330	275	245	200	200	150	90	90	100	100	100	100	100	
2. LIGHT PATROLLING	90	120	140	180	200	180	180	120	110	70	90	80	80	80	80		
3. HEAVY PATROLLING	40	38	45	60	60	65	45	70	60	100	90	70	70	80			
4. ENCADREMENT		2	8	20	35	45	45	70	60	70	60	60	60				
5. CONSTRUCTION			2	8	20	35	40	45	60	60	70	70					
6. RALLY				2	8	20	35	40	45	45	60	60					
7. CONSOLIDATION	100	90	65	23	2	8	20	35	40	45	60	60	70	80	80	100	100
8. CLEAR	300	310	335	377	400	402	410	430	465	505	550	610	670	740	820	900	1000

RESOURCES

(A indicates primary constraint, B indicates secondary constraint)

		1	2	3	4	5	6	7	8	9	10	11	12	13	14	15	16	17
1. PACIFICATION TROOPS	used:	1700	1980	2290	2600	2750	2950	3150	3300	3400	3700	3850	3100	1400	500			
	avail:	1700	2100	2300	2600B	3200B	3200B	3200A	3300B	3400A	3700	4000	4400	4880	5360	5920		
2. PACIFICATION GEN. CADRE	used:		30	150	430	865	1300	1450	1775	2025	2250	2550	2715	3060	1900	500		
	avail:		30A	150A	450A	900	1350A	1800	2050	2150	2325	2550	2750A	3050A	3350	3700		
3. RURAL POLICE	used:		20	50	100	150	200	281	385	480	560	640	720	820	880	560	200	
	avail:		30A	50	100B	150	150	300	400A	500	600	700	760	825B	915	1110		
4. INFORMATION CADRE	used:		8	20	40	66	66	72	91	82	111	113	128	126	66	50		
	avail:		9	50B	100B	150	150	300	400A	500	600	700	760	825B	915	1005	1110	
5. HEALTH CADRE	used:		10	20	40	60	80	80	80	121	130	140	150	165	183	171	126	82
	avail:		10	20	60	80	80	80	92	120	122	140	142	151	165	165B	183	201	222
6. AGRICULTURAL CADRE	used:		15	12	17	40	60	80	120	120	130	140A	150B	165B	183	201	222	201
	avail:		15	15	40	80	80B	120A	120	130	120A	70	81	87	99	78	54	
7. REFORM CADRE	used:					10	20	36	47	62	70	81	87	99	78	54	30	
	avail:						60	80	80	80	90	100	110	120	134	148		
8. BUDGET (net of dist. level) (in $000)	used:	200	850	1050	1300	1851	1700	1297	1484	1603	2024	1948	1631	1522	828	374	122	
	avail:	600	900	1200	1500	1800B	1800B	1800	1800	1800	2100	2100	2100	2100	2100	2100	2100	

BASIC COEFFICIENTS

OTHERS*

	UCQ	UCM	MTQ	MRV
Pacification Troops	$150	$1500	300	8
Pacification Gen. Cadre	120	700	450	5
Rural Police	140	1200	100	1.5
Information Cadre	160	1000	20	.3
Health Workers**	400	1500	40	.3
Agricultural Cadre	130	800	30	.3
Reform Cadre	130	1000	30	.3

PER VILLAGE BY STAGE:

	2	3	4	5	6	7
Pacification Troops	10	20	10	5	5	2
Pacification Gen. Cadre		15	15	15	5	
Rural Police			1	4	5	
Information Cadre			.2	.7	.5	.2
Health Workers**			.2	1	.3	.3	.1
Agricultural Cadre			.3	.3	.3	.3
Reform Cadre				.4	1.	
Construction Budget		$150	$150	$650	$370	$800
Materiel & Misc. Budget		500	500	800	800	800
TOTAL BUDGET	$1500	$3110	$4630	$5100	$2760	$1220

*UCQ = Unit Cost per Quarter per man, personnel & materiel
UCM = Unit Cost of Mobilization training & eqpt. per added man
MTQ = Maximum Trainees per Quarter
MRV = Maximum Recruitees per Village (stages 7 & 8 only)

**UCQ includes medicines

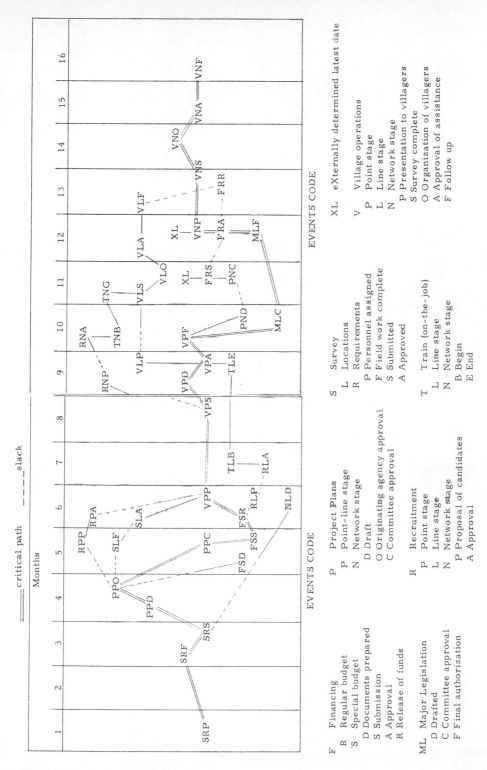

FIGURE 25.3. Pacification program: reform PERT schedule.

EVENTS CODE

F   Financing
  R Regular budget
  S Special budget
    D Documents prepared
    S Submission
    A Approval
  R Release of funds

ML Major Legislation
    D Drafted
    C Committee approval
    F Final authorization

P   Project Plans
  P Point-line stage
  N Network stage
    D Draft
    O Originating agency approval
    C Committee approval

R   Recruitment
  P Point stage
  L Line stage
  N Network stage
    P Proposal of candidates
    A Approval

S   Survey
  L Locations
  R Requirements
    P Personnel assigned
    F Field work complete
    S Submitted
    A Approved

T   Train (on-the-job)
  L Line stage
  N Network stage
    B Begin
    E End

EVENTS CODE

XL eXternally determined latest date

V   Village operations
  P Point stage
  L Line stage
  N Network stage
    P Presentation to villagers
    S Survey complete
    O Organization of villagers
    A Approval of assistance
    F Follow up

511

point-line-network field work. Along with the field work goes
recruiting, training, planning of further stages, and legislation.
During the first six months the critical path is largely on surveying and planning. Then the critical path follows the point
stage field operation. During the line stage the critical path
switches to legislation.

One can see from this that the evolution of the reform program can come in time to make the necessary stage advances
in the overall program possible.

GEOGRAPHIC ALLOCATION

The above procedures have determined overall targets,
staffing, and budget for each quarter. These must now be
divided up geographically.

The first step is to give every district, commune, and village a sequence number, indicating its priority and degree of
security. The priorities are assigned on the basis of two factors. The first is the minimum perimeter rule; the expansion
of the program should always enclose the maximum population
with the minimum outer patrolling perimeter. This will depend on the pattern of population density and also on terrain
features--a kilometer of forest and hills represents a longer
patrolling perimeter, in effect, than a mile of open field.

The second factor is the geographic strategy. This is in
large measure a matter of compromise between two options,
oilspots and vectors. One can either gradually enlarge a ring
around secure centers or run a line or belt of secure villages
that gradually rings the insurgent base area. The former is
sounder if the insurgency has already moved into most of the
districts of the region.

Once the priorities are set, there are two allocation options, assuming that the strategy is basically oilspot: one can
have more or fewer oilspots. One can allot all the stage advances and thus all the pacification resources that the No. 1
district can absorb and then give the balance to the No. 2 district. Or one can observe priority in a somewhat looser

manner, alloting more to the higher priority districts but
spreading resources over several districts. Assuming that
districts 1, 2, and 3 are largely in stages 7 and 8, all of the
stage advances beyond stage 3 in the first three quarters
might be given to district 4. Or they might be divided between districts 4, 5, and 6.

Within each district, again, there is some option between
concentrating in fewer or more communes. This is somewhat more limited by the miminum perimeter rule. Within a
commune all villages should be advanced from stage 3 to
stage 4 in no more than two periods, except in sparsely populated areas where villages are widely scattered.

Some measure of decentralization can be applied to the
planning of the final allocation. District chiefs can be invited
to submit plans and based on the common village strategy on
a hyperbudget, an allocation of resources to each high priority
district such that the sum of these hyperallocations is substantially greater than the total available. These plans would
then be trimmed back at the center to match total resources.
The basis of the cutback might be to minimize total perimeter;
areas of better concentration would receive a larger share of
their hyperbudget.

FEEDBACK AND REVISION

The reporting system should serve two main functions:
it should signal trouble spots and indicate how coefficients and
possibly strategy should be revised.

For the first objective, the reporting form (based on the
principles set forth in Chapter 17) should be laid out as follows. Districts and communes should be listed vertically, in
order of priority. Intrastage benchmarks should be established and alpha-coded; within stage 4 there would thus be
stages 4A, 4B, and 4C. Horizontally after each commune
should be written the planned substage, the actual substage
achieved, and a brief explanation of any failures to reach the
target. One can thus spot quickly what substages are causing
problems generally, and what high-priority locales are lagging.

Effort can then be concentrated on the more generally occurring problems and on the lagging locales with the highest priority.

Toward the second reporting objective, districts should submit reports on a format showing: planned vs. actual; villages in each stage; manpower resources and budget (planned, released, and spent); and recruitment planned and realized.

It is not excessive work to do a revised projection each quarter of the next four quarters at least. The first quarter's experience will generate a lot of revised thinking. Operating strategy revision is a time-consuming process, involving much high-level conferencing, but revised programming based on the original strategy can be accomplished in a few days if it is done systematically. Once a year the strategy should be updated to reflect experience.

A FINAL WORD

Counterinsurgency has one particularly notable feature in common with the general process of peaceful rural development: it succeeds through a systematic decentralization of initiative. It succeeds when the people of the villages themselves are able and willing to take the full responsibility of defending their community, just as rural economic development succeeds when villages and then individual farmers can plan their own diversification and seek out the necessary technical and financial support. To provide the villagers with the environment, the motivation, and the competence to take on this responsibility is a complex, laborious, and, indeed, agonizing process, requiring enormous patience, sophistication, and disciplined working method.

CHAPTER **26** COMPUTERIZATION

The procedures of the preceding chapters have been largely manual, requiring the following set of equipment: pencils, accounting spreadsheets, rotary desk calculators or (preferable because they are cheaper) adding machines plus slide rules, wide-carriage typewriters, stencil or hectograph duplicators (the latter are cheaper), blackboards and, possibly, overhead projectors. Organizations which have really exhausted the full planning capability of the pencil and its complementary equipment are rare indeed, perhaps nonexistent.

Nevertheless, the paperwork explosion has its casualties everywhere; developing nations with great pools of cheap clerical labor resources find themselves unable to keep up on routine accounting with purely clerical methods. As a result, third-generation computers, IBM 360's or the equivalent, are now at work in every country of Latin America and in all the major nations of Asia and Africa, as well as in many minor ones.

Planning as well as routine accounting can fall victim to the paperwork explosion. The manual methods of the previous chapters have major limitations. ICM (Information Constrained Maximization) cannot be applied multiregionally, to optimize or maximize net benefits among regions. It is difficult to apply sensitivity analysis to many of the procedures. Consideration of alternatives is largely limited to systematic elimination of alternatives. Each alternative strategy examined positively and fully requires just as much work as the formulation and programming of the basic strategy.

Updating of plans by the manual procedures of this book is far easier than with conventional narrative-based planning documentation. Nevertheless, it requires a lot of work, for which staff may or may not be available when needed. Use of feedback data in updating plans is also limited under manual techniques. The formats porposed (Form A-18 of Appendix A in particular) are good for practicing management-by-exception and they provide all the raw data for revision of planning coefficients. The processing of that raw data, however, requires some statistical analysis beyond the capabilities of the pencil and the slide rule.

In considering how the computer can be used to move rural development planning beyond the limitations mentioned above, this chapter will first review some of the basic features and problems of computers. It will consider possible applications, first agricultural development programming and simulation and then a variety of feedback applications. Finally, this chapter will take up the problem of the relationship of manual and computer planning techniques, and how the two should evolve together.

COMPUTER FEATURES
AND PROBLEMS

This section should serve as an introduction for those unfamiliar with computer work and as a review with some possible updating for those who have had some programming experience.

Basic Characteristics

The most notable and at times dramatic feature of a computer is its speed. Today's machines do upwards of 100,000 word or number manipulations per second. The other massive capability of computers is data storage. Depending on the number of secondary memory units, they can store millions of digits of information. The third feature is computation, not only addition, subtraction, multiplication, and division but extraction of roots, exponential multiplication, and a wide variety of standard mathematical functions. The computer also has the capacity to do logical manipulations, making moves on the basis of comparison of numbers and also using Boolean algebra. Finally it can receive data or print out data with a wide variety of media.

It can perform all its operations according to preset or
in-process instructions, or programs as they are generally
called. These come in three forms. The machines themselves work only in the binary number system, so they are
sometimes instructed directly in machine language. This
takes less machine time but is very time-consuming and difficult for the person writing the instructions. To circumvent
this difficulty, standard programming languages have been
established. These are standardized wordings and sequences
of instructions which are converted into machine language by
compilers stored in the machine. Finally there are standard
routines for solving certain types of problems, which are
called programs. These packages of standard instructions
are generally written in program languages. The machines
themselves are generally called the hardware of the computer
system; the programming languages and standard programs
are generally called the software.

Software Characteristics

The advances in software have been almost as important
to the computer as the advances in hardware. Indeed, without them the hardware improvements would be useless.

Programming Languages--Perhaps the most commonly
used programming language today is FORTRAN (for FORmula
TRANslation),[1] but the more recently developed PL/1 (for
Program Language 1) is more flexible and easier to understand.[2] Figure 26.1 is a sample of PL/1; it is one subroutine
of the simulation model found in Appendix B. This particular
subroutine is the key equation of the model described in Chapter 14. Figure 26.2 is the subroutine's flow chart.

It should be noted that the standard instructions of the
program language, in the example given, provide for standard
computations, addition, multiplication, etc., and also two
distinctive types of instructions known to programmers as DO
statements and IF statements. The DO statements command
the machine to execute a certain succeeding number of statements (down to END followed by the DO statement label, e.g.,
END PROJECTS) sequentially for each of the values of a particular subscript. If the statement says DO I = 1 TO 3, the

```
1  /PROCEDURE FOR SETTING PACE OF GROWTH OF PARTICIPATION OF FARMS
2        IN NEW CROP INNOVATIONS/
3  PROJECTS:  DO I = 1 TO 20;
4        IF MAX_FARMS (I) = 0 GO TO END PROJECTS;
5        STAGES:  DO J = 2 TO 30;
6                   IF FARMS (I, J-1) = MAX_FARMS (I)  GO TO LIMIT;
7                   NEW_FARMS(I, J) = OLD_FARMS_COEFF(I)  *  FARMS (I, J-1)
8                              + DEMO_COEFF (I)  *  NEW_DEMONSTRATIONS(I, J-1);
9              FARMS (I, J) = FARMS (I, J-1) + NEW_FARMS (I, J);
10             IF FARMS (I, J) > MAX_FARMS (I) GO TO LIMIT;
11                    ELSE GO TO END STAGE;
12        LIMIT:  FARMS (I, J) = MAX_FARMS (I);
13                 NEW_FARMS (I, J) = FARMS (I, J) - FARMS (I, J-1)
14     END STAGES:
15 END PROJECTS:
```

FIGURE 26.1. A sample of PL/1 (Computer Program Language 1); subroutine of a simulation model.

Explanation:

> /XXX/ indicates a comment not affecting the program
> (X, X) indicates subscripts
> * indicates multiplication, X

Line

3   Do all the operations down to line 15 first for i=1, then around again through all of them for i=2, etc., through i=20, i being the subscript denoting the project.

4   If MAX_FARM (I), the number of farms per district to which project$_i$ is suited, = 0, i is not a crop project, so skip to the next i.

5   J is the stage subscript. Do the following operations to line 14 first for j=2, then around again for j=3, etc.

6   FARMS (I, J) is the number of farms which have adopted the innovation of project i by stage j. If it has reached the maximum in the previous stage, skip to line 12.

7-8   This is the key equation of the model, as explained in Chapter 4.

$$\Delta f_{ij} = d_{fi} f_{ij-1} + d_{di} \Delta d_{ij-1}$$

9   In terms of the above equation: $f_{ij} = f_{ij-1} + \Delta f_{ij}$

10   If lines 7-8 have pushed FARMS (I, J) beyond the limit of MAX_FARMS (I), do lines 12 and 13, otherwise skip 12 and 13 and go to 14.

12-13 Definitions applied instead of lines 7 and 8, if those lines have pushed the value of FARMS (I, J) over the limit.

14-15 Terminal points for the DO loops started in lines 5 and 3, respectively.

Note: Except in IF statements, the = sign indicates that the value of the right-hand side is being assigned to the variable on the left-hand side.

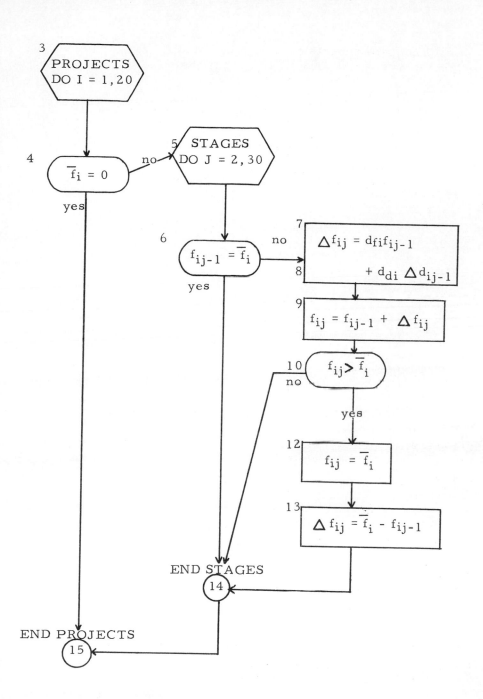

FIGURE 26.2. A sample of flow charting, based on the sub-routine shown in Figure 26.1.

succeeding statements are executed first for i=1, then for i=2, then for i=3. This simplifies operations on large vectors and arrays.

The IF statements permit logical switching and application of decision rules. They say that IF x is so, go to one set of operations, if not then continue below or go to another set. The "is so" part is generally a comparison of two values. This makes it possible to apply rules such as: "If the return on capital is less than a set minimum ratio, drop the project."

In addition, PL/1 and other programming languages have a wide variety of built-in functions. LOG or COS followed by the number will generate the logorithm or the cosine. The programming languages also have the capability of calling subroutines from other programs stored in the machine into a routine with a single instruction. All these features considerably reduce the detail involved in writing programs, as well as improving the compactness and communicability of programs. PL/1, using as it does full words and phrases to identify variables and coefficients, may be a better way of communicating models than conventional mathematical symbols.

Standard Program Packages--Ready-to-apply standard programs have been compiled for particular types of problems, types of planning situations, and types of systems techniques. These may be classified in two categories: generalized and specific.

The generalized programs usually contain a number of modularized subroutines applying specific techniques or variations on techniques. Perhaps the most useful in rural development is MPS/360 (Mathematical Programming System) for linear and other programming.[3] It can handle a linear program of up to 4,000 equations with 4,000 constraints. To illustrate the compactness of these ready-to-apply packages, one need only feed in the data, signal some 5 or 10 statements to set up the problem and then state PRIMAL to generate the primal solution. DUAL generates the dual solution. Similar single statements generate parametric variations.

Some other generalized programs of possible use in rural development planning are PMS/360 (Project Management System, which contains CPM, PERT, and PERT/Cost)[4] and

GPSS (General Purpose Systems Simulator, which applies
queueing theory to highly complex queue structures).[5] There
are also some generalized programs for statistical analyses
(for correlations by multiple regression analysis).

Specific packages have been compiled for planning tasks
in various industries and for problem-solving in various academic disciplines. In economics, for example, IBM provides
program IB 9 FES (Forecasting by Econometric Systems).[6]

THE APPLICATION TO
AGRICULTURAL PROGRAMMING

Appendix B gives a computerizable mathematical model
of agricultural development based on the concepts of Parts I
and III. The computer application procedure is briefly flow
charted in Figure 26.3, a linear program for maximizing net
benefits (present discounted value) over a multiregional multiyear program; the coefficients are derived by simulation of
farm and district modules.

The Nature of Simulation

The term simulation is often applied to all model-building,
but it is a more meaningful term when more narrowly defined.
Here it will mean building a computer model and moving it
over time.

The general simulation procedure is to generate inputs or
events, solve the equations for period one, use the values of
period one as inputs to period two, solve period one, and so
on. At any point one may take a readout of the values of the
state variables to "observe the state of the system." Thus
one learns how the system behaves and how it responds to
changes in the environment.

General Problems--Computers might be described as
expensive, fast-counting idiots.

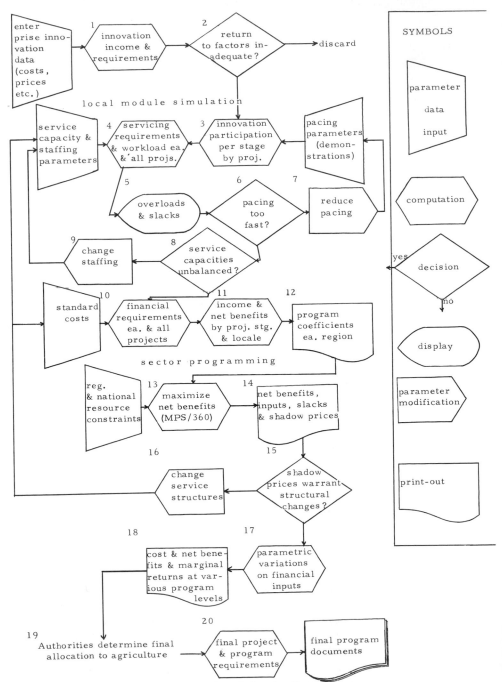

FIGURE 26.3. Computerized agricultural planning flow chart.

One of the formidable qualities of human intelligence that impresses anyone who has worked with computers is its ability to function with garbled data and instructions. The human mind can (though it does not do so invariably) reach correct conclusions and decisions on the basis of ambiguous, misleading, or totally inadequate instructions and information. Not so the computer. Insignificant programming ambiguities, illogicalities, and trivial data gaps result in output that is pure garbage. Programming must be zero-defect. Data input must be of far higher quality than that required for manual methods.

For this reason debugging of a computer program is arduous. A program for a simulation system such as that described later in this chapter, running from 600 to 800 lines, may require many man-months to debug, although the operating time on the machine may be measured in minutes. Even ready-to-apply packages require perfect handling and may require scores of test runs before usable output is generated.

The equipment is expensive, running into the millions of dollars for moderate size 360 installations (prices vary with peripheral equipment and accessories, numbers of auxiliary memory units, and features of the core units). Supporting personnel and other operating requirements are expensive. For this reason purchase of new equipment could never be justified on the basis of planning applications alone. All the planning applications considered later in this chapter could not possibly use more than a few days computer time a year, plus several hours each month.

The general accounting and routine administrative applications use vastly more time than planning applications. These frequently justify the use of computers in developing nations, keeping them busy 8 to 10 hours a day. Planning applications can only be considered if there is idle time on existing equipment (optimum usage of computers is 20+ hours a day, considering their cost).

One drawback of the computer can have positive results. Its stupidity forces men to be that much smarter. It is a stern disciplinarian and enforces rigorous thinking, thorough logic, and coherence in the planning system.

The Limitations of Simulation--Note that, unlike linear programming, simulation does not generate an optimum solution. It can produce a solution which satisfies certain decision rules, but it cannot produce a combination of activity levels which, according to given criteria, is assured to be optimum.

This, in a sense, reduces the quality of a programming model whose coefficients are derived by simulation. It reduces the optimization of the linear program to a narrow range of options. In the model in Appendix B, the linear program itself decides only how many districts in each region are to be launched into the first stage of that region's program each year. Regarding the content of each regional program there is no optimization. There is no optimization between promotion of different crops, between different combinations of structures of services, or between project activities and policy alternatives such as subsidization.

This limitation is unavoidable for two reasons. First, to use a standard linear programming software package, it is necessary to keep the number of equations down to 4,000; structuring the equations of the modules as parts of the master linear program would raise the number of equations for one region alone to well above 4,000. Secondly, purely quantitative optimization is not possible. Before the coefficients can be accepted for programming, the state of the system must be examined with an eye to its qualitative as well as its quantitative aspects. This requires some human interaction in midprocess, which is possible in simulation but not in linear programming.

This combination of simulation and linear programming can be used to evaluate a variety of specific structural alternatives, as will be noted below. The last part of this section, furthermore, presents a number of "second generation" modifications that can increase the model's flexibility and realism. The practical limitations of the model are not as rigid as its technical limitations would imply.

The Simulation Procedure

In Figure 26.3 the flow chart starts with the farm module.

Step 1 is simply the solving of the F series equations in Appendix B. For each enterprise, given the average scale, recommended inputs and their costs, yield, home consumption, and market prices, it determines net income and other single farm coefficients to be used later.

Step 2 asks if the ratio of net income to land, labor, and credit requirements is adequate to make the innovation attractive to farmers. This can be done by human intervention, by judging and evaluating a readout on step 2, or by the machine. For each of the three criteria a minimum acceptable ratio could be set. The program might read:

IF NET_ENTERPRISE_INCOME (I) / ENTERPRISE_SCALE (I)>

MIN_RETURN_TO_LAND

GO TO KEEP_PROJECT; ELSE GO TO DROP_PROJECT;

(etc.)

Step 3 is the subroutine presented in Figure 26.1, applying the L1 equations in Appendix B.

Step 4 applies the L2 series equations, to determine whether the pace set in Step 3 can be supported by the various institutional projects, applying also equation L7.1 to determine staging.

Step 5. The differences between the workloads generated in Step 3 for the service institutions and their initially planned capacities are read out at the console.

Steps 6-9. Project coordinating staff is assumed to be gathered at the console. If several institutions are overloaded the number of demonstrations on certain projects is reduced (step 7) thus recycling the operation back through step 3. If one or two institutional projects have far too little or far too much capacity relative to the general level of

activity, their staffing and other service parameters are
changed (step 9), thus recycling the operation back through
step 4. Results are again displayed (step 5), and after a few
changes the display should indicate to the coordinating group
that the projects are all in balance, in the local module.

Step 10. First the commercial projects are run through
the L3 series of equations. These may apply to cooperatives
and also to submodels of private supply and marketing operations. Then all projects are run through the L4 equations,
and the commercial projects are run through the L5 series.
The L7.2 equations determine when financial support to projects from the development budget terminates.

Step 11. This does a summary like that found on Form
A-13 in Appendix A (Local Cost Benefits Summary) and then
computes the present discounted value of net benefits for the
total module for each stage in each starting year.

Step 12. All the coefficients having been computed, they
are summarized on a listing that would contain the same data
as Form A-14 (Program Coefficients Table), and they are
also listed on a tape, for speedy input into the next step.

Linear Programming Procedure

Step 13. The 14 equation types of the linear program in
Appendix B are applied on MPS/360 to derive a primal and a
dual solution. A program of 10 regions and 20 crops over
five years would require about 500 equations. It would probably be advisable to do this operation three times, once for a
low level of financial allotments, once for a medium level,
and once for a high level. This will give a picture of possible
input bottlenecks.

Steps 14-16. The results of step 13 are printed out. The
shadow prices, in particular, are examined to see if any
strategy or structural changes are warranted. The shadow
price of a particular type of cadre, for example, might be so
high that it would be worth while importing them at a high
price from abroad or spending the money to give them a lower
level assistant to increase their servicing capacity. Such

decisions are cycled back (step 16) into step 4, making appropriate cost changes at step 10. One thus may come up with different coefficients for different ranges of total program scale, using higher cost inputs beyond certain bottleneck points.

Steps 17-18. Parametric variations, primal and dual solutions over a range of values of a parameter, are performed on the financial inputs: budget, credit, and foreign exchange. From these the marginal revenue product of these inputs are computed. The final printout gives the maximum net benefits and marginal revenue product for a range of financial allocations to the agricultural sector.

Step 19. The national planning authority, whatever it may be, uses this data plus data on other sectors to determine how much budget, credit expansion, and foreign exchange to allot to agriculture.

Steps 20-21. On the basis of the final allocation decision, which determines the number of districts in each region to be launched into the regional program, requirements of individual projects are computed. Final documents, such as the Form A-10's and A-11's are printed out.

Alternative and Complementary Programs

The machine time on a single run of steps 1 through 13 is on the order of minutes. Additional uninterrupted runs can provide some useful by-products, in addition to programming the overall sector program.

Policy Measures--Nonproject measures such as subsidies can be evaluated with the model. Such evaluations require, of course, assumptions on several parameters. On a subsidy for fertilizer, for example, one would lower the input price parameter and then perhaps assume that this would make it feasible, as in Pakistan, to do without institutional credit arrangements. One would then add a high interest charge to the cost of the input to compensate for borrowing from traditional sources at 5 percent a month and eliminate or postpone some credit activities. The run would indicate whether additional innovations

were feasible, whether faster or broader coverage and participation was made possible by the elimination of credit cadre
requirements, and what the total impact would be on net benefits and marginal returns for the sector. One can thus assay
the tradeoff between policy and nonpolicy measures, as well
as test the cost-effectiveness of the policy measure.

   Alternative Institutional Options--Cadre parameters can
be easily changed. One can add more functions to a multipurpose cadre, for example, and give them assistants, while
reducing the number of special purpose cadre. The simulation and programming will then show what the difference
will be in terms of utilization of manpower resources, cost,
and total maximum net benefits with the same resources.
Alternative strategies, in other words, can be assayed in
terms of their relative net benefits from the same inputs,
financial and human.

   By making certain assumptions it is also possible to
evaluate the possibility of private versus public or public-
supported supply and marketing channels. One must assume
that private firms need a substantial possible gross margin
as an inducement. This might lower the net income per
farmer and require some subsidy to compensate. By running
the model with these changed assumptions one can see if the
budget requirements are reduced under this alternative and if
the net result will be higher or lower coverage and net benefits.

   Capital Projects--The effect of a large scale road or irrigation project is to increase the number of districts in which
certain innovations are possible. It should be noted that the
maximum number of farms to which an innovation is suited in
the modular district, $\overline{f}_i$ in the model, is based on the number
of districts to which the innovation is suited:

$$\overline{f}_i = \overset{*}{f_i}\left(\frac{\overline{C}_i}{\overline{C}_r}\right)$$

where $\overset{*}{f_i}$ = farms to which suited in the average district to
which suited, $\overline{C}_i$ = districts in the region to which innovations
of proj. i is suited, and $\overline{C}_r$ = total districts in region.

A transportation or irrigation project, by increasing $\overline{C}_i$, increases f_i. One can thus find the payoff on such a project by the resulting increased net benefits in the agricultural sector. Note that this simulation also shows what complementary cadre and other expenses in the agricultural sector are necessary to make a transportation or irrigation project pay off--considerations that have been fatally neglected on some projects in the past.

Second Generation Modifications

Computer programs, like good plans, are of modular construction. Generalized programs are built up from subroutine modules, which can be used in varying combinations for specific tasks. More modules can be added to them to broaden their capabilities. The model in Appendix B should be considered a first generation program; it has some obvious over-simplifications which can gradually be overcome by adding new subroutine modules which will make the total program more realistic.

One should not try for perfection on a first generation model, however. One is constantly getting ideas that might improve it, but at some point one must freeze the model and put what one has to work. After at least one year of operation and feedback of the starting model, one can then add in all the ideas for improvement that have been collected.

The model in Appendix B is a first generation design that was frozen at a certain point, partly so as not to add more complications to a presentation that is already difficult to grasp in one sitting. Some obvious improvements suggest themselves for the second generation model:

The Farm Level--It is possible to build a model of the farm module that is considerably more useful than the simple definitions in Appendix B. First of all, one might distinguish more than one farm system in each region by a farm system subscript f, such that $\overline{f}_r = \sum_f \overline{f}_{rf}$, where $\overline{f}_r$ is the average farms per district in the r-th region and $\overline{f}_{rf}$ is the average number of farms per district of the f-th farm system in region r.

One can than apply a linear program at this level to optimize the long-run cropping pattern. To do this one must establish variables one level lower, for units of land or breeders of livestock, of a given quality class: h''_{rfhi}, the quantity of land used by the modular f-th type farmer in the r-th region of the h-th class of land for the i-th crop. A second type of quantitative variable must now be introduced: workdays $\left(w''_{im}\right)$, the number of days required in the m-th month to produce the i-th crop on one unit of land. Using the double prime superscript to denote coefficients and values applying to one unit of land, the linear program for maximizing income by region would read:

Maximize

$$\sum_f \sum_h \sum_i y''_{fhi} h''_{fhi}$$

subject to:

Land

$$\sum_i h''_{fhi} \overset{/}{=} \bar{h}_{fh}$$

Labor

$$\sum_i \sum_h w''_{im} h''_{fhi} \overset{/}{=} \bar{w}_{fm}$$

Market
Capacity

$$\sum_f \sum_h v''_{hi} h''_{fhi} \overset{/}{=} \bar{\bar{M_i}} \\ \overline{fC}$$

Home Con-
sumption

$$\sum_h v''_{hi} h''_{fhi} = \bar{c}_{fi}$$

The regional subscript is understood to apply to all expressions. In the objective function the coefficient y''_{fhi} is income per unit of land quality $\underline{h}$ under farm system f for the i-th crop. The land constraint $\bar{h}_{fh}$ is land of quality h available to the average farm of type f. The labor constraint is total workdays available in month m. The coefficients used in the market capacity and home consumption equation v''_{hi} is the yield of crop i per unit of land type h. The market capacity constraint is the maximum quantity the region can market (an arbitrarily high figure used to prevent outlandish solutions) divided by the number of farms in the region, since all equations are in terms of an average farm. The constraint of the last equation is $\bar{c}_{fi}$, home consumption of farm type f of crop i.

Using the coefficient h_{fi} for average enterprise scale of farm system f for the i-th crop, one then derives the number of farms to which an innovation can apply from the above program's solution:

$$\bar{f}_{fi} = \bar{f}_f \frac{h''_{fi}}{h_{fi}}$$

Obviously the data necessary to apply the above program will take a few years of farm management research.

The local Level--It is possible to be more realistic about service capacities and workloads of institutions, first by adding a month subscript m into the L2 series. Beyond that, it might be possible to apply a queueing theory model to this step of the operation.

It could be possible to add another level of local aggre- gation, say, a commune module in addition to the district module. This would go by a different staging sequence than the district, as the community development and agricultural engineering projects in Appendix A have three-stage programs at the commune level. It could also be possible to have dif- ferent categories of districts within each region, to recognize differences in size or differences in dominant farm systems. All these additional nuances involve basically the addition of more subscripts.

A simple improvement that can improve considerably the quality and the realism of the targets for early stages of the program is the phasing in of innovations on farms over two or more years. Farmers frequently, perhaps generally, try innovations on existing enterprises on only half or a fraction of their land in the first year. This phenomenon might be expressed in the following manner:

$$\triangle y_{ij} = .4y'_i \triangle f_{ij} + y'_i f_{ij-1}$$

Perhaps the most important but most difficult improvement that can be made is improved behavioral theory regarding innovation. In the first generation model the pace of adoption of a feasible and profitable innovation is purely a function of the number of demonstrations. These coefficients should also be a function of net income per hectare of per manday; obviously a highly profitable innovation will be adopted faster, other things being equal. Accumulated feedback may permit the planner to derive more complex and realistic coefficients to predict the rate of technological innovation on the farm.

Third Generation Modifications

As institutional structure moves well into stage III of rural development, the model can be modified in many ways and, on balance, simplified. It is no longer necessary to coordinate the staging of projects; the various service institutions are also sufficiently qualitatively developed; they can all handle any kind of innovations. One can assume that the key local module in stage III becomes the commune. The unit of increment then becomes c_{irs}, the number of communes or region, r, into which the i-th project is introduced in the s-th starting year (projects retain internal staging).

At this stage it is possible to combine the individual and the sector models in the program shown in Figure 25.3 if a quadratic program algorithm can be applied. Some quadratic program computer packages are available but their use to date has been limited. One can expect, however, that by the time a few more countries have the institutional structure and the data to support such an approach, good generalized computer programs will be available.

INFRASTRUCTURE AND
FEEDBACK APPLICATIONS

There are a number of computer feedback applications which apply equally well to complementary sectors and decentralized infrastructure programs and to agriculture programs. Infrastructure programming, however, is quite different.

Infrastructure Scheduling

The object of infrastructure project scheduling, under the decentralized procedure described in Chapter 20, is to satisfy the priority preferences of the villagers while neither overloading or grossly underutilizing support capacity, inspection, design, and construction equipment capacity. The priority preferences of numerous locales cannot be boiled down to a single maximand or a single objective function so linear programming cannot be applied. Simulation is necessary.

Satisfying individual job priorities with constrained resources is essentially the problem faced by any industrial "job shop," which manufactures custom engineered products to order. Generalized computer packages are available for industrial job shop scheduling which could probably be adapted to infrastructure scheduling.

Report Processing

The management-by-exception quarterly or monthly reporting forms discussed in Chapters 17 and 20 can be posted by machine to cumulative planned-vs.-actual records, such as Form A-17 (Project Annual Plan) or the Malaysian schedule/report checkerboard format. Once the data is in the machine, it can provide a variety of other analyses. First of all, it can print out the percentage of variance of planned vs. actual. It can also arrange the information in different ways, year-to-date cumulative, current year vs. last, and totals by province and region, all at over 500 lines a minute.

The computer can go beyond useful rearranging of data and provide useful quantification of relative performance. The ratio of planned vs. actual participation divided either by the ratio of planned vs. actual cadre available, for example, or by the sum of the ratios of planned vs. actual cadre and money available, can indicate the relative efficiency and effectiveness of units. A printout of the top and bottom 10 percent performing units can be of particular use to management-by-exception. The object of management-by-exception reporting, it should be emphasized, is to reduce the amount of detail that must be examined in order to understand what is happening. The computer does this by boiling a number of statistics down to one ratio and then printing out only the exceptions.

Such reporting must be used, however, as a tool for further investigation rather than as a final answer. If ratios are used as the final indicators of the performance of individuals, those individuals will work together to contrive some means of producing ever-victorious statistics. Statistics must be considered a tool and a guide to understanding rather than a final answer.

Improvement of Coefficients

One of the most important functions of feedback is the improvement of the quality and the realism of the coefficients used in further planning. Two types of coefficients are particularly important. First, the operating coefficients which link pacing factors to output, such as the ratio of cadre to participants, are often based on guesses founded on a small amount of poorly structured experience. A number of standard computer programs can do multiple factor regression analysis, which can correlate outputs properly with pacing factors, net of the influence of extraneous factors. Such analysis, for example, can indicate how much of the variance in cadre-realized participation ratios in various locales is due to differences in cropping conditions, and can isolate the actual ratio under average cropping conditions.

The second important coefficient to be analyzed, refined, and updated is cost, particularly construction cost. As mentioned in Chapter 20, plans based on obsolete cost data can

cause serious delays, as every project gets held up for high-
level approval of expenditures greater than the original budget.

Updating of Plans

Here again, the problems and possibilities of agricultural
and infrastructure projects differ.

On agricultural development projects the main reason for
frequent updating of plans is to reflect improved coefficients.
It may be useful to get a new five-year projection every six
months, reflecting work to date and more realistic coefficients.
Such revisions need not be made official or submitted to top
levels for approval, but they are nevertheless very useful as
unofficial documents. They show what problems can be anticipated in reaching the targets that were originally set. They
forecast which projects will not be able to use the money originally alloted. They show certain projects whose probable
failure, based on current plans and their implementation, may
jeopardize other plans. In brief, frequent revision of forward
projections can signal problems of great importance to top-
level authorities at the earliest possible moment.

Manual reporting procedures can signal needs for current
troubleshooting. Computerized revisions of plans can signal
problems well in advance, and thus avoid a lot of frantic last-
minute troubleshooting.

On infrastructure programs the frequent revision of plan
books by computer can be most useful in preventing rapid ob-
solescence due to changing priorities. During the course of
the year some projects will prove unfeasible and others will
suddenly become unexpectedly urgent. Priorities as shown
in plan books tend to get rapidly out of date. With the basic
data that goes into a computerized planning or reporting system, plus some signals of changed priorities, the computer
can update the plan books at more than 500 lines a minute.

A word of caution about this and other feedback functions:
such reporting is never completely up to date, and reported
figures are always imprecise. Fortunately, many good decisions can be made on the basis of imprecise or slightly out
of date information.

THE PHASE-IN OF
SYSTEMS-BASED PLANNING

The computer takes up where the pencil leaves off. It should not be used until the possibilities of the pencil have been exhausted. This means that planning should not be computerized until it has been "pencilized" to the maximum, and additional data and computations are required which the pencil cannot handle.

Planning, like projects, must be phased in. Of the various routines and subroutines presented in this book, the sequence of possible introduction would depend heavily on the preceding system and its weaknesses and strengths, and on the problems of planning which were particularly urgent. In any event the transition to comprehensive computerized planning would have to be a multiphase evolution. Indeed, the transition to comprehensive planning based on manual techniques would have to be executed over several phases. The following is a schema of how the phasing might be executed, based on the nature of the procedures themselves (each phase taking anywhere from six months to two years).

Phase I

The easiest and most immediately useful procedure is the single project plan, Form A-11 of Appendix A, applied to institutional projects without the backing of a staged local module. The education and family planning projects shown in Tables 18.1 and 18.3 are illustrative of this basic format. It can be applied at any time in the planning cycle without major new decisions on project structures, and its application will in itself sharpen the agency's thinking about the activity.

Phase I starts, then, with preparation of project plans on Form A-11's of all institutional projects in agriculture. Along with these, annual and subannual documentation (the Project Annual Plan on Form A-17 and the Quarterly Report on Form A-18) can start. Preparation of local modules on Form A-10's starts at the same time, with staging unrelated to other projects (as in Chapter 12). Since the definition of multiproject stages may require some high level strategy decisions, these may not be issued till the end of Phase I.

Crop project definition starts at the beginning of this phase with the Farm System Analysis on Form A-1, and the organization of one crop working group to prepare an Innovation Package Analysis on Form A-4. This results in one crop project on Forms A-10 and A-11.

Phase II

Crop Working Groups are established for other main crops. An organizational strategy working group is started, centering its deliberation on the agricultural services structure charts, A-7.1 and A-7.2.

The feasible innovation packages for one region are analyzed on Form A-4 and summarized on Form A-5. A strategy for one region, plus some alternatives, is set forth on Forms A-7.3, A-8, and A-9. From these a complete program is drawn up for one region on Form A-10's and A-11's, with the pace of the total campaign determined by ICM on the Program Summary (Form A-16). In brief, the total system on manual forms is tried out on one region. Simplified PERT is applied to plan in the first campaign of the program. Annual and subannual documents are also initiated for that region (Forms A-17 and A-18.)

At this point computerization can be initiated with the net benefits computation, step 11 on Figure 26.3. Computing the net benefits for various stages and starting years is a very simple computer program that can save a great deal of manual work. Programming of the simulation is initiated with steps 3, 10, and 11. These are the easiest and most useful steps of the simulation, as they can be used to determine financial requirements of alternatives.

Phase III

The A-series forms and manual programming is expanded
to all regions in stage IIb. Computer simulation and linear
programming is applied to one region. PERT is applied to all
campaigns. Statistical analysis of feedback is begun.

Phase IV

Simulation and linear programming by computer is applied
to all regions. The computer updating of projects begins.
Second generation modifications of the program are tested on
one region.

Phase V

The second generation program is applied to all regions.
Infrastructure planning must go through similar phasing,
laying the foundation for decentralized planning of agriculture,
once all the agricultural service institutions are in place. At
that point distinctive rural development planning begins to
fade at the central echelon, as the local echelon takes on more
and more initiative. Rules of program discipline can be relaxed. The staging of projects no longer must be coordinated.
The local community and then the individual farmer exercise
an increasingly wide range of options.

Thus standardization generates diversity. By planning on
the basis of farm and local modules (based on the fiction that
all farms and communities in a region are alike), the institutions of increasing diversification are built.

There is an interesting parallel in industry. It has been
said that mass production is giving way to modular production,
that emphasis is changing from mass production at lowest cost
to producing maximum variety at reasonable cost. The key is
mass-producing a variety of multiusable parts (modules),
which can be combined to custom tailor what the customer
wants. The company which initiated mass production on the

basis of highly standardized components by offering the customer his choice of any color, provided it was black, now offers any basic model in literally thousands of combinations of
options.

So in rural development, rigid standardization of detail
lays the foundation for diversification. The Model T must precede the offer of the Mustang in x different colors, with y different engines, and z different interior trims. The farmers
must be offered the chance to own a Model T before trade-ups
can be considered. To get the cost of rural institutions down
to the mass market price, institutions and innovations must be
rigorously standardized and simplified.

NOTES

1. E. I. Organick, A FORTRAN IV Primer (Reading,
Mass.: Addison-Wesley, 1966).

2. IBM System/360, Disk and Tape Operating Systems,
PL/1 Subset Reference Manual (IBM Systems Reference
Library, 1969).

3. Mathematical Programming System/360 (360A-CO-
14X), Linear Programming User's Manual (White Plains,
N.Y.: IBM, 1966).

4. Project Management System/360, User's Manual
(White Plains, N.Y.: IBM, 1966).

5. General Purpose Simulation System/360, User's
Manual (White Plains, N.Y.: IBM, 1967).

6. H. Eisenpreis, Forecasting by Econometric Systems,
IB-9-FES, (White Plains, N.Y.: IBM, 1963).

APPENDIXES

APPENDIX A HYPOTHETICAL
AGRICULTURAL
DEVELOPMENT
PROGRAM

The forms presented on the following pages have been prepared for a hypothetical "Southern Region" for the years 1968-
1972. They are discussed in a general way in Chapter 11.
Detailed discussions of each form and its contents will be
found in subsequent chapters, as indicated below.

FORM A-1

Farm Systems Analysis

Total land: 3. 3 ha.   In crops: 2. 7 ha.

C r o p s Enterprise	Av. ha.*	Yield per ha.	Production Consume	(kg)* Sell
Rice-- 1st Season	1.8	1,400	1,600	900
2nd Season	.8	1,200		960
Kenaf	.7	1,000		700
Sugar	1.0	30,000		30,000
Corn	1.0	1,800	300	1,500
Bananas	.1	4,250	100	325
Coconuts***	.1	1,500	30	120
Vegetables	.2	900	70	110
Others				

Livestock Enterprise	Ave. No. of Breeders*	Production** Consume	Sell
Cattle	1	.5	.5
Hogs	.5	2	2
Chickens	4	10	20
Eggs & Other			

Non-Agricultural Labor

Employment Calendar (workdays per average farm)

Purpose	Jan	Feb	Mar	Apr	May
Rice Production	10	2	3	5	20
Other Crops	5	5	10	10	15
Livestock	10	10	10	10	5
Non-agricultural Off-farm	10	15	15	10	10
Total Workdays	35	32	38	35	50
Days Unemployed (basis 60 days/mo.)	25	28	22	25	10

System: Rice Growers

Price per ton	In-come*	% Farms Raising	Net Cash Income**	
$70	$63	100%	$63	* For average farm
84	81	15	12	raising that crop.
85	42	45	18	
3	90	10	9	** Income per enter-
50	75	15	11	prise X % of farms
60	20	30	6	in that crop.
6/100	7	40	3	
85	9	85	8	*** Production in fruit
			7	rather than kg.
		Total	128	

Price per head				
$45	$23	70%	16	* Cows, sows, hens.
25	50	30	15	
.30	6	85	5	** In head.
			3	
		Total	39	
			42	

Total Income per Ave. Farm $209

Jun	Jul	Aug	Sep	Oct	Nov	Dec	Total
35	5	30	10	10	15	70	215
10	10	5	5	15	20	5	115
5	5	5	5	5	5	5	80
5	5	5	5	5	5	5	85
55	25	45	25	35	45	85	505
5	35	15	35	25	15	-25	175

FORM A-2

Present Institutional Structure and Coverage.

Institutions Central & Local	Functions	Level
Ag. Extension Dept. Vill. Farm Clubs	Demonstration Seed Distribution	Dist.
Livestock Dept.	Inoculation Breeding	Dist.2/
Community Dev. Dept. Commune Dev. Councils	Leader Training Self Help Project	Dist. Cmne.
Cooperative Dept. Coops (Cmne. & Vil.)	Supply & Mktg. Short Term Loans	Dist.
Ag. Dev. Bank	Coop Financing Med/Long T. Loans	Prov.

Ag. Engineering Dept.
   Irrigation Societies
   (commune & village)
	Soil Survey
	Irrigation
		Prov.

Kenaf Marketing Board	Warehousing Marketing	Dist.

Cadre Grade System
Educ. Experience & Gd.*

Level	0	5	15
18 yr.	2	1	1
16	3	2	1
12	4	3	2
10	5	5	4
6	6	6	5
4	7	7	6

Coverage

Grade	Provs.	Dists.	Communes	Villages	Partici-pation[1]
4	10	45		900	50,000
4	8	23			100,000[2]
4 5	6	30	250	1,500	80,000
4	10	40	40	750	25,000
1-2[4] 1/4-3	8				4,000[3]
1-2 1-3 1/2-4 2/4-5	10				12,000
1-4 1-5	7	30			120,000 (clients)

[1] Number of farm families active members of local institution.
[2] District veterinary technician & no. of families serviced.
[3] Number of direct loan clients.
[4] Means 1 grade 2 officer and 1 to 4 grade 3 officers.

* Usual attained grade level of cadre with corresponding education after 0, 5, and 15 years.

Market Demand Projection

(partial listing)

	RICE tons paddy	KENAF tons washed	SORGHUM tons	HOGS head*	COTTON gross tons**
1966 Total Demand	3,500,000	220,000	5,000	2,000,000	250,000
1967 Total Demand	3,400,000	200,000	10,000	1,800,000	260,000
1968 Total Demand	3,700,000	190,000	20,000	2,300,000	270,000
Domest. Consump.	3,000,000	50,000		2,200,000	270,000
Export/Import (-)	600,000	140,000	20,000	100,000	-250,000
Other Regions	2,100,000	60,000	20,000	1,700,000	20,000
Southern Region	1,500,000	130,000		500,000	
1969 Total Demand	3,800,000	180,000	100,000	2,450,000	290,000
Domest. Consump.	3,200,000	55,000	20,000	2,300,000	290,000
Export/Import (-)	600,000	125,000	80,000	150,000	-210,000
Other Regions	2,250,000	55,000	60,000	2,000,000	60,000
Southern Region	1,550,000	125,000	40,000	550,000	20,000
1970 Total Demand	3,900,000	170,000	200,000	2,600,000	300,000
Domest. Consump.	3,300,000	55,000	50,000	2,400,000	300,000
Export/Import(-)	600,000	115,000	150,000	200,000	-170,000
Other Regions	2,325,000	50,000	100,000	2,100,000	80,000
Southern Region	1,575,000	120,000	100,000	600,000	50,000
1975 Total Demand	4,300,000	160,000	800,000	3,500,000	400,000
Domest. Consump.	3,900,000	60,000	400,000	3,000,000	400,000
Export/Import (-)	400,000	100,000	400,000	500,000	-150,000
Other Regions	2,500,000	55,000	300,000	2,200,000	120,000
Southern Region	1,700,000	115,000	500,000	1,300,000	130,000
1980 Total Demand	5,000,000	170,000	1,000,000	5,000,000	600,000
Domest. Consump.	4,700,000	70,000	500,000	4,000,000	600,000
Export/Import (-)	300,000	100,000	500,000	1,000,000	-150,000
Other Regions	2,800,000	55,000	400,000	3,000,000	150,000
Southern Region	2,200,000	115,000	600,000	2,000,000	300,000

* Excluding on farm consumption and intra-village sales.
** Converts to lint at 33%.

FORM A-4.1

Innovation Package Analysis: Rice 1.

(Existing enterprise--fertilizer, pesticides and market improvements)

MARKET
Structure   Exists but inadequate.
               Too many middlemen... commune & province dealers not needed
               excess seasonal fluctuations due to lack of credit & storage
               no grading.
               Structural improvements can raise price to farmer 25-30%.

Demand   Can absorb additional 500,000 tons by 1980 at steady prices.

TECHNOLOGY
Adaptation   Already adopted successfully by 3,000 farmers at current market.

Compatability No problems, additional labor required negligible.

SUPPLIES   Requires fertilizer & pesticides, $26.

Problems   No specialized farm supply dealers in region.
               Now sold through general merchants uninterested in pushing farm
                 supplies.
               Cooperatives too small for efficient distribution.

TRANSPORT   No problem for 80% of villages.

INCENTIVE   62% increase in cash income of enterprise, assuming market changes.
               142% return on investment.
               $10 a day return to labor.

EDUCATION   Requires results plus 1 application demonstrations.

CREDIT   Short-term $26 per enterprise for production loan.
               Marketing credit $50 per enterprise, to hold stocks 3 months.

LAND   No problems.

GROUP ACTION   Minimum 1,500 customers needed for efficient supplies distribution.
               Minimum 2,000 customers needed for efficient marketing.

551

FORM A-4.2

Innovation Package Analysis: Rice 2.

(Existing enterprise--a comprehensive package of
inputs, practices, and marketing)

MARKET
  Structure   See Rice 1.
  Demand   See Rice 1.

TECHNOLOGY
  Adaptation   Proven on experimental stations.
                  First on-farm trials this season.

  Compatability   3 days additional labor in June may cause some shortages.
                  Additional labor July-November can easily be provided.

SUPPLIES   Requires fertilizer, seed, pesticides, $50.

  Problems   See Rice 1.
                  Also may have seed production bottleneck.

TRANSPORT   No problem for 80% of villages.

INCENTIVE   37% increase in cash income over Rice 1.
                  136% return on investment over Rice 1.
                  $1.70 per day return to labor.

EDUCATION   Requires results demonstration.
                  Requires 5 cultural practice demonstrations.

CREDIT   Production loan $50 per enterprise.
                  Marketing finance, see Rice 1.

LAND   No problem.

GROUP ACTION   See Rice 1.

FORM A-4.3

Innovation Package Analysis: Small Irrigation

(Existing enterprise--irrigation projects under 200 hectares)

MARKET   See Rice 1.

TECHNOLOGY
  Adaptation   Many successful trials
                    but need further work on optimum water level for improved varieties.

  Compatability   Requires special early variety for first crop.
                    No labor problem.

SUPPLIES   Production supplies similar to Rice 2.
                    Also need pumps & tubing, $50 to $200 per enterprise.

  Problems   Pump distribution and maintenance facilities very inadequate.

TRANSPORT   No problem for 80% of villages.

INCENTIVE   58% increase in cash income over Rice 2.
                    30% return on investment.
                    $.80 per day return to labor.

EDUCATION   Requires results and practice demonstrations.
                    Requires special training in organization & maintenance.

CREDIT   Short-term similar to Rice 2.
                    Medium-term $40 per enterprise for pumps.
                    Long-term $250 for ten years for land improvements.

LAND   Requires land use and water resource surveys.
                    Requires special engineering design of each project.
                    Estimated maximum 20% of paddies suitable for double-cropping.

GROUP ACTION   Minimum project size 20 farmers.
                    Must have minimum 20 projects per district for efficient service.
                    Group must have a few years experience at cooperative action.

FORM A-4.4

Innovation Package Analysis: Sorghum

(A new enterprise for farmers with marginal land available)

MARKET
  Structure   None marketed at present.

  Demand   Growing international demand and also a potential.
                     Regional demand from Hog Project, #31-S-275.
                     No danger of market saturation.

TECHNOLOGY
  Adaptation   Proven on experimentation station.
                     Now being tested in one village.

  Compatability   Suited to any farms with 1.5 to 4.5 ha. unused land.
                     Within 3 kilometers, unless the farm is already
                         growing corn; provided custom plowing available.*

SUPPLIES   Seed, fertilizer, pesticides $18 average.
                     Single-axle plow for custom operators $750.
                         1 plow per 40 farms needed.

  Problems   No present distribution on supplies.
                     2 equipment distributors ready to supply tractors
                         through FA's or motorbike dealers.

TRANSPORT   Needs major highway link to metropolis, available to
                         30 districts, plus all-weather truck link to village,
                         available to 65% of villages in those districts.

INCENTIVE $80 net income.
                     66% return of fixed investment.
                     210% return on annual costs.
                     $2.50 per day return on labor.

EDUCATION   Requires results demonstrations plus three practice
                         demonstrations.

CREDIT   Medium-term loan on land clearing $120.
                     Production loan $38.

LAND   Average 2.2 ha. of marginal, presently uncultivated land
                         requires commune land use survey and plan before clear-
                         ing. Suitable land available to estimated 150,000 farms
                         in 25 districts.

GROUP ACTION   Minimum 20 farms per village and 500 per district needed
                         for efficient servicing.

*Plowing season overlaps rice plowing season so outside plowing services
required; small single-axle tractor considered more suitable than larger
tractors because it can operate in fields which have not been perfectly
cleared, which have stumps remaining.

FORM A-4.5

Innovation Package Analysis: Hogs

(A new enterprise for farmers with inadequate land)*

MARKET
  Structure   Only a few districts have agents regularly assembling hog shipments
                               for urban markets.
                               Existing agents purchase by the head rather than by weight.

  Demand   Growing urban demand and export market can absorb 300,000 head
                               by 1980.

TECHNOLOGY
  Adaptation   Already adopted by farmers of other regions, using sorghum as
                               major element of feed diet.

  Compatability   Limited to families of average size with less than 2.5 ha. because
                               of heavy year-round labor requirement.

SUPPLIES   Feed $300 per enterprise.
                               Materiel for pen construction $100.
                               Breed stock 2 sows $100.

  Problems   No feed or feed supplement distributors.
                               No production of breed stock in region.

TRANSPORT   Village must have year-round cart access.
                               Commune must have year-round truck access.

INCENTIVES $140 net income.
                               70% return on fixed investment.
                               35% return on annual costs.
                               $.80 per day return on labor.

EDUCATION   Requires results demonstration plus four practice demonstrations.
                               Requires three day training course.
                               Requires initial supervision of operator.

CREDIT   Production loan $300.
                               Medium-term loan $200.

LAND   No problem.

GROUP ACTION   Minimum 500 farmers per district for efficient servicing.

*Differs from present hog enterprises: a) larger scale, b) for shipment to other areas,
c) improved heavier breed, d) use of feed and feed supplements, e) comprehensive
sanitation practices.

FORM A-5

Summary of Feasible Innovations

	Old Enterprises	
Data per average applicable farm	RICE 1	RICE 2
1 Enterprise Scale (hectare or head)	2.0	2.0
2 Yield (kg./ha. or head/sow)	1800	2200
Production & Income		
3 Total Production (line 2 x line 1)	3600	4400
4 Kg. Sold (line 3 less consumed)	1900	2700
5 Price (per ton or head)	x$80	x$80
6 Gross Cash Income	$152	$216
Investments Required & Terms		
7 Land--20 years @5%		
8 Structures & Eqpt.--5 years @10%		
9 Breed Stock--5 years @10%		
Production Supplies Qty. & Prices		
10 Fertilizer (kg./ha.)	130 @ 8¢	250 @ 8¢
11 Pesticide (kg./ha.)	12 @14¢	40 @20¢
12 Seed (kg./ha.)		15 @10¢
13 Feed (kg./head)		
Annual Costs per enterprise		
.14 Amortization of Investment		
15 Plowing & Other Services		
16 Supplies (lines 10-13)	$26	$50
17 Interest	2	4
18 Total	28	54
Effect on Net Income		
19 Net Income per Enterprise	124	162
20 Increase over Prev. Enterprise**	41	38
21 % Farms in Region Applicable	x96%	x92%
22 Ave. Net Incr. Income per Farm	$ 32	$ 30
23 Cumulative Increased Income	32	62
Net Return per Year		
24 Per day of labor	$10	$1.70
25 On fixed investment		
26 On annual investment	142%	138

*   Land clearing on 5 year loans.

**   Rice 1 over traditional culture, Rice 2 over Rice 1, etc.

*** 74% increase over present average cash income of $209.

			New Enterprises		
IRRI-GATION	KENAF improve	KENAF cease growing	SORGHUM	HOGS	COTTON
1.0 2000	.5 1800	0	2.2 1600	2 sows 10 head	1.5 1800
2000 2000 x$80 $160	900 900 x$40 $36		3400 3400 x$45 $152	20 head 15 head x$38 $575	2700 2700 x$120 $330
450 150			120*	100 100	90* 10
250 @ 8¢ 40 @20¢	160 @10¢ 16 @20¢		62 @ 8¢ 12 @20¢ 15 @ 6¢	300 @6¢	135 @15¢ 200 @15¢ 12 @20¢
$30 10 25 15 80	$10 1 11		$24 20 18 10 72	$ 40 360 35 435	$20 20 80 15 135
80 80 x20% $ 16 78	25 -7 x35% $ -3 75	-32 x15% $ -5 70	80 80 x30% $ 24 94	140 140 x15% $ 21 115	195 195 x20% $ 40 155***
$.80 15% 100%			$2.50 66% 111%	$.80 70% 35%	$3.50 155% 145%

FORM A-6

Innovation Promotion Requirements

	RICE I	KENAF	SORGHUM	RICE II	COTTON	IRRI-GATION	HOGS
Priority Considerations							
Year Ready for Extension	1967	1968	1968	1969	1969	1969	1970
Districts Suitable*	100%	90%	50%	100%	50%	80%	90%
Farms Suitable*	90%	25%	30%	90%	20%	20%	15%
Increased Income/Av. Farm	$ 32	$ '-3	$ 24	$ 30	$ 24	$ 16	$ 21
R e q u i r e m e n t s							
Education							
Practice Demonstrations (no)	1	2	3	5	5		
Training Course						1 wk	1 wk
Supplies							
Fertilizer	x		x	x	x	x	
Pesticide	x	x	x	x	x	x	x
Seed			x		x	x	
Equipment			x		x	x	
Feed & Other							x
Marketing							
Improved Volume	x	x	x	x	x	x	x
Improved Timing	x		x	x	x		x
Buying on Grade			x	x	x	x	x

558

	$26	$10	$38	$24**	$100	$25	$360
Credit							
Short Term	$26	$10	$38	$24**	$100	$25	$360
Medium Term			120		100	150	180
Long Term						450	
Engineering							
Land Use Survey			x		x	x	
Design						x	
Ratio of farms adopting innovation *							
To previous innovators.	2	2	2	2	2		1
To previous new demonstrations.							
village level	20	25	35	25	25		
commune level						100	10

*   Percentage of total districts and farms in the region suited to the innovation package.

** Over credit requirement of Rice 1 package.

*** Number of new farms in a district adopting an innovation package as a coefficient of a) farms practicing the innovation the previous year, and b) new demonstration plots started the previous year.

FORM A-7.1

Agricultural Services Structural Analysis: Present Structure

Echelon

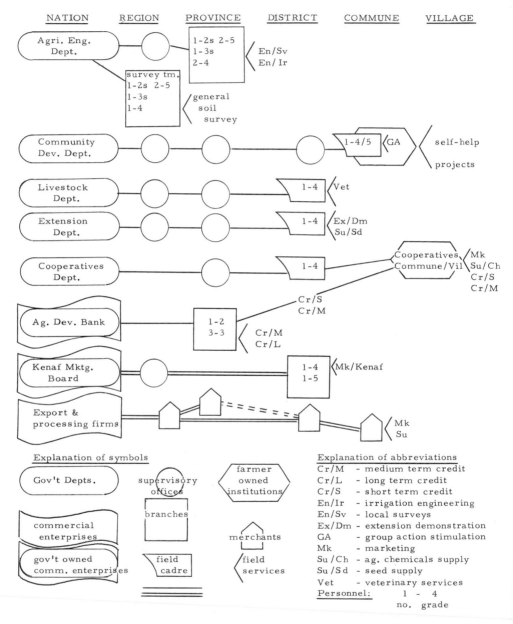

NATION   REGION   PROVINCE   DISTRICT   COMMUNE   VILLAGE

Explanation of symbols

Gov't Depts.

supervisory
offices

branches

field
cadre

commercial
enterprises

gov't owned
comm. enterprises

farmer
owned
institutions

merchants

field
services

Explanation of abbreviations
Cr/M   - medium term credit
Cr/L   - long term credit
Cr/S   - short term credit
En/Ir - irrigation engineering
En/Sv - local surveys
Ex/Dm - extension demonstration
GA   - group action stimulation
Mk   - marketing
Su/Ch - ag. chemicals supply
Su/Sd - seed supply
Vet   - veterinary services
Personnel: 1 - 4
              no. grade

560

FORM A-7.2

Agricultural Services Structure Analysis: Objective Structure

Echelon:

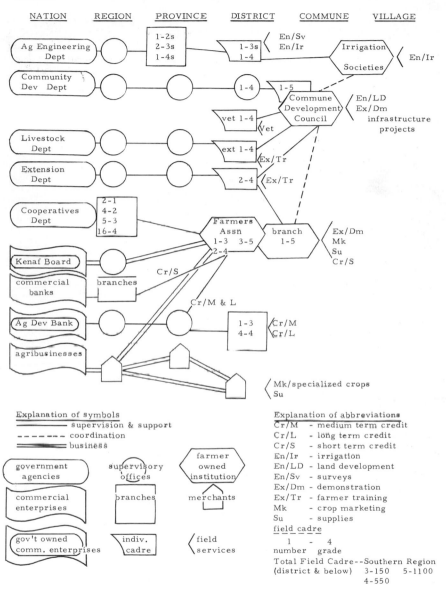

| NATION | REGION | PROVINCE | DISTRICT | COMMUNE | VILLAGE |

Explanation of symbols

————— supervision & support
------- coordination
══════ business

government agencies

supervisory offices

farmer owned institution

commercial enterprises

branches

merchants

gov't owned comm. enterprises

indiv. cadre

field services

Explanation of abbreviations

Cr/M - medium term credit
Cr/L - long term credit
Cr/S - short term credit
En/Ir - irrigation
En/LD - land development
En/Sv - surveys
Ex/Dm - demonstration
Ex/Tr - farmer training
Mk   - crop marketing
Su   - supplies

field cadre

1 - 4
number grade

Total Field Cadre--Southern Region
(district & below)   3-150   5-1100
                     4-550

561

FORM A-7.3

Agricultural Services Structure Analysis: Transitional Structure

Echelon:

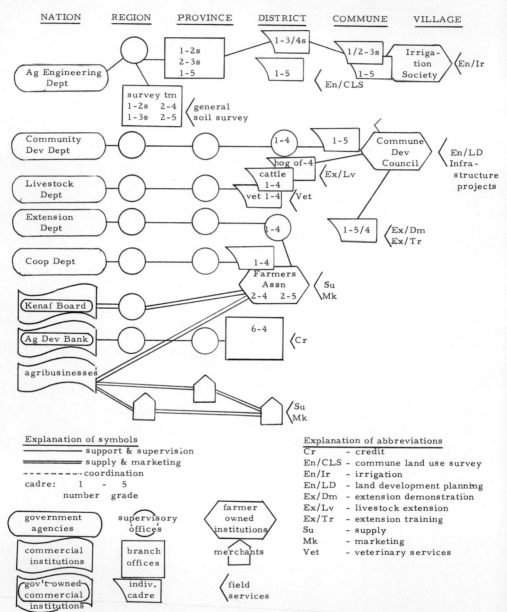

Explanation of symbols
========= support & supervision
========= supply & marketing
-------- coordination
cadre: 1 - 5
       number grade

government agencies
commercial institutions
gov't-owned commercial institutions
supervisory offices
branch offices
indiv. cadre
farmer owned institutions
merchants
field services

Explanation of abbreviations
Cr   - credit
En/CLS - commune land use survey
En/Ir   - irrigation
En/LD   - land development planning
Ex/Dm   - extension demonstration
Ex/Lv   - livestock extension
Ex/Tr   - extension training
Su   - supply
Mk   - marketing
Vet   - veterinary services

FORM A-8

Local Development Strategy Diagram

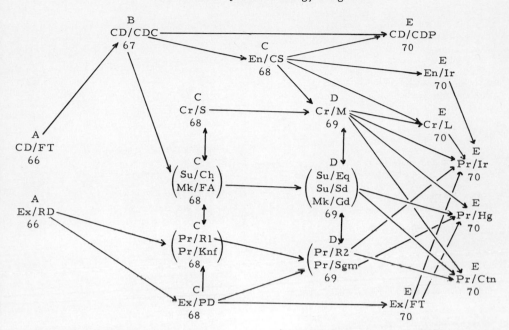

Explanation of symbols

C = stage of district development
Cr/S = event
68 = year initiated

Events Code *

CD/	Community Development	Mk/	Marketing
FT	Farmer Training	FA	Farmers Assn. organized
CDC	Commune Dev. Council	Gd	marketing by Grade
CDP	Commune Dev. Plan		
		Pr/	Production by farmers
Cr/	Credit	R1	Rice 1 program
S	Short term	R2	Rice 2 program
M	Medium term	Knf	Kenaf improvement
L	Long term	Sgm	Sorghum
		Hg	Hogs
En/	Ag. Engineering	Ctn	Cotton
CS	Commune Land Survey		
Ir	Irrigation	Su/	Supply business
		Ch	agri. Chemicals
Ex/	Extension	Eq	Equipment
RD	Results Demonstrations	Sd	Seed (certified)
PD	Practice Demonstrations		
FT	Farmer Training courses	* point at which activity began

FORM A-9

Local Development Activity and Staffing Schedule

Elements stages:	A	B	C	D	E	F	G	H-I	Misc. Notes
Community Development									
1 Staff: dist. & commune	6	11	— — — — — — →						
2 Village Leader Training	5	10	— — — — — →						no. of
3 Commune Dev. Councils		5	10 — — — — →						communes
4 Commune Dev. Plans					5	10 — — — — — →			
Extension									
5 Staff: district level	1	1	1	1	2	3 — — — — →			
6 commune level		5	10	10	5				
7 ext. trained CLW & CA*					10	20 — — — →			see below
8 development		X results demonstrations							
9 of the			X practice demonstrations						
10 program					x farmer training				
Farmer Association									
11 Staff: dist. level ofrs.			2	3	— — — — — →				
12 commune agents					5	10 — — — — →			
13			X supply & marketing						
14 development				X marketing by grade					
15 of the				X equipment sales					
16 program				X certified seed sale					
Agriculture Dev. Bank									
17 Staff: Loan Officers			2	3	4	6	6	4	
18 development			X short term loans						
19 of the				X medium term loans					
20 program					X long term loans				
Ag. Engineering Dept.									
21 Staff: Survey Engineers			2	2	1				
22 Survey Ass'ts.			2	2	1				
23 Irrig. Engineers					1/2	1/2	1/2	1/2	
24 Irrig. Ass'ts.					1	1	1	1	
25 Soil & Land Use Survey			5	10					communes
26 Commune Land Use Plan				5	10				completed
27 Commune Water Dev. Plan					3	6	9	10	
Commodity Programs									
28 Rice 1	d	d	P (replaced by Rice 2)						d=demonstration
29 Kenaf		d	d P	d P	P				
30 Rice 2			d	d P	d P	d P	P		P=Production
31 Sorghum			d	d P	d P	P			increase
32 Hogs				d	d P	d P	P		
33 Cotton				d	d P	d P	P		
34 Legumes) -no project yet					d	d P	d P	P	
35 Pasture)					d	d P	d P	P	

* Commune Level Workers (CD) and FA Commune Agents will be trained to take over the function of the commune level Extension Agents.

FORM A-10.1

District Plan: Community Development
Community Development Department

ELEMENT	s A	t B	a C
Leader Training (no. trainees)			
1 Initial 1 week	150	150	
2 Program Bldg. 2 weeks		200	200
3 Special 1 week			250
Coverage of Commune (No.)			
4 Phase 1: Self-help Projects	5	5	
5 Phase 2: Works Budget		5	10
6 Phase 3: Total Dev. Program			
Subsidies ($000) per Commune			
7 Phase 1 $2,000	10	10	
8 Phase 2-3 4,000		20	40
9 Phase 3 6,000			
District Staff	No. $000	No. $000	No. $000
10 Commune Level Workers (CLW)	5 7.5	10 15	10 15
11 Supervisor	1 2.5	1 2.5	1 2.5
Equipment Purchases			
12 Motorbikes	5 2.5	5 2.5	
13 Jeep	1 2.5		
14 Audiovisual & Misc.	1.0	.5	
Operating Budget	$000	$000	$000
15 Training	14	14	16
16 Staff Salary & Expenses	10	18	18
17 Equipment	6	3	
18 Miscellaneous Expenses	2	4	5
19 total	32	39	39
20 Commune Budget Subsidy	10	30	40

566

g D	e E	s F	ADDITIONAL EXPLANATIONS
			Subject of Training Sessions
	200	200	- formulation of village needs
500	250	500	- budgeting for phases 2 & 3
			- special interests of villagers
			explanation of phases
			- hamlets do individual projects
10	5		- Commune Dev. Council has works budget
	5	10	- CDC has complete dev. program
			including extension budget
			) preliminary estimate only
40	20		) - will vary from year to year depending
	30	60	) on budget availability

No. $000	No. $000	No. $000	qualifications & training
10 15	10 15	10 15	10 yr. grads., 1 yr. training
1 3	1 3	1 3	12 yr. grads., min. 3 yrs. CLW
2 1	2 1	2 1	
.5	.5	.5	
.3	.3	.3	

$000	$000	$000	
10	16	22	- @ $25 per man/week
18	18	18	
2	2	2	
5	5	5	Note: Expenses all transferred to
35	41	47	admin. budget after stage F
40	50	60	charged to infrastructure
			sector of Dev. Budget

District Plan: Agricultural Extension
Dept: Extension Dept.

		Stages				
		A		B		C
1	Farm Club Membership		500		1500	2400
2	Coverage: Villages		15		30	60
3	Communes	1		5		10
	Demonstrations (no.)	c'mun	vill	c'mun	vill	c'mun vill
4	Rice 1	5	30	10	60	
5	Rice 2					10 80
6	Kenaf	3	10	5	20	5 30
7	Sorghum					
8	Cotton					
9	Hogs					
10	Total Project Planned	8	40	15	80	15 110
11	Other Projects					
12	Commune Sponsored					
	Cadre	no	$000	no	$000	no $000
13	Village Volunteers	10		30		100
14	Ag. trained CD Workers					
15	Commune Extension Agents			5	7.5	10 15.4
16	Livestock Agents					
	Equipment	no	$000	no	$000	no $000
17	Jeep with trailer	1	3.3			
18	Tractor					1 6.5
19	Motorbikes			5	2.5	5 2.5
20	Total		3.3		2.5	9.0
	Training	no	$000	no	$000	no $000
21	Farmers	30	1.5	60	3.0	120 6.0
23	Commune Ext. Agents	10	10.0			
24	CD & FA Agent Training					
25	Total		11.5		3.0	6.0
	Project Costs		$000		$000	$000
26	Training		12		3	6
27	Staff				8	15
28	Equipment		3		3	9
29	Miscellaneous		2		4	6
30	Total		17		18	36

project # 31-S-235

	Stages			
D	**E**	**F**		

D	E	F	Notes
4500	6000	9000	- based on Rice 1 project participation village level groups
90	100	100	
10	10	10	

c'mun	vill	c'mun	vill	c'mun	vill	Notes
10	90	10	100	10	100	- commune & village demonstrations derived from specific crop projects & funded under those projects
5	30					(note: number of demonstrations under specific projects x percentage of
2	10	4	15	4	40	total districts covered by those crop
2	8	3	16	3	24	projects)
2	16	4	40	6	64	
21	154	21	171	23	228	
		5	50	10	150	- after stage F other projects & commune
		5	50	10	100	programs should maintain total at F level

no	$000	no	$000	no	$000	Notes
200		200		200		- number & cost
		5		10		- farmers trained & running demonstrations
10	15.8	5	8.1			in stages E & F CD Workers & Farm
1	1.5	2	3.1	2	3.2	Assn. Agents replace Commune Extension Agents

no	$000	no	$000	no	$000
1	3.3		1.0	1	1.0
1	.5	2	1.0	2	1.0
	3.8		2.0		2.0

no	$000	no	$000	no	$000	Notes
180	9.0	300	15.0	400	20.0	- training in general practices
						- six months preservice training
10	2.0	10	2.0			- three months inservice training
	11.0		17.0		20.0	

$000	$000	$000	All Years $000
11	17	20	69
17	11	3	121 - excl. Dist. Ext. Ofr. (charged to Admin. Budget)
4	2	2	23
6	6	6	30
38	36	31	243

569

District Plan: Farmers Associations
Agency: Dept. of Cooperatives

	Stage:	C		D		E	
1	Participating Farmers	600		2,400		7,200	
	Sales Volume ($000)	Sply	Mrktg	Sply	Mrktg	Sply	Mrktg
2	Rice	16	54	110	296	337	900
3	Kenaf	3	150	10	130	30	110
4	Sorghum					6	37
5	Hogs					16	92
6	Cotton					16	66
7	Other			10		20	
8	Total	19	204	130	426	425	1,205
9	Contribution to Fixed Costs	5,800		15,200		45,000	
	Fixed Expenses	No.	Cost	No.	Cost	No.	Cost
10	Manager	1	2,200	1	2,500	1	2,900
11	Assistant Managers	1	1,300	2	2,800	3	4,500
12	Commune Agents					5	6,500
13	Clerks	3	2,100	3	2,900	4	3,700
14	Other Employees	3	1,200	4	1,700	6	2,600
15	Misc. Operating Expenses		4,000		8,000		12,000
16	Amortization		2,400		4,700		9,200
17	Interest		400		2,100		11,600
18	Total		13,600		22,700		53,000
19	Net Profit		-7,800		-7,500		-8,000
20	Assets Working Capital (peak)		27,000		148,000		450,000
21	Equipment		10,000		15,000		20,000
22	Buildings & Land		11,000		43,000		130,000
23	Total		48,000		206,000		600,000
24	Liabil- Short Term Debt (peak)		19,000		104,000		315,000
25	ities Long Term Debt						120,000
26	Government Subsidy		37,000		113,000		171,000
27	Membership Capital				4,000		16,000
28	Earned Surplus		-8,000		-15,000		-23,000
29	Total		48,000		206,000		600,000
30	Annual Project Budget		39,000		77,000		58,000
31	Annual Project Loans						120,000

	F			G		
		9,500			9,500	same as Rice 1 project participation
	Sply	Mrktg	Sply	Mrktg		Supply & Marketing business
	468	1,223	468	1,223		60% of crop market
	30	110	30	110		100% of crop market
	28	167	54	320		70% of crop market
	71	350	180	400		up to 200 hd./wk.
	56	185	156	515		80% of crop market (100% of 1st yr.)
	30	50	50	100		
	683	2,085	948	2,668		
		69,200		98,800		gross margin = 3.5% on supplies
						= 2.5% on marketing
	No.	Cost	No.	Cost		
	1	3,300	1	3,800		@ 2,200 + 15% increase per year
	3	5,200	3	6,000		@ 1,300 + 15% increase per year
	10	14,000	10	15,000		@ 1,300 + 15% increase per year
	5	4,500	6	5,300		@ 700 + 3% increase per year
	8	3,500	10	4,400		@ 500 + 3% increase per year
		16,000		20,000		
		11,800		12,800		@ 5 yrs. on eqpt., 25 yrs. on bldgs.
		16,400		15,000		@ 2% on short term,* 5% on long term
		75,000		81,400		
		-5,800		17,400		
		611,000		611,000		50% of Rice marketing volume
		25,000		30,000		
		171,000		171,000		@ 1.2m^2 per member x $15/m^2 cost
		807,000		812,000		
		428,000		428,000		70% of Wrkg. Cap. @ 8% for 3 mo.*
		157,000		126,000		max. 80% of fixed assets
		211,000		211,000		
		40,000		57,000		$1 per new member, $2 ann. per
		-29,000		-12,000		old mmbr.
		807,000		812,000		
		30,000		5,000		subsidy + $1,000 training per
		37,000		-21,000		new cadre

571

District Plan: Agricultural Development Bank
Agency: Agricultural Development Bank

		C No.	C Vol.	D No.	D Vol.	E No.	E Vol.
LOAN BUSINESS							
1 Short	Project	2,400	72	7,200	265	9,500	489
2 Term	Other			1,000	50	1,000	100
3 Loans	Total	2,400	72	8,200	315	10,500	589
4 ($000)	Gross Margin		1.5		6.6		12.4
5 Medium	New Loans: Sorghum					380	46
6 Term	Tractor					18	14
7 Loans	Hogs					160	61
8 ($000)	Cotton					200	20
9	Other					200	30
10	Total					960	171
11	Volume Outstanding						171
12	Gross Margin						5.1
13 Long	New Loans: Project						
14 Term	Other						
15 Loans	Volume Outstanding						
16 ($000)	Gross Margin						
17 Total Gross Margin Earned					6,600		17,500
18 District	Manager	2	7,000	1	3,800	1	4,200
19 Branch	Senior Loan Officers	2	7,000	2	7,400	2	8,100
20 Staff	Junior Loan Officers			2	4,600	2	5,100
21 &	Clerks	2	1,400	3	2,200	5	3,700
22 Other	Vehicles	1	2,500	3	7,500	3	
23 Expenses	Rental						6,000
24	Other		3,000		4,000		6,000
25	Total		13,900		29,500		33,000
26 District Contribution to Profits			-12,400		-22,900		-15,500

	F		G	
No.	Vol.	No.	Vol.	
9,500	745	9,500	1,097	Maximum $1,133,000
1,500	150	2,000	200	
11,000	895	11,500	1,297	One agent can handle 1200 increase
	18.9		27.	av. 5 mo. x (12%-7%) = 2.1% earned.
1,225	159	1,425	185	
62	47	70	53	
450	171	900	342	
500	50	1,250	125	
200	30	200	30	
2,435	457	3,845	735	One agent can handle 400 loans.
	553		1,057	
	16.6		31.7	10% - 7% = 3% gross margin
300	108	300	108	
50	25	100	50	
	132		158	
	1.6		3.2	7% - 5% = 2%
	37,100		61,900	
1	4,600	1	5,100	Selected from senior loan officers.
2	8,900	3	9,800	G3@ $3,500 + 10% for 5 years.
3	7,900	3	8,700	G5@ $2,300 + 10% up to
7	5,200	8	6,100	G6@ $700 + 4%
3		4	2,500	
	6,000		6,000	
	8,080		8,000	
	40,600		46,200	
	-3,500		-15,700	Total gov't. subsidy per district $54,000

FORM A-10.5

District Plan: Agricultural Engineering and Small Irrigation
Agricultural Engineering Department

ELEMENTS	B		Stages C		D	
Small Irrigation						
1 Farms						
2 Hectares						
3 Net Additional Income ($000)						
Communes Covered						
4 Soil Survey	5		10			
5 Land Development Plan			5		10	
6 Water Development Plan					3	
Investment in Irrigation ($000)						
7 Earthworks						
8 Equipment & Piping						
9 Total						
Cadre	No.	$000	No.	$000	No.	$000
10 Soil Survey Engineers	2	10	2	10	1	5
11 Soil Survey Assistants	2	5	2	5	1	3
12 Irrigation Engineers					.5	3
13 Irrigation Assistants					1	2
14 Total		15		15		13
Farmer Training						
15 Land Use			100	2	100	2
16 Irrigation					300	3
Total Project Cost						
17 Cadre		15		15		13
18 Training				2		5
19 Miscellaneous		3		3		3
Total		18		20		21
20 Credit Expansion						

574

E		F		I		ADDITIONAL COMMENTS & EXPLANATIONS
new	cumul	new	cumul	new	cumul	note: from small projects only
300	300	300	600	300	1,500	
300	300	300	600	300	1,500	
	24		48		120	
						Commune scale surveys
						- on 1:20,000 scale, soil types & land use
						- projected optimum land use plan
	6		9		10	- irrigation & water reservoir plan
						investments financed by bank loans
135	135	135	270	135	675	may be subsidized from commune
45	45	45	90	45	225	development budget
180	180	180	360	180	900	
No.	$000	No.	$000	No.	$000	all cadre attached to prov. office
.5	3	.5	3	.5	3	
1	2	1	2	1	2	
	5		5		5	
						2/village, 1 wk.
300	3	300	3			1 wk. for all irrig. participants
						Stages B-I note: G & H have some
	5		5		5	68 activities & costs as
	3		3			19 stage F.
	4		4		4	15
	12		12		9	102
	180		180		180	

District Plan: Rice 2
Agency: Extension Dept.

Applicable to 50 districts and 480,000 farms

		C			D		
	Outputs	New	Total		New	Total	
1	Farms Participating*				2,000	2,000	
2	Hectares				4,000	4,000	
3	Production (Tons)					1,800	
4	Net Increased Income					76,000	
5	Crop Marketing (Tons)					1,800	
	Demonstrations	New	Total	Cost	New	Total	Cost
6	Village	80	80	$5,600	10	90	$6,300
7	Commune	10	10	5,000		10	5,000
	Supply Requirements	New	Total		New	Total	
8	Fertilizer					500	
9	Pesticides					80	
10	Seed					30	
	Farm Assn. Business						
11	Supplies					68,000	
12	Marketing					76,500	
13	Credit					68,000	
	Marginal Cost per District						
14	Budget for Demonstration		11,000			11,000	
15	Seed Production Investment		36,000			192,000	
16	Credit Expansion					68,000	
	Total		47,000			271,000	

*New farms = 2 (prev. farms) + 25 (prev. new demonstration)

	E			F		all lines = increase over Rice 1
	New	Total		New	Total	
	4,250	6,250		2,950	9,200	
	8,500	12,500		5,900	18,400	2 ha./farm
		5,625			8,300	900 kg./farm
		237,000			394,600	
		5,625			8,300	900 kg./farm
New	Total	Cost	New	Total	Cost	
10	100	$7,000		100	$7,000	1 ha. @ $70
		5,000		10	5,000	1 ha. @ $100
	New	Total		New	Total	
		1,562			2,300	250 kg./ha.
		250			368	40
		94			138	15
		192,000			250,000	$24 per farm
		240,000			352,000	60% of market
		192,000			250,000	$24/farm +$10/new farm/or a sprayer
		12,000			12,000	$46,000 total
						$1,200/ton of 1st & 2nd yr. req.
		124,000			56,000	
		136,000			78,000	

FORM A-10.7

District Plan: Sorghum
Agency: Extension Dept.

Applicable to 25 districts
and 150,000 farmers.

	D		E	
Outputs	New	Total	New	Total
1 Farms Participating*			700	700
2 Hectares			15,400	15,400
3 Production				
4 Net Increased Income			56,000	56,000
Demonstrations	No.	Cost	No.	Cost
5 Village	20	$2,000	50	$5,000
6 Commune	4	2,000	8	4,000
Contract Plowing Units				
7 New			18	
8 Cumulation			18	
Supply Requirements (kg.)				
9 Fertilizers				43,400
10 Pesticide				8,400
11 Seed				11,200
Credit	New	Outstndg.	New	Outstndg.
12 Short Term			26,600	26,600
13 Medium Term (3 yr.)			84,000	84,000
14 Plow Loans (3 yr.)			13,500	13,500
FA Business				
15 Supplies				6,000
16 Crop Marketing				37,000
17 Total				
Marginal Cost per District				
18 Budget for demonstration		4,000		9,000
19 Credit Expansion				124,000
20 Seed Production Investment		4,400		15,600
21 Total		8,400		148,600

*New farms = 2 (previous farms) + 25 (last year new demonstrations)

	F		G	
New	Total	New	Total	
2,450	3,150	2,850	6,000	
53,900	69,300	62,700	132,000	2.2 ha. per farm
				3,400
196,000	252,000	252,000	480,000	$80 per farm
No.	Cost	No.	Cost	
80	$8,000	80	$8,000	2.2 ha. @ $100
8	4,000	8	4,000	12 ha. @ $500
62		70		1 per 40 farms, 2 wheel type
80		70		@ $750
	195,300		372,000	62 kg. per ha.
	37,800		72,000	12
	50,400		96,000	16
New	Outstndg.	New	Outstndg.	
93,100	119,700	108,300	228,000	$ 38 per farm Stage H - $289,000
294,000	344,400	342,000	543,600	$120 per farm Stage I - $217,000
46,500	54,600	52,500	84,500	$750 per unit Stage J - $118,000
	28,000		54,000	
	157,000		320,000	70% of mkt.
	12,000		12,000	Total $37,000
	394,300		337,200	See Note lines 29-31
				$400/Ton of seed incr.
	406,200		349,200	

District Plan: Hogs
Agency: Extension Dept.

Applicable to 40 districts & 76,000 farms.

	D		E	
Output	New	Total	New	Total
1 Farms Participating			200	200
2 Breed Sows			400	400
3 Production (head)			4,000	4,000
4 Net Increased Income			28,000	28,000
Demonstrations	No.	Cost	No.	Cost
5 Village	20	6,000	30	9,000
6 Commune	3	4,500	5	7,500
Supply Requirement				
7 Feed (Tons)				1,200
8 Breed Sows				400
Credit	New	Outstndg.	New	Outstndg.
9 Short Term			36,000	36,000
10 Medium Term			76,000	76,000
Farm Assn. Business				
11 Feed				5,000
12 Breed Sows				10,000
Marginal Cost per District				
13 Budget		10,000		17,000
14 Credit Expansion				112,000
Total		10,000		129,000

*New farms = 1 (old farms) + 10 (new demonstrations previous stage)

F		G		
New	Total	New	Total	
560	760	1,340	1,900	
1,120	1,520	2,640	3,800	2 per farm
11,200	15,200	16,400	38,000	20 head per farm (15 marketed)
18,400	106,400	187,600	266,000	$190 per farm (cash)
No.	Cost	No.	Cost	
80	24,000	80	24,000	
7	10,500	7	10,500	
	4,560		11,400	300 kg. per head production
	1,120		2,640	
New	Outstndg.	New	Outstndg.	
100,800	136,000	241,000	342,000	$180 per farm
212,800	258,000	209,200	659,700	$380 per farm
	19,000		47,500	@ $ 25 per farm
	56,000		134,000	@ $100 per new farm
	35,000		35,000	Stage H $290,000
	283,000		607,000	Stage I $217,000
	338,000		642,000	Stage J $153,000

Project Plan: Community Development
Agency: Community Development Dept.

	1966-67		1968		1969		1970	
1 Leader Training	7,500		7,600		8,350		13,750	
2 Coverage A	A 15		A 15		A 14		A 14	
3 of B	B 15		B 14		B 10		B 12	
4 Districts C			C 1		C 5		C 10	
5 by D					D 1		D 5	
6 Stage E							E 1	
7 F								
8 Total	30		30		30		42	
9 Cadre Commune Workers	225		225		230		350	
10 Dist. Supervisors	30		30		30		42	
11 & Province Officers	6		6		7		9	
12 Staff Specialists	10		12		14		16	
13 Staff Others	20		25		30		35	
Cadre Training								
14 CLW Preservice					120		110	
15 CLW Inservice					10		50	
Program Development								
16 Commune Budget Regulation	D M		C					
17 Comm. Dev. Plan Regulations			D M		C			
Project Costs (in $000)	Total	Fixed	Total	Fixed	Total	Fixed	Total	Fixed
18 District Operation	915		915		928		1,382	
19 Cadre Training Cost		10	10	10	122	20	120	20
20 Prov. & Region. Staff		68	79	79		93	110	110
21 Misc. Overhead		50	60			70	80	80
22 Total		128	1,064	149		183	1,692	210
23 Commune Subsidies	600		610		680		1,160	
24 Foreign Exchange	150		20		40		110	

1971	1972	End Year 1976	
19,450	23,100		
A 8			
B 14	B 8		
C 12	C 14		
D 10	D 12		
E 5	E 10		
F 1	F 6		
50	50	50	
			Grade & Cost/Yr.
460	500	500	5 charge to dist.
50	50	50	4 project budget
10	10	10	3 $3000
18	20	25	3 $3000
40	45	50	6 $1000
40			@$1000
100	120		@$ 200 at Stage D
			D=drafted, M=Ministry approval,
			C=Cabinet approval

Total	Fixed	Total	Fixed	All Years	
1,792		1,923		11,650	
52	20	24	20	700	
124	124	135	135	609	
90	90	110	110	460	
2,058	234	2,192	265	13,419	
					charge to infrastructure Dev.
1,900		2,360			Budget; will vary with
					availability of funds.
100		40			

FORM A-11.2

Project Plan: Agricultural Extension
Agency: Extension Dept.

		1967		1968		1969		1970	
1	Farm Club Membership	4,000		14,900		37,500		77,500	
2	Coverage	A 5		A 10		A 12		A 14	
3	of	B 1		B 5		B 10		B 12	
4	Districts			C 1		C 5		C 10	
5	by					D 1		D 5	
6	Stage							E 1	
7									
8									
9	Total	6		16		28		42	
	Cadre & Staff								
10	Commune Extension Agents	6		35		111		222	
11	Ag. Trained CD & FA Agents					10		70	
12	District Ext. Officers	45		50		50		50	
13	Prov. Offrs. & Specialists	15		20		25		30	
	Training								
14	Commune Extension Agents	30		70		110		110	
15	CD & FA Agents					10		60	
	Ext. Trng. Cntr. Constr.								
16	Stage A	P	C						
17	Stage B					P	C		
	Program Development								
18	Commune Ext. Agent Manual			P		F			
19	Local Program. Bldg. Manual						P		F
	Project Costs (in $000)	Total	Fixed	Total	Fixed	Total	Fixed	Total	Fixed
20	District Operation	113		316		626		1,068	
21	Trng. Cntr. Construction	50	50	60	60	200	200		
22	Trng. Cntr. Operation	10	10	30	30	50	50	60	60
23	Miscellaneous	50	50	60	60	70	70	80	80
24	Total	223	110	466	150	946	320	1,208	140
25	Foreign Exchange ($000)	25		60		120		200	

	1971		1972		End Year 1976	
	137,800		213,600		450,000	
	A 8					
	B 14		B 8			
	C 12		C 14			
	D 10		D 12			
	E 5		E 10			
	F 1		F 5			
			G 1			
	50		50		50	
	337		396		100	Charged to district budget
	220		420		1,000	On admin. budget, not
	50		50		50	charged to project
	35		40		50	
	160					@ $1,000
	150		200			@ $300
						P = planning, C = construction
						Issuance deadlines.
						P = preliminary
						F = fixed
	Total	Fixed	Total	Fixed	All Years	
	1,427		1,619		12,150	Incl. variable training cost
					310	$243,000 per district
	60	60	60	60	270	
	90	90	100	100	450	
	1,577	150	1,779	160	13,180	
	230		235		1,200	

FORM A-11.3

Project Plan: Farmers Associations
Agency: Coop Department

	1967	1968	1969	1970
1 Participating Farmers		5,400	5,400	25,400
2 Sales : Supply Business		19,000	225,000	1,265,000
3 Volume: Marketing Business		204,000	1,471,000	5,375,000
4 Total		223,000	1,695,000	6,640,000
5 Coverage		C 1	C 5	C 10
6 of			D 1	D 5
7 Districts				E 1
8 by				
9 Stage				
10 Total		1	6	16
11 Cadre : Managers	1	5	10	12
12 Training: Asst. Managers	1	2	11	25
13 Commune Agents			5	30

Program & Legislation

	1967	1968	1969	1970
14 Pilot District Plan	D M	C		
15 Prelim. Expansion Plan		D M C		
16 Operations Manual			D M	
17 Permanent Legislation			D	M C

Project Staff

	1967 No	1967 Cost	1968 No	1968 Cost	1969 No	1969 Cost	1970 No	1970 Cost
18 Project Manager	1	5,000	1	5,000	1	5,000	1	5,000
19 Supply & Mktg. Specialists			2	11,000	6	48,000	8	64,000
20 Training Officers			1	3,000	2	6,000	2	6,000
21 Field Specialists					1	3,000	3	8,000
22 Auditors & Lawyers			1	4,000	2	7,000	3	10,000
23 Other Personnel			2	2,000	4	4,000	6	6,000
24 Total		5,000		25,000		49,000		99,000

Project Costs ($000s)

	1967 Total	1967 Fixed	1968 Total	1968 Fixed	1969 Total	1969 Fixed	1970 Total	1970 Fixed
25 District Variable			39		272		833	
26 Staff	5	5	25	25	73	73	99	99
27 Misc. Overhead	5	5	25	25	30	30	40	40
28 Total	10	10	89	50	375	103	962	139

	1967	1968	1969	1970
29 Project Loans ($000s)				120
30 Foreign Exchange ($000s)		10	75	210

586

	1971		1972	End Year 1977	
	76,000		166,000	475,000	same as Rice 1
	4,336,000		10,439,000	47,000,000	
	14,818,000		33,111,000	133,000,000	
	18,154,000		43,550,000	180,000,000	
	C 12		C 14		
	D 10		D 12		
	E 5		E 10		
	F 1		F 5		
			G 1		
	28		42	50	
	14		8		@ $1,000 largely in
	22		40		@ $1,000 pilot districts
	75		110		@ $ 500
					deadlines
					D = drafted
					M = ministry approval
	L				C - Council of Ministers approval
					L = Law passed
No	Cost	No	Cost		
1	5,000	1	7,000		
8	64,000	8	64,000		
2	6,000	2	6,000		
7	20,000	9	25,000		
4	14,000	4	14,000		
8	8,000	10	10,000		
	119,000		126,000		
Total	Fixed	Total	Fixed	All Years	
1,558		2,205		10,450	$225,000/district
119	119	126	126	520	
50	50	60	60	280	
1,727	169	2,391	186	11,250	
637		1,364		7,000	
420		630		3,600	incl. $76,000/dist.

587

Project Plan: Agricultural Development Bank
Agency: Agricultural Development Bank

	1967	1968	1969	1970
1 Loan Short Term		72,000	648,000	2,884,000
2 Volume Medium Term				171,000
3 Outstanding Long Term				
4 Total		72,000	648,000	3,055,000
5 Dist. Contribution to Profit		-12,000	-85,000	-254,000
6 Coverage Stage C		C 1	C 5	C 10
7 D			D 1	D 5
8 of E				E 1
9 F				
10 Districts G				
11 Total		1	6	16
Loan Officers				
12 Senior		2	13	33
13 Junior			2	12
Program Development				
14 Production Credit	P	X	T M	
15 Medium Term Credit		P	X	T M
16 Long Term Credit			P	X T
Regional Fixed Costs				
17 Provincial Branch Operation	80,000	80,000	80,000	100,000
18 Loan Officer Training		2,000	11,000	23,000
19 Regional Office & Staff	30,000	40,000	40,000	50,000
20 Miscellaneous	10,000	10,000	10,000	20,000
21 Total	120,000	132,000	141,000	143,000
Reg. Contribution to Profit				
22 By Year	-120,000	-144,000	-226,000	-447,800
23 Cumulative	-120,000	-264,000	-470,000	-917,000
24 Foreign Exchange		3,000	19,000	50,000

1971	1972	End Year 1979	
7,854,000	28,786,000	64,850,000	Assumes loan volume per
1,408,000	5,532,000	27,600,000	district will remain
132,000	758,000	3,790,000	constant after current
9,394,000	35,076,000	96,300,000	projects end.
-459,000	-464,000		
C 12	C 14		
D 10	D 12		
E 5	E 10		
F 1	F 5		
	G 1		
28	42	50	
57	86		Grade 3.
33	62		Grade 4.
			P = planning
			X = experiment in 1st dist.
			T = 1st training
M			M = issuance of manual
		All Years	
100,000	120,000	700,000	Expenses chargeable to
30,000	50,000	200,000	project only.
60,000	70,000	300,000	
20,000	30,000	200,000	
210,000	270,000	1,400,000	
-675,000	-734,000		
-1,592,000	-2,320,000	-3,500,000	Maximum under All Years
76,000	94,000	500,000	

FORM A-11.5

Project Plan: Agricultural Engineering and Irrigation

		1967		1968		1969		1970	
	Irrigation (cumulative)								
1	Farms Participating							300	
2	Hectares Irrigated							300	
3	Net Increased Income							24,000	
4	Coverage	B 1		B 5		B 10		B 12	
5	of			C 1		C 5		C 10	
6	Districts					D 1		D 5	
7	by							E 1	
8	Stage								
9									
10	Total	1		6		16		28	
	Investments (new)								
11	Earthworks							135,000	
12	Equipment & Piping							45,000	
13	Total							180,000	
	Cadre								
14	Engineers	10		10		20		47	
15	Supervisors	15		15		15		15	
16	Assistants	5		12		32		55	
	Program Development								
17	Commune Soil Survey	P____ X____		M					
18	Land Use Plan			P___X____		M			
19	Water Resources Plan				P____	X____T____		M	
20	Irrigation Financing					P___F			
	Project Cost ($000 s)	Total	Fixed	Total	Fixed	Total	Fixed	Total	Fixed
21	District Variable Costs	18		110		299		523	
22	Cadre Training	30		7		30	5	55	5
23	Equipment	10	10	20	20	35	5	85	5
24	General Overhead	20	20	30	30	50	50	60	60
25	Total	78	30	167	50	414	60	723	70
26	Foreign Exchange ($000 s)	10		20		35		120	

590

1971		1972		End Year 1981	
2,100		6,900		75,000	using Rice 2 techniques on
2,100		6,900		75,000	second crop hectarage
168,000		552,000		6,000,000	
B 14		B 8			
C 12		C 14			
D 10		D 12			
E 5		E 10			
F 1		F 5			
		G 1			
42		50		50	
					to be financed by Ag. Dev. Bank
810,000		2,160,000		33,750,000	
270,000		720,000		11,250,000	
1,080,000		2,884,000		45,000,000	
62		54		20	1967 cadre available to be
16		28		50	shifted gradually to new dists.
78		84		50	
					P = planning
					X = experiment in pilot district
					T = training of first cadre
					M = manual issuance
					F = financing approved
Total	Fixed	Total	Fixed	All Years	
754		841		5,800	
44	5	23	5	189	$1,000 per new cadre
53	5	41	5	244	$3,000 per new engineer &
70	70	70	70	300	supervisor
921	80	975	80	6,533	
300		750			

Project Plan: Rice 2
Agency: Extension Dept.

		1965-67	1968	1969
	Outputs			
1	Farms Participating			2,000
2	Hectares			4,000
3	Crop Marketed (tons)			1,800
4	Net Increased Income			76,000
5	Coverage C		C 1	C 5
6	D			D 1
7	by E			
8	F			
9	Stage G			
10	Total		$\overline{1}$	$\overline{6}$
	Supply Requirements (tons)			
11	Fertilizer			1,000
12	Pesticide			160
13	Seed			60
14	Value (40)			48,000
	Seed Production			
15	Hectares		20	160
16	Investment		90,000	142,000

	Project Staff	No.	Cost	No.	Cost	No.	Cost
17	Manager	1	4,000	1	4,000	1	4,000
18	Extension Specialists	1	3,000	1	3,000	5	15,000
19	Agronomists	2	6,000	2	6,000	1	3,000
20	Seed Production Managers	1	3,000	2	6,000	3	9,000
21	Supply Specialists			1	3,000	2	6,000
22	Others	2	2,000	3	3,000	9	9,000
23	Total		$18,000		$25,000		$46,000

	Project Costs ($000)	Total	Fixed	Total	Fixed	Total	Fixed
24	District Budgets			11		66	
25	Seed Production			90	10	142	30
26	Staff	18	18	25	25	46	46
27	Equipment	40	40	20	20	20	20
28	Other	20	20	10	10	15	15
29	Total Total	78	78	156	65	289	111
30	Foreign Exchange ($000)	20		10		50	

	1970	1971	1972	End Year 1976	
	16,000	60,000	142,000	460,000	
	32,000	120,000	284,000	920,000	
	14,400	54,000	127,000	414,000	900 kg. per farm over Rice 1.
	608,000	2,280,000	5,396,000	17,480,000	$38 per farm over Rice 1.
	C 10	C 12	C 14		
	D 5	D 10	D 12		
	E 1	E 5	E 10		
		F 1	F 5		
			G 1		
	10	28	42	50	
					Incl. Rice 1 requirements.
	8,000	30,000	71,000	230,000	
	1,280	4,800	11,360	36,800	
	480	1,800	4,200	13,800	
	384,000	1,440,000	3,408,000	11,040,000	= credit requirement
	600	1,400			
	332,000	700,000			

No.	Cost	No.	Cost	No.	Cost
1	4,000	1	4,000	1	4,000
5	15,000	4	12,000	3	9,000
1	3,000				
3	9,000	2	6,000	1	3,000
1	3,000				
7	7,000	4	4,000	2	2,000
	$41,000		$26,000		$18,000

Total	Fixed	Total	Fixed	Total	Fixed	All Years
177		314		466		2,300
332	60	700	60	60	60	1,444
41	41	26	26	18	18	174
						80
10	10	10	10	10	10	75
560	111	1,046	96	554	88	4,073
300		1,200		3,100		

Imports of fertilizer.

Project Plan: Sorghum
Agency: Extension Dept.

		1968		1969		1970	
	Outputs						
1	Farms Participating			700		5,000	
2	Hectares			1,540		11,500	
3	Production (tons)						
4	Net Income			56,000		420,000	
5	Coverage			D 1		D 3	
6	of					E 1	
7	Districts						
8	by						
9	Stage	Total		1		4	
	Supply Requirement						
10	Fertilizer (tons)			95		714	
11	Pesticide (tons)			8		63	
12	Seed (tons)			11		84	
13	Small Tractors (new units)			15		108	
14	Credit Expansion					124,000	
	Seed Production						
15	Hectares	8,000		56		214	
16	Investment	4,000		24,000		76,000	

	Project Staff	No.	Cost	No.	Cost	No.	Cost
17	Manager	1	4,000	1	4,000	1	4,000
18	Agronomist 1	2	6,000	2	6,000	1	6,000
19	Extension Specialist	2	6,000	2	6,000	4	12,000
20	Equipment Specialist	1	3,000	2	6,000	2	6,000
21	Others	5	5,000	10	10,000	10	10,000
			24,000		32,000		35,000

	Project Costs ($000)	Total	Fixed	Total	Fixed	Total	Fixed
23	District Variable			4		21	
24	Seed Production	9	5	24		76	
25	Staff	24	24	32	32	35	35
26	Equipment	20	20				
27	Overhead	10	10	20	20	20	20
28	Total	63	59	80	52	152	55
29	Foreign Exchange					20	

1971		1972		End Year 1977	
	19,000		38,500	150,000	av. 2.2 had farm
	41,650		83,000	330,000	av. 2.2 had farm
					3,400 kg. per farm
	1,520,000		3,080,000	12,000,000	$80 per farm
D 5		D 6			
E 3		E 5			
F 1		F 3			
		G 1			
8		14		25	
	2,584		5,236	20,400	136 kg. per farm
	228		462	1,800	26 kg.
	304		616	2,400	33
	350		488	3,750 cumul.	1 per 40 new farms
	766,000		2,139,000	7,193,000	
	410		600		1500 kg. per ha.
	98,000		100		$500 per ha.
No.	Cost	No.	Cost		
1	4,000	1	4,000		
4	12,000	2	6,000		
1	3,000	1	3,000		
5	5,000	2	2,000		
	25,000		15,000		
Total	Fixed	Total	Fixed	All Years	
59		117		925	$37,000 per district
98		100		306	
25	25	15	15	131	
				20	
10	10	5	5	65	
192	35	237	20	1,447	
160		500			Fertilizer Imports

FORM A-11.8

Project Plan: Hogs
Agency: Extension Dept.

		1968		1969		1970	
1	Farmers Participating					200	
2	Marketing (head)					3,000	
3	Net Income					28,000	
4	Coverage Stage: D			D 1		D 4	
5	E					E 1	
6	of F						
7	G						
8	Districts Total			1		5	
	Supply Requirements						
9	Feed (tons)					1,200	
10	Breed Sows					400	
	Credit ($000)	New	Outstg.	New	Outstg.	New	Outstg.
11	Short Term					36	36
12	Medium Term					76	76
	Construction						
13	Prov. Hog Breeding Center						
14	Reg. Hog Breeding Centers		1		1		2
	Project Staff	No.	Cost	No.	Cost	No.	Cost
15	Manager	1	5,000	1	5,000	1	5,000
16	Veterinarians	1	5,000	2	9,000	2	9,000
17	Animal Nutrition Spec.	2	8,000	3	12,000	1	4,000
18	Extension Specialists	1	3,000	1	3,000	1	3,000
19	Provincial Officers			1	3,000	2	6,000
20	Other	5	5,000	10	10,000	12	12,000
21	Total		$20,000		$42,000		$39,000
	Project Costs ($000)	Total	Fixed	Total	Fixed	Total	Fixed
22	District Variable			10		57	
23	Prov. Center Op.			26	26	32	32
24	Construction	160	160	20	20	20	20
25	Misc. Equipment	30	30	20	20	10	10
26	Other	10	10	20	20	30	30
27	Total	220	220	96	86	149	92
28	Foreign Exchange ($000)	25		15		15	

596

	1971		1972	End Year 1977	
	1,600		6,500	76,000	
	24,000		97,500	1,140,000	15 head per farm
	224,000		910,000	10,640,000	$140 per farm
D 8		D 10			
E 4		E 8			
F 1		F 4			
		G 1			
13		23		40	
	9,600		39,000	456,000	6 tons per farm
	2,800		9,800		2 per new farm
New	Outstg.	New	Outstg.	Outstg.	New loans & outstanding balances
245	281	932	1,213	13,680	$180 per farm
517	562	1,968	2,230	14,000	$380 per new farm
	3		3		
No.	Cost	No.	Cost		
1	5,000	1	5,000		
1	5,000				
1	4,000	1	4,000		
2	6,000	2	6,000		
4	12,000	7	21,000		
16	16,000	18	18,000		
	$48,000		$50,000		
Total	Fixed	Total	Fixed	All Years	
183		411		3,880	$97,000 per district
44	44	62	62	400	
40	40	60	60	300	
15	15	20	20	110	
30	30	40	40	170	
312	129	593	182	4,860	
30		50		150	

FORM A-12

Project Narrative: Farmers Associations
Min. Ag., Dept. of Cooperatives, Southern Region

1. Objectives

   This project organizes district-level farmer supply
and marketing cooperatives, called Farmers Associations
(FA's), initially in the Southern Region and later in other
regions, in order to:

   a. Promote use of production supplies, agricultural
      chemicals, improved seed, and also farm equip-
      ment, which now have no adequate production
      network.

   b. Improve crop marketing, to yield the farmer the
      best possible price, by eliminating excess layers
      of middlemen, by organizing efficient lot sizes, by
      introducing grading, and by providing storage.

   c. Promote new cash crops, largely by contractual
      arrangements with major processing and distri-
      bution firms.

   d. Bring farmers into active participation in the plan-
      ning and management of agricultural development.

2. Local Operation

   a. Organize FA's--The first step is to consolidate
      existing village-level units into a district-level unit
      with sufficient clientele to conduct an efficient com-
      mercial operation. The district-level unit is called
      the FA to distinguish it clearly from village coopera-
      tives. The district administration invites representa-
      tives of all existing village cooperatives, or farmer
      clubs in villages having no cooperatives, to an initial
      organizational meeting. This meeting adopts a
      charter (based on a standard Coop. Dept. format) and
      bylaws, and files a standard request for Coop. Dept.
      assistance.

b. Name Officers--The first general meeting elects a
   nine-man executive board and a seven-man auditing
   board. The executive board elects its chairman and
   secretary. The first two years the executive board
   is elected for one-year terms, after which members
   are elected to staggered three-year terms.

c. Select Employees--The executive board selects a
   manager from among suitable candidates in the district having, among other requirements, at least 10
   years education and some commercial as well as
   farming experience. It also selects an assistant
   manager, with at least eight years education and
   some commercial experience; districts having a
   Kenaf Agent must designate them as assistant manager. In later stages the board selects additional
   assistant managers. The manager selects clerks
   and other employees, subject to board approval.

d. Train Employees--On-the-job training and in-service
   training are stressed. The Coop. Dept. does give each
   manager and assistant manager two weeks preservice
   training at the Coop. Center in the capital, plus a
   week at the Southern Regional Research and Extension
   Center (SRREC). Each year it gives them at least 10
   days of in-service training, largely at the pilot FA by the
   SRREC. The Coop. Dept. also gives clerks a standard
   two week preservice course.

e. Build and Equip Warehouse--Adequate warehouse
   space and crop loans enable farmers to get a 20 percent better price by avoiding dumping all their crop
   right after harvest. Upon approval of the initial subsidy, the Province Engineer let a contract for construction of the basic FA warehouse and office. As
   part of the subsidy, the Coop. Dept. provides equipment, initially including two trucks. Where they
   exist, kenaf agencies are used as the core of the office
   and warehouse. The second year (stage D) the FA itself contracts for construction of additions. Expansion
   after the second year is financed to the maximum by
   mortgage loans from the Ag. Dev. Bank.

f. Distribute First Farm Supplies--Commercial opera-
    tions in stage C, the first year, are based on projects
    Rice 1 (31-S-225) and Kenaf (31-S-227). Local per-
    sonnel of the Coop. Dept., Extension Dept., Com-
    munity Development (CD) Dept., and the Ag. Dev. Bank
    lead an intensive preparatory campaign to sell farmers
    on use of agricultural chemicals and make loan appli-
    cations. Farm Leaders, CD Workers and other volun-
    teers are trained to canvass farmers and assist them
    make loan applications. The loans are in kind, dis-
    tributed by the FA.

g. Market First Crops--A similar preparatory campaign
    is made before harvest to get farmers to market their
    rice through the FA. A substantial number of parti-
    cipating farmers is essential to give the FA the volume
    to market crops efficiently. The FA contracts with a
    local miller to mill the paddy and sells it directly to
    large firms in the capital, to avoid middlemen. The
    Ag. Dev. Bank advances short term loans to the FA's
    to make crop storage loans to farmers who wish to
    hold crops off the market, the crop being held at the
    FA as collateral.

h. Initiate Diversification--New commercial operations in
    the second year (stage D) are based on projects Rice 2
    (31-S-237) and Kenaf. Commune and village coverage
    is increased. Under Rice 2, improved seed sales and
    marketing of graded crops is introduced. Before har-
    vest time, the FA holds mass meetings to plan the
    program for the third year (stage E). Representatives
    of agribusiness firms visit these meetings, presenting
    their companies' products and crop contracting plans
    to the farmers.

i. Expand FA Business--Diversification in the third year
    (stage E) is based mainly on projects Sorghum (31-S-
    239), Cotton (31-S-241) and Hogs (31-S-245). Demon-
    stration and field days the previous year prepare for
    this. In addition to diversifying its line of agricultural
    chemicals, the FA introduces the sale of new farm
    equipment and feed supplements, based on these

projects. FA's in hog areas may contract with metropolitan dealers for shipment of regular truckloads of
hogs. Many FA's also go into supply and marketing
for horticultural crops in the third and fourth years
(stages E and F).

j. Establish Commune Branches--Once sufficient volume
   is achieved, better service and participation can be
   gained by decentralization. In the third and fourth
   years (stages E and F) a branch office and warehouse
   are established in each commune, with an agent having
   the same prerequisites and training as an assistant
   manager. The commune agent is also trained under
   the Extension project (31-S-235) to manage the commune demonstration program. The Agricultural Committee of the Commune Development Council is
   responsible for planning the demonstration program
   and any special supply and marketing programs undertaken by the FA at the commune level.

k. Attain Financial Independence--The FA is expected to
   start showing a profit in its fourth or fifth year, after
   which no further subsidies are granted.

3. Project Development

   1967--An interministerial evaluation of rural marketing
   indicated need for consolidating village cooperatives
   into larger units. A working group proposed a trial
   of a district level FA, which was approved by the
   Council of Ministers. The Coop. Dept. named a
   project manager, who planned a pilot operation and
   subsequent expansion, as part of the 1968-72 Plan.
   Cooperation agreements were signed with the Kenaf
   Board, the Ag. Dev. Bank, and the Extension Dept.

   1968--The Coop. Dept. will operate and evaluate stage C
   in the district adjoining the SRREC. The project manager will be given a temporary section with supply and
   marketing specialists and a lawyer and a training officer. An aid donor agency has agreed to furnish business specialists. The section will draft an FA law.
   Upon evaluation of the pilot supply operation, a plan
   will be negotiated for initiating several more district
   FA's in 1969.

1969--The pilot district will operate at stage D and several
districts will initiate first year FA operation. All
operations will continue under temporary arrangements,
with property held by the department. Kenaf agencies
will continue to be owned by the Kenaf Board. The FA
section of the department will be expanded by several
specialists, including more foreign advisers. The
Ministry and the Council of Ministers will consider the
FA Law and, if acceptable to them, it will be submitted
to the Assembly. The section will also draft an operations manual and a training manual. The first commune branches and first crop diversifications will be
tested in the pilot FA.

1970--On passage of the FA Law, all assigned assets will
be turned over to FA's which have had one successful
year of operation. As many new FA's as possible will
be launched in this and following years, until all districts of the region are covered. The Coop. Dept. will
establish a permanent FA Division. The Division will
establish a regular training program, preservice and
inservice, for FA employees at the SRREC in cooperation with the Extension Dept.

1971--FA's will be initiated in other regions. The Division will draft legislation authorizing a Regional FA
Federation.

1972--Upon passage of authorizing legislation, a Regional
FA Federation will take over training and business
promotion functions from the FA Division of the Coop.
Dept.

FORM A-13

Local Cost Benefits Summary

Stage No.	Comm Dev cost	Extension cost	Farm Asn. cost	Ag Bank cost	Ag Eng. cost	Ag Eng. ben	Rice 1 cost	Rice 1 ben	Rice 2 cost	Rice 2 ben
1 A	32	19					21	25		
2 B	39	18			18		51	98		
3 C	39	36	39	12	20		130	295	47	
4 D	35	38	77	23	19		65	389	271	76
5 E	41	36	174	16	192	24		389	136	238
6 F	47	31	42	4	174	48		389	68	395
7 G			-15		153	72		389		395
8 H			-21		135	96		389		395
9 I			-21		117	120		389		395
10			-21		-90	120		389		395
11			-21		-90	120		389		395
12			-21		-90	120		389		395
13			-21		-90	120		389		395
14					-90	120		389		395
15					90	120		389		395
16					72	120		389		395
17					54	120		389		395
18					-36	120		389		395
19					18	120		389		395
20						120		389		395
						120		389		395
						120		389		395
						120		389		395
30						120		389		395
**	233	178	332	55	810	2,760	267	14,638	822	14,139

all figures above in $000

* Net = Costs - Benefits; Disc = Net Benefits discounted at 6%.
** Cost totals are for maximum cumulative outlays, before 6% debt repayments become greater than outlays.

604

Kenaf cost	Sorghum cost	Sorghum ben	Cotton cost	Cotton ben	Hogs cost	Hogs ben	Total Costs	Total Ben	Net*	Disc*
							51	1	-51	-48
2							98	25	-73	-65
12							256	98	-158	-133
3	4		2		8		610	371	-239	-189
2	75	28	23	39	103	22	863	740	-123	-92
	203	126	42	137	270	85	881	1,175	299	207
	175	240	96	380	514	213	923	1,689	766	507
	-145	240	-21	390	-232	213	-293	1,713	2,006	1,254
	-109	240	-27	390	-174	213	-223	1,737	1,960	1,153
	-59	240	-15	390	-122	213	-307	1,737	2,044	1,136
		240		390		213	-111	1,737	1,848	968
		240		390		213	-111	1,737	1,848	915
		240		390		213	-111	1,737	1,848	864
		240		390		213	-90	1,737	1,827	805
		240		390		213	-90	1,737	1,827	758
		240		390		213	-90	1,737	1,827	716
		240		390		213	-72	1,737	1,809	670
		240		390		213	-54	1,737	1,791	626
		240		390		213	-36	1,737	1,773	585
		240		390		213	-18	1,737	1,755	547
		240		390		213				
		240		390		213				386
		240		390		213		1,737	1,737	
19	457	5,914	163	8,580	895	5,219	3,931	51,250	41,949	15,044

Program Coefficients Table
(In $000 unless otherwise noted.)

Financial Input Coefficients per District per Stage

Project Budget

	A	B	C	D	E	F	G
Community Dev.	37	43	39	35	41	47	
Ag. Extension	24	23	36	38	36	31	
Ag. Eng. & Irrigation	2	18	20	19	12	12	9
Farmers Assns.		2	40	78	59	10	5
Ag. Dev. Bank		3	15	23	17	4	
Rice 1	1	21	10				
Kenal		2	12	3	2		
Rice 2			47	204	12	12	
Sorghum				8	25	12	12
Cotton				2	11	12	12
Hogs				10	17	35	35
Total	64	112	219	420	220	175	61

Credit Expansion

	A	B	C	D	E	F	G
Community Dev.							
Ag. Extension							
Ag. Eng. & Irrigation					180	180	180
Farmers Assns.					120	37	
Ag. Dev. Bank							
Rice 1			72	130	65		
Kenal							
Rice 2				68	124	56	
Sorghum					124	394	337
Cotton					12	30	250
Hogs					112	283	607
Total			72	248	817	1,030	1,374

Foreign Exchange

A	B	C	D	E	F	G
6	3		2	2	2	
3	3	9	4	2	2	
	5			45	45	45
		10	15	20	25	
		3	4			3
	4	31	105	230	230	230
			60	170	220	220
				20	100	200
				20	50	125
			D	E	F	G
9	15	53	215	509	674	823

Increased Personnel for District per Stage (no. of persons)

	Grade 3							Grade 4						
	A	B	C	D	E	F	G	A	B	C	D	E	F	G
Community Dev.								1						
Ag. Extension														
Ag. Eng. & Irrigation		2		-1	-1						1			
Farmers Assns.									1					
Ag. Dev. Bank			2	1			1			2	1			
Total		2	2		-1		1	1	1	3		1		

Grade 5

A	B	C	D	E	F	G
5	5					
	5	5	1	-4	-5	
	2		-1			
		1	1	1	5	5
5	12	6	1	-4		5

Increase in Crops Marketed per District*						
	A	B	C	D	E	F	G
Rice			510	3,840	11,800	16,400	16,400
Sorghum					960	4,240	8,160
Cotton					216	1,600	2,120
Hogs					3,000	11,400	28,500

*Tons or head per <u>av.</u> dist.

Annual Total Project Fixed Costs						
Project & Launch Stage		1968	1969	1970	1971	1972
Community Dev.	(A)	159	183	210	234	255
Ag. Extension	(A)	150	320	140	150	160
Ag. Eng. & Irrig.	(B)	50	60	70	80	80
Rice	(B)	21				
Kenal	(B)	30	50	10		
Farmers Assns.	(C)	50	103	143	169	186
Ag. Dev. Bank	(C)	56	50	70	100	110
Rice 2	(C)	55	81	51	36	28
Sorghum	(D)	59	52	55	35	20
Cotton	(D)	109	107	63	62	55
Hogs	(D)	220	81	62	113	164
Total		733	1,077	875	979	1,058

Sum of Net Benefits per District discounted @ 6%						Annual Income	Participating Farms
Stage	1968	1969	1970	1971	1972		(no.)
A	14,914	14,529	14,169	13,827	13,512		
B	16,129	15,809	15,469	15,109	14,727	25	600
C	17,472	17,151	16,811	16,451	16,069	98	2,400
D	18,918	18,597	18,258	17,897	17,517	311	7,200
E	20,541	20,221	19,881	19,521	19,139	740	9,500
F	22,348	22,027	21,687	21,327	20,945	1,175	9,500
G	24,139	23,819	23,479	23,119	22,737	1,689	9,500
H	25,597	25,276	24,936	24,576	24,194	1,713	9,500

Marginal Revenue*	1968	1969	1970	1971	1972
	385	360	342	315	287

*Loss from postponing Stage A 1 year.

FORM A-15

Intraproject Constraint Application

	1967	Low Option 1968	Low Option 1969	Low Option 1970	Low Option 1971	Low Option 1972	Low Option 1973	High Option 1968	High Option 1969	High Option 1970	High Option 1971	High Option 1972
Coverage by Stage (A–H)	A 15, B 15	A 8, B 5, C 1	A 8, B 8, C 5, D 1	A 11, B 8, C 8, D 5, E 1	A 9, B 11, C 8, D 8, E 5, F 1	A 8, B 9, C 11, D 8, E 8, F 5, G 1		A 12, B 5, C 1	A 16, B 12, C 5, D 1, E	A 16, B 16, C 12, D 5, E 1	A 16, B 16, C 12, D 5, E 1, F	A 16, B 16, C 12, D 5, E 1, F
		14	22	33	42	50		18	33	50	50	
Training Capacity — C.D. CLWs need		0	50	100	100	85			135	160	80	
limit		60	60	100	100	100		60	160	160	160	
Ag. Ext. Agents need		30	65	80	95	100		30	85	140	160	80
limit		60	80	100	100	100		60	100	160	160	150
Personnel — Engineers need		10	25	35	44	46		12	35	61	76	38
limit		15	25	35	45	55		15	50	100	100	100
Seed (tons) — Rice need			490	1,430	2,000	4,750			490	1,670	3,240	4,000
limit		60	500	1,500	3,008	5,000		100	1,000	2,000	4,000	5,000
Cotton (50% of districts) need			1	11	50	147			1	11	60	177
limit			10	30	100	200			10	30	100	200

608

FORM A-16

Program Summary

	1968		1969		1970	
Net Benefits disc. @ 6%	247,257,000		436,550,000		660,131,000	
1 Ann. Increased Income	223,000		1,111,000		3,875,000	
Crops Marketed						
2 (incr. in Rice	510		6,390		36,100	
3 tons Sorghum					960	
4 or Cotton					210	
5 head) Hogs					3,000	
6 Farmers Participating	5,400		25,200		76,700	
7 Coverage	A 10 limit: 12		A 12 limit: 16		A 14 limit: 16	
8	B 5 5		B 10 12		B 12 16	
9 of	C 1 1		C 5 5		C 10 12	
10			D 1 1		D 5 5	
11 Districts					E 1 1	
12						
13						
14 Total	16		28		42	
Constrained Resources	Used	Limit	Used	Limit	Used	Limit
15 Personnel: Grade 3	12	50	30	50	43	50
16 4	13	40	20	60	39	80
17 5	126	200	211	250	270	300
Credit Expansion ($000)						
18 Annual	72	1,000	608	1,500	2,990	2,000
19 Cumulative	72		680	2,500	3,670	4,500
20 Foreign Exchange ($000)	495*	2,000	608	3,000	2,420	5,000
Program Budget ($000)						
21 Variable	1,574		3,353		6,750	
22 Fixed	733		1,077		875	
23 Residual*	1,200					
24 Total	3,507	4,000	4,430	6,000	7,625	8,000
25 Cumulative	3,507	4,000	7,937	10,000	15,562	18,000

* Cost of extra districts in stages A & B, Community Development Project.

1971	1972	
720,379,000	871,838,000	max.
10,111,000	20,998,000	85,650,000
120,000	270,000	
9,000	38,500	
2,680	12,300	
26,400	115,500	
166,200	276,800	
		Prior Years
A 8 limit:	limit:	5
B 14 16	8	1
C 12 16	14 16 C	
D 10 12	12 16 D	
E 5 5	10 12 E	
F 1 1	5 5 F	
	1 1 G	
50	50	

Used	Limit	Used	Limit	
47	50	35	50	
51	100	55	120	
271	350	162	400	
8,459	7,500	18,678	18,000	
12,129	12,000	30,807	30,000	Maximum
6,287	8,000	12,725	15,000	
10,183		12,138	13,000	
979		1,058	1,058	
11,162	12,000	13,196	14,000	
26,724	30,000	39,920	44,000	

611

FORM A-17

Project Annual Plan: Farmers Associations
(All figures in $000 unless otherwise noted.)

#33-S-315/1970
Dist: Yakyak

		1st Qtr.		2nd Qtr.		3rd Qtr.		4th Qtr.		total year	
		plan	act'l	plan	act'l	plan	act'l	plan	act'l	plan	act'l
1	Members	4,000	3,800	6,800	6,200	7,200		7,200		7,200	
2	Crop — Rice	200	150	75	65	25		700		900	
3	Mar- — Kenaf					110				110	
4	keting — Sorghum			37	15					37	
5	Cotton	92	105	33	50	33				92	
6	Other									66	
7	Total	292	255	145	130	168		700		1,205	
8	Gross Margin	7.5	6.4	3.2	3.1	4.2		16.1		31	
9	Supply — Fertilizer			200	160	100				300	
10	Sales — Pesticides			25	30	50				75	
11	Other	10	15	20	20	20				50	
12	Total	10	15	245	210	170				425	
13	Gross Margin	.3	.4	8.6	7.4	6.1				15	
17	Total Gross Margin	7.8	6.8	11.8	10.5	10.3		16.1		46	
	Personnel (no.)										
18	Manager	1	1	1	1	1		1		1	
19	Assistant Managers	3	3	3	3	3		3		3	
20	Commune Agents	5	4	5	4	5		5		5	
21	Clerks	4	4	4	4	4		4		4	
22	Other	6	6	7	6	6		7		7	
	Expenses										
23	Manager	.7	.7	.7	.7	.7		.8		2.9	
24	Assistant Managers	1.1	1.1	1.1	1.1	1.1		1.1		4.5	
25	Commune Agents	1.6	1.3	1.5	1.3	1.6		1.7		6.5	
26	Clerks	.9	.9	.9	.9	.9		1.0		3.7	

	1	2	3	4	5	6	7
27 Other Employees	.5	.5	.6	.5	.5	1.0	2.6
28 Interest	2.0	1.6	.8	.8	2.2	7.0	11.4
29 Miscellaneous	5.0	5.2	5.0	5.3	5.0	6.0	21.0
30 Total	11.8	11.3	10.9	10.8	12.0	18.6	53.4
31 Profits	-4.0	-4.5	-.9	-.3	-1.7	-2.5	-8.0
32 In- Crops	150	130	75	60	25	420	420
33 ven- Fertilizer			100	120	50	20	20
34 tory Other			30	30	30	10	10
35 (peak) Total	150	130	205	190	155	450	450
36 Warehouse Space (m²) Occupied	2,900	2,400	2,300	2,100	2,800	8,700	8,700
37 Available	2,900	2,900	2,900	2,900	8,700	8,700	8,700
38 Construction: Stage			25%	16%	100%		
39 Spent			22	14	65		87
40 Assets Net Working Capital	148	128	80	75	150	450	450
41 Equipment	15	15	20	20	20	20	20
42 Building	43	43	65	57	130	130	130
43 Total	206	186	165	152	300	600	600
44 Liabilities Short Term Debt	108	90	43	41	120	280	
45 Long Term Debt					19	120	120
46 Earned Surplus	-19	-21	-17	-21	4	-23	-23
47 Membership Capital	4	4	4	4		16	16
48 Subsidy	113	113	135	127	171	171	171
49 Total	206	186	165	152	300	600	600
50 Project Released	0	17	22	14	37	58	58
51 Subsidy Spent	0	17	22	14	37	58	58

FORM A-18

Quarterly Report: Farmers Associations
(All figures in $000 unless otherwise noted.)

#33-S-315/1970
Dist: YAKYAK

Qtr: Apr-June

Stage E		Plan	Actual	Explanation of Divergences
1	Members (no.)	6,800	6,200	1 commune still stg. D from '69 flood
2	Crop Rice	75	65	'69 flood damage
3	Mar- Kenaf			
4	keting Sorghum	37	15	#1* and '69 sorghum participants shortfall
5	Cotton			
6	Other	33	50	success of special local tomato mktg.
7	Total	145	130	
8	Gross Margin	3.2	3.1	
9	Supply Fertilizer	200	160	#1 and late rains
10	Sales Pesticides	25	30	#9
11	Other	20	20	
12	Total	245	210	
13	Gross Margin	8.6	7.4	
17	Total Gross Margin	11.8	10.5	
	Personnel (no.)			
18	Manager	1	1	
19	Assistant Managers	3	3	
20	Commune Agents	5	4	#1
21	Clerks	4	4	
22	Other	7	6	
	Expenses			
23	Manager	.7	.7	
24	Assistant Managers	1.1	1.1	
25	Commune Agents	1.5	1.3	#20

614

#	Item				Explanation
26	Clerks		.9	.9	
27	Other Employees		.6	.5	
28	Interest		.8	.8	
29	Miscellaneous		5.0	5.3	truck repairs
30		Total	10.6	10.6	
31	Profits		.9	-.3	
32	In-	Crops	75	60	#2
33	ven-	Fertilizer	100	120	#9
34	tory	Other	30	30	
35	(peak)	Total	205	190	#35
	Warehouse Space (m²)				
36	Occupied		2,300	2,100	
37	Available		2,900	2,900	
38	Construction:	Stage	25%	16%	#1, 1 commune warehouse postponed
39		Spent	22	14	also const, start 5 wks, late
	Assets				
40	Net Working Capital		80	75	
41	Equipment		20	20	
42	Building		65	57	#39
43		Total	165	152	
	Liabilities				
44	Short Term Debt		43	41	
45	Long Term Debt				
46	Earned Surplus		-17	-19	
47	Membership Capital		4	4	
48	Subsidy		135	127	
49		Total	165	152	
50	Project Released		22	14	
51	Subsidy Spent		22	14	

*Numbers in this column indicate lines above in which explanation found.

615

APPENDIX $\quad$ B $\quad$ AN AGRICULTURAL DEVELOPMENT PROGRAMMING MODEL

GENERAL STRUCTURE

This model is a linear program at the regional and national level for an agricultural sector multiyear development program whose coefficients are derived by simulation of modular farms and modular districts for each region. (If more appropriate, the commune may be used as the local modular.) The program has four levels:

The Sector--The agricultural sector program consists of r regional subsector programs run over t years. The objective is to maximize the present value of discounted net benefits (defined as net cash income to farmers less budget outlays and credit expansion), subject to resource constraints and some administrative constraints. The program has i projects, some institution-building and some innovation-package promoting. Some fixed costs are aggregated at the sector level. The principle constraints are at the sector level: financial including budget outlays $\overline{B}_t$, credit expansion $\Delta \overline{K}_t$, and foreign exchange $\overline{E}_t$; market demand on crops promoted $\overline{M}_{it}$; higher level personnel recruitment $\Delta \overline{P}_{gt}$; training capacity $\overline{T}_{git}$ (g denoting the class of personnel in terms of civil service grades); and domestic production of crop production inputs $\overline{Z}_{cit}$ (c denoting the class of input: fertilizer, pesticide, etc.).

The Region--The r-th region has a total of $\overline{C}_r$ districts (or communes), all of which are considered identical to the modular district for planning purposes. Each region has a different selection from among the i projects (though certain projects may be found in all regions) and each region has different coefficients within the same projects. Fixed costs for project administration and support and for research are largely aggregated at the regional level. Medium-grade personnel have regional level constraints ($\Delta \overline{P}_{rgt}$).

The District--The district (or commune) is the unit of increment of the program. Each year t of the program a certain number of districts are launched into the program to advance through j modular stages. Each stage has its coefficients of input requirements, and, for crop projects, income y_{irj} and marketed production m_{irj} (derived by simulation from the farm level). All districts launched into stage j=1 in starting year s (=t, the year launched) are designated C_{rs}, (the number of districts launched in the r-th region in s-th year of the program). Thus, in the program displayed on Form A-16 in Appendix A, C_{rs} takes the following values:

$$s = \quad -1 \quad 0 \quad 1 \quad 2 \quad 3 \quad 4 \quad 5$$

$$C_{rs} = \quad 1 \quad 5 \quad 10 \quad 12 \quad 14 \quad 8 \quad 0 \quad (\overline{C}_r = 50)$$

The Farm--For each region there is a modular farm, which gains an increase in net cash income y'_{ri} when it adopts the innovation promoted by the i-th project. The modular district has a maximum number of farms $\overline{f}_{ri}$ to which the innovation of the i-th project is suited. Net benefits are thus maximized in a district by bringing the number of farmers who have adopted the innovation of the i-th project in the j-th stage f_{ij} up to the maximum $\overline{f}_{ij}$ as quickly as possible.

General Notational Features

Capital letters denote regional or national level variables, endogenous and exogenous, e. g., X_t. Constraints are denoted by bars, e. g., $\overline{X}_t$. Values for the district module are denoted by lower-case letters, e. g., x_{rij}. If the expression does not have an i subscript, then implicitly it is understood to be the value for the sum of the i's: $x_r = \sum_i x_{ri}$. Farm level variables are denoted by a prime: x'_i. For simplicity the regional subscript r is omitted from the simulation equations but is understood to apply to all of them. Greek letters denote structural coefficients or parameters.

THE PROGRAM

Maximize:
(1)

$$\sum_r \sum_s n_{rs} C_{rs}$$

where
(1a)
and

$$n_{rs} = \sum_{t=s}^{30} y_{rj} - \frac{(b_{rj} + \Delta k_{rj})}{(1 + R)^t}$$

(1b)

$$j = t + 1 - s$$

subject to:

(2) Budget

$$\sum_r \sum_s b_{rj} C_{rs} + \sum_r B_{urt}$$
$$- S_{Bt-1} \leq \bar{B}_t$$

(3) Credit Expansion

$$\sum_r \sum_s \Delta k_{rj} C_{rs} - S_{Kt-1} \leq \Delta \bar{K}_t$$

(4) Foreign Exchange

$$\sum_r \sum_s e_{rj} C_{rs} - S_{Et-1} \leq \bar{E}_t$$

(5) Market Demand

$$\sum_r \sum_s m_{irj} C_{rs} + \overset{*}{M}_{it} \leq \bar{M}_{it}$$

(6) Personnel Top Grades

$$\sum_r \sum_s \Delta p_{grj} C_{rs}$$
$$+ \Delta P_{gut} - S_{gt-1} \leq \Delta \bar{P}_{gt}$$

(7) Personnel Med. Grades

$$\sum_s \Delta p_{grj} C_{rs} - S_{grt-1} \leq \Delta \bar{P}_{rgt}$$

(8) Specialized

$$\sum_r \sum_s \Delta p_{girj} C_{rs} - S_{git-1} \leq \Delta \bar{P}_{git}$$

(9) Training Capacity

$$\sum_r \sum_s \Delta p_{girj} C_{rs} \leq \bar{T}_{git}$$

(10) Input Production Capacity

$$\sum_r \sum_s z_{crij} C_{rs} \leq \bar{Z}_{cit}$$

(11) Point stage

$$\{C_{rs-1} = 0\} \qquad C_{rs} = \bar{C}^a$$

(12) Line Stage

$$\{C_{rs-2} = 0\} \qquad C_{rs} \leq \bar{C}^b$$

(13) Political Minimum

$$\{C_{rs-2} > 0\} \qquad C_{rs} \geq \bar{C}^c$$

(14) Total Districts in Region

$$\sum_s C_{rs} \leq \bar{C}_r$$

Notation

s   o = dist. level value
t   O = reg./nat. level value
y
1   $\bar{Q}$ = constraint
e$\overset{*}{O}$, $\overset{*}{o}$ = exogenous

B, b = budget
C   = coverage of districts
        $\bar{C}^a$ = point stage max.
        $\bar{C}^b$ = line stage max.
        $\bar{C}^c$ = politically required
                minimum
E, e = foreign exchange
K, k = credit outstanding
M, m = crop market volume
    n = net benefit discounted
P, p = personnel
R   = rate of discount
S   = slack variable
T   = training capacity
y = net cash income
Z, z = production inputs

Subscripts

c = subcategory of variable
g = personnel grade
i = project
j = stage of district
    development
r = region or regional program
s = year dist. in stage j=1
t = year of program
u = fixed cost

Further notation features

a) if expression does not have an
   i subscript, then implicitly

$$^o_r \qquad \sum_i {}^o_{ri}$$

b) 1b applies to all equations

c) Implicitly

$$\sum = \sum^n$$
$$o=1$$

THE PROGRAM

Notes on the Programming Model

The Objective Function--The solution values of C_{rs} are
the number of districts launched into stage j=1 in the r-th
region in the s-th starting year. The derivation of n is discussed in Chapter 14. The relationship between j, t, and s
in (1b) can be illustrated in the following table:

Year   Starting Years of Districts (s)
 (t)   1   2   3   4   5   6   7   8   9

 1   1
 2   2   1   corresponding
 3   3   2   1
 4   4   3   2   1   values
 5   5   4   3   2   1
 6   6   5   4   3   2   1   of
 7   7   6   5   4   3   2   1
 8   8   7   6   5   4   3   2   1   j
 9   9   8   7   6   5   4   3   2   1

The j values in all equations are determined by (1b).

Financial Constraints--In the budget equation b_{rj} is the
budget required per district for stage j in the r-th region.
B_{urt} is the fixed budget for the r-th region in the t-th year.
Money unspent from the previous year, S_{Bt-1}, can also be
used. Likewise Δk_{rj} is the credit expansion (or contraction)
per district in the j-th stage in the r-th region, and lags in
planned credit expansion, S_{Kt-1}, can be carried over and used
in the following year. As loans are repaid, Δk_{rj} becomes
negative. In some cases it may be possible to combine
equations (2) and (3).

Market Demand--m_{irj} is the increase in the volume of
the crop marketed as a result of the i-th project (the crop and
project i numbers being the same), in the r-th region in the
j-th stage. $\overset{*}{M}_{it}$ is the anticipated marketed volume of the i-th
crop in year t not related to project activity. $\overline{M}_{it}$ is the

maximum volume of the i-th crop in the t-th year that the market can absorb without the price dropping below γ'_i (see equation (F1) below).

Personnel Constraints -- ΔP_{grj} is the change in the number of cadre of the g-th grade per district in the r-th region in the j-th stage. ΔP_{gut} is the increase or decrease in central personnel of the g-th grade in the t-th year. Personnel available but not recruited in the previous year, S_{gt-1}, can be recruited in the current year. Equation (6) assumes that personnel in higher grades can be recruited nationwide, so the constraint $\Delta \overline{P}_{gt}$ does not have the regional subscript r. Equation (7) applies to those categories whose supply is limited to the region. Equation (8) applies to those categories of personnel which are limited to one project. The training capacity equation (9) states that the coverage C_{rs} is limited by the $\overline{T}_{git}$, the training capacity of the i-th project in year t for personnel in grade g, divided by ΔP_{girj}, the increment in personnel of the g-th grade and the i-th project district in the r-th region and the j-th stage. This constraint may be regional or multiregional, and it can be modified by expanding training facilities.

Input Production Capacity--The coefficient z_{crij} is the amount of input of the c-th category--a certain type of fertilizer or pesticide or seed or equipment--required per district in the r-th region and the j-th stage by the i-th project. $\overline{Z}_{cit}$ is the maximum production capacity in-country available in year t for input type c and project i. The constraint may be multiproject, as for fertilizer used on many crops. In that case the i is dropped from the constraint expression.

Policy Maxima and Minima--Equations (11) and (12) express the maximum districts that can be covered by a program in the point stage ($\overline{C}^a$), and in the line stage ($\overline{C}^b$). In these equations an important administrative limitation is applied to the program. Equation (13) expresses the common political reality that, no matter what the relative payoff, no region can be deprived completely of rural development activity in a given year. Frequently, due to political pressure, some expansion must be financed in every region.

DERIVATION OF
THE PARAMETERS

The Individual Farm

(F1) <u>Net Cash Income</u> $y_i^! = \pi \,' (v_i h'_i - c_i^!)$

   production costs $-\sum \left\{ (\tfrac{1}{\tau} + r_\tau)_z \sum v_{zi} z' z\tau_i h'_i \right\}$

   previous income $- \overset{*}{y}_!$

(F2) <u>Market Volume</u> $m'_i = v_i h'_i - c'_i - \overset{*}{m}'_i$

(F3) <u>Inputs</u> $z'_{\tau zi} = y_{zi} h'_i$

(F4) <u>Credit</u> $k'_{\tau i} = \chi_{zi} v_{zi} z_{\tau zi} - \overset{*}{k}_{\tau i}$

<u>Notation</u> (all values for average farm)

h' = enterprise scale (hectares or head)
c' = home consumption
k' = credit
m' = kg. or head marketed
r = interest rate
y' = net cash income
z' = quantity of input used

y = quantity of input recommended
χ = % of cost of input on credit
v = price of input
π = price of crop
τ = term of loan
v = yield

Subscripts
i = project or crop
z = type of input
τ = term of loan
$\overset{*}{o}$' = indicates value previous to project

In the above expressions, and in all equations and expressions below, the regional subscript r has been left out. All parameters, however, must be computed separately for each region. The r subscript, though absent here for the sake of compactness, is implicit.

The Local Level

The next level of aggregation is the locale, a district or, possibly, a commune. This is the structural variable in the program. At this level, four types of projects must be distinguished:

    A. Crop promotion
    B. Noncommercial institutions (extension, agricultural engineering, etc.)
    C. Credit agencies and enterprises
    D. Marketing enterprises (assumed supported by subsidy or equity investment)

Five sets of equations apply to the above types of projects as follows:

Equations	Project types
L1:　Income	A
L2:　Services and Personnel	B　C　D
L3:　Business Volume and Gross Margin	C　D
L4:　Expenses	A　B　C　D
L5:　Assets and Liabilities	D

Income--The following equations determine the gross benefits of projects, which are defined in this model as net cash income to farmers resulting from project activity:

(L1. 1)　Income
$$y_{ij} = y'_i f_{ij}$$

(L1. 2)　Participants
$$\Delta f_{ij} \leq \delta fi f_{ij-1} + \delta di \Delta\, d_{ij-1}$$

(L1. 3)　Maximum Participants
$$f_{ij} \leq \bar{f}_i = \emptyset_i \bar{f}$$

Notation

d = demonstrations

f = farmers

y = net cash income

α = ratio of previous activity to adoption

$\emptyset$ = % of farmers in suitable district to whom applicable

Subscripts

i = project

j = stage

(L1.2) is the key dynamic equation of the model. It is the initiation of demonstrations in a district that starts farmers adopting the innovation package promoted by a project; the pace of expansion of demonstrations determines the rapidity of adoption. The number of participants, f, is defined as the number of farmers in a district who have adopted the innovation package of a project.

Services and Personnel--Each institutional project provides certain services which are essential to successful adoption of innovations, services such as community organization, farmer training, demonstration, land survey and titling, credit, supply sales, and crop marketing. The units of these services may be the individual farmer, the village, or the commune. The service provided by a particular institutional project, s_{cij}, will limit the number of participating farmers according to one of the following equations:

(L2.1a) Service
$$\sum_i \Delta f_{ij} \le \sigma_{ci} s_{cij}$$

(L2.1b) Limitations
$$\sum_i \Delta f_{ij} \le \sigma_{ci} s_{cij-1}$$

(L2.1c) Limitations on Participation
$$\sum_i f_{ij} \le \sigma_{ci} s_{cij}$$

(L2.2) Max. Pace of Expansion
$$s_{cij} \le \xi_{ci} s_{cij-1} \{ s_{cij-1} \quad 0 \}$$

(L2.3) Personnel Limitation
$$s_{cij} \le \varepsilon_{cgi} p_{gij}$$

Notation

f = farmers participating	α = ratio of participants to service	Subscripts
p = project personnel	ϵ = ratio of personnel to service	c = subcategory of variable
s = service		g = personnel grade
		i = project
		j = stage

Equation (L2.2) is a policy limitation, stating that the expansion of any service in a district will be limited to a pace that can be adequately administered. Equation (L2.3) indicates the number of personnel, generally field cadre, necessary to provide a given volume of service or, conversely, the maximum service that can be provided by the assigned staffing of the project.

The above equations provide the key links between institutional projects and crop promotion projects; (L1.2) is a variation on (L2.1b).

Business Volume and Gross Margin--The first three equations of this set apply to supply and marketing projects; the last three apply to credit projects:

(L3.1) Marketing Volume $v_{imj} = \mu_{im} \pi_i m'_i f_{ij}$

(L3.2a) Supply $v_{izj} = \mu_{iz} v_i z'_\tau z_i f_{ij}$ $\{\tau = 1\}$

(L3.2b) Volume $v_{izj} = \mu_{iz} v_i z'_\tau z_i \triangle f_{ij}$ $\{\tau > 1\}$

(L3.3) Supply and Marketing Gross Margin $g_{ij} = \sum_m \gamma m^{v_{imj}} + \sum_{z_3} \gamma_z v_{izj}$

(L3.4a) Short-Term Credit Outstanding $k_{\tau ij} = \mu_\tau k'_{\tau i} f_{ij}$ $\{\tau = 1\}$

(L3.4b) Med./Long-Term Credit Outstanding $= k_{\tau ij-1} + \mu_\tau k'_{\tau i} \quad f_{ij}$

$$= -\sum_{j=j-}^{i-1} \frac{\mu_\tau k'_{\tau i} \quad f_{ij}}{\tau} \quad \{\tau > 1\}$$

(L3.5) Credit Gross Margin $g_{ij} = \sum \gamma \, k_{ij}$

(L3.6) Change in Credit $\triangle k_{ij} = \sum (k_{\tau ij} - k_{\tau ij-1})$

Notation

		Subscripts
f = farmers participating	= rate of gross	
g = gross margin	= share of	i = project
k = credit	market	j = stage
m = kg. or head marketed	= price of input	m = type of crop
z = quantity of input used	= price of crop	= term of loan
	to farmer	

It should be noted first that the i subscripts to the left refer to the institutional projects, while those to the right refer to crop projects. The share of market coefficients and the gross margin coefficients apply to the institutional projects; the two price coefficients apply to crop projects. The o' notation refers to the individual farm level. Equations (L3.2a) and (L3.4a) apply to current production needs; equations (L3.2b) and (L3.4b) apply to investments; they therefore are governed by the increase in participants rather than the absolute number.

The rather long equation (L3.4b) states that credit outstanding of a given term-of-loan category equals the credit outstanding of the previous year (first expression) plus new loans (second expression) less repayments (third expression).

Use of a share-of-market coefficient makes it possible to have competing commercial service agencies or enterprises in one district. It is assumed that their gross margins will be the same for any given type of merchandise or credit.

Operating Expenses--The following equation applies to all projects. Most projects, however, will use only a few expressions. A crop project will probably only use the first expression, the service being demonstrations. A supply and marketing institution will probably use all the expressions.

(L4.1) Operating Expenses

$$x_{ij} = \underset{c}{c_i{}^s c_{ij}} + \underset{m}{mi^v mij} + \underset{z}{zi^v zij} + \underset{g}{gi^p gij}$$

services

handling

personnel

Notation

a_a = profit
b = project budget
k = debt outstanding
p = personnel
q = equipment
r = rate of interest
s = service
v = volume of business
x = operating expenses

new

equipment $\begin{cases} + \quad \Delta q_{uij} \\ + q'_{gi} \, \Delta P_{gij} \end{cases}$

or

amorti-

zation $\begin{cases} + \dfrac{q_{ij}}{q} + \dfrac{h_{ij}}{h} \end{cases}$

interest $\quad + \sum r \; h_{ij}$

misc. fixeu $\quad + x_{uij}$
costs

Subscripts
c = class of service
g = grade of personnel
h = buildings and land
i = project
j = stage
m = type of crop marketed
q = equipment
z = type of product supply
τ = term of loan
Coefficients
β = unit expense
τ = term of amortization
q' = equipment per man

(L4.2) Government $b_{ij} = x_{ij}$
        Agency
        Budget

(L4.3) Profit $\Delta a_{aij} = g_{ij} - x_{ij}$

The preceding expressions should be largely self-explanatory. β_{gi}, it should be noted, includes not only salary but any other expenses which would vary with the number and type of personnel assigned to a project: per diem, travel, housing, etc. The expressions q_{ij} and h_{ij} represent current value of assets.

Assets, Liabilities, and Subsidies--The following set of equations are for computing capital requirements of supply and marketing projects. The first three provide a simplified statement of assets. The rest compute the more complex liabilities side of the balance sheet.

(L5.1) <u>Working Capital</u>

$$w_{ij} \geq \rho_{mi} v_{mij} \quad \{v_{mij} > v_{zig}\}$$

$$\text{o r} \quad \geq \rho_{zi} v_{zij} \quad \{v_{zij} > v_{mij}\}$$

<u>Notation</u>
w = working capital, net
v = business volume
ρ = maximum ratio
i = project
j = stage
m = crop } line of business
z = input } with largest volume

(L5.2) <u>Equpiment</u>

personnel
variable

$$q_{ij} = \sum_{g} \beta_{gi} P_{gij}$$

volume
variable

$$+ \beta_{mi} v_{mij}$$

general

$$+ q_{uij}$$

amortization

$$- \sum_{j=1}^{j} \frac{q_{ij}}{\tau q}$$

<u>Notation</u>
a = capital
a_a = earned surplus
a_b = subsidy to date
a_p = paid in capital
b = project budget
h = buildings and land
k = debt outstanding
p = personnel
q = equipment
v = volume of business
w = net working capital
  (peak need)

(L5.3) <u>Building and Land</u>

$$h_{ij} = \chi_{mi} v_{mij}$$

$$+ h_{ui}$$

$$- \sum_{j=1}^{j} \frac{h_{ij}}{\tau h}$$

λ = maximum ratio of type of
  debt to type of assets
τ = term of amortization
χ = ratio of buildings to peak
  business volume

(L5.4) <u>Short-Term Debt</u>

$$k_{\tau ij} = \lambda_w w_{ij} \{\tau - 1\}$$

<u>Subscripts</u>
g = personnel grade
h = building and land
i = project
j = stage
m = maximum business line
q = equipment
w = working capital
u = fixed

(L5.5) <u>Med.-Term Debt</u>

$$k_{\tau ij} = \lambda_h h_{ij} \{2' = \tau' = 5\}$$

(L5.6) <u>Long-Term Debt</u>

$$k_{\tau ij} = \lambda_h h_{ij} \{6' = \tau' = 30\}$$

(L5.7) <u>Total Debt</u>

$$k_{ij} = \sum_{\tau} k_{\tau ij}$$

(L5.8) <u>Capital Account</u>

$$a_{ij} = a_{ij} + a_{pij}$$

$$+ a_{bij}$$

(L5.9) <u>Capital Subsidy</u>

$$a_{bij} = w_{ij} + q_{ij} + h_{ij}$$

$$- (k_{ij} + a_{aij} + a_{pij})$$

(L5.10) <u>Project Budget</u>

$$b_{ij} = \triangle a_{bij}$$

627

Most of the preceding equations express policy decisions or simplifications of requirements determination formulas. The coefficient would be a management decision, the β and $\varkappa\psi$ coefficients likewise. The λ coefficients would be determined by the bank or authority providing credit to the project. It should be noted that the short-term lending for working capital should provide sufficient marketing credit to give the farmers their money at harvest time and hold crops off the market within the district. The w variable thus is the channel of marketing credit in this model.

Equation (L5.10) applies only if, as is often the case with cooperatives, the government commits itself to all financial support necessary to get them financially self-sufficient. The previous equations can also be used to simulate a private venture, with credit and some equity capital from publicly controlled agencies, or from private sources.

Miscellaneous Coefficients--Two project coefficients remain to be derived:

(L6.1) Market Volume $\quad m_{ij} = m'_i f_{ij}$

Notation
e = foreign exchange

(L6.2) Foreign Exchange $\quad e_{ij} = \epsilon_q \triangle q_{ij}$
$\quad\quad\quad\quad\quad\quad\quad\quad + \epsilon_c z_{cij}$

f = farmers
    participating
m = marketed crop vol.
    (tons)
m' = crop marketed
      per farmer
q = equipment
z = production inputs

Subscripts
c = type of input
i = project
j = stage
q = refers to equipment

The market volume equation applies only to crop projects; the foreign exchange equation applies to all projects; ϵ is the percentage of total requirement which must be imported.

Project Launch and Phase-out Rules--A predetermined strategy, such as that shown on Form A-9, determines the time interrelationships of projects, particularly when they are

to start, and the stage. For computerization the initial stage
formula can be stated:

(L7. 1) <u>Launch Stage</u> $b_{ij}, k_{ij}, p_{ij}, d_{ij} = 0 \} j < j_i \}$

where j_i is the designated first stage of the project. The final
stage of budget support may be designated arbitrarily or according to a signal showing that the objective of support has
been accomplished:

(L7. 2a) <u>Crop Project</u> $b_{ij} = 0 \ \{ f_{ij-1} = f_i \}$
       <u>Phase-out</u>

(L7. 2b) <u>Commercial</u> $b_{ij} = 0 \ \{ \triangle a_{aij-1} > 0 \}$
       <u>Project</u>

(L7. 2c) <u>Phase-out</u> $b_{ij} = 0 \ \{ a_{bij} \leq a_{bij-1} \}$

The first phase-out rule states that a crop project is to be
phased out fater the number of participating farmers reaches
the maximum. The first commercial project phase-out rule
ends support after profit becomes positive; the second rule
ends support after the balance sheet shows no further need of
support.

   <u>Consolidation of Projects</u>--For purposes of programming,
all projects in the modular district are consolidated, so that,
for each region,

$$y_{rj} = \sum_i y_{ij} \quad b_{rj} = \sum_i b_{ij} \quad k_{rj} = \sum_i k_{ij} \quad P_{grj} = \sum_i P_{gij}$$

Regional and Sector Levels

   Only two expressions in the program express purely regional or sector level aggregation: fixed costs, B_{rut}, and
central personnel, P_{gut}. These expressions are simply the
sum of the requirements of each individual project. Fixed
costs here are all aggregated at the regional level; there
might, in addition, be significant fixed costs aggregated at the
sector level, B_{ut}. This would not affect the functioning of
the program.

The level of fixed costs may determine the training capacity, T_{git} in equation (9) or the input production capacity,
Z_{cit}, in equation (10).

APPENDIX   **C**   SYSTEMS
TERMINOLOGY

A SYSTEM is a set of <u>entities</u> and their <u>attributes</u>, bound
together by a defined set of <u>interrelationships</u> and a defined
set of common <u>objectives</u> within a definable <u>boundary</u>. A
meaningful system has a greater density of interrelationships
within than across the boundary. A system may be a conception of an object or a process. <u>Systems engineering</u> deals
with the design of equipment conceived as systems. This
book deals with social processes conceived as systems.

ENTITIES may be objects, flows, activities, or events,
taken individually or as groups or classes. A single entity
may constitute a <u>subsystem</u> with its own objectives contributing to the overall systems objectives.

ATTRIBUTES are the types of relevant mathematical or
logical values of the entities. The <u>endogenous variables</u> of
the system are the set of values of attributes within the system boundaries. Taken together, they constitute the <u>state of
the system</u> and are sometimes called the <u>state variables</u>.

The OBJECTIVES of a system are the set of criteria for
the optimum solution of the problem at hand, by which system
performance is judged. The size and complexity of a system
depend on the breadth of the problem being considered. The
broader the objectives, the more relevant entities and interrelationships must be considered.

The ENVIRONMENT of a system is the set of all entities
whose changes in attribute may affect the state of the system
or whose attributes may be affected by changes in the system.
These attributes are sometimes called the <u>exogenous vari-
ables</u>. The <u>inputs</u> of the system are those changes in the exogenous variables which affect the state of the system and which
are subject to control or are the primary generators of change

within the system. The <u>outputs</u> of the system are those
changes in exogenous variables caused by changes in the state
of the system.

A MODEL is an abstracted, simplified statement of the
system as it exists in the real world, identifying those entities, attributes, and relationships which are essential to
specific decisions.

APPENDIX D THE MALAYSIAN
REDBOOK (Excerpts)

The following pages are reproduced verbatim from the so-
called "Redbook," which contains guidelines for the planning
of the Malaysian Rural Development Program (the Redbook
and the program itself are discussed in detail in Chapter 7):

RURAL DEVELOPMENT PLANNING

PURPOSE

A District Rural Development Plan, if carefully thought
out, and actively implemented, will benefit the livelihood of
many thousands of people in the District; it will contribute
considerably to the future prosperity of Malaya; it therefore
deserves the very best effort that can be put into its preparation.

Careful co-ordinated planning will save time, tempers,
energy, and funds when projects are in progress. Time spent
in careful planning is well worthwhile.

Departmental differences can be the death of development.
Co-ordination and co-operation are the life-blood of all action
on development. All departmental officers must play their
part and work together as a team.

MAIN ESSENTIALS OF RURAL DEVELOPMENT

There are two main aspects of Rural Development: --

(1) The improvement of existing kampongs;

(2) The opening up of new areas of land with new
kampongs.

The following are the basic physical essentials of Development which need careful planning: --

      (a) Roads and Bridges
            (i) To give access to existing kampongs;
           (ii) The opening up of new areas of land
                 with new kampongs.
      (b) Land development;
      (c) Water supplies;
      (d) Processing and Marketing facilities for Rural produce;
      (e) Rural industries;
      (f) Schools, Health Centres; and Playing Fields;
      (g) Irrigation for padi areas;
      (h) Electricity and Telecommunications, where possible.

There may be other essentials, different districts have different needs; these should be included in the District Plan.

PRIORITY

Rural Development planning and subsequent action on the Plan takes priority over all other work in the District.

All officers are hereby charged with the duty of faithfully implementing the detailed instructions which follow for the production of this plan.

RESULTS ARE WHAT WE WANT.

Tun Abdul Razak Bin Hussain

Deputy Prime Minister and
Minister of Rural Development

DISTRICT RURAL
DEVELOPMENT COMMITTEE

A "Committee" is a group of persons to whom a task is committed.

The District Rural Development Committee is a team to which is committed the task of improving the conditions of the Rural people in the District.

MEETINGS

The purpose of meetings is, by discussion: --

(1) To examine given problems/proposals for development;
(2) To ensure that no aspect of such problems/ proposals has been ignored;
(3) To reach agreement;
(4) To decide necessary action.

PRINCIPLES IN COMMITTEE

(1) Talk is only a means to an end;
(2) Discussion in itself will not produce results;
(3) Discussion must be translated into decision;
(4) Decision must be translated into action.

SINGLENESS OF PURPOSE

(1) Every member of a Committee during general discussion has a right--indeed a duty--to state his views with the utmost frankness.
(2) Once discussion has been completed every member equally has a duty to support the majority decision: --
    (i) Persistently to reiterate independent views after discussion is closed is un- intelligent;
    (ii) To do so after majority agreement has been reached is irresponsible;

(iii) To do so after a formal decision has
       been recorded is disloyal.
(3) Once action is under way anything less than
     full support is sabotage.

TEAM SPIRIT

Gunong tinggi sama di-daki
Lautan dalam sama di-renang
Mari-lah kita bersatu hati
Perkara yang susah menjadi senang.

NOTE: More detailed instructions on procedure for District
       Rural Development Committee Meetings are given at
       Appendix "A".

PREPARATION OF THE PLAN

Rural Development problems and proposals must first
be studied on the ground. Mere paper planning from a
desk is useless.

ACTION BY DISTRICT RURAL DEVELOPMENT COMMITTEE

1. First collect all outstanding requests from the ra'ayat,
    e.g., kampong roads, bridges, etc.

    (1) Requests which are not practicable: --
         Reject these and inform kampong applicants
         with regret.
    (2) Requests which are practicable: --
         Retain these for consideration in the Plan.

2. Next collect and consider all proposals by Government
    Departments and integrate these with kampong requests
    in a single co-ordinated plan.

3. The method of planning is to be as follows: --

    (a) First take stock of what already exists and where.
    (b) Summarize what improvements can be made to
         what exists.
    (c) Consider where new areas can be opened up and
         list proposals to achieve this.
    (d) Show location of all proposed improvements and
         new proposals on tracings.

4. Officers responsible for planning will avoid exchange of
    correspondence. They will in all cases proceed by per-
    sonal discussion and joint consultation.

THE BOOK PLAN

1. The results of the above co-ordinated action are then to
    be reduced to graphic form in the series of tracings and
    summaries listed below: --

    I.   Basic District Map
   II.   Land Map
  III.   Road Map
   IV.   Rural Water Supplies
    V.   Minor Irrigation Works
   VI.   River Clearing Proposals
  VII.   Schools, Health Centres and Playing Fields
 VIII.   Rural Processing and Marketing Facilities
   IX.   Rural Industries
    X.   Co-operative Development
   XI.   Telecommunication Facilities
  XII.   Rural Electricity Supplies

2.   Detailed instructions for the preparation of these Tracings
      and Summaries are given in the printed pages numbered
      I-XII bearing the above headings.

3.   Should it be found necessary to include further subjects,
      additional pages of instructions will be issued numbered
      XIII onwards.

PRODUCTION OF THE BOOK PLAN

Three copies of the Book Plan will be prepared.   Each will consist of: - -

DISTRICT MAP
TRACINGS
SUMMARIES OF PROPOSALS

DISTRICT MAP

(1) On the back cover of each Book, a map of the District will be mounted in such a way that it can be folded over and inter-leaved below particular Tracings as required.

(2) This Map could normally be a rectangular portion cut from the State Map but, where a map on that scale would be too small to show all necessary detail, a map on a larger scale should, where available, be substituted.

(3) The Survey Department will be responsible for mounting this Map on linen and for fixing it to the back cover in the correct way.

TRACINGS

(1) Map Tracings for each of the Headings I - XII will be inter-leaved opposite the respective printed page.

(2) Care must be taken to ensure that a Map Tracing is placed so that it will fall directly over the District Map when the latter is folded below it.

(3) The purpose of these Tracings is to show, at a glance, the broad essentials of each subject.

(4) It is a clear diagrammatic picture which is required. Meticulous accuracy of detail is NOT essential.

(5) The special instructions on each of the printed pages I - XII will be followed implicitly.

(6) Where such special instructions require that concrete proposals be shown in a Tracing, each proposal is to be labelled with the number by which it is listed in the relevant summary. [See below - Summary item (2)].

(7) The preparation of each Tracing is the joint responsibility of the Officers of the Departments listed in the appropriate printed page of instructions.

(8) Each Tracing is to be signed by each of the Officers responsible for its preparation. The precise official title of such signatory will be shown below his name.

SUMMARIES

(1) Under each Head I - XII a Summary will be drawn up stating clearly:
    (a) All specific proposals for new development.
    (b) The approximate cost of each proposal.

(2) The order in which the proposals are to be listed is the order of priority as assessed by the District Rural Development Committee.

(3) Reasons in support of each proposal will be given in brief, clear and forceful language.

(4) ALL SUMMARIES WILL BE PREPARED IN DUPLICATE AND BOTH COPIES PLACED IN THE PLASTIC POCKET.

USE OF THE
COMPLETED BOOK PLAN

(1) The Book Plan is to be used as the basic source of information on all Rural Development projects when under consideration by State or Federal Governments.

(2) In seeking approval for specific proposals the District or State Authority will describe such proposals by reference to the Summaries in which they appear, quoting their reference number.

(3) No facts or arguments already covered in the Summaries need then be repeated.

(4) Necessary correspondence will be kept to a minimum and written briefly and to the point.

(5) Unnecessary correspondence will not be written at all.

DISTRIBUTION

The three copies of the Book Plan will be distributed as follows: --

(i)   One copy to be retained by the District Rural Development Committee for use as a working plan;

(ii) One copy to be sent to the State Rural Development Committee for the consideration of proposals and for the inclusion of approved proposals in the overall State Rural Development Plan;

(iii) One copy to be sent direct to the Ministry of Rural Development: this will be kept for information.

No action on any proposals will be taken at Federal level until these have been considered by the State Rural Development Committee concerned.

I. -- BASIC DISTRICT MAP

The purpose of this tracing is to show, at a glance, those areas in the District which are available for large-scale development.

DETAIL OF MAP

The following areas are to be outlined with black line
boundaries: --

    (i)   Areas already developed;

            To be coloured-in in B r o w n .

    (ii) Areas incapable of Agricultural development for
        physical reasons, e. g., mountainous country,
        swamp, mangrove, tin tailings, etc;

            To be coloured-in in G r e y .

The resulting uncoloured areas will be those within which
new development is possible. They will be limited by the
above black line boundaries and these boundaries are to be
reproduced for reference purposes on each of the succeeding
Tracings.

The following additional information is to be inserted on
this tracing: --

    (iii) Gazetted Reserved Forests are to be indicated
         by g r e e n   l i n e boundaries, the whole area
         cross-hatched in G r e e n .

    (iv) Gazetted Game Reserves are to be indicated by
        y e l l o w   l i n e boundaries, the whole area cross-
        hatched in Y e l l o w .

    (v)   Mukim boundaries are to be shown in t h i c k
        b l a c k   l i n e . Each mukim is to be labelled
        with its name and the number, if any, by which
        it is known in the Land Office.

    (vi) The Rural population of each mukin is to be in-
        serted in brackets below the name of the mukim;
        the population of any town which may lie within
        the mukim is to be excluded.

RESPONSIBILITY

The production of this Map is the joint responsibility of the following: --

> (a) Forest Department
> (b) Agricultural Department
> (c) District Officer/Collector of Land Revenue.

The appropriate representative of each Department concerned will sign each Tracing.

IMMEDIATE ACTION

> (i) The Basic District Map is the first essential to the Plan since without it none of the more detailed maps such as road maps can be attempted.

> (ii) The Basic District Map must be produced without delay.

> (iii) As soon as it is ready a single copy is to be sent direct to the Ministry of Rural Development.

NOTE: The single copy required by (iii) is in addition to the copies ultimately required in the three plans in book form.

II. -- LAND MAP

The purpose of this Tracing is to show graphically the probable general trend of new development within the District.

DETAIL OF MAP

1.   The following areas are to be outlined with thin black line boundaries: --

(a) Areas available for large-scale agricultural development . . .

. . .   . . . to be coloured-in in R e d .

(b) Areas available for supplementing uneconomic
holdings in existing Kampongs

. . .   . . . to be coloured-in in B l u e .

(c) Areas within which mining development is projected,
as follows: - -

(i) Alluvial tin mining . . . to be coloured-in in
B l a c k Indian ink.

(ii) Other mining   . . . to be coloured-in in
B r o w n line.

2.   Where areas in 1 (a) and 1 (b) above cannot be developed
without previous large scale irrigation or drainage projects
the area should be hatched across with B l a c k line.

3.   The areas in 1 (a) above should, in particular, show the
sites in which residential villages will be established.

4.   The areas in 1 (b) above will comprise both fringe areas
lying within the area available for large-scale development
and also pockets of State land which may have been left un-
developed within the general alienated and developed area.

N o t e :   In either case the Kampong which they are proposed
to supplement should be shown: the distance between
the Kampong and the supplementary land area should
not exceed two miles.

SUMMARIES

1.   Details of proposals (in duplicate) of all block settlement
schemes should be listed in o r d e r of p r i o r i t y and enclosed in plastic pocket.

2.   These lists should include all areas both in 1 (a) and 1 (b),
and on the Tracings these areas should be labelled with the
corresponding number on the lists.

RESPONSIBILITY

1.   The production of this Tracing and the Summaries are the
joint responsibility of the following Departments: --

> (a) Agricultural Department
> (b) Drainage and Irrigation Department
> (c) Mines Department
> (d) Survey Department
> (e) District Officer/Collector of Land Revenue

2.   The appropriate representative of each Department concerned will sign each Tracing.

III. -- ROAD MAP

POLICY

1.   The key to Rural Development is an adequate network of
access roads of a width and surface capable of taking heavy
lorry traffic in all weathers.
2.   Metalled roads cannot be expected all at once but earth
roads are entirely satisfactory provided that they conform to
the minimum standards specified in App. B.
3.   ROADS NOT UP TO THIS STANDARD ARE USELESS.
4.   Accordingly: -- (i) Existing roads, if not of this standard,
                    must be raised to it.
                (ii) New roads must be built to this stan-
                    dard from the first.
5.   The District Rural Development Committee has the
responsibility to decide where road improvements or new
roads are required but the Public Works Department alone is
capable of designing and planning them.
6.   The precise route to be taken by a new or redesigned road
must therefore be a compromise between social and economic
requirements and topographic necessity.

DETAIL OF MAP

1.   The Road Map, in addition to showing new proposals, will
include in diagrammatic form all existing roads--whether

metalled or not--and including P. W. D. main roads. The purpose of showing these existing roads is to provide a frame of reference.

2.   Existing roads and new roads will be indicated respectively in single line and in double line as below: --

    (a)   Existing roads.
        (i)   Roads of full standard and above: in
           single continuous black line   ——————
        (ii)   Sub-standard roads: in single broken
           black line   — — — — —
    (b)   Proposed roads.
        (i)   New roads: in double continuous
           black lines   ═══════
        (ii)   Improvements to sub-standard roads:
           in double broken black lines   ═════════

3.   Proposed roads will be coloured between the double lines according to function: --

    (a)   To provide or improve access to existing Kampongs:
        Blue.
    (b)   To provide access to new areas: Red.

4.   All proposed roads and improvements are to be numbered to correspond with the serial number in the Summary and the position and names of relevant Kampongs are to be shown.

5.   It is essential that all new roads should be connected to a standard road. The point of junction should be marked with the number of the nearest mileage post.

SUMMARY

    Summaries of the proposals, listed in order of priority, are to be prepared under each of the above heads b (i) and b (ii) in the form below:

    These Summaries (in duplicate) are to be enclosed in the plastic pocket.

Serial No.	Road From: To:	Distance	Estimated Cost including bridges and culverts	Brief Description of proposed work-- w/reasons

RESPONSIBILITY

1.   The preparation of this Tracing and Summary is the joint responsibility of the following Departments: --

(a) Public Works Department

(b) District Officer/Collector of Land Revenue

2.   The appropriate representative of each Department concerned will sign each Tracing.

IV. -- RURAL WATER SUPPLIES

The purpose of this Tracing is to show the location of
proposed improvements to water supplies of existing
Kampongs.

PROCEDURE

Rural Development Committees in considering improvements to Kampong supplies of water must necessarily take
into account all the following factors: --
(a) Present population of area.
(b) Approximate percentage increase of population per
annum.
(c) Approximate assessment of present minimum daily
requirements in gallons additional to existing supply
(based on 5 gallons total consumption per head per
day).
(d) Present source(s)--river, stream, well--assess
draw-off from each source.
(e) Nearest treated supply and distance.
(f) Name of nearest large stream/river and distance--
assess maximum draw-off available in the wet and
dry seasons.
(g) If existing wells are inadequate a survey is required
on the lines of the standard Geological Survey Proforma at Appendix "C".

DETAIL OF MAP

The following are to be shown: --
(a) The location of the proposals in the Summary denoted
by the corresponding serial number within a circle.
(b) The location of the source of supply where this is
some distance away.

SUMMARY

A Summary of the proposals, listed in order of priority is to be prepared in the form below. This Summary (in duplicate) is to be enclosed in the plastic pocket.

Serial No.	Name of Kampong or Area	Population of Kampong	Estimated Cost	Brief Description of Proposed Work --with reasons

RESPONSIBILITY

The preparation of this Tracing and Summary is the joint responsibility of the following Departments: --
(a) Public Works Department
(b) District Officer/Collector of Land Revenue
The appropriate representative of each Department concerned will sign each Tracing.

WATER RESOURCES FOR NEW DEVELOPMENT

The existence of adequate water resources will be proved before the site for a new Kampong is determined.

DISTRICT RURAL DEVELOPMENT COMMITTEE PROCEDURE

GENERAL

In each District there will be a Rural Development "Operations" room. This may, if necessary, be the District Officer's own office.

A map of the whole District on the scale of one inch to the mile, and mounted in one piece, will be displayed permanently in the Operations Room.

The District copy of the Book Plan, when completed, will be kept permanently in this Room.

Meetings of the District Rural Development Committee
will invariably be held in this Room.

PROCEDURE

Routine meetings, though informal, must be conducted in
a business-like manner.

All items discussed will be recorded concisely in the
Minutes with a clear statement of the decision reached.

Each item will be the subject of a separate paragraph in
the Minutes and these paragraphs will be numbered in a continuous series throughout each year, i.e., numbering will
NOT recommence from "one" for each meeting.

It is not necessary for the Minutes to be formally confirmed at the following meeting. If corrections are necessary
they will form the subject of a separate paragraph in the
Minutes of the next meeting.

The Minutes of each meeting will conclude with a paragraph giving the time and date of the next meeting.

Two copies of the Minutes will, within three days of the
meeting, be sent to the State Rural Development Committee.

SPECIAL PROCEDURE DURING A VISIT BY HON'BLE
MINISTERS/MENTRI[2] BESAR/CHIEF MINISTERS AND
OTHER IMPORTANT PERSONS

   (a) A brief by the District Officer giving:-
      (i) a general review of Rural Development proposals,
          following the sequence of subjects in the Plan;
     (ii) the review will commence with a more particular
          description of the progress made in land develop-
          ment;
    (iii) a clear statement of all problems and difficulties
          encountered.
   (b) A brief by each of the Departmental Officers stating
      his particular problems, if any, and summarizing
      the progress made in projects;
   (c) Each brief on each subject will be followed by ques-
      tions and discussions;

(d) A summary note will be made of the main points
     raised during the visit and a copy sent within three
     days to: - -
         (i)   The Ministry of Rural Development
         (ii) The State Rural Development Committee.

FINANCIAL POLICY

1. In planning, the important thing is not to consider whether
or not funds will be available. Make a co-ordinated plan and
ensure that every proposal included in the plan is essential
and worthwhile for the benefit of the Rural Areas.

2. Do not worry at the planning stage as to what the total
estimate of proposals come to.

3. Ensure that every proposal is listed in order of priority
and that an estimate is given.

4. The provision of Federal funds will be considered when
State Governments have completed the following action: -

    (a) made a detailed plan for Rural Development within
         the State;

    (b) made an estimate of the amount of money required to
         implement such a plan;

    (c) made absolutely certain that all expenditure possible
         has been met from State funds.

5. In brief, the Policy is that Federal funds will be made
available, provided that State Governments show that they
have geared their own Policy, Funds and Efforts towards
giving the maximum to the development of the Rural Areas.

6. When it is abundantly clear that the State has given of its
best, every effort will be made by the Federal Government to
make up the balance of the funds.

7.   The National Policy of Rural Development is not a matter
of paper battles between the State and Federal Governments
but it is a co-ordinated and determined effort to which both
Federal and State Governments will give of their best in a
combined effort, to ensure that in the next few years the utmost is done for the Rural people.

TOURING THE DISTRICT

PAST PRACTICE

Departmental Officers have in the past usually toured the
Rural Areas individually, on their own programmes, in dis-
charge of their own duties.

FUTURE PRACTICE

Although individual visits must continue where circumstances make them necessary, most of the problems of Rural
Development require joint discussion and co-ordinated action.
Officers jointly concerned in any Rural problem will therefore
find it convenient to tour together and work as a team.

TEAM TOURING

Wherever it is at all possible the District Rural Development Committees will therefore tour the Rural Areas as a
Team. This practice will: -

  (i)   facilitate immediate consultation and joint decision;

  (ii)   make it possible, when visiting important kampongs,
         to organize a public meeting in the nature of a "forum"
         in which there will be a free and frank discussion with
         the ra'ayat of all problems;

  (iii) make it possible to explain the full reasons why cer-
         tain proposals must be rejected and so clear up mis-
         understandings in an atmosphere of good-will.

APPENDIX E A STANDARD ALPHA-
MNEMONIC CODE FOR
RURAL DEVELOPMENT
PERT.

CODE SYSTEM

First letter -- general type of activity ⎱ the work
Second letter -- more precise description ⎰ package
Third letter -- specific event

FIRST LETTER CODES

A = Agreements which must be negotiated
B = Building of structure or road or earthwork
C = Commodity procurement
D = Demonstration
F = Financing, other than by agreement
L = Land improvement
M = Major law or decree
O = Organize agency, enterprise, or committee
P = Plans and procedures
R = Recruitment
S = Study or survey
T = Training
V = Village mass canvass
X = eXternally given date

CATALOGUE OF EVENTS

First Letter	Second Letter	Third Letter
A = Agreement	C = Central gov't	D = Drafted
	L = Local gov't	O = Originating agency approval
	I = International	B = Bilateral approval

652

First Letter	Second Letter	Third Letter
	P = Private firm	C = Committee approval
		A = Authorizations complete
B = Building	B = Bridge	L = Location determined
	C = Clinic	D = Design completed
	H = Housing	A = Authorized
		B = Bids invited
	M = Meetinghouse	C = Contracted
	O = Office	M = Materiel ordered
	R = Road	F = Foundation laid
	S = School	S = Structure completed
	W = Warehouse	O = Occupied or operating
C = Commodity procurement	E = Equipment	R = Requirements determined
	S = Supplies	S = Specifications written
		D = Documents signed
		C = Contract awarded
		P = Produced, ready to ship
		W = Warehoused
		A = Arrival on site
D = Demonstration	C = Commune level	L = Location decided
	D = District level	C = Cooperators secured
	R = Regional	P = Ploughed or planted
	V = Village	H = Harvested
		T = Toured
		R = Reported and analyzed
F = Financing	B = Budget	N = Needs determined
	L = Loan	S = Source selected

First Letter	Second Letter	Third Letter
	S = Special fund	C = Commitment received D = Documentation complete R = Release of funds
L = <u>Land improvement</u>	C = Conservation I = Irrigation N = New land clearing	R = Requested S = Surveyed A = Authorized M = Materiel ordered E = Equipment on site B = Basic earthwork complete F = Final work complete U = Usage begins
M = <u>Major authorization</u>	D = Decree L = Law	D = Drafted O = Originating agency approval M = Ministry approval C = Council of ministers approval L = Legislature approval P = Publication
O = <u>Organizing</u>	A = Agency C = Committee	P = Purpose approved S = Structure and staffing approved C = Call for first meeting O = Officers elected F = Functioning
P = <u>Plans and procedures</u>	G = Guidelines P = Project S = Standards or SOP L = Long range	D = Drafted O = Originating agency approval C = Concurrences received A = Authorizations completed

First Letter	Second Letter	Third Letter
R = <u>Recruitment</u>	A = Advisers	R = Requirements determined
	D = Detail (temp.)	D = Documents completed
	P = Professional staff	P = Proposal of candidate
		A = Acceptance of candidate
	F = Field workers	C = Contract signed
	V = Volunteers	O = On board
S = <u>Study or survey</u>	F = Feasibility	P = Personnel assigned
	E = Evaluation	F = Fieldwork completed
	M = Means available	D = Data collected
	L = Locations	P = Processing and analysis of data complete
	P = Problem	
	R = Requirements	S = Submission for comment
		A = Approval of report
T = <u>Training</u>	A = Academic	M = Materials prepared
	F = Farmers	O = Organization completed
	M = Managerial	S = Selection of participants
	O = Observation tour	D = Documentation complete
	T = Technical	P = Precourse training
	V = Volunteers	B = Begin course
		F = Finish course
V = <u>Village mass canvass</u>	B = Beginning village	V = Volunteers selected
		P = Program presented in village

First Letter	Second Letter	Third Letter
	E = Ending village	S = Survey of farms or land
	P = Pilot village	O = Organize village group
		R = Request loans or projects
		A = Approval of assistance
		D = Distribution of materiel
		U = Usage of materiel
		F = Follow-up
X = eXternally determined	(determined by)	B = must Begin
	C = Crop season	F = must Finish
	B = Budget cycle	E = Earliest date possible
	O = Other program	L = Latest date possible
	W = Work season	

PROCEDURE

1. Use the above catalogue of first-letter codes as a pre-liminary checklist of work packages.

2. Use the suggested second-letter codes to identify the work packages within each first-letter category.

3. Change the second-letter code as necessary to make the coding more literal and clear.

4. Apply the third-letter codes while drawing the network.

BIBLIOGRAPHY

BOOKS

On Economic Development in General

Adelman, A., and Thorbecke, E., The Theory and Design of Economic Development, Johns Hopkins Press, Baltimore, 1966.

Agarwala, A. N., and Singh, S, eds., The Economics of Underdevelopment, Oxford U. Press, London, 1963.

Baldwin, R., Economic Development and Growth, Wiley, New York, 1966.

Frank C., and Van Arkadie, B., Economic Accounting and Development Planning, Oxford U. Press, Nairobi, 1966.

Hirschman, A., The Strategy of Economic Development, Yale U. Press, New Haven, 1958.

Hirschman, A., Development Projects Observed, Brookings Institution, Washington, 1967.

King, J. A., Economic Development Projects and Their Appraisal, Johns Hopkins Press, Baltimore, 1967.

Lewis, W. A., Development Planning, Harper & Row, New York, 1966.

Myrdal, G., Asian Drama, Twentieth Century Fund, New York, 1968, 3 vols.

Waterston, A., Development Planning, the Lessons of Experience, Johns Hopkins Press, Baltimore, 1965.

On Agricultural Development

De Wilde, J., Experience in Agricultural Development in
    Tropical Africa, Johns Hopkins Press, Baltimore,
    1967. 2v.

Dumont, R., Bad Start in Africa, Praeger, New York, 1966.

Gittinger, J. P., The Literature of Agricultural Planning,
    National Planning Association, Washington, 1966.

Johnson, B. F., and Southworth, A. M., Agricultural Devel-
    opment and Economic Growth, Cornell U. Press, Ithaca,
    1967.

Mellor, J., The Economics of Agricultural Development,
    Cornell U. Press, Ithaca, 1966.

Mosher, A., Getting Agriculture Moving, Praeger, New York,
    1966.

Schultz, T., Transforming Traditional Agriculture, Yale U.
    Press, New Haven, 1964.

On Special Problems of Development

Doob, L., Becoming More Civilized, Yale U. Press, New
    Haven, 1960.

Galula, D., Counterinsurgency Warfare, Praeger, New York,
    1964.

Geertz, C., Agricultural Involution: The Process of Ecological
    Change in Indonesia, U. of California Press, Berkeley,
    1963.

Wilson, G. W., Bergmann, B. R., Hirsch, L. V., and Klein,
    M. S., The Impact of Highway Investment on Development,
    Brookings Institution, Washington, 1966.

Doxiadis, C., Architecture in Transition, Oxford, New York,
    1963.

On Systems Analysis

Baumol, W. J., Operations Research and Economic Theory, Prentice-Hall, New York, 1965.

Heyel, C., Ed., The Encyclopedia of Modern Management, Reinhold, New York, 1963.

McMillan, C., and Gonzalez, R., Systems Analysis: A Computer Approach to Decision Models, Irwin, Homewood, 1965.

Novick, D., Ed., Program Budgeting, Harvard U. Press, Cambridge, 1965.

Société Francaise de Recherche Opérationelle, Recherche Opérationelle et problemes du tiers monde, Dunod, Paris, 1964.

Theil, H., Boot, J. C. G., and Kloek, T., Operations Research and Quantitative Economics, McGraw-Hill, New York, 1965.

On Individual Countries

Birkhead, G., Administrative Problems of Pakistan, Syracuse U. Press, Syracuse, 1966.

Gittinger, J. P., Planning for Agricultural Development: The Iranian Experience, National Planning Association, Washington, 1965.

Haq, M., The Strategy of Economic Planning, Oxford U. Press, London, 1963.

Haroun er Rashid, East Pakistan: A Systematic Regional Geography, Sh. Ghulam Ali & Sons, Lahore, 1965.

Jacoby, N., U.S. Aid to Taiwan, Praeger, New York, 1965.

Ness, C. D., Bureaucracy and Rural Development in
    Malaysia, U. of California Press, Berkeley, 1967.

Fisk, Silcock, T. H., and Fisk, E. K., Eds., The Political
    Economy of Independent Malaya, U. of California Press,
    Berkeley, 1963.

Waterston, A., Planning in Pakistan, Princeton U. Press,
    Princeton, 1965.

UNITED NATIONS PUBLICATIONS

ECLA, "Manual on Economic Development Projects," 1958.

FAO, "Agricultural Planning Course," 1963.

FAO, "Farmers Associations on Taiwan," by M. H. Kwoh,
    1964.

UNESCO, "Agricultural Planning and Village Community in
    Israel," 1964.

GOVERNMENT PUBLICATIONS
AND DOCUMENTS

France

"Planification en Agrique--Serie rouge,"Min. de la Cooper-
    ation, Paris, 1964, 12 vol.

Madagascar

"Groupement pour l'Opération Productivité Rizicole--Rapport
    de campagne, 1966-7," Min. d'Etat Chargé de l 'Agricul-
    ture, de l'Expansion Rurale et du Ravitaillement, 1967.

Malaysia

"First Malaysia Plan, 1966-70, " Jabatan Chetak Kerajaan,
    1965.

"Report on the First Seminar on Development, " Malaysian
    Center for Development Studies, 1966.

Pakistan

"Outline of the Third Five-Year Plan, " Government of
    Pakistan, 1964.

"68/9 Annual Plan, " Government of Pakistan, 1968.

"Approved Annual Development Programme of the Government
    of East Pakistan, " Government of East Pakistan, 1967.

"East Pakistan Food Self-Sufficiency Program, 1968, "
    Government of East Pakistan, 1967 (mimeo).

Owen, E., "Democratic Development in East Pakistan, "
    Embassy of Pakistan, Washington, 1966.

"Rural Works Reporting Manual, " Government of East
    Pakistan, 1965.

"Manual of Reporting Procedures, " Pakistan Family Planning
    Council, 1967.

"Manual of Rural Public Works, " Pakistan Academy of Rural
    Development, 1962.

Senegal

"Projet de programme de développement accéléré de la pro-
    ductivité d'arachide et de mil, dans les régions de Thies,
    de Kaolack, et de Diourbel, " Min. de l'Economie Rurale
    et de la Coopération, 1964.

"Programme de développement accéléré de la productivité
     d'arachide et de mil, dans les régions de Thies, de
     Kaolack, et de Diourbel--Rapport annuel, " Société de
     l'Assistance Technique et de Coopération (SATEC), 1967.

Taiwan

"Taiwan Statistical Year Book, 1967, " Committee for Inter-
     national Economic Cooperation and Development (CIECD),
     1967.

"The Republic of China's Fourth Four-Year Plan for Economic
     Development of the Province of Taiwan, 1965-68, Agri-
     cultural Sector, " Agricultural Production Committee,
     CIECD, 1965.

United States

"Rural Development in East Pakistan (The Rice Goal Plan), "
     USAID/Dacca, 1966 (mimeo).

BROCHURES

Hapgood, D., Ed., "Policies for Promoting Agricultural
     Development, " Massachusetts Institute of Technology,
     1963 (mimeo).

"Mathematical Programming System/360, " IBM, 1966.

"Project Management System/360, " IBM, 1966.

"General Purpose Simulation System/360, " IBM, 1967.

Eisenpreis, H., "Forecasting by Econometric Systems, "
     IBM, 1963.

Gillespie, R. "Family Planning on Taiwan, " Taiwan Popu-
     lation Study Center, 1967.

ARTICLES

On Economic Development

Enke, S., "The Economic Effects of Slowing Population Growth, " Economics Journal, 70(301): 44-66, 1966.

Johnston, B. F. and Mellor, J. W., "The Role of Agriculture in Economic Development, " American Economic Review, 51: 566-93, 1961.

Mosher, A. T., "Administrative Experimentation as a Way of Life for Development Projects, " International Development Review, June 1967, pp. 38-41.

Notestein, F., "Approaches to Population Control, " Development Digest, 6(2): 13-19, 1968.

Rostow, W. W., "Unsolved Problems of Economic Development, " International Development Review, March 1966, pp. 2-8.

Waterston, A., "What Do We Know about Economic Planning?" International Development Review, Dec. 1965, pp. 2-9.

On Systems Analysis

Ackoff, R., "Management Misinformation Systems, " Management Science, 14(4): B147-56, 1967.

Black, G., "Systems Analysis in Government Operations, " Management Science, 14(1): B41-58, 1967.

Dorfman, R., "Operations Research, " American Economic Review, 50(4): 575-623, 1960.

El Moghraby, S., "The Role of Modeling in Industrial Engineering Design, " Journal of Industrial Engineering, 19(6): 292-305, 1968.

Laue, H., "Operations Research as a Tool of Decision Mak-
    ing," Journal of Industrial Engineering, 18(9):539-49,
    1967.

Nelson, R. R., "Uncertainty, Learning, and the Economics
    of Parallel R&D Efforts," Review of Economics and
    Statistics, 43:351-64, 1961.

Sattinger, I. J., "Systems Analysis in Development Programs,"
    International Development Review, Sept. 1963, pp. 20-24.

Smalter, D., and Ruggles, R., "Six Business Lessons from
    the Pentagon," Harvard Business Review, March-April
    1966, pp. 64-75.

Starr, M., "Planning Models," Management Science,
    13(4):B128-41, 1966.

ABOUT THE AUTHOR

An industrial engineer and systems analyst, Earl M. Kulp joined AID in 1962 as Assistant Program Officer, serving as adviser to the Cambodian, Vietnamese, and Thai governments. In that capacity, he helped to innovate the first South East Asian program in which private commercial banks made loans to farmers without collateral. He has observed rural development in many other South East Asian countries. Mr. Kulp received his B.A. from Harvard College and his M.B.A. from Harvard Business School. He was awarded a Systems Analysis Fellowship by Princeton University for 1967-68. Mr. Kulp is now a senior consultant with Peat, Marwick, Mitchell & Co.